MARRIAGE TODAY

"Graciously hear our petition, Lord, and in Your loving kindness further Your own design for the continuance of mankind. Let the union made by Your warrant be preserved by Your help."   *Richard Cardinal Cushing*

"For this cause a man shall leave father and mother and cleave to his wife, and the two shall become one flesh. Therefore now they are no longer two, but one flesh."
Mark 10:7-8

MARRIAGE TODAY

A Commentary on the Code of Canon Law

By

Bernard Andrew Siegle, T.O.R., J.C.D., S.T.M.,

THIRD REVISED EDITION

1979

ALBA · HOUSE   NEW · YORK

SOCIETY OF ST. PAUL, 2187 VICTORY BLVD., STATEN ISLAND, NEW YORK 10314

Library of Congress Cataloging in Publication Data

Siegle, Bernard Andrew.
   Marriage Today.

   Bibliography: p.
   Includes index
   1. Marriage (Canon law) I.Title.
Law   262.9'33   79-18786
ISBN 0-8189-0384-8

Imprimi Potest:
Edmund Carroll, T.O.R.

Nihil Obstat:
Robert Senetsky, J.C.D.

Imprimatur:
†*Michael J. Dudick, D.D.*
Bishop of Passaic Diocese
April 25, 1979
The Nihil Obstat and Imprimatur are
a declaration that a book or pamphlet is considered
to be free from doctrinal or moral error. It is not implied
that those who have granted the Nihil Obstat and
Imprimatur agree with the contents,
opinions or statements expressed.

Designed, printed and bound in the United States of
America by the Fathers and Brothers of the
Society of St. Paul, 2187 Victory Boulevard,
Staten Island, New York, 10314, as part of their
communications apostolate.

1 2 3 4 5 6 7 8 9 (Current Printing: first digit).

ACKNOWLEDGEMENT

With sincere gratitude and appreciation I wish to thank Reverend Jordan Hite, T.O.R., for his painstaking effort in assisting me in this work. Also, Reverend Francis Morrisey, O.M.I., Reverend Robert Sanson, Reverend Lawrence G. Wrenn, Reverend James I. O'Connor, S.J., Monsignor Marion Reinhardt, Reverend Donald E. Heintschel, Executive Coordinator C.L.S.A., Reverend Adam Maida, Our Sunday Visitor, Studia Canonica, Saint Paul University, Ottawa, Canada, the many dioceses of the U.S.A., and all other colleagues for their contributions and cooperation in this work.

DEDICATION

This book is proudly dedicated to my dear father and mother, Paul and Anna, who made unselfish and untiring endeavors during their lifetime for the honor and glory of God, their family and society.

CONTENTS

CHAPTER I

General Principles

CHAPTER II

Preliminaries to Marriage

CHAPTER III

Impediments in General

Prohibiting Impediments

CHAPTER V

Diriments Impediments

CHAPTER VI

Matrimonial Consent

CHAPTER VII

Form of Marriage

CHAPTER VIII

Consequences of Marriage

CHAPTER IX

Separation of Married Persons

CHAPTER X

　*These cases have been carefully selected for the convenience of the teachers, students and others interested in canonical matters as examples of contemporary jurisprudence.
　**Numbers in parentheses refer to the Canons of the Oriental Code. Abbreviations:
　　　T.R.　　= The Tribunal Reporter
　　　M.J.　　= Marriage Jurisprudence
　　　C.L.D.　 = Canon Law Digest
　　　N.C.C.B. = National Council of Catholic Bishops of the USA
　　　D.S.M.　 = Diagnostic and Statistical Manual of Mental Disorders

CONTENTS

APPENDIX I
DOCUMENTS OF THE HOLY SEE ON MARRIAGE

MARRIAGE TODAY has been written as a handbook for seminarians, priests and others who might be interested in the preliminaries and fundamental basic factors of Canon Law on Marriage. It is not intended to be an exhaustive work. Those interested should have their own basic library of canonical works, such as: *The Tribunal, Reporter, Marriage Jurisprudence, The Jurist, Studia Canonica, Annulments, Canon Law Digest, and others.*

This is a time of transition. Canon Law exists and is being revised constantly even though we do not have a new Code of Law as yet. Canon Law is not in a vacuum as some might think. Immediately after Vatican Council II in the sixties, many presumed that we would have a new set of laws, but nothing appeared on marriage as such. We are still waiting. Codification is a long process.

This handbook, then, is being published to fill that void somewhat and to fulfill the requests of students who wish to update their knowledge on the latest positions in law.

This is a challenge, but as everyone knows, as soon as a book is published, it is criticized. This is good. Constructive criticism is a factor every writer welcomes, but no writer can please everyone. Moreover, those who could write a handbook are hesitant to do so. "Better something doubtful or overbold, and therefore in need of forgiveness, than nothing at all" says Karl Barth. Therefore, I accept the challenge.

Marriage Today, III Edition, contains all the laws of the Code of 1918 and some of the proposed new laws of the Code Commission. The basic canons are retained in the old and proposed new laws to uphold "What God hath joined together, let no man put asunder."

Since the Pastoral Constitution on the Church in the Modern World (*Gaudium et Spes*) is the cornerstone of this era and is of supreme importance for everyone, it is presented here with the *Humanae Vitae* for the convenience of the reader.

Commentaries are made on important issues which should provoke discussion with the hope of establishing a good theology of law. We will find examples of this under Canons 1012, 1014, and others.

It must be noted that the term "contract" is used throughout this work because it is existing law but it is not the existing jurisprudence and theology of law since Vatican Council II which recognizes marriage as a "covenant." For this reason, I have used substantial material from noted authors as Morrisey, Sanson, LaSage, Wrenn, Maida, Bevilaqua and others. This is being done for the benefit of all the readers of this book especially for those in other countries who do not have access to this current material. Therefore, with the permission of the renowned authors, their commentaries are used.

A cross-section of the best nullity cases on marriages expedited in the USA and Canada, including the Roman Rota, will be found in the Appendix based upon the impediments, defective consent: mental illness, immaturity, lack of due discretion, etc.

As an official of the Metropolitan Archdiocese of Pittsburgh, Pennsylvania (Byzantine Rite) for the past 25 years (10 years as Officialis), many interritual problems have come to my attention, which I discuss in this work.

A bibliography of important authors, books, articles will be included at the end of this work.

One might think that the exhaustive report on consanguinity might seem unnecessary, however, students and priests of other countries who use the book requested that this section should be retained because consanguinity problems do exist.

Jurisprudence is discussed also because it is very important as an interpretation of the law today and will eventually become law.

We must remember that Canon Law is a universal law binding both Catholics of the Latin rite and Catholics of the Oriental rite. It is necessary to state that law in general is divided into two categories, namely, (1) Divine Law and (2) Human Law. Divine Law is subdivided into (a) Divine Natural Law which is the participation of the Eternal Law of God, placed in the very nature of things when created by God; and (b) Divine Positive Law which is made known by God himself through divine revelation. (2) Human Law is subdivided into Ecclesiastical Law and Civil Law.

The Church teaches that all authority comes from God because in God's plan we find an orderly government of the world. The Church upholds that God delegated his authority to two perfect sovereign societies independently and exclusively competent to regulate the affairs of mankind within its own sphere. These two societies we call the Church and the State.* The Church was established by God for the spiritual welfare of man in the world to help him attain his salvation. The State, on the other hand, was established by God for the temporal welfare of mankind.

---

* This is debated in Lex Fundamentalis.

Within the Church's exclusive realm of jurisdiction come the seven Sacraments instituted by Christ. Moreover, the Roman Catholic Church considers itself as divinely appointed guardian and interpreter of the Divine Positive and Natural Law. It considers the State the legitimate civil authority which God grants the authority to make laws, carry them out and pass judgment upon all things which pertain to the temporal welfare of mankind.

Since marriage is the foundation stone of human society, the Church considers this institution most sacred because it was instituted by God not man.

God made certain positive regulations concerning marriage, but all the other important detail requirements and restrictions follow from the very nature of marriage itself for the benefit of mankind. All marriages should be governed by the precepts of divine-positive and natural laws, regardless of the tenets or belief of the individuals contracting marriage.

Marriage is a contract (covenant) between a man and a woman, who are juridically capable of contracting marriage, by which each gives and accepts the perpetual and exclusive rights to acts suitable for the generation of offspring. This definition pertains to all marriages, regardless of the subjective beliefs, or the lack of belief, of the parties who contract marriage. Therefore, all persons, regardless of their religious belief, who are not juridically capable, who do not give and accept the rights to acts suitable for generation, or who do not give and accept the right perpetually and exclusively, do not make a valid contract. Therefore, unity and indissolubility are the essential qualities of every true marriage by the Natural Law and by the very definition and nature of marriage. Because of this, a valid marriage contract is much different from every other contract; the marriage contract results in a bond and relationship sealed by God, who instituted it, between the two parties.

Therefore, the marriage contract cannot be broken by mutual agreement of both parties; although the two made the mutual contract, they cannot undo or break this bond since this contract is governed by Divine. Law. It is principally with this end in view that this work has been written, and now revised as the third edition, in order to bring up-to-date all the new legislation according to the recommendations of Vatican Council II, the Synod of Bishops, and the Ecumenical Age. This work is intended for every priest and clergyman, as well as the teacher, lawyer and other members of the laity to whom it may concern who wish to be more knowledgable about the marriage regulations in this modern age.

A recent report from the Bureau of Census in Washington, D.C. tells us that for every 1,000 persons living with their spouses, there are 84 divorced persons. Since 1970, the divorce ratio increased by 79 percent, compared with 34 percent increase during 1960 to 1970. Most of the increase has been among younger couples.

For those of Asia, Africa, Europe, India and elsewhere who have reported to me in Rome on the lack of progress in their tribunals, I can only recommend these words from the Allocution of Pope Paul VI to the Auditors of the Roman Rota: "The ministry of the ecclesiastical judge is pastoral because it comes to the aid of the members of the People of God who find themselves in difficulties. For them the judge is the one who has erred, recognizes the rights of one who has suffered harm, been calumniated, or unjustly humiliated. The judicial authority is in this way an authority of service, a service consisting in the exercise of a power entrusted by Christ to his Church for the benefit of souls.

"Prudence is not in fact to be identified with slowness which sometimes results in real injustice to the great harm of souls."

The teaching of the Church regarding the Sacrament-Mystery of Marriage and especially their canonical dimension, normally strikes the laity as being complex and difficult to understand. This is further complicated by the constant flow of new decrees and decisions concerning marriage. The publication of the third Revised edition of *Marriage Today*, which incorporate recent jurisprudence with the theologically maturing spirit of post Vatican II, should be a welcome aid to those involved in pastoral ministry, who must contend with the reality of today's world.

Emerging in the Church during the past several years is a growing awareness of its mission to the divorced and separated. Advancements in the behavioral sciences have given new insights into resolving the difficult state of life in which the divorced find themselves. Since there have been so many changes both in law and in the spirit of the Church, priests often find themselves in a quandry when confronted with a marriage problem. To rely upon their seminary training, especially if ordained more than ten years, is like trying to solve a computer problem with high-school algebra.

While in every diocese there are experts in canon law, the visible presence of the Church for the People of God is the parish priest. He is the one whom they first approach. He enjoys the opportunity to offer his knowledge and pastoral concern for their spiritual welfare. Father Bernard Siegle's *Marriage Today, Revised III Edition* is a practical guide and informational source meant to assist priests in bringing the peace of Christ into the hearts of many troubled people.

As presiding judge of the Tribunal of the Byzantine Catholic Archdiocese of Pittsburgh, Father Siegle has experienced a daily encounter with marriage law. He has witnessed its developments and lived with the changes on a personal basis. *Marriage Today, Revised III Edition* shares these insights and adds a particularly useful dimension. It treats not only the matrimonial jurisprudence of the Roman or Latin rite but also includes commentary on the Motu Proprio *Crebrae Allatae*, the matrimonial law of the Eastern Catholic Churches. Promulgated in 1949, *Crebrae Allatae* is of more recent vintage than the C.IC. and included some up-dated interpretations of the universal law. Several decisions of the Commission for the Authentic Interpretation of the Code of Canon Law have been rendered since 1949, which are of prime importance for inter-ritual relations.

Diocesan officials and those engaged in pastoral ministry will find

Father Siegle's book useful when dealing with marriage of different rites. Frequently, they encounter cases involving Catholics of the Eastern Churches and are in need of a reference source. *Marriage Today, Revised III Edition* is a readily available and up-dated source to meet their needs.

✠ Michael J. Dudick, D.D.
Eparch of Passaic

We have come to the crossroad in the field of law, where hopefully all the sources that are available must be utilized at this point in time to present Canon Law on marriage in its proper perspective. Therefore we begin (1) with the important key points of the doctrine on marriage as presented to the world by Vatican Council II in the Pastoral Constitution on the Church in the Modern World Gaudium et Spes; (2) the traditional format of the Code of 1918; (3) the salient points in "communicationes" and (4) the prevalent publicized recommendations of the Code Commission.

Doctrine on Marriage (Gaudium et Spes)

48. The intimate partnership of married life and love has been established by the Creator and qualified by His laws; rooted in the conjugal covenant of irrevocable personal consent. God Himself is the author of matrimony, endowed as it is with various benefits and purposes. All of these have a very decisive bearing on the continuation of the human race, on the personal development and eternal destiny of the individual members of a family, and on the dignity, stability, peace, and prosperity of the family itself and of human society as a whole. By their very nature, the institution of matrimony itself and conjugal love are ordained for the procreation and education of children, and find in them their ultimate crown.

Thus a man and a woman, who by the marriage covenant of conjugal love "are no longer two, but one flesh" (Mt. 19:6), render mutual help and service to each other through an intimate union of their persons and of their actions. Through this union they experience the meaning of their oneness and attain to it with growing perfection day by day. As a mutual gift of two persons, this intimate union, as well as the good of the children, imposes total fidelity on the spouses and argues for an unbreakable oneness between them.

Marriage as a Sacrament

Christ the Lord abundantly blessed this many-faceted love. The Savior of men and the Spouse of the Church comes into the lives of married Christians through the sacrament of matrimony. He abides with them thereafter so that, just as He loved the Church and handed Himself over on her behalf, the spouses may love each other with perpetual fidelity through mutual self-bestowal.

Graced with the dignity and office of fatherhood and motherhood, parents will energetically acquit themselves of a duty which devolves primarily on them, namely education, and especially religious education. The Christian family, which springs from marriage as a reflection of the loving covenant uniting Christ with the Church, and as a participation in that covenant, will manifest to all men the Savior's living presence in the world, and the genuine nature of the Church.

Marriage and Conjugal Love

49. The biblical Word of God several times urges the betrothed and the married to nourish and develop their wedlock by pure conjugal love and undivided affection. This love is an eminently human one since it is directed from one person to another through an affection of the will. It involves the good of the whole person. Therefore it can enrich the expressions of body and mind with a unique dignity, ennobling these expressions as special ingredients and signs of the friendship distinctive of marriage. This love the Lord has judged worthy of special gifts, healing, perfecting, and exalting gifts of grace and of charity.

Such love merging the human with the divine, leads the spouses to a free and mutual gift of themselves, a gift proving itself by gentle affection and by deed. Such love pervades the whole of their lives. Indeed, by its generous activity it grows better and grows greater. Therefore it far excels mere erotic inclination, which, selfishly pursued, soon enough fades wretchedly away.

This love is uniquely expressed and perfected through the marital act. The actions within marriage by which the couple are united intimately and chastely are noble and worthy ones. Expressed in a manner which is truly human, these actions signify and promote that mutual self-giving by which spouses enrich each other with a joyful and a thankful will.

Sealed by mutual faithfulness and hallowed above all by Christ's sacrament, this love remains steadfastly true in body and in mind, in bright days or dark days. It will never be profaned by adultery or divorce. Firmly established by the Lord, the unity of marriage will radiate from the equal personal dignity of wife and of husband, a dignity acknowledged by mutual and total love.

The steady fulfillment of the duties of this Christian vocation demands notable virtue. For this reason, strengthened by grace for holiness of life, the couple will painstakingly cultivate and pray for constancy of love, largeheartedness, and the spirit of sacrifice.

Marriage and its Purpose

50. Marriage and conjugal love are by their nature ordained toward the begetting and educating of children. Children are really the supreme gift of marriage and contribute very substantially to the welfare of their parents. The God Himself wished to share with man a certain special participation in His own creative work. Thus He blessed male and female, saying: "Increase and multiply" (Gn 1:28).

Hence, while not making the other purposes of matrimony of less account, the true practice of conjugal love, and the whole meaning of the family life which results from it, have this aim: that the couple be ready with stout hearts to cooperate with the love of the Creator and the Savior, who through them will enlarge and enrich His own family day by day.

Parents should regard as their proper mission the task of transmitting human life and educating those to whom it has been transmitted. They should realize that they are thereby cooperators with the love of God the Creator, and are, so to speak, the interpreters of that love. Thus they will fulfill their task with human and Christian responsibility.

Marriage and Circumstantial Norms

They will thoughtfully take into account both their own welfare and that of their children, those already born and those which may be foreseen. For this accounting they will reckon with both the material and the spiritual conditions of the times as well as of their state in life. Finally, they will consult the interests of the family group, of temporal society, and of the Church herself.

The parents themselves should ultimately make this judgment, in the sight of God. But in their manner of acting, spouses should be aware that they cannot proceed arbitrarily. They must always be governed according to a conscience dutifully conformed to the divine law itself, and should be submissive toward the Church's teaching office, which authentically interprets that law in the light of the gospel. That divine law reveals and protects the integral meaning of conjugal love, and impels it toward a truly human fulfillment.

Marriage to be sure is not instituted solely for procreation. Rather, its very nature as an unbreakable compact between persons, and the welfare of the children, both demand that the mutual love of the spouses, too, be embodied in a rightly ordered manner, that it grow and ripen. Therefore, marriage persists as a whole manner and communion of life, and maintains its value and indissolubility, even when offspring are lacking—despite, rather often, the very intense desire of the couple.

51. This Council realizes that certain modern conditions aften keep couples from arranging their married lives harmoniously, and that they find themselves in circumstances where at least temporarily the size of their families should not be increased. As a result, the faithful exercise of love and the full intimacy of their lives are hard to maintain. But where the intimacy of married life is broken off, it is not rare for its faithfulness to be imperiled and its quality of fruitfulness ruined. For then the upbringing of the children and the courage to accept new ones are both endangered.

To these problems there are those who presume to offer dishonorable solutions. Indeed, they do not recoil from the taking of life. But the Church issues the reminder that a true contradiction cannot exist between the divine laws pertaining to the transmission of life and those pertaining to the fostering of authentic conjugal love.

For God, the Lord of life, has conferred on men the surpassing ministry of safeguarding life—a ministry which must be fulfilled in a manner which is worthy of man. Therefore from the moment of its conception life must be guarded with the greatest care, while abortion and infanticide are unspeakable crimes. The sexual characteristics of man and the human faculty of reproduction wonderfully exceed the dispositions of lower forms of life. Hence the acts themselves which are proper to conjugal love and which are exercised in accord with genuine human dignity must be honored with great reverence.

Marriage: Doctrine and Objective Standards

Therefore when there is question of harmonizing conjugal love with the responsible transmission of life, the moral aspect of any procedure does not depend solely on sincere intentions or on an evaluation of motives. It must be determined by objective standards. These, based on the nature of the human person and his acts, preserve the full sense of mutual self-giving and human procreation in the context of true love. Such a goal cannot be achieved unless the virtue of conjugal chastity is sincerely practiced. Relying on these principles, sons of the Church may not undertake methods of regulating procreation which are found blameworthy by the teaching authority of the Church in its unfolding of the divine law.

Everyone should be persuaded that human life and the task of transmitting it are not realities bound up with this world alone. Hence they cannot be measured or perceived only in terms of it, but always have a bearing on the eternal destiny of men.

Objective standards according to the Church teaching were issued by Pope Paul, July 29, 1968 in his encyclical *Humanae Vitae*. The following excerpts from this document are important for consideration because they contain the traditional teaching of the Church and emphasized once again by Vatican Council II:

Humanae Vitae

. . . These (conjugal) acts, by which husband and wife are united . . . are, as the Council recalled, "noble and worthy". . . not every conjugal act is followed by a new life . . . nonetheless, the Church calling men back to the observance of the norms of the natural law as interpreted by her constant doctrine, teaches that each and every marriage act (quilibet matrimonii usus") must remain open to the transmission of life.

12. Indeed, by its intimate structure, the conjugal act, while most closely uniting husband and wife, capacitates them for the generation of new lives, according to laws inscribed in the very being of man and of woman. By safe-guarding both these essential aspects, the unitive and the procreative, the conjugal act preserves in its fullness the sense of true mutual love and its ordination toward man's most high calling to parenthood.

Faithfulness to God's Design

13. It is in fact justly observed that a conjugal act imposed upon one's partner without regard for his or her condition and lawful desires is not a true act of love, and therefore denies an exigency of right moral order in the relationships between husband and wife. Hence, one who reflects well must also recognize that a reciprocal act of love, which jeopardizes the responsibility to transmit life which God the Creator, according to particular laws, inserted therein, is in contradiction with the design constitutive of marriage, and with the will of the Author of life. To use this divine gift destroying, even if only partially, its meaning and its purpose is to contradict the nature both of man and

of woman and of their most intimate relationship, and therefore it is to contradict also the plan of God and His will.

Illicit Way of Regulating Birth

14. In conformity with these landmarks in the human and Christian vision of marriage, we must once again declare that the direct interruption of the generative process already begun, and, above all, directly willed and procured abortion, even if for therapeutic reasons, are to be absolutely excluded as licit means of regulating birth.

Equally to be excluded, as the teaching authority of the Church has frequently declared, is direct sterilization, whether perpetual or temporary, whether of the man or of the woman. Similarly excluded is every action which, either in anticipation of the conjugal act, or in its accomplishment, or in the development of its natural consequences, proposes, whether as an end or as a means, to render procreation impossible.

To justify conjugal acts made intentionally infecund, one cannot invoke as valid reasons the lesser evil, or the fact that such acts would constitute a whole together with the fecund acts already performed or to follow later, and hence would share in one and the same moral goodness. In truth, if it is sometimes licit to tolerate a lesser evil in order to avoid a greater evil or to promote a greater good it is not licit, even for the greatest reasons, to do evil so that good may follow therefrom, that is, to make into the object of a positive act of the will something which is intrinsically disorder, and hence unworthy of the human person, even when the intention is to safeguard or promote individual, family or social well-being. Consequently it is an error to think that a conjugal act which is deliberately made infecund and so is intrinsically dishonest could be made honest and right by the ensemble of a fecund conjugal life.

Church Guarantor of True Values

18. It can be foreseen that this teaching will perhaps not be easily re ceived by all: Too numerous are those voices—amplified by the modern means of propaganda—which are contrary to the voice of the Church. To tell the truth, the Church is not surprised to be made, like her divine founder, a "sign of contradiction," yet she does not because of this cease to proclaim with humble firmness the entire moral law, both natural and evangelical. Of such laws the Church was not the author,

nor consequently can she be their arbiter; she is only their depositary and their interpreter, without ever being able to declare to be licit that which is not so by reason of its intimate and unchangeable opposition to the true good of man.

In defending conjugal morals in their integral wholeness, the Church knows that she contributes toward the establishment of a truly human civilization; she engages man not to abdicate from his own responsibility in order to rely on technical means; by that very fact she defends the dignity of man and wife. Faithful to both the teaching and the example of the Savior, she shows herself to be the sincere and disinterested friend of men, whom she wishes to help, even during their earthly sojourn, "to share as sons in the life of the living God, the Father of all men."

Chapter One

GENERAL PRINCIPLES

Nature and Purpose of Marriage

Canon 1012—1. Christ our Lord elevated the matrimonial contract between two baptized persons to the dignity of a sacrament. **2.** Therefore every valid marriage contracted between baptized persons is by that very fact a sacrament.

1. *Marriage as a Sacrament:* It is a visible sign instituted by Christ to give sacramental grace; this he did by making the contract the instrument by which sacramental grace is conveyed to the parties. The sign consists of *matter* and *form*: "The mutual and lawful surrender of the bodies indicated by *words* or *signs* expressing the interior which is the *matter* of the sacrament while the mutual lawful acceptance of the bodies is its *form*" (Pope Benedict XIV[1]).

The matter, then, is the mutual offer made by the words or signs expressing genuine internal consent to the contract, while the form is the mutual acceptance expressed in a similar manner. For a valid contract, consent must be both interiorly genuine and mutually expressed externally.

The sacred quality of any marriage is emphasized by Pope Pius XI when he said: "The light of reason alone—above all, if we study the ancient records of history, if we question the unchanging conscience of peoples, if we examine the institutions and moral codes of nations—is enough to establish that there is in marriage itself a sacred and religious quality" (*Casti Connubii*). Even Pope Innocent III and Pope Honorius III "felt able to affirm without rashness and with good reason that the sacrament of marriage exists among believers and unbelievers," says Pope Leo XIII. What he means is that the act of marriage itself is holy as a fact of nature willed by God.

---

1. **Benedict XIV, Paucis Abbino, March 19, 1758.**

Pope Pius XI continues: "The sacred character of marriage, intimately linked to the order of religion and of holy things, is the effective result of its divine origin and also of its purpose which is to bring children to birth and to form them for God, and at the same time to bind husband and wife to God in Christian love and mutual help; and finally it is the result of the duty which is mutual to married union itself, instituted as it is by the all-wise providence of God the Creator, the duty to serve as a sort of medium for the transmission of life, by which parents become as it were the instruments of the almighty power of God." To emphasize still further that the sacred character of marriage is inherent in its nature Pius XII reminds us that "even among those who are not baptized, legitimately contracted marriage is, in the natural order, a sacred thing" (Allocution to the Sacred Roman Rota, October 6, 1946).

2. Is every contract a sacrament for validly baptized Christians?

During the Commission deliberations in revising the Code of Canon Law after the Vatican Council II, it has been significantly noted that this canon was challenged. Where there is a contract, there we also automatically find a sacrament whether we willed it or not, whether we were suited for it or not, whether we were a believing Christian or not at the time of marriage.

Since we are always trying to improve our laws by a good sound theology, we should be acquainted with this dilemma. The proposed new law of the Commission (C. 242, 1.2.) contains this conflict. Faith is important to all Christians. A literal definition of faith can be found in Hebrews: ". . . it is impossible to please God without faith, since anyone who comes to him must believe that he exists" (6:6) and rewards those who try to find him. In other words, a "saving faith" is necessary, one should have a firm belief in the Incarnation and Redemption of Christ. Marriage, to be called sacramental, should be contracted in faith in order to receive grace, otherwise, we are putting false labels, as it were, on products which are absent. For example, we can have two non-Catholics, baptized in infancy, but never had, or have no connection with Christianity whatsoever. Could we put a label on such a marriage saying that it is sacramental? The same can be said for two non-practicing Catholics who have abandoned their Christian ideals. The Canon should read: When two *believing*, validly baptized persons contract marriage, this marriage becomes by the very fact a sacramental marriage.

The Purpose of Marriage

Canon 1013—1. The primary purpose of marriage is the procreation and education of children. The secondary end is the mutual support and allaying of concupiscence. 2. The essential properties of marriage are unity and indissolubility, which gives stability to a Christian marriage by virtue of the sacrament.

Essential Properties

Unity: This is one of the essential characteristics of every marriage whether Christian or non-Christian. By unity is meant oneness. A husband has only one wife; a wife has only one husband. In other words unity means that marriage can take place only between one man and one woman. Another word for unity would be monogamy. The opposite is polygamy which is twofold: (a) polyandry—which exists when one woman has several husbands; (b) polygeny—which exists when one man has several wives. Polyandry is opposed to the primary concept of natural law; it is also opposed to the primary ends of marriage since it not only interferes with the love and companionship of the spouse, but is also the potential cause of sterility. If there are children, the paternity is doubtful in which case the education of children is uncertain.

Indissolubility: This is the second essential characteristic of marriage which means that the contract of marriage cannot be dissolved at will or with the consent of the contracting parties but only through death of one of the parties.

Commentary

This canon as stated is the traditional teaching of the Church. If this canon had been studied in depth during the codification of the law (1904-1912), the result might have been different because over the years there has been very much controversial discussion over this teaching, namely, the primary and secondary ends of marriage. Canonists and theologians find it difficult to provide an adequate explanation of the nature of marriage; these experts claim that if the term "primary" is retained, then there is more than one primary end of marriage as will be illustrated.

The secondary end of marriage, says the canon, is mutual support and allaying of concupiscence. This also is the traditional teaching of the Church. However, this secondary end of marriage known as the "remedy of concupiscence" is, to say the least (in its terminology), very misleading and offensive. It gives one the impression that God instituted marriage to remedy concupiscence. The notion which *remedium concupiscentiae* conveys is offensive because it gives the idea that marriage is a permission to *engage in activities which are shameful, sinful and improper*. This concept of *remedium* arises in part from the historical and cultural background of theologians who fostered this idea from a failure to appreciate the insights of modern psychology which sees this in a different light. The desire for marital relations *is fully normal and good*. Yet, to speak of it as "concupiscence" or a desire in need of a remedy, namely marriage, is to imply that it is a human weakness, or that something is lacking, or that something is defective in man.

Therefore to answer the question: what are the ends of marriage? we *put aside the traditional answer* and state that there are many *subjective ends of marriage*: such as *companionship, security, love, etc.;* there are also objective ends which flow from the marital act itself: namely *procreation*, mutual love and education of *the offspring*.

Vatican Council II deliberately left out the terminology of primary and secondary ends of marriage because of the mistaken notion it once *conveyed*. In the pastoral Constitution of the *Church in the Modern World* we find the following: "Marriage *to be sure is not instituted solely for procreation;* rather, its very nature as an unbreakable compact between persons, and the welfare of children, both demand that the mutual love of the spouses be embodied in a rightly ordered manner, that it grow and ripen. Therefore, marriage persists as *a whole manner and communion of life*, and maintains *its value* and *indissolubility*, even when despite the often intense desire of the couple, offspring is lacking." With this we can discard the traditional expression of "primary" and "secondary" ends of marriage and simply state that the ends of marriage are the procreation and education of offspring and mutual love between the spouses.

Marriage as a Contract

Since Vatican Council II, there is a new concept of marriage, not so much as a *contract*, but as a *covenant*. Francis Morrisey, O.M.I., gives an excellent commentary on this new concept.[2]

In recent years there have been a number of significant developments in the understanding of the nature of Christian marriage. They are centered on three particular areas of concern:

1) While marriage was formerly considered only as a contract requiring the same essential conditions for validity as any contract, today it is presented as a *covenant* or pact establishing an intimate partnership of conjugal life and love.

2) It was generally taught (C. 1013) that the primary end of marriage was the procreation and education of children, while the secondary ends were mutual help and remedy for concupiscence. Today, following the teachings of the encyclical "Humanae Vitae," *conjugal love* is considered as an essential element of marriage, with no reference to primary or secondary ends.

3) The essential giving in marriage was the right to those acts apt for the generation of children (the ius in corpus"). Today, the emphasis is placed on the *total giving of self* ("donatio") rather than just the right to physical acts.

These three shifts in emphasis call for the elaboration of a renewed theology of marriage, based on the Church's most authoritative statements and on a better understanding of what is entailed in the community of conjugal life and love.

This will be necessary to develop canonical insights, for as Pope Paul VI stated, canonists must "deepen the work of the Spirit which must be expressed in the Church's law" (September 17, 1973, in *Origins*, p. 272).

The development of a renewed theology of marriage will also be the result of the acceptance or recognition of the contribution that the psychological and psychiatric sciences have given us as we strive to understand better the structure and make-up of the total human person.

Marriage as a covenant (Sanson, p. 10-20)

The three developments mentioned above do not, in any way, destroy or weaken the traditional teaching of theologians and canonists that the essential properties of Christian marriage are its unity and indissolubility. Rather, it was from using these characteristics as a background

---

2. Morrisey, Francis; **Handbook on Marriage,** St. Paul's University, Ottawa, Canada. (A compilation)

that later developments were possible and that any future understandings must stem. To understand the position of the Church's marriage courts today, it is essential to grasp the principles underlying their practice.

Marriage has been described by Bernard Häring as the "great sacrament of God's covenant with his people" (in L. Wrenn, *Divorce and Remarriage in the Catholic Church*, New York, Newman, 1973, p. 16). To understand this notion of covenant it is necessary to refer briefly to some of its scriptural foundations, realizing that we do not yet have an adequate theology of covenant.

The heart of the covenant is the approach by God, and the response of man: "This day you have accepted God's commitment, and God has accepted yours" (Dt 26:17).

Covenant is a form of contract, but in it the details are not always fixed at once, nor are the duties carefully spelled out from the beginning. There are fundamentally no formal legal terms. The law becomes secondary and continuous—a contingent expression of the commitment. The legalistic prescriptions of rights and duties are secondary, and must not be allowed to overshadow the basic commitment of persons in fidelity and spontaneity (cf. Jos 24: 19-20).

It is only in the classic passage of the New Testament covenant-theology (Ep 5:2132) that we have the *explicit* application of the mystery of Christ's covenant love to the reality of human marriage. Sacramental theologians today are centering on this key passage in the New Testament theology of marriage not just to defend marriage as one of the seven sacraments, but to reflect further how "Paul presents the marriage of two believers as a reflection of Christ's covenant of redemptive love and fidelity with the Church, and as a sign or sacrament of that covenant. Thus marriage is a sign or symbol of Christ's covenant precisely because marriage is itself a covenant mystery if seen in relation to Christ's covenant with His Church" (P. Palmer, *loc. cit.*, p. 624).

Covenant is seen in Scripture *primarily* as a personal relationship and mutual commitment, even though from a human point of view it must be specified by legal terms and prescriptions, and have warnings of what will happen if it is violated. It is also to be seen primarily in the light of God's two great covenant virtues: his *faithful-promise* which will never be broken (cf. Jr 31: 31-34), and his *loving-kindness* in which he never stops extending not only selfless, creative love, but also forgiving and reconciling love (Mal 2:14).

In law, the three goods (*bona*) of marriage proposed by St. Augustine, have expressed this reality clearly. However, today, presented in the context of the Conciliar constitution *Gaudium et Spes* (no. 48), we could now state that:

1) the *bonum prolis* is the right to the intimate sexual union with an openness to fecundity. The capacity to be responsible parents, not only procreating, but properly raising and educating a family.

2) the *bonum fidei* is the right to a marital love special to this exclusive and lifelong union. The possibility of loving and being beloved as the "only one."

3) the *bonum sacramenti* is that Christian love which signifies and partakes of the mystery of that unity and fruitful love which exists between Christ and His Bride, the Church. The *capacity for life*, of *all* the essentials of marriage.

In this perspective, marriage becomes the interpersonal human relationship most closely mirroring the covenant of God and His people, and Christ and His Church. It may be defined as "a graced covenant of love and fidelity between two baptized persons which, when ratified and sealed in the flesh, has God as its author, witness, and guarantor of the indissoluble bond" (P. Palmer, *loc. cit.*, p. 624).

The idea of a "covenant" which the Council fought so resolutely to maintain against those who wanted marriage defined as a "contract" (over 190 *modi* against the text), corresponds to an understanding of marital intercourse as mutual self-giving. It is not the single act, but the whole community of life and love which is viewed as mutual self-giving. The stability of the covenant is explained by the divine ordination, which is more than a merely factual arrangement.

A description of Christian marriage from the aspect of *covenant* may be found by paraphrasing *Gaudium et Spes*:

> Marriage is the intimate partnership of conjugal life and love which is rooted in the conjugal covenant or irrevocable personal consent. The relationship of this sacred bond arises by that human act whereby spouses mutually bestow and accept each other. The marriage covenant of conjugal love is ordained for the procreation and education of children. In the total communion of life and love, the partners render mutual help and service to each other by an intricate union of their persons and of their actions (R. Sanson, *op. cit.*, p. 18).

The importance of conjugal love (R. Sanson, p. 21-29)

The role of conjugal love as an essential element of Christian marriage is not something that has always been recognized as having great importance.

In the Code of Canon Law, marriage was presented as a contract giving rights to the "ius ad corpus," without any direct reference to conjugal love.

In 1930, Pius XI, in his encyclical *Casti connubi* spoke of conjugal love within two definitions of marriage. In the contractual definition, conjugal love is presented as a secondary end. The other definition refers to marriage as a "communion of life" between husband and wife and places love in the higher dimension of mutual sanctification in the supernatural order, referring to it as the "primary cause and reason" for marriage (*A.A.S.*, 22(1930), p. 547-548).

In 1935, Herbert Doms, when writing of the meaning and purpose of marriage, stated that the meaning or essence of marriage was first and foremost a communion of life, and its purpose must be placed in this context: "the purpose of marriage is the community of two persons who make but one person, a community of life embracing the whole human being, from the spiritual sphere, through that of sense, and into the bodily." However, on April 1, 1944, the Holy Office stated that it could not be admitted that the secondary ends are not essentially subordinate to the primary end, but are equally principal and independent (*A.A.S.*, 36 (1944), p. 103).

In 1963, Ford and Kelly (*Contemporary Moral Theology*, Vol. II) taught that conjugal love was an essential end of marriage: "conjugal love is the virtue by which man and wife wish to communicate to each other the benefits proper to marriage" (p. 110). Among the benefits they list "the sharing of each other's lives in the work to which the very instinct of paternal love impel father and mother" (*Ibid*).

The second Vatican Council, in *Gaudium et Spes*, issued an outstanding compromise statement on the theology of marriage which provides a very important development in the understanding of the nature of Christian marriage. A remarkably strong emphasis is placed upon conjugal love. The intimate union which is a consequence of conjugal love demands permanence and exclusivity, a sharing of actions and the creation of a common conscience. The sacramentality of marriage is explained in terms of a transforming effect firstly upon the parties and then extended to the family.

The Council sedulously avoids the terminology of primary and secondary ends in Nos. 48 and 50 where a clause is phrased with so much care: "non posthabitis ceteris matrimonii finibus" (while not making the other purposes of marriage of less account).

According to the Conciliar doctrine, conjugal love must be productive of intimacy, of mutual fulfillment and sanctification, and also be open to fruitful love. Conjugal love, and the procreation and education of children, are not two disparate and separate elements, but intertwined, interrelated and *both* essential.

The covenanting of love described in *Gaudium et Spes*, no. 49, will be a primary source of sacramental theology for years to come. This love will be evaluated in terms of compatibility (personality), comprehension (intelligence), agreement (willpower), affection (sensitivity) and charity (grace).

In 1967, Pope Paul VI issued the encyclical *Humanae vitae*. Unfortunately, the beautiful theology of marriage which it contains was effectively ignored because of the "birth control debate." Pope Paul does not use the term "ends" at all. Instead, he gives the characteristics of human love; the first time, it seems, that an official document of the magisterium applies the new understanding of marriage initiated by the Council. The encyclical gives five characteristics of conjugal love (nos. 9-10):

> —it must be *fully human*, that is an expression of the senses and of the spirit, arising from the unity of heart and soul, presented in the light of an integral vision of human perfection;
> —it must be *total*, generously sharing everything, with oblative love that excludes selfishness and undue reservations;
> —it must be *faithful* and *exclusive until* death;
> —it must be *fruitful*, ordained toward the raising up of new life;
> —it must be *moral*, in the sense that the responsible exercise of parenthood implies that husband and wife recognize fully their own duties toward God, toward themselves, toward the family and toward society, in a correct hierarchy of values.

In view of the renewed teaching, it is easily seen that, as a consequence of a "covenant theology" of marriage, conjugal love is not seen only as a "secondary end" of marriage. Rather, it is even more than an integral part. It becomes essential since it is necessary to the developing communion of life and love.

The two elements of "covenant" and "conjugal love" are both outside the juridical sphere. The third new element will enable Canon Law to apply the teachings of the renewed theology: the gift of oneself in a communion of life and love.

The gift of oneself in a communion of life and love
(R. Sanson, op. cit., pp. 30-41)

While no theologian can yet give a definite answer as to what is the essence of marriage, the key is found again in the conciliar Constitution, *Gaudium et spes*, when it speaks of the conjugal community of life and love.

While it is impossible to determine accurately the immediate contribution of the conciliar teaching to the ordinary jurisprudence of the Rota because the collection of sentences is not published until ten years later, we are at least able to glean from those decisions published in canonical periodicals, some indication of the influence this new doctrinal approach had in determining the outcome of certain marriage cases.

While for many years the aptitude to perform a connatural conjugal act was considered in Canon Law as the sign and proof of a valid marriage, the time had come for a different approach to be adopted by judges. The former approach was based on the premise that law must be grounded in facts or realities which can be perceived and demonstrated. In former days, love, which is something intimate and changing, did not seem to provide a reliable and stable criterion of life in common. However, with the development of the psychological sciences and the perfectioning of testing techniques, specialists are now able to know better some of the secrets of personality with its characteristic traits, with its weaknesses and impulses. In view of this, conjugal love can enter into the canonical sphere as an "aptitude for the community of conjugal life" (G. Lesage, *Evolution* . . . , p. 18).

The conjugal community of life and love
(no. 48 Gaudium et Spes)

On February 25, 1969, a decision given by the Rota, *coram* Msgr. Lucien Anné brings the conciliar teaching to the level of law and marks an important breakthrough in juridical practice. He writes: "The statement of the second Vatican Council has juridical significance. Indeed, it is concerned with the establishment of the community of life, but rather with the right and obligation of this intimate community of life, which has as its most specific element the intimate union of persons by which a man and a woman become one flesh, and to which, as a summit, this community of life tends" (*loc. cit.*, p. 429).

Anné then proceeds to define matrimonial consent as "an act of the will by which a man and a woman constitute between themselves a mutual covenant, or by an irrevocable consent, a perpetual and exclusive community of conjugal life, ordered by its very nature to the generation and education of children. Thereby, the formal substantial object of this consent is found not only in the perpetual and exclusive ius in corpus, but it also includes the right to a communion of life, or a community of life which, properly speaking, is matrimonial, and gives rise to correlative obligations or the right to 'an intimate conjunction of persons and works' by which they complete each other and associate their action to God in the procreation and education of new lives" (*Ibid.*, p. 430-431).

While Anné had broken the ice in this matter, the sailing was still not clear. Indeed, for a short period of time, it seems that other Rotal judges did not care to admit this new interpretation of law. We find a strong stand taken against conjugal love in a decision by Pinto, July 30, 1969, in *Monitor ecclesiasticus*, 96(1971), p. 510-512, and in another by Palazzini as late as June 2, 1971 (unpublished to date).

Likewise, the recent lengthy decision of C. Raab, contests the interpretation given to the Conciliar and Rotal decisions by a number of canonists.

Nevertheless, there now appears to be greater uniformity with conjugal love accepted as a capacity to commit oneself to a life-long union and a capacity to share a significant degree of one's life with a marriage partner. (See, for instance, *S.R.R.*, Dec., C. Fagiolo, October 30, 1970, unpublished to date).

Thus, the interrelated fundamental finality of marriage can be seen —not in the mere multiplication of human life, nor in the human development of spouses—but rather in the fulfillment and diffusion of a value which transcends and incorporates these particular aspects: love, in imitation of its supreme source, God, who is love.

Proposed changes in the law

The law of the Church has not yet put this teaching and practice of the courts into formal legislation. However, the *Schema*, of the canons on marriage for the new Code of Canon Law clearly intends to incorporate these new notions. It is proposed to define marriage as "an intimate partnership of the whole of life between a man and a woman, which by its very nature is ordered to the procreation and education of children" (cf. P. Huizing, *loc. cit.*, 1971, p. 70, new canon 243, par. 1). If this descriptive definition is compared with the text of canon 1013 as it now stands, we can appreciate the great progress that has taken place since 1917: "The primary end of marriage is the procreation and education of children; its secondary end is mutual help and the allaying of concupiscence."

Other developments

A further step in jurisprudence was the recognition of the "*donatio*" the giving of the right to the community of life. At first, the Rotal judges accepted this in the sense that if the couple *could* not give the right, the marriage was invalid (*S.R.R.* Dec., C. Fagiolo, October 30, 1970); this practice later evolved into the idea that if they *did* not give the right, whether they could or not, the marriage again was invalid (cf. C. Murtagh, *loc. cit.*).

The latest development in jurisprudence seems to be the recognition of an important point made by Msgr. J. Serrano of the Rota: the necessity of capacity of entering an interpersonal pact of marriage: marriage requires that both parties be able to accept the full interpersonal relations of the marriage state; each partner has a *right* to interpersonal friendship through interpersonal conjugal understanding.

d. The rights entailed in the community of conjugal life

In the Rotal decision given by Msgr. Lucien Anné on February 25, 1969, he mentions the rights pertaining to the "consortium vitae conjugalis" as outlined in *Gaudium et Spes*, No. 48.

However, no detailed analysis is given in this decision of the rights which should be considered essential to any Christian marriage in the true sense of the word, and as described in the encyclical letter *Humanae vitae*.

An attempt to do so was made in a decision given by the Montreal Appeal Tribunal on April 20, 1972 (Prot. No. AQ 5/72). The substance of this decision was reprinted in *Studia Canonica*, 6(1972), p. 99-104: G. Lesage, O.M.I., *The 'Consortium Vitae Conjugalis': Nature and Applications*. Father Lesage listed some 15 elements, the absence of which to a vital degree would deprive the partner of an essential right of marriage.

In his more recent study, "Evolution récente de la jurisprudence matrimoniale," he has reworked these rights, grouping them into headings which would make them more easily distinguishable.

While some canonists might not agree with each of the points given in these articles, we must recognize that they constitute one of the first attempts to determine more precisely what rights are truly involved in a Christian marriage, and as such merit very serious consideration.

Quoting then, at least indirectly, from Father Lesage, we could describe as follows the elements of the community of conjugal life, the absence of which, to a serious degree, would render the consent null and void:

Balance and maturity required for truly human conduct

The person as an individual must be able to function as a rational being: a maturity of personal conduct in the relationships of daily life; a self-mastery, which is indispensable for any reasonable and human conduct; a stability of conduct and ability to adapt to circumstances.

The relationship of interpersonal and heterosexual friendship

The person must be capable of acting as a social being: an oblative love, which is seeking not only for egotistical satisfaction, but the good and happiness of the partner; a respect for the personality or sensitivity of the parties within the affective and sexual orders; kindness and gentleness of character and manners in mutual relationships.

The aptitude to cooperate sufficiently for conjugal assistance

The person must be capable of heterosexual and conjugal love: the respect for Christian morality and for the partner's conscience in sexual and conjugal relationships; respective responsibility of husband and wife in conjugal friendship; mastery of passions, impulses or irrational instincts which would place mutual understanding or life in peril.

Mental balance and the sense of responsibility required for
the material welfare of the family

Needed are: respective responsibility of both husband and wife in providing for the material well-being of the home, stability in employment, budgetary foresight, etc; mutual sharing and consultation on important points of conjugal and family life; objectivity and realism in the evaluation of happenings and events of family or conjugal life; lucidity in the choice and determination of the ends and means to attain them.

Psychic capacity to participate, each in his own way,
in promoting the welfare of the children

The person must be capable of being a parent: with moral and psychological responsibility in the generation of children; parental responsibility in the care for, love and education of children.

If one of the spouses is *radically unable*, in spite of his good will, to meet these needs sufficiently, he is depriving his partner of an essential right of Christian marriage; he is incapable of fulfilling the object of his promise, and, consequently, enters into an invalid union. More will be said on this matter when we consider the defects of consent.

If other courts could devise similar working criteria, I believe that it would not only simplify their work, especially in dealing with cases of lack of due discretion, but it would also enable the jurisprudence of the Church to develop in accord with the conciliar teaching and the recent advances found in Rotal decisions. The points mentioned above could be expressed in different terms; some might be more readily accepted than others, but I sincerely believe that they merit very careful consideration.

Marriage Favored by Law

Canon 1014—Marriage enjoys the favor of the law; hence in case of doubt the validity of the marriage is to be upheld until the contrary is proved, without prejudice to the prescription of Canon 1127.

Whenever a doubt arises concerning the validity of a marriage that was certainly celebrated, the marriage is considered valid until the contrary is proved with moral certainty. If there is a doubt of fact that the marriage was celebrated but the parties are in possession of decent public reputation as a married couple, the marriage is considered valid until it is proven otherwise. In all cases the presumption is in favor of marriage both in the internal and external forum. Since every presumption is a probable conjecture in an uncertain matter, the presumption holds whether the marriage is valid or invalid until proven definitely. This theory is based on the fact that one would take the risk of violating the natural law by making either decision. In the case of marriage, the Code Commission gave a decision in such cases that the presumption of the validity of a first marriage (in which a doubt arose) is sufficient to justify a declaration of nullity of a subsequent marriage, provided the case is being handled according to the ordinary course of law. This canon is applicable especially in the U.S.A. in the ligamen or bigamy cases.

The exception in this canon is provided for in Canon 1127. In case of doubt, the privilege of the faith enjoys the favor of the law. In other words, the presumption of Canon 1127 takes precedence over the presumption of Canon 1014 because the privilege of the faith enjoys the favor of the law, when there is doubt as to the validity of a marriage contracted by the non-baptized; in other words, the doubt is to be resolved in favor of the faith, or in favor of the convert.

Doubt of Law Favors the Institution rather than the Individual
An opinion—

In his talk at the meeting of the Canon Law Society of America in Denver, 1967, Monsignor Stephan Kelleher, J.C.D. brought to light some interesting facts about Canon 1014 which are worthy of consideration. He says: "The canon goes on to state that in case of doubt a marriage is to be considered valid unless the contrary is proved. This is the heart of our subject. When there are strong reasons favoring the invalidity of a marriage, must its validity be upheld because there is a probability that it may be valid? It is with this question that we are primarily concerned. . . . Granted that marriage enjoys the favor of the law, what action may a person take to try to free himself from the bond of an unhappy marriage? What steps can be taken so that the force of presumption of Canon 1014 may be reduced? Can steps be taken so that, where the presumption stands, marriages may be dissolved? These answers are offered: (a) a revised judicial procedure whereby a judicial official grants annulments; (b) a judicial or administrative procedure whereby an ecclesiastical official grants a divorce; (c) a personal decision by a party, or parties, to a marriage that the marriage is null.

Some of the complaints (which are justified) of Monsignor Kelleher were against our judicial process of three judges and the mandatory appeal. This fortunately has been simplified through the new provisional faculties granted for three years by the Holy See, through the Canon Law Society of America.

"However, the question is asked: 'Can there be a judicial or administrative procedure whereby the Church will grant divorces, including divorces in sacramental, consummated marriages?' The answer to this question lies with the teaching authority of the Catholic Church, guided, in large part, by scripture scholars and theologians. The ideal of the indissolubility of marriage is not at stake. Every divorce has elements of tragedy. There is a potential tragedy in any marriage if the parties do not initially intend a permament marriage. . . . Granted the validity of the indissolubility of every marriage, is every marriage an ideal marriage? Given the fact that divorce is, in fact, almost as common among Catholics as among non-Catholics, does the present teaching of the Church contribute to the common good? My response to these questions inclines to the negative. In view of the number of persons who cannot go to the sacraments, does our present teaching derogate from the common good and adversely affect the spiritual lives of many individual persons? If the Church permitted divorce, would Catholics be in a more realistically effective position to influence civil legislation to sustain individual rights and to foster the common good? My response to these questions inclines to the affirmative.

"Canon 1014 states that, for the welfare of the community, the stability of the institution of marriage is to take precedence over the rights of individual persons. In our culture there is a fundamental error in a juridical system which is more concerned with protecting what it conceives to be the stability of a given institution than the safeguarding of rights of the human persons involved in that institution.

"The present law looks upon marriage as a 'thing,' a sacred 'thing,' but nevertheless, a 'thing.' This concept is in opposition to contemporary theological thought which looks upon the sacrament as a personal relationship. . . . Canon 1014 is concerned primarily with marriages whose validity is in some way doubtful. There is an inconsistency between what this canon requires of Christian souls and what we have consistently been taught to require of souls in other moral situations. For example, when the Church recognizes the moral system of probalism to be used in the sacrament of Penance, it is saying that we have no right to impose the more strict obligation upon a Christian soul when there is a reasonable doubt concerning the immorality of a certain action. In such matters the Church does not look primarily to the protection of the institution; she looks primarily to safeguarding the basic right of the Christian to be free from obligations other than those that are certain.

"Consistent logic, as well as the present conciliar teaching on the meaning of Christian freedom and responsibility, call for change in our outlook concerning doubtfully valid marriages. It would be well if we adopt the principle that where there is a preponderance of evidence that marriage is invalid, or where there is solidly probable evidence that marriage is not viable the individual who so desires could be declared free of such a marriage."

Kinds of Marriage

Canon 1015—1. A valid marriage of baptized persons is called *ratum* if it is not yet completed by consummation. Matrimonium *ratum et consummatum*, if there has taken place between the parties the conjugal act to which the marriage contract is by nature ordained and by which the parties become one flesh. 2. After the celebration of marriage, if the parties have lived together, the consummation of the marriage is presumed until the contrary is proved. 3. A marriage celebrated validly between unbaptized persons is called *legitimate*. 4. An invalid marriage which has been celebrated in good faith on the part of at least one of the parties is called *putative*, until both parties become certain of nullity.

This canon gives the legal terms which are constantly used when discussing the question of marriage.

1. *Ratum:* A *ratum* marriage is a sacramental marriage which takes place between two validly baptized persons (Catholics as well as Protestants) but which has not been consummated by the conjugal act.

2. *Ratum et Consummatum:* This is a marriage which is both sacramental and consummated by the conjugal act. A marriage is not considered consummated by sexual intercourse which may have occurred prior to a valid marriage. Neither is onanistic intercourse a complete act.

3. *Consummatum et Ratum:* Whenever two unbaptized persons enter into matrimony and later, after their marriage is consummated, they receive baptism together, is considered in the *consummatum et ratum* category.

4. *Legitimum:* This is a marriage between two non-baptized individuals.

5. *Naturale:* This is a marriage between a baptized and an unbaptized person. This is not used by the Code but by the Holy Office in one of its decisions (S.C.S. Office, Nov. 5, 1924). This is not a sacramental marriage because the sacrament cannot exist in one party and not in the other.

6. *Putativum:* This is an invalid marriage which was contracted in good faith by at least one of the parties, and it remains putative until

the parties become aware of its invalidity. Children born of a putative marriage are considered legitimate. This is due to the principle that because of the ignorance of one or both parties regarding an impediment which invalidated the marriage, and because of the absence of malice on the part of the parties. It is this which makes the putative marriage differ from the ordinary invalid marriage. The Code Commission was asked whether the word *celebratum* of Canon 1015:4 is to be understood only by a marriage celebrated before the Church. The reply was: In the affirmative. Jan. 26, 1949.[3] Therefore, a marriage of a Catholic and a non-Catholic contracted outside the Church, though the Catholic was in good faith, cannot be called putative.

7. *Attempted Marriage:* This is an invalid marriage, strictly speaking, when the contract is made whereby at least one of them is cognizant of an invalidating impediment, e.g., ligamen, or a marriage takes place without the proper form according to Canon 1094.

8. *Public Marriage:* This is a marriage celebrated in the external form or in some public way and recognized by the Church as valid.

9. *Clandestine Marriage:* This is a marriage that is contracted without the presence of the pastor and two witnesses.

10. *Secret Marriage,* also called *Marriage of Conscience:* This is a marriage which is contracted before the pastor and two witnesses *secretly* for some very grave reason. These marriages are not entered into the regular matrimonial register in the parish but entered in the secret archives in the Chancery (C. 1107). One must have special permission to perform such a secret marriage (C. 1104).

Laws Governing Marriage

Canon 1016—The marriage of baptized persons is governed not only by Divine Law, but also by Canon Law, without prejudice to the competency of the civil power in regard to the civil effects of such a marriage.

I. *Divine Law:* Whatever is required by the natural law for all marriage contracts is also necessary for a Christian marriage. All marriages are governed by the natural and divine positive law. Moreover, it must be remembered that marriage was restored to its pristine category (unity and indissolubility) by Christ not only for all Christians but for all men.[4]

---

3. **AAS 41-158.**

II. *Canon Law: Marriage is a sacrament.* Because of this the Church claims independent and exclusive right over marriages of all that are baptized validly, Catholics as well as Protestants. This power of authority has been given to the Church by Christ (Leo XIII, Encycl. Arcanum). The Church as such is the official custodian and interpreter of laws governing marriage. This jurisdiction—legislative, judicial, and coercive—includes all marriages in which at least one of the parties is baptized. It has the power to establish both diriment and prohibitive impediments. It is competent to render decisions on matrimonial cases within the limits of the natural and the divine laws.

Although the Church does not legislate directly for the unbaptized persons (C 12), nevertheless, whenever one of the parties is Catholic it claims direct jurisdiction over the entire contract of marriage and, as such, indirectly over the unbaptized.

The question is disputed, however: Whether such a marriage would be valid is argued from the fact that the contract which is indivisible must be governed by the one power or another, namely, the Church or the State. *According to jurisprudence, the right of the Church is upheld.*[5] The reason is that the contract is considered indivisible. Canon Law concerns itself with marriage under both aspects as a contract and as a sacrament.

The contract and sacrament cannot be separated; they are one and the same. The priest present at the marriage does not contribute anything to the matter and form of the sacrament. The bodies of the spouses constitute the MATTER *of the* sacrament, the words they express represent the FORM. The matter and form are found in the natural contract itself. Christ added nothing external to that contract. He merely raised the natural contract to the dignity of a sacrament.

III. *Civil Law:* According to this canon the civil power has jurisdiction over the mere civil effects of marriage, but not over the bond itself, or what is essential to marriage. The civil effects are those which are separable from the substance of the marriage contract, e.g., a dowry, the tenure of property, the right of succession, the right of the wife to use the husband's name (Vidal No. 10). If there is no infringement upon divine or canon law, the civil power may prescribe regulations which

4. Joyce, George, **Christian Marriage**, Sheed & Ward, New York, 1933. (Mostly historical and doctrinal).
5. Bouscaren, T. Lincoln, S.J., **Canon Law**, Bruce, 1957, p. 455.

safeguard health and public order, just as it requires a license or the registration of marriage must always be just and reasonable.[6]

IV. *Form of Marriage for the Unbaptized:* Since the Church does not claim the right over the non-baptized, they must be subject to some authority; otherwise it would be detrimental to peace and public order. The good of the family and of society would suffer. Therefore, within the realm of the natural law, the state can determine the form of marriage for the unbaptized for the valid marriage contract.

V. *Orientals:* The Oriental or Eastern Church is governed by the motu proprio, *Crebae Allatae* of Pope Pius XII, February 22, 1949, regarding its marriage legislation. This codification went into effect May 2, 1949. All marriages celebrated on or after this date are governed by *Crebrae Allatae.* All marriages celebrated before that date are governed by the Latin Code when the legislation is derived from divine law and the particular discipline in force in the rites to which the parties belonged. For example, some Maronites would come under the Synod of Lebanon, while others would not, after May 2, 1949.

VI. *Oriental Dissidents:* The Orthodox faithful are not subject to *Crebrae Allatae,* (even though there are authors who think otherwise—Coussa, Pospishil, Herman, etc.). The Orthodox Church is not bound by *Crebrae Allatae* because 1) there are no conciliar or papal statements extant denying the Orthodox hierarchy the authority to make or change their disciplinary legislation. As a matter of fact, there are innumerable statements to the effect that the Latin Church is committed to uphold the laws, rites, and customs of the Oriental Churches. 2) Clement Pujol, of the Oriental Institute, who studied the preparatory acts and the motu proprio, *Crebrae Allatae,* concluded that it was not the intention of Pope Pius XII to legislate for the Orthodox. Motivated by the pleas of Catholic bishops, the Pope promulgated the new legislation in 1949 *only for those Orientals in union with the Holy See.* To legislate for the Orthodox would have separated the Catholic Church even more than it is at present. Pujol holds that the technical term: *"christifideles"* refers only to Catholics—the same term that was used in other previous documents with this same meaning. (Moreover, *leges quae ... liberum iurium exercitum coarctant ... strictae subsunt interpretationi.*) It is a general principle of the Roman Church not to legislate for he Orthodox Church.

6. Goldsmith, J. W., **The Competence of Church and State over Marriage,** Catholic University Press, 1944.

CHAPTER TWO

PRELIMINARIES TO MARRIAGE

THE ENGAGEMENT CONTRACT

Canon 1017—1. A promise of marriage, whether it is unilateral or bilateral which is called an engagement, is null for both the internal and external forum, unless it is made in writing signed by the parties and by either the pastor or Ordinary of the place or at least two witnesses.

2. In case both parties, or either party have never learned to write or cannot write, it is required for validity that this fact be noted in the writing itself, and that an additional witness sign the document with the pastor or Ordinary of the place or with the two witnesses mentioned in §1.

3. From a promise of marriage, even if it be valid and there be no just cause excusing from its fulfillment, there arises no right of action to compel the celebration of the marriage; but there is a right of action for damages, if any are due.

Nature of Engagement

An engagement is a contract whereby two persons mutually promise to marry each other in the future. They must be capable of making this contract; for example, an engagement by minors would be valid but illicit. It is possible to have a conditional engagement.[1]

Form of Engagement

1. The promise of marriage must be (a) in writing, (b) signed by the parties, (c) signed by the pastor or local Ordinary or two witnesses, in order to be valid.

---

1. Mathis & Meyer, S.J., **The Pastoral Companion**, Chicago, 1961, p. 170.

2. If either or both parties are unable to write, an additional witness must sign the above-mentioned document for validity.

3. This contract may be made by proxy.

4. All parties involved must sign in each other's presence.

Binding Force of Engagement

The parties involved have a grave obligation in justice to fulfill the terms of the contract; e.g., to marry at the time specified in the contract.

An obligation of fidelity to one another arises to the exclusion of any third party; i.e., fornication with a third party would be unjust.

Although the engagement contract is valid, it does not give rise to the right of legal action in compelling the celebration of the marriage.

If one of the parties suffers harm, financial or any other, by the breaking of this contract, he may sue for damages.

Dissolution of the Contract

The contract can be dissolved by: (a) mutual consent of the contracting parties, (b) papal dispensation, (c) a subsequent invalidating impediment which cannot be dispensed, (d) entrance into a religious institute, (e) reception of Sacred Orders, (f) inability to change the object of the contract; i.e., one becomes a heretic, an alcoholic, mentally ill, or mutilated.

Introduction

1. With almost 1 out of 3 marriages ending in divorce in the United States, many priests have successfully initiated a program to reduce the number of divorces in this country by using the protective Canon 1017 regarding the solemn engagement. Although this Canon has been with us since 1918, it has so seldom been used that priests who have been approached by prospective couples have turned them away because he was not acquainted with the betrothal contract and ceremony. This laudable ceremony which is sanctioned by the Church should be introduced into our pastoral work and employed for all couples contemplating future marriage. Since it is found in every Canon Law and Moral Theology book, much emphasis has been placed on this ceremony in an attempt to help cut down the leakage in the field of marriage in the United States.

2. Historically, formal engagements were considered a "promise of

future marriage" by Roman law and the Roman Pontiffs. St. Thomas referred to this engagement contract as a "quasi-sacramental." The Code of 1918 treats engagements as either bilateral or unilateral contracts; i.e., when the contract is made and accepted by both parties, it is *bilateral;* when made by only one party and accepted by the other, it is called *unilateral.*

3. The pastor is not bound to insist on a formal engagement contract, but with so many attempted divorces in the Church today, use of the solemn engagement contract may serve to help correct this abuse. If canonical betrothals were more common during the period of the Second World War, we would have had fewer divorces, broken homes, so-called parentless children (from divorced parents); we would have fewer regrets, heart-aches, and nervous breakdowns.

4. The betrothal contract is a safety measure which provides an excellent opportunity for proper preparation and anticipation of many obligations, cares and responsibilities which every marriage presents to those entering this particular state of life.

5. It must be understood that the Natural Law requires no special formality, but that such a special formality or solemnity is required by the positive law found in Canon 1017. For this solemnity and for validity, the several conditions specified must be observed; it must be signed by both parties and by either the pastor or the local Ordinary or at least two witnesses, i.e., women, non-Catholics, and even children with the use of reason can act as witnesses. The contract should be dated, and the place should also be indicated; this is not necessary, however, for validity.

ORIENTAL LAW

Unlike the Latin Church, the Oriental Church has retained the ordinary practice of formal engagement for centuries as far as the contract and ceremony are concerned. The new Oriental Code specifically treats of this solemn engagement in Canons six and seven.

Canon 6–1. The promise of marriage, even though bilateral, or in the nature of a mutual espousal, is null in both forms, unless made before the pastor of the local hierarch, or before a priest to whom the faculty of assisting has been given by either of these.

2. #1. The same pastor or local hierarch or priest designated by either, can validly assist at a promise of marriage, who, by pre-

scription of Canons 86 and 87, can validly assist at the marriage.
#2. He who assists at a promises of marriage is by obligation bound to see to it that the celebration is entered into his book of espousals.
3. However, from the promise of marriage, no judicial action is made available for seeking the celebration of marriage; such action is granted for the repairing of damages if any be due.

Canon 7—The priest assisting at the promise of marriage must not neglect to impart to the Catholic parties the blessing prescribed by the liturgical books, if particular law provides for this.

This canon is practically the same as in the Latin Code, except that it *need not be made in writing.* If a couple belonged to different rites, either pastor may have a choice in the matter. However, it may be more advantageous for the pastor who will eventually assist at the marriage to handle this matter.

SUGGESTIONS FOR THE LATIN RITE CEREMONY

An engagement ceremony may take place as follows:
1. A brief talk can be given by a priest who is dressed in surplice and stole, standing at the altar rail, telling the couple that the promise they will make to each other does not bind under sin. It is well that they come to make it publicly and to ask the Church's blessing on such an important occasion in preparation for the great sacrament of matrimony. The priest can also tell them that an individual who enters a religious community prepares for his life by a novitiate. Candidates for the Priesthood spend many years in study and prayer. So also Matrimony should be entered into with great care and consideration. Some instructions could be given regarding their sincerity and devotion to one another.

2. *The Reading of the Formula of Engagement:* Kneeling at the communion rail or at the altar of the Blessed Virgin, they should listen attentively to the words of the priest. Then standing they read the document together aloud and then sign it. The priest adds his own signature, stating that he has been witness to this proposal and declares them engaged in the name of the Father, of the Son and of the Holy Spirit. And then he should sprinkle them with holy water.

3. *The Blessing of the Engagement Ring:* The formula: *Our help*

is in the name of the Lord/who made heaven and earth. The Lord be with you/And with your spirit. Let us pray: Bless, O Lord, this ring which we bless in thy name, that she who will wear it, keeping full faith with her betrothed, may abide in thy peace and in thy will, through Christ our Lord. Amen. He then sprinkles it with holy water. The man then takes the ring and puts it on the ring finger of the woman with the words: *"In the name of the Father, and of the Son, and of the Holy Spirit."* If it is a double ring ceremony, the woman does the same thing to the man.

4. If further solemnity is desired, the priest may read the Gospel of St. John 15, while all stand. This may be followed by an appropriate hymn sung by the assembled attendants of the couple.

5. Then the engaged couple kneel before the priest who places his stole over their clasped hands and says: *"May God bless your bodies and your souls. May he send His blessing upon you as He blessed Abraham, Isaac, and Jacob. May our blessed Mother keep you in her motherly care. May the Guardian Angel protect you from all harm and lead you on to the path of holiness. Go in peace in the name of Christ. Amen."*

Engagement Contract

We, the undersigned, being of sound mind and understanding full well the obligations to be assumed, do hereby freely and mutually promise to enter into Matrimony on the day........ month................, 19........

In testimony whereof, we affix our signature on this day ...., month ...., 19.........

Signature of man...
Signature of woman..
Signature of pastor..

(Church Seal)

INSTRUCTION OF THE PASTOR

Canon 1018—The pastor must not fail prudently to instruct the people regarding the Sacrament of Matrimony and its impediments

1. Every pastor is a teacher—he must instruct. Therefore, he must have the right knowledge and understanding of the principles of Christian marriage, since the general morality and the common good depends on this.

2. Today, when pornography and sex information of all kinds are being freely distributed to the young, the proper approach to instruction in sexual matters is different from what it was in past generations. Again, with almost one out of three marriages ending in divorce in the United States, a definite stand must be taken by pastors to counteract this deluge of bad information which is distributed daily.

3. This canon uses the word *prudenter,* which cautions the pastor to avoid abruptness or embarrassing situations. There are various means and techniques of dealing with such a delicate subject. The priest instructor should first acquaint himself with the person to be instructed and proceed according to the circumstances; e.g., a different approach would be required in the case of a nurse, or an ordinary layman, or that of an illiterate person, even though the same essential doctrine must be given to each. This is stressed here because unfortunate mistakes have been made in the past in this regard.

4. Every priest has had sufficient training to use good common sense and good judgment. He must face facts; he must explain the principles of marriage and the responsibility married people have to society. He must stress the fact that marriage is not a private matter; that the common good plays an important role in this particular phase of life.

5. Pope Pius XI[2] recommends the study of the encyclical *Casti Connubii,* which deals with the nature and dignity of marriage; and it is imperative that a thorough course in this matter be given in high schools as well as colleges. By all means it should be given to high school students; they are certainly not too young for this instruction, and many of them will not go on to college to be exposed to this at a more mature age. Many modern philosophies, false as they are, are diabolical in their tendency to undermine the good of society. It is the pastor's duty to offset this by insisting on the proper instruction both to the young as well as to those about to be married.

Canon 1018 obliges the pastor to give proper instruction to the parties wishing to enter marriage. In other words, he is to lay the foundation for their future happiness and keep in mind that society is plagued by too many invalid marriages today, and that "an ounce of prevention is worth a pound of cure." Many failures in marriage have been traced to priests who have been a failure in counselling, or have been disinterested, or gave no counsel at all. It would be well if all priests encouraged

---

2. Pius XI, **Casti Connubii** (Christian Marriage), 1930, America Press, New York.

young people to seek counsel and help before deciding to get married.

THE PRENUPTIAL INVESTIGATION

Canon 1019—1. Before a marriage is celebrated it must be certain that nothing stands in the way of its valid and licit celebration. 2. In danger of death, if other proofs cannot be had, and there are no indications to the contrary, the sworn testimony of the contracting parties that they have been baptized and are under no impediment, is sufficient.

1. *The Prenuptial Investigation:* (a) examination of each party privately, (b) publication of the banns.

After giving the parties the proper instructions (cf. C. 1018), the pastor will interrogate privately each party carefully after which he will publish the banns. The reason for such a thorough investigation is to prevent an invalid marriage as well as to show respect for the sacrament of matrimony in the interest of the family and society (cf. Inst. 1941).[3]

2. In danger of death, the law is not so strict for the parties. They merely declare under oath that they are baptized and that they are not under any impediment of marriage. Should there be any impediments, Canons 1043-44-45 should be invoked.

Canon 1020—1. The pastor who has the right to assist at a marriage shall inquire diligently at an opportune time beforehand whether there is an obstacle to the celebration of marriage. 2. He must interrogate both the bridegroom and the bride, even separately and carefully, whether they are under any impediment, whether they are giving their consent freely, and whether they are sufficiently instructed in Christian doctrine, unless in view of the quality of the persons this last question should seem unnecesssary. 3. The local ordinary has the right to establish specific norms for this investigation by the pastor.

Introduction: Too many marriages have failed in our generation due to the negligence of pastors in making the proper investigation before

---

3 S. C. of the **Sacraments:** Instruction on Canonical Investigation. June 29. 1941. **AAS** 33-297.

marriage. These findings are prevalent in so many instances when a search is made in parochial files. Some cases reveal that the pastor had no time to be bothered. Yet, if he had taken the time out to check each couple according to this canon, he would have discovered that they were either not sufficiently instructed, or did not have the proper intention.

1. All pastors have the very grave responsibility to make the proper investigation, even though someone else performs the marriage through his delegation.

2. If the party or parties involved are living away from the parish, the pastor of their residence will investigate the matter and send all his findings to the pastor who will assist at the marriage. Sometimes this is feasible because of the distance and inconvenience.

3. Each party should be interrogated separately. Many things are revealed when they are free to talk. (This is true also when a married couple is having trouble.) Separate investigations are invaluable. We must be prudent in making the investigation, especially when we are dealing with non-Catholics. Priests should be open-minded, discreet and tactful.

4. Historically speaking, the Holy See has tried to impress pastors of this great responsibility.

In 1670, the Holy Office gave definite instructions regarding prenuptial investigations; they were to check carefully to see if there were any impediments and to determine whether they are entering the marriage freely; this question must be directed to the woman especially. It further demanded that priests and bishops comply with this regulation strictly.

In 1911, the Sacred Congregation of the Sacraments again issued a decree regarding this matter and spoke out against careless pastors in this regard. In 1921, a few years after the promulgation of the Code, pastors again were reminded of the evils connected with poor and improper investigations; they were also reprimanded for this laxity. The decree contained the following items of importance:

(1) Ordinaries were instructed to remind all pastors to refrain from assisting at marriages unless they had *satisfactory proof* of the freedom of the parties to marry according to Canons 1020, 1097: 1, n. 1, and above all, to demand certificates of baptism of both if they were baptized in another parish.

(2) The pastor who assisted at the marriage must *promptly* inform

the pastor of baptism of this marriage (C. 1103:2).

(3) For security sake and expediting the matter better, pastors were exhorted to send all necessary documents through their respective chanceries.

(4) Pastors were to consult the Ordinary regarding vagi and immigrants, and migrant workers, except in case of necessity, or danger of death.

(5) If the pastor of baptism received a notice of marriage to be entered into the record and found that the party was married before, he is to consult the Ordinary immediately.

(6) Ordinaries were instructed to impose the necessary canonical sanction on those pastors that were negligent in making the proper prenuptial investigations.

(7) Later in 1941, the Sacred Congregation of the Sacraments sent out detailed instructions on how the pastor was to conduct the prenuptial investigation of the parties; it also gave the form to be used.

From the instructions given above, it is obvious that the Church is concerned about this grave obligation. Negligent pastors had to be reminded from time to time.

Suppose one of the parties or both were totally ignorant of the principles of Christian doctrine, should the pastor delay the marriage until they are sufficiently instructed? The Code Commission answered by saying that the pastor should give them as much instructions as is possible under the circumstances, but if they refuse to come for instructions, the marriage should not be delayed. Because many difficulties do arise after marriage, chanceries are using special forms to cover any and all possibilities.

The Sacred Congregation of the Sacraments, on June 29, 1941, issued an Instruction on the manner of making this investigation. In summary, it indicated that (1) the pastor of the bride has the right and grave duty to investigate whether there are any obstacles to the marriage; he may conduct the inquiry regarding the groom or request the groom's pastor to do so; (2) when the parties are from different dioceses, documents of investigation should be transmitted through the groom's diocesan chancery to the pastor of the bride, or if the marriage is to take place in the domicile of the groom, then the documents should be sent in the same manner to the groom's pastor. It is also suggested that the *nihil obstat* be obtained by the chancery of the place of marriage. Many chanceries have drawn up their matrimonial forms according to this Instruction.

THE ESSENTIAL DOCUMENT-BAPTISM CERTIFICATE

Canon 1021–1. Unless baptism was conferred in his own territory, the pastor shall require proof of baptism of both parties, or from the Catholic party only, if the marriage is to be contracted with a dispensation from the impediment of disparity of cult.
2. Catholics who have not yet received the sacrament of confirmation should first receive this sacrament before being married, if they can do so without grave inconvenience.
Proof of baptism is most essential in the prenuptial investigation.

If the parties were baptized in the same church where the marriage will take place, the proof of baptism can be found in the parish baptismal record. The pastor usually checks the records. If the parties were baptized elsewhere, then they must secure proof of the baptism from the church of baptism. The certificate, will indicate whether the parties are free to marry. It will indicate whether the person was married before, received the order of subdeaconate or solemn religious vows.

Canon 470 obliges all pastors to record in the baptismal register of the parish all these important facts. For this reason Canon 1103 demands that pastors who assist at a marriage send a record of this marriage with the names, dates, witnesses, dispensations received, etc., to the church of baptism. Hence, a certificate of baptism will show whether there was a previous marriage, etc. Information of any marriages that have been declared null by the ecclesiastical court should also be included.

Sometimes we find that baptismal books have been destroyed by fire. One trustworthy witness would suffice to prove reception of baptism, e.g. the Godparent or the priest who baptized. In litigated cases, more proof is needed. *The pastor of a marriage must insist on a baptismal certificate which is issued at least within the past six months. Old certificates must never be accepted.*

Non-Catholics: Pastors must also demand a certificate of baptism from non-Catholics. This will determine just what type of dispensation is needed. If the parties were unbaptized it might be well to ask further questions. This information may prove valuable later on to some matrimonial tribunal.

PUBLICATION OF THE BANNS

Canon 1022—The pastor must announce publicly the names of those persons who are about to contract marriage.

1. In order to safeguard the marriage contract, every possible precaution must be taken. The Council of Trent laid down a law announcing the banns of marriage. The banns of marriage are to be published by the proper pastor of the parties. Athough banns are not required for validity, the pastor should nevertheless in every case discharge this duty to be morally certain that there is no impediment to the marriage.[4]

Place of Publication

Canon 1023—1. The banns of matrimony must be announced by the pastor of the parties.
2. If a party has lived in another locality for a period of six months since attaining puberty, the pastor shall consult his ordinary, who in his prudent discretion will either demand that the banns be announced in that place, or, other proofs of presumptive evidence regarding freedom of the party be gathered
3. If there is any suspicion that an impediment has been incurred, the pastor, even for the case of a briefer period of residence, should consult the ordinary who should not permit the marriage until the suspicion has been removed.

The pastor who is bound to publish the banns is the one in which the parties have their domicile or quasi-domicile (The Catholic acquires a proper parish and pastor either by domicile or quasi-domicile). A domicile is acquired by residence in any parish with the intention to stay there permanently unless something calls one away or one's residence must extend over a period of ten years. A quasi-domicile is acquired by residence in a parish with intention to stay there for the greater part of a year unless something calls the person away, or, by having actually lived there for the greater part of the year, at least more

---

4. (a) Canon 21: Laws are made for the purpose of safeguarding against common danger, bind, even though in a particular case there is no danger.
(b) In some dioceses faculties have been given whereby pastors may dispense from one, two or three banns. Cf. **Diocesan Faculties in the U.S.,** Woodstock College Press, Md., 1948, pp. 22-23

than six months. Canon 92:2 states "If the parties have several domiciles or quasi-domiciles the publication of the banns should be made at the parish churches of each."

It is possible that one could have incurred an impediment or impediments in a place where he or she lived for six months. After reaching the age of puberty,[5] however, it is left to the local ordinary whether the banns should be published in all these places. A difficulty may arise when people have been moving about from place to place because of business or for other reasons and would not be known to the people there, in which case the announcement of the banns would be useless. In such a case the Ordinary may demand testimony of a reliable witness or witnesses. In any case all necessary information regarding the parties should be obtained. Regarding a pending urgent marriage wherein there is not sufficient time to make the necessary investigation the pastor should consult the ordinary; the Code Commission suggested that reliable witnesses and the parties should be questioned on the matter and have them take the suppletory oath (Canon 1829: "This is better than nothing at all.")

Time of Publication

> Canon 1024—The publications are to be made on three successive Sundays or other days of obligation in the church during the solemnities of the Mass or during other divine services at which many people are in attendance.

The code does not specify the manner in which banns are to be published. One should follow the custom of the place. Publication should be made in the vernacular language and specifying the name or names and residences of the parties. The faithful should also be informed that they have a grave obligation to make known any impediment of the parties to the pastor if they know of any.

Form of Publication

> Canon 1025—The ordinary may, for his own territory, substitute for the publications the public posting of the names of the parties on the doors of the church, or near the door of the pa-

---

5. Canon 88: 2. A boy is regarded as having reached the age of puberty when he completes his 14th year; a girl is regarded as having reached the age of puberty when she completes her 12th year.

rochial church or another church for at least eight days provided, however, that within this time two feast days of precept are included.

Although this is a new form of publication of the banns, historically we find it used in the case of necessity with special permission. The oral announcement was customary because many people could not read. The names must be posted at the door of the parish church or another church within the parish limits, e.g., a church of religious if there is one.

Publication for Mixed Marriages

Canon 1026—Publications are not to be made for marriages which are contracted with a dispensation from the impediment of disparity of cult or mixed religion, unless the local ordinary in his prudent judgment, in the absence of scandal, deems it advisable to permit them, provided that the apostolic dispensation has been obtained previously and no mention is made of the religion of the non-Catholic party.

This prohibition is had because otherwise the publication might encourage others to mixed marriages. Here in the U.S. it has been the custom not to make such announcements. In one large city in the U.S. where there is a great non-Catholic population, out of 53 marriages that occurred, 50 were mixed marriages and announcement of banns was made only three times in that year. Publication of banns in mixed marriages is very seldom done although it is known that permission can be granted by Rome. The publication of banns is also prohibited in marriages of conscience and in marriages in danger of death.

Duty of the Faithful

Canon 1027—All the faithful are bound to reveal to their pastor or local ordinary impediments, if they know of any, before the celebration of marriage.

This is a grave obligation on the part of the faithful stemming from the natural and divine law and for the benefit of the common good. No exception is made for a relative or friends. Only a grave reason would excuse them from divulging this information. Historically, in 1886, the

Synod of Baltimore[6] inflicted excommunication on persons who neglected to reveal such impediments. This is an indication of the gravity of the matter. One would be excused from revealing this information if the information came from a sacramental confession. If the knowledge came through some particular profession as, for example, a doctor or a lawyer or a priest outside of confession, there is no need to reveal it because the common good may suffer or that particular profession might suffer because of this. Although some authors hold that if it is not revealed, harm would come to a third party.

Dispensations

> Canon 1028—1. The local ordinary of the parties can in his prudent judgment for a legitimate cause dispense from making the publications even in another diocese.
>
> 2. If there are several proper ordinaries, that one has the right to dispense in whose diocese the marriage takes place; if the marriage takes place outside the parties' own diocese, then any ordinary of either party can dispense.

When we speak of legitimate reasons for the local ordinary to dispense his subjects in a strange diocese, we may enumerate among these: (a) danger of civil marriage; (b) fear of scandal; (c) a business trip; (d) transfer from one military post to another. Of course, it is presumed that freedom to marry has been established.

C A S E

(Domiciles or Quasi-Domiciles) *A wishes to marry B in Washington, D.C.* A has a domicile in Boston and a quasi-domicile in Connecticut. B has a domicile in Reno and a quasi-domicile in Los Angeles. The ordinaries from any of these dioceses of the domiciles or quasi-domiciles can grant the dispensation. Since a pastor may marry parties who have stayed in his parish for at least one month without acquiring a domicile or quasi-domicile, it seems a fortiori (C. 1097: 1, no. 3) that the pastor's ordinary would also have the right to dispense from the banns even though he is not mentioned among the ordinaries in this particular canon. Woywood is hesitant in admitting this.[7]

---

6. Synodus Diocesan Baltimorensie 9, p. 51.
7. Woywood, S., O.F.M., **A Practical Commentary on the Code of Canon Law**, Wagner, Inc., New York, p. 664.

Canon 1029—If another pastor has conducted the investigation or the publications, he must immediately by an authentic document send information as to the result of the same to the pastor who must assist at the marriage.

This sometimes happens when parties move about the country and belong to several dioceses. According to the instructions of 1941, the *nihil obstat* should be given by the respective chanceries.

After Publication

Canon 1030—1. After the investigation and the publications the pastor shall not assist at the marriage, until he has received all the necessary documents, and unless a reasonable cause warrants it, not until *three days have elapsed* since the last publication. 2. If the marriage is not contracted within six months, the publications must be repeated unless the ordinary of the place decides otherwise.

The pastor must wait three days so that any documents, reports, dispensations, receipts, that are necessary will be in his possession before the marriage takes place. For a serious reason of inconvenience, the pastor may go ahead with the marriage without consulting the ordinary to dispense with these three days.

Canon 1031—If a doubt has arisen concerning the existence of some impediment: (1) The pastor shall investigate the matter more thoroughly by questioning, under oath at least two trustworthy witnesses, unless the impediment is one which if known would injure the good reputation of the parties, and if necessary he shall also question the parties in the same way. (2) He shall make or finish the publication if a doubt arose before they have been begun or before they are finished; (3) If he prudently judges that the doubt still exists he must not assist at the marriage without consulting the ordinary.
2. If a certain impediment has been discovered: (1) If the impediment is occult, the pastor shall continue or complete the publications and refer the matter, without mentioning the names, to the local ordinary or to the Sacred Penitentiary; (2) If the impediment is public and is detected before the publications are

begun, the pastor shall not proceed further until the impediment has been removed, even though he may know that a dispensation has been obtained in the forum of conscience alone, if it is detected after the first or second publication of banns, the pastor shall finish the publications and refer the matter to the local ordinary.

3. Finally, if no impediment has been detected, either doubtful or certain, the pastor, the publication having been completed, shall admit the parties to the celebration of marriage.

The pastor usually encounters no difficulties such as are mentioned in this canon because he usually knows the individuals and their families. When the pastor does not know the parties, he should proceed cautiously. He will, of course, have many investigations before publishing banns. The law states that if a doubt arises before the publication of the banns, he should endeavor to solve that doubt before beginning the publication. If the doubt cannot be solved, the law does not forbid him to go ahead with the announcement. Someone might be present who knows more about the parties and this impediment, and can inform the pastor if they are aware of this impediment. If the doubt arose just before the official announcement, the code specifies that he go ahead. If the doubt arose during the period of the time of the announcement of the banns, he must go ahead and complete them. Should the doubt still remain after the publication, the pastor should consult the Ordinary before proceeding with the marriage. The necessary precautions are taken here, otherwise, the sacrament of matrimony might be exposed to danger of nullity and lead the parties into a union which would be sinful. Every effort should be made to remove any doubts that might occur, in which case interrogation of the witnesses is in order. If the pastor finds that the impediment is occult, the publication of the banns continues and in the meantime the pastor should write for the proper dispensation. If the impediment happens to be public, nothing should be done without obtaining a dispensation.

V A G I

Canon 1032—Except in the case of necessity, the pastor should never assist at the marriage of vagi, as described in Canon 91, unless, after he has referred the case to the local ordinary or to the priest delegated by him, he has obtained permission to assist.

A vagus is one who has neither domicile nor quasi-domicile (Cs. 91 and 92). This is not an unusual occurrence but if it happens, the pastor should consult the ordinary. In danger of death, an oath of their freedom to marry would suffice. Proper instructions for parties, according to the various needs of the individuals on the sanctity of the sacrament of matrimony, initial obligation and the obligation of parents toward their children should be given. The pastor shall earnestly exhort them before the marriage to make a good confession of their sins and to receive Holy Communion devoutly.

FORMULA IN ANNOUNCING THE BANNS OF MARRIAGE IN A PARISH

Banns of Marriage

Be it Known to All Here Present That the Following Parties, God Willing, Purpose to Marry. Therefore, We Advise Each and Everyone to Whom it Concerns That if Any Person Knows of Any Impediment of Consanguinity, Affinity, Spiritual Relationship, or Any Other Impediment, or Any Other Reason Which Would Prevent These Parties from Entering into the State of Matrimony, He is Hereby Bound to Advise the Pastor or Any Other Priest, of This Fact as Soon as Possible.

First Time: *John A. Brown*, son of Maurice C. Brown and Mary Baker of St. James Parish and *Anna M. Smith*, daughter of Michael Smith and Mary Jones, of St. Rita's Parish. [Same, second and third times]

INSTRUCTIONS TO THE SPOUSES

Canon 1033—The pastor must not omit, with due regard to the condition of the persons concerned, to instruct the parties on the sanctity of matrimony, their mutual obligations, the obligation of parents toward their children; he shall earnestly exhort them to make a careful confession of their sins and receive with devotion the Most Blessed Eucharist.

Through the investigation of marriage cases, it has been found that many couples have not been given the proper instruction by their pastors. Perhaps the instructions would have saved the marriage. If pastors would take this canon seriously, they would give all the instructions necessary. Every case is different. Some parties need more than other parties. Giving instructions to the people on Sunday is very good but this canon has reference to private instructions. This canon is connected with Canon 1018, and all the recommendations given there should be followed in such an instruction. To receive so great a sacrament as matrimony and to venture into a new profession for a lifetime, the parties need all the graces and blessings that are possible. Hence, this canon strongly exhorts the pastor to persuade the parties to make a good confession and to receive Holy Communion. Confession and Communion are not obliged by any law; it is highly recommended. To receive sacraments in mortal sin only aggravates the situation. It could result in sacrilege.

TEENAGE CASES

In one such case, we found that a girl, 16, who was pregnant wanted to marry the boy of 17. The girl's parents would not hear of it. The parents of the boy were in favor of it, because they knew many people who married at such an age with success; the couple presented a marriage license to the pastor and threatened to have a civil ceremony if he would not marry them. Although the couple were sixteen and seventeen, the license indicated that they were twenty-one. The pastor called the chancery and got the permission to marry them. The problem arose whereby the father of the girl was going to sue the pastor, for even though he knew this, the official civil license gave him the right to marry them. According to civil law, this judgment was passed by the civil official that they were of age; the pastor merely had a permission to marry them, not to investigate them. The father of the girl was informed that a perjury charge could be brought against his daughter. The case was dropped.

Pastors must point out to all parents and teenage individuals that venturing into the field of matrimony at this age, without any formal training makes it difficult to face the economic problems of providing a home, and to raise a family; one is trying to compete with many skilled professional men who are unemployed. After putting up with this situation for a time, the young couple becomes disgruntled and upset and eventually are seeking a way out of their marriage. The result of one third of the divorces stems from such a source.

Due to the fact that 50% of all teenage marriages end in divorce, California has introduced a state law (Nov. 1970), designed to make it more difficult for teenagers to marry:

"To marry, any boy or girl under 18 must get: Superior Court's permission; permission from parents or guardian; and premarital counseling can be required by the court (court permission was formerly required only for girls under 16)."

JUSTICE OF THE PEACE AND MARRIAGE

QUESTION: Is a justice of the peace obligated to perform all marriage ceremonies that come to his attention?

A justice of the peace is not required by law to perform a marriage ceremony. *It is a privilege of his office to do so.* Most judges of our Common Pleas Court refuse to perform marriage ceremonies stating publicly that this is a matter peculiarly for a cleric. They too have the right to officiate at a wedding. A justice of the peace is not obligated to offer his services to all callers nor can he be required to perform a marriage ceremony against his will. Before performing a marriage ceremony, a justice of the peace is not required to make any investigation other than to be satisfied that the parties are of age and that a marriage license has been issued. Before a justice of the peace may perform a ceremony, the parties must present to him a marriage license which they have previously obtained from the marriage license clerk in the Orphan's Court Office. It is the duty of the license clerk to ascertain whether the parties are of age and otherwise free to marry, i.e., whether either party has a spouse in being from whom no divorce has been granted. A justice of the peace may marry anyone in his office who brings to him the marriage license regardless of whether the parties reside outside of the county or state. He himself can perform the ceremony any place within the Commonwealth.

A priest who also holds the office of Justice of the Peace can refuse, as a justice of the peace, to perform the ceremony. Indeed, it would be his duty to do so. The same holds true for a Catholic layman who holds the office of Justice of the Peace.[8]

MARRIAGE OF MINORS: TEENAGERS

Canon 1034—The pastor must seriously exhort minors from contracting marriage without the knowledge or against the reasonable wishes of their parents; but if they refuse to obey, he should

---

8. Moore, Thos., Esq., Legal Reply, Luzerne County, Penn.

not assist at their marriage without having first consulted the local ordinary.

Rights and Duties of Minors

1. This law is based on the legislation of the Council of Trent and adopted by the codifiers who uphold the rights of minors to marry, but emphasize their duty to parents.

2. The implication is that minors can marry validly without their parents' consent; although they should consult their parents, it in no way gives them absolute right to command them in the choice of a partner. If the parents have a reasonable cause to oppose the marriage and they are insistent, the pastor should consult the Ordinary of the diocese. Want of consent of the parents is in no way a prohibitive impediment. However, pastors and diocesan authorities are urged to give the matter utmost consideration because even though minors have a right, it is not always feasible to use this right for economical, psychological, and spiritual reasons. *The best answer to this situation is deferment.*

Due to the fact that many teenage marriages do not succeed, it is necessary to legislate some more stringent laws to curtail this problem. For those who feel reluctant to curtail such marriages, we recommend Father Anthony Bevilaqua's excellent survey. (*Problem Areas in Chancery Practice; Refusal or Deferral of Baptism and Marriage*). Cf, this section on Marriage is included in the Appendix).

THE POLICY OF ORLANDO DIOCESE RE: TEENAGE MARRIAGE

1. Concern for Welfare

The Catholic Church is deeply concerned about the welfare of her members. She wants them to be happy and satisfied in this world and to be united with God, our Father, in heaven after death. One of the greatest obstacles toward achieving happiness and satisfaction is the breakup of family life. This is especially true of families whose marriage began at an early age.

According to the National Center of Health Statistics, 56% of all divorces occur before the parties reach the age of 24. 33% of all divorced couples are teenagers. 62% of all divorced men, and 75% of all divorced women were under twenty-five years of age at the time of their marriage. Norms for statistical evidence differ, but the inference is made: the lower the age of marriage, the greater the probability of divorce. The experience of Family Life Directors leads them to the same conclusion. Msgr. James T. McHugh of the Family Life Bureau of the National Catholic Conference of Bishops indicated that 7 out of 10 marriages involving teenagers end in separation or divorce. In teenage marriages where pregnancy was a factor, 90% break up.

Church officials are very much aware of the fact that in marital marriages requiring a dispensation of some kind, premarital pregnancy is on the increase. This "factor" puts extreme pressure on the teenagers to see "Marriage as a solution." In the "Lack of Form" cases handled by diocesan tribunals, it becomes clear that well over *half* of the "Broken Marriages" began with a pregnant girl.

These facts are understandable. They corroborate the legitimate presumption that many teenagers are not mature enough, emotionally, spiritually, intellectually, financially to handle the rights, the obligations, and the responsibilities of marriage in contemporary society. This seems true even when one does not consider the factor of religion. Even a sturdy Catholic faith will not adequately compensate for the pressure put on youngsters trying to fulfill the responsibility of adults.

The right to marry is a natural right of high priority. It is not, however, an unrestricted right. Both Church and State can establish legitimate restrictions. Such restrictions must be founded in serious causes, whereby the proposed marriage is shown to be in conflict with Christian Revelation, or posing a threat to the common good of society.

The Church takes a minimum view of essential personal requirements and sums it all up by saying: "all persons who are not prohibited by law, can contract marriage" (c. 1035). Canon 1067 establishes a minimum age for marriage. This law is keyed to an understanding of marriage which concentrates on the biological capability of reproduction. This law was enacted at a time when the way of life provided a setting in which one might hope for marital stability. Today, in our present American culture, these guarantees are frequently absent.

Many priests feel helpless where the legal and the minimal and/or pregnancy factor leads the priest to believe that marriage has little hope for success. Even though the priests may try to dissuade the couple, they feel that the *Natural Right to Marry*, and the established *Canonical Age* make it impossible for them to refuse, or even to postpone the marriage.

Because of the ultra-romanticism to which couples are subject, many couples do not come to terms with the realities and the responsibilities of married life. Sexual and emotional involvement blur their picture of the future, and the demands that marriage will put on them. When the girl becomes pregnant, there is very little tendency for her, or the boy, to seek counsel, or to search for possible alternatives to marriage. To protect their rights, to assure their future happiness and stability, every possible assistance should be given to help them understand, if they now are, or now are not ready for marriage. Marriage is not a solution to problems. All too often it causes greater problems.

Marriage entails serious responsibilities: *moral, spiritual, sexual, familial, financial, societal.*

It takes a certain minimal level of maturity to fulfill those responsibilities. One who gives positive indications of possessing this minimal maturity should not be excluded from marriage. Anyone who does not give positive indications of possessing such minimal maturity is *Precluded by the Natural Law* from marrying, since no one has a right to enter into a contract which he is incapable of fulfilling.

The fact that the individual *"Thinks"* he is capable, or insists to the Church that he is, does not relieve the Church of the obligation to make its own judgment in individual cases.

Canon 1039:1 advises that "Ordinaries of places can forbid marriages in a particular case, but only temporarily, for a just cause, as long as the just cause continues." This canon would supply the legal basis on which a policy of selective postponement of an indissoluble sacramental marriage of some ill-prepared teenagers would be founded.

The policy devised attempts to guarantee these objectives:

Upholding the right to marry where both parties, though quite young, give evidence of required minimal maturity.

Wide enough consultation with experienced persons of good judgment, to insure that the evaluation is objective. This consultation should include both lay and clergy.

The opportunity for the couple to avail themselves of prudent counselors who will help them face up to the serious aspects of the lifelong commitment that marriage demands.

Postponement of sacramental marriage until such time as an adequate level of maturity is reached by both parties.

2. Diocesan Policy for Youthful Marriages

When either party requesting marriage has not yet reached his/her nineteenth (19) birthday, the following norms will be observed in the Diocese of Orlando:

The date of the wedding may *not* be set until all the steps required herein have been taken.

There will be a three (3)-month mandatory waiting period from the time of the first interview with the priest.

The priest and couple will have an in-depth interview(s).

Both parents of the boy and of the girl will be interviewed by the priest.

The couple will be referred to Catholic Social Services for evaluation by a professional counselor.

The couple must attend the Pre-Cana Program.

The Tribunal will authorize the marriage in writing to the referring priest.

3. Guidelines for Priests

When the couple first approach the priest to make preparation for marriage, he should inform them of the Diocesan policies regarding youthful marriages and assist them through its various stages.

The priest should conduct an in-depth interview with the couple (separately and together) in order to understand better their motives for marriage, level of maturity, and readiness to receive the sacrament.

This interview will investigate factors which are influencing the decision to marry, such as pregnancy, family back-ground, parents' attitudes, desire to escape an unpleasant home situation, degree of infatuation, etc.

The interview will also consider the financial status of the couple including salary, savings, debts, ability to handle money, and budget planning.

The spiritual status will be reviewed, emphasizing church attendance, reception of the sacraments, fidelity to religious instruction, and attitudes toward divorce.

Other topics for this interview include: courtship, sexuality, pregnancy, family relationships, personal goals and leisure-time activities.

The attached *Suggested Guide Questionnaire* provides an outline for developing a fruitful dialogue with the couple. Not all questions are apropo for all couples but the material covered is generally applicable to most couples.

Following the interviews with the couple and their parents, the priest completes a form which records his judgment of the couple and his recommendation regarding the suitability of the marriage at this time. A copy is sent to the Catholic Social Services office which will be evaluating the couple.

Although this procedure is required only in the case of a premarital pregnancy or when either party has not yet reached the 19th birthday, the priest may desire to use it in situations where the parties are older but the level of maturity and understanding is seriously limited.

4. Evaluation by Professional Counselors

After the priest has interviewed the couple and their parents, he will refer them to Catholic Social Services for evaluation by a professional counselor.

The couple is to be referred to the Catholic Social Services office most convenient to them. Offices are located in Orlando, Daytona Beach, Cocoa and Lakeland. When the couple arrange the appointment, they may request that the interview be held in their city if they reside in an outlying area and are unable to travel to one of the above offices. This would apply to residents in such areas as Fort Pierce, Vero Beach, Ocala, Leesburg, Sebring, etc.

Catholic Social Services personnel may find it necessary from time to time to call on others in the Diocese to assist in this evaluation process. This might occur when staff are on vacation, or during particularly busy periods, or for the convenience of the couple, or for purposes of confidentiality, etc. In such circumstances, a counselor would be selected from the following.

(Names and addresses listed.)

The fee for the first counseling interview will be paid by the couple at the time of the interview. It is anticipated that the majority of the couples will require one or two interviews.

A summary of the counselor' assessment of the couple will be sent to the referring priest who will send the completed file to the Tribunal.

The Catholic Social Services staff will be available for on-going counseling, especially for those couples with negative evaluations.

The tribunal will request an additional report from a second counselor when there is one positive evaluation and one negative evaluation from the priest and the first counselor. Following review of these reports, the tribunal will notify the referring priest of the decision.

5. Suggested Guide Questionnaire for Fruitful Dialogue

PRESENT (*Courtship*)
1. When did you begin dating?
2. What attracted you to your fiancé(e)?
3. What kind of activities do you share together?
4. How often have you been seeing each other?
5. How did the subject of marriage arise?
6. When did you definitely decide to marry (formal engagement)?
7. Have you broken up during your courtship? Why?
   How do you deal with differences of opinion between you?
   Who usually gives in? Why?
8. Have you made any preparations for the wedding?
   Who? What?
9. What motives do you have for considering marriage now?
   Any hesitations about your decisions?
10. Is a pregnancy involved?

(*If Pregnant*)
   How long (have you/has she) been pregnant?
   Who is the father?
   Were you considering marriage before the pregnancy?
   Are your parents aware of your plans?
   Have you thought of other solutions?

(*Religious Attitudes*)
1. Describe your own religious beliefs and practices
   as well as those of your fiancé,e).
2. How does religion influence your present relationship?
3. Why have you come to the Church to be married?
4. What in your opinion are the most important elements
   of a (Christian) marriage?
5. Does the statement that marriage is a commitment for life
   have meaning for you?

PAST (*Family Background*)
1. Describe your own parents; brothers; sisters.
2. How do you get along with them?
3. Which of your parents is more dominant?

4. Which of your parents do you get along better with? Why?
5. Do you presently live at home? If not, why not?
6. What has been the degree of happiness or unhappiness of the relationship of your parents in their marriage? (Separated or divorced?)
7. How are the differences of opinions or quarrels solved by your parents?
8. What in your family experience do you resent most? What do you treasure most?
9. Describe your fiancé(e)'s family life. How does he/she get along with his/her parents? Which parent is dominant?
10. Do you think your fiancé(e) is marrying to escape unhappiness at home?
11. What do both sets of parents think of the marriage?
12. Has anyone tried to dissuade you from marriage?
13. What sort of relationship do you anticipate having with your parents and in-laws after the marriage?

(*Education*)
1. How far did you go in your formal education?
2. Did you enjoy school?
3. If further education is needed, how would you manage that?

(*Life Experience*)
1. Have either of you dated others? Did either of you ever decide to marry someone else?
2. How much sexual experience have you had? Is this known to your fiancé(e)?
3. Do you both have close friends? How long have you known them?
4. Do you know many happily married couples?
5. Have either of you had any significant medical history (physical or psychological)?
6. Do either of you have any problems with alcohol, drugs, gambling?

FUTURE (*In General*)
1. Would you tell me why you and your fiancé(e) believe that you are mature enough to assume the lifelong responsibilities of marriage?

2. What are your strengths and weaknesses as you see them? How do you think they will affect your marriage? What are your fiancé(e)'s strengths and weaknesses? How do you think they will affect your marriage?

4. Does your fiancé(e) have any characteristics that you would like to change after you get married?

(In Particular—Finances)

1. Are you or your fiancé(e) working? Have you had many jobs? How much do you earn? How much have you saved? Any debts? How much?

2. How often do you speak about your future home? aboutfur niture? future recreational activity?

3. Where do you plan to live? If with parents, what effect will this have on your relationship?

4. How will you help and assist one another in the beginning of your marriage?

5. What decision have you come to in regard to budgeting? What experience have you had in budgeting? Who will look after the budget?

6. How much do you think you will need in the beginning for living expenses per week?

7. Do you feel that you and your fiancé(e) have planned well enough for your economic future?

(Sexuality)

1. Have you and your fiancé(e) spoken about the number of children you will have? Do you both agree?

2. How many children do you plan on having? (Good opportunity to present the teaching of the Church on family planning)

3. What are your ideas concerning the place of sexuality in your forthcoming marriage?

4. How would you react to the possibility that your loved one would need affection and sexual expression more than you? What would be your responsibilities in this area?

5. What are some of the chief duties you will have as (Christian) parents? Do you look forward to these obligations?

6. Do you believe that you and your fiancé(e) have decided to marry after sincere and mature deliberation with complete freedom of choice and because you truly love one another?
7. What will your exchange of marriage vows mean for you?

In addition to the recommendations on teenage marriages, there are several new developmtnts in the area of marriage preparation in general which are being used in a number of dioceses (Cleveland, Newark, Denver (1977), Cheyenne, etc.) They are willing to assist others who are in need of such information.

CHAPTER THREE

IMPEDIMENTS IN GENERAL
KINDS OF IMPEDIMENTS

Canon 1035—All persons may contract marriage who are not prohibited by law. All persons have a natural right to marry. Natural society is founded by God for the propagation of the race. Hence, this right must be honored, unless there is some prohibition of the divine or ecclesiastical law. Since marriage between the baptized is a sacrament, the ecclesiastical authority must always safeguard the sanctity of holy matrimony. Hence, the Church must determine how, when, and where the marriage will be celebrated. The prohibition mentioned in this canon occurs when there is some impediment which could render a marriage illicit or invalid.

Canon 1036—1. A prohibiting impediment contains a grave prohibition against contracting marriage, which, however, is not indeed invalid if it is contracted notwithstanding the impediment.
2. A diriment impediment both gravely prohibits the marriage and prevents it from being concluded validly.
3. Although an impediment exists only on the part of *one party*, nevertheless, the marriage is illicit or invalid.

Commentary

1. Impeding Impediments: simple vows; mixed religion; relationship through adoption if forbidden by law.
2. Diriment Impediments: want of age; impotency; existing bond of previous marriage; disparity of cult; sacred orders; solemn religious vows; abduction; crime; consanguinity through adoption, if according to

itual relationships; legal relationship through adoption, if according to the law of the states, it invalidates marriage.

3. Impediments are said to be absolute if they prohibit marriage with any person; they are said to be relative if they prohibit a marriage with some particular person only.

Canon 1036: 1, prohibits marriage; however, if it is contracted, it does not invalidate the marriage, that is, it forbids marriage under the pain of sin but does not invalidate it.

A diriment is one which not only gravely prohibits any marriage contract but makes the marriage null and void.

Furthermore, the canon mentions that if an impediment exists in only one of the parties it presents an obstacle because the marriage contract is indivisible. Consequently, if it is invalid for one, it is equally as invalid for the other to make the contract. An impediment could effect one or both parties: *one party:* impediment of age, impotency, ligamen or sacred orders. *Both parties:* consanguinity, affinity, adoption or spiritual relationship. In other words, both parties must be qualified to make the contract.

PUBLIC AND OCCULT IMPEDIMENTS

Canon 1037—An impediment is considered as public, if it can be proved in the external forum; otherwise it is occult.

A public impediment is one which can be proved in the external forum, that is, the circumstances from which it arises are public. Facts can be proved in the external forum in most cases either by authentic public documents (C. 1816) (e.g., sacred orders, religious vows, disparity of cult, consanguinity, affinity, etc.) OR, two trustworthy witnesses (C. 1791:2) who can testify because of their personal knowledge, OR one exceptional witness with regard to official acts (C. 1791:1).

The reason why we have a distinction between public and occult impediments, because (with the former) after a dispensation, this fact must be put in the public record. Confessors therefore should be very careful in dispensing from such impediments. A conflict may arise between the internal and the external forum. (An impediment *occult by nature* would be, e.g., a private vow, crime arising from adultery or conjugicide, ocult consanguinity.) We have an *occult case* when an impediment is *public by nature and occult in fact*, e.g., consanguinity which is *public by nature but not known* in a new domicile - city or town.

Canon 1038—1. The Supreme Authority of the Church has the sole right to declare authentically in what instances the divine law forbids or invalidates marriage.
2. The same Supreme Authority has the exclusive right of establishing impedient or diriment impediments for baptized persons either by universal or particular law.

Canon 1039—1. Local ordinaries can forbid marriage in a particular case, but only temporarily, for a just cause, and as long as the cause continues, to all persons actually sojourning in their territory, and to their subjects even outside their territory.
2. Only the Holy See has the power to add an invalidating clause to the prohibition.

The ordinary of the place may forbid a certain marriage only as long as the cause exists; for example, if there is danger of scandal, doubtful impediment, etc. *The ordinary cannot prohibit a marriage under pain of nullity.* If, for instance, an ordinary enacts a law that no marriage whatsoever can be celebrated in his diocese after 6:00 p.m., would the marriage be invalid if this law were disobeyed, viz., performing the marriage at 8:00 p.m.? *This canon forbids such a sanction,* therefore the marriage would be valid but illicit.

Canon 1040—No one except the Roman Pontiff can abrogate or derogate impediments of ecclesiastical law whether they be impedient or diriment; nor dispense from the same unless this power has been granted either by the common law or by special indult from the Holy See.

This canon deals exclusively with ecclesiastical law for no human authority can abrogate or dispense from impediments of the divine law. The Holy Father can abrogate an impediment—take it out completely from the Code, or derogate it by taking out only part of the law as he did in 1949 regarding Canon 1099:2. (Motu Proprio, Pius XII, August 1, 1948)

Canon 1041—A custom which introduces a new impediment or one which is contrary to an existing impediment is reprobated.

Canon 1042—1. Some impediments are of minor, others of major grade.

2. Impediments of minor grade: (1) *Consanguinity in the third degree* of the collateral line; (2) *Affinity* in the second degree of the collateral line; (3) *Public propriety* in the second degree; (4) Spiritual relationship. (5) Crime resulting from adultery with a promise OR attempt at marriage, even by a merely civil act.

3. Impediments of a major grade are all the others.

This distinction is made to indicate that those of minor grade are more easily dispensed. Note: Although all these are minor degree, they are diriment impediments. In the new proposed laws this canon is omitted.

MARRIAGE IN DANGER OF DEATH

Canon 1043—In the danger of death, the local ordinaries *for the peace of conscience, and,* if the case warrants it, for the *legitimation of offspring,* both to *the form observed in the celebration of marriage* and as to all *ecclesiastical impediments,* public or occult even multiple, *except impediments* arising from the *sacred order of priesthood* and from *affinity in the direct line of a consummated marriage* can dispense their own subjects wherever they may be, and all persons actually staying in their territory, provided that scandal be removed, and, if a dispensation of disparity of cult or mixed religion is granted, the usual prescribed promises must be given.

Canon 1044—In the same circumstances as mentioned in Canon 1043 and only for cases in which the local ordinary cannot be reached, the pastor as well as the priest who assists at the marriage, according to Canon 1098:2, and the confessor for the internal forum and in the act of confession only, have the same faculties of dispensing.

1. To clarify these canons, it is best to study all the elements involved separately. We all know that the Church grants extraordinary faculties on extraordinary occasions. From the common law, Canon 882, in danger of death, grants to any priest all the faculties necessary to absolve the dying person from all censures, sins, even though the

priest has no faculties in that particular territory. This (C. 1043-44) is a complicated canon, but it can be made clear if each part is studied separately. The Church gives these very extensive powers of dispensation to the local ordinary and also to the priest mentioned there, when there is danger that a party may die before the priest can in the ordinary mode of communication get a dispensation from the Holy See. By an ordinary communication we mean a personal interview, letter, cablegram, etc.

What about telephone or telegraph? It is not absolutely impossible to contact the Holy See in our day and age. However, the committee for the authentic interpretation of code, Nov. 12, 1922, condemned the use of the telephone or the telegraph in such cases, because these are extraordinary means; and, moreover, are not safe. Furthermore, in 1891, the Papal Secretary of State, had declared that "the Supreme Pontiff *orders* that all applications or favors made to the Roman Curia by telephone or telegraph shall be ignored, and that he wants the bishops to do the same."

2. Ordinaries of places are those mentioned in Canon 198, viz, bishops, (residential) not merely a titular bishop or an auxiliary, unless he is also a vicar general; an abbot nullius; vicar general; apostolic administrator, papal apostolic; prefect apostolic; or temporary administrator during a vacancy.

3. The circumstances requisite for the use of the powers here granted are: (a) *danger of death;* (b) *for the sake of relieving a person's conscience;* (c) for the *legitimation of children;* (d) *dispense from the form of marriage;* (e) *dispense from all and each ecclesiastical impediments,* public, occult or multiple; (f) *that all scandal be removed;* (g) *that the cautiones or guarantees be given if the dispensation from disparity of cult or mixed religion be given at the time.*

4. Canon 1040 explicitly states that "no one except the Holy Father has the power to dispense from prohibitive or diriment impediments, unless it has been granted him by common law or by special apostolic indult.

The primary factor of this canon is the salvation of souls. Therefore, the law is set up for this particular purpose. *Due to certain circumstances, the distance of the Holy See, the urgent necessity, as well as the danger of death,* Canon 1043 provides a means whereby the Ordinary of the Place and others do not have permission from the Holy Father or the Holy See, neither does he need a special indult to grant certain important dispensations. Why? Because the common law gives the Ordinary these faculties, these same faculties are given to the pastor and other priests mentioned in that Canon.

5. *Danger of death is one of the requisites to use these faculties;* this *does not mean immediate or extreme danger* (articulo mortis) but any *ordinary danger* which arises from (1) *internal cause* and (2) *external cause.* An *internal intrinsic cause* such as an accident, where injury is sustained, disease, illness, or a serious operation, such as surgery. *Extrinsic or external* might be special or unusual circumstances that place persons in danger of death. These may come from two sources; (1) *natural causes* and (2) *social causes.*

Natural causes, such as catastrophes, i.e., earthquakes, epidemics, mine disasters, innundations.

Social causes, i.e., a serious disturbance of peace and public order from bloody revolutions, insurrections, invasion by enemies, mobilization, civilians who reside in war zones carryng on battle, civilians exposed to air attacks, dangerous missions, prisoners awaiting capital punishment.[1]

6. *Must we be certain of death?* Certainty is not required but the law of probability is sufficient to use these faculties. *If no actual danger of death is present objectively,* but prudently determined probable, the faculties are valid and can be used. Other requisites for the valid use of these faculties are either *peace of conscience* or *legitimation of children* or both together. Peace of conscience is sufficient in itself. The ordinary, pastor, etc., who uses these faculties should keep in mind that *it is unnecessary that both parties seek peace of mind.* If only one of them seeks this, this party does not have to be the one who is in danger of death, nor the one who has the impediment to the marriage.[2] The reason for peace of mind need not be the need for sacramental absolution.[3]

It is not necessary that the confession be *Sacramentally Valid.* Nor is it necessary that absolution be given (by the confessor) from an impediment in the Internal Forum. It may be, for example, to remove the proximate occasion of sin, or some grave cause of contention, such as a legal controversy over property, reparation of injury or loss of reputation. An example of *peace of mind: Mrs. Smith, a Catholic, calls you about her husband, an unbaptized, who is dying.* They are not married validly. Mr. Smith does wish to become baptized, and he is willing

---

1. Dowdell, **Celebration of Marriage in Danger of Death,** Vatican Press, Rome, 1944, p. 529.
2. Clays Bowaaert-Simenon, **Manuale Juris Canonis,** Gandae et Leodin, No. 250.
3. Bouscaren-Ellis, **Comm. on Code of Canon Law,** Bruce, 1956, p. 487.

to do anything to give peace of mind to Mrs. Smith. Mrs. Smith does not want to go to confession. The pastor can't get in touch with the ordinary. Mrs. Smith was in a convent before and was never dispensed from vows. She is also related to Mr. Smith as a second cousin. The dispensation can be granted and the marriage validated.

Legitimation of Children:[4] (1) When peace of mind is not sought, but merely the legitimation of children, there is a rare case. Authors do not agree on this. 2. Suppose the children were spurious, i.e., *adulterine* (born while one of the parties was in vows or sacred orders), in virtue of Canon 1051 the children could not be legitimated. Canon 1051 "a dispensation from a diriment impediment. . . ." "There is granted also *ipso facto* the legitimation of children in case any have already been born *or* were conceived by the parties who are being dispensed, *with the exception, however, of adulterine and sacrilegious children.*" Now, this canon deals with normal cases and not cases in danger of death.

(2) Nor could the children already born, by subsequent marriage of the parties, be legitimized according to *Canons* 1114 and 1116, when the only reason for granting the dispensation is the legitimation of offspring. *Canon* 1114: "Children who are conceived or born, of a valid or putative marriage, are considered legitimated *unless*, at the time of conception the *marriage contracted was forbidden to the parents* because of *solemn religious profession* or *the reception of sacred orders.*" *Canon* 1116 "by a subsequent marriage of the parents whether a true marriage or a putative marriage (one in good faith), whether newly contracted or validated, even though not consummated, the children are legitimated provided that the parents were free to marry." Wernz-Vidal, Gasparri, Ojetti, De Smet and others. It must be noted that in case of sacrilegious offspring, that a dispensation from the diriment impediment of solemn vows or sacred orders at the hour of death, secures the legitimation of the children *not yet born.*

For adulterine and sacrilegious children already born: Some authors claim that the faculties of Canons 1043 and 1044 can be used even in the case of adulterine and sacrilegious children *already born*, because it could facilitate (after marriage is contracted) in obtaining an indult of legitimation from the Holy See. The phrase "*ad consulendum legitimationi prolis*" is the reason for using the 1043 and 1044 Canons which contain the faculty to dispense from such marriage impediments. Moreover, there are other authors who hold the *probable opinion* that adulterine or

---

4. **The Jurist,** "The Philosophy of Legitimacy," Jan., 1943, pp. 64-116.

sacrilegious children already born is included in this extraordinary faculty of 1043 and 1044. It is safe to follow this opinion until the Holy See declares otherwise. According to this viewpoint then such *children already born or to be born* are legitimized immediately even though one of the parties should die before the marriage contract is made, or, for some other reason, the marriage does not take place.

7. *Dispensation from Impediments:* (1) This canon is dealing with ecclesiastical law, therefore, any impediment of divine or natural law cannot be dispensed, e.g., a previous bond of marriage, consanguinity, etc. (2) The power to dispense includes all impediments prohibitive and diriment, public and occult of ecclesiastical law except the priesthood and affinity in the direct line arising from a consummated marriage (affinity in the direct line would mean the wife's mother, grandmother, daughter, and vice-versa). The Church sometimes (rarely) does dispense from affinity in the direct line for a man and his mother-in-law, a stepfather and a daughter of his wife by another man (refer Lydon, Canon Law, page 178). A dispensation would be needed in the collateral line, second degree inclusive. The dispensation is needed for affinity in the collateral line, second degree inclusive, e.g., Jack and Mary, catholics, are married, Mary dies, Jack needs a dispensation to marry his sister, which is the first degree, her first cousin, her aunt, her niece. He would need no dispensation for a second cousin marriage. This canon gives faculties for dispensations which are rarely given by the Holy See under normal circumstances, e.g., sacred orders or third degree of crime.

In danger of death: to be sure that no consummation took place and proof cannot be had for this, the sworn testimony or statement by the parties that they have been baptized and are under no impediment would suffice.

8. *Avoid Scandal:* If the scandal results, this alone would not invalidate the dispensation. If the impediment is public, the dispensation should be public, e.g., the parties lived in public concubinage. In an occult case, when people consider their marriage as valid, it seems that no scandal could result. Scandal could result if the person would be in sacred orders or vows and lived in this condition in the territory in which he is known.

9. *Disparity of Cult or Mixed Religion:* Here the cautiones or guarantee is required for validity of the dispensation. The Holy See did require this promise explicitly, but since 1941 it is sufficient that the promise be given at least implicitly. (AAB 33-294). In the case of *children*

already born the controversy existed until 1941, are these included in the guarantee made by the non-Catholic party? The Holy Office in 1941 says that it did not pertain to *children already born*. The guarantees are made for children *to be born*. However, the parents should try to bring up all children already born into the Church. Canon 1061 requires that all the guarantees be made in writing. Since this prescription is for *liceity only*, the marriage would be valid. In case of grave necessity, there is not time to discuss the promises to the parties, the dispensation would be valid, all things being equal. In case of necessity when one must hurry, one may use the dispensation from the diaconate, etc. Notification of this dispensation should be sent to the chancery if given in the external forum, or sent to the Sacred Penitentiary or the chancery for the secret archives as the case warrants, if given in the internal non-sacramental forum.

FACULTIES GRANTED BY THESE CANONS

Canons 1043 - 1044 - 1045 - 1098:

1. *ORDINARY OF THE PLACE* - has ordinary power
2. *PASTOR* - has ordinary power
3. *ASSISTANT PASTOR*
    has delegated power from the Ordinary through letter, or
    has delegated power through statutes, or
    has delegated power from the pastor.
N.B. Oriental rite assistants have this *a jure*. It was included in *Craebrae Allatae*, 1949. (Why the new Latin proposed law omits it is a mystery).

4. *STRANGE PRIEST*
    acts as assisting priest simply according to 1098 because even without him a marriage before two witnesses is valid.
    acts as confessor having jurisdiction from Canon 882. No ordinary jurisdiction here because a confessor does not have an office as such.
    acts as pastor with power given him *a jure* by Canon 1044. Since he does not have an office, does not have ordinary jurisdiction.

5. *CONFESSOR* has power from diocesan facilities a jure - Canon 882

The above list includes all the clerics mentioned in Canons 1043-45 and 1098 who are *qualified to act in danger of death.*

ORIENTAL LAW

It is of particular interest to note that in Canon 34 which is the parallel of our Canon 1044, but differs in substance insofar as *curates or assistant priests* in a parish are explicitly mentioned to have the same power as the pastors. ". . . eadem dispensandi facultate pollet tum parochus, *tum vicarius cooperator* . . ." of whom no mention is made in the Latin Code, Canon 1044. Hence, it is that many canonists have a good opinion that a curate that has general delegation to assist at marriages, though not explicitly mentioned in Canon 1044, would possess the same power as that given to the pastor and the non-delegated priest of Canon 1098. To argue otherwise is to create an anomaly in law of a non-delegated priest who would actually have more power than a legitimately delegated priest.

Another interesting fact is that the Oriental Code, Canon 34:2, includes the substance of the response of the Code Commission given in 1922, that it is to be considered impossible to reach the ordinary in the circumstances of this canon and Canon 35, (C 1045) CIC, if the only means of contacting the ordinary is by telephone or telegraph.

Again in Canon 36 (1046) CIC the curate (vicarius cooperator) is explicitly mentioned among those who granting a dispensation in the external forum in virtue of the preceding canons and are exhorted to inform the ordinary immediately and that a record be made in the matrimonial register. It is only logical that he (curate) be explicitly mentioned here.

CASE: SICK CALL

You are an assistant at St. Mary's Church. The telephone rings at 2:00 a.m. Mrs. White tells you that her husband, Mr. White, is at the point of death and would like to have a priest come to him as soon as possible. Mr. White is a Catholic. You hear his confession. Through the confession you learn the following:

1. Mr. and Mrs. White were married in the Baptist Church and the marriage was never validated.

2. There are three children (6 - 8 - 10) and one child on the way. The three children attend the Catholic school.

3. Mrs. White, non-baptized is Mr. White's second cousin.

4. After this, Mr. White mentions that he was also in the seminary and received the subdeaconate, but due to an argument with his bishop, he left the seminary without getting a dispensation and later entered into this marriage. Mrs. White does not know of this fact; moreover, Mr. White wished to conceal this fact from her.

Now, Mr. White is very sorry for what he did and wishes to die in peace. He begs you to straighten out this marriage, and he also tells you that Mrs. White will cooperate but is ashamed of witnesses being present. How should this case be handled?

MARRIAGES IN URGENT NECESSITY

Canon 1045—1. Ordinaries of Places can, under conditions laid down at the end of 1043, grant a dispensation from all the impediments mentioned in the said Canon 1043, whenever an impediment is discovered; *when everything is already prepared for the marriage*, and the marriage cannot, *without probable danger of great harm*, be deferred until a dispensation is obtained from the Holy See.

2. *This faculty* can be used also *for the validation of a marriage* already contracted, if there is the same danger in the delay and there is not sufficient time for recourse to the Holy See.

3. *In the same circumstances* all the persons mentioned in Canon 1044, have the same faculty, but only for occult cases in which not even the local ordinary can be reached or in which he could not be reached without great danger of violating a secret.

1. *The Ordinary:* Whenever all things are prepared for the wedding and one discovers an impediment which is diriment, the ordinary may dispense from all ecclesiastical impediments, except those two mentioned in Canon 1043, whenever there is not enough time to approach the Holy See; scandal must be avoided; and whenever it is a mixed marriage, requiring a dispensation of mixed religion or disparity of cult, the necessary promises must be made. According to the probable opinion, they can dispense from the juridical form of marriage (priest and two witnesses).

2. *The same privilege is given to others besides the Ordinary:* Pastors, the strange priest of Canon 1098, and confessors have the same faculty, in the same circumstances whenevr the ordinary cannot be

reached, OR, whenever he can be reached but would involve the danger of disclosing the secret.

3. Impediments discovered only before the wedding *not yet dispensed:* In this case it need not be the day of the wedding when they have already arrived at the church, or a few days before the wedding which would cause grave injury through postponement. If the wedding must be celebrated within a shorter time for some reason, this canon may be used. If the ring is not engraved or the invitations have not been sent out as yet, we can still use the privilege if other preparations are made. Even if the parties withheld the fact of the diriment impediment until the day of the wedding, a dispensation could be given according to Canon 1045.

Lack of Time

If the lack of time to make the recourse is present, then this canon could be used. Of course it must be kept in mind that any extraordinary means, as telephone or telegraph, are not to be used.

Probable Danger of Great Harm

Absolute certainty is not required; the probable danger of great harm is sufficient. The probability depends on a reasonable estimation of the matter, which may result in serious consequence, as e.g., scandal, family feuds, loss of finances, danger of breaking the sixth commandment, loss of reputation. If there is a doubt whether the reasons are grave enough, this doubt is sufficient to grant the dispensation. This dispensation is for their own subjects, taking all the precautionary measures that no scandal will result; and the guarantees must be given if the marriage deals with a mixed marriage or disparity of cult. It must be noticed that the pastor's faculties are limited by "occult cases" whenever the ordinary cannot be reached, or if he can be reached it would be violating a secret, e.g., (a) natural secret; (b) professional secret; (c) sacramental secret (Jone, Oesterle).

According to some authors, if the pastor approaches the ordinary for a dispensation and the ordinary failed to respond, the pastor may go ahead according to Canon 1045:3, whenever a grave and urgent cause is present. In such a case, he should notify the ordinary at once of the dispensation and circumstances of the case. This also includes impediments *public* in nature and *occult* in fact, which we call an *occult case,* as e.g., the pastor forgets to get the dispensation and realizes this only on the day of the wedding, he may go ahead.

CANONS 1043-1044-1098

An Opinion on the New Proposed Canons

It is difficult to understand why the Code Commission of the Western (Latin) Church left this Canon unresolved. The Oriental Law of 1948 (*Craebrae Allatae*) remedied the situation by inserting in this law that the (vicar cooperator) assistant pastor also has these powers in danger of death. My question is why did not the Latin Codifiers utilize this same legislation? This would avoid the legal gymnastics which an assistant pastor must do. Ordinarily, he has no jurisdiction to marry anyone (unless delegated). He can only act in the internal forum. Instead he must act in the capacity of the strange priest of Canon 1098, to perform a death bed marriage. The insertion of (vicar cooperator) assistant pastor would have eliminated this problem.

JURISDICTION

A FORUM is a place for the transaction of official business— *judicial* or *administrative.*

External Forum is *Forum of External Government of the Church*
   Here one is Innocent or Guilty in the eyes of the Church
   Non-Sacramental, exercised publicly
   Exercised outside the Sacrament of Penance
   Has Juridical Effects - *Always Recorded*[5]
   No Secret

Internal Forum is *Forum of Conscience*
   Here one is Innocent or Guilty in the eyes of God
   Non-Sacramental, exercised privately
      Exercised outside Sacrament of Penance
      Has Juridical Effects - Is Recorded[6]
      Professional Secret!
   Sacramental, exercised privately
      Exercised in the Sacrament of Penance
      Has no Juridical Effects - Never Recorded
      Sacramental Seal!

---

5. Always recorded in the Parochial records and the Diocesan Chancery.
6. Recorded in the Secret Archives: Diocesan or Sacred Penitentiary, Rome.

MODE OF RECORDING DISPENSATIONS

Canon 1046—The pastor or the priest mentioned in Canon 1044, shall notify the ordinary of the place as soon as possible regarding the dispensation granted for the external forum; and the dispensation must be recorded in the marriage register.

Whether it is a new marriage, or a validation, it must be recorded. This marriage must also be recorded in the baptismal book, if the party or parties were baptized in that parish; otherwise, it must be recorded in the parish of baptism.

Canon 1047—Unless the rescript of the Sacred Penitentiary provides otherwise, a dispensation from an occult impediment, granted for the internal non-sacramental forum must be registered in a book to be carefully kept in the Secret Archives of the diocese referred to in Canon 379; nor is any other dispensation necessary for the external forum, even if the occult impediment afterwards becomes public; but one is needed if the dispensation has been granted only in the internal sacramental forum.

This canon is clear when the dispensation from the impediment is given by the Sacred Penitentiary. However, when this dispensation is given in connection with the sacramental forum, another dispensation is needed. This is so, not because the dispensation in the internal forum is invalid but because there is no way in proving this in the external forum. If a dispensation was given outside of confession in the internal non-sacramental forum, a record of this should be made in the secret archives of the chancery, and if this cannot be done for some reason, then it should be sent to the secret archives of the Sacred Penitentiary.

Canon 1048—If a petition for the dispensation has been sent to the Holy See, ordinaries of places must not use their faculties, if they have any, except as provided in Canon 204:2.

If the ordinary has power and perhaps through forgetfulness wrote for a dispensation, and later realizes that he has such power, he should wait until he hears from the Holy See. But if an urgent or grave cause arises requiring action, he may go ahead and grant the dispensation. He need not wait. If no grave cause arose and the ordinary did grant the dispensation, it would be valid, but *illicit*. In this case he should notify the Holy See afterwards that he dispensed according to Canon 204:2.

Canon 1049–1. When there is a question of marriages already contracted or *to be contracted*, one who has a general indult to dispense from some particular impediment, unless the indult itself expressly provides otherwise, can dispense from it even if the same impediment is multiple.

2. One who has a general indult to dispense from several impediments of different kinds, diriment or impeding, can dispense from the same even though they are public, when they occur in one and the same case.

This may arise when a dispensation is needed for the impediment of consanguinity which is multiplied, or the impediment of affinity and one of mixed religion. This would not be so if the faculties were given for a particular case.

Canon 1050–If it happens that together with a public impediment or public impediments from which a person can dispense in virtue of an indult there concurs another impediment from which he cannot dispense, he must apply to the Holy See for all of them; if, however, the impediment or impediments from which he can dispense are discovered after the Holy See has granted the dispensation, he may use his faculties.

Canon 1051–By a dispensation from a diriment impediment granted either in virtue of ordinary power in virtue of Canon 1043-44, or power delegated through a general indult, not however by a rescript in particular cases, legitimation of children also is granted in case any have been already born or conceived by the parties who are being dispensed, with the exception of adulterine and sacrilegious offspring.

Legitimation takes place automatically regarding children already conceived or born when a dispensation is given from a diriment impediment by ordinary power or in virtue of a general indult, but not by rescript in a particular case. In other words, by the act of dispensing a diriment impediment, legitimation takes place ipso facto which is implicitly contained in the dispensation. Before the Code (1918) a declaration had to be explicit regarding legitimation. This is not necessary now. Whenever a dispensation is given in view of marriage, if the marriage does not take place, and it is not the fault of the parties, (e.g., one of the parties dies suddenly) legitimation takes place. Some authors claim that if the marriage does not take place because of the *fault of the parties* legitimation takes place just the same. (Payen, 291; Cappello, 358, Bous, 496). It must be noted here that children born at the time parents are incapable of marrying, e.g., prior marriage, solemn vows, sacred orders, these children are not legitimized. One must write to the Holy See for such legitimization.

IMPLICIT DISPENSATIONS

Canon 1052 A dispensation from an impediment of consanguinity or affinity, granted for a certain degree of the impediment, is valid, even though in the petition or grant there be an error about the degree, provided the degree really existing is inferior, or even though another impediment of the same kind, in an equal or inferior degree, has been concealed in the petition.

If, for example, the petitioner asked for a dispensation of consanguinity in the third degree (second cousins) and mentioned that they were first cousins (second degree in the collateral line) it is considered as valid because the greater includes the lesser; but if the dispensation was asked in the reverse order, it would not be valid. Sometimes we have a case of double consanguinity or affinity, in the same degree or in an inferior degree, if this is not mentioned the dispensation will be valid. Jack and Jill may be second cousins in two ways, when they have two common ancestors, first cousins in one way and second cousins in another. The dispensation would be valid in this case even though they did not mention it in the petition. It is good to remember that when the relationship is mixed in some way as third degree touching the second, the *longer line determines the degree* (C 96:3), in this case it is satisfactory to say that they are related in the third degree. It is another question when we deal with relationship of second degree touching the first (uncle and niece); it would not be satisfactory to say that it is second degree of consanguinity alone according to the interpretation of the Sacred Congregation; the ordinary himself must apply for such a dispensation and say that they are related *second* touching the *first* and indicate that it is an *uncle-niece case*, in order to be sure of the validiy of the dispensation.

Canon 1053—A dispensation granted by the Holy See from a marriage *Ratum non-Consummatum*, or permission granted to contract another marriage on account of the presumed death of the other party, always implies a dispensation from the impediment arising from *adultery with the promise*, or *attempt at marriage*, if the case warrants it, but by no means from the impediment mentioned in Canon 1075; 2 and 3.

Just in case this particular impediment existed in any of these two cases, which is common to these cases, this canon implicitly grants the dispensation.

ORIENTAL LAW

Canon 1053 (43) It is interesting to note that both disciplines grant the implicit dispensation from the *impediment of crime which arises from adultery with a promise, or attempt of marriage* in two cases, namely, (1) when the Holy See grants a dispensation from a non-consummated marriage, and (2) whenever permission to re-marry has been granted on the presumed death of a spouse. However, the Oriental case contains the words: ". . . etiam ab iis qui potestatem habent infra Sedem Apostolicam, licentia . . ." which are not found in Canon 1053 (CIC). However, after the promulgation of the Oriental Code in 1949, the Code Commission explained that the implicit dispensation of Canon 1053 is valid and effective also when the permission to remarry on the presumed death of a spouse is given by the ordinary of the place. *In other words, the implicit dispensation, from the impediment of crime in the presumption of death case handled by the ordinary of the place, was not included in the permission to remarry until this was included in the Oriental Code in 1949 and later for the Latin ordinaries when the Code Commission gave this interpretation.*

OBREPTIO ET SUBREPTIO

Canon 1054—A dispensation granted from a minor impediment is not invalidated by any defect, whether of misstatement (obreptio) or omission (subreptio) even though the only final cause stated the petition is false.

1. This canon deals with Minor Impediments exclusively (cf. C. 1042:2).

2. *Obreptio* is a misstatement, or statement of a falsehood; while *subreptio* is an omission or concealing a fact in the petition.

3. According to Canon 40, truth is an essential condition for the validity of every rescript; however, this canon makes an exception for the minor impediments, which is an extraordinary concession.

4. The dispensation must be asked for a specific impediment, otherwise the dispensation is not granted and would be invalid, e.g., if one asks for a dispensation of public propriety and it was actually one of affinity, the impediment would still remain undispensed, and sometimes when a dispensation is valid, when they conceal a truth or state a falsehood, but the petitioner may be punished for so doing.

> Canon 1055—Dispensations from public impediments committed to the ordinary of the petitioners are to be executed by the ordinary who gave the testimonial letter or who forwarded the petition to the Holy See, even though the parties, at the time when the dispensation is to be executed, have left their domicile or quasi-domicile in his diocese and have departed to another diocese, never to return, notification should be sent to the ordinary of the place in which the parties intend to contract marriage.

Today when people move around frequently, it is possible that a rescript may come to the ordinary of the petitioner. Since these dispensations are granted usually for the external forum *in forma commissoria* it is to be executed by the same ordinary who asked for it. This same ordinary may, even though the parties moved to another diocese, execute this rescript and send notification of it to the ordinary where the marriage is to take place. There are no restrictions on the rescript (Bouscaren, 499). For a dispensation in the internal forum, an approved confessor would handle this.

> Canon 1056—With the exception of some small offering to defray the expenses of the chancery in dispensations for persons who are not poor, ordinaries of places and their officials are forbidden, and any contrary custom is reprobated, to demand any payment on the occasion of granting a dispensation, unless the

faculty to do so has been expressly given them by the Holy See; and if they do exact anything, they are bound to restitution.

Canon 1057—Those who grant a dispensation in virtue of the power delegated to them by the Apostolic See must expressly mention the pontifical indult in the dispensation.

This is also done when a dispensation is granted in virtue of the quinquennial faculties.

4

PROHIBITIVE IMPEDIMENTS

IMPEDIENT IMPEDIMENTS

Canon 1058—1. A marriage is rendered illicit by the following simple vows: (1) of Virginity; (2) of perfect Chastity; (3) not to marry; (4) to receive Sacred Orders; (5) to embrace the religious state.

2. No simple vow renders a marriage invalid unless this has been decreed for certain persons by special provision of the Holy See.

Vows: Impediment to Marriage

I. Definition: A vow is a free deliberate promise made to God to do something which is possible. It is an act of religion, differing from a simple resolution insofar as it binds under pain of sin (Lv 27; Si 5:3). A vow is *public* when it is accepted by a competent ecclesiastical authority, otherwise it is private. Vows are either simple or solemn. A vow is solemn when it is recognized by the Church as such and when taken in a religious order approved by the Holy See. As to their effects, solemn vows render certain acts invalid, e.g., one in solemn vows who marries contracts marriage invalidly, whereas one in simple vows marries illicitly.

II. Simple Vows: *Prohibitive Impediments to Marriage:*

(1) *Vow of Virginity:* The object of this vow is to keep one's virginity intact; the state of virginity is lost irrevocably by a consummated solitary sin or by the first deliberate act of sexual intercourse. This vow is usually taken along with the vow of chastity and the vow not to marry.

(2) *Vow of Perfect Chastity:* is one whereby a promise is made to refrain either perpetually or temporarily from every sexual pleasure, complete or incomplete, of mind and body. If one should contract mar-

riage while he is bound by this vow, such marriage is illicit until dispensed; moreover the right to conjugal act is forfeited unless the other party demands his debt in which case the one in vows must render it.

(3) *Vow not to Marry:* This vow has celibacy for its object. If one contracts marriage, he sins against this vow, but not in exercising his marital rights. If the marriage bond is dissolved, the vow still remains.

(4) *Vow to receive Sacred Orders:* This vow has for its object the reception of Sacred Orders which are the subdiaconate, diaconate, and priesthood. If one with such vows marries, he indirectly violates the vow because it would make the fulfillment of the vow impossible.

(5) *Vow to enter Religious Life:* This impediment arises when one makes a vow to enter a religious order or congregation of solemn vows. However, if one did all in his power to become a religious, but failed to meet with the requirements necessary for the religious life or for some other reason after making an honest effort, the vow would not be binding.

No simple vow invalidates marriage unless it has been declared as such by special precept of the Holy See, (CIC C. 1058:2). The Society of Jesus has such a precept and thereby becomes a diriment impediment.[1]

III. Oriental Law: The legislation is similar to the Latin Code; however, the vow of receiving the subdiaconate (which is a minor order) or major orders is an impediment only when a particular rite demands the observance of celibacy for these orders. This is the case for the reception of the subdiaconate among the Armenians, Italo-Albanians and Malabar rites; for the reception of orders (Major) among the Syrian and Coptic rites.

IV. Dispensation: Vows can be dispensed by the Church. Due to their character, vows are established by the Church as impediments and as such only the Church can dispense from these vows (CIC C. 1307-15). Among the private vows, *only two* are reserved to the Holy See: (a) Vow of perfect chastity and (b) vow to enter a religious order. Vows taken in a religious order of Solemn Vows cannot be dispensed except by the Holy See. Vows (simple) taken in a diocesan congregation must be dispensed by the local ordinary. Although, when the congregation is of Pontifical right, not the ordinary but the Holy See dispenses. *In danger of death*, the ordinary, pastor and others may dispense.

---

1. Gasparri-Seredi, **Fontes**, N. 153, Vol. 1, p. 269.

Canon 1059—In those regions where a legal relationship arising from adoption renders marriage illicit according to civil law, the marriage is also illicit by canon law. (Cf. 1080)

For Christian marriage, the Code gives canonical force to the civil law in each state or country. Whatever the law of the state determines regarding this impediment is usually accepted by the Church. If the state or country enacts a law making legel adoption a diriment impediment, the Church recognizes it also as a diriment impediment. Some countries as Italy, Spain, Poland, consider it as a diriment impediment. France, Germany, Hungary, Switzerland and Belgium consider it a prohibitive impediment. Puerto Rico retains it as a diriment impediment.[2]

The Former Law

A person excommunicated who contracts marriage before a non-Catholic minister with the religious rites (*communicatio in sacris*)[3] with heretics, which implies approval of heresy (C. 2319). Regarding the doubt of two Catholics who would go through such a ceremony (the Code was silent about this), Pope Pius XII in his Motu Propio, Dec. 25, 1953 (AAS, 46-88; Digest, Vol. IV, C. 2319) expunged from Canon 2319: 1, #1, the qualifying clause, *contra praescriptum canonis 1063: #1*. As a result, this penalty is now incurred *by any marriage contracted or attempted by Catholics* before a non-Catholic minister as such, e.g., if both parties were Catholic, OR if one was unbaptized, OR if no Catholic marriage took place beforehand. (The excommunication of the Third Council of Baltimore, no. 127, is no longer in effect.)

DECREE ON MIXED MARRIAGE—March 18, 1966

Due to the fact that this decree *has been abrogated*[4] in part, since the promulgation of *Matrimonia Mixta, of* March 31, 1970, we find it worthwhile to reiterate number seven of this decree.

"The excommunication provided for by Canon 2319, 1, 1, for those who celebrate a marriage before a non-catholic minister is abrogated. The effects of this abrogation are retroactive."

The Code has no penal law for those marrying before a civil officer,

2. Ayrinhac-Lydon, SS., **Marriage Legislation,** 2nd ed., Benziger Brothers, New York, 1952, p. 98.
3. Orientals, Cf. New Legislation under C. 1094.
4. Canons 1061, 1062, and 1063 were abrogated in 1970.

judge, magistrate or Justice of the Peace. However, we must check the synodal law of each diocese. Some have enacted a penal law for excommunication of those who attempt marriage before a civil magistrate; these laws are enacted because of the frequent abuse in particular territories. Canons 1061, 1062, 1063 were abrogated in 1970.

NORMS FOR MIXED MARRIAGES (March 31, 1970)

(Cf. Appendix for Motu Proprio)

The history of mixed marriages is rather peculiar because many different policies have developed on this type of marriage over the years. In some instances, certain bishops were wont to grant a limited number of dispensations over a certain period of time; norms were given for the performance of such marriages in the rectory or sacristy of the church; later developments found such marriages performed in the church but outside the altar rail, and in some dioceses without flowers on the altar, without music, without lighted candles; as time went on permissions were granted for the wedding to take place inside the altar rail, with music but no singing and with flowers on the altar; finally we have new norms which permitted the Mass in which the Catholic party alone received Communion during the service.

Today, with the Norms of March 18, 1966 abrogated or, rather supplanted by the Motu Proprio, *Matrimonia Mixta*, the Apostolic Letter of Pope Paul VI, March 31, 1970, we find very broad privileges regarding mixed marriages. Due to the changing times and conditions in our modern pluralistic society, the results of Vatican II and the rise in mixed marriages in general, Pope Paul deemed it necessary to promulgate these norms March 31, 1970, which became effective August 1, 1970 in Canada and became effective on October 1, 1970 in the United States. These changes came about because the former legislation on this matter did not lead to Christian unity. Although the Pope continues to discourage mixed marriages, he felt that these norms were necessary to promote Christian unity.

Laws should be clearly known and understood by all concerned. In this case not only the Catholic priest and Catholics in general, but also the non-Catholic minister as well as the non-Catholic layman and civil officials should be acquainted with these new norms. It is essential then to know what these norms are: the changes in the law, how they are applied to each individual, and all the circumstances surrounding each case.

Since mixed marriages are increasing, Pope Paul VI has shown his pastoral concern for them by issuing these norms, trying to safeguard, however, the existing principles of divine law, and the inherent natural right of men and women to contract marriage and beget children.

These norms do prescribe a twofold obligation upon the Catholic party to a mixed marriage according to the circumstances instituted by divine law for the salvation of souls. The Catholic has the duty "of preserving his or her own faith; nor is it ever permitted to expose oneself to a proximate danger of losing it." "Furthermore, the Catholic partner in a mixed marriage is obligated . . . as far as possible, to see to it that the children be baptized and brought up in that same faith and receive all these aids to eternal salvation which the Catholic Church provides for her sons and daughters." These are not merely ecclesiastical mandates but divine commands.

The only dilemma in such a mixed marriage is that of the children's upbringing and education. Both parties have equal responsibility in this matter, and, as such, could lead into difficulty between two believing Christians, namely, the one Catholic, the other non-Catholic. Because of this, Pope Paul VI points out that there cannot be a uniform canonical discipline on mixed marriages as in the past. By issuing this Apostolic Letter on mixed marriages, Pope Paul VI wished to bring this new legislation up to the proper perspective with the teaching of Vatican II as expressed especially in the *Decree on Ecumenism* and the *Declaration on Religious Freedom.*

MIXED MARRIAGE

Author's Commentary

The impediment of mixed religion or disparity of cult comes from the divine law to safeguard the danger of perversion of the Catholic party or their offspring. Both of these impediments are prohibitive by the divine law; but in view of ecclesiastical law, mixed religion is merely a prohibitive impediment, while disparity of cult is a diriment impediment, and as such, would render a marriage invalid if this dispensation would be lacking.

In issuing this norm 4, Pope Paul is attempting to preserve the divine law obligation of Catholics while at the same time he is keeping in mind the principles of ecumenism and of religious freedom. Hence, for every Catholic this is a grave obligation: to live his faith and to pass it on to his offspring.

It must be remembered that this obligation is imposed upon the Catholic only in the degree to which this is concretely possible. This obligation is qualified according to the norm; it (the obligation) "is imposed according to the various situations." The Catholic baptism and the education of the children is to be undertaken "as far as possible." In other words, the Catholic promises "to do all in his power" because no one is bound to do the impossible. This is a departure from the law of 1918 which stated that no dispensation could be given unless a **guarantee** was given. These norms do not require a guarantee.

A Catholic is asked to respect the sincere conscience of his non-Catholic partner, just as he wants his own conscience to be respected. Harmony must be sought in the family, especially when it comes to the education of the children. Here there must be the **give** and **take** idea. A Catholic is asked only to do **what is possible**, and no more in a given situation.

Therefore, dispensations may be granted even when it is uncertain that the children will actually be raised as Catholics. The norm seems to imply more the sincerity, the attitude and intention of the Catholic rather than the actual raising of children. The success in raising the children as Catholics may vary according to the attitude of the non-Catholic party. Sometimes it will be possible and in other situations it might be impossible, in which case the Catholic is not obliged to do the impossible.

The norm "to do all in his power" does not mean that the Catholic must exert pressure or undue strain on the non-Catholic party which would destroy the harmony of the marriage, or contribute to the breaking up of the marriage. Is the promise also a guarantee? These norms do not insist on a a guarantee that children will be **baptized and brought up Catholics.** It is merely a promise. It merely indicates that the Catholic should be aware of his obligation and be ready to fulfill his duty to the best of his ability in the situation. More than this is not demanded. Not even moral certitude is needed that the children will be brought up in the Catholic faith. This drastic change has taken place in respect to the sincere conscience of the non-Catholic party.

Vatican II declared:"All men are to be immune from coercion on the part of individuals or of social groups and of any human power, in such wise that no one is to be forced to act in a manner contrary to his own beliefs, whether privately or publicly, whether alone or in association with others, within due limits . . . parents, moreover, have the right to determine, in accordance with their own religious beliefs, the kind of religious education that their children are to receive" (Declarations on Religious Freedom, 2-5), and, insofar as other Christians are concerned the Second Vatican Council decreed that "Catholics must gladly acknowledge and esteem the truly Christian endowments from our common heritage which are to be found among our separated brethren . . . nor should we forget that anything wrought by the Holy Spirit in the hearts of our separated brethren can be a help to our own edification. Whatever is truly Christian is never contrary to what genuinely belongs to the faith; indeed it can always bring a deeper realization of the mystery of Christ and the Church" (Decree on Ecumenism, no. 4).

ORIENTAL LAW

This law includes legal guardianship (which the Latin Code omits) if this is an impediment in civil law.

Mixed Religion — Law of 1918 to March 31, 1970

Canon 1060—The Church everywhere most strictly forbids the contracting of marriage between two baptized persons of whom one is a Catholic and the other is a member of a heretical or schismatic sect; and if there is danger of perversion for the Catholic party and the children, the marriage is forbidden also by Divine Law.

COMMENT: Although the principles of mixed marriage remain the same, nevertheless some elements of this canon have been mitigated; for example, we could say: "The Church everywhere permits the contracting of marriage between two baptized persons—one Catholic and the other Protestant."

1. Mixed religion in general could mean (a) a marriage between a Catholic and a baptized non-Catholic person, or (b) a marriage between a Catholic and a non-baptized person. However, canonically speaking, *mixed religion* is restricted to a marriage between a *Catholic and a baptized non-Catholic*.

2. Whenever the baptism of the non-Catholic is doubtful, we have here an impediment either of mixed religion or disparity of cult. What it actually is we do not know. *After* a marriage, the burden of proof rests upon the presumption in favor of the validity of the baptism and of the marriage until it is proven otherwise. *Before* marriage, when applying for a dispensation it is granted for *mixed religion and disparity of cult ad cautelam*.

3. In this precautionary method, all the possibilities are covered in such a doubtful case. If in the eyes of God the person is baptized validly in the Protestant sect, the *mixed religion* dispensation would apply and takes effect, the other would not. And if in the eyes of God, the person is not actually baptized, the *disparity of cult* dispensation would take effect, the former would not. The precautionary phrase *ad cautelam* then prevents any further difficulties.

4. Communism or Atheism: If any person belongs to any atheistic sect, (Communism is in this category), those persons are considered as belonging to an atheistic sect. The dispensation of *mixed religion* or *dis-*

parity of cult is needed according to whether the person is baptized or not.

5. Danger of Perversion: Whenever there is danger of perversion of the Catholic party or the children of a mixed marriage, the divine law gravely prohibits such a marriage. As long as such danger exists, the Church cannot grant a dispensation. The necessary conditions must be fulfilled before a dispensation is granted.

DUTIES OF THE ORDINARY AND PASTORS

Canon 1064—Ordinaries and other pastors of souls:

1. must deter the faithful from mixed marriages insofar as it is possible;

2. if they cannot impede them, they shall strive by all means lest they contract in violation to the laws of God and the Church;

3. after mixed marriages have been celebrated either in their own territory or outside of it, they shall carefully see to it that the parties faithfully discharge the promises they have made;

4. in assisting at such marriages, they must observe the prescriptions of Canon 1102.

Canon 1065—1. The faithful must also be deterred from contracting marriage with those who have either notoriously abandoned the Catholic faith even without joining a non-Catholic sect, or with those who have become members of societies condemned by the Church.

2. The pastor must not assist at above-mentioned marriages unless he consulted the ordinary, who after considering all the factors, may permit him to assist at the marriage, provided there be a grave reason and the ordinary in his prudent discretion judges that adequate measures have been taken to insure the Catholic education of all the children and the removal of danger of perversion from the other party.

An unworthy party to marriage does not necessarily mean that this is an impediment. Whenever a non-Catholic becomes a convert and is a member of the Masons, permission can be obtained from the Aposolic Delegate for him to retain *passive membership.*

PUBLIC SIN AND CENSURE

Canon 1066—If a public sinner or one who is notoriously under censure refuses to go to sacramental confession, or to be reconciled with the Church beforehand; the pastor must not assist at his marriage, unless there be a grave reason, concerning which, if it is possible, he should consult the ordinary.

All these precautionary measures are taken to prevent the individual from committing a sacrilege. If the matter is known only through the confessional, and he will not become reconciled, nothing can be done because of the seal of confession.

BURIAL FOR CATHOLICS INVALIDLY MARRIED

The common problem of burial in a mixed marriage case is the request to have permission to bury the non-Catholic party in a Catholic cemetery in order that both parties and their offspring could share a common plot. According to a survey made in the United States, it was discovered that some dioceses permit the non-Catholic to be buried in consecrated ground.

Catholics, invalidly married, who died without the sacraments or without any sign of repentance, but who brought up their children in the faith, and who themselves attended Mass regularly, cannot be buried with a Christian burial ceremony according to Canon 1240:1. These are usually ligamen cases that could not be validated. The survey found that some dioceses permit prayers at the funeral parlor or at the grave, with burial in consecrated ground. Others were more strict, by permitting non-liturgical prayers at the funeral parlor, or at the grave, but denying burial in consecrated ground. Since Vatican II, each diocese has a different policy. Some are more lenient than others. One would have to consult the guidelines of his own diocese.

CREMATION

The Church, in 1963, removed the punitive measures previously associated with cremation in view of the changing mental attitude and the removal of danger to religion, the Church and Christian morals. But the Church did not withdraw completely its opposition to cremation. Nor did it put it on equal terms with burial in the ground or entombment in special burial facilities. A responsibility was placed upon the bishops to discourage the practice of cremation except in cases of necessity and if there is no danger of scandal and religious indifferentism. They were to encourage their faithful to retain the "old and better custom which the Church has always guarded with solicitude through the centuries." In addition, Christian burial was to be excluded for those who deny Christian dogmas in choosing cremation and for those who chose cremation "because of a sectarian spirit," for reasons "inimical to the Christian way of life."

Since it is the responsibility of the bishop of the diocese to discourage cremation and to promote the retention of bodily burial, formal permission must be obtained from our diocesan offiices to permit cremation for any of our subjects. Permission is granted only in cases of necessity and for grave reasons, and with no danger of scandal and irreligion. The bishop has this prerogative when he considers it opportune for serious pastoral reasons.

CHAPTER FIVE

DIRIMENT IMPEDIMENTS

INTRODUCTION

1. A diriment impediment is some definite fact of circumstances which renders a person incapable of making a valid marriage contract.

2. There are 13 diriment impediments:
   1 Want of Age (C. 1067)
   2 Impotence (C. 1068)
   3 Previous and Existing Marriage (C. 1069)
   4 Disparity of Cult (C. 1069)
   5 Sacred Orders (C. 1072)
   6 Solemn Vows (C. 1073)
   7 Abduction (C. 1074)
   8 Crime (C. 1075)
   9 Consanguinity (C. 1076)
   10 Affinity (C. 1077)
   11 Public Propriety (C. 1078)
   12 Spiritual Relationship C. 1079)
   13 Legal Relationship (C. 1080)

DIRIMENT IMPEDIMENTS

Want of Age

1. A man before completing his sixteenth year, and a woman before completing her fourteenth year cannot contract a valid marriage.

2. Although a marriage contracted after the aforesaid age is valid, yet pastors of souls should try to deter young people from marrying before the age at which, according to the received customs of the country, marriage is usually contracted.

A man before the completion of his sixteenth year and a woman before the completion of her fourteenth year cannot contract a valid marriage. Although the marriage is a valid contract after the aforesaid age, nevertheless, pastors of souls should deter young people from making such a contract before an earlier age than is commonly the custom in their respective country.

(1) The impediment of age arises from physical capacity. The restriction is one of ecclesiastical law because by the natural law children who have sufficient discretion and have a general knowledge of what marriage means and are willing to enter the contract may marry validly. The theory is that actual power to generate is not necessary since it is consent of the parties, not carnal relation, that makes the marriage contract. Mental capacity is required for making a valid matrimonial contract.

(2) The canonical impediment of age binds only the baptized, whereby, it recognizes a marriage valid only when the parties have completed the canonical age - 16 for a male, 14 for females. The age must be determined by Canon 34, Section 3, whereby a boy who was born on September 1, 1940, has canonically completed his sixteenth year only after midnight of the sixteenth birthday, namely, September 2, 1956. He could not get married on the day itself of the sixteenth birthday. It would be invalid. It must be after his sixteenth birthday. What could be said of the girl? She cannot contract a valid marriage, only the day after her fourteenth birthday.

(3) Dispensation. If parties marry under the established age, the impediment ceases with the lapse of time; however, the marriage remains invalid; a validation is necessary according to the form of marriage.

Impotency

> Canon 1068–1. Impotence, antecedent and perpetual, whether on the part of the man or the woman, whether known to the other party or not, whether absolute or relative, invalidates marriage by the law of nature itself.
> 2. If the impediment of impotence is doubtful either in law or in fact, the marriage is not to be hindered.
> 3. Sterility neither invalidates marriage nor renders it illicit.

(1) What is impotency? The codifiers did not define it. Canonists do not agree as to its real definition. All agree, however, that when

there is an incapacity or inability to have natural sexual intercourse, this case would constitute impotency and would invalidate marriage. The inability to perform a natural sexual act (Human Act - copula) namely, penetration of the vagina by the male organ and the emission of true semen in it, is called impotency. For example, on the part of the man: When the man is deprived of both testicles; when he cannot have an erection; or if the sex organs are out of proportion. On the part of the woman: the absence of a vagina, the vagina is out of proportion or prevents penetration.

(2) *Sterility.* All agree that sterility is the case when natural sexual intercourse can take place, while at the same time both parties possess all the organs necessary for generation, but are not capable of generating offspring. For example, the parties are too old; women who have reached the age when ovulation ceases; women who have no ovaries; no uterus.

(3) *Generation is a twofold process:* First, the *human act* called *copula;* and second, the *physiological process,* that is, the natural process of generation which takes place in a man or woman for the generation of children. The *physiological* includes the development of the ova in the ovaries of the female and the sperm in the testicles of the male. When copula takes place, during a fertile period, the sperm goes from the vagina to the uterus and on to the fallopian tubes of the female. At the same time the ovum or female germ cell released from ovary of the female meets the sperm somewhere enroute. When the sperm penetrates it, they are united. *This union we call fecundation.* Here we have a human being in its embryonic stages. This embryo descends from the tube and enters the uterus. Here it attaches itself to the wall of the uterus, develops to maturity, after approximately nine months, a child is born.

(4) From what has been said, we have first, the human act of generation, controlled by the will, that is copula; the penetration of the vagina by the male organ and the emission of true semen into the vagina; the natural process of generation, which cannot be controlled directly by the will. *Whatever hinders the human act of generation, that is, normal copula is considered* impotency. Whatever hinders the *physiological process is considered sterility.* (In the medical profession, this distinction is not accepted. At times our definition of sterility is considered impotency by the medical profession.)

(5) Impotency is commonly defined as the incapacity to perform the marital act, that is, when the parties are incapable of "having copula

which is in itself suitable for generation."

How do we determine *when copula* is in itself suitable for generation? This is not clear. If a woman lacks ovaries or has a hysterectomy, her acts are not suitable for generation. In other words, the controversy concerns the case when intercourse is possible, but the organs are lacking which are essential to beget offspring. The decisions of the Holy See must be our guide. As long as a married couple are capable of having normal conjugal relations, they are not impotent. What is considered here is that the conjugal act depends on the human will, not on the physiological process which follows the act. If the parties are able to have the conjugal act, that is sufficient; the fact that they are incapable of having children is a defect of nature.

TYPES OF IMPOTENCY

a) *Antecedent* is that which existed before the marriage.
b) *Subsequent* if it arose after the marriage.
c) *Perpetual* if it cannot be cured by licit means and is not dangerous
d) *Temporary* if it disappears naturally or can be cured by licit
e) *Absolute* whereby the marital act cannot be had with any person
f) *Relative* is an impediment only in regard to certain persons.

(6) *Doubtful Impotency:* a) If the impotency is doubtful by either doubt of law or doubt of fact, marriage can take place even though this impediment is of natural law. The reason for this is because it is difficult to solve such doubts, the Church maintains that it is a probable and prudent doubt; the Natural Law to marry prevails.

b) If there is a doubt regarding the impediment of impotency *before the marriage*, an investigation must take place. After the investigation, if the doubt persists, marriage could take place.

c) If *after the marriage*, a doubt of the impediment of impotency arises, after the parties have tried marital relations, an investigation as to whether the impotency was antecedent and perpetual must be made. If it is certain that antecedent and perpetual impotency is present, action should be taken to begin process for declaration of nullity.[1]

The Code Commission for the revision of Canon law has been considering various aspects of interpretation on this canon regarding impotence of the male and female. Whether these aspects will be included

---

1. Bouscaren, I. Lincoln, S.J., **Canon Law Digest**, Vols. II, III, IV.

in the new law remains to be seen. (cf. *Communicationes* 6 (1974),
pp. 177-198. Some of these interpretations are as follows:

1. The husband's penis must be capable of penetrating wife's vagina.
2. The ejaculate need not contain true semen.
3. Ordinary insemination is required, without consideration of the nature of the seminal fluid.
4. The copula need not be accompanied by complete orgasm or sexual satisfaction on the part of both husband and wife.
5. True copula does not exist if it occurred violently.
6. True copula does not exist even if aphrodisiac means are required.
7. True copula exists even if the wife experiences great pain, provided she consented to the act.
8. True copula and consummation do not exist when anti-conceptual devices affect the physical act itself.
9. True copula and consummation exist when the anticonceptual devices do not affect the physical act itself.
10. Double vasectomy does not constitute masculine impotence.
11. A woman who has an artificial vagina inserted before marriage is to be considered potent.
12. A woman who has simply a closed vagina or one that is equivalent to closed is not to be considered impotent.
13. A woman who has had a tubal ligation is to be considered potent.
14. It is not yet decided whether functional impotence constitutes a diriment impediment of impotence.
15. It is not certain whether impotence is an impediment of the natural law or an impediment arising from the very nature of marriage (new canon 283, 1).
16. If the impediment of impotence is doubtful, either by doubt of law or doubt of fact, marriage is not to be prohibited, nor, as long as the doubt remains, is it to be declared null (new canon 283, 2).
17. Sterility does not prohibit marriage or render it invalid, unless the sterility was fraudulently concealed (new canon, 3).[2]

CONGREGATION FOR THE DOCTRINE OF THE FAITH

DECREE: Concerning impotency as a diriment (invalidating) impediment for marriage [translation]

2. Cf. Questions & Answers, (H.P.R.), Jan. 1978, pp. 65-68, Carr., Aidan. "Sexual Impotency & Sterilization."

This Sacred Congregation always holds that those who have undergone a vasectomy cannot be impeded from marrying just as others in similar circumstances cannot be impeded when their impotency is not shown to certainly exist.

Now, however, having reviewed this position and after study by this sacred Congregation and by the Commission for the Revision of the Code of Canon Law, in a plenary meeting on Wednesday, May 11, 1977, the most eminent and reverend Fathers of this Sacred Congregation, postulating for themselves the following questions, decreed the answers:

1) Whether the impotency which invalidates marriage, consists in an antecedent and perpetual incapacity, either absolute or relative, for accomplishing conjugal copulation? Answered: Yes.

2) Given an affirmative answer, whether there is necessarily required for conjugal copulation, the ejection of semen produced by the testicles? Answered: No.

And in the Audience of Friday, May 13, 1977, given to the undersigned Prefect of this Sacred Congregation, the Supreme Pontiff, Pope Paul VI by divine Providence, approved this decree and ordered its publication.

Given at Rome, from the Palace of the Congregation for the Doctrine of the Faith, May 13, 1977.

Prior Bond of Marriage

> Canon 1069—1. One who is bound by a previous marriage bond, even though it was not consummated, invalidly attempts marriage, without prejudice however to the Privilege of the Faith.
> 2. Even though the prior marriage be invalid or dissolved for any reason, it is not lawful to contract another until the nullity or dissolution of the former shall have been established according to law and with certainty.

1. This impediment is of the divine law and binds all men both Christian and pagan. There is no exception. One who was married before, is forbidden to marry again, unless the first marriage is declared null or has been dissolved. The Privilege of the Faith is the only exception to this rule insofar as the first marriage is dissolved, not before, but at the very moment the second is contracted.

2. A prior marriage is dissolved by the death of one of the parties,

whereby the surviving party is free to marry. *This freedom must be verified by:*

    (1) Authentic documents: death certificate, ecclesiastical or civil; where the ordinary does not require a *nihil obstat*, the pastor may allow the new marriage to take place.

    (2) Gathering proof from witnesses when authentic documents are not available; this, of course, is submitted to the ordinary for the *nihil obstat*.

    (3) Having recourse to presumptions mentioned in an Instruction of the S.C. of the Holy Office, May 13, 1868.[3] Strict proof is impossible in some cases and in such circumstances, the proper authorities can decide with moral *certainty* on the basis of the presumption that the party is dead.[4]

    (4) *Cases decided by the Sacred Congregation of the Sacraments:* AAS III-26 (1911); AAS VII-40, 235:476 (1915); AAS VIII-151 (1916); AAS IX-120, (1917); AAS XIV-96 (1922); Instruction AAS III-102 (1911); Instruction AAS XIII-348 (1921).

It must be noted that in *Presumption of Death* cases, the validity of the second marriage depends upon the fact whether the *former spouse is actually dead. Permission is by no means a dispensation.* If it happens that the spouse is still living, *the Second Marriage is Invalid.* Permission is given only under these circumstances. "What God has joined together let no man put asunder."

INSTRUCTION OF THE HOLY SEE ON PRESUMPTION
OF DEATH CASES

1. Prolonged Absence or Civil Declaration is Insufficient: The mere lapse of time, prolonged absence, e.g., the five or seven year period established by civil authorities or other presumptions of death considered by civil law, is insufficient.

2. Official Documents: Interested parties should obtain, if possible, official documents proving the death of the party concerned, e.g., the church, hospital, army or other institutional records. The Department of Vital Statistics which operates in each State sometimes pro-

---

3. Instruction of the Holy See: AAS 2-199.
4. "Presumption of Death Case," **The Jurist**, July 1959, Vol. XIX; also **Canon Law Digest**, Vol. I, p. 508.

vides important information of this kind. This department is usually located in the State's capital city.

3. Two Witnesses: When official documents cannot be obtained, the testimony of two trustworthy witnesses should be obtained, provided these witnesses:
    (1) knew the deceased;
    (2) know the fact of his death:
    (3) agree on the circumstances, e.g., the time and cause of the death.
    (4) state whether they were related to each other, or were friends or associates of the deceased.

4. First Class Witness: One first class witness of the deceased may suffice if this witness can provide adequate circumstantial evidence.

5. Hearsay Evidence:[5] Sometimes hearsay evidence may suffice (*tempore non suspecto*) and it coincided with information already available.

6. Conjectures: Presumptions based on:
    (1) age;
    (2) moral character;
    (3) physical or mental status;
    (4) affection for his or her family;
    (5) correspondence (letters);
    (6) any circumstances which would give reasons to presume he or she would be heard from if they were alive at the time.

7. Rumor: One should resort to rumor if there is any foundation here.

8. Newspapers, Radio, TV, Government Agencies, FBI: The results of investigations through these media could be used if sufficient grounds are present for the presumption.

9. Holy See: Whenever any other doubts that are serious are present, the matter must be referred to the Holy See (H.O. July 2, 1898, AAS XXXI, 252).

10. References to Other Cases:
    (1) *Earthquake in Messina 1908:* The Sacred Congregation of the Sacraments demanded that each case be investigated separately according to the decree of 1898.

---

5. Fraenkel, F., **Missing Persons,** New York, 1950.

(2) *Russian-Japanese War:* A decree of 1910 gave the same instructions. Incidentally, lapse of time in this case was only three years. The decision gives a good review of circumstances in wars, flood, earthquakes, etc.

SOURCES OF INFORMATION

Cases of Servicemen or Former Servicemen

Whenever a tribunal is handling a case of this kind, it may be necessary to conduct a special investigation in order to obtain information or additional information on a case already started about the party in question. The following address may be helpful: Military Ordinariate, 1011 First Avenue, New York, N.Y. 10022.

DECLARATION OF NULLITY

I. Lack of Form

A prior attempted marriage is proclaimed invalid by the *declaration of nullity* because of the *defect of form* (C. 1097). No formal process is used here. The ordinary after close examination is the competent authority to declare the nullity. The following documents are sent to the ordinary for this *Declaration of Nullity:*

(1) Certificate of Baptism;
(2) Certificate of Confirmation and of First Holy Communion;
(3) Record of the Civil Marriage;
(4) Record of the divorce (photostat from the clerk of the Circuit Court);
(5) Sworn statement that the marriage was never validated in the Church, that is, celebrated in the form prescribed by the Church.

II. Diriment Impediment

The ordinary may grant a nullity on a prior marriage by simple summary judicial process (C. 1990) which is based on the following diriment impediments:

(1) Disparity of cult;   (2) Holy Orders;
(3) Solemn Vows;   (4) Ligamen;
(5) Consanguinity;   (6) Affinity;
(7) Spiritual Relationship.

When these impediments (or impediment) can be proved by

authentic documents and one is certain that no dispensation had been obtained (C. 1990).

Another impediment could arise from *Crime:* A marriage could be declared invalid, if a person bound by a previous marriage *commits adultery* and *promised*, or *attempted marriage* with this same person.

III. Nullity of Marriage Arising from Other Causes

To grant a nullity on a previous marriage arising from other causes, would be *defective consent*, impotence, force and fear; in these cases a formal *judicial trial must take place and two concordant sentences rendered.* Cf. Instr. of S. C. Sacr. August 15, 1936, Art. 220.

The question of a presumed death is considered not directly under the impediment of ligamen (a previous and existing marriage) but it is a corollary because many of these cases are introduced for processing without any direct reference to this impediment (ligamen).

COMMON LAW MARRIAGE

A *Common Law Marriage* is one that omits the canonical form (C. 1094), as well as the civil form of marriage and the parties live together as husband and wife. This is a marriage without any ceremony whatsoever, that is, it is one without either minister or witnesses assisting; the man and woman live together as husband and wife and act as such before society.

Whenever a *Common Law Marriage* is permitted, the civil law requires (when there are no impediments) that (1) the *parties exchange their consent mutually.* (The manner and form is not determined by civil law and hence considered immaterial); (2) *they must have the intention* to contract a marriage here and now (*de presenti*); (3) the parties must cohabit with each other. This third condition required by civil law seems to be a contradiction. It is difficult to see how this condition can be a constituent of a Common Law Marriage. Objectively speaking and also from the canonical point of view, the *mutual consent* and the *proper intention* are sufficient. *Cohabitation* is merely a proof of such a marriage. To retain it as a condition to constitute marriage is a contradiction.[6]

With the trend of "shacking up" or living together without marriage so prevalent throughout the Western World, we might overlook

---

6. Long, Jos., **A Treatise on the Law of Domestic Relations**, 3rd ed., Indianapolis, 1948, p. 91.

the fact that some of these cases could be common law marriages and could be helpful in solving some of our cases. One must study each case separately.

Principles

1. The fact that a man and woman may live together for many years cannot be construed that this relationship automatically becomes a valid common law marriage with the lapse of time. The first two conditions mentioned above: *mutual consent and intention* must take place, otherwise this relationship amounts to *mere concubinage*, even though people publicly consider them married.

2. It is also erroneously believed by clergy and laymen alike, that relationships of this kind *are not valid* common law marriages, when they actually are. These cases should be carefully checked. After a divorce, individuals easily change their minds then choose (*post factum*) the type of opinion that suits their needs here and now; they may change their story.

3. Catholics cannot contract a valid common law marriage.

4. *Unbaptized parties must observe the prescribed form of the civil law.* If common law marriages are recognized by the state, then the unbaptized contract a *valid* common law marriage in that state. If it is forbidden by the state, then the common law marriage would be invalid. The state regulates the form of marriage for them.

A common law marriage is recognized as *valid* by the Church between *two baptized non-Catholics* as well as between an *unbaptized person* and a *baptized non-Catholic*, irrespective of the civil law of a particular state, because these people are subject to the laws of the Church. Therefore, these cases must be carefully scrutinized by pastors and especially by the chancery to ascertain whether such common law marriages constitute an impediment of a prior bond, in which case it would invalidate a subsequent marriage. We should keep in mind that the solution of such cases is *not* determined by the fact that the civil law recognizes such marriages as valid, but rather by the very fact that mutual consent and proper intention in virtue af the natural law *was* or *was not given*. It must be kept in mind that for such people no legislation exists requiring a specific formality for the celebration of their marriage.[7]

5. When the parties to a common law marriage wish to become

---

7. Cloran, Owen, M., **Previous and Practical Cases on Marriage,** Vol. I, Bruce. 1960, pp. 231-235.

Catholics, (in those states that prohibit a common law marriage) they must obtain a license and renew their consent in order to fulfill the requirements of civil law. It is also advisable that the same procedure be followed even in those states that recognize common law marriages despite the fact that they do not require it.

6. Regarding convalidation of a marriage in civil law, this is done by reason of the theory of *consent persevering* and this applies only to the marriage of the unbaptized.

7. The unbaptized persons who contract a common law marriage are bound by the diriment impediments of civil law.

8. If one or both of the parties to the common law marriage is a *baptized* non-Catholic, they are not bound by the impediments of the civil law, but are bound by the diriment impediments of the ecclesiastical law.

Proving a Common Law Marriage

1. According to Canons 1081 and 1014, a common law marriage of a baptized non-Catholic enjoys the presumption that it is valid. When such a marriage lacks proof, registration of witnesses to same, the testimony given with an oath of the parties themselves can be accepted as proof of their marriage, provided no other marriage is prejudicial to this testimony.

2. *Cohabitation:* Cohabitation and the public knowledge of the marital status establishes a presumption of such a marriage contract. This presumption is corroborated by various concomitant circumstances:

   (1) whether both parties registered as husband and wife at hotels when traveling;
   (2) whether the man introduced the woman in social circles as his wife;
   (3) whether they acted as husband and wife in legal matters, for example:
       (a) having a joint bank account;
       (b) filing their income tax together;
       (c) registering together when voting;
       (d) making out their last will and testament in such a way that he legally considered her his wife;
       (e) taking out insurance policies declaring one of the parties as beneficiary;

(f) whether the income tax report of the man had any reference to the woman as his wife;

(g) whether they referred to themselves as Mr. and Mrs. in public;

(h) whether they were registered in the post office or in the telephone directory as husband and wife;

(i) whether they intended to live this way until death.[8]

FORM TO DETERMINE COMMON LAW UNIONS

1. Do you believe in the sanctity of an oath? ....
2. Do you realize the gravity of perjury and its serious consequences? ....
3. Do you solemnly swear to tell the whole truth and nothing but the truth in answering all the following questions? (Touching the Holy Gospels) ....
4. Name? ....
   Address? ....
   Place of Birth? .... Age? ...... Occupation? ....
5. Father's name? .... Mother's maiden name? ....
6. Were you ever baptized, sprinkled, or christened in any religion? When? .... Where? ....
   What denomination? ....
7. Have you ever lived with anyone in a common law union? ......
   With whom? ....
   Was this party married before he (she) lived with you? ....
   When? .... Where? ....
   With whom? ....
   Was the former spouse living at the time you cohabited? ....
8. What is the present name and address of the person with whom you lived in common law? ....
9. Was this party ever baptized, christened or sprinkled in any religion? ....
   When? .... Where? ....
   What denomination? ....
10. How long did you live together? ....
11. When did you begin living together? ....
12. Where did you spend this time together? ....
13. Why was there no marriage ceremony? ....
14. Did you look upon yourselves as husband and wife? ....
    What was the opinion among your relatives, friends, neighbors, trades folk, etc.? ....
    Give names and addresses: ....
15. Did you call yourselves Mr. and Mrs? ....
    Did you ever register at work or for income tax purposes, charge accounts, insurance, mail box, and telephone directory, as Married? ....
    ....
16. Did others consider you as married to each other? ....
    Who? ....
    What is their present name and address? ....

---

8. Doheny. **Canonical Procedure in Matrimonial Cases,** Vol. I. Bruce, 1937

Why did they consider you married? ....

17. Did you consider that you had a right to him (her)? ....
    Why? ....

18. Did you ever tell him (her) that this was no marriage? ....
    Did you ever tell anyone else? ....
    Who? .... Address? ....
    Why did you do this? ....

19. Did you ever mention that you really should get married? ......
    To whom? ....
    What is their present name and address? ....
    ....
    Why did you mention this? ....
    What was the answer to this? ....

20. Did you intend to live this way until death? ....
    Did either of you make a will? ....
    How did you provide for the other party? ....

21. Did you own property together? ....
    In what name is it listed? ....

22. Did you have any children? ....
    Were they registered as children of Mr. and Mrs? ....

23. Did you think it was a sin to live thus? ....

24. Did the other party consider it a sin to live thus? ....

25. Did you ever go through any kind of a marriage form together,
    i.e., in which marriage consent was expressed, even privately? ...

26. Additional Questions: ....
    ....

27. Do you swear to the truth of the above statements? ....

Disparity of Cult

Canon 1070—A marriage contracted by a non-baptized person with a person who was baptized in the Catholic Church or who has been converted to it from heresy or schism, is null.

2. If a party at the time of the marriage was commonly regarded as baptized, or if his or her baptism was doubtful, the marriage must be regarded as valid according to Canon 1014, until it is certainly established that one of the parties was baptized and that the other was not.

A marriage is considered null when contracted between a non-baptized person and a person who was baptized in the Catholic Church, or who has been received into the Church from heresy or schism.

If the party at the time of the marriage was commonly held to have been baptized, or if his or her baptism was doubtful, the marriage must be considered doubtful (C. 1014) until it is proved with certainty that one party was baptized and one was not.

This canon deals with three items: (1) persons born in the Catholic Church; (2) persons received into the Catholic Church from heresy and schism; and (3) a doubtful baptism.

Historical Aspect

1. The natural and divine laws govern the impediments of *mixed religion* and *disparity of cult* because of the consequent danger to the faith and morals of the Catholic party.

2. In the Old Testament we have a positive law which forbids marriage between a Jew and a Gentile (Ex 34:16 and Dt 7:3).

3. Marriages between Jews and Christians, in the early Church, were considered legitimate by Christian emperors and they then influenced many of the Church councils.

4. From the 12th century to the new Code of Canon Law in 1918, all marriages were considered invalid which were contracted between a baptized person and a non-baptized person, unless a dispensation was obtained. This included baptized Protestants. Because of this legislation, many marriages were null.

5. This impediment is from divine law if there is a danger of perversion either to the Catholic party or their offspring, and a dispensation cannot be given until the danger is removed. However, this is considered a prohibitive impediment of the divine law only, because we have no positive proof that such a marriage is invalid by divine law.

Ecclesiastical Law

According to ecclesiastical law, it is a diriment impediment regardless of whether there is a danger or not. For example, from the facts and circumstances that children are being raised Catholics and the wife practices her Catholic religion without any interference from her unbaptized husband is not sufficient in itself of the guarantee. Canon 21 must be followed: "A law passed to guard against some danger remains binding even for individual cases in which the danger does not exist." The danger of perversion is a serious matter. The removal of the danger is a condition for the dispensation from the ecclesiastical law.

In summary, before 1918 and the New Code, the diriment impediment existed in all marriages of one probably baptized or for heretics and schismatics, and the non-baptized. After 1918, the impediment exists only in marriages where one party is not baptized and the other is baptized in the Catholic Church, or converted to it from heresy or schism.

The Oriental Code

It may be well to point out here the differences between the Latin Code and the Oriental Code of Law. Canons 60, 61 states: "A marriage contracted by a non-baptized person with a baptized person is null." This implies that baptized non-Catholics validly cannot marry a non-baptized person; this includes Oriental schismatics. Hence, the Oriental Code, dealing with the impediment of disparity of cult, is more restrictive than the Latin Code. In other words, the Oriental Code is similar to the Latin legislation before 1918. This impediment is retained according to the particular discipline. It also includes Oriental schismatics and retains the impediment of disparity of cult.

In ecclesiastical circles there are discussions about returning to this legislation as it was before 1918, because of the high divorce rate which results among the great number of non-Catholics who enter into such a marriage, or wish to enter a marriage with Catholics. They must resort to the complicated and involved process of the Privilege of the Faith. If we had the pre-Code legislation, our chanceries would not be tied down to all the necessary paper work and routine which is involved now. It would all be solved simply by the declaration of nullity, as it is done in the Oriental Church.

Conversion to the Catholic Church

The second item considered in this canon is conversion to the Catholic Faith from heresy, schism, or any other religion.

The manner in which conversion takes place into the Catholic Church (after which the member is called a convert): the so-called ABC formula is used: (A) Adjuration of heresy and profession of faith, (B) Baptism which is given conditionally, and (C) Confession sacramentally with conditional absolution. If the individual was baptized validly in a heretical sect, A and C are used. If one was never baptized, he is baptized absolutely.

The third element in this canon—*The Non-Baptized Party. There is a basic disparity or inequality regarding religion between a Catholic and a non-baptized person.* After questioning the party concerned, relatives, friends and acquaintances should be questioned, and records of churches where the non-baptized party lived for more than six months should be investigated.

One should investigate: if other members of the family were baptized, and if the parents were baptized and whether they were religiously inclined. If there is a doubt then there is a strong presumption that the party may have been baptized; if the parents were religious, we can presume they were baptized. Baptism is not usually presumed if the parents of the non-Catholic party frowned on baptism, did not have any children baptized, or had no records in the church.

Cases of Orientals and Non-baptized Persons

Case No. 1. C. 1070: *Mary, a Byzantine (Ruthenian) Catholic* was raised from childhood in the Roman Catholic Church. She attended Mass and received her Holy Communion there. Later when she planned her marriage with a non-baptized person, the pastor of the Latin Church obtained a dispensation from the disparity of cult. The Latin pastor performed the ceremony. Some time later the marriage ended in separation and divorce. Mary then married another non-baptized person outside the Church, but now this person wishes to take instructions and come into the Catholic Church. Mary wishes to have her second marriage validated. *This marriage can be validated* due to the fact the Latin rite ordinary invalidly granted the dispensation from the disparity of cult which resulted in an invalid marriage because the Latin ordinary has no subject and therefore no jurisdiction in the case, even though Mary attended the Latin Church during her lifetime.

Case No. 2: The ordinary of the Military Ordinariate in the USA enjoys faculties for Catholics of both the Eastern and Latin Rite subjects in the service. Chaplains may obtain the necessary dispensations from the Military Ordinariate, for example, for a Byzantine Catholic and a non-baptized person.

Susan, a Byzantine Catholic in the U. S. Army, plans to marry a non-baptized person in the city where they are sojourning. The chaplain went to the local ordinary of the place, who lived close by and obtained the dispensation from disparity of cult. The chaplain performed the marriage in the parish church. Some years later Susan separated and got a divorce. Her marriage was declared invalid on the score that the Latin ordinary did not have jurisdiction for either of these two parties. If the chaplain would have obtained the dispensation from the Military Ordinariate, the marriage would have been *valid.*

Canon 1071—The presciptions of Canons 1060-1065 pertaining to mixed marriages must also be applied to marriages in which an impediment of disparity of cult exists.

Who are the persons born in the Catholic Church?

(1) All adults who are validly baptized in the Catholic Church.

(2) All children of Catholic parents, also those of a mixed marriage, who have been baptized with the intention of belonging to the Catholic Church.

(3) All persons in danger of death who have been baptized by a Catholic. This may be baptism conferred by a layman or a priest, even though the party was unconscious.

(4) Children born of non-Catholics or were born of an invalid marriage are validly baptized in the Catholic Church when their parents' consent is given and a promise that the child will be brought up as a Catholic.

Manner of Baptism

The baptism takes place with the remote matter: water, and the proximate matter: the washing or ablution by infusion, immersion or aspersion. When any of these are used, the one baptizing must use the form simultaneously; "I baptize you, in the name of the Father...." The moral unity must exist between the ablution and the form. *Re: Protestant ministers:* They must have the *proper intention*, regardless of what their opinion might be. As long as the minister has the general intention: *to do what Christ instituted*, or he follows the Scripture as *all the Christians do in conferring Baptism.* When the proper ritual of Baptism is used, we can presume the proper intention. This brings up the question: *Are non-Catholic baptisms valid?* This question is frequently asked. We must distinguish. For a general principle, we could use this: If the minister used the proper matter and form and does what *Christ intended,* the baptism is valid. Hence, we cannot say, as some erroneously believe, that all non-Catholic baptisms are invalid. Ordinarily doubtful baptisms are considered valid. According to the response of the *Holy Office* to certain ordinaries in the U.S.:

Whether baptism conferred by the Disciples of Christ, Presbyterians, Congregationalists, Baptists, Methodists, is to be presumed invalid, when the necessary matter and form were used, because the minister did not have the intention to do what the Church does, or what Christ instituted, or whether such baptism is to be considered valid, unless the contrary is proved in a particular case. REPLY: In the *negative to the first part;* in the *affirmative to the second part.*[9] In other words, *in practice, baptism*

---

9. S. C. Holy Office, Dec. 28, 1949, AAS 41-650.

in these particular sects is considered valid until the contrary is proved, which means that each baptism could be subjected to a careful investigation of a particular locality at the time of the baptism, as well as the method and practice of the individual minister in the administration of the sacrament. These investigations are not easy but, when done, are rewarding.

Cases exemplifying deceptive records and circumstances of Baptism

Case No 1: Father *A* was sufficiently satisfied with a beautifully embossed baptismal certificate stating from a certain non-Catholic church that the person concerned was baptized. Father *B* doubted the baptism of the church. An investigation took place. The rector of the church of the baptism directed the investigators to his curate who took care of such matters. When asked what form he used, he was confused. "Do you have a baptismal font?" he was asked. He replied he did not use one. "Do you issue certificates?" His answer was: "All the members of our church are baptized in this church when they sign our golden book of baptism. We then issue the certificate of baptism. This was the case regarding your party."

Case No. 2: One non-Catholic minister stated that he baptized more solemnly than Catholics do. He exclaimed that while he poured the rose water on the person to be baptized, his wife sang with the accompaniment of the organ from the choir loft. He issued a certificate of baptism. We must be very careful in accepting baptismal certificates from non-Catholic churches.

Case No. 3: This case is very interesting. Mary had been married and divorced and now, after taking instructions, wished to marry a Catholic, if her Privilege of the Faith was granted in Rome. In the process it was discovered that her minister issued a baptismal certificate, thus making her first marriage a *ratum* marriage, since the other party was also baptized. Mary protested that she was never baptized. Investigation was made in the parish where she was baptized. Fortunately, the minister was courteous in permitting the examination of the baptismal record. The records showed that the former minister entered the baptism several times at different times. Mary's baptism was recorded only partially and not like the others. The records showed that Mary was baptized a day after the wedding when she was on her honeymoon. Moreover, the date October 12 (which was in the record), the date of marriage, was made into a 13, i.e., October 13, whereby baptism was to have been conferred on October 13. He was asked if the former minister was forgetful. He said he was 80 and very forgetful, the reason for his retirement. "How did you know?" said the minister. He replied: "Well, the records indicate forgetfulness." What really happened was that the minister began entering the marriage record into the baptismal book and realized that it was the wrong book. He left it go and did not finish entering the names, etc. Some one later changed the date which was written in blue ink, and a 3 out of 2 with black ink. The fact that the entry was incomplete, the minister forgetful, the date changed, the time of baptism listed when the party was away, and additional evidence was given by relatives. Therefore, from this internal evidence, we concluded that she was never baptized, thus substantiating her statement and the Privilege of the Faith case was carried through.

The Impediment of Mixed Religion of the Synod of Trullo (691)

Due to the controversy of the impediment of disparity of cult (mixed religion[10] enacted by the Council of Trullo (A.D. 691), which went on for several years, it is necessary to clarify some of these issues. In the Latin Church the impediment of mixed religion has not been an invalidating prohibition of marriage since the thirteenth century. In the Eastern Churches, the severity of the prohibition was once sharpened by conflicts regarding christological heresies, but here, too, the impediment has not been considered diriment for hundreds of years. However, a gradual development in Catholic and Orthodox teaching over the many years of separation parallels this fact. Since Vatican II it coincides in a shared acceptance of the sacramentality of marriages of baptized persons and the intimate relationship existing between Christian marriage and the eucharistic community of the Church.

Since there is a common bond of belief today in the sacramental hier-archical dimensions of marriage, it is difficult to understand the contra-diction between the publicized jurisprudence of the Roman Rota and the pastoral practice of the Orthodox Church regarding the impediment of "mixed religion." The discordance exists between the interpretation of the binding force of Eastern law derived from the Canon 72 of the Council of Trullo (691) and some Canonists. (In summary, Canon 72 stated that marriage between the Orthodox and heretics are forbidden, under the

---

10. **Canon Law Digest,** V, 13-14.

penalty of excommunication, and must be dissolved.) On the basis of a canonical theory of jurisdiction followed in recent years, the Orthodox faithful are considered still bound to the impediment enacted by this council.

The earliest use of the impediment of the Council of Trullo as a possible ground of nullity is found in a private reply given to the Bishop of Worcester by the Sacred Congregation of the Oriental Church on December 1959.[11] Since that we have public record of the fact that this impediment has been upheld by the Oriental Congregation, and used to invalidate many marriages by the Congregation of the Doctrine of the Faith, and more recently by the Roman Rota. Two cases ("documentum libertatis") were granted by the Holy Office, Feb. 10, 1960.

Five such cases were reported in the Roman Replies for 1965. The Canon Law Digest Supplement, through 1965, records three cases. In each of these cases one party was a validly baptized member of the Orthodox Church and the other was validly baptized as a Protestant. All these marriages occurred before motu proprio Crebrae Allatae, May 2, 1949. It was Cardinal Coussa's contention that after this motu proprio Canon 72 of Trullo was abrogated for the Orthodox. He was wrong.

Therefore, it can be stated that motu proprio Crebrae Allatae was not intended for the Orthodox and as such, Canon 72 of Trullo still holds. Moreover, a rescript dated May 22, 1969 declared invalid a marriage of an Orthodox with a validly baptized Protestant contracted in 1956: Constare de invaliditate matrimonii in casu ex 72 Concilii Trullani quod adhuc suam vim tenet.[12] This now clearly contradicts the former theory and sustains the opinion that the motu proprio did not affect the matrimonial law of the Orthodox Churches.[13] To understand the controversy better, one should read The Impediment of Mixed Religion.[14]

---

11. The terminology "Mixed Religion" was never used in the time of Trullo. This term was unknown; instead, "disparity of Cult" was used, which has a different meaning today, but it is still used, at least until 1967, according to this letter of the Holy Office.
Letter of S.C. Doctrine of the Faith—Rome, June 8, 1967 Prot. N. 1155/67
Exc.me ac Rev.me Domine:
Litteris die 22 februarii a.d. datis, Excellentia Tua Rev.me postulavit facultatem declarandi nullum matrimonium contractum a Greco-orthodoxa N-N cum lutherano baptizato N-N anno 1942 ob impedimentum disparitatis cultus.
Ad rem Tecum communico hanc S. Congregationem decrevisse: "Ordinarius procedere poterit, vi can. 72 Concilii Trullani, ad declarationem nullitatis matrimonii de quo supra ad normam can. 1990.   A. Card. Ottaviani, Pro Pref.

12. Pro No. 2911/59m.
13. The Jurist, XXIX, 1969, p. 387.
14. Bassett, The Jurist, Vol. XXIX, Oct. 1969, pp. 383-415.

At first, decisions regarding Canon 72 of Trullo were handled administratively and reserved explicitly to the competency of the Holy Office; subsequently in particular cases local ordinaries (Latin and Oriental) were instructed to decide the cases. By virtue of the apostolic constitution *Regimini Ecclesiae Universae* of August 15, 1967 and the decree *Integrae servandae* of December 7, 1965, these cases should now be handled judicially, with appeal to normal tribunals of second instance and then, if necessary, to the Roman Rota.

Sacred Orders

Canon 1072—Clerics in Sacred Orders who attempt marriage do so invalidly.

1. Sacred Orders are the Subdeaconate, Deaconate, Priesthood, and Bishopric.

2. This is an ecclesiastical impediment which became established for the Latin Church at the Council of Trent, stemming from the Lateran Council of 1139.

3. Celibacy had been encouraged in the Church for centuries, since the fifth century.

4. Since it is only an ecclesiastical impediment, it could be dispensed by the Holy See, but this is seldom done for the priesthood. The *Deaconate and Subdeaconate:* in danger of death, Canons 1043 and 1044 provide for such dispensation out of the Subdeaconate and Deaconate.

5. Clerics who are constituted in Major Orders when they attempt marriage even by a civil ceremony, incur an *ipso facto* excommunication which is reserved simply to the Holy See. Canon 2388: By common law such clerics lose their ecclesiastical office which they may hold (C. 188:5). In addition, they become irregular *ex delicto* (C. 985:3).

6. On May 4, 1937, the Sacred Penitentiary added a more severe penalty for an attempted marriage by a priest; it is now a *specialissimo modo* censure reserved to the Holy See.

7. *Oriental Law:* This legislation is similar to the Latin code, however, the Subdiaconate is still retained in the Oriental Churches. It is a major or minor impediment depending upon whether the particular rite demands the observance of celibacy.

8. The Order of Subdiaconate was discontinued in the Latin Church September 14, 1972.

Solemn Vows

Canon 1073—Likewise marriage is invalidly attempted by religious who have pronounced either solemn vows or vows which by special provision of the Holy See are endowed with the power of invalidating marriage.

1. Anyone who attempts marriage in solemn vows: this marriage is rendered invalid by this canon. Here we exclude Sacred Orders.

2. Vows taken in a religious institute are public and are either simple or solemn. The distinction between these is the fact that a simple vow renders an attempted marriage illicit or unlawful, while solemn vows render an attempted marriage invalid (C. 529). This is one of the ecclesiastical prohibitions.

3. By special provision of the Holy See, the Jesuits have a simple vow whereby an attempted marriage is rendered invalid.

4. *Penalty:* A person in solemn vows who attempts marriage incurs an excommunication simply reserved to the Holy See. The guilty partner incurs the excommunication also (C. 2388: 1). Solemn vows are so-called because they are recognized by the Church as such. The solemnity is considered not so much in the external ceremony but in their object or effects; *whereby solemn vows render certain actions invalid whereas simple vows render them illicit.* Ecclesiastical law gives this invalidating effect.

5. *Dispensation:* A person in solemn vows can obtain a dispensation from the Holy See. The obligation of solemn vows arises from the divine law and as such cannot be dispensed while the vow is in effect. But by

Letter of National Conference of Catholic Bishops USA, January 14, 1974
Your Excellency: In the past few years there have been several questions presented to the Committee on Canonical Affairs regarding the processing of marriages cases involving Eastern Orthodox with non-Catholic Christians. The Committee asked the Canon Law Society of America for assistance, and we have now received an extensive report from a committee headed by Father Edward J. Luca of the Diocese of Cleveland. The report makes two conclusions:
1) That cases **probably can** no longer be processed under Canon 72 of the Synod of Trullo. This conclusion is supported by recent Rotal jurisprudence, a decision of the Apostolic Signatura, and most recent canonical literature.
2) That **local tribunals may handle by ordinary administrative procedure** cases of "defectus ritus sacri" in the marriage of an Eastern Orthodox with another (non-Catholic) Christian that was not blessed by an Orthodox priest.
Bernard J. Flanagan, Bishop of Worcester
Chairman: Bishop Committee on Canonical Affairs

exercise of jurisdiction, which the Holy Father has, he can relax this vow, and in so doing relax the obligation.

Abduction

> Canon 1074—1. Between the abductor and the woman abducted with the intention of marriage, there can be no marriage as long as she remains in the power of the abductor.
> 2. If the woman, after having been separated from the abductor and put in a free and safe place, consents to have him as her husband, the impediment ceases.
> 3. As regards the nullity of marriage, the violent detention of a woman is held equivalent to abduction; that is, when the man, for the purpose of marriage, violently detains a woman in the place where she is staying or to which she has freely come.

1. This is an ecclesiastical impediment: the factors herein considered came under force and fear before the Council of Trent; this invalidated the marriage. In other words, the Council of Trent considered the factor of abduction along with force and fear. The Code includes not only abduction but also the violent detention of a woman.

2. The second paragraph also indicates that if she freely consents in the place of detention, the marriage is still null because she must be brought to a safe place to make the consent freely.

3. A distinction should be made here. Suppose a man abducts a person for reason of sexual relations and not for marriage. The woman afterwards consents to marry him. In this case, there is no impediment; but if she is abducted for sexual relations and afterward is detained for the purpose of marrying, the impediment would be there. Since this is an ecclesiastical impediment, it would not affect the unbaptized.

Crime

> Canon 1075—The following persons cannot validly contract marriage:
> 1. Persons who, during the existence of the same lawful marriage, have consummated adultery together and have mutually promised each other to marry, or have attempted marriage even by a mere civil act;
> 2. Those who, likewise during the existence of the same lawful marriage, have consummated adultery together, and one of

whom has killed the lawful spouse;

3. Those who, even without committing adultery, have by mutual cooperation, physical or moral, killed the lawful spouse.

A valid marriage cannot be contracted in the following cases of crime:

I. *First Degree of Crime:* (1)*Adultery* - Adultery must be taken in the true sense, namely, one party at least is bound by a valid marriage.

(2) *Adultery must be consummated* - That is, the penetration of the vagina and the depositing of the seed therein. The use of contraceptive devices during intercourse would eliminate this impediment. Of course, the parties would have to prove this.

(3) *Formal Adultery* - This means that at least one of the parties is a married person. Affected ignorance, that is, when something is done, but not enough to find out if the other party is married, on the part of one of the parties, if the other party is married would excuse.

Crass or supine Ignorance (i.e., indifference), when one realizes the gravity of the obligation and should find out, but does not, probably excuses in this case because of the doubt of law and fact.

Condition - The promise must be absolute and sincere; it must be serious and mutual, exteriorly manifested and accepted during the existing marriage. The promise of marriage must be upon the fact of the dissolution of the present marriage by the death of the party espoused, not by divorce (Cipos, par. 123).

Today, divorced persons who marry again during the lifetime of the other party, and consummate the attempted marriage, fall under this degree of the impediment of crime. If one is validating such a marriage later, a dispensation from this impediment is needed and one should apply for it in the chancery.

II. *Second Degree of Crime:* The second degree of crime is when adultery is committed and one of the adulterers kills the lawful spouse. Two factors make up this impediment: First: true adultery, and second, one adulterer kills either his own spouse or the spouse of the other party or both spouses. The adultery must precede the killing of the spouse. There must be murder with the intention of marrying. We say it must precede the murder because after the murder one cannot call it adultery because the party is already dead. To kill one's spouse for the purpose of collecting insurance or to inherit property is no impediment (Cipos, par. 123).

III. *Third Degree of Crime:* The third degree of crime is when no adultery takes place but the cooperation to murder the lawful spouse takes place. First, both must be accomplices, physical and moral, to the murder. The intention to marry must be present. This is presumed unless the contrary is proved. If adultery took place, this would be an additional impediment. In practice, give the entire case to the chancery so they would understand the situation.

Dispensation: Ordinaries can give a dispensation which they have from the *quinquennial faculties* for the first degree of crime. The *Apostolic Delegate grants a dispensation* for the *second degree of crime.* The ordinary can grant it in the second degree only in occult crime cases. For the third degree of crime, dispenastion must be obtained from the Apostolic Delegate. Ordinaries and pastors and all those listed in Canons 1043 and 1044 may dispense from all three in danger of death.

Consanguinity

Canon 1076—1. In the direct line of consanguinity, marriage is invalid between all the ancestors and descendants *whether legitimate or natural.*
2. In the collateral line, marriage is invalid up to the third degree inclusively, but the understanding is that the matrimonial impediment is multiplied only as often as the common ancestor is multiplied.
3. Marriage must be permitted if there exists a doubt that the parties may be related by consanguinity in any degree of the direct line or in the first degree of the collateral line.

Consanguinity is the relationship between persons, based on carnal relationship, or carnal generation. Consanguinity does not arise from blood transfusions. Consanguinity exists in the *direct line,* if one of the persons is the *direct* ancestor of the other, that is, persons who descend from each other. For example, *Father, Daughter, Granddaughter, Great-granddaughter,* etc.

Father—Daughter 1° — Granddaughter 2° Great-granddaughter 3°

Consanguinity in the Indirect Line

This indirect line is also called *oblique line, transverse line* but usually it is called the *collateral line,* if neither person is the direct ancestor of the other, but both are descended from a common ancestor, as for example, brother and sister, first cousins, etc.

	JOHN		is the *Common Stock* (stipes)
1°	Joseph	Mary	(brother and sister)
2°	Peter	Anna	(1st cousins)
3°	Andrew	Jane	(2nd cousins)
4°	Jack	Jill	(3rd cousins)

(No dispensation needed.)

In the preceding diagram: *Joseph and Mary are brother and sister* and 1° removed from the common stock (Peter); *Peter and Anna are first cousins and* 2°; *Joseph and Anna* are in the 2° 1°, second degree touching the first (*in secundo gradu tangente primum*) OR Uncle and Niece: *Andrew and Anna* are in the third degree collateral mixed with the second degree 3° 2°, that is (*second cousins-first mixed*); *Andrew and Jane* are in the 2° degree, or a second cousin degree. Since 1918, there is *no dispensation needed for third cousins 4° collateral of consanguinity.* Marriage between *Brother —and Sister is Probably Null* in the natural law itself. The Church never grants a dispensation in such a case or even when it is probable that the parties are related in this manner. If nonbaptized people are related in this way and already married, the Holy Office does not forbid a priest to baptize them.

Uncle-Niece Marriages

We have a special instruction of the Sacred Congregation of the Sacraments, August 1, 1931, regarding such marriages. No dispensation will be granted without very special reasons. The ordinary himself must write the petition to Rome for such a dispensation, *or*, at least, sign the petition, *and* give his views on the reasons for asking such a dispensation (AAS XXIII, 1931, p. 413). These marriages should be discouraged, as well as cousin marriages.

Diagramming

It must be kept in mind that there is no impediment of consanguinity unless one of the parents, of one party wishing to get married, was at least a first cousin of one of the parents of the other party.

When determining the degrees of relationship, use the following:

(1) To make two persons *Brother and Sister*, give them a common ancestor.

(2) To make two persons *First Cousins*, give them a common Grandparent.

(3) To make two persons *second cousins*, give them a common Greatparent.

(4) To make brothers,

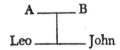

(5) To make brothers *Half-Brothers*,

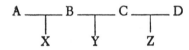

MANNER OF COMPUTING THE DEGREES
The degrees are computed in this way:

Direct Line: Compute it according to the *number of generations,* or, according to the *number of persons* in the line, *without counting the ancestor* (Stipes).

Collateral Line: Compute it according to the *number of generations* in one branch, *if the branches are equal;* if the two branches are *unequal, count the longer branch* (C. 96).

CONSANGUINITY

Case No. 1: Jack and Mary come to your rectory to arrange for their marriage. Jack tells you that he is the *first cousin* to Mary's mother; he is also a *nephew* to Mary's father. Do you need a dispensation?

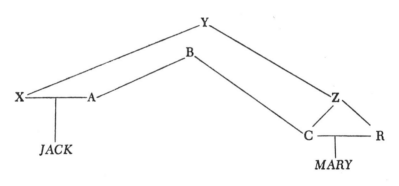

```
JACK -- A -- B )            2° Collateral
MARY -- C -- B )
JACK -- X -- Y              2° )
MARY -- R -- Z -- Y -- 3° ) 3° 2° Collateral
            (Dispensation needed.)
```

Case No. 2: While *Peter* and *Eva* are going over **their** marriage plans with the pastor, they mention that they are related; their *fathers* were *first cousins,* and *Peter's mother* was a *second cousin* to *Eva's father.*

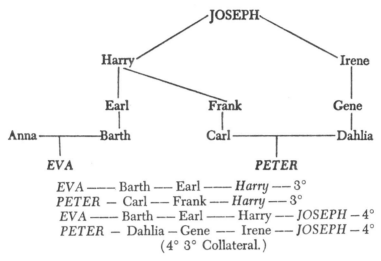

EVA —— Barth —— Earl —— *Harry* —— 3°
PETER — Carl —— Frank —— *Harry* —— 3°
EVA —— Barth —— Earl —— Harry —— *JOSEPH* — 4°
PETER — Dahlia — Gene —— Irene —— *JOSEPH* — 4°
(4° 3° Collateral.)

Case no. 3: Father John of St. Joseph's encounters this dilemma. *Susie* and *James* wish to marry, but their *fathers* were *half-brothers* and their *grandmothers* were *full sisters.*

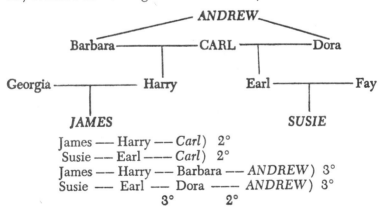

James —— Harry —— *Carl*) 2°
Susie —— Earl —— *Carl*) 2°
James —— Harry —— Barbara —— *ANDREW*) 3°
Susie —— Earl —— Dora —— *ANDREW*) 3°
           3°   2°

Case No. 4: **Joseph** and *Rosemary* wish to marry but they present the pastor with this consanguinity problem. Joseph's father is Rosemary's *uncle* on the *father's* side and Rosemary's mother is Joseph's *aunt* on the *mother's* side. (Their fathers are brothers and their mothers are sisters.)

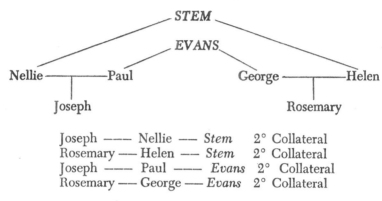

Joseph —— Nellie — *Stem*	2° Collateral
Rosemary — Helen — *Stem*	2° Collateral
Joseph —— Paul —— *Evans*	2° Collateral
Rosemary — George — *Evans*	2° Collateral

Case No. 5: Donald and Teresa signed the engagement contract a year ago; now they are preparing for their wedding. In the investigation the pastor discovers that their *grandfathers* are *brothers*, their *fathers* are *brothers*, and their *mothers* are *sisters*.

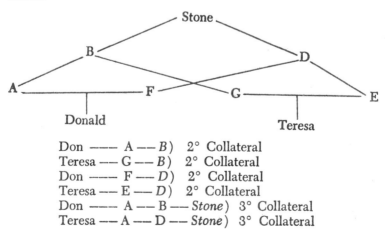

Don —— A — B)	2° Collateral
Teresa — G — B)	2° Collateral
Don —— F — D)	2° Collateral
Teresa — E — D)	2° Collateral
Don —— A — B — *Stone*)	3° Collateral
Teresa — A — D — *Stone*)	3° Collateral

Case No. 6: Owen plans to marry *Lea*, but they are related. Their mothers are *first cousins* and their fathers were *brothers.*

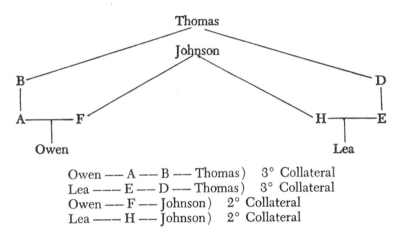

```
Owen —— A —— B —— Thomas)   3° Collateral
Lea ——— E —— D —— Thomas)   3° Collateral
Owen —— F —— Johnson)       2° Collateral
Lea ——— H —— Johnson)       2° Collateral
```

Case No. 7: After filling out the preliminary investigation papers, *Ted* and *Zia* left the rectory, but returned later to find out how he was related to Zia (which he forgot to mention). Their father married two *first cousins* successively.

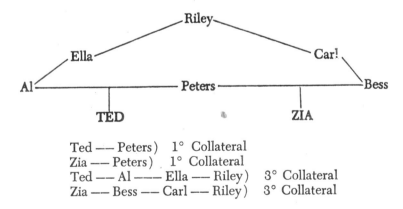

```
Ted —— Peters)              1° Collateral
Zia —— Peters)              1° Collateral
Ted —— Al ——— Ella —— Riley)   3° Collateral
Zia —— Bess —— Carl —— Riley)  3° Collateral
```

Case No. 8: Peter and *Julia* are engaged. Father Thomas discovers that they cannot marry unless a dispensation is obtained. Julia's father, Christian, is Peter's *brother,* and Julia's mother is *first cousin* to both Peter and Christian.

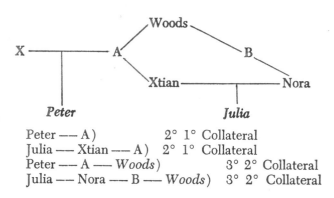

Peter — A)   2° 1° Collateral
Julia — Xtian — A)   2° 1° Collateral
Peter — A — *Woods*)   3° 2° Collateral
Julia — Nora — B — *Woods*)   3° 2° Collateral

Case No. 9: In a discussion before marriage, the parents of the couple reveal to *Matilda* that it might be impossible to marry *Blane* because she is related to him. Matilda's grandfather was a *brother* to Blane's grandfather and Matilda's grandmother was a *sister* to Blane's grandmother.

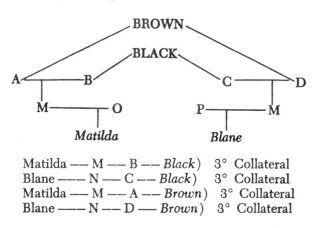

Matilda — M — B — *Black*)   3° Collateral
Blane — N — C — *Black*)   3° Collateral
Matilda — M — A — *Brown*)   3° Collateral
Blane — N — D — *Brown*)   3° Collateral

Case No. 10: **Father Charles encountered some difficulty** with the couple *Pat* and *Lulu* when they came to arrange for their wedding. Lulu's father was a *brother* to Pat's grandfather on his father's side; Lulu's mother was a *sister* to Pat's grandmother on his mother's side and Lulu's father was a *brother* to Pat's grandfather on his mother's side.

In other words, three sisters, G, H and D Denby marry three brothers F, E and C Smith. Peter the son of the first pair F and G Smith marries Joanne, the daughter of the second pair, E and H; this couple PETER AND JOANNE have a son, Patrick who plans to marry Lulu, the daughter of the third pair C and D.

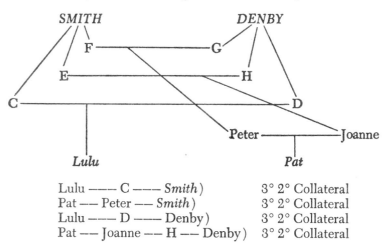

Lulu —— C —— Smith)	3° 2° Collateral
Pat —— Peter —— Smith)	3° 2° Collateral
Lulu —— D —— Denby)	3° 2° Collateral
Pat —— Joanne —— H —— Denby)	3° 2° Collateral

Case No. 11: *Clement* and *Jenny* have been dating for several years. They now plan to marry. In their conversation with their pastor, he is dubious whether it is possible but told them he would work out a solution. Checking the family tree he finds the following.

Clem's grandfather, Tom Fulton, and Joe Fulton are *brothers.* Rose, Jean and Fay Jones are *sisters.* Tom marries Fay and they have a child Rita. Joe marries Jean and they have a child, Nicholas. Rita and Nick marry and have a daughter, Jenny. Fay dies (Tom Fulton's wife). Tom now marries Rose, the other Jones sister. The grandson, *Clement*, now wishes to marry *Jenny*. Give the schema.

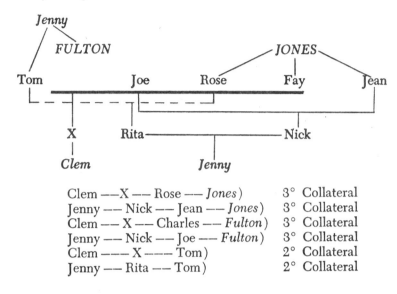

Clem —X — Rose — *Jones*)	3° Collateral
Jenny — Nick — Jean — *Jones*)	3° Collateral
Clem — X — Charles — *Fulton*)	3° Collateral
Jenny — Nick — Joe — *Fulton*)	3° Collateral
Clem —— X —— Tom)	2° Collateral
Jenny — Rita — Tom)	2° Collateral

Case No. 12: *Dora* and *Bob* plan on getting married, but they are related. Their fathers are *brothers*, and Bob's mother is *first cousin* to Dora's father.

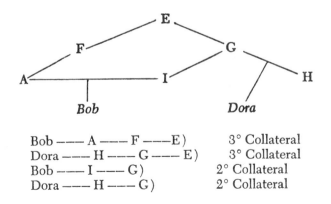

Bob —— A —— F ——E)	3° Collateral
Dora —— H —— G —— E)	3° Collateral
Bob —— I —— G)	2° Collateral
Dora —— H —— G)	2° Collateral

Case No. 13: *Fay* and *George* are in doubt whether they can get married because they are related. Fay's father is the *grandfather* of George by a former marriage, he is also an *uncle* of Fay's mother.

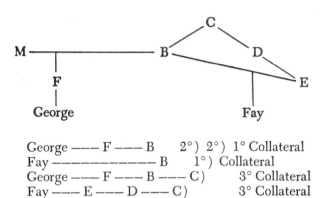

George ——— F ——— B   2°) 2°) 1° Collateral
Fay ————————————— B   1°) Collateral
George ——— F ——— B ——— C)   3° Collateral
Fay ——— E ——— D ——— C)   3° Collateral

Case No. 14: *Sam* and *Rose* decided to get married. They have a problem. Sam's father was the *grandfather* of Rose by a former marriage, and Sam's mother was the *grandmother* of Rose by a previous marriage.

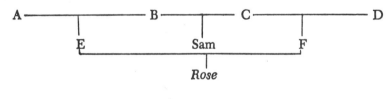

Rose ——— E ——— B - 2°)   2° 1°
Sam ————————— B - 1°)   2° 1°
Rose ——— F ——— C - 2°)   2° 1°
Sam ————————— C - 1°)   2° 1°

Case No. 15: Steve, a widower, and his son *Junior* get married to *Kate* and her daughter, *Jane*, respectively. The daughter of Steve and Kate now wants to marry Leo, the son of Junior and Jane.

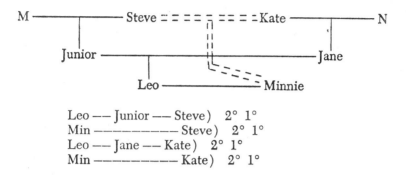

Leo — Junior — Steve) 2° 1°
Min ———————— Steve) 2° 1°
Leo — Jane — Kate) 2° 1°
Min ———————— Kate) 2° 1°

ORIENTAL COMPUTATION

Case No. 16: John of the **Melchite rite** wishes to marry Helen of the Byzantine rite. Helen is John's second cousin, once removed. Can they marry without a dispensation? Would the case be the same if John and Mary were of the Latin rite?

Canon 66: 2. Marriage is invalid in the collateral line to the 6°: Examples:

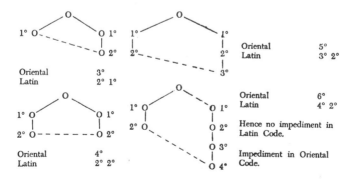

Oriental Law

The diriment impediment of consanguinity and affinity differ as to the manner of computation and applicability. Canon 66 of the Oriental Law provides that marriage between blood relatives in all degrees of the direct line are null and void; furthermore, blood relations in the collateral line nullifies marriage up to the sixth degree inclusive; in case of a doubt concerning relationship in any degree of the direct line or up to the second degree of the collateral line inclusive, marriages are never permitted. Canon 66 has a fourth provision not to be found in its Latin counterpart, Canon 1076. This provision gives the Oriental version of the Canon 96 CIC, namely, the manner in which the degrees of consanguinity are to be computed.

The Oriental code computes the degree of consanguinity by taking into consideration *all generations on both sides* of the collateral line, whereas the Latin Code takes into consideration only the one, *the longer line*. At first sight the casual observer might be inclined to think that this computation is the same as the third degree in the Latin Code, but this would be true only if there would be an unequal number of generations on both sides of the line. However, if one side of the line should have four or five generations and the other one or two, the Latin Code would permit marriage in the fourth and fifth generations whereas the Eastern Code would prohibit the same. Interritual marriages frequently take place and hence a situation might take place where a Latin would plan to marry an Oriental to whom he might be related in the fourth or fifth degree of consanguinity often in the collateral line. According to his own law, the Latin may contract marriage validly whereas the Oriental could be disqualified from contracting a valid marriage without a dispensation. Which law prevails? Cappello proposes the principle of communication of freedom from the Latin subject to the Oriental party; moreover, if there still remains doubt regarding this (doubt of law), Canon 15 CIC could be applied, namely, that the law does not oblige of laws creates a doubt, we are free to follow this (Canon 15 CIC) until here.[15] E. Herman disagrees with this interpretation.[16] Since this conflict the Holy See declares otherwise. We might add that some authors suggest that the safest would be to obtain a dispensation from the proper Eastern Hierarch (Ordinary) who can dispense the Oriental party.

15. Cappello, F., **De Matrimonio**, VI, 1947, pp. 487-488.
16. Herman, Emil, "Adnotationes," **Periodica de Re Morali Canonica Liturgica,** Rome, 1949.

Affinity Code

There are also some differences regarding the affinity (unlike the Latin Code). The Oriental Code recognizes as a diriment impediment affinity between blood relations of the spouses and the so-called affinity (ex trigeneia) which arises from two valid marriages (even if not consummated) when the spouses contract marriage successively with the same third party or with two different persons related to each other by blood. For example; John marries a widow, Margaret, who had a son Joseph by her first marriage. Some time after Margaret dies and John marries another person, Susan. John subsequently dies. *Later Susan wishes to marry Joseph.* In this case, we find that there exists the impediment of affinity arising from trigeneia: *the degree of affinity of Susan's late husband John to Joseph. The degree of John's affinity to Joseph then depends upon the degree of consanguinity of John's first wife to Joseph.* Since Margaret was Joseph's mother (1°) between John and Joseph we have simple affinity in the first degree and we find then that Susan is related in the same degree of affinity to Joseph arising from *trigeneia*, or a successive marriage with the same third party, namely, two different persons related to each other by blood.

John	*Margaret*	*Xavier*
Susan		*Joseph*

In the direct line affinity nullifies marriage in all ascending and descending degrees similar to the Latin Code but, unlike the Latin Code, marriage contracted in the fourth degree inclusive in the collateral line is considered null.

Affinity (*ex digeneia*) which exists between the blood relatives of the two parties nullifies marriage up to the fourth degree inclusive.

Affinity

Canon 1077—1. Affinity in the direct line in any degree invalidates marriage; in the collateral line it invalidates it up to the 2° degree inclusive.

2. The impediment of affinity is multiplied: 1° as often as the impediment of consanguinity from which it arises is multiplied; 2° whenever marriage is repeated —successively with a blood relative of a deceased spouse.

Canon 97—1. Affinity arises from a valid marriage, either ratified or ratified and consummated.

2. It exists only between the man and the blood relatives of the woman and likewise between the woman and the blood relatives of the man.

3. It is computed in such a way that the same persons who are blood relatives of the man are related by affinity in the same line and degree to the woman and vice versa.

1. Affinity comes from a valid marriage. It extends to all degrees in the direct line. A man could not, e.g., marry his wife's mother, grandmother, daughter, or granddaughter, and vice versa.

Grandmother

Mother

Daughter

Granddaughter

2. The brothers of the husband are not related by affinity to the sisters of the wife.

3. The Church rarely dispenses from affinity in the direct line.

4. *Henry VIII of England:* Henry VIII got a dispensation to marry Catherine, his sister-in-law, who was his brother's wife; Arthur never consummated the marriage, is the alleged opinion. When Henry VIII decided to marry again, he claimed that the affinity dispensation was invalid, even given by the Pope of Rome, because it was an impediment of the Divine Law.

5. Canon 1043-44 grants the faculty to dispense with all ecclesiastical impediments but affinity in the direct line of a consummated marriage is restricted here.

6. In 1957 the disputed question among authors was presented to the Holy See: whether affinity contracted in infidelity became an impediment for marriage which was entered into after baptism even of only one of the parties. The answer was Affirmative (AAS 49-77).

Affinity: Twenty-six states in the United States do not have affinity as an impediment. The following have degrees of affinity that annul marriages: Alabama, Georgia, Iowa, Kentucky, Maine, Maryland, Massachusetts, Connecticut, Delaware, Michigan, Mississippi, New Hampshire, Oklahoma, Pennsylvania, Rhode Island, South Carolina, Tennessee, Texas, Vermont, Virginia, Washington, West Virginia and District of Columbia. Every state varies regarding this impediment. Alabama, e.g., forbids the son to marry his stepmother or the widow of his uncle. The father may not marry the widow of his son. The father may not marry the daughter of his wife, or the daughter of his son. It is best to check the laws and statutes of each state.

Cases of Affinity

Case No. 1: Joseph marries Mary who dies within a year. Joseph then wants to marry Mary's sister, Ann.

Miller

Joseph   Mary   Ann

Case No. 2: Susie and Lea are sisters. Helen and Rose are sisters. Susie and Lea are first cousins to Helen and Rose. John marries Lea. How is he related to the other three in virtue of the impediment of affinity?

Joseph

W   S

Susie   Lea   John   Helen   Rose

1. Lea and John marriage
   John to Susie———1^0
   John to Helen———2^0
   John to Rose———2^0

2. John and Helen marriage
   John to Rose———1^0

Public Propriety

Canon 1078—*Public Propriety*

The impediment of public propriety arises from an invalid marriage, whether consummated or not, and from public or notorious concubinage; it annuls marriage in the first and second degree of the direct line between the man and the blood relations of the women and vice versa.

1. It must be noted that this impediment arises from an invalid marriage, consummated or not consummated, and it must be from concubinage which is public or notorious. Thereby, any attempt at marriage in the first and second degree of the direct line between the man and the blood relations of the woman would render this attempted marriage invalid.

2. What kind of invalid marriage are we considering here? The code does not distinguish; neither shall we.

3. In 1929 the Code Commission did give a definition regarding public propriety insofar as it settled the question that this impediment does not arise from the mere fact of a civil marriage when there is no cohabitation (Chap. AAS. 21-170).

4. An invalid marriage is one that has the appearance of marriage but is invalid because of some diriment impediment or force or fear or lack of consent, etc.

5. What is concubinage? When two people live as husband and wife with the intention of having sexual relations and this union does not even have the appearance of marriage. If this is publicly known, the impediment arises; if it is not publicly known, there is no impediment. For example: John and Mary live in concubinage in a hotel. They are thought to be man and wife; therefore, there is no impediment - the crime is not public.

6. *The Unbaptized:* The unbaptized are not bound by this —ecclesiastical impediment. If one is baptized, it binds directly the baptized and indirectly the unbaptized party. However, the unbaptized are not bound by the impediment if they give up their concubinage at the time of conversion; if they continue after the baptism, they incur this impediment.

7. *Dispensation:* This is not like affinity insofar as it extends to the direct line only and not to the collateral line. Hence, this would be concubinage, provided it is public or notorious.

An invalid marriage is different technically from concubinage. They are both similar insofar as both are *immoral* because these people have *no right* to the conjugal act. They are different insofar as an *invalid marriage* has some juridic act involved (the ceremony which accompanied it), whereas in *concubinage* no such act took place. A marriage is considered *invalid* only when the prescribed form is used and a diriment impediment is present. It must be remembered that we can obtain a *sanation for an invalid marriage,* but we cannot sanate a case of *concu-*

---

17. Monitor Eccles. 1962, pp. 541-555.

binage. In the former (invalid marriage) some form of juridic act took place, whereas in concubinage people are living together as married people, preceded by no celebration of marriage or, in other words, lacking this juridic act. No consent was given to marriage in concubinage. When a sanation is given, the consent to marriage must be persevering at the time it is granted. In applying for a *sanatio in radice*, every priest should keep this in mind, namely, the difference between concubinage and an invalid marriage. A dispensation for a *sanatio* for a concubinage case would be invalid.[17]

Spiritual Relationship

Canon 1079—The only spiritual relationship which invalidates marriage is that mentioned in Canon 768.

1. That spiritual relationship annuls marriage only which is mentioned in Canon 768: "The minister of baptism and the sponsor contract spiritual relationship from baptism with the person baptized only." In other words, because of baptism the minister and the sponsor or sponsors contract spiritual relationship whereby the impediment to marriage arises with the baptized person.

2. The Code does not distinguish whether this pertains to solemn or private baptisms. Therefore, we do not consider this question. There is, however, no impediment between the parents and the minister, or parents and sponsors.

3. On one baptismal certificate, we found the minister of baptism was also the sponsor. Is this possible? According to the Sacred Congregation of Rites, 1873, if the bishop wants to be sponsor in confirmation, he can appoint a proxy to act as sponsor. One author (Wernz)[18] states there is a double relationship; the proxy sponsor does not contract any spiritual relationship whereby it would become an impediment. Does one incur the spiritual relationship if he acts as sponsor at a conditional baptism? No, he would incur spiritual relationship with the person if the same individual were present for the first baptism, as well as the conditional baptism. If a non-baptized person acted as sponsor, did he become related spiritually to the baptized if he was baptized in the Church? No, because it is an impediment of ecclesiastical law and he was not held by the law at the time he acted as sponsor.

18. Wernz, Jus. Decretal., IV, no. 492, ftn. 67.

4. Dispensation: The ordinary can dispense from this impediment by his quinquennial faculties.[19]

Legal Relationship

Canon 1080—Legal Relationship
Persons who according to the civil law are regarded as incapable of marrying each other because of a legal relationship arising from adoption, cannot validly contract marriage together according to canon law.

All persons who by civil law are disqualified in marrying certain persons because of legal adoption are likewise disqualified in contrcting a valid marriage according to canon law. Such invalidating laws are found in Puerto Rico; also in Massachusetts, Rhode Island and Connecticut (Cf. Alford, *US MAT. Comparatum* No. 163, N58, ch. 15). A dispensation from this impediment must be obtained from the Apostolic Delegate.

Adoption and Guardianship as Impediments

This canon provides that, where civil law makes the relationship arising from legal adoption an impediment, i.e., merely prohibitive, impediment, the same relationship constitutes for that civil jurisdiction, a canonical impediment of the same nature.

In a recent (1976) study of 100 nations on this subject:

1) the following nations have *no* law on adoption as any kind of marriage impediment: Afghanistan, Algeria, Cambodia, Cameroun, Canada, Ceylon (Sri Lanka), China, Cuba, Cyprus, Ecuador, Egypt, Gambia, Ghana, Hungary, Jordan, Liberia, Madagascar, Malawi, Malaysia, Morocco, Nigeria, Pakistan, Saudi Arabia, Sierra Leone, Singapore, Somali Republic, Sudan, Sweden (former prohibitive impediment abrogated in 1973), Syria, Tanzania, Thailand, Tunisia, Uganda, United States of America.

2) *Adoption* is a *diriment* impediment to marriage in: Albania, Argentina, Australia, Bolivia, Brazil, Chile, Colombia, Czechoslovakia, Dominican Republic, East Germany, El Salvador, Ethiopia, Great Bri-

---

19. Oriental Law: In the new code for the Orientals, the sponsor contracts relationships with the person baptized and with this person's parents. However, spiritual relationship does not arise between the minister and the person baptized. This is an important point when dealing with Orientals.

tain, Greece, Indonesia, Italy, Japan, Liechtenstein, Mali, The Netherlands, New Zealand, Nicaragua, Paraguay, Philippines, Poland, Rumania, Russia, San Marino, South Korea, Spain, Switzerland.

3) *Adoption* is an *impedient* impediment to marriage in: Austria, Belgium, Denmark, Finland, France, Guatemala, Haiti, Iceland, Ivory Coast, Luxembourg, Mexico, Norway, Peru, Portugal, South Africa, Turkey, Venezuela, West Germany, Yugoslavia.

4) *Guardianship* is an *impedient* impediment to marriage in: Albania, Argentina, Brazil, Costa Rica, Guatemala, Honduras, Mexico, Nicaragua, Panama, Peru, Portugal, Rumania, Spain, Uruguay, Venezuela, Yugoslavia.

5) *Guardianship* is a *diriment* impediment to marriage in: Greece, Taiwan. Reported in article in *Periodica*, 65 (1976), pp. 141-158 (Prader).

CHAPTER SIX

MATRIMONIAL CONSENT

MATRIMONIAL CONSENT

Introduction

Historically a great debate existed in the Church on what was the essential factor constituting a marriage. The Canon Law School in Bologna maintained that *consummation* was this factor; this made the marriage. While the School of Paris at the time, maintained it was *consent* which made the marriage valid. Eventually this debate was settled when Pope Alexander III 1159-1181), using tradition as his basis, stated that *consent was* the essential factor that made the marriage valid. This is still the authoritative teaching of the Church today. Therefore, consent in marriage is of utmost importance to all canonists.

From the number of documents from the Holy See, the Decrees of Vatican Council II, and the ongoing jurisprudence of Rotal decisions over the years since the Code of 1918; (Cf. Appendix) we have seen a significant development in the theology of Canon Law regarding the role *consent* plays in the nature of marriage. The approach of de-emphasizing the traditional concept of marriage as a *contract* and putting more emphasis on the concept of *covenant* proposed by Vatican Council II, is indeed a great step forward in the theology of Canon Law redounding to the salvation of souls and the promotion of justice. Here we present the traditional Laws of the 1918 Code which are still valid as interpreted by the Rotal decisions and according to the Vatican Council II. Later an explanation of the law will be given at the end of this chapter. We should take cognizance of scholars and excellent canonists who have written papers in this field. For this reason I am inlcuding in the Appendix an enlightening address given by Rev. Francis Morrisey, O.M.I., on this matter. These we must read in the light of past rotal decisions on consent and the proposed new laws.

QUALITIES

Canon 1081—1. Matrimony is effected by the consent of the
parties legitimately expressed between persons capable according to law; which consent no human power can supply.
2. Matrimonial consent is an act of the will by which each
party gives and accepts a perpetual and exclusive right over the
body, for acts which are of themselves suitable for generation
of children.

The Proposed new Canon of the Commission of CIC was prompted
by Vatican Council II, therefore it is inserted here[1]

1. Marriage is effected by the consent of the parties lawfully
expressed between persons who are capable according to law;
and this consent no human power can supply. 295.1
2. Matrimonial consent is that act of the will whereby a man and
a woman by means of a mutual covenant constitute with one
another a communion of conjugal life which is perpetual and
exclusive and which by its very nature is ordered to the procreating and education of children. 295.2

1. *Contract of the parties:* Every contract made by individuals
comes under the law of reason whereby it implies a transfer of rights
and obligations; as such, there can never be a marriage without real
consent of both parties.
2. In order that this contract produce effects, the parties must be
juridically qualified. The marriage consent is an act of the will with
a definite object. The act of the will must really exist, (actually or
virtually). Act of the intellect, the disposition of one's mind, various
opinions, errors of judgment are considered only insofar as these affect
the will. The consent must be mutual. The object of this consent is
the perpetual and exclusive right over each other's body for the exercise
of actions that by their very nature pertain to the procreation of children. This right is the essential object of the true marriage contract
by virtue of the natural law and the divine positive law. Custom, circumstances of the times, state or ecclesiastical laws can never change
this.

---

1. Due to the influence of Vatican Council II, and for evaluative reasons the
proposed New Canons of the Code Commission will be cited in this chapter
on consent.

3. The consent must be lawfully expressed as determined by Canon 1094. However, there are also state laws which must be considered. The capacity of the persons is determined by natural law; for the *baptized by canon law;* for the *unbaptized by the state law.*

4. Even though a marriage has been contracted invalidly because of an impediment, the consent which has been given is presumed to persevere until its revocation shall have been proved (C. 1093)

This Canon states a presumption that consent exists unless revoked. A good example of this is the application of the Sanatio in Radice, whereby an invalid marriage becomes a valid marriage without the renewal of consent.

5. When all the conditions mentioned above are fulfilled in the external forum, we consider the marriage contract valid because every act: (the giving and accepting, the holding of hands, the words expressed) was in perfect order externally. However, if we examine the act itself—the essential factor or marriage, namely, the mutual consent to marry according to the established standards (unity, indissolubility, procreation of children, etc.) we find that sometimes the interior dispositions of the contractants do not correspond exactly to those of the exterior acts. In order to have a valid marriage, the interior dispositions must conform to the external, otherwise it is possible that the contract would be invalid.

6. Before a marriage, the pastor seldom meets with such a problem. These conditions are withheld and usually arise when, after a separation or divorce, one of the parties claims nullity on the grounds that the consent was not mutual or for some other condition made at the time of the contract, and asks permission to enter into a new marriage.

7. True consent is very important so much so that the contract would be invalid if certain obstacles were present, such as:

(1) Insanity (1081) (2) Ignorance (1082)
(3) Error (1083) (4) Fraud (New Proposed law)
(5) Sexual Anomalies (Rotal Decisions)
(6) Simulation: Total or partial (1086)
(7) Force and Fear (1087)

Those incapable of contracting matrimony:

1. Those so affected by a mental illness or a serious disturbance of the mind, that lacking the use of reason, they cannot give matrimonial consent; 296:1

2. Those suffering from a serious defect of discretion of judgment

on the matrimonial rights and obligations to be mutually given and received. 296:2

DEFECTIVE CONSENT

INSANITY

Insanity cases seem to be increasing more and more in our generation as shown statistically in our marriage tribunals. Why this is so, is difficult to say. It is generally known that there are more people in mental institutions than there are students in all our colleges and universities in the United States. The study of mental illness among the insane belongs to the field of medicine, but it also becomes an object of study for ecclesiastical and civil lawyers because of the great influence it has upon the ability of persons in this state in placing legal acts. Mental illness is such that it can diminish or even totally destroy a person's capacity for legal acts, and as such, it can disqualify him for marriage.[2]

Insanity is an obstacle to making a valid contract of marriage because the mental defect deprives one of the use of reason and therefore, renders one incapable of acquiring knowledge. It is the act of the will that constitutes consent, and one cannot will what he does not know. Moreover, a person, who enjoys the use of reason, would be incapable of proper consent to marriage, due to his mental condition, because he could not realize the substance of the marriage contract. The use of reason was the norm used by the Roman Rota in former times due to the insecure nature of psychiatry and psychology; but due to the growing refinement of both psychiatry and ecclesiastical jurisprudence we find that ("usus rationis non sufficit)[3] this norm is outdated.

The investigation and scrutiny of insanity in matrimonial cases strictly speaking belongs to the experts in the matrimonial tribunals who gather their information from professional psychiatrists and other medical experts. However, every pastor or marriage counselor should be acquainted with some of the basic principles which surround these difficult cases of mental illnesses. There are some very good articles written in recent years on this subject.[4]

The Code of Canon Law contains *explicit* substantive laws regarding cases of insanity (Amentia—as it is called by the Rota). Canons 1081 and 1082[6], however, contain implicitly the substantive law under

---

2. Van Ommeren, Mental Illness Affecting Matrimonial Consents, CUA, 1961, p. 45.
3. S.R.R. Dec. XXVI, 1934, p. 709.

which insanity cases are considered. These canons merely restate the natural law which is our source for an invalid marriage, due to insanity. Canon 1082[5] states the need of using experts (psychologist and psychiatrist) in adjudication of insanity cases. Articles of Provida Mater Ecclesia, and the Allocution of Pope Pius XII recommended the use of these experts. At present the best source for processing and adjudicating insanity cases is to study the decisions of the Sacred Roman Rota. Here we learn how to use and evaluate the opinions of the experts. Since the latest decisions contain the best opinions, we should go to this source.

We have very few decisions from the Roman Rota on Insanity cases. Between 1937-1946, only twenty-two cases were decided. In the year 1943, only four cases were tried. Authors wondered why so few diocesan tribunals simply did not feel prepared to cope with the situation. Since that time, a new and successful approach has fortunately opened up the avenues in this category. For further information: *Canon Law Digest:* Vol. I, p. 518, Vol. II, p. 299, Vol. III, pp. 429-430, Vol. IV, pp. 435-436, Vol. VI, pp. 331-332; *Jurist*, Vol. XVI, 1956, pp. 251-266; *Tribunal Reporter* (Cases) pp. 317-474

REQUISITE KNOWLEDGE

IGNORANCE

Canon 1082–1. In order that matrimonial consent be given properly, it is necessary that the contracting parties fully understand that marriage is a permanent union between a man and a woman for the procreation of children.

2. This ignorance is not presumed after puberty.

---

4. The Jurist Vols. XVI, e, July, 1956; XX, 3, July, 1960 XXII, October 4, 1962. Bulletin of the Guild of Catholic Psychiatrists, Vol. VII, April, 1960: the following four articles: Kubitschek, M.D., "Psychopathic Personality and Annulment," pp. 83-85; Rt. Rev. John Hayes, "Mental Disease and the Ecclesiastical Courts," pp. 76-83; J. W. Higgins, M.D., "Schizophrenia as a Consideration in Annulment of Marriage," pp. 87-96; John R. Cavanagh, M.D., "Homosexuality as an Impediment to Marriage," pp. 96-110.
John R. Keating, "Marriage of the Psychopathic Personality," "Chicago Studies, 1963; Cuschieri, O.F.M., "Paranoia—Partial or Integral Insanity," The Jurist, IV, 69; Rev. John Keating, "Marriage Nullity Trials," "Studia Canonicum, Vol. IV, 1, 1970; and Lawrence G. Wrenn, Third Edition Revised, "Annulments," Canon Law Society of America, 1978.

5. In order that matrimonial consent may be possible it is necessary that the contracting parties be at least not ignorant that marriage is a permanent society between man and woman for the procreation of children.

6. Instruction, **Provida Mater Ecclesia**, August 15, 1936, AAS XXVIII, pp. 312-370.

1. Lack of knowledge may be due to: (1) ignorance, (2) error, or (3) fraud.

Ignorance is the lack of knowledge. In reference to marriage, if one of the parties did not know that marriage is a permament union of a man and woman for the purpose of begetting offspring, such a marriage would be invalid. Ignorance, of course, would have to be proven without a doubt. The contract of marriage requires consent in the transfer of rights. In this serious transaction there cannot be a true and valid marriage without the real consent of both parties. The consent, freely given, alone constitutes marriage. Such was the teaching of the Roman law, Church Fathers (regarding the Blessed Mother and St. Joseph), the teaching of St. Thomas and the Council of Trent. Consent is an act of the will regarding a definite, specific object. Therefore, regarding a definite, specific person in the contract of marriage.

2. It is not necessary to know the way in which children are procreated, provided that the parties know that it is done by their own mutual and bodily cooperation (Rotal Case, January 20, 1926). In other words, a distinct and explicit knowledge either of the sexual act, or of the way in which, or the organs by which it is exercised, is not required. (Rotal Case, July 30, 1927). If however, one party thinks that children are born as a result of kisses, through the stork, etc., and has a confused, vague knowledge that some kind of bodily union is required, this party apparently would lack sufficient knowledge for valid consent in a marriage (Abbo-Hannon II, no. 1082).

ERROR

ERROR OF FACT

Canon 1083—1. Error regarding a person renders marriage invalid.

2. Error regarding the quality of the person, even if it is the cause of the contract, invalidates marriage *only:* (a) if the error regarding the *quality amounts to an error of person;* (b) if a free person contracts marriage with a person whom he or she considers free, but who is on the contrary in a condition of slavery in the proper sense.

1. Here we have two types of error of fact: (1) Error of Person, and (2) Error of the Quality of the Person. The first invalidates marriage; the second invalidates marriage only under certain conditions.

2. If the error concerned the identity of the other party as, e.g., Joseph marries Mary thinking she is Rose. Today, this is hardly possible; but if he does the marriage would be invalid.

3. If the error concerned some quality or characteristic of the other party, provided that this certain quality or characteristic expected is such that it amounted to *error concerning the person*, e.g, marrying a slave girl thinking she was free.

4. *The Essence of the Marriage Contract Is the Consent. The Essential Object of the Consent Is the Person; it is not the qualities of the person. Qualities are something accidental to marriage; these qualities, even though insignificant in themselves are sometimes very important to the other party.* It is true that the injured party *hoped, wished, thought, believed* that his spouse possessed this or that quality, but the *"die is cast," the consent was given—the contract was made—the marriage is valid.* This is an *error* or *false judgment made by the injured party* regarding the personal qualifications of the other spouse. The Church could make such an error a nullifying factor but it does not because this factor would only cause greater confusion. Human beings are not perfect, as we all know; therefore, it is self-evident that there would be no end to such problems. In practice, it is almost impossible to prove that an error in quality amounts to error of the person. This is possible *only* when the injured party can give full proof that the quality of the party amounted to a *conditio sine qua non.* However, in the last few years a new interest has been created in this lack of consent because of error. This new interest arose especially after two canonical decisions of nullity, one of the appellate court of Sens, dated April 22, 1968 and the other of the Sacred Rota, *coram* Canals, dated April 21, 1970.[7]

In the Sens case, Edward, a Catholic, aged 35, entered a civil marriage from which two children were born. Ten years later he abandoned his children and his civil consort. After the second World War he was found guilty of crime and sentenced, among other things, to twenty years of forced labor. At the age of 58, under an assumed name, and posing as a single person, a nephew of a high government official, a doctor of medicine, and a member of the faculty of Louvain, he married Colette. The marriage was a failure and Colette obtained a civil annulment in France on the grounds that she had been completely deceived about Edward's identity and that she would never have married him if she had known the truth. She then took her case to the Tribunal of Moulin on the same grounds, e.g,, error as to the person.

Moulin gave an affirmative decision, arguing according to the principles of St. Alphonsus that the marriage was null because of error inasmuch as the consent of the Plaintiff had been directly and principally about a person who was single, a doctor of medicine, of good repute, etc. The appellate court of Sens, after having stated that it was necessary to redefine our concept of person by taking into account the findings of anthropology and psychology, also found for nullity on the grounds of error.

It is reported that this decision of Sens of April 22, 1968 was appealed by the Defender of the Bond "pro sua concientia" to the Sacred Roman Rota, but the Defender of the Bond of the Rota refused to pursue the appeal in which case the Plaintiff was free to remarry. If this is true, it would not necessarily mean that the Defender of the Bond approved of all of the reasoning of the prior two cases. It could be that he merely thought that the appeal would be futile inasmuch as in his estimation the marriage was null and void for some other canonical reason, e.g., error as to qualities which amounted to implicit conditions.

The second case which recently provoked thought about the concept of error of the person originated in Niteroi, Brazil. The Plaintiff requested a declaration of nullity of her marriage on the grounds of error as to person. Two months after her canonical marriage, her husband was taken into custody and charged with bigamy. He had previously entered into a canonically invalid civil marriage. Three children had been born of this marriage. He had fraudulently concealed knowledge of his prior civil marriage from the Plaintiff. The trial court found for nullity on the grounds of error of a quality which redounded into error of a person. The appellate court reversed as far as the original grounds of error were concerned, but found for nullity because of an incapacity on the part of the Defendant to oblige himself to the essential property of fidelity in marriage. The case then found its way to the Sacred Roman Rota. The Rota found for nullity on the grounds as the trial court, i.e, error of the person. It reasoned that a moral, social, or a juridical quality which is so intimately connected with the physical person that the person would be altogether different if that quality did not exist, can be the grounds of nullity because of error. Canals, writing the opinion of the court, after citing the traditional strict opinion that

---

7. **"Error Qualitatis in Errorem Personae Redundans"** M. J. Reinhardt, CLSA Praceedings, 1973, pp. 60-63.

a quality which amounts to a quality about the person must be the only possible means of establishing the identity of an otherwise unknown person, and after recognizing the opinion of Thomas and Alphonsus that an error as to a quality which was directly and principally intended, cause nullity, cites a third opinion:

> The third interpretation considers the case of a moral, social, or juridical quality which is so intimately connected with the physical person, that the person would be altogether different if that quality did not exist. Thus, if someone enters marriage with a person whom he believes to be free from all ties, but who is already civilly married, the contract would be invalid according to this third interpretation. The reason for this invalidity would not arise from any implicit condition, but rather be due to an error of quality amounting to an error concerning the person understood in a more complete and integral way. Civil marriage cannot be considered in the same way as concubinage. The former is recognized by the Church as valid for non-Christians and for baptized non-Catholics. Because of the defect of form, a merely civil marriage does not share this recognition when entered into by Catholics, nor in the union of a Catholic and non-Catholic. Nevertheless, even in these cases, Canon Law accepts the fact that a civil union produce certain juridic effects, as for example, establishing the basis for a sanation, or the impediments of public honesty or crime, or for resulting in a possible excommunication. Moreover, in those places where a complete separation exists between the civil and religious marriage the faithful to contract the civil marriage first, thereby indirectly protecting the religious marriage with civil laws of indissolubility, legitimacy of children, and protection of property. Therefore, we must admit that although civil marriage is rejected in principle, it does establish a status of the person and consequently an error about such a status amounts to an error of the person. The Church's opposition to civil marriage is also opposed to slavery and yet Canon 1083 #2, explicitly declares null a marriage contracted in error regarding that matter.

Canals gives credit for his reasoning to Jemolo from whom he quotes:

> The formula, drawn up with canonical tradition in mind, does not correspond to real life. The tradition itself is a relic from the past,

as a glance at ecclesiastical jurisprudence will reveal. It refers to the pre-Tridentine era when there were merely civil acts, when marriages were imposed by parents with hardly any period of engagement or mutual acquaintance of the intended partners and at a time when proxy marriages were not uncommon in the upper classes. Under such conditions, it may have been possible to have the situation where one who was to marry Bertha intended to marry her as the King's daughter, identifying her solely as the daughter of the King of Cyprus, without caring whether she was beautiful or deformed, educated or illiterate, talented or otherwise.

But all this is far removed from our situation today. Rather, we should ask ourselves what are those qualities which are generally considered as constituting the identity of a person, without its being even necessary (providing the ignorance or error is established) to investigate further into the reaction of the person at the discovery of his mistake. If we pursue this approach, it is almost impossible to deny the importance of error . . . even in the case where, for example, a woman marries a man thinking he is honest when actually he has a long criminal record or where a man marries a woman thinking she is a virgin when in fact she is a prostitute.

The most noteworthy point about this decision of Canals is that it does not require for a finding of nullity that error be concerned about such a quality which would be the only possible means of establishing the identity of an otherwise unknown person. Eliminated is the rigid distinction between person or substance on one hand and accidents on the other with the result that any error about an accidental quality would not pertain to the person or to the substance. As has been pointed out by many canonists, a quality which by its specific detail can point to one person alone is merely another means of naming that particular person. Consequently, many canonists, following the very rigid interpretation of the phrase "error qualitatis in erroram personae redundans" as meaning that the error had to be about a quality which definitely specifies a certain person, are of the opinion that this phrase should be removed from the Code as having no value. The value of the decision of Canals is that it recognizes that there are such qualities in persons which, although they are accidental, are so important as to be means of identifying the person, even though there might be other persons having the same qualities. A particular quality or a combination of particular qualities identifies the person in the particular case. This is most natural. If we maintain the hylomorphic theory of substance and accidents on which the traditional exclusion of all qualities as basis for nullity is founded, we must admit that the only way that we have of knowing a person is through the qualities, or accidentals, of that person. By reason of substance, all persons are alike. They differ exclusively by accidentals. It is through the qualities or accidentals that we must identify persons. There is a basis for this in the teaching of Thomas who said that the meaning of this word, person, is not essence or nature but personality. Thomas also affirmed that the person in whatsoever nature means that which is distinct, just as in human nature it means this flesh and these bones and this soul which are the things which distinguish one person from another.

Another noteworthy point about the Niteroi decision is that nullity because of error does not require the substitution of one physical person for another physical person. This was the understanding of error, generally speaking, in Gratian, in decretal law, and in the commentators following the Code. It was for this reason that it was said that it was very difficult for error to be realized unless the marriage was contracted by proxy. The proper person would be readily recognized. The Niteroi decision puts the emphasis on the subjective intention. The question is whether the qualities which were principally intended are actually in existence in the other person at the time of marriage.

In this case of Niteroi, decided by Canals, the only case where the Rota found for nullity because of an error of a quality, which did not specify a definite individual? There are a number of cases where the Rota came to the conclusion that although an expressed condition had not been made by the Plaintiff, impliedly a condition actually existed about a quality, causing nullity. However, there is one case which makes special reference to the third rule of St. Alphonsus concerning error which redounds into the person. This was decided on June 21, 1941. The decision was written by Heard. It concerned a marriage which took place in Pakistan where, according to the local custom, women are divided for the purposes of marriage, into virgins and non-virgins. A higher price was demanded for virgins than for non-virgins. The Plaintiff in the case paid the higher price to have a virgin as his wife, but later found out to his dismay that she was not a virgin. The court recognized the marriage as null because of error in a quality which was directly and principally intended. In a few other cases, the rule of

Alphonsus of a quality being principally and directly intended was quoted to find for validity inasmuch as the quality had not been directly and principally intended.

John marries Jane *under the condition* (in writing or before qualified witnesses) that Jane is a wealthy woman, or that Jane is of noble birth which she claimed; or that Jane was never in a mental institution. *After the marriage*, John learns that Jane is not a wealthy woman, nor is she of noble birth, etc. This marriage would be considered invalid.

FRAUD

Fraud or deception in which a person is misled into error could happen through misrepresentation through one's conduct, by deceptive speech or even silence. In *civil courts*, fraud, *if proven*, invalidates marriage. But in *ecclesiastical courts*, fraud does not invalidate a marriage no matter what grave injustice or injury was incurred by the other party *because a valid marriage is indissoluble*. What measures could one take against a fraudulent marriage? A prolonged courtship is one way. A lifetime project should always be carefully planned and evaluated. The sexual aspect of marriage is only one phase of the married life, and young people lose sight of all the other important aspects. Too often young people marry each other without knowing too much about one another. During the war years this was a common occurrence. Soldiers away from home were lonely, had a casual meeting and married immediately and were sorry later. Prolonged courtship is one way to offset fraud. If a *party fears* that he is being deceived by the party he intends to marry, he should *put this condition into writing or before witnesses;* make this statement on what he expects of the other, or what he does not expect of the other party. Only in such a case would fraud invalidate the marriage. It is a quality of the person which is considered in this error.

ERROR OF LAW

Canon 1084—Simple error regarding the unity, or indissolubility, or sacramental dignity of marriage, even though it is the cause of the contract, does not vitiate matrimonial consent.

Whenever a person makes a civil contract, he is bound by all the obligations contained therein and he cannot be excused from these because these obligations are much different than what he thought them to be. So too, all the principles and characteristics which constitute marriage *as instituted by God* remain intact and stable regardless what a married person thinks, wishes, or believes them to be. His way of thinking does not change these principles. Errors, mistakes, judgments or private opinions of persons regarding the principles of marriage cannot be given any consideration in judging marriage cases. While ignorance is a lack of knowledge, error is mistaken knowledge or the making of a false judgment.

1. *Concomitant Error:* An error when there is *no real influence on the consent,* that is, the consent would have been given even though the error existed at the time.

2. *Antecedent Error:* An error which has such influence that if the truth had been known, the consent would not have been given. If a person was in such a frame of mind that he would refuse to give consent if the condition had been known, this is called an *interpretative will.* Since it actually did not take place the marriage is valid. The case is such that we consider *not what would have been done, but what actually did take place.*

3. *Simple Error:* Error is simple when it remains in the mind (intallect) without passing over the will. We have *simple error in the mind* when it exists *there* in a *speculative way* without actually becoming incorporated in the choice made by the will. For example, a person may have a *simple error in the mind* regarding indissolubility, unity, the sacramental character of a marriage; nevertheless, the will wishes to contact a marriage that is valid according to the law of nature. (The speculative factor in the intellect did not pass over into the category of the will). *The actual fact is that the will selected marriage without any conditions or reservations.*

A non-Catholic, wishing to come into the Church as a convert and in order to marry a Catholic, asks for a declaration of nullity on his first marriage he always *thought* (as all Protestants do) that he could divorce his wife anytime. This is *simply* an *erroneous idea* about the indissolubility of marriage (remaining speculatively in the intellect); this simple error always carries with it the *presumption that one wishes to get married according to God's plan.* Therefore, if this non-Catholic *merely thought* he could get a divorce[3] or *believed* he could get a divorce, or *wished* he could get a divorce, or *hoped* he could get a divorce, *this simple speculative error remains in the intellect* and *never passed over into the will.* This marriage is valid. As long as the error remains in the mind (intellect), *no positive act of the will is placed* regarding it. This is also called *theoretical error. A positive act if a fact which must be proved.* It is never presumed!

4. *A Qualified Error:* A qualified error is opposed to simple error. When the simple error passes over from the *intellect to the will* and becomes an *intention,* this error is called *qualified error.* Since this *process is invisible,* the party entertaining this *process must make it visible.* This is done by bringing it into the external forum. This is possible and can be done when this same party has the final product—this Qualified Intention *in writing* or *can prove it with the help of witnesses.* If the above mentioned convert can prove[9] that he married with the agreement that the marriage could be dissolved by a civil divorce at the will of either party, the marriage would be considered *invalid.* Here the general notion of divorce which Protestants hold passes from the so much the error that causes the invalidity of the marriage as the *presence of two conflicting intentions: one to contract a real marriage,* the other *to contract a dissoluble marriage* (with the intention of a divorce).

> Canon 1085—The knowledge or opinion of the nullity of marriage does not necessarily exclude matrimonial consent.

Here again is a repetition of the former laws stressing the principle that an error concerning one's opinion or belief does not invalidate a marriage contract. This prevails over one's private opinion. For example, John contracts marriage with Anna on June 10, 1950, knowing that he left a wife in Europe; he knows that a diriment impediment exists and this marriage to Anna will be invalid; at the same time he does everything to contract marriage, thus giving matrimonial consent. John learns later that his wife died in Europe on May 30, 1950. Is his marriage to Anna valid despite the fact that he thought he had a diriment impediment? John and Anna are married validly despite the fact of what he *thought.* In any case, the validity or invalidity of the marriage does not depend upon what the parties *believe* or *think* at the

---

8. The same is true if a woman marries a man whom she **believed** or **hoped** to be temperate and after the marriage turns out to oe a confirmed alcoholic. A man marries a woman **thinking** or **believing** she is a virgin, but after the marriage, learns that she is one of loose morals or a prostitute.

9. Proof: In writing or before a qualified witness.

time of the marriage, but rather what actually and objectively takes place according to the principles of law.

The intention to contract a real marriage is always presumed unless the contrary is proved. When a Catholic contracts a mixed marriage before a civil magistrate, he generally knows that it is invalid. However, when a *sanatio in radice* is granted, it presupposes that a natural valid consent was given at the time of this marriage, and that this valid consent is still persevering; therefore, there is no need for a renewal of consent. If a mere mock marriage took place, the valid consent would be absent.

SIMULATION

INTERNAL CONSENT

Canon 1086—1. The internal consent of the mind is always presumed to be in agreement to the words or signs used in the celebration of marriage.

2. But if one or other of the parties by a positive will exclude marriage itself, or all the rights to the conjugal act, or any essential property of marriage, *the contract is invalid.*

1. This canon expresses the presumption of law regarding the existence of the internal consent, when the words expressed and the signs shown externally, in the celebration of marrige, take place. This internal consent must exist in the parties at the same time. If the positive act of the will regarding consent was excluded, this fact must be proved in the external forum. We exclude here the simple error of the mind, or an interpretative will.

2. A positive act of the will opposes the very nature of the matrimonial contract, or opposes the essential properties of marriage, makes the marriage null and void. If the parties cannot prove this fact in the external forum, the law presumes this marriage a *valid contract.* In the forum of conscience, it is not a valid marriage, in which case an ecclesiastical court could grant a separation. If the case exists whereby they must live together for some reason, they have an obligation to validate this marriage by giving their consent. If the lack of consent was merely *internal* it suffices that the party who did not give the consent, give this consent *now* by an internal act. If the lack of consent was shown publicly or outwardly, the consent should be given in the same way:

publicly or outwardly as the case may be (C. 1136).

(a) Total Simulation

3. We may have total simulation (or a fictitious marriage) if the positive act of the will (the intention) is not to contract marriage at all. The acts are merely done without giving internal consent. This could happen if one marries merely to inherit a property or to gain a high social position, etc.

(b) Partial Simulation

4. We may have *partial simulation* when one excludes some of the essential obligations of marriage, for example, one does not wish to have the conjugal act which is *per se* suitable for generation of offspring; or excludes the essential properties of unity and indissolubility. In this case, partial simulation makes the marriage invalid.

5. Simulation is difficult to prove. The testimony of the interested party taken under oath is not accepted as sufficient proof; neither is the testimony of the two parties accepted as sufficient proof. Conjectures from the circumstances may throw some weight on the case itself. If, for example, man ran off immediately after the marriage ceremony and made a declaration that he never gave his consent to this marriage, we would have a very good and a strong presumption that his consent was simulated. When there is a doubt, the presumption of law is in favor of the validity of the marriage (C. 1014).

A Dilemma

6. We may have a matrimonial dilemma. We might have a case in which the parties are *certain* and the confessor *certain* that this particular marriage is null for lack of consent. But it is impossible to prove it satisfactorily in an ecclesiastical court. A second marriage is not permitted. Cohabitation might be obligatory, but conjugal relations would be unlawful. Hence, we have a conflict between the internal and external forum.

7. Such a conflict is even worse if a person who simulated consent, later, being free of the first wife, contracts a valid marriage with another party. In the external forum, wife #1 would be his legitimate wife, he would be bound to live with her but could not have marital relations with her. Wife #2, which is his second wife would be his

real wife (in the forum of conscience) in the eyes of God, with whom he could have marital relations, and there is no possibility of revalidating the first marriage.

8. Much research has been done on this conflict between the *internal* and the *external* forum. It is a dilemma recognized by canonists and theologians alike.

Today we find all kinds of moral delinquents, sexual perverts, psychotics, neurotics, sociopaths, etc. *It is the belief of many psychiatrists and canonists that those individuals afflicted with sexual anomalies should not enter into marriage.* The unfortunate part about these people is that the problem really begins after marriage when the partner is unable or unwilling to accept the responsibility of an indissolube union. The result is separation and divorce. What is the solution of so many problems today?

Arguments that Homosexuality is Incompatible with Marriage

1. When considering Canons 1081 and 1086, the homosexual could not have the proper intention and the will to enter a true marriage due to the fact that under the outward appearance of marriage he retains the desire to continue his homosexual relations.

2. In considering the same Canons (1081-1086), the homosexual proposes to commit sins against matrimonial fidelity, and these propositions can be substantiated by the gathering of evidence *before and after* the said marriage.

3. Moreover, in virtue of Canon 1081, the true matrimonial consent is not given in the sense that the man and woman reciprocally hand over and receive the perpetual and exclusive right to each other (*ius in corpus*).

According to Canon 1086, any person who externally manifests consent but inwardly does not invoke the corresponding act of the will would simulate consent, since the contract of marriage requires four elements: (1) the intention to make a true contract, (2) the intention to bind oneself to the matrimonial contract (3) the physical and moral capacity to bind oneself, and (4) to fulfill the obligations that are undertaken. *How then could a homosexual physically and morally be able to make a contract binding him to the object of the contract?* We are certain that a person cannot enter into a valid contract who cannot dispose freely of the object of the same contract. Moreover this must be an object which is both physically and morally possible. Since we know that no one is obliged to the impossible, nor is he able to oblige himself to it; therefore, we can state that for these reasons the marriage of a homosexual is invalid: (1) the homosexual is incapable of restraining himself from homosexual relationships; (2) the homosexual does not permit the exclusive right to marital intercourse, and often excludes it entirely. Thus, we can conclude that homosexuality is incompatible with marriage.[10]

HOMOSEXUALITY[11]

Homosexuality is a strong preferential erotic attraction to members of one's own sex.[12] DSM III D does not regard homosexuality in itself as a mental disorder. However, when the homosexuality is accompanied by consciously perceived distress resulting from an internal conflict over the fact that homosexual stimuli are incompatible with the person's conscience, then DSM III D recognizes this as a disorder. It is called dyshomophilia and is listed among the paraphilias or sexual deviations.

Kinsey and his associates in 1948 suggested the following scale that would describe points on a heterosexual–homosexual continuum:

0 exclusively heterosexual, only incidentally homosexual
1 predominantly heterosexual, only incidentally homosexual
2 predominantly heterosexual but more than incidentally homosexual
3 equally heterosexual and homosexual
4 predominantly homosexual but more than incidentally heterosexual
5 predominantly homosexual, only incidentally heterosexual
6 exclusively homosexual

Those people who are 1 and 2 on the scale are sometimes referred to as *facultative homosexuals;* those who rate 3 and 4 as *bisexual;* and those who are 5 and 6 on the scale as *obligatory homosexuals.*

Homosexuality seems most often to result from a combination of causes, some of them genetic, others environmental. The genetic causes, the study of which has been spurred by the development of modern genetics and endocrinology, would be hormonal or chromosomal imbalances. The environmental causes would consist primarily in the psychosexual influence of the parents on the child. Freud held that all hetero-

10. **The Jurist,** Vol. XXIII, October 1963, pp. 394-422.
11. **Annulments,** L. G. Wrenn, CLSA, Toledo, Ohio, pp. 50-52, 1978.
12. DSMD refers to: **Diagnostic and Statistical Manual of Mental Disorders.**

sexuals have latent homosexual tendencies, that all persons go through a homoerotic phase in chidhood in the regular course of development, that one grows out of that stage entirely, and that adult homosexuality is often simply the result of an arrest of normal development. Bieber, on the other hand, takes almost the opposite point of view. He holds that all homosexuals are latent heterosexuals, that heterosexuality is the norm in all mammals, and that the development of homosexuality is always a pathological consequence of fears of heterosexual functioning that have been produced by unfavorable life experiences. Chief among these experiences, according to Bieber, at least for the male homosexual, is the parental constellation of a detached, hostile father and close-binding, seductive mother who dominates and minimizes her husband. Specific environmental causes of female homosexuality are unclear except that generally there is a strong antiheterosexual pattern in the home.

Donald Webster Cory, himself a homosexual, lists in his book, "The Homosexual in America" twelve reasons why the homosexual marries:

1. Desire for children.
2. Need for permanent family relationship.
3. Inability to create permanent relationships with male companion or lover.
4. Fear of loneliness of older years.
5. Desire or hope to escape from homosexual life.
6. Deep affection for the girl.
7. Latency or repression of homosexuality.
8. Hope of finding companionship in marriage; disappointment at inability to find it outside of marriage with male friends.
9. Desire to create facade of married life, and hope to find protection against gossip and its concomitant evils.
10. Aspiration for economic and social gain.
11. Desire to please family.
12. Inability or unwillingness to take the strong stand in order to put an end to drift toward marriage.

The four areas of investigation in incompetence cases merit the following observations relative to homosexuality:

Severity. In speaking of the severity of homosexuality several points must be clarified. First of all we are speaking always of genuine homosexuals and not pseudo homosexuals (heterosexuals who, in circumstances where opposite sex partners are not available, turn to persons of the same sex for gratification). Secondly whereas alcoholism is defined as including overt acts of drinking, homosexuality is defined apart from any overt acts, simply as "a strong preferential erotic attraction." This obviously involves the jurisprudential judgment that the erotic homosexual attraction, even without there being any overt acts, is likely to interfere substantially with functioning in an intimate heterosexual relationship, whereas totally controlled alcoholism is not. Thirdly, it can be said, as a rule of thumb, that obligatory homosexuals and bisexuals would probably be incapable of those acts which are per se apt for the engendering of the community of life, whereas facultative homosexuals would probably be capable of them. Here again, though, an attempt must be made in every individual case to determine the competence of the homosexual to function in a heterosexual relationship.

Antecedence. When a person is known to be homosexual, the homosexuality may always be presumed antecedent to marriage since a person's psychosexual preference is always fixed at least by early adolescence.

Perpetuity. Assuming that the homosexual disposition did, in fact, render a person incompetent for marriage, the question here is whether that disposition could have been turned around at the time of marriage, whether, in other words, a genuine shift in preferential sex choice could have been effected. Given a strong motivation to change one's sexual preference, given a youthful age and a history of previous heterosexual responsiveness, given a low rating on the Kinsey continuum, and given no overt acts or a fairly recent onset of infrequent overt homosexual acts, the chances of altering sexual preference are perhaps fairly good. Given their opposites the chances are bad. A Court must make a judgment in light of the particular facts in each instance.

Relativity. The choice of marriage partner by a homosexual can sometimes be significant. A female homosexual, for example, might function less well with an aggressive husband than with a gentle, passive man. It is always possible, therefore, that a homosexual condition not invalidating in itself could, given the wrong partner, result in an inability of the two parties to relate.

FORCE AND FEAR

Canon 1087—1. Likewise is invalid a marriage entered into through FORCE or grave FEAR which was unjustly exercised by an external agent such that in order to escape from it a party was compelled to choose marriage.

2. No other fear, even though it be the cause of the contract, entails the nullity of marriage.

1. Force and fear are correlative terms. *Force* is the physical impulse from an external agent which cannot be overcome, as for example, when an unjust moral force with blows or threats is used. *Fear* is the trepidation of the mind because of an impending evil.

2. *Absolutely grave fear* is such that will overcome the mind and will of a normal firm and steadfast person because of a grave injury or loss he or she would suffer. For example, the loss of life or limb, fortune, liberty or reputation from an external agent. (*Internal fear*— such as one's own imagination, would be ruled out in this case).

3. *Relative grave fear* is such that will overcome the mind and will of certain individuals according to their capacity. *Reverential fear* would be *one* of these. For example, the fear of being ejected from the parental home; the fear of offending one's parents or one's superiors; for certain over-sensitive people, this could amount to grave fear.

4. *Fear must be unjustly inflicted from an external agent.* Natural causes are excluded. We have this fear when human justice is violated in forcing a certain marriage. If, for example, a young man is threatened with his life or with bodily harm, and he has no way of escaping except through marriage, his marriage would be considered null. Threat of a seducer with imprisonment or marriage could not be considered as unjustly inflicted. This is a *just penalty*, but a better alternative would be to impose a fine or demand support of the child. *A principle one should use in evaluating force and fear cases is to judge whether there was any other alternative than marriage.*

5. It is questionable whether force and fear is an impediment of the natural or of ecclesiastical law. We have various opinions in this matter.

PROXY MARRIAGE

Canon 1088—1. In order that marriage be contracted validly it is necessary that the contracting parties be present either in person or by proxy.

2. The parties must express matrimonial consent in words, and they may not use equivalent signs if they are able to speak.

This canon applies to both Catholics as well as non-Catholics who are baptized. Before the Council of Trent, it was possible to contract marriage by means of a letter. After the Council of Trent, authors disputed whether this was possible for a valid marriage. We have proof of this even as late as 1910, in which the Roman Rite upheld the validity of such a marriage. The man gave his consent to marriage by letter which he sent to the girl. The girl went to her pastor with a witness and expressed her consent there. The marriage took place in 1900.[13] The Code ruled out this form of marriage; although it states explicitly that marriage can be contracted through a proxy.

> Canon 1089—1. Without prejudice to the status of the diocese, which may be imposed in addition hereto, in order that marriage may be contracted by proxy, a special mandate is required to contract it with a certain person, which mandate must be signed by the principal and by either the ordinary of the place, the pastor where the mandate is given, or by a priest delegated by either of these, or by at least two witnesses.
> 2. If the principal cannot write, this fact must be indicated in the mandate itself and another witness must be added who shall himself also sign the document; otherwise, this mandate is invalid.
> 3. If the principal who gave the mandate should have revoked it, or he became insane before the proxy contracted the marriage in the principal's name, this marriage would be invalid, even though the proxy or the party to the marriage knew nothing about this revocation.
> 4. In order that the marriage be valid, the proxy must fulfill this office in person.

According to Clark, proxy marriages are not recognized in the United States. However, we have an unusual case in which Federal Judge Lowell of Boston, Mass., upheld the validity of a marriage contracted in this way. This case happened in 1924 in which a United States citizen went to the Portuguese Consulate in Philadelphia and obtained a certificate whereby he contracted marriage by proxy to a person in Portugal.[15]

---

13. Woywood, Commentary, p. 750.
14. AAS II, pp. 297-309.

MARRIAGE THROUGH INTERPRETERS

Canon 1090—Marriage can also be contracted through an interpreter. [All things being equal, if the pastor is satisfied with all the other preliminaries, he may go ahead with the marriage; but if there is time he should consult the ordinary.]

Canon 1091—The pastor must not assist at a marriage which is to be contracted by proxy or through an interpreter, unless there is a just cause and there is no doubt regarding the authenticity of the mandate and the veracity of the interpreter, and if there is time, he must have the permission of the ordinary.

CONDITIONAL MARRIAGE CONSENT

Canon 1092—When a condition is attached to the marriage contract and not withdrawn before the marriage, the following rules govern the case: A condition once placed and not revoked: (1) If it is a condition concerning a *future* event which is *necessary*, or *impossible*, or *immoral*, but not contrary to the substance of marriage, it is to be considered as not having been made.
(2) If it concerns the *future* and *is contrary to the substance of marriage*, it renders the marriage invalid.
(3) If it concerns the *future and is licit*, it suspends the validity of the marriage.
(4) If it concerns the past or the present, the marriage will be valid or not, according as the matter concerning which the condition is made, exists or not.

1. We usually do not meet marriages based on conditions.[17] In most cases, conditional marriages remain a secret, because it is unlawful to

---

15. Clark, **Contracts**, p. 381.
16. Proxy Marriage: (1) Most authors agree that the principal party of proxy marriage cannot authorize a proxy to substitute another proxy for himself. (2) One must make out a special mandate for a proxy marriage; it is not proper to give a general mandate to place all the legal acts of the marriage. (3) The mandate must indicate the specific person that will marry by proxy. It would be unlawful to give the proxy a mandate to choose a partner and marry her for him (by proxy). (4) The date and name of the place should be indicated where the proxy marriage is to take place.
17. In the year 1930, the Roman Rota received thirteen such cases; it accepted one and rejected the rest. AAS XXIII, 1931.

have a condition. If it was made before the marriage *in writing or before two witnesses* whereby it can be proven in the external forum, the marriage would remain valid until the contrary proof is obtained by the ecclesiastical authorities.

2. If the pastor discovers that a condition was placed, he must warn the parties not to cohabit. The pastor should investigate the case and act prudently in the matter in order to avoid any scandal. Sometimes the Church permits a marriage to be contracted conditionally for grave reasons.

3. A condition is some circumstance which is attached to the consent and upon which the contract of marriage depends. We must distinguish between a *cause* and a *condition* of marriage. A woman marries a man because she *believes or thinks* that he is a millionaire. Here we have no condition; it is a *cause*. *This* is merely an error and the contract would be valid despite the fact that she *would not have married* had she known the true facts that he was not a millionaire (*error dans causam contractui*).

I. Illustrations of Future Conditions

1. Those not contrary to the substance of marriage:

(1) *Necessary Future Conditions*: "I marry you now on condition that the sun rises tomorrow." If this is a serious statement, the marriage is valid only on that condition. If the sun did not rise, it would be invalid. People usually do not make such conditions seriously.

(2) *Impossible Future Conditions*: "I marry you on condition that you learn the Russian language within a week."

(3) *Immoral Future Conditions*: "I marry you on condition that you have an abortion; or on condition that you kill your father." The marriage would be valid only when this condition is fulfilled.

(4) *Licit Future Conditions*: "I marry you only on condition that you pass your Ph.D. examination." The marriage is valid when this condition is fulfilled.

2. Those contrary to the substance of marriage:

(1) "I marry you now on condition that you agree like all

non-Catholics, that I can divorce you any time during the marriage." "I marry you now on condition that I could live with other women."

Note: *If the parties agree to practice birth control, this may be gravely sinful, but it does not invalidate the marriage.*

II. Illustrations of Past Conditions:

(1) "I marry you now on condition that you have had a hysterectomy or vasectomy." If this is not true, the marriage would be invalid.

III. Illustration of a Present Condition:

(1) "I marry you on condition that you are wealthy." If the party is not, the marriage is invalid.

All these cases are true on condition that these statements are made seriously. Furthermore, to prove that such conditions were made, proof must be given of this in *writing (tempore non suspecto)*, or *before two witnesses;* otherwise, such conditions would be valid only in the internal forum (forum of conscience).

Canon 1093—Even though a marriage had been contracted invalidly because of an impediment, the consent which has been given is presumed to persevere until its revocation shall have been proved.

It is argued among authors whether marriage consent could be present if only one of the parties knew of a diriment impediment, and thus knew that a valid marriage could not be contracted. They here declare that the marriage consent is here presumed to exist in such a case.

A NEW CONCEPT OF CONSENT IN MARRIAGE ACCORDING TO VATICAN II

The new concept of Consent of marriage has been adopted since Vatican II through Rotal decisions and jurisprudence. It is important to know the law of 1918 which is still in vogue as well as the new concepts which are presently utilized in Rotal decisions and most tribunals. Therefore, both are present here:

Francis G. Morrisey, O.M.I., and Germain Lesage, O.M.I., give an enlightening explanation of the nature of Christian marriage as it is now understood by the Church. They begin by stating that the traditional teaching has always been that "consent makes the marriage." However, consent does not simply refer to the ceremony of marriage, but to a number of elements which make it possible for the marriage partners to live the graced covenant of conjugal life and love. It is these elements of marriage that we will now consider, namely, the elements of matrimonial consent in positive terms.

1. The Nature and Object of Matrimonial Consent

a. *The nature of matrimonial consent*

The present law of the Code, canon 1081; 2 (CICO. 72, 2) states that "matrimonial consent is an act of the will by which each party gives and accepts a perpetual and exclusive right over the body, for acts which are of themselves suitable for the generation of children.

It can easily be seen that this definition does not take into account the developments of thought that followed the Second Vatican Council, and so, the Commission for the Revision of the Code of Canon Law has proposed a new definition to express better the nature of matrimonial consent.

New Proposed Law

"Consent is an act of the will whereby a *man and a woman by means of a mutual covenant* constitute with one another a communion of conjugal life *which is perpetual and exclusive* and which by its very nature is ordered to the procreating and education of offspring" (new canon 295:2). This gives a broader notion of consent and a broader scope of nullity actions. A number of remarks could be made concerning this definition:

i. The use of the word "covenant," taking into account the long-range dimensions of marriage, not limiting ourselves to the event and situation occuring at the time of the actual ceremony itself (i.e., the "contract"). It refers to the capacity of carrying this out in the future.

ii. The definition incorporates the notion of a perpetual and exclusive community of conjugal life. Conjugal love is not referred to, because, as mentioned elsewhere it is not an element that can be directly evaluated by law.

iii. The community of conjugal life is ordered by its very nature to the procreating and education of offspring.

In general, consent is a pact or a covenant, in this case binding to the Christian state of marriage. Juridically it is a pact by which the parties are publicly bound to keep the laws of the Christian institution of marriage.

A number of *qualities* must be found in matrimonial consent: truth, deliberation, and maturity:

i. *Truth* (cognitive element). The deficiency of truth, or of a correct intellectual apprehension and knowledge, may be rooted in *ignorance* or *error* about the actual reality of Christian marriage.

ii. *Deliberation* (volative element): The act of consent must be a fully deliberate act which requires that one proceed with sufficient discretion and act with an enlightened and mature judgment. The consent of the contracting parties as related to the role of the act of the will may be defective in different ways: it may be defective because of *force* or *fear;* it may be so because of a positive *refusal of consent;* it may be deficient by reason of a *condition* attached to the contract (cf. Dennis J. Burns, *Matrimonial Indissolubility:* Contrary *Conditions,* Washington, CUA, 1963, no. 377, pp. 54-67).

iii. *Maturity* (psycho-somatic element): the mental maturity required for a valid consent comprises: (1) *a normal personality* with the following elements or traits: relationship with the milieu; (2) a normal state of mental health comprising a capacity for adaptation, an aptitude for happiness, and an acceptance of sexual instincts. (e.g., Absence of personality disorders)?

b. *The object of matrimonial consent*

The present law, in canon 1086; 2, refers to the exclusion of the conjugal act or of any essential property of marriage as necessary and sufficient for the invalidity of the marriage. However, since consent is now said to consist in a mutual covenant for a communion of conjugal life, it follows that the willful exclusion of the community of life or of one of its essential elements, renders the covenant void. Consequently, if the right to an intimate, life-long conjugal partnership is not mutually given and accepted, there is no marriage (cf. new canon 303; 2).

In positive terms, the parties must offer each other the following elements which constitute the object of matrimonial consent:

1) the right to the community of life;

2) the possibility of living this community of life;

3) the right to conjugal acts;

4) the other essential properties of marriage: exclusivity, indissolubility, fecundity.

In some authors consider the constitutive elements of the community of life: (1) maturity and balance, (2) capacity for interpersonal and heterosexual friendship, (3) conjugal complementarity, (4) sense of material responsibility, (5) mental capacity to contribute as father and mother, to the good of the children. There are also a number of constitutive elements to be found in the procreation of *offspring:* (1) the conjugal act must be the ultimate expression of conjugal love, and (2) an act connaturally apt to beget offspring.

2. Cognitive elements of consent

The knowledge necessary for consent must cover a number of elements: knowledge of the contract, of the person, of the object of the bond itself.

a. *Knowledge of the contract (substantial error)*

The present Law (canon 1082:1) as expressed in canon 1082:1 states: "In order that matrimonial consent may be possible, it is necessary that the contracting parties be at least not ignorant that marriage is a permanent society between man and woman for the procreation of children."

New Proposed Law

The Commission for revision proposes to have the new law read: "In order that matrimonial consent may be possible, it is necessary that the contracting parties be at least not ignorant that marriage is a permanent community between man and woman, ordered to the procreation of children through some physical cooperation" (new canon 298:1).

Since marriage requires the community of conjugal life and the right to acts apt for the procreation of children, it would be a substantial error to believe that marriage is 1) a purely friendly society, 2) a work pact for family needs, 3) a companionship for mutual help. It would be sufficient for validity to know that the parties are obliging themselves to an action or union of the sexual organs.

b. Knowledge of the person (factual error)

Present Law. The present law (C. 1083) states in part: "Error regarding the person makes marriage invalid. Error regarding a quality of the person, even though it is the cause of the contract, invalidates marriage in the following cases only: if the error regarding the quality amounts to an error regarding the person," etc.

New Proposed Law

In the new Code, it is proposed to state that an "error in the quality of the person, even though it is the cause of the contract, does not invalidate marriage unless it amounts to an error regarding the person" (new C. 299:2).

Likewise, it is proposed to add a new canon: "The person who enters into matrimony deceived by fraud perpetuated to obtain consent, on some quality of the other party, which could seriously disrupt the community of conjugal life, contracts invalidly" (new C. 300).

Error, a false or insufficient apprehension of reality, may be either simple (not affecting the will) or prudential (affecting the intention of the party).

Ignorance is a lack of personal information that causes a false apprehension of reality (error). Deceit is dishonest information that also causes a false apprehension of reality.

Error, caused either by ignorance or by deceit, invalidates a marriage if it affects: (1) the physical person itself, or (2) a personality trait which amounts to a substantial condition, in the sense that the quality desired and missing in the partner is preferred to the physical person: if it deprives the partner of a trait which in his mind is the only individuating note of the other, or is morally and socially individuating the other, or if it introduces in the other party a trait which, because of its nature precluded the physical presence of the consort

c. *Knowledge of the object (doctrinal error)*

Present Law. The present law states (C. 1084): "Simple error regarding the unity, or indissolubility, or sacramental dignity of marriage, even though it is the cause of the contract, does not vitiate matrimonial consent."

New Proposed Law

The new law would read: "error regarding the unity or indissolubility of marriage, as long as it does not influence the will, does not vitiate matrimonial consent" (new C. 301).

A prudential error, affecting the intention of the party, can influence the intention in three ways: (1) if it takes the form of a mutual pact, (2) if it amounts to a condition for the contract, (3) if it affects the knowledge on which the will power bases its decision, or forms its intention, either because of a personal reflexive thinking, or of a pervading influence of the surrounding milieu.

d. *Knowledge of the bond* (*juridical error*)

Present Law. The present law states (C. 1085) that "The knowledge or belief that the marriage is null does not necessarily exclude matrimonial consent." No change is proposed in the text of this canon (new C. 302).

If the nullity does not really exist, the involved party commits an error either in law or in fact. In both cases, the intention of marrying can subsist either because he forgets about the invalidity, or because he reflexively decides to disregard the law of the Church, and marries anyway.

If the nullity does really exist, the marriage is invalid because of the existing cause of nullity, not because of a defect of consent, since this consent might be valid, if the intention to marry prevails against the known nullity (a very rare case).

3. Volitive elements of consent

a. *Adequate personal consent* (C. 1086)

Canon 1086:2 was referred to in the first part of this chapter. As reworded it would read: "If either party or both parties by a positive act of the will exclude marriage itself, or the right to the community of life, or the right to the conjugal act, or any essential property of marriage, they contract invalidly (new canon 303:2), e.g., unity and indissolubility.

i. *Consent.* The external expression is presumed to convey the internal intention (C. 1086:1). The object must be the community of life and the right to the body.

A defect of consent is the *absence* of consent due to a voluntary abstention (total simulation) or mental incapacity (lack of human responsibility).

Likewise, consent could be defective because of *voluntary distortion* (partial simulation), either abstention from consenting to an element, or excluding it, or because of a *lack of mental capacity* to perform a true contractual act because of lack of discernment of judgment, of freedom of the will, firmness of decision, or, of the capacity to fulfill the obligations connected with the object of the contract.

ii. *Nullifying intentions.*

1). *Against the bond* (*total simulation*). Simulation is an external manifestation of consent, notwithstanding an internal decision not to marry really. The elements would be an intention to fake the marriage, or not really to consent, following one's concept of marriage in opposition to Christian doctrine by rejecting in practice the consequences of this doctrine or accepting the consequences of the intention (ignoring the invalidity following the simulation).

2) *Against the community of conjugal life.* Community of life includes two elements: the *physical capacity* to cohabit in an assiduous way and to perform the conjugal act, and the *psychic or mental capacity* to realize true heterosexual *friendship*, or conjugal complementarity both morally and psychologically, and provide for the material welfare of the home and for the good of the children.

3) *Against fecundity.* An intention against fecundity can be expressed by either a refusal of the object of marriage or a refusal of one of its ends. The refusal of the object of marriage is found in either total refusal of the connatural act (non-consummation), or limitation of the right by following personal fancy, excluding certain periods, or using unnatural devices.

The refusal of the end of marriage can occur either by denying procreation through birth prevention (abortion) or killing born children, or by denying education of children.

4) *Against fidelity. An* intention against fidelity is a positive prev-

alent act of the will that excludes the obligation of conjugal fidelity, and includes a perverse intention of sharing either the conjugal act or the community of life with a third party.

5) *Against indissolubility.* An intention against indissolubility is a positive intention of terminating the marriage before death. It may be either an actual intention of divorcing that bears on the individual marriage to be contracted, or an habitual belief in divorce, due to a permanent state of mind. (e.g., "Divorce Mentality").

b. *Freedom from external influence Force and Fear* (CICO 178)

Present Law. The present law states that "a marriage entered into through force or grave fear unjustly inspired from without such that in order to escape from it a party is compelled to choose marriage, is invalid. No other fear, even if it furnish the cause for the contract, entails the nullity of marriage" (C. 1087).

New Proposed Law

The revised law intends to add the expression "even without advice" after the word "unjustly" (new canon).

Force is an external influence used to induce fear in a person; fear is a perturbation of the mind on account of an impending evil. Fear may be either *common* (physical or moral threats) or *reverential* (indignation on the part of parents or superiors).

Force and fear invalidate a marriage if they are grave, unjustly induced from without, and unavoidable except through marriage.

4. Psycho-somatic elements - Elements of Maturity or Psychic Balance

New Proposed Law
The new law (Cs. 296-297) will supplement a deficiency in the present Code by providing for a recognition of the influence of psycho-somatic defects on matrimonial consent.

a. *The proposed new canons would read as follows:*
"They are incapable of contracting matrimony—
1° who are so affected by a mental illness or a serious disturbance of the mind, that lacking the use of reason, they cannot give matrimonial consent; (296).
2° who suffer from a serious defect of discretion of judgment

on the matrimonial rights and duties to be mutually given and received.

They are unable to contract marriage who are unable to assume the essential obligations of matrimony because of a serious psycho-sexual anomaly." (297)

As Msgr. Lucien Anne stated, "the abnormal conditions of the future spouses that radically prevent the establishment of any community of conjugal life,—in such a way that the principles whereby it may be established are missing—are: either a very grave distortion or perversion of the sexual instinct, or an abnormal paranoiac disturbance of the affectivity, or one that is equal to them" (*Ephemerides Iuris canonici*, 26 (1970), p. 432).

b. *JURISPRUDENCE*

i. *The incapacity of reasonable conduct* is the traditional (incurable) ground of insanity. Ex-Schizophernia (296:1)
  ii. *The incapacity of contractual act lack of due discretion.*
    The responsibility essential to the validity of the contract supposes in the spouses: (e.g., Lack of due discretion, Pregnancy, alcoholics, epilepsy. (296:2)
    (1) an affective maturity that enables them to grasp the deep meaning of the conjugal covenant and to give it a permanent value; (e.g., Psychological state at time of marriage).
    (2) a discernment of judgment proportionate to the importance of the pact being concluded;
    (3) an internal free choice of the will, without coercitive impulsions or repulsions; (e.g., A father got four daughters pregnant—ran away and married the first man she saw; he married her and the marriage broke up.
    (4) a firmness of character or personality that is capable of an effective decision;
    (5) a normal sexuality, without perversions or troubles that vitiate the perception of values and attractiveness of marriage.
  iii. *The incapacity of assuming obligations.* In order that their marriage be valid, the spouses must have the mastery of the homosexuality, multiple sclerosis, sadism object of the contract, in the sense that they be in a position to discharge, later on, their conjugal responsibilities. This incapacity to assume the

obligations of marriage is that of a person, undermined by a psychic ailment, independent of his will, the connatural evolution of which would eventually jeopardize, permanently or even transitorily, the practice of a true community of conjugal life. Being incapable of realizing the essential object of the contract, this person cannot assume the obligations and consequently, cannot conclude a valid covenant.

c. *Philosophical approach*

Whatever is sufficient to disrupt this marriage: relative incapacity, multiple sclerosis, homosexuality, sadism, etc.

As a voluntary and free act, the matrimonial covenant must be exempt from constringent psycho-somatic pressures or tensions. Certain pathological defects of the personality make the patient "impotent to act indifferently": he is impelled by the internal dynamics of his pulsional system to act beside or against moral rules. The person who is thus affected cannot reach maturity either of his psychological or of his moral conscience.

Such pathological defects affecting the act of the will are, e.g.: perversion, alienation, obsession, impulsion, depression, phobia, immaturity.

d. *Contribution of Psychiatry*

Mental frailties that may affect marriage come under the general heading of psychoses, neuroses and personality disorders. (the law does not require a specific diagnosis).

i. *Psychoses.* In general disorders labelled psychoses differ from the other groups of psychiatric disorders in one or more of the following aspects:

(1) *severity*: psychoses are major disorders that tend to affect all areas of the patient's life.

(2) *withdrawal*: objective reality is perceived in a distorted way;
(3) *affectivity*: emotions are often qualitatively different from the normal;
(4) *intellect*: judgment often fails; hallucinations and delusions may appear;

(5) *regression:* there may be generalized failure of functioning and falling back to early behavioral levels.

ii. *Neuroses.* General symptoms of the neurotic conflict include:

(1) *specific avoidances;*
(2) *inhibitions* of marital instincts, of aggressiveness, of sexualized functions, and of emotions;
(3) *sexual disturbances* such as impotence, premature ejaculation, and frigidity;
(4) *lack of interest* in the environment and general impoverishment of the personality;
(5) *use of emergency discharges* for the relief of tension;
(6) *sleep disturbances*

iii. *Personality disorders.* The most significant forms of pesonality disorders are:

(1) *personality disorders:* paranoid, cyclothymic, schizoid, obsessive-compulsive, hysterical, asthenic, antisocial, immature, inadequate, and psycopathic personalities.
(2) *Sexual deviations:* homosexuality, sadism, hyperaestheaia.
(3) *alcoholism*
(4) *drug dependence*

These are deeply ingrained, chronic, and habitual patterns of reaction that are maladaptive in that they are relatively inflexible: they limit the optimal use of potentialities and often provide the very counter-actions from the environment that the subject seeks to avoid.

5. *The contractual act*

a. *Exchange of consent* (C. 1088)

The parties must be present either in person or by proxy. The consent must usually be expressed in words.

b. *Marriage by proxy* (C. 1089)

c. *Marriage through an interpreter* (C. 1090-1091)

The veracity of the interpretation must be beyond all doubt.

d. *Conditional consent* (C. 1092))

Present Law. The present law authorizes conditional consent provided it is not related to a future, necessary, impossible or immoral event, or concerns a future event contrary to the substance of marriage.

New Proposed Law

In the new Code, it is stated that marriage may not be contracted validly with a condition regarding a future event; the Ordinary's written permission will be required in each case.

A condition is a clause or stipulation in the matrimonial contract which provides that the essential obligations of marriage may be qualified or nullified under stated circumstances for certain stipulated reasons.

e. *Perseverance of consent* (C. 1093)

"Even though a marriage has been contracted invalidly because of an impediment or a defect of form, the consent which has been given is presumed to persevere until its revocation shall have been proved." It is proposed to leave this unchanged in the new Code (C. 310).

The word "impediment" is to be taken in a very broad sense here, not in the sense of a diriment impediment, but of any obstacle to the marriage itself.

This canon is used as a basis for convalidations without renewal of consent (i.e., a *sanatio in radice*).

Conclusion

Consent is a multi-faceted reality which reaches into the innermost sectors of every marriage. Without consent, no marriage could exist. The Church teaches that once given, consent lasts forever, although some authors today are starting to speak of the death of a marriage when consent no longer exists (cf. S. KELLEHER, *op. cit.*, p. 45). This theory has not yet received recognition, and understandably so, in Church law; indeed, if it were accepted, the entire approach to the study of marriage would necessarily be changed. Only time will tell what directions this new school of thought will take and what following it will receive.

CHAPTER SEVEN

FORM OF MARRIAGE

HISTORICAL SUMMARY

Canon 1094—Only those marriages are valid which are contracted before the pastor or the ordinary of the place, or a priest delegated by either of these, and at least two witnesses, but according to the regulations of the following canons, and with the exceptions mentioned in Canons 1098 and 1099.

As mentioned elsewhere, whenever two people (man and woman) contract marriage without any formality and without any witnesses (clandestine marriage) but they mutually express their matrimonial consent externally, such a marriage is valid according to the natural law. In the early days of the Church, there were no general laws requiring that a marriage be celebrated before an authorized priest for validity, although the Church Fathers did forbid secret marriages and were insistent upon having all marriages contracted *publicly* and in *church*.

1. *Council of Trent* (1545-1563): This Council specified the form of marriage which is contained in the *Tametsi decree*. It stated that all marriages were invalid unless they were contracted before one's own pastor, or another priest delegated by the pastor or local ordinary *and* at least two witnesses.

Before the Council of Trent marriages contracted without a priest present were valid but illicit. After the Council of Trent, marriages contracted without a priest present were invalid where the *Tametsi* decree was published[1] in the places where the decree was not promul-

---

1. Published in the Provinces of New Orleans, San Francisco, parts of Utah, Vincennes (Indiana) and St. Louis. It was not promulgated in the rest of the USA. Hence, a marriage contracted in the USA before 1908 in any other place without a priest—such a marriage was valid.

gated, the marriage was valid even without the priest but this marriage was illicit. All baptized persons, including heretics, who were married in the place where the decree was published were bound by this form. Therefore, heretics marrying in such a place married invalidly. The pastor of the domicile or quasi-domicile of the parties to be married had *personal jurisdiction* over them whereby he was able to assist *validly* at any marriage of his subjects *anywhere*. (Today it is territorial, except in the case of danger of death C. 1044). The pastor also was able to delegate this same power to any other priest to assist at a marriage of his subjects anywhere.

2. *The Benedictine Declaration* (1741): Due to the fact that the *Tametsi* decree caused some hardship upon heretics marrying among themselves or with Catholics, Benedict XIV modified the *Tametsi* decree, exempting heretics from this legislation. *In the United States of America* the *Tametsi* decree or the *Benedictine Declaration* was in force only in places where it was published. A baptized person (Protestant or Catholic) who married a non-baptized person without a dispensation of disparity of cult married *invalidly*. (This was followed until 1918.)

3. *Ne Temere* (1908): In 1908 a new decree of Pius X, the *Ne Temere*, was published everywhere and bound every Catholic everywhere. Heretics were excluded unless they wished to marry a Catholic. The *Ne Temere* was incorporated into the New Code of Canon Law in 1918.

The Church claims the right of power to prescribe the form of marriage. According to Canon 1016, here the power extends to the entire contract which is subject to the natural and the divine law, leaving to the State the right of power over the civil effects alone.[2]

Oriental Law: The form of marriage is precisely the same for the Oriental Church, with the exception that the marriage must be contracted with the so-called sacred rite, namely the *blessing of the priest*. Although this sacred rite is not a certain liturgical rite, but a simple blessing, nevertheless this blessing is required for *validity*.

PASTORS: Pastors mentioned in this canon include all clerics mentioned in Canons 451:1; 216:3; 451:2; 1°. Canon 1095: 1, 1° must be observed regarding the canonical possession of a parish and the territorial limits.

---

2. **Anachronism or Pastoral Necessity? (Studia Canonica).** Vol. 12, 1978, p. 41 E. Dunderdale.

WITNESSES: This canon mentions that *two witnesses must be present physically and morally (simultaneously) with the priest* and capable of giving testimony that a marriage was performed.

4. *Matrimonia Mixta* (March 31, 1970): This is a new legislation regarding mixed marriages. (Cf. Appendix and section on mixed marriage.)

ORIENTALS

The Form of Marriage in relation to *Ne Temere* and Orientals in the United States:

The Sacred Congregation of the Council, on March 28, 1908, stated that Orientals were only obliged to the decree *Ne Temere* when they married Latin Catholic. Generally speaking (with one exception) up to May 2, 1949, Oriental Catholics *marrying among themselves*, outside of their Patriarchate, or an *Oriental marrying a non-Catholic*, were not held to the form of marriage (except Disparity of Cult cases).

The exception mentioned above refers to the Orientals (Ruthenians) of the Byzantine Rite who were bound to the form of marriage prescribed by the *Ne Temere* decree, not from 1908, but rather from August 17, 1914, when Bishop Ortynsky made a request of the Holy See that, for the sake of uniformity of discipline, the decree *Ne Temere* should be extended to all Uniate Greek Ruthenians in the United States (Decretum, *Cum Episcopo*, AAS, VI, 1914, 458-463). From this time on Orientals (Greek Ruthenians) were bound to contract marriage under the pain of nullity before a pastor or their ordinary or delegated priest and two witnesses as called for by the decree *Ne Temere*. This canonical form obliged those Ruthenians when they married among themselves and when they married with other Orientals who were heretics. The Decree of 1914 refers only to the United States. Ruthenians of other countries became obligated to the *Ne Temere* at different times.[2]

A New Marriage Form for the Orientals

The II Vatican Council promulgated this new form on November 21, 1964; it went into effect in the United States on January 21,

---

3. Cf. Pospishil, **Law on Marriage**, pp. 185-187, should such information be required, on the latter. / Marbach, F. Joseph, J.C.D., **Marriage Legislation for Catholics of the Oriental Rites in the U.S. and Canada**, Catholic Univ. Press, Washington, D.C.

1965.[4] This new marriage form is found in Article 18 of *Orientalium Ecclesiarum*, the Decree on the Eastern Catholic Churches of Vatican II, Article 18 states the following:

"To obviate invalid marriages when Eastern Catholics marry baptized Eastern non-Catholics, and in order to promote the stability and the sanctity of marriage, as well as domestic peace, the Sacred Council determines that the canonical form for the celebration of these marriages obliges only for liceity; for their validity the presence of a sacred minister is sufficient, provided the other prescriptions of law are observed."[5]

The introduction of this new marriage form for Orientals affects the validity of a marriage, therefore it is very important that the date (January 21, 1965) be kept in mind when dealing with cases involving *a Byzantine Catholic and a baptized non-Catholic of an Eastern Catholic rite*. Chancery and tribunal officials must keep this new legislation in mind when dealing with cases involving individuals of this category.

*Liceity:*The liceity of such marriages remains in effect as found in the former law (*Crebrae Allatae* - May 2, 1949) whereby censures and other penalties are incurred if the regular prescriptions of the law are not observed. Neither can ordinaries dispense from this marriage form whereby they would grant permission for a Catholic to contract marriage *solely* or *first* before a non-Catholic minister (*communicatio in sacris*). It must be noted that Pospishil gives his opinion and makes a fine distinction when he states that although *communicatio in sacris* is forbidden, nevertheless, after such a couple has exchanged the marriage vows before a Catholic priest, thereby becoming recipients of the sacrament of matrimony, the rites performed in the Eastern dissident church cannot lead to a sacrament; therefore this is an extra-sacramental *communicatio in sacris*, which is permissible according to the above mentioned principle.

A New Marriage Form for the Latin Church

The Decree *Orientalium Ecclesiarum*, Art. 18, was promulgated only for the Orientals, but the Latin bishops requested the same privilege for their subjects. It was granted three years later and went into

---

4. Cardinal Joseph Slipy, the Byzantine Archbishop of Lwiw in the Ukraine who possesses quasi-patriarchal power and jurisdiction declared that the Decree would begin its legal force at a later date, namely April 7, 1965, due, probably, to the difficulties existing behind the Iron Curtain.
5. The translation of the text is taken from the Decree of the unofficial translation of the NCWC.

effect March 25, 1967. Therefore this date is important because all marriages between a Latin Catholic and an Orthodox person in the Orthodox Church, *with* or *without* the Latin Ordinary's permission, is considered valid. The marriage would be considered only illicit if no permission was granted.[6]

EASTERN CHURCHES OF THE U.S.A.

When reference is made to Eastern Oriental Catholics in the U.S.A., this refers to the Ruthenians and Ukrainians of the Byzantine Rite and others. We have four such ecclesiastical jurisdictions:

1. The Metropolitan Ruthenian Province
   a. Archdiocese of Pittsburgh, Pennsylvania
   b. Diocese of Passaic, New Jersey
   c. Diocese of Parma, Ohio

2. The Metropolitan Ukrainian Province
   a. Archdiocese of Philadelphia, Pennsylvania
   b. Diocese of Stamford, Connecticut
   c. Diocese of St. Nicholas, Chicago, Illinois

3. Maronite Exarchate of Detroit[7]
   (Established in March, 1966)

4. Melchite Exarchate of West Newton, Massachusetts[8]
   (Established in March, 1966)

Other Eastern Rites in communion with Rome do not have Ordinaries of their own in the U.S.A. Consequently, they are under the juris-

---

6. Decree issued February 28, 1967.
7. DIOCESE OF ST. MARON, DETROIT
Very Reverend and Dear Fr. Siegle:
   This is to thank you for your letter of October 15, 1976, regarding the promulgation of the Decree on mixed marriages between Maronite Rite Catholics and Orthodox church members. The following is the letter that I received from the Maronite Patriarchate. I translated it from the Arabic for your understanding and convenience.
   BKERKE, December 16, 1974 — Prot. no. 11/74
   "Reverend and Dear Msgr. Joseph Abi-Nader: In reply to your letter, Prot. no. 807/73 dated December 21, 1973, may I inform you that according to the minutes of the Patriarchal Synod held on Friday, April 29, 1966 the Bishops of the Synod and His Eminence Paul Peter Cardinal Meouchi, Patriarch of Antioch of All the East have decided to promulgate the Decree on mixed marriages on this date (April 29, 1966) and to consider hereafter the marriage of a Maronite to an Orthodox before a non-Catholic priest, and in the Orthodox Church VALID, but UNLAWFUL. — With best wishes for health and success," BISHOP NASRAL-LAH SFEIR, PATRIARCHAL VICAR

diction of the local Latin Ordinary. The following Eastern rites come under such jurisdiction: Armenian, Bylorussian, Chaldean,, Romanian.

VALID ASSISTANCE AT MARRIAGE

Canon 1095—1. The Pastor and Local Ordinary Validly Assist at Marriage:

1° Only from the day on which they took canonical possession of their benefice according to Canons 334, 3 and 1444; 1 or entered upon their office, and provided they have not been excommunicated, placed under interdict, or, suspended from office or been so declared by a declaratory sentence;

2° Only within the limits of their own territory, in which, they can validly assist at all marriages, *not only of their own subjects but also of non-subjects;*

3° Provided that they ask and receive the consent of the contracting parties without being coerced either by force or by grave fear.

2. The pastor and local ordinary who can validly assist at a marriage can also give another priest permission to assist validly at marriage within the limits of their respective territories.

3. Deacons: The power of the deacon to officiate at marriage celebration: A deacon who will not remain in this grade, but will advance to the priesthood, has those offices which are enumerated in n. 29 of the Dogmatic Constitution of Vatican II, *Lumen gentium,* and in no. 22 of the Apostolic letter, *Sacrum diaconatus ordinem* of June 18, 1967.[9] No. 22 states that it is

---

8. EXARCHATE FOR THE MELKITES, WESTON, MA
Dear and Very Reverend Father Siegle, In reply to your letter of December 17, 1976, I have the pleasure to answer with the following:
1. Until the erection of our own Diocsee (1966) we abode with the directives of Rome concerning the "form" in the United States. 2. Consequently the marriage between a Melkite and an Orthodox was always considered valid. 3. However, the Decree effective May 2, 1949, was applied in the United States, but never accepted generally in the Middle East. 4. That is why the Decree on the Catholic Churches of the Eastern Rite of Vatican II was hailed with enthusiasm in relation to no. 18 by all Melkites (November 21, 1964). In reality we never needed a Decree from Rome to regulate our discipline. The directives of the Synod were more than sufficient.
In summary we can say that the Melkite Synod has always demanded the presence of an ordained priest to make the marriage valid. The non recognition of a marriage performed by the "Moslem Cheikh" or by a Protestant Minister" illustrate the idea that the presence of an Orthodox priest to bless a marriage was of a different calibre altogether.
Rt. Rev. Archimandrite Lucien Malouf, Vicar General.

the office of the deacon, but only insofar as the local Ordinary has commissioned him, to expedite a number of matters. Among these matters, in places where a priest is lacking (*ubi sacerdos deest*), the deacon may assist at and bless marriages in the name of the Church, by delegation of the bishop or the pastor, the norms of Canons 1095:2 and 1096 being also observed. Canon 1098 remains in force, and what it says of the priest is to be understood also of the deacon. The cause "*ubi sacerdos deest*" mentioned above is *not* required for the validity of the delegation given to the deacon to assist at marriages.[10]

PROPER DELEGATION

Canon 1096—1. The permission to assist at a marriage granted in accordance with Canon 1095, §2, must be given expressly to a *certain priest for a certain determinate marriage*, all general delegations being excluded except to the regularly appointed assistants of the parish for the parish to which they are attached, otherwise it is invalid.[11]

2. The pastor or local ordinary must not give permission unless all the canonical requirements for proving the freedom of the parties to marry have been fulfilled.

1. *Express delegation* (licentia) must be given to a certain specified priest for a particular marriage. General delegation is sometimes given to the assistants (vicarii cooperatores) for the parish to which they are assigned.

2. *Valid Assistance:* Pastors or local ordinaries can validly assist at all marriages *only within* the limits of their territory (in danger of death 1043-44, of their subjects anywhere) not only of their own subjects but also of those who are not their subjects.

9. Pont. Comm. for Interp. Decr. Vat. II — AAS 60, p. 363.
10. Ibid., AAS, 1969, p. 348.
11. General Delegation for Deacon Assigned to Parish (Com. Vat. II Interp., July 19, 1970) AAS 62-571.
   The Fathers of the Pontifical Commission for the Interpretation of the Decrees of the Second Vatican Council decided to reply to this question proposed in a plenary session:
   Whether a deacon who is firmly and lawfully assigned to a certain parish, can be equated with assistant pastors (for the parish to which they are assigned, in accord with the intent of canon 1096, sec. 1) as regards general delegation or permission relative to assisting at a marriage according to the norm in canon 1095:2? Reply: **In the affirmative.**

3. *National Parishes:* Authors[12] are divided on this type of parish. The Code did not change the status of such parishes (S.C. of Conc. Feb. 1, 1908). This Congregation stated that such pastors who have no exclusive territory hold it together cumulatively with another or other pastors. These might be Italian, Slovak or German. One should acquaint himself with the particular diocesan laws or the documents on the establishment of the parish or church. The Code did not change the status of these parishes and the local ordinaries are not to make any changes without consulting the Holy See (C. 216).

Military Chaplains are such that they have this jurisdiction over military persons without regard to territory; they can assist at marriages of these persons anywhere without regard to territory, provided it is on the military base.

Orientals: The law is practically the same. However, they cannot assist validly at a marriage of two Latin Catholics; neither may the Latin pastor or Latin local ordinary assist validly at a marriage of two Oriental Catholics. If the particular Orientals do not have a hierarchy in this country, the jurisdiction to assist at marriages belongs to the Latin local ordinary. The Holy See sanctions this in many instances (Cf. New Legislation for Orientals under C. 1094).

General Delegation to an assistant may come from (1) *Diocesan Faculties:* (2) from *The Pastor:* (3) or by *Letter of Appointment to a Parish* from the Ordinary.

Particular Delegation: This can be done by a (1) temporary administrator; (2) by the vicar substitute, (3) by the priest supplying for, and appointed by the pastor who for some reason or other leaves the parish suddenly, even without the approval of the ordinary as long as the notification is sent to the ordinary. All these faculties are given with the power to subdelegate; further subdelegation may not be involved unless granted by the pastor or the local ordinary. *Delegation is invalid,* if the pastor calls a monastery asking the prior or superior to send *someone* (not delegated) to perform a marriage in the parish. *This delegated power must be given to a priest.* It seems that it could also be given to a deacon just before ordination when the marriage is to take place after the ordination because this assistance at marriage is merely a quasi-jurisdiction, it is not the power of orders as such that is required to assist at marriage. Delegation must be expressed, orally or in writing; or by

---

12. Woywood, **Canon Law, p. 759.** DeSmet, Leitner, Fanfani, Blat, Chelodi, Ayrinhac.

certain signs or facts surrounding the situation. Presuming delegation or assuming tacit delegation because one is a good friend of the pastor, etc., would render the marriage invalid. Oriental Law is the same unless a mixed rite is involved.

Inter-Ritual Marriages: We refer here to marriages between a Latin Catholic and a Byzantine Catholic. The previous requirement of seeking permission from the Apostolic Delegate for such marriages to take place in the rite of the bride has been changed. These cases are provided for by Canon 88:3 of the Oriental Code, *Crebrae Allatae*, and Canon 1097:2 of the Latin Rite Code. An interpretation from the Cardinal Pro-Prefect for the Sacred Congregation for the Doctrine of the Faith, Feb. 1, 1967 states that the local Ordinary can now dispense from these provisions. In other words, the local Bishop is now competent in inter-ritual marriages, to grant permission for the marriage to take place in the rite of the bride. For example: John, a Byzantine Catholic is going to marry Mary, a Latin Catholic. According to the law, this marriage should take place in the Byzantine Church because the husband is Byzantine. However, the bride prefers to have the marriage in her Latin Church. The Latin pastor may get this permission from his Latin Ordinary to do this; he need not apply to the Apostolic Delegate as it was done in the past. Neither must he apply to the Oriental Ordinary. The Latin Ordinary has this faculty. This works both ways; the Oriental Ordinary has the same privileges for a Byzantine bride and Latin groom, should they seek such a privilege.

Interritual Marriages of Oriental Catholics and Protestants

According to the present law, whenever a Byzantine Catholic marries a Protestant (e.g. Lutheran), the Latin pastor must obtain the necessary permission from the respective Byzantine Ordinary for validity; otherwise, such a marriage would be invalid. This is due to the fact that the Latin pastor has no subject in this particular case. Several such cases have been referred to the Apostolic Delegate and to the Oriental Congregation. In reply, the Holy See said such a marriage is invalid.

According to several authors, Wojnar, Pospischil, Besondorfer, they conclude that such a marriage is valid per *accidens* or *secundum quid*. It seems we have two completely opposite answers. The argumentation of these authors seems to have some validity but until the Holy See decides this question, we must abide by the decision of the higher authority that such a marriage is invalid; namely, a marriage between a Byzantine Catholic and a Protestant (e.g., a Lutheran) by a Latin pastor without proper permission is invalid.[13]

CANON 1138
Without Knowledge of Parties Concerned, Marriage Sanated in Case of Original Lack of Jurisdiction (Holy Office, Nov. 17, 1962) Private.

The following was first sent to the U.S. Apostolic Delegate who, in turn, forwarded it to the Holy Office.

CASE: On July 29, 1961, John Doe, a non-Catholic baptized in the Baptist sect, entered marriage with Mary Smith, a Catholic, before a Latin-rite priest with a dispensation from *mixtae religionis et ad cautelam disparitatis cultus.*

Recently, her mother's marriage was brought to the attention of this office, at which time it was discovered that Mary canonically is a member of the Byzantine-Slavonic Rite, since both her father and mother belonged to this Rite. Mary was baptized in a Latin-rite church and because the spelling of her name was changed, it was not discovered until now that she is a member of the Byzantine-Slavonic Rite.

It is evident that the dispensation granted for the marriage between John Doe and Mary Smith was invalid, since it was granted by the Latin-rite Ordinary. However, since John was a baptized non-Catholic, this would not make the marriage invalid. There is the additional question that the marriage might be invalid due to lack of jurisdiction on the part of the Latin-rite priest. In spite of this, the marriage would be valid if canon 209 (152, *Cleri sanctitati*) would apply in this case.

In the light of the above, can we consider this a valid marriage? If not, would it be possible to obtain a *sanatio in radice?*

PETITION: The Ordinary humbly requests from Your Holiness a radical sanation of the marriage invalidly contracted by Mary Smith,

REPLY: From the Holy Office, His Holiness, Pope John XXIII, through special faculties granted to the S. C. of the Holy Office and in view of the particular circumstances of the case, graciously remands the petition to the prudent judgment and conscience of the Reverend Ordinary who, provided the consent of each party still continues, can, without the knowledge of the parties, radically sanate the marriage invalidly

---

13. Reply of Holy Office, Rome, November 17, 1962.
Catholic, with John Doe, non-Catholic.

contracted by Mary, Catholic, with John, non-Catholic.

Canon 1097–1. The pastor or the local Ordinary may *assist* at a marriage:

1° After they have legitimately ascertained according to law, the freedom of the parties to marry;

2° After they have ascertained moreover, that one of the contracting parties has a domocile or quasi-domicile, *or a month's residence;* or in the case of a vagus (itinerant) who is actually staying in the place where the marriage will be contracted.

3° Provided that, if the conditions mentioned in n. 2 are wanting, the permission is had from the local ordinary of the domicile or quasi-domicile or place of a month's residence of one of the contracting parties, unless it is a question of itinerants (vagi) who are actually traveling and have no place of sojourn anywhere, *or unless some grave necessity occurs which excuses from asking the permission.*

2. In every case let it be taken as the rule that the marriage should be celebrated before the pastor of the bride-to-be unless a just reason excuses therefrom; marriages, however, between Catholics of different rites are to be celebrated before the pastor of the groom and according to the ceremony of that rite, unless some laws provide otherwise.

3. A pastor who assists at a marriage without the permission required by law, has no right to the stole fee and must return it to the proper pastor of the parties.

This canon deals with the *liceity, not the validity.* Should such permission be lacking, the marriage is valid but illicit. It is the pastor and local ordinary who are obliged to see that the individuals are free to marry. The proper pastor of the investigation is usually the pastor of the bride; the pastor of the groom could do this also, but it belongs to the bride's pastor.

Month's Residence: When circumstances warrant it, one month's residence is sufficient. This brief stay is equivalent to a domicile or quasi-domicile, and this residence need not be made physically for 30 continuous days; a *morally* continuous month suffices before marriage is contracted.

Non Subjects: To perform a marriage validly and licitly of a non-subject, a pastor should have the permission of the proper pastor with (1) the pastor of the bride-to-be, or (2) the pastor of the groom.

Permission is not needed for itinerants (vagi) who have no domicile or place of permanent residence; therefore, there is no one from whom to get the permission. However, the pastor should consult the local ordinary before assisting at such a marriage (C. 1032). Permission is not needed in case of necessity.

Case of Necessity: If a business man, or a government employee, or soldier, is leaving on an urgent business or other business and there is no time to get in touch with the proper pastor, (all things being equal) all the canonical aspects cleared, the pastor may go ahead with the marriage.

It must be kept in mind that all pastors can assist at all marriages of *non-subjects* in their own territory (C. 1096) validly, also licitly, if they have the proper pastor's permission (*not delegation*) unless they are vagi or in case of necessity.

Orientals: Conditions for lawful assistance are the same as in the Latin Code. However, a Latin pastor can assist at a marriage of an Oriental man and Latin woman validly but illicitly, because such a marriage belongs to the pastor of the groom. The Latin pastor would have full right if the groom was of the Latin rite. The marriage must take place in the parish of the groom when there is a marriage between a Latin and an Oriental. In the case of an Oriental woman of the *Byzantine Ruthenian rite and a non-baptized person*, the Byzantine bishop is the only one competent to grant the dispensation and the marriage is to take place in the Byzantine Church. Otherwise, the dispensation would be invalid and the marriage would also be invalid (*Diriment Impediment*).

Witnesses at a Catholic or Non-Catholic Marriage

Members of the Orthodox Church and also Protestants of other denominations may act as bridesmaid or best man at a wedding in a Catholic Church. A Catholic too can be best man or bridesmaid at a marriage properly celebrated among our separated brethren or celebrated in any Protestant Church.

LACK OF FORM CASES

Since the so-called "Lack of Form Cases" are on the increase in the United States, as many as 800 in one large diocese in one year, which causes so much alarm, the Fathers of the Ecumenical Council gave some consideration as to whether a change should be effected regarding the form of marriage. Some countries such as Germany and Holland are having high casualty rates in this regard. In dealing with the Universal Law—Canon Law—it is the opinion of most canonists that the Church could allow some special way in handling these situations, but it would not be feasible to make the law whereby the universal Church would be obligated. It is the general consensus of opinion among canonists, especially those of the United States, that the form of marriage be retained despite the fact that we have many cases coming to the attention of our Tribunals. To do away with the present legislation of the form of marriage would only increase the number of ligamen cases and we would be in a worse state than the first.

Because of the prevalent unfortunate situation, every priest should be acquainted with the essential items that are considered in the Lack of Form cases. Ordinarily this is a case which is handled in the administrative process in the Tribunal. Some of the essential items would be:

1. That at least one of the parties was held to the Catholic form of marriage at the time of the marriage;
2. That the marriage did not take place before a Catholic priest;
3. That the marriage was not later validated or sanated in some church.

The following documents in general are necessary to establish the Lack of Form cases:

1. The petition which should clearly state the facts of the case.
2. A recent copy of the baptismal record of the Catholic party.
3. A First Communion record *or* Confirmation record *or* proof of Catholic parentage or training when the marriage took place before January 11, 1949, for a Latin Catholic.
4. A certified copy of the marriage certificate.
5. A decree of the civil divorce or annulment.
6. There should be a sworn testimony of the Catholic party that the marriage was not validated.
7. The testimonial of character

Lack of Form (C. 1097)

On August 14, 1928, John Beck married Mary White before Rev.

George Black of the Christian Alliance Church. John is a member of the Evangelical Church in Albany, New York. John claims that his wife was unfaithful. They lived together from 1928 until 1932. They were divorced in August, 1950. One child was born of this union. Mary White is married again.

John Beck wishes to marry again. The woman he plans to marry is Mary Day, a Catholic of St. John's parish. She has been a parishioner at St. John's since 1943. This church wedding which he is planning is merely a validation because he and Mary Day were married by a Justice of the Peace. John Beck was a baptized Catholic before 1928.

1. What is necessary for the pastor of St. John's to do in the investigation of this case?
2. List the necessary documents which must be obtained before handling this case.
3. How would you handle this case?

EXTRAORDINARY FORM OF MARRIAGE

Canon 1098–1. If it is impossible without grave inconvenience to have or reach the pastor or local ordinary, or a delegated priest, who can assist at the marriage in accordance with canons 1095-96:

1° In danger of death, marriage is valid and licit when celebrated before the witnesses alone; and even *outside the danger of death*, provided it be prudently foreseen that these circumstances (difficulty to get an authorized priest) will last for a month.

2° In both cases, if another priest who can be present is available he must be called and must assist at the marriage, together with the witnesses, without prejudice however to the validity of the marriage contracted before the witnesses alone.

1. *In Danger of Death:* The reasons would be the same as those enumerated in Canons 1043-45.

Inconvenience: This could be bad highways, rough seas, distance (e.g., in mission territories - Brazil, India), too great expense (on part of the people or priest); sickness, bad weather (ice and snow in northern countries); great fear of being apprehended (e.g,. living in communistic territory); during persecutions, floods, disasters, etc. One is not obliged to use the telephone or telegraph. The inconvenience could be either physical or moral and could be on the part of either the priest or the parties wishing to contract marriage.[14] If there is any diriment impediment, without a priest, nothing is provided whereby this impediment could be dispensed, i.e., when two witnesses are had. If any priest is present, he could invoke Canons 1043-44 and absolve and dispense the couple from the impediment.

Outside the Danger of Death: When it is foreseen that they will not be able to approach a priest for a month, the parties may contract marriage before two witnesses. However, if they wish to marry and wish to have it recognized by the civil law (because of property rights. etc.) they would be justified to go to the Justice of the Peace or any civil magistrate (as the judge), who is entitled to assist at marriages. If any of these would be unavailable the parties would be justified to go to any minister (who would not act as a minister of religion) who would merely perform the ceremony without any religious ceremony. according to his right given him by civil authorities.[15]

2. *In both cases, in danger of death and outside the danger of death.* if another priest (not authorized as such) can be had, he may assist at the marriage as an official witness. Further, he may use the faculties of Canons 1043-44-45 as a norm for dispensing from impediments of marriage, if necessary. The general rule is that *in danger of death or outside of danger of death as mentioned* in the conditions above, a priest should be called if it is possible; otherwise, the two witnesses would suffice for a valid and licit marriage.

PERSONS BOUND BY THE FORM

Canon 1099–1. The aforementioned law on the form of marriage obliges the following:

1° All persons baptized in the Catholic Church and those who have converted to it from heresy or schism, even if the former or latter afterwards fall away, whenever they contract marriage among themselves.

2° The same aforementioned persons when they contract marriage with non-Catholics, either baptized or non-baptized, even when a dispensation has been obtained from the impediment of mixed religion or disparity of cult.

3° Orientals, if they contract with Latins bound by this form.

---

14. Code Commission, May 3, 1945.
15 Woywood, op. cit., p. 777.

2. Without prejudice to the prescriptions of paragraph 1, n. 1, non-Catholics whether baptized or non-baptized, if they contract among themselves, nowhere are bound to observe the Catholic form of marriage.

The law is clear in itself. When non-Catholics marry among themselves, it makes no difference who assists at the marriage, minister, Justice of the Peace, etc., this marriage is considered valid. The clause "likewise exempt are persons born of non-Catholic parents, even though they have been baptized in the Catholic Church, who have grown up from infancy in heresy or schism or infidelity, or without any religion, when they contract with a non-Catholic party" was abrogated by the *Motu Proprio* of Pope Pius XII, August 1, 1948, and took effect January 1, 1949. The phrase: *children of non-Catholics* refers canonically to children of apostates.[17] Children of non-Catholic parents and those of apostate parents, even though they be *baptized in the Catholic Church*, were not obliged to the Catholic form of marriage, if they grew up from infancy *without any religion*, and married non-Catholics.

Without any Religion: What is meant here? If one receives instructions for First Communion, or if one knows the Our Father and Hail Mary, or if one went to church occasionally, would we consider this as sufficient to constitute *some religion*, some religious training, which would oblige one to the form of marriage? This is the question that puzzled canonists since 1918 to 1949. Since January 1, 1949, *anyone baptized in the Catholic Church* regardless how much religious training he had, or if he had none whatsoever, *is bound by the form of marriage*. One can readily see the importance of this date in reference to the people mentioned in this canon.

CASE: John and Mary came to their pastor to see if they could be married. John was married before and was divorced. He and his wife had been baptized in the "Church with the Lighted Cross" (non-Catholic). He knew nothing of his wife's background, but upon investigation it was found that his wife was born in a Catholic hospital and had an emergency baptism. Her mother, a Catholic, died at childbirth. Since the marriage of this baptized Catholic took place after 1949, even though she had no religious instructions in the Catholic religion, (she was brought up by her Lutheran grandparents as a Lutheran) her marriage

17. AAS XXI, 1929, p. 573; AAS XXII, 1930, p. 195.

to John was invalid because of Lack of Form *due to the revision in the code* in 1949. If this revision or deletion had not taken place, her marriage would have been valid. John and Mary were permitted to marry.

RITE

Canon 1101—1. The Pastor shall take care that the parties receive the solemn Nuptial Blessing which may be given them even after they have lived for a long time in the married state, observing the special rubrics.

2. The solemn blessing can be given either in person or through a representative, by that priest alone who can validly and licitly assist at the marriage.

NUPTIAL BLESSING

In a Catholic marriage, the wedding ceremony takes place not at the beginning (as was customary), but *after the Lord's Prayer in the Nuptial Mass*. In the marriage of two Catholics, the nuptial blessing is always given, even if, for good reasons, the marriage takes place outside the Mass, in which case the Nuptial Blessing is given following the Blessing and Exchange of Rings. The Nuptial Blessing is always given for both a Catholic and a Mixed Marriage, even when it takes place during Lent or Advent (Decree MR. 23/969, March 19, 1969, S.C.R. Card. Gut). It may be given more than once, and even for a mixed marriage.

MIXED MARRIAGES

Canon 1102—1. In marriages between a Catholic and a non-Catholic party, the questions regarding the consent must be asked according to the prescriptions of Canon 1095:1., no. 3.

2. But all sacred rites are prohibited; if however, it is foreseen that greater evils were likely to result from this prohibition, the ordinary can permit some of the usual ecclesiastical ceremonies excluding always the celebration of Mass.[18]

---

18. Decree March 18, 1966, no. 4. As an exception the Local Ordinaries may permit the celebration of a mixed marriage using the Sacred Rites with the usual blessing and discourse.

ORIENTALS

The Nuptial Blessing or Crowning

Interpretation issued by the *Pontifical Commission for the Redaction of the Code of Oriental Canon Law* on May 3, 1953.[19]

Question: Is the word "blessing" in can. 85 ≠ 2 to be understood as a simple blessing or is a certain liturgical rite required? Answer: Affirmative in respect to the first part, negative to the second.

1. MARRIAGE FORMS IN GENERAL

1. In discussing ecclesiastical marriage forms of the past often not sufficient attention is paid to the fact that they must be distinguished in accordance with the legal sanctions which were attached with willful disregard of an obligatory ecclesiastical marriage form was gravely sinful, the marriage itself could have been valid.

The marriage ceremony in the Ancient World was a public contract also, and an occasion for a religious rite. However, no public official, religious or secular, was commissioned to represent the state. The Church of the Apostolic era had therefore no special interest in strictly demanding that the marriage contract be concluded in the church and in a liturgical rite, particularly when the parties alone were the ministers of the sacramental action. Nonetheless, it was ruled very early that no marriage should be celebrated without the bishop (St. Ignatius the Martyr to St. Polycarp, 107 A.D.). This does not mean the establishment of an ecclesiastical form, but merely that the presence or approval of the bishop should be secured.

Tertullian (197-217) spoke of a liturgical rite of marriage, and ecclesiastical legislators of the following centuries are even more explicit; without it they considered a marriage contracted outside the Church invalid. Later centuries made it even clearer: who ever married without an ecclesiastical rite committed a sinful act, which sometimes was even punished by an excommunication *latae sententiae*, but the marriage was thereby not invalidated. This was an obligatory ecclesiastical marriage form, which was not, however, sanctioned with invalidity of the marriage contract.

In some parts of the Oriental Church the liturgical marriage form

---

19. AAS, 1953, p. 313.

was made obligatory for the marriages only of the nobility or freemen while serfs could marry without the ceremony of coronation. The last stage of the development of the marriage form, i.e., when it became obligatory and its neglect invalidated the marriage contract, was reached in the Latin rite Church with the Council of Trent (Decree *Tametsi*). However, even here a limitation remained: *Tametsi* was not in force everywhere, but solely in certain places. Only the Motu Proprio *Ne Temere* (1907 and the CIC (1917) made the obligatory marriage form with a sanction of invalidity applicable everywhere for Latin rite Catholics. This strict obligatory form was established also for all Oriental Catholics by the motu proprio *Cr. All.* (1949).

Canon 1112:2 of the Latin Code is not included in the Oriental legislation. If a priest of the Latin rite lawfully assists at a marriage of an Oriental Catholic and a non-Catholic (either baptized or non-baptized) he must follow the Latin rite liturgical formula according to Canon 1102:2, and not that of the Oriental ritual (C. 85). Likewise, if a priest of the Oriental rite lawfully assists at a marriage of a Latin-rite Catholic and a non-Catholic (baptized or non-baptized), he must follow the Oriental ritual according to Canon 85 of the Oriental law and not of Canon 1112:2.

2. "If the religious form (blessing or crowning) is required for validity of a marriage, it must be proved that such legislative authority had been granted by the Church, either by specific enactment or by tacit recognition of a legal custom. Neither of these has ever been done."[20] The argument has been brought forward that the obligatory marriage form among dissident Orientals may have been in existence before the schism and therefore continues its legal force which it acquired then. However the studies of E. Herman, S.J., on the historical evolution of the marriage form within the many Oriental groups, the Byzantine rite, showed the conviction that the act of exchanging consent must be accompanied by a religious, liturgical rite, was not customary all the time or did not apply to all classes of the faithful and was never a general practice in all Byzantine territories. The same may be said, but more strongly, for the other Oriental rites.[21]

"It might be advanced," says Pospishil, "that the Oriental dissidents by themselves could evolve a legal custom introducing an obligatory

20. Pospishil, **Law on Marriage, pp.** 135-136.
21. Herman, E., S.J., "De Benedictione nuptiali quid statuerit ius Byzantium sive ecclesiasticum sive civile," found in **Orientalia Christiana Periodica,** 1938, **pp.** 189-234.

marriage form sanctioning marriages contracted in defiance of it be null and void, but this would have to be proved in each single community; the argument can never be raised higher than to a mere hypothesis. Practically it was never adopted or followed by any office of the Catholic Church, and will not contribute to the solution of problems in practice, that is, will not overcome the presumption enunciated in Canon 3, Cr. All. (C. 1014) *in dubio standum est pro valore matrimonii*, in doubt the validity of the marriage must be upheld.

As to the blessing itself, required by Canon 85:2 as an essential part of the Oriental marriage form, the Pontifical Commission for the Redaction of the Oriental Code resolved that *any blessing suffices as far as the validity is in question*, and no specific liturgical act is required. For the lawful assistance at marriage the respective liturgical formularies must be followed Many dirrident Orientals consider the solemn coronation of the spouses, which consists in an imposition of wreaths or crowns on their heads by the priest, the essential form of marriage, an assumption not substantiated by historical documentation, even though the coronation ceremony belongs to the age old custom of the marriage rite.[22]

In other words, the Oriental law requires the simple blessing of the priest assisting at marriage; it is essential but only for *liceity;* it would still be *valid.*[23]

DISPENSATION FROM THE FORM FOR SPECIAL CASES

The Instruction "Matrimonii Sacramentum" of March 18, 1966 of the Sacred Congregation of the Doctrine of the Faith on *Mixed Marriages* establishes a new discipline for mixed marriage. Certain options were possible and normally should be taken. Many dioceses have already published their own directives and made their options. Montreal has published its own directory on mixed marriages.

The same Instruction provides for recourse to Rome in cases where dispensation from the form or from the "cautiones" are necessary in certain cases. It may be of interest to know that Montreal has obtained various dispensations from Rome in particular cases described below.

a) Dispensation from the form
1) For a Catholic and an Orthodox
with Catholic baptism and education of children,

---

22. **Ibid.**
23. Pospishil, loc. cit.

with Orthodox baptism and Catholic Schooling of children,
with Orthodox baptism and Orthodox education of children.

2) For a Catholic and an Anglican
with Catholic baptism and education of children,
with Anglican baptism and Anglican education of children.

3) For a Catholic and a Presbyterian
with Catholic baptism and Catholic education of children.

4) For a Catholic and a member of Dutch Reformed Church
with Reformed Church baptism and Catholic education of children.

5) For a Catholic and a Jew
with Catholic baptism and Catholic education of children,
with Jewish circumcision and Jewish education of children.

b) Marriage permitted in spite of refusal of Cautiones

1) As above with Orthodox, Anglican, Presbyterian, United Church, Dutch Reformed, Jew.

2) Cautiones refusal
of baptism only, of Catholic baptism and education with, acceptance of Catholic schooling,
of Catholic baptism and education and,
Catholic schooling.

3) Minimal Condition for granting dispensation
that the Catholic party do his or her best to see to the Catholic baptism and education of the children.

c) Place of celebration
In several cases the *Ordinary* has permitted, in special circumstances, that a mixed marriage take place in a non-Catholic Church or chapel *with a Catholic priest officiating* and the non-Catholic doing only what is allowed in the Instruction Matrimonii Sacramentum i.e. congratulate, exhort, pray with the assembly for the happiness of couple after the marriage has been solemnized by the Catholic priest alone.
Conditions: 1) least possible publicity. 2) that the non-Catholic minister and higher authorities of his Church agree to the arrangement.

d) Sanatio:
We have obtained permission to grant a Sanatio in a case where the non-Catholic party refused to agree to the Catholic

baptism and education of future children on condition that the Catholic party do his best.

e) Double ceremonies:

permission to be married in both Churches granted in the U.S.A.–in two cases–exchange of matrimonial consent in both churches.

Has not been granted here yet. Two ceremonies permitted. Catholic marriage first followed by ceremony in non-Catholic Church where renewal of consent had to be omitted. (Impractical, not applicable).

f) Catholic priest officiating with non-Catholic minister in non-Catholic (Orthodox) Church.

requested once - permission refused.

REGISTRATION OF A MARRIAGE

Canon 1103–1. After the celebration of marriage, the pastor or one who is taking his place shall, as soon as possible, enter the names of the contracting parties and witnesses, the place and date of the celebration of the marriage and other items according to the method prescribed in the ritual books and by his local ordinary; and this must be done even though another priest, delegated by the pastor or by the ordinary, assisted at the marriage.

2. Moreover, according to Canon 470:2, the pastor shall also note in the baptismal register that the party has contracted marriage in his parish on a certain date. If the party was baptized elsewhere, the pastor of the marriage shall send notification of this marriage to the pastor of baptism either himself or through the episcopal Curia, in order that the marriage may be recorded in the baptismal register.

3. Whenever the marriage is contracted according to Canon 1098, the priest, if he assisted at it, otherwise the witnesses are bound in solidum with the contracting parties to take care that the marriage be recorded as soon as possible in prescribed books.

The Council of Trent (Sess. XXIV, c. 1) commanded pastors to have a book in which to enter marriages which took place in their parishes and include the names of the parties and the witnesses, the day and the place of the contract. We find the same prescriptions in the Roman Ritual[24] giving the forms to be used and stressing the fact that the parish priest should enter the marriage which took place as soon as possible. It further prescribed that he put this in his own handwriting, even when another priest (if he was delegated by him to the ordinary) took care of the marriage. The law of 1908 contains the same prescriptions and added new ones. This law stressed the fact that it was a grave obligation on the part of the parish priest to have the marriages that took place in his parish to be registered into the marriage record as soon as possible. It also stressed the fact that *one must be careful to avoid omissions and inaccuracies. The record must contain the names of the contracting parties, place and date of the marriage, and other particulars. The priest who officiated, if he was delegated, the dispensations that were obtained, the promises that were made in a mixed marriage, the publication or omission of banns.* If for some reason the marriage was declared null later on, this fact should be recorded also (C. 1918). A marriage should be entered into the baptismal record of the parties, if any of them were baptized in another parish. According to the new baptismal record, there is a margin left for such notations. This notation notification could be sent directly or through the Chancery Office, (Instr. 1941), to get better results it is best to send it through the Chancery or episcopal curia, if the marriage was celebrated according to the norms of Canon 1098. If a priest was present at such a marriage, it is his obligation to send in the information. If no priest was present, the obligation rests with the witnesses and the parties themselves. The record of all marriages should be kept in order to prevent bigamy or fraudulent unions. The Catholic Church has this wonderful system because by cross-checking a pastor can very easily find out whether a person was married before or not. All one has to do is to consult the baptismal register, or the baptismal certificate, which must be issued at least within the last six months, and presented to the pastor who is going to marry the parties; the baptismal record should contain all the items which are found in the baptismal records. Sometimes there is a double record: in the baptismal and the matrimonial register.

MARRIAGES OF CONSCIENCE

Canon 1104—Only for a very grave and a very urgent reason and by the local ordinary in person, not even the Vicar General without a special mandate, can it be permitted that a marriage

---

24. **Roman Ritual** Trt. 7, Ve. Sap. Mt. 2.

of conscience be contracted, that is, that a marriage be celebrated without the publication of Banns and in secret according
to the norm of canons which follow.

A marriage of conscience is one in which a marriage is contracted
without the publication of banns, in which the priest and witnesses
who assist at the ceremony, are bound to strict secrecy. After careful
investigation, the local ordinary may permit a marriage of conscience.
In such a case the information regarding the parties must be gathered
secretly without revealing the identity of the parties. The reasons for
such marriages of conscience might be, e.g., (1) a widow has to raise
a number of children and conduct a business (which forbids marriage);
if it were known that she was married it would put the business in
jeopardy; or perhaps a person who is in the Army and is forbidden to
marry while he is in this position, has a grave reason to get married.
In conditions such as these, marriages of conscience are permitted.

> Canon 1105—The permission to celebrate a marriage of con-
> science imposes a promise and grave obligation to observe the
> secret on the part of the priest assisting, the witnesses, the
> ordinary and his successors, and also the other contracting party
> as long as one does not consent to the divulgation of the mar-
> riage.

> Canon 1106—The obligation of this promise on the part of the
> ordinary does not extend to a case in which any scandal or grave
> injury to the sanctity of the marriage is imminent as a result
> of the observance of secrecy, or of the children born of such a
> marriage, or have them baptized under fictitious names, unless
> in the meantime notifying the ordinary within 30 days of the
> birth of the children, giving notice of birth and baptism of the
> child, and the true indication of the parents, or if the parents
> neglect the Christian education of the children.

Regarding the permission for a marriage of conscience, the local
ordinary must insist on the obligation of secrecy about this marriage
and all those connected with its celebration. He is also bound implicitly
to the secret in such a way that it is a conditional promise, for if there
is some danger to the common good, or if some evil should follow

from such a marriage, he would be bound to reveal the secret. This is the local ordinary's prerogative. Children that are born of marriages of conscience at times must be given fictitious names; precautions must be taken that the names of the parents do not appear on the baptismal register, nor the proof of the legitimacy of the children. All this information is kept in the secret archives of the Chancery.

Whenever the ordinary permits a marriage of conscience to a couple who are forbidden to marry by civil law because of some impediment of civil law, all the necessary precautions and care must be taken that this does not become known publicly, because the state can impose a fine or imprisonment upon the priest assiting at such a marriage. Some marriages are permissible under the laws of the Church but might be forbidden by some civil laws; therefore, it is necessary to handle this matter with great caution. In the final analysis, marriage is governed objectively by the divine law and the Church who is the custodian of the divine law.

> Canon 1107—Marriages of conscience should not be recorded in the usual matrimonial and baptismal register, but in a special book to be kept in the secret archives of the curia mentioned in Canon 379.

Some kind of notification should be made in the church of baptism; perhaps this should be put in the secret archives of the respective chancery.

TIME

> Canon 1108—1. Matrimony can be contracted at any time of year.
> 2. Only the solemn nuptial blessing is forbidden from the first Sunday of Advent to the day of the Nativity of our Lord inclusive, and from Ash Wednesday to Easter Sunday inclusive.
> 3. However, ordinaries of places can, observing the Liturgical laws, permit the nuptials even during the above mentioned time, for a just cause and admonishing the parties to abstain from excessive festivity.

1. *Marriage may be celebrated at any time of the year.*
2. It can also be celebrated any time of the day unless the ordinary has some diocesan legislation, enacted for some good reason, forbidding

marriage at a certain time or on a certain day. *This particular law would only be for liceity, not for validity.* The ordinary must obtain a special indult from the Holy See to enact a law forbidding it under the penalty of invalidity.

PLACE

Canon 1109—1. Marriage between Catholics should be celebrated in the parish church; it may however take place in another church or oratory whether public or semi-public, only with the permission of the local ordinary or the pastor.
2. Ordinaries can permit that marriage be celebrated in a private home only in an extraordinary case and always on condition that there be a just and reasonable cause; but ordinaries must not permit it in churches or oratories of a seminary or of religious women, unless in case of necessity and with proper precautions.

Canon 1113—Parents are bound by a most grave obligation to provide for religious and moral as well as for the physical and civil education of their children and also to provide for their temporal welfare.

Parents must attend to their welfare that (1) they receive catechetical instructions, (2) they receive the sacraments often, especially to make their Easter duty each year, and (3) they attend a Catholic school.

LEGITIMATION

Canon 1114—Children who are conceived or born of a valid or putative marriage are legitimate, unless *at the time of conception,* the use of the marriage theretofore contracted was forbidden to the parents because of solemn religious profession or the reception of a sacred order.

PATERNITY

Canon 1115—1. The father is he who is indicated by a lawful marriage unless the contrary be proven by conclusive arguments.
2. Children born at least six months ofter the celebration of marriage or within 10 months after the date when conjugal relations ceased are presumed to be legitimate.

Canon 1116—By the subsequent marriage of the parents whether true or putative, whether newly contracted or validated, even though it was not consummated, the offspring become legitimate provided the parents were legally capable of contracting matrimony together at the time of conception, or of pregnancy, or of birth.

Canon 1117—Children legitimated by a subsequent marriage, as regards canonical effects, are equal to legitimate children, unless the contrary is expressly provided.

CHAPTER EIGHT

CONSEQUENCES OF MARRIAGE

RATUM ET CONSUMMATUM MARRIAGE

Canon 1118—Marriage which is *ratum et consummatum* cannot be dissolved by any human power nor by any cause except death.

This canon is precise and clear indicating that marriage cannot be dissolved by the parties themselves (*intrinsic indissolubility*); neither can a marriage be dissolved by any human power by secular or religious authorities (*extrinsic indissolubility*).[1] Natural law is the basis for indissolubility as an essential property of marriage whereby every marriage is indissoluble but not absolutely. *Extrinsic indissolubility* is possible when the marriage is *non consummatam*. A ratified and consummated marriage is one in which two baptized persons (Catholic or non-Catholic) perform the human action of copula whereby there is the penetration of the vagina by the male organ and the emission of true semen therein; hence, such a marriage is indissoluble and even beyond the power of the Supreme Pontiff.

The ultimate reason for this inflexibility may be found in the mystical signification of Christian marriage; according to St. Paul (Ep 5:32), marriage between Christ and his Church. Now this reproduction is achieved in its perfection in marriage between baptized persons which has been consummated. Common sense teaches us that by the use of the conjugal right, marriage receives a sort of completion; something irreparable has taken place; the affective and verbal self-surrender has been supplemented by an actual physical one which justifies the expression, very significant in itself, of "consummated marriage." *It is consummated*

---

1. The existence of this power was clearly and explicitly taught only in the 13th century and, with the exception of cases of Solemn Religious Profession, only in the 15th century was the power knowingly used. Pope Martin V (1417-31) and Pope Eugene IV (1431-47).

in the symbolical and mystical order, in which it represents the indefectible union between Christ and his Church. In a perfect representation of this union, the indefectibility of the union must have its own symbol; and it has it in the absolutely indissoluble marriage.[2]

It is interesting to note that the question here is not the controversy of fact but the controversy of the question of law (*questio iuris*) and from time to time authors boldly step forward with their opinions. We find one such opinion in *Ephemerides Theologicae Lovanienses.*[3] "Does it follow then that what the Church has bound today she can loose tomorrow through the exercise of the same power of the keys? ... Inasmuch as all marriages are contracts, even though some of them are sacramental and consummated, they all come under the power of the keys. ... In *actu primo*, therefore, even ratified consummated marriages form no exception to this unlimited power of the Church. In *actu secundo*, however, these marriages are extrinsically indissoluble *de iure divino* simply because the *Church has used her divinely given binding power upon them instead of her loosing power*.... Having once committed herself to its intrinsic indissolubility, there need be no fear that at some future time she may reverse herself and dissolve a marriage of this kind."

According to this opinion, a ratified and consummated marriage was within the ambit of the ministerial power of the Church; in other words, such marriages are, by divine law, extrinsically indissoluble, simply because up to the present day, the *Church has always used her binding power rather than her loosing power*. It is the opinion of authors[4] that there is nothing against holding the opinion that the Church by some dint of the same ministerial power by which today she declares indissoluble a *ratum et consummatum marriage* of two baptized, can tomorrow change her attitude and allow dissolution.[5] Although in recent years the Church has granted a dissolution of the matrimonial bond in cases where, in the past, she never conceded a dispensation should be a caution to us regarding such a warning to us not to make or formulate categorical assertions. It is only through, or after some practical experience with actual cases that we know the precise limits of the ministerial

2. Vermeersch, **What is Marriage?**, no. 68, p. 26.
3. O'Connor, W. R., **The Indissolubility of a Ratified, Consummated Marriage,** Ephemerides, Theologiae Lovanienses, XII, 1936, pp. 720-722.
4. Abate, Antonius, O.P., **The Dissolution of the Patrimonial Bond in Ecclesiastical Jurisprudence,** Desclee, New York, pp. 25-29.
    Bride, A., "Le Pouvoir du Souverain Pontif sur Le Marriage des infideles," **Revue de Droit Canonique,** X-XI, 1906-61, pp. 98-99.

power derived from the divine law. However, it is possible to believe that in some future date the Church can intervene in a ratified and consummated marriage, not by extending its power, but by specifying and revising the notion of non-consummation extending this term also to the case where conjugal copulation, though having taken place, has, because of permanent sterility, never attained the primary end of marriage, namely, the generation of offspring.

"It is certain that consummation, like sacramentality, does not add any fuller perfection to the indissolubility of the validly contracted bond. What it does is to *actuate* in a more adequate manner, the symbolism existing in a marriage between the baptized. The marriage that is solely sacramental represents the union of Christ with the soul through grace, a union which can be destroyed by mortal sin. The marriage crowned by consummation, however, represents the unbreakable union of Christ with human nature. It is only on account of this element that the ratified and consummated marriage is asserted to be absolutely indissoluble, both extrinsically and intrinsically."

Essential Facts in Dealing With non-Consummated Marriages

There is no *consummation of marriage* unless there is the actual penetration of the vagina by the male organ and the emission of the *true semen* in it. There is no consummation if this is lacking.

2. There is no true consummation if contraceptive devices are used. However, each case must be thoroughly investigated and studied before making a decision.

3. A marriage is considered as non-consummated if intercourse takes place *only* before a marriage.

4. The investigation of the fact of *non-consummation of marriage* and of the *existence of a just cause for granting a dispensation belongs solely* to the Sacred Congregation of the Sacraments. Therefore, no ordinary may constitute a tribunal and conduct a test trial with the questioning of the parties and witnesses in the form of a judicial process until he has received express authorization to do so from this Sacred Congregation. (Permission is no longer necessary.)

5 What right then, or what is the source of power which the Church exercises to dissolve such marriages, since marriage is naturally indissoluble by the parties themselves or by any other human power?

---

5. **Ibid.**

Marriage is *intrinsically* *indissoluble* but *extrinsically dissoluble* in certain cases. Theologians have discussed this question for a long time whether the dissolution of the marriage bond by religious profession depends upon the *natural law*, the *ecclesiastical law*, or the *positive divine law*. The Church has never given an official pronouncement on this matter. The Council of Trent condemns anyone who claims that the Church has no such power. The history of this case and the reasons which prove that the Supreme Pontiff has this power has been under discussion by theologians. The conclusion of these discussions end in saying that this matter has reference to Christian morality and that the Supreme Pontiff cannot err in matters of faith and morals; therefore, we can reasonably conclude that the Pope has this power.

DISSOLUTION OF THE MARRIAGE BOND

Canon 1119—A non-consummatum marriage between baptized persons, or between a baptized and a non-baptized person, is dissolved by solemn religious profession, and by a dispensation granted by the Apostolic See for a just cause, at the request of both parties, or either party, even though the other be unwilling.

1. Canon 1119 deals with two methods in dissolving a *ratum et non-consummatum* marriage, namely, (a) by Solemn religious profession and (b) by dispensation of the Holy See. Consummation is the conjugal copula or intercourse, that is the physiological elements: penetration of the vagina by the male organ and the emission of the true sperm in it. A marriage that is *ratum et consummatum* (C. 1118) cannot be dissolved. For "What God has joined together, let no man put asunder."

2. *Solemn Religious Profession* dissolves a *non-consummatum marriage* not only for a Christian but also for the non-Christian (unbaptized).

3. *Dispensation of the Holy Father:* The Pope can dissolve a *ratum et non-consummatum* marriage of Christians by papal dispensation, if it can be proven to the matrimonial court that the marriage was not consummated. Such cases are long and very involved.

THE PAULINE PRIVILEGE

Canon 1120—1. Legitimate marriage between unbaptized persons, even though it has been consummated, is dissolved in favor of the faith by the Pauline Privilege.

2. This privilege does not apply in a marriage between a baptized and an unbaptized person entered into with the dispensation from the impediment of disparity of cult.

1. Canons 1120 to 1126 deal with the Pauline Privilege, although Canon 1025 (Constitutions) deals with marriages between unbaptized parties (a requisite in the Pauline Privilege); nevertheless, some of the other requisites of the Pauline Privilege are lacking. Canon 1127 deals with the privilege of the Faith in doubtful cases, that is, when a doubt arises in a Pauline Privilege category.

2. When we speak of the privilege of the Faith, we do so in generic terms for the privilege of the Faith is a *genus*, whereas the Pauline Privilege and the Petrine Privilege are the *species* of this *genus*.

3. *Pauline Privilege:* This is a privilege whereby a legitimate marriage between two unbaptized persons, even though it is consummated, is dissolved in favor of the Faith.

4. *Requisites for the Pauline Privilege:* To utilize this privilege, it is required that (1) two persons be unbaptized at the time of the marriage; (2) that one of these persons be validly baptized after that marriage; (3) that the baptized person interpellate the other unbaptized party according to Canon 1121; (4) when the new marriage is contracted the former marriage is automatically (*ipso facto*) dissolved.

5. *Petrine Privilege:* This is a privilege whereby the Roman Pontiff dissolves a legitimate consummated marriage between a baptized person and an unbaptized person in favor of the Faith.

6. *Baptism of Heretics:* Regarding the valid baptism of heretics, it is morally certain that this baptism would be a sufficient foundation to use this privilege. However, the Church does not use it. It is a difficult procedure to handle such a case. It would simplify matters if the heretic became a convert to the Catholic religion. In such a case, we could call it the dissolution of a "natural bond" of marriage rather than the Pauline Privilege.

7. *Departure of the Unbaptized:* This departure must be proved by (1) interpellations (C.S. 1121 to 1122) from the circumstances whereby a dispensation is granted from making the interpellations. The departure of the unbaptized party must not be the fault of the converted party after baptism. The Pauline Privilege gives the new convert the right to marry a Catholic. However, in recent years, the Holy See has granted permission to marry another infidel or a baptized non-Catholic.

THE INTERPELLATIONS

Canon 1121—1. Before the party who has been converted and baptized can validly contract a new marriage, he or she must, except as provided in Canon 1125, interpellate the unbaptized party:
(1) whether he or she is also willing to be converted and to receive baptism; (2) or at least be willing to live peacefully without offense to the Creator.
2. These interpellations must always be made unless the Apostolic See shall have declared otherwise[6]

Canon 1122—1. The interpellations are to be made regularly, at least in a summary and extrajudicial form, by authority of the ordinary of the converted party, and the same ordinary shall also grant the unbaptized party, if he or she asks for it, an extension of time to think over the matter, warning the same party however that in case there is no reply within the specified time, a negative reply will be presumed.
2. Interpellations, even when made privately by the converted party himself, are valid, and indeed even licit in case the form above prescribed cannot be observed; but in this case they must be proved for the external forum by at least two witnesses or by some other lawful manner or proof.

Canon 1123—If the interpellations have been omitted by declaration of the Holy See, or if the unbaptized party has expressly or tacitly given a negative answer, the baptized party has the right to contract a new marriage with a Catholic person, unless since baptism he or she has given the unbaptized party a just cause for departing.

Canon 1124—The baptized even though since baptism he or she may have lived in matrimonial relations with the unbaptized party, does not thereby lose the right to contract a new marriage with a Catholic, and can therefore make use of this right in case

---

6. Pope Paul VI has declared otherwise. Cf. **Pastorale Munus I, 23** in the Appendix.

the unbaptized party changes his or her mind and departs without just cause or ceases to cohabitate peacefully without offense to the Creator.

1. *Departure of the unbaptized party:* This is understood if, when he does cause offense to the Creator by giving scandal (moral departure), or threaten the party with physical harm or causes life to be miserable, e.g., by quarrelsome dispositions, outbursts of anger, causes perversion, forces the person to onanism or commits some grave sin, the baptized convert may make use of the privilege.

2. *Infidel wishes baptism but not cohabitation with the baptized convert:* In this case we consider the matter a physical departure; however, it would be best for the convert to use this privilege before the other spouse is baptized; otherwise this would result in a *ratum* marriage causing complications and another intervention with the Holy See. Sometimes it happens that the infidel party (while separated and married) receives baptism (heretical sect) while the Pauline privilege case is being expedited, unknown to the newly baptized convert; when the interpellations are made, this is then discovered. The case becomes a *ratum* matter and is referred to the Holy See. We could also have a physical departure of the infidel when, for example, one is given a long term or when an infidel who already married for the second time is considered as a physical departure.

3. *Dispensation from the interpellations:* Ordinaries did not have this faculty from their Quinquennial faculties, but have them now from Pope Paul VI: *Pastorale Munus.*

4. *Time of interpellations:* After the baptism and before the conversion of the other party. If the interpellations were made before the baptism, the action would be valid provided that the non-baptized party did not change his mind.[7] Moreover, in a summary or extra-judicial form, the ordinary must give an extension of time if the infidel asks for it according to C. 1122.

Factors of Importance: (1) If the unbaptized person gives the necessary guarantees to let the newly baptized convert practice his religion freely, etc., and later violates this promise, the Catholic party is not

---

7. **Pastorale Munus** I, 23, grants faculties to the Ordinaries, "permitting them, for a grave cause, to make the interpretations **before the baptism of the party who is being converted** to the faith; also dispensing from the same interpellations before the baptism of the party . . . when the interpellations cannot be made or it would be useless."

obliged to live with that party and may get a divorce provided that the interpellations are made, or again a dispensation is obtained.

(2) It must be kept in mind that the legitimate marriage is not dissolved at the time of baptism of one party, but only after at the very moment of the new marriage of the convert.

(3) If the case is such that the interpellations cannot be made because it would be useless to make them, or the party cannot be found, or because the party is already married, *nevertheless, the invalidating canonical law* would render the new marriage invalid if they are not made. Canon 1121 is clear: "that the interpellations must always be made *unless the Holy See declares otherwise.*" *Pastorale Munus* changed this, since this faculty has been granted to ordinaries. We have canonists who discuss this speculative question whether the interpellations can be omitted if the party is already married or cannot be found. Practically the interpellations are useless in this case. Nevertheless, we must submit to the law and let the *Ordinary declare otherwise.*

INVESTIGATING THE NON-BAPTISM OF BOTH PARTIES

In dealing with a Pauline Privilege case, one must investigate and obtain conclusive evidence with moral certainty of the non-baptism of both parties of this legitimate marriage. Proving negative facts is very difficult, yet by a process of elimination this can be done as follows:

1. Check the religious affiliation and background of the parents or guardians. We have a very good and strong presumption of non-baptism of the party, if the parents belong to a *sect which rejects baptism,* if the parents belong to a sect which *believes only in adult baptism* (they reject infant baptism), or if the parents have no *religious affiliations whatsoever.*

2. If some of the children were baptized and the party claims no baptism, inquiry should be made why baptism did not take place. Also check the belief or practice of the parents regarding the baptism of their children. A search for possible records of baptism in the church or churches in the place of domicile.

3. Besides inquiring from the parents, one should check with the sisters, brothers, relatives and friends as to the possible baptism.

PAULINE PRIVILEGE EXTENDED

Canon 1125—Those things which pertain to marriage in the Constitutions: *Altitudo* of Paul III, June 1,1537; *Romani Pontificis* of Pius V, August 2, 1571; *Populis* of Gregory XIII, January 25, 1585, which were decreed for particular territories are *extended to other regions that have the same circumstances.*

In addition to the provisions of Canons 1120-1124, we have an extended privilege in Canon 1125, which can be used in regions in which particular circumstances exist. It may also be said that Canon 1125 is practical application of Canon 1127.

I. Constitution - *Altitudo*, Paul III:

(1) If a convert becoming baptized had several wives, but does not remember which he married first may, after his conversion to the faith, choose anyone and marry her, excluding all the others.

(2) If he remembers the first one he married, he must keep her and dismiss the rest. He cannot use the privilege of this Constitution. He may then use the Pauline Privilege if she is not baptized, but if she refused to live with him peacefully without offense to the Creator, he may use the Pauline Privilege.

Some of the important factors of this Constitution are:

(1) This constitution contains a dispensation (*ipso jure*) from the impediment of consanguinity and affinity.[8]

(2) No dispensation is needed from the impediment of disparity of cult; however, the *cautiones* required by the divine law are imposed.

(3) No interpellations are necessary.

II. Constitution - *Romani Pontificis*, St. Pius V:

(1) If a man, before receiving baptism, chooses from among his wives the one who wishes to be baptized with him and keep her to the exclusion of all the rest, even though she was not the first one he married, he may do so.

(2) No interpellations are made whatsoever.

III. Constitution - *Populis*, Gregory XIII.

Local Ordinaries,[9] pastors and confessors of the Jesuits *can dispense from the interpellations in Pauline Privilege cases, and provided that a summary and an extrajudicial investigation took place, when the party*

---

8. Ordinaries of Place-Now have the faculty from **Pastorale Munus**, December 3, 1963.

9. Mathis & Meyer, **Pastoral Companion**, p. 283.

cannot be interpellated; or was interpellated and did not make known these intentions within a certain specified time:

(1) whenever his whereabouts is unknown;
(2) whenever his whereabouts is known but cannot be reached;
(3) whenever his whereabouts is known but he is inaccessible;
(4) whenever the interpellations have been made and no answer is given.

Many authors agree that the ordinary of the pastor can *use this faculty* in favor of his subjects *anywhere*, and also for non-subjects within their own territory. Since this privilege comes from ordinary power, it can be delegated to others[10] All religious orders who held the communication of privileges may use this privilege. For the confessors of the Jesuits and others (religious orders) this faculty is not restricted to the internal forum; it may be used in the external forum.

When the newly baptized convert obtains his dispensation from the interpellations, the Constitutions permit him to marry. This marriage is valid even if the former party appears on the scene and gives the excuse that there was no opportunity to answer.

A dispensation from a legitimate consummated marriage between two infidels, which later became a ratified marriage but was not consummated after the ratification is also included in this Constitution *Populis* of Gregory XIII.

Theoretical Factors: Some authors claim that these Constitutions are an extension of, and an application of the Pauline Privilege; while others claim that it is really a *special vicarious power of the Supreme Pontiff,* apart from the Pauline Privilege, and because the latter Constitution dispenses with the interpellations.[11]

The circumstances considered here need not characterize a whole territory, but could be applied to individual cases. It would be sufficient in the case of a couple who is separated (when the other party cannot be found) that the ordinary or the pastor could utilize this Constitution in such a case.

When speaking of polygamy, it need not be simultaneous because successive polygamy would be sufficient. For example, we have cases in the United States in which non-baptized people get divorced and marry

---

10. Winslow, Vromont, no. 355, pp. 75-82.
11. Ayrinhac-Lydon, p. 32.

many times successively. This Constitution could be used in this particular case. Furthermore, these powers enumerated in Canon 1125 are actually *common law itself* and can be used without consulting the Holy See, when one is assured that all the conditions are verified. It is most unfortunate that this Constitution is not utilized more here in the United States by the ordinaries and pastors to whom it is directed.

Canon 1126—The bond of the former marriage contracted in infidelity, is dissolved *only* at the time when the baptized party contracts a *new marriage* validly.

If the newly baptized convert does not get married, the former marriage is considered valid; neither can the other (infidel) party marry validly again because of ligamen.

THE PRIVILEGE OF THE FAITH

Canon 1127—In doubt, the privilege of the Faith enjoys the favor of the law.

Dissolving Non-Sacramental Marriages and Privilege of the Faith:

Strictly speaking, the privilege of the faith signifies a faculty granted to a convert from infidelity through the vicarious power of the Roman Pontiff, whereby after the reception of baptism, the convert may contract a second marriage if the infidel party departs. In this sense, the privilege of the faith is synonymous with the Pauline privilege. Non-Sacramental marriages can be dissolved according to Canons 1119, 1120 and 1125, and the granting of dispensations in cases not directly contained in the Pauline privilege. Here, too, contrary to what seems to be the widespread misconception, Canon 1127 cannot be applied in a case in which a party who is certainly unbaptized with one who is certainly baptized in heresy. Canon 1127 deals with the question of doubt; in this case there is no question of doubt. The validity of this marriage as well as the baptism of one party is certain. Today the privilege of the faith, has been broadened to include the vicarious power of the Pope over such consummated legitimate marriages. This dispensation from the bond of marriage is given in circumstances not covered directly by Canons 1120 and 1125.

1. This power is exercised first in the three constitutions mentioned

---

12. Winslow, p. 55.

in Canon 1125 and all the conditions required for a Pauline Privilege were absent. This is especially true of the Constitution *Populus*, of 1585 of Gregory XIII.

2. In the Helena Case of Montana, 1924: A non-baptized man who contracted marriage with a baptized non-Catholic woman before a non-Catholic minister, the Holy Office petitioned the Holy Father to dissolve the *natural bond* of this marriage in favor of the faith. This marriage was dissolved. This case differs from the Pauline Privilege because the latter (Pauline privilege) deals with a valid marriage of two non-baptized persons; it also differs from the cases considered by Canon 1127, which deals in doubtful cases in favor of the faith. For example, whenever there is a doubtful baptism involved. It is clear that the dissolution of the Helena Case is due to the power of the Roman Pontiff, since a valid sacramental marriage which is consummated cannot be dissolved by any human power (Canon 1118), we can conclude as certain that a valid marriage between a certainly baptized person and a non-baptized person is not a sacrament and for grave reason the Holy Father can dissolve such a marriage.

3. In the Fresno Case, the Roman Pontiff dissolved a valid marriage of a baptized Catholic with a non-baptized person, contracted with a dispensation from disparity of cult; since this is not a sacramental marriage but a natural contract, there is no intrinsic difference between these cases and those of a baptized non-Catholic and a non-baptized person. This latter dispensation is a departure from the former policies. The Church had this power; nevertheless, was reluctant to act in these cases. The reason for this reluctance in which a prior marriage was celebrated after the granting of a dispensation from the impediment of disparity of cult is that some authors claim the Church would undo what she herself sanctioned to do previously. However, these are dogmatic truths; and basically the dogmatic aspects also have practical application. In the hierarchy of values, a sacramental union is to be preferred to a non-sacramental union. *Salus animarum* is the principle involved. A marriage of a Catholic contracted with a non-baptized person with a dispensation given by the Church for the disparity of cult is no more a sacrament than a marriage contracted by two non-baptized persons, since we cannot have half a sacrament. Moreover, it is no more sacramental than a marriage between a baptized non-Catholic and an unbaptized person. The granting of a dispensation by the Church for such a marriage does not render it intrinsically different. It is understood that

some who are concerned with such problems do not look with favor upon granting such dispensation for reason of scandal, laxity on the part of Catholics; but it may be that the meaning of the phrase *in favorem fidei* is sometimes misunderstood.

We cannot deny that the privilege of the faith means in some cases that a person who is baptized enjoys more favors in the Church than an unbaptized person. Moreover, the privilege also means that a person who receives baptism acquires a more favorable position legally than he had formerly. According to an Allocution of Pope Pius XII to the Sacred Roman Rota, he remarked that in approaching this type of case, we are not to be too lenient, nor too strict. The *via media* should be chosen, first things should be put first; *salus animarum* is to be preferred to the letter of the law. In the words of St. Paul, "The letter killeth, the spirit quickeneth." Pope Pius XI, who was a great defender of Christian marriage, has revealed in *Casti Connubii*, that he too was greatly concerned with the sacrament of marriage but was never reluctant to use the privilege of the faith when cases were presented to him. Therefore, *salus animarum* should be the principle governing such cases.

Pastoral Aid or Consideration of a Non-Sacramental Marriage and What is Necessary in Gathering Documents

1. A history of the case. This history should set forth all the facts, showing who is the baptized party, who the unbaptized party, the time of the marriage, the history of their marital difficulties, the time, place, and petitioner of the divorce. The certificate of marriage and divorce must be sent in. If the parties desire to keep the original certificates, then a certified copy should be obtained from the County Clerk. The complete history should be written on a separate sheet of paper.

2. The full name and address of the petitioner.

3. The names and addresses of the parents of the petitioner.

4. The name and address of the unconverted party.

5. Names and addresses of the parents of the unconverted party.

6. The names and addresses of people who can give testimony about the baptism or absence of baptism of either party, specifying for which party the witness appears. The witnesses for the unbaptized party should be the parents and relatives who lived in the vicinity during the infancy of the person, and who know the whole life of the person. In case an authentic baptismal record can be furnished no witnesses need be brought forward to substantiate the baptism.

7. Names and addresses of several people, preferably Catholics, who can testify concerning the truthfulness of the above mentioned witnesses, especially concerning those who testify to show the non-baptism of one of the principals.

8. The Catholic baptismal record of the convert.

9. The names and addresses of at least seven witnesses who can give testimony to show that the couple had no marital relations after the baptism of the spouse who had never been baptized. This is very important when the convert is the one who had not been baptized previously.

10. The name of the pastor.

11. The name or names of the priest who gave the instructions to the convert.

Non-Catholic as Plaintiff

The Instruction *Provida Mater*, August 15, 1936, 35, 3, states that non-Catholics, whether baptized or not, cannot act as plaintiffs in marriage cases without recourse in each case to the Congregation of the Holy Office. However on January 20, 1970, a letter from the Apostolic Pro-Nuncio to Canada to Archbishop Plourde expressed the opinion of the Signatura that marriage cases initiated by non-Catholic plaintiffs may be heard by a diocesan tribunal since non-Catholics, whether baptized or not, no longer need to request the ability to act as a plaintiff in marriage cases because of the promulgation of the apostolic constitution *Regimini Ecclesiae Universae*.

In a letter from the Congregation of the Doctrine of the Faith to the Bishop of Portland, dated October 15, 1968, it was stated that the Ordinary who is competent to process a case in the first instance can allow a non-Catholic the faculty to stand in court. A similar letter is found under c. 1646 in Volume VI of the Canon Law Digest, New York: Bruce, 1969, page 827. Dated February 12, 1966, it is a private reply from the Congregation of the Doctrine of the Faith that "the Ordinary who is competent to draw up the process in the first instance can grant to the petitioner the faculty to sue in court even though the person is a non-Catholic, and this is true also in a case of nullity."

Chapter Nine

SEPARATION OF MARRIED PERSONS

GENERAL PRINCIPALS

Canon 1128—Married persons are obliged to observe the community of conjugal life unless some just reason excuses them. The Church admits separation of spouses for reason of (1) adultery, (2) heresy or schism, (3) grave bodily or spiritual danger, (4) mutual consent.[1]

ADULTERY

Canon 1129—1. Whenever one party is guilty of adultery, the other party, the bond remaining intact, has a right to terminate the community of life even permanently, unless he consented to the crime, or was the cause of it, or condoned it expressly or tacitly, or himself committed the same crime.

2. Tacit condonation is had, if the innocent party, after learning of the adultery, of his own accord receives the other with conjugal affection: Condonation is presumed, unless the injured party within six months expels or deserts the adulterer, or brings a legal accusation against him.

To separate because of adultery the act must be (1) formal, (2) complete, (3) morally certain, and it must not be attributed in any way whatsoever (refusal of the marital debt, desertion, etc.,) on the part of the other party.

---

1. Gasparri, **De Matrimonio, II,** no. 1363.

The tacit condonation must be spontaneous, it must not arise from fear or danger of grave inconvenience. After six months, if the party does not separate or bring legal action, condonation is presumed, unless the contrary is proved.

THE RETURN OF THE GUILTY PARTY

Canon 1130—The innocent party who has separated legally, whether by judicial decree or on his own authority, is never bound to admit the adulterous partner again to conjugal life, but he may either receive or recall the party, unless the latter, with the consent of the innocent party has in the meantime embraced a state of life incompatible with the married state.

SEPARATION - RECONCILIATION

Canon 1131—1. If the other party has joined a non-Catholic sect; or educated the children as non-Catholic, or is leading an ignominious and criminal life; or is causing grave spiritual or corporal danger to the other; or makes the common life too difficult by cruelty; these and other things of the kind, are so many lawful reasons for the other party to depart, on the authority of the local ordinary, and also on his own authority if the reasons are certain and there is danger in delay.
2. In all these cases, when the cause of the separation has ceased to exist, the common life is to be restored; but if the separation was decreed by the ordinary for a definite or indefinite time, the innocent party is not bound to the common life unless by decree of the ordinary or upon expiration of the time.

It is always best to handle separation cases through the local chancery because here the experts can evaluate the cases and situations surrounding the trouble. Here the parties are interrogated privately and separately. Reconciliation is always the objective, especially if there are children involved. In too many instances these cases go on too far to salvage them. The pastor should know his people and should enter into these conflicts and try to settle them. He is considered the pastor of souls and it is his obligation. If he gets the case in its early stages the chances are that he will be contributing much not only to the family but also to society in general.

Separation can also be made on the party's own initiative, if the legal cause is certain and there is danger of delay. Here again many times the innocent party is upset and is not able to evaluate the circumstances. In all cases and whenever possible, they should take the case to a priest; all priests should make themselves available for such cases and situations. A priest who would be deliberately avoiding such cases would be guilty of a grave sin of omission; after all, he is the shepherd of his flock and has a given responsibility before God.

CHILDREN OF SEPARATED PARTIES

Canon 1132—When the parties are separated, the children are to be educated by an innocent party, or, if one of the parties is a non-Catholic, by the Catholic party, unless in either case the local ordinary has declared otherwise for the benefit of the children themselves, always keeping in mind their Catholic education.

In some of the dioceses there is no established procedure to handle separation cases. It is usually left up to the pastor, but if the pastor also is indifferent, little is done and disaster follows. It is the prerogative of every ordinary in his administration and judicial capacity to adjudicate marriage cases. Better administration would result. Because divine and ecclesiastical law is never specific on the nature and indissolubility of marriage, these laws must be kept.

JUDGES, LAWYERS AND DIVORCE

I. The Judge

Every judge before entering upon the duties of his office usually takes an oath or affirmation, swearing (or affirming as the case may be) in some such terms as these that he will support the Constitution of the United States and the Constitution of the state in which he will preside, and will faithfully discharge the duties of judge in the particular court to which he is assigned, according to "the best of his ability." *Could a judge in conscience take such an oath if he knows that he cannot grant a divorce decree in the manner in which the state understands it?* We can assuredly answer in the affirmative that he could take such an oath; this is so because every oath taken by any man is understood in such a way that there is no intention to violate the law of God.

It would be blasphemy to think otherwise. Moreover, there is no civil law which requires that the judge must share the intention of the legislator—the lawgiver. Consequently, when the judge grants a divorce he is not coerced or forced in any way *to intend* to dissolve the bond of marriage, in any way. He must stress the civil effects, however, in the decree or in the admonishment. Despite all this, the State, the public, and the divorced parties will look upon the decree as a means of breaking this bond of marriage. Nevertheless, the judge has the right to grant the divorce, if statutory evidence warrants it and there are *grave reasons* for his action and cooperation.

What would be considered a grave reason *for a judge to cooperate in such a case? Judges are public officials who are working for the common good.* In looking further, what does a judge do but hear the case presented to him in court; he weighs it on the "scale of justice"; and, in turn pronounces the verdict according to all the evidence which is presented to him. It would be wrong to ask all upright and conscientious judges to give up their offices in order to prevent them from granting a divorce decree. The judge on the bench holds a very important position. In this position he can offer his advice, counsel and possibly the ways and means for proper reconciliation. It is a known fact that many such judges have been very successful in this way. The judge is doing a service to the common good and at the same time is preventing a greater evil which is a justifying reason for permitting the judge to cooperate *materially* in granting a divorce.

It must be kept in mind, however, that a judge should never be guilty of *formal* cooperation in granting a separation or divorce decree; he must never act as if the case really pertains solely to the competency of the civil court; otherwise, he would be considered as *formally* cooperating and really usurping the power of the Church. This would be true in the case of a complete divorce, annulment, a separation maintenance, or even if he is denying such a petition. This would also be true even if the Church already declared that the marriage in question was null and void, because of some impediment of the natural or divine law. Every judge whether he be Catholic or non-Catholic should endeavor to persuade and assist the parties in becoming reconciled for the common good and the lessening of evil in the world.

II. The Lawyer

The lawyer is in a different category than the judge. A lawyer is called a private attorney because he is just that. As a private professional individual he has an option to take or refuse a case that comes to his attention; whereas, a judge is a *public official* in a public office and has no choice in the matter. He must act on the cases that are presented to him.

According to Canon 31 of the Statutes of Professional Ethics issued by the American Bar Association, we find: "No lawyer is obliged to act either as advisor or advocate for every person who may wish to become his client. He has the right to decline employment. Every lawyer upon his own responsibility must decide what business he will accept as counsel, what cases he will bring into court for plaintiffs, what cases he will contest in court for defendants. The responsibility for advising as to questionable transactions, for bringing questionable suits, for urging questionable defense, is the lawyer's responsibility. He cannot escape it by urging as an excuse that he is only following his client's instructions. The ecclesiastical norm of moral conduct is the same regarding divorce and separation. *By the very fact that the lawyer represents and speaks for his client, he may licity do only what his client may licitly do in regard to divorce and separation.* The lawyer is considered by the public as the "alter ego" of the client. Moreover, he is the necessary cooperator with the client in the case which he petitions or defends. As a result, in these divorce and separation cases, he is the cooperator, at least materially, in all the evil that would follow from the divorce, as for example, the unjust usurpation of competency in marriage cases on the part of the State, and in the violation of the divine law on the indissolubility of a valid marriage. However, just as the judge may be morally justified in cooperating materially with such evils, so also may the lawyer if he has a proportionately grave reason for such cooperation in the case. This will be determined on what the client may do licitly in regard to seeking a civil divorce or separation.

A person may licitly seek a civil divorce in the following circumstances: (1) when the Church declares a marriage null and void which is nothing more than dissolving the civil effects of an invalid contract; (2) when the Church decides that there is sufficient reason for a permanent or indefinite separation in a valid marriage and merely permits the civil divorce to protect the civil rights of the party. Two conditions must be verified by the client: (a) that there is a just cause for the separation and (b) that the party obtain the permission of the ordinary of the place to bring the matter to the civil court to obtain separate maintenance. If all of these conditions are fulfilled the lawyer may licitly represent his client. If the client is seeking the real dissolution of a valid marriage in order to remarry, the lawyer cannot represent him. Neither could he take it because another lawyer will take the case. The lawyer must be objective in dealing with his clients. Subjectivism has no place for the good lawyer. He must obey *his conscience*, not that of his client.

CHAPTER TEN

CONVALIDATION OF MARRIAGE

SIMPLE CONVALIDATION

Canon 1133—1. For the convalidation of a marriage which is invalid because of a diriment impediment, it is required that the impediment cease or be dispensed, and that consent be renewed at least by the party who is aware of the impediment.
2. This renewal of consent is required by ecclesiastical law for the invalidity of the marriage even though both parties gave their consent in the beginning and have never revoked it.

CONVALIDATION
    Ordinary (simple)
        Diriment Impediment
        Defect of Form
    Extraordinary, i.e., Sanatio in radice
        Convalidates
        has retroactive effect

Diriment Impediment: This impediment must first cease or be dispensed before convalidation takes place by renewal of consent. This renewal is required by ecclesiastical law. It is not required by the natural law. For example, a non-baptized person marries and later is divorced, but marries again. This person has a ligamen (bond) impediment and his second marriage is considered invalid while he is living with his second wife. His first wife dies but he continues to live with his second wife. Since his marriage is governed by the natural law, he need not renew consent; but if he were a Catholic, he would have to renew his consent since it is required by Canon Law. When it is impossible to get a non-Catholic party to renew the consent again and from the circumstances of the case we find that the children are being brought up Catholic, one can apply the *Sanatio* in this case, as explained later on.

A pastor should never be too hasty in getting a marriage validated and should never be too quick to tell the parties that their marriage is invalid. When it is discovered that there is no hope to validate the marriage, they should separate, but if the parties are in good faith, in extraordinary circumstances, we should let them go.

RENEWAL OF CONSENT

Canon 1134—The renewal of consent must be a new act of the will having for its object the marriage which is known to be invalid from the beginning.

MANNER

Canon 1135—1. If the impediment is public, the consent must be renewed by both parties in the form prescribed by law.

2. If the impediment is occult and known to both parties, it is sufficient that both parties renew their consent privately and secretly.

3. If it is occult and not known to one of the parties, it is sufficient that only the party who is aware of the impediment renew his consent privately and secretly, provided the other party perseveres in the consent once given.

When the impediment is occult and known to both parties, they need not go before the priest (C. 1094) but should renew their consent *explicitly*, externally, and through a mutual act. The conjugal act would not necessarily supply this; however, if they agreed to this way of giving mutual consent, this act would suffice.

If the impediment is occult and known to only one of the parties, all that is required is to make an internal act of the will; the confessor who might be handling the case, would simply ask the party to express his consent explicitly.

Canon 1136—1. A marriage which is invalid for want of consent is validated if the party who had not consented, *consents now*,

provided the consent given by the other party continues to exist.
2. If the lack of consent was merely internal, it is sufficient that
the party who had not consented, give his consent interiorly.
3. If it was external also, it is necessary to manifest it externally
also, either in the prescribed form by law, if the lack of consent
was public, or in some other way privately or secretly, if it was
occult.

Here we have three types of lack of consent cases: (1) internal,
(2) external but occult, and (3) external and public. If the person withheld his consent by a positive act of the will regarding, e.g., the conjugal right or the essential properties of marriage, the marriage would
be null. But this fact could never be proved in the external forum.
Since this fact comes up in the confessional, the confessor should have
the party elicit the consent then and there explicitly.

If the party withheld the consent by an external act, which would
be impossible to prove in the external forum, he need merely to express
his consent externally, not necessarily publicly.

If the lack of consent is both public and external, it must be renewed in the same manner, otherwise the marriage would be invalid.

Canon 1137— A marriage which is invalid for lack of form must
be contracted again in the form prescribed by law in order to be
made valid.

SANATIO IN RADICE

Canon 1138—1. The "healing in the root" of a marriage is its
convalidation involving, besides the dispensation or cessation of
an impediment, a dispensation from the obligation of renewing
the consent, and retroactivity through fiction of law, as regards
canonical effects, to the past.
2. Convalidation takes place at the moment when the favor is
granted, but retroaction is understood as going back to the beginning of the marriage, unless there are express provisions to
the contrary.
3. The dispensation from the law concerning renewing the consent can be granted even without the knowledge of one or both
parties.

A sanation implies three different items: (1) a dispensation or cessation of an impediment; (2) a dispensation from the law (C. 1094) which requires the renewal of consent; and (3) retroactivity.

NATURE OF THE SANATION

When a marriage has been contracted invalidly due to some impediment or for lack of the proper form; the consent which was given in the invalid marriage must continue or persevere. The dispensation of the sanation removes the impediment, if there is any, and the necessity of observing the form of marriage, or renewing the consent. The original consent which had no effect canonically, is now canonically made effective.

By retroactivity we mean that when the sanation is given, by fiction of law, the marriage is considered as valid from the very beginning. The dispensation *sanates* it. Children who were born illegitimate to such an invalid marriage are hereby legitimated canonically even as far as the canonical effects are concerned.

Our most common case is where there is a mixed marriage: when the non-Catholic party refuses to come to the church to have his marriage validated because he claims that he was married once; nevertheless, he does not disturb the Catholic party, he allows the practice of their religion and the Catholic education of the children. He will not go before a Catholic priest to renew his consent. Since this creates a problem, the church allows this dispensation in favor of the Catholic party in order to receive the sacraments, when the request is made to *sanate* the marriage.

TYPES OF SANATIONS

We have two kinds of sanations:

(1) *Perfect:* If there is a dispensation from renewing the consent by both parties and this makes it retroactive.
(2) *Imperfect:* If any of these items is absent, the sanation is imperfect:
    (a) *when one party only renews the consent;*
    (b) *when a sanation is given after the death of the party,* the bond of marriage is not there, but the other effects can take place by fiction of law, e.g., legitimation.

(c) *if the retroactive effect does not go all the way but only partially.*

Canon 1139—1. Any marriage which was contracted with the consent of both parties which was naturally sufficient but juridically ineffective because of a diriment impediment of ecclesiastical law or because of the defect of form, can be sanated, provided that the consent perseveres.
2. But a marriage that was contracted with an impediment of divine or natural law, even if the impediment has since ceased to exist, *cannot be sanated by the Church*, even from the time of the cessation of the impediment.

According to this Canon, whenever an impediment ceases, the consent must be given again. Gasparri claims that the sanation could be given up to the time that the impediment ceased. But the Church does not do so. The Code does not say that it cannot. We have evidence of such cases being granted by the Holy See.[1]

CONDITIONS FOR SANATION

Canon 1140—1. If the consent is lacking on the part of both parties or in either party, the marriage cannot be sanated "in the root," regardless whether the consent was lacking in the beginning or was originally given and later revoked.

If consent was lacking in the beginning, but was afterwards given, a sanation can be given from the moment when the consent was given.

Canon 1141—A sanation in root can be granted only by the Apostolic See.

When the Code of Canon Law is revised at some future date, this Canon will be revised, because this faculty has been granted on a permanent basis to all bishops throughout the world. They need no longer go to Rome for these faculties.

With the Motu Proprio, *Pastorale Munus*, of Pope Paul VI, Nov. 30, 1963, "*all bishops, both resident and titular, have the special privilege to grant this sanation, provided that the consent perseveres, in marriages*

---

1. Gasparri, **De Matrimonio**, **II**, nos. 1215-19; Cappello, **De Matrimonio**, no. 854.

*that are invalid because of minor impediments, or defect of form, even
if there is a question of mixed marriage, but in this last case, Canon 1061
of the Code must be observed." no. 21. no. 22: They can also grant
"the sanation in radice provided that the consent persevered in a marriage that is invalid because of the impediment of disparity of cult, even
if they are invalid because of the lack of form, as long as Canon 1061
of the Code is observed."* (Canon 1061 deals with the necessary promises).

SECOND MARRIAGES

Canon 1142—Although a chaste widowhood is more honorable,
nevertheless, second and further marriages are valid and licit,
without prejudice to the provision of Canon 1069, p. 2.
Canon 1143—A woman who has received the nuptial blessing
once cannot receive it again in a subsequent marriage.

BROTHER AND SISTER ARRANGEMENT

(The Last Resort)

We find very little written about the Brother and Sister arrangement among the authors. Yet such arrangements have been made for
almost two thousand years since the time of Christianity. Of course,
it is only within recent years that this method has been adopted on
a wider and bigger scale whereby the external forum has a better
control of this age-old arrangement. Although we still have some of
the clergy who frown upon this arrangement, nevertheless, it is a universal solution to many unfortunate cases. It requires very little reasoning to understand that such an arrangement is possible and feasible.
To illustrate a case, a woman who lived in an invalid marriage for
years and after ceasing marital relations for some ten years, asked a
priest why she could not receive the sacraments. She explained that she
was married by a justice of the peace; there were no children of the
marriage and she lived in a large city where no one knew of her status.
She further stated that for the past ten years she was living as any
housekeeper does. She wondered why she could not go to the sacraments under these conditions after reasoning the matter out. She asked
for the priest's advice. Her case was none other than those we handle
now as a Brother and Sister case. It did not require much reasoning for

this simple woman to draw the practical conclusions

More and more cases of this kind are coming to our attention. We must be prepared to meet them. With the necessary and proper precautions we can be of immense assistance to many souls who are in an invalid marriage but, for some reason or other, cannot separate. *For the best method, in handling such cases, is through the diocesan chancery or tribunal.* Here the experts could scrutinize the case with care and greater success than would the parish priest who might not be fully aware of the dangers which lurk in handling such a case. Scandal is the great factor that must be considered here.

Some dioceses are not too anxious to handle these cases through diocesan channels in which case, the parish priest is at a loss on what to do. In 1950 when this kind of case was being discussed and brought out into the open, we found that some bishops frowned upon this arrangement. Today we have thousands who have found their salvation through this particular channel. A few years ago a book was published by a Catholic woman with an *imprimatur* explaining the "brother and sister" case which she discovered after searching for a solution of her own marital problem for many years.[2] With this information which was made public, there is no way in which this system can be suppressed. It is no longer the secret it once was; therefore, those priests who cannot handle this case through their diocesan chancery or tribunal, and are forced to take care of the matter themselves could use the following formula:

BROTHER AND SISTER ARRANGEMENT

After Careful Investigation of the Case One Must be Sure That:

1. Validation of the marriage is impossible.
2. Separation of the parties is extremely difficult (children and property).
3. Scandal will not result from this arrangement.
4. Danger of incontinence is removed (advanced age, illness or serious operation).

---

2. McAuley, Clair, **Whom God Hath Not Joined**, Sheed & Ward.

QUESTIONNAIRE FOR THE MAN

1. Name ....
2. Address ....
3. Date of Birth .... Place of Birth ....
4. Religion ....
   If (Catholic), when did you go to the Sacraments the last time?
   ....
   If (non-Catholic) what church do you attend? ....
   Where? ....
   Do you wish to become a Catholic? ....
5. Did you ever ask for such permission before? ....
   When? .... Were you ever refused? ....
   Explain? ....
6. Where were you married? ....
   When? .... Before whom? ....
7. Did many people know at that time your marriage was invalid?
   .... How many? ....
8. How many children were born of this marriage? ....
9. How long have you lived in this town? ....
10. How many neighbors and friends know your marriage is invalid?
    List them on a separate sheet. ....
11. How many relatives and friends know your marriage is invalid?
    List them. ....
12. How many know that your marriage cannot be validated? ......
    List them. ....
13. Is it at all possible for you to separate? ....
    If not, why? ....
14. What type of illness do you have? ....
15. How many times were you married before? ....
16. What is the date and place of your wife's death? ....
17. Her name (if living) .... Religion? ....
    Catholic? .... Non-Catholic? ....
18. When were you married? .... Where? ....
    By whom? ....
19. How many children were born of this marriage? ....
    List them ....
20. Why did you separate? ....
21. Where did you get your divorce? ....
    When? .... Where? .... By whom? ....
22. Give the name and address of your former wife. ....
23. Did she remarry? ..... When? ... Where? ....
24. If you had more than one wife, list them ....
25. Are you sure that you can keep your promise to live as brother and
    sister? .... Why are you so certain? ....
26. Have you ever tried to live in such a manner? ....
    How long have you tried this? ....
27. Would you be able to support your wife if she would separate
    from you? ....
28. Would there be scandal, if she separated (if people considered you
    married)? ....
29. If the answer is no, check on the financial standing. ....
30. Where will you go for confession and communion? ....
    (Here the priest would advise the party where to go without
    causing any scandal)
31. Do you realize that you will have to forfeit your right to Christian
    burial? ....

QUESTIONNAIRE FOR THE WOMAN

This questionnaire could be the same as that for the man except to change the wording where this will be necessary.

PROMISES

(Have both read the following together)

I. We, the undersigned, knowing full well that our marriage is invalid in the sight of God, and realizing that it is sinful to live in the manner of husband and wife, and realizing that it would be difficult for us to separate, We hereby beg for permission to live together as brother and sister and to be readmitted to the sacraments of the Church. (Leave out last part for Non-Catholic.)

OATH

(This will be made by each party separately in the others presence.)

II. I .... realizing full well the sacredness of an oath, and my obligation before God, touching the Holy Gospels, I solemnly swear;

1. That I will not attempt to live as husband and wife with my present consort.
2. That I will separate, and refer the matter to the (bishop) or priest before I receive the sacraments again.
3. That I will receive the sacraments only in the churches where my marital status is unknown to the parishioners.
4. To explain my status to my regular confessor and will report to him regularly.
5. That I will take every precautionary measure to avoid scandal in using this privilege, so help me God and these Holy Gospels which I touch.

Signatures   .... (Man)
                         .... (Woman)
                         .... (Priest)

Date: ....
Seal:

INTERNAL FORUM CASES

*Intolerable Marriage Situations: Conflict between the
External and the Internal Forum*

The Code of Canon Law has numerous laws that govern and protect the institution of Christian marriage. The procedure of handling informal and formal marriage cases are all found in the laws on marriage in Canons 1012-1143, 1552-2194, the Instruction *Provida Mater Ecclesia* (1936) and the *23 Provisional Norms on Procedure* (1970). The purpose of this legislation is to protect and promote the values of Christian marriage. As members of the Catholic Church, these laws must be upheld if we are to be faithful to Christ and his Church, at least in our present understanding of what Christian marriage is.

Since the codification of Canon Law in 1918, drastic changes have taken place throughout the world especially in the last five or ten years. These changes occurred in the development of jurisprudence regarding the grounds of annulment of marriage, such as psychic-incapacity, alcoholism, sociopathy, homosexuality, etc. Annulments on such grounds are granted today; ten years ago this was an impossibility.

No law is ever perfect because the human law maker of church laws is subject to imperfections. We must admit that we live in an imperfect and a changeable world. Even St. Thomas admitted this when he stated: *"because the human acts with which law deals are surrounded with particular circumstances which are infinitely variable, it is impossible to establish any law that suffers no exception; law makers observe what generally happens, and legislate accordingly; in some instances, to observe the law would violate the equality of justice and hurt the very welfare which law is meant to serve."* This is also the reason why we have such things as *epikeia*, rescripts and dispensations of all sorts. We must look to new insights from theological and scriptural sources and from the secular sciences, such as sociology, psychology, anthropology, etc., which are so intimately connected with human beings.

Everyone is aware of the changes that have come about and are continuing since Vatican Council II. The recent legislative norms to come from the Holy See (1970) are the *Twenty-Three Norms of Procedural Law*. Since they are only provisional is an indication that the law-giver is acting with caution and therefore are given by way of experimentation, which is a great step forward in the field of justice. So too, the long awaited answers to our present day intolerable marriage situations are being given to a hungry and large segment of our Catholic population through the "Good Faith Solution."

Before venturing into this category, for the sake of the would-be critic who will claim that the private good must suffer to preserve the common good, we reply that a balance must be maintained between the common good of the society and the justice and rights due to any individual within that society. Even Christ, who had a great respect for Jewish law and order, as well as the common good, made many exceptions to that law when human beings were suffering. For example, he healed the sick on the Sabbath, which was directly opposite to the Jewish law, and caused great scandal among the people. In reference to the common good, did he not suggest that we leave the ninety-nine and go in search of the one that was lost? Or, the woman who was caught in adultery was to be stoned to death according to the law, but Christ stepped in on the scene and opposed the law; and, instead of reprimanding the adulteress Samaritan woman, he talked to, and accepted a drink from her; this certainly was against the Jewish law.

Pope John XXIII also spoke clearly on this issue and about the definition of the common good in which we see the ultimate concern must be the welfare of the person, namely: "the sum total of those conditions of social living whereby men are able to achieve *their own* integral perfection more fully and more easily."

Marriage as we know it, is indissoluble. This we uphold; but there must be a marriage first in order to speak of indissolubility. We cannot take apart something that has not been molded together. We have seen many marriages that have failed because they were not true marriages to begin with. According to our marriage laws, marriage is a public act, not a private act. Marriage enjoys the favor of the law by legal presumption, and therefore considered valid until someone can prove it to be invalid.

If an ecclesiastical annulment could be obtained more reasonably than the present code of law permits, the problem would be lessened. The following illustration will show the conflict which can arise between a just law and the private good of an individual conscience:

Mary Jones was abandoned by her husband shortly after their marriage. He left telling her that he only married her to give the baby a name and that he never intended to remain with her permanently. In this case, Mary would have good grounds for an ecclesiastical annulment, but she must prove these facts in an ecclesiastical court. According to the law, she would have to bring two or more witnesses to establish conclusively that her husband lied to the priest before the marriage when he was asked: "Do you intend a permanent union?" The difficult burden of proving that he lied at the time of the marriage falls on her. Mary was deceived by her husband, but she is not able to produce the necessary evidence to convince the Church officials of the invalidity of her marriage. She can find no witnesses; she can offer no legal proof. Tribunal officials are satisfied that they have done all they can under the circumstances. Mary finds herself stranded to the frightening alternatives of living alone for the rest of her life (according to the law), or of marrying again outside the Church. She wants neither. She is doomed.

Later on, however, Mary falls in love and is married outside the Church; she is denied the sacraments because she is considered a sinful woman. Is she really a sinful woman? Is this second marriage really an invalid marriage? This is the question.

Ayrinhac-Lydon give their version of this dilemma in the following example, which fits our case: "The conflict would be more serious of the man who simulated consent had afterwards, being really free, contracted a valid marriage with another woman. In the external forum the first woman would be considered his legitimate wife; he would be bound to live with her and forbidden to have relations with the second one. In conscience, before God, the second woman would be his real wife, and there would be no possibility of revalidating the first marriage."[3]

The dilemma is self-evident. Our attempt is to maintain a healthy attitude towards the laws governing marriage and to look into the possibilities that would allow for a just and reasonable way of handling these situations where we find the legal system of the Church inadequate, unprepared or incapable of handling it. We must look elsewhere for the solution. In the past years, the Canon Law Society of America and Canada, theologians and canonists have looked elsewhere in their search for an answer. We have also learned that for many years this solution was obtained through the internal forum from the Sacred Penitentiary and for this reason is called the "Internal Forum Solution." However only a few priests knew about it or did anything about this problem. Today it is referred to as the Canonico-Moral solution, or pastoral solution, and is being used in many dioceses throughout the United States. It has been used, e.g., by the Chicago Tribunal for 20 years under three

---

3. Ayrinac-Lydon, **Marriage Legislation**, 1959, New York.

different Cardinal Archbishops.[4]

Our problems concern primarily the conflicting situation between *truth internally known* and truth *externally unknown;* secondly, it concerns the difficulty that arises from apparently genuine irregularity on the one hand, and a desire to be in line with the community, on the other. In other words, the problem concerns primarily the conflicting situations that arise when a marriage is invalid before God but it cannot be proved to be so before a human tribunal. Secondly, it concerns the situations when a marriage was a sacrament before God and the community, and the person now desires to receive the sacraments while remaining faithful to his second marital union. This is really the case of those who are divorced and remarried and are now anxious to return to full communion with the Church but cannot do so either because their first marriage was invalid, but invalidity cannot be proved, or because the first marriage, valid as it was, ended in divorce and there is now another marital union.

The aforementioned dilemma has puzzled Canonists over the years. The "Internal Forum Solution" recommended by the Holy See is the only possible manner to settle this conflict. In years past, solutions were offered by the Sacred Penitentiary; (such cases have appeared in the Canon Law Digest). The bibliography below is offered for those interested in this matter. Because of the controversy that existed in the U.S.A., the Holy See intervened and sent a reply in 1975 regarding the "internal forum" cases. This letter follows:

Letter of S. C. Doctrine of the Faith
March 21, 1975: Prot. N. 1284/66

Dear Archbishop Bernadin,

As you reminded us in your recent letter of December 31, 1974 and also during your recent visit of March 11, Cardinal Krol, when he was President of the National Conference of Catholic Bishops, wrote to this Sacred Congregation requesting an official interpretation of the phrase used in the circular letter of April 11, 1973, "probata praxis Ecclesiae." This phrase referred to Catholics living in irregular marital unions.

I would like to state now that this phrase must be understood in the context of traditional moral theology. These couples may be allowed

---

4. **The Jurist**, Vol. XXIX, October 4, 1969, p. 428.

to receive the sacraments on two conditions, that they try to live according to the demands of Christian moral principals and that they receive the sacraments in churches in which they are not known so that they will not create any scandal.

Sincerely yours,

(signed) Archbishop Hamer

BIBLIOGRAPHY OF BOOKS AND ARTICLES ON INTERNAL FORUM

Basset, William, **The Bond of Marriage**, University of Notre Dame Press, 1968.

Bresnahan, James F., "Problems of Marriage and Divorce," **America**, May 25, 1968, pp. 706-709.

Carey, Raymond G., "The Good Faith Solution," **The Jurist**, Vol. XXIX, Oct. 1969.

Catoir, John T., "Church and Second Marriages," **Commonweal**, April 14, 1967, p. 113. "What is the Marriage Contract?" **America**, Vol. 118, no. 7, p. 229.

Constitution on the Church in the Modern World, nos. 12, 17.

Council Daybook, Vatican II Session 4, pp. 71-72, An Address by Archbishop Elie Zoghbi.

Doherty, Denis, "Problem of Divorce and Remarriage," **Marriage** 28, 1966, pp. 12-18.

Häring, Bernard, **The Law of Christ**, Newman Press, 1966. Vol. III, p. 327.

Hertel, James R., O.D.M., **When Marriage Fails**, Paulist Press, Paramus, N.J.

Hertel, James, "Save the Bond or Save the Person," **America**, Vol. 118, no. 7, Feb. 17, 1968, pp. 217-220.

Hurley, M., S.J., "Christ and Divorce," **Irish Theol. Quarterly** 35, 1968, pp. 56-72.

"Indissolubility of Marriage, The," **The Theological Tradition of the East**, pp. 97-116.

Kelleher, S.J., "The Problem of the Intolerable Marriage," **America**, September 14, 1968, pp. 178-182.

Krebs, A. V., "American Catholic Marriage and the Church," **America**, Feb. 1969, p. 228.

Mahoney, John, "Do They Intend Marriage," HPR, 67, 1966.

Monden, Louis, S.J., **Sin, Liberty and Law**, Sheed & Ward, New York, 1965, pp. 135-136.

Montserrat, J. Torrents, **The Abandoned Spouse**, Bruce, 1969.

Pope John XXIII, Pacem in Terris, no. 58.

Pospishil, Victor J., **Divorce and Remarriage**, Herder and Herder, New York, 1967, pp. 40-73. / "The Damned Millions: The Problem of Divorced Catholics," HPR, 1968, pp. 95-104.

"Sacraments: An Ecumenical Dilemma, The," **Concilium** 24, Paulist Press, New York., 1967, pp. 113-138.

Shaner, Donal, **A Christian View on Divorce**, E. J. Brill 1969, Leiden, pp. 14-25.

Sullivan, Jos. Deuel, "Divorce and Psychological Change," **Catholic Theological Society of America Proceedings**, Vol. 22, 1967, pp. 245-252.

The Jurist, January 1970 contains these excellent articles:
(1) "Intolerable Marriage Situations: The Conflict between the External and Internal Forum," by Ladislas Orsy, S.J.
(2) "Law, Conscience and Marriage," by Peter Huizing.
(3) "Internal Forum Solutions to Insoluble Marriage Cases," by Bernard Häring.
(4) "The Pastoral Care of Those Involved in Canonically Invalid Marriages," by Anthony Kosnik.
(5) "Toward 'An Immediate Forum Solution' For Deserving Couples in Canonically Insoluble Marriage Cases," by Leo C. Farley and Warren T. Reich, S.J.

"The Tragedy of Broken Marriages," **Jubilee**, March 1966, p. 48.

Cf. **Chicago Studies**, Vol. 15, no. 3, 1976, pp. 300-303.

INDICES

Marriage Cases

Case #1

CANON 1013 (M.J.)
CONTRA BONUM PROLIS

No. 1/Michelle vs. Kevin

Michelle, a baptized Protestant, aged 18, contracted marriage with Kevin, a baptized Catholic, aged 29, in a northeastern diocese, in the presence of a Catholic priest. The marriage took place in 1948.

The parties knew each other for a period of eight months and dated approximately once a week during this time. Kevin was described as an only child who had a good home background, and who was very close to his mother. Michelle, on the other hand, did not enjoy a close relationship with her family, particularly with her father whom she considered to be over-restrictive and harsh. Escape from this situation was not a major motive, however, in her decision to marry.

The marriage was reasonably successful and satisfying to the parties for over 10 years. It was only after this time that serious problems began to coalesce, although there were problems from the beginning. One of these was Kevin's insistence that they not have any children. After they had been married a couple of years and following Michelle's insistence, Kevin relented and agreed that they could have one child. Apart from this, artificial methods of birth control were used up to the time when marital relations ceased altogether, which was approximately eight years before the final separation.

Kevin was something of a loner, and consequently, they had little social life. He had little interest in bettering their position financially. It was alleged that this was due to psychological reasons. A Medical Expert examined both parties and concluded that Kevin had a personality which could be classified generally as a schizoid type. The Expert did not think that this affected his ability to consent to marriage or his actual performance in the marriage.

During the course of the marriage, Michelle became a member of the Catholic Church. This took place around the time of the birth of their child. The picture of their relationship from that time on indicates a steady deterioration, although the parties themselves did not really become aware of the magnitude of their problem until some six years later.

Finally, after a total of approximately 20 years, they separated. Michelle filed for a civil divorce and, at the same time, filed a petition to the Church Court for annulment on the grounds that Kevin entered the marriage with an intention contra bonum prolis.

The methods of proof and evaluation of evidence used in this case are not out of the ordinary. What is of interest is the way the Judges developed the law on partial simulation relative to an intention limiting the number of children which would be permitted in the marriage.

In defining the law relative to an intention contra bonum prolis, the Court begins with Canon 1081: 1, stating that "it is essential that the object of this consent be clearly defined, and should this object be totally withheld or substantially restricted, then the contract cannot be considered valid and binding for life."

That object is substantially restricted not only by a permanent exclusion of children but also by a temporary exclusion and, thus, either one will invalidate a marriage. The Court's decision points to recent Rotal decisions supporting this view, quoting from a decision of Pinna, May 30, 1956, where he states that "temporary exclusion can certainly pertain to the essence . . . (S.R.R. Decisions, XLVIII, 494)." The temporary nature of such an exclusion is seen in the limitation of children by reason of either time, e.g., no children for the first two years of the marriage, or by number, e.g., will have only two children. The Court's decision points out: "Thus, if there is an exclusion of children, it could either be permanent or temporary in its duration. Either of these exclusions would violate the right to children which the marriage contract must give to both parties."

There is a distinction between the granting of the necessary right and an intent to abuse that right. This decision declares that distinction to be outmoded, basing this on the lack of such a distinction in "the parlance of the layman, especially if he be little acquainted with Catholic doctrine," and on more recent Rotal decisions. At the same time, the decision does go on to show that the distinction between the right itself and an intention to abuse that right is real. It points to a practical application of the distinction:

> If there should remain a doubt whether the right to children or acts productive of children was excluded, or whether an abuse was intended, this doubt can be resolved by examining the circumstances and means by which the contraception is planned on being attained. Should both parties by mutual consent agree that they have a right to children in their future marriage, but will abstain from exercising this right by some means of contraception, then there is a recognition by them that they have a right to children but are not willing to use it. If, on the other hand, one party plans on excluding children and at the same time pretends to his proposed partner that he is willing to have children, then such a deception already belies the fact that the right of the other party is going to be withheld. If, furthermore, during the course of the marriage, the party who has practiced such a deception continues to insist on the practice of contraception contrary to the other party's desires and expressed will, and is able to overpower, as it were, the other party by moral force to have relations only with contraceptives, then the exclusion of the right is further evident. It is impossible to reconcile the granting of a perpetual and exclusive right to the other party with such deception and moral force which overpowers the other party's continued protestations.

In this particular case, Kevin agreed to have one child and went into the marriage with the intention of so limiting his family. The decision declares:

> The very fact that the Petitioner definitely knew at the time when she was carrying her first and only child that this would be the only child, and that all plans on his part were made in such a way that there would be no other children because of what he so consistently indicated to her, shows without doubt that the intention that the Respondent had prior to the marriage was to exclude children to the point of permitting only one child and no more.

The Court found sufficient evidence to establish that this, indeed, was his definite intention at the time of the marriage. It then proceeded to raise the question: "Does such an intention of wanting to have one child and only one child in marriage and excluding all others make the marriage invalid"? The answer given is:

> Definitely an invalidity of marriage exists when an individual enters into marriage with such an intention. The marriage contract calls for the perpetual and exclusive exchange of rights over the body for those acts by which procreation can take place. The intention for contraceptive relations and the determination for refusal to have proper relations when contrary to the expressed wishes and plans of the other partner certainly is a violation of this right even if such is practiced only partially or temporarily. When two people agree to abstain or to use contraceptives, their very agreement denotes the recognition of each other's rights and the acceptance of the other person's procedures of abusing the act of marriage. If there is no such agreement and if on the contrary there is deception practiced by one party who intends not to have children or not to have more than one child while the other party wants to have other children, then there is a definite violation of the right which marriage should hand over.

Based on this understanding of the law, the Court found that Kevin's intention to have, at most, one child was a limitation of Michelle's right to normal marital relations. It was, therefore, an invalidating intention.

DECISION: FIRST INSTANCE—affirmative
              SECOND INSTANCE—affirmative

CANON 1013 (T.R.)
INTENTION AGAINST CHILDREN

No. 11/Frank vs. Louise

The Facts:

The petitioner, Frank, a Catholic, entered into marriage in a Catholic Church on January 1, 1961, with a certain Louise, a Lutheran, hereinafter referred to as the defendant. The petitioner had not been raised a Catholic. He contracted a civil marriage in 1941 with Helen J. This union was invalid by reason of defect of form. He met the defendant in the fall of 1960. At this time he was forty-four years old and she was approximately thirty-eight years old. The defendant wanted the marriage in her own Church but did not object to marriage in the Catholic Church. Before the marriage the defendant stated she did not want children. The petitioner thought he could change her mind. She even wrote a letter before the marriage, in which she stated she did not want children and gave her reasons, mainly her age. She agreed to avoid children through the use of rhythm rather than through artificial birth control, so that the petitioner would not violate the laws of his Church. A few months after the marriage a great number of arguments arose. The question of children came up. She was adamant—she would have nothing to do with them. She refused to have marital relations except during the safe period. The union lasted until March of 1963, when she left. For a great number of reasons she has filed for a divorce. She says there are no witnesses who knew of her intention before the marriage. She did discuss this with her family, but refuses to allow them to be contacted. On the 23rd of August, 1964, the Tribunal of the Archdiocese accepted a petition from Frank that this marriage be declared null and void, because the defendant positively excluded and permanently excluded the possible marital rights from her marriage contract.

The Law:

The primary end of marriage is the education and procreation of children: its essential qualities are unity and indissolubility (canon 1013). Without these elements even the very concepts of marriage cannot be brought forth, or, in other words, these elements belong to the very substance of marriage, by reason of the contract insofar as it expresses the general will of contracting marriage (Canon 1082:1). Every person marrying assumes at least implicitly the substantial obligations of marriage. When such a general desire or will of contracting marriage is absorbed by a contrary and overcoming act of the will, then matrimonial consent is lacking. Now this takes place according to the norm of law when a contracting party either by a positive act (Canon 1086, 2), or by a condition (Canon 1092, 2), rejects the marriage itself or the marriage in its substance. Such a positive act as described in (Canon 1086:2) can be defined as that act by which a contracting party, on account of an overpowering will, excludes the very marriage itself or all right to marriage relationship of some essential property of the marriage. Such a positive act differs from a condition (*S.R.R.* Dec., Vol. XV p. 275, no. 2), and by all the authors is called a mental condition or something retained in the mind. For a condition against marriage, or against something belonging to the substance of marriage is nothing more than a positive act manifested externally in some conditional form; e.g., I'm not contracting marriage except that I exclude children. In the positive act described above, the consent depends upon a contrary intention of the contracting party which is developed on account of an imposing will of excluding marriage or its substance. However, in a condition, the contracting party makes his consent depend upon that intention, not only on account of the imposing will, but because it is also manifested externally. He places it not only in his mind but in a very express way exteriorly as a circumstance governing his consent. If this should occur, then that positive act is in all regards a *conditio* (Staffa, *De conditione contra matrimonii substantiam*, ed. 2a, p. 32). With the exclusion of the substance of martimony, the contrary intention on the part of the person contracting must enter into this matrimonial consent in order to limit it and to vitiate it, because marriage arises from the consent of the parties, who are determined persons, with definite obligations (Canon 1081). Such an intention does not enter the consent of the parties unless it is placed as a condition at least retained in the mind as is described above. Once it is placed as a condition, it necessarily limits and vitiates the consent, so that the marriage must be held to be invalid and may not be presumed as valid. For once the consent has been limited, the given right and the assumed obligation are also limited because this is the source of them.

It is of the very essence of marriage, of course, that it be indissoluble and you never find marriage without indissolubility, and this is called the good of the sacrament. It follows that an intention against the good of the sacrament, just as an intention against the marriage itself, from its very nature, is always a condition at least retained in the mind. Whoever simulates this consent wishes with a prevailing will not to contract marriage. Whoever has the intention of contracting a dissoluble marriage excludes true marriage by his prevailing will. The situation is somewhat different when there is a question of children or fidelity. In this case there must be a distinction between the right and the exercise of the right, the obligation and the fulfillment of the obligation. An intention against children or against fidelity by its very nature does not take on the design of a condition at least retained in the mind. The person can assume all of the obligations of marriage and at the same time have the intention of violating this obligation by avoiding children or by not observing fidelity. In this case the marriage would be valid.

The marriage is invalid when the right to conjugal acts are excluded. This takes place only when the contrary will on the part of the contracting person prevails against the general will of contracting marriage. When the intention of avoiding children takes on the nature of a positive act or condition in the mind of the person doing the contracting, in such a case, and only in such a case, will the intention against children enter the consent, limit it, and vitiate it. Whoever contracts with the intention or the condition of avoiding children, very rarely would say, "I exclude the right to true conjugal acts," because in most cases, maybe not always, he does not know the distinction between the right and the exercise of the right, between the obligation and its fulfillment, or at least he does not even advert to it. Hence, the exclusion of the right itself to children directly and immediately can hardly ever be proved. Such an exclusion can only be proved indirectly from the prevailing will in the contracting party of avoiding children. The more cogent and emphatic the will or desire of avoiding children is, then the less important is the will of contracting a true marriage. And contrariwise, the more emphatic is the will or desire to contract a true marriage, the less emphasis can be given or placed upon the intention of avoiding children, so that such an intention must be considered as really accompanying the matrimonial consent, not really limiting it and vitiating it.

The existence of the prevailing will or desire on the part of the contracting parties is proved directly from the confession of the party who contracted with a contrary intention, and from the depositions of the other party, from witnesses, and from documents. It can be proved indirectly from a proportionate cause, from the circumstances preceding, accompanying, and following the marriage. Direct and indirect proofs supplement one another. The best key is the proportionate reason or cause which exists in the opinion or mind of the contracting party. This furnishes the principal proof, for example, if a contracting party cannot escape some particular circumstance, and then he enters the marriage with the intention of avoiding children, and after the marriage observes this design with a great tenacity, the conclusion is in order that the will of contracting a true marriage was absorbed by the will of avoiding children (*Monitor Ecclesiasticus*—Fasc III, 1961, pp. 387-390).

The Argument:

Petitioner, Frank, baptized a Catholic but raised a Protestant, came to the practice of his faith during the service. He met the defendant in July of 1960. He then was a practicing Catholic. She was a Presbyterian. Before the official engagement, she said she did not want children. He did not take her seriously. She discussed this even with her family. She said she was well aware of the method of rhythm and would practice it, so that he would not be violating his religion. He thought he could change her mind after about a year, when he made her secure in their home and when she would not be too concerned with her jobb. She wrote him a note prior to the marriage, in which she definitely expressed her mind regarding children. The next time he saw her he mentioned the note. After this discussion she softened her attitude completely. She did not say that she would have children; in fact, she still insisted on birth control by way of rhythm. Probably the reason for her attitude was that she was established in her work and looked forward to her career. This would continue until retirement age. She was getting along in age and did not want a family. The petitioner knew from general knowledge that she discussed this with her father. She placed a great deal of importance on her job. She had allegiance to the people for many years. She was close to her family. The marriage was consummated, the night of the marriage in all probability. She would not permit relations at any time other than the so-called safe period based on the rhythm method. She knew the rhythm method well, because she worked with two physicians and a gynecologist. She did not object to relations during her sterile period; however she would never permit relations during a fertile or non-sterile period. There was no exception, and she refused even to discuss the matter. She expected to avoid children through the use of rhythm; also, she refused to adopt a child. The note and the discussion after it were a stipulation, but the petitioner thought she might change her mind. She never retracted the statement in the letter, but seemed more lenient in her views. She left in approximately May of 1963. By that time she was refusing him completely at all times. She obtained a divorce on the grounds of desertion in September of 1964. The description of the defendant, as given by the petitioner, is fairly clear insofar as her complete and definite refusal to have children. It would seem that her reasons are based on her age and desire to pursue her career.

She refused further testimony. For this reason it was necessary to incorporate her preliminary testimony. She did agree before the notary of the tribunal that she had positive intentions of never having any children with the petitioner or with anyone else. She identified the letter as being written in her hand, although it is not dated or posted. In the letter she clearly evidences that she shall plan to prevent children. Since she mentions it at this time of life, it is certainly indicative that this would be a permanent plan. She indicates that she wants no future with him, if the condition is that there be children. She has been consistent in this, because she again just before the plea for nullity told Father McNeil that she never wanted any children. She also told various doctors, such as Dr. Martin, from State University, a marriage counselor.

Father McNeil, a Catholic priest, has the impression that this woman was telling the truth, that she definitely did not want children because she thought they were too old, and she had her own career. The petitioner had told Father McNeil of her attitude before marriage, and she discussed it at length with him. The petitioner thought he would be able to change her mind after marriage. The priest was persuaded that the petitioner, perhaps within a few years, would be able to change her mind, because the petitioner is persevering and persistent. She said she put the condition of not having children in writing, and this was done also vocally. There was no agreement on his part though hw was aware of it. He thought it might have been mentioned before her sister also, but she denies that anyone else knew. This resolve on her part was definite and permanent. She placed considerable importance on the fact that she was going to continue her career after marriage. Children were to be avoided by rhythm or contraception. Their married life was one of tolerance, and the petitioner was reserved and reticent, closed-in. Mrs. Hanson was highly controlled, a highly emotionally controlled type of personality. It was not an open communication. The comments of Father McNeil and his particular capabilities as a psychologist enable him to give strength to the fact of the exclusion of the right to have children on the part of the defendant.

Father Clark, a priest of the archdiocese, made preparations for the marriage to be held at St. Athanasius. He thinks of the petitioner as kind of devious. He thinks of the defendant as being truthful. He did not know these people very well. He says the defendant talked about the Church's teaching on children, and she was agreeable to following such. He recalls nothing negative about her regarding children and birth control. She espressed no objections to having children. After the marriage, the petitioner said that the marriage broke up because she did not want children. The testimony of Father Clark can add nothing to the alleged grounds of the case, because nothing of the intent of the defendant was made known to him.

The defendant had claimed consistently that there were no witnesses to her intention of excluding children. Later she changed this and said that her father was a witness to this intention. She re-emphasized her stand and asked that no more people be contacted. The father of the defendant refused to give any formal testimony. However, he did issue an affidavit certifying that, for a considerable time prior to participating in the marriage ceremony, the defendant, Louise Hanson, had stated to him categorically that she was about to enter the marriage relationship, but that she would not have any children and would do all things necessary to avoid any pregnancy for the reason that she was emotionally and physically incapable of having or raising children.

The defendant's attempt to keep her father out of the case is regrettable, but does not substantially weaken, in our judgment, the credibility of the respondent. Nor does it, contrary to the opinion of the defender of the bond, really call into question the reliability of the sworn statement of the respondent and her father.

Simulation of marital consent takes place when one or both of the parties deny one of the substantial and essential elements of the contract. Certainly the primary end of marriage is the education and procreation of children. The essential qualities are unity and indissolubility. This is clearly indicated in Canon 1013. Without such elements even the concept of marriage is impossible. These elements belong to its very substance and by that same token the contract must, of necessity, express the general will of the party who is contracting marriage. Any person marrying assumes at least implicitly the substantial obligations of the marriage contract. When the general desire or will of contracting marriage is absorbed by a contrary or overcoming act of the will, then the matrimonial consent is lacking. If either party, by a positive act of the will or by condition, rejects the marriage itself or the marriage in its substance, then this contract is not valid. This is an act by which a contracting party, because of an overpowering will, excluded the very marriage itself or all right to marriage relationship of some essential property of it. This positive act differs from a condition. It is something retained within the very soul and mind of the party and militates against the actuality of the contract. Theoretically, it can be argued that the respondent placed a definite condition to her consent, a condition which would limit and vitiate the consent itself. However, it appears to us that the respondent in the case did not put her marriage on a conditional basis. She wanted and did intend to contract marriage, but at the same time she had a very positive intention ot exclude children. Hers was a distorted concept of what marriage really is, but the kind of marriage she was contracting was more described and influenced by the exclusion of the right to have children than by the giving of herself in the contract. It was a facet governing her consent. Actually she excluded part of the very substance of what a marriage must be, and in this her consent was vitiated.

From all of the circumstances that led up to this marriage, from the confession of the respondent herself, from the evidence of the petitioner, from the witnesses after the marriage including the priest, Father McNeil, we must conclude that the prevailing will of this defendant in contracting marriage was that children always and forever be excluded. This will was more cogent and emphatic than the will to marriage. The letter written in the respondent's own handwriting, the circumstances of her age and her career, her knowledge of children from her work, all these confirm the fact that the respondent knew precisely what she wanted, and what she wanted was to exlude children permanently. Therefore, despite the fact that more ample testimony would be desirable, the testimony obtained, coupled with the circumstances and documentary proof, is sufficient for us to conclude that the Hanson-Southerly marriage is null and void because of the exclusion of the right to have children on the part of the respondent.

Having considered all of these things and having maturely studied all the adjuncts in law and in fact, we the undersigned judges of the Chicago Tribunal, keeping God alone before our eyes, after invoking the name of Christ, decide, declare and definitively pronounce this sentence:

The nullity of this marriage has been proved because of the intention of the respondent against the good of offspring.

And so we proclaim, commanding the execution of this our sentence to those local ordinaries and ministers to whom it belongs according to the norm of the sacred canons.

CANON 1013 (M.J.)
INTENTION AGAINST PERMANENCE

No. 21/Louise vs. Rene

The Facts

Louise, a Catholic, made the acquaintance of Rene, a baptized non-catholic, in June, 1959. They began to keep company and despite a courtship which left much to be desired, they considered themselves engaged on New Year's Day, 1960 although there was no formal canonical engagement. Certain aspects of ene's personality prompted Louise not to contract marriage with him but she felt that she had no alternative because of sexual intimacies which had taken place between them.

The marriage was celebrated on November 1, 1960. In December of the same year there was a temporary separation of two weeks. A reconciliation was effected but not for long. Arguments and physical violence erupted, and the final separation took place on February 10, 1961. On Ortober 9, 1962 Louise presented to our tribunal a libel requesting a declaration of nullity of her marriage and alleging that Rene had excluded from the marriage contract the essential property of indissolubility. The libel was admitted to trial, the parties were summoned, and the doubt was formulated, and the question was proposed to us for decision:

Whether the marriage in question is null and void because of an intention on the part of R. Gaskins to exclude the permanency of marriage?"

The Law

Canon 1013: 2. The the essential properties of marriage are unity and indissolubility and these, in Christian marriage, are given special support in virtue of the sacrament.

Canon 1081: 1. A marriage is made by the consent of the parties, i.e. lawfully manifested persons qualified in law; this can be supplied by no human power. 2. Matrimonial consent is an act of the will by which each party surrenders and accepts a perpetual and exclusive bodily right to the end that acts may be performed which as such are adequate for the generation of offspring.

Canon 1086: 1. The internal consent of the mind is always presumed to be in conformity with the words or signs used in the contracting of marriage. 2. But if either party or both parties by a positive act of the will should exclude . . . any essential property of marriage, he contracts invalidly.

Indissolubility is an essential property of marriage. As such, it is so closely joined to the essence of marriage that it can not be separated from it. Consequently, who excludes indissolubility, also excludes marriage itself.

The words of the marriage contract as they are found in the ritual explicitly state that the marriage is indissoluble. He who pronounces these words must be prepared to intend their ordinary meaning. Also, generally speaking, people contracting marriage understand and intend that it be a permanent union. Anyone entering marriage should be presumed to intend what people ordinarily understand by marriage and what marriage is in itself. This is what is intended, this is what is desired. The thought that marriage is indissoluble does not necessarily destroy the fundamental intention to enter marriage as people ordinarily do. Error is in the intellect but matrimonial consent is an act of the will.

Error about the indissolubility of marriage can cause invalidity if it causes to be merely in the intellect and if it excludes indissolubility from the matrimonial consent. This is realized in the case of one who erroneously believes that marriage can be dissolved and who foresees that he will not be able to live peacefully for a long period of time with his intended spouse. If he contracts with the attitude of mind that he is contracting but that he does not wish to bind himself except for a period of time, or as long as their mutual love will endure, then his error is no longer merely in the intellect but it so affects the will that the will positively excludes permanency from the contract. Such error causes a marriage to be null and void. Coronata, *De Sacramentis Tractatus Canonicus (ed. 2, 1947), Vol. III, no. 459.*

In the canons cited above it must be noted that it is specifically the exclusion of the indissolubility which causes nullity. Certainly the intention to obtain a divorce can be a fact from which a court can infer the intention to exclude indissolubility. *S.R. Rotae Decisiones, Vol. XIX (1927), p. 549, coram Massimi, 30 Dec. 1927, Dec. LXI, no. 2; Vol. XLI (1949), p. 438, coram Staffa, 29 iul. 1949, Dec. LXXI, no. 3; XLV (1953), p. 571, coram Heard, 4 Aug. 1953, Dec. XLI, no. 3.* But the intention to exclude indissolubility and the intention to obtain a divorce are not necessarily one and the same thing. It is altogether possible for a person to exclude without having, at least explicitly, an intention to obtain a divorce. In other words the intention to obtain a civil divorce can be contained implicitly in the intention to dissolve all of the matrimonial rights and obligations which were brought into the marriage contract.

When a party who is accused of defective consent is said to have manifested that defect of consent by such expressions that he intended to leave his spouse after a certain period of time or under certain conditions, special care must be taken. Ordinarily the intention to leave the other party can be interpreted in terms of separation, or in not observing marital fidelity. The court must determine whether there was a true exclusion of indissolubility, i.e. a positive determination not to enter a permanent bond. *S.R. Rotae Decisiones Vol. XXXI (1939), p. 391, coram Wynen, 10 Iun. 1939, Dec. XLI, no. 3; Vol. XXXI (1939), pp. 546-547, coram Heard, 26 Oct. 1939, Dec. LIV, no. 4; Vol. XL (1948), p. 396, coram Julien, 8 Nov. 1948, Dec. LXII, no. 3.*

The Argument

We find as a fact that when defendant, Rene contracted marriage with plaintiff, Louise Tauirella he excluded from his consent the essential property of indissolubility of marriage, and that he thereby caused this marriage to be null and void. We base this finding on the judicial confession of Rene before our court on December 7, 1962; on the extra-judicial statements made by Rene before the marriage, and to which for the satisfaction of the court we have the testimony of various witnesses; and on the circumstances, preceding and subsequent to the marriage among which can be found one in particular which motivated Rene Gaskins to intend only a dissoluble union.

When Rene appeared before our court, he testified that before the marriage he had determined that if Louise ever became obese he would leave her and get some one else. Immediately we are met with the question as to his meaning when he said that he would "leave her." Did he intend that he would separate himself from her and carry on his life as he wished, continuing to recognize her as his wife but refusing to abide by his obligation to fidelity? Or did he mean that leaving her, he would terminate all his ties with her and go about his life free to do as he wished, even to assume new marital ties if he so desired?

It is our finding that when he said that he would leave her, he meant that he would leave her and all his rights and obligations toward her. He quoted himself as having warned her, "Don't get fat, or else I will leave you and find someone else." It is our understanding of this that he meant that he would find someone else and put her in the exact same relationship to him that plaintiff had been, i.e. as his wife. Louise would be gone, his ties to her would be broken, and he would be free. This he explicitly stated in his answer to a special question—that he would "find another woman and get married."

To this understanding of defendant's meaning of "leaving," it might be objected that he also spoke of the possibility of finding another girl "on the side."

It must be admitted that these words sound more of infidelity to marital vows than of limitation on the duration of the marital bond. But, looking further, we see that these words of finding another girl on the side were uttered in response to a question as to what he meant when he told the plaintiff that whether or not he would leave her would depend on how many children they had. He saw that if there were children, especially if there were numerous children, the situation would be more complex because provisions would have to be made for the children. In this event he might have to remain and only have "another girl on the side." But this forced situation, in the event that there would be a large family, did not take away the determination to leave and to marry again but it only added another condition. We understand him to have determined that after his marriage he would reassume his absolute liberty if his wife ever became obese and if they did not in the meantime have a large family; if they had a large family, he might have to content himself with "another girl on the side." Such an intention excludes indissolubility under the conditions mentioned. The added condition of a large family does not render the marriage indissoluble but merely lessens the possibility of its being dissolved. The marriage remained dissoluble in the mind of the defendant.

It might also be objected that the fact that the defendant did not believe in divorce, and the fact that he did not recall having spoken of the possibility of a divorce, and the fact that he thought the marriage would be permanent, show that he had no plans for a divorce and he did not intend to dissolve the marriage.

First of all, the intention to dissolve a marriage does not necessarily include the intention to obtain a divorce from the civil authority. Marriage is rendered invalid by an intention to bind oneself to marital obligations only for a pre-determined period of time or as long as certain conditions exist. In fact we see that in Rene's manner of thinking and acting marriage is something more than the civil bond that is terminated by a court action. A divorce is just something which must be obtained under certain conditions so that the legal status corresponds to the reality. This is evident from his remark that if she would become obese he would find another woman and get married, and that in so doing he would have to divorce Louise. The realities of the marriage are, the leaving, the finding of another girl, and the remarriage. The divorce is a mere legal technicality. The same way of thinking is shown in his letter of April 7, 1962 in which he complained that he has been without a wife but that the State says he had a wife. For Rene the obtaining of a divorce is not the cutting of the marital tie it is not the dissolution of the marriage. For him the walking away, being free to find another, the leaving behind of the past are the actual dissolution. This is what he intended to do—to be free if his spouse should become obese.

Secondly, the fact that he did not plan a divorce does not indicate that he ruled out a dissoluble union. Although he might have been content to continue with plaintiff without marriage, he was content with having her as his wife. She had assured him that he had nothing to fear about her gaining weight. He found her physically attractive and he even thought that he was in love with her. There was no reason to suspect that he would have to leave her; he would be happy not to leave her because he had no liking for the formalities of a divorce. Although he felt that he had been trapped into marriage, that circumstances had closed in on him, he acquiesced in the situation; he was content with his wife and it was his hope that it would last; but if she did not live up to what he expected of her, he would have his freedom.

It is impossible for us to accept as in any manner probable that Rene intended to bind himself to an indissoluble union. The circumstances render this untenable. He was a Protestant. Although he had a dislike for divorce, he regarded the termination of marriage at will and remarriage a possibility, and even as desirable under certain conditions. He was imbued with a philosophy of life that there was no existence beyond the grave, and that it was most desirable to obtain the maximum of pleasure here upon earth. Sexual enjoyment was the optimum of such pleasure, and the physical beauty and attractiveness of his spouse was a very important element of his sexual enjoyment. He seriously considered before the marriage that his spouse might lose her appeal by becoming obese; he was concerned over this and he determined that he would leave her and find another if she became unattractive by added weight. If Rene were of the Catholic religion we could see the possibility that he could have foreseen that he would "leave" his wife and be unfaithful to her if she became obese but that he intended always to regard her as his wife. As Brennan points out, the intention to leave one's spouse does not necessarily indicate an intention to dissolve the bond.

For Rene this might have been a practical necessity if there arose the question of supporting children, but in the absence of children his mentality was that if Louise became unattractive, he would replace her with someone else.

The testimony of plaintiff agrees substantially with the judicial confession of the defendant. Louise testified that on a number of occasions Rene had said to her that if she ever got fat he would leave her and divorce her.

This was not specifically placed as a condition subsequent or even as part of the marriage pact but was a simple unilateral determination made before the marriage. At the times when defendant mentioned it before marriage, the plaintiff did not take him seriously, but from his conduct after the marriage she knew that he was serious.

The witnesses, Fanny, Sonny and Ramsey all confirm plaintiff's allegation that defendant determined before marriage to leave her if she became obese. Sonny and Ramsey witness that Rene was very much concerned about the possibility that his wife would eventually come to look like her mother and sister; others had mentioned this possibility to him; this was something which definitely was not to his liking.

There is some disagreement among the witnesses as to exactly what words were used by Rene. According to Fanny he spoke both of leaving and of divorcing the plaintiff; Ramsey also testified that Rene spoke specifically of divorcing his wife as well as of leaving her. Rene was not certain that he ever spoke of divorce, and Sonny seems not to have heard him mention the word "divorce." But even if Sonny did not hear him use the word divorce, he understood him to mean that he would get a divorce if that was a necessary thing to do.

This confirms our finding that although Rene might not have spoken specifically of divorce, he intended a complete break with plaintiff if she became obese, and that if a divorce was necessary to complete the break, he would not hesitate to obtain a civil dissolution. The witnesses who testified that Rene made specific mention of divorce at least by that testimony show that this was his intention as they understood it, and that according to them he was not speaking merely of physical separation *permanente vinculo*.

What about the motivating cause of the exclusion of the *bonum sacramenti?* This we find in the personality and philosophy of life of Rene of which we have already spoken and to which he himself bore witness. Temporal pleasure was the only enjoyment of which he could be certain; sexual was a very important part of the pleasure he sought on earth, and the beauty of his spouse was a necessary means to this end. He was not going to be frustrated in attaining his end by a wife who would permit herself to lose her physical beauty. The history of their married life as given by plaintiff indicates how important a motive sexual pleasure was in his life. Sonny was not intimately acquainted with Rene so as to understand his motivation, especially of such a personal nature, he did testify that when the defendant spoke of his intention to leave plaintiff if she became obese, he was very serious and he made himself very clear. Sonny could discern when Rene was serious because he would become "firey in the face," a characteristic mentioned by other witnesses. Ramsey was closely associated with defendant from childhood days and understood him more deeply. He knew that defendant was motivated principally by the physical enjoyments of life and especially by feminine physical beauty.

Considering the motivation of Rene, his judicial confession, the testimony of the witnesses who verify statements made by him before the marriage, the precedent, concomitant and subsequent circumstances of his marriage with plaintiff, we find that it has been conclusively proved that defendant excluded from his marital consent the essential property of indissolubility.

Wherefore, having thoroughly examined all these matters, both as regards the law and as regards the facts, and invoking the Name of Christ, we the undersigned judges, sitting as a Tribunal of First Instance, and having only God before our eyes declare, decree, and define in answer to the proposed doubt: *"Whether the marriage in question is null and void because of an intention on the part of Rene to exclude the permanency of marriage?"*

A F F I R M A T I V E L Y,

or, in other words, *the nullity of the marriage has been proved in the present case.*

We decree further that this our definitive sentence be published according to the second method prescribed by canon 1877.

CANON 1013 (T.R.)
INTENTION AGAINST PERMANENCE
No. 24/Kent vs. Lara

The Facts

Alice, a Catholic by birth, and Paul, baptized a Catholic on August 12, 1960, by the Rev. Lawrence, at St. John's Church, Hartford, Connecticut, were married on August 20, 1960, in the presence of the Rev. Lawrence, New Haven, Connecticut.

The couple were introduced to one another by a mutual friend in May of 1955, when both parties, it seems, were finishing their junior year in high school. They dated occasionally that summer but towards the end of the summer Alice discovered that Paul was anti-Catholic and broke off with him. During the following school year they began dating again and Paul wanted to be married in May but Alice did not take this seriously. Nevertheless, by the time Alice was in her sophomore year in college, it was mutually understood that they would one day marry. That spring, however, Paul and Alice broke up again because Paul stated that he did not want children from the marriage. After four or five months they resumed company keeping until the following June. June of 1959, they again broke up for the same reason. They finally resumed the courtship after three months when Paul professed a change of heart. Paul actually proposed when Alice was a senior and by the end of her senior year, Alice definitely accepted. This was June of 1960. Paul was then 22, Alice 21, and they had known one another for five years.

The marriage took place on August 20, 1960, and the couple was divorced about a year and a half later in December of 1961. They only lived together, however, for about five months and at that their cohabitation was sporadic.

On September 7, 1963, Alice petitioned this tribunal to declare null her marriage to Paul on the double grounds of *contra bonum prolis et sacramenti* and on November 8, 1963, the *Contestatio Litis* was conducted.

The Law

A. THE PERTINENT CANONS
Canon 1086: 1. The internal consent of the mind is always presumed to correspond with the words or signs employed in the marriage ceremony.

2. If, however, either one or both parties by a positive act of the will refuse the marriage itself, or all rights to the conjugal act, or any of the essential qualities of marriage, the marriage is invalid. (cf. Canon 1013).

Canon 1092: 2. Conditions attached to the marriage consent, and not revoked, . . . if the condition is of the future and is contrary to the essence of marriage, it renders the marriage null and void. (cf. Canon 1013).

B. RELATIONSHIP BETWEEN THE CANONS

Since "consent makes marriage," if the consent is either lacking or intrinsically limited, there is no marriage. Now consent is limited, that is to say, conditioned, by an act of the will, and the generic term which includes all such limiting will acts is called a "condition."

C. RELATIONSHIP BETWEEN *IUS* AND *USUS*

1. Contra Bonum Prolis

    a. Obviously the *ius* and the *usus* in respect to the *bonum prolis* are distinct. The *ius*, for example, is always present whereas the *usus* is not.

    b. Nevertheless, the *ius* in marriage *is* a *ius ad usum* is that the distinction in real law about the *ius radicale* and the *ius utile* cannot be transferred to marriage law. There is only one *ius* in marriage and that is the *ius utile*, the *ius ad usum*.

    c. This means that the distinction between a condition by which the *ius* is excluded or limited is completely illusory. If the *usus* is really limited as part of the contract (where the *ius* is granted), the *ius* is intrinsically limited and the contract is vitiated.

    d. It does not however mean that every time the *usus* is limited, *eo ipso* the *ius* is limited. But in every case one must determine whether such a limitation put on the nature of a condition, whether it became part of the contract, and so limited the *ius* itself. A couple may, for example, intend, when entering marriage, to use contraceptives for the first month. This is a limitation of the *usus*. It is not, however, a limitation of the *ius* unless it was a constitutive part or a condition to the contract. Which would be true, it seems, if either party would consider a request for *non-condomistic* relations by the other party during that first month as a real extension of the contract, a violation of rights, an infringement on the agreement. If this were true, then obviously the limitation of the *usus* was part of the contract and the marriage would be null. Otherwise, the limitation of the *usus* would have to be considered extrinsic to the contract itself and the marriage would be valid.

2. Contra Bonum Sacramenti

    a. If the *bonum sacramenti* referred to the inseparability of the spouses then the *ius* and *usus* would obviously be distinct. Indeed the *ius* would be present but not the *usus* at every description. This, however, is not what the *bonum sacramenti* means. It does not refer to the inseparability of the spouses but rather to the indissolubility or perpetuity of the marriage bond, and here there is no distinction between the *ius* and *usus*. They are identical. The *usus* is lived every moment and is always operative, no matter what has intervened between the spouses, until one or the other dies.

b. As regards the *bonum sacramenti*, therefore, one does not speak about the *ius* and the *usus*. This may be a legitimate distinction in the *bonum fidei*, for example, where an intention to *abuse* (e.g., keeping a mistress) does not necessarily destroy the right of exclusivity truly given to the wife. But in the *bonum sacramenti* it would be double talk to say that indissolubility could be abused without being utterly destroyed. Obviously, if one intends a temporary marriage, he does not intend simply to *abuse* indissolubility. He intends a *dissoluble* marriage. The point is that in the *bonum sacramenti* we are talking not so much about the rights of spouses as we are about the nature of marriage. And here any real limitation is necessarily drawn into the heart of the contract and must be considered as an intrinsic limitation.

c. This is true even of a hypothetical limitation as, for example, if one intended at the time of marriage to leave his wife and find someone else *if* his wife put on more than twenty pounds. Even this would invalidate a marriage.

D. THE SUBSTANCE OF THE CANONS
1. *Contra Bonum Prolis*

a. Since the "right to conjugal acts" is a right which binds forever and at all reasonable times, if the *right* is excluded or limited, even for a short time, the marriage is valid. The same is true, as noted above, if the *use* is intrinsically limited for a short time. The marriage is null.

b. The "right to conjugal acts" is clarified somewhat in Canon 1081: 2, where the right is described as a *"ius in corpus, perpetuum et exclusivum, in ordine ad actus per se aptos ad generationem."* Since the basic physical education of the child is considered a kind of extension of generation, it is irrelevant whether the intrinsic limitation be contraceptive, abortive or educationally privative. Any such limitation constitutes invalidating partial simulation.

2. *Contra Bonum Sacramenti*

The *bonum sacramenti* refers to the indissolubility of marriage. It has been called the *bonum sacramenti* because of that special permanence enjoyed by the consummated sacramental marriage. Nevertheless, it is a property of all marriages, even non-sacramental ones, since perpetuity belongs to the essence of marriage itself.

E. PROOF OF SIMULATION

Obviously, for a marriage to be declared null in the external forum, consensual limitation must have been externally manifested, so that the nullity of the marriage is demonstrable. The principal ways of demonstrating or proving nullity are two: 1. The judicial confession of the simulator; 2. The testimony of the witnesses and petitioner.

1. *The Judicial Confession of the Simulator:*

Although each confession must be judged on its own context and on its own merits (because of the variable factors of credibility of and profit to the simulation), a few basic rules can be stated

a. a confession never suffices;

b. a confession is normally required;

c. a denial by the simulator eliminates the possibility of proof unless:

    1) he can be proved to be lying *and*

    2) the combined weight of all other proofs results in moral certitude.

2. *The Testimony of the witnesses and the Petitioner:*

    a. *In every case the canons under De testimoniorum fide* are worth reviewing:

    Canon 1789. In weighing the dispositions of witnesses the judge shall keep in view the following points:

    1° The status of the witness, his reputation for probity and the position he holds;

    2° Whether his testimony is based on personal knowledge, especially sight or hearing, or whether it is based on rumor, public report, or things which he heard from others;

    3° Whether the testimony is consistent and coherent or contradictory, uncertain, and vacillating;

    4° Whether other witnesses corroborate the testimony, or it is unsupported.

    Canon 1790. If the testimonies are at variance, the judge shall consider whether the depositions are mutually contradictory, or whether they merely cover different facts or circumstances of a case, and therefore supplement each other.

    Canon 1791: 1. The deposition of one witness does not constitute full proof, unless he is a so-called qualified witness who testifies as to things done in his official capacity.

    2. If two or three absolutely trustworthy witnesses testify in court under oath as to some affair or fact, and do so of their own personal knowledge and their testimony is strictly concordant, it is considered sufficient proof. If however, in view of the very nature of an affair or because of indications which create doubt as to the truth of things asserted, the judge believes it necessary, he may demand more complete proofs.

    b. The pertinent article regarding the petitioner's testimony is Article 117 and reads as follows: *"Despositio Iudicialis coniugum non est apta ad probationem contra valorem matrimonii constituendam."* Father Doheny's translation of this article ("The judicial deposition of the consorts is not admissible as proof against the validity of the marriage." cf. p. 283) seems to say more than the Latin but it is true, no doubt, that the article does not wish to grant to the combined concordant testimony of the parties the same weight enjoyed by the testimony of two less interested witnesses (Canon 1791: 2). Nevertheless, the judicial deposition of a trustworthy petitioner can certainly be considered corroborative evidence.

    c. The witness and petitioner, of course, cannot directly testify to the simulation since simulation is an internal act of the will. They can, however, testify to *extrajudicial confessions* to certain *indicia*, to a sufficient *motive* for simulation and to certain facts which result in *presumptions* regarding the validity of marriage.

1) *Extrajudicial confession.* An extrajudicial confession made at a non-suspect time is usually considered stronger than a judicial confession. As stated above, some confession, judicial or extrajudicial, is normally required. If neither is had, the judges must determine whether the combined weight of all other proofs results in moral certitude.

2) *Indicia (seu conjecturae).* These are circumstances (e.g., the aversion of one spouse for another or the non-consummation of the marriage as regards the *contra bonum prolis* and an extremely short period of cohabitation joned with another marriage as regards the *contra bonum sacramenti)* which cast suspicion on and if serious enough, disprove the validity of the marriage.

3) *Motive for simulation.* Simulation cannot be considered demonstrated unless it is apparent from the acts that there was a sufficient motive for simulating. Motives for excluding children would be an inordinate fear of childbirth on the part of the woman or fear of transmitting hereditary diseases, an aversion to children or, given a sufficiently selfish person, just plain irresponsibility. Motives for excluding indissolubility would be an excessive love of liberty and independence, a passion for a girl who would not permit extra-marital relations, etc.

4) *Presumptions.* Oftentimes it will be the testimony of the witnesses and petitioner which will enable the judges to arrive at a sufficiently detailed knowledge of the case so that certain presumptions will come into play.

a) As regards the *bonum prolis,* for example, if it is learned that the *usus* was perpetually excluded, it is presumed that the *ius* itself was excluded. So too, a tenacity or prolonged resistance to a partner wanting children gives rise to a presumption that the *ius* itself is excluded. Contrariwise, a temporary or untenacious exclusion of children creates the presumption that only the *usus* was in question. Testimony can also reveal whether the alleged simulator ever indicated awareness that such an action was invalidating. This does not have the importance in partial simulation that it does in total simulation (where from ignorance of invalidity is presumed validity) but in the case of a very well instructed Catholic (who knows the essentials of marriage) the same presumption might be operative.

b) As regards the *bonum sucramenti,* if it is learned that one of the parties intended to obtain a divorce or at least to reserve that hypothetical right, it is not presumed that the party simply intended separation from bed and board. Rather the presumption is that something more is intended, namely an intention to enter a new marriage (which may be either *contra bonum sacramenti* or *contra bonum fidei,* depending on whether or not the simulator considers the first marriage dissolved by the divorce). On the other hand, if it is shown that the person was in simple error regarding the indissolubility of marriage, it is not presumed that indissolubility was furthermore positively excluded since this would ordinarily be superfluous. Again, if it is clear from the acts that the alleged simulator truly loved the other party, a presumption is immediately established in behalf of permanence since love of its nature yearns for eternal expression. As regards the awareness of the simulator mentioned above under the presumptions affecting the *bonum prolis*, the same observance could be made as regards the *bonum sacramenti*.

The Argument

A. CONTRA BONUM PROLIS

1. This court is of the opinion that the allegation of the nullity of this marriage on the grounds of an intention *contra bonum prolis* has not been demonstrated.

2. First of all there does not seem to be present here a credible confession of the simulator. It is true that Paul Lara does on five different occasions offer statements which tend to favor the nullity of marriage on these grounds. These statements are found scattered throughout the various testimonies given by Paul. One such statement appeared in the preliminary testimony, one appeared in Session A and three are found in Session B. Over against these five statements, however, there are seven places in Paul's various testimonies which favor the non-exclusion of children and therefore the validity of the marriage: six in Session A, and one in Session B.

It is not really, it seems, so much a matter of Paul being truthful in one session and untruthful in another on this question of children. Rather it seems that Paul's intellect is a very bemused, subtle and not entirely consistent instrument when it turns to the question of an intention *contra bonum prolis*. His testimony on this issue is the perfect labyrinth that leads nowhere, a potpourri of conflicting conjecture, and remains completely inconclusive.

3. We must turn then to the testimony of the plaintiff and witnesses. Alice Kent, of course, offered in her testimony many helpful *indicia,* motives and presumptions favoring the invalidity of the marriage.

On the other hand, it is the opinion of the court that the other witnesses are less helpful. Didi, Paul's sister, was of little assistance since she only saw Paul a couple of times in the year and a half before his marriage and on neither occasion discussed with him the subject of marriage. Mr. and Mrs. Joseph L.'s preliminary testimony is certainly clear and strongly in favor of nullity, but appears considerably modified and weakened by Mr. L.'s formal testimony. Linda B.'s testimony about Paul's not wanting more than one child must be considered detrimental to the cause of nullity. Cecil K.'s answer to a question creates the hope that John A. actually heard from Paul before the marriage, that Paul planned never to have children from his marriage to Alice. But Mr. K. does not actually say this and as a matter of fact no such conversation transpired between Paul and Mr. A. Mr. A. does say that he doubts that Paul planned to have children and Mr. K. says that Paul specifically told him this several months after the marriage.

4. The court, of course, agrees that Paul did, somewhere along the line, decide definitely not to have children by Alice. What is not clear is that this intention was

present at the time of marriage. There are indications that it was. But there are also contradictions and, on the basis of all the evidence, it is the judgment of the court that such an intention has not been demonstrated.

5. Wherefore, we the undersigned judges of the tribunal, having invoked the divine name and having only God before our eyes; seated in the hall of the tribunal; having considered and weighed the law and the facts pertaining to this case; by these presence define, declare and decree answering the proposed *dubium quoad intentionem contra bonum prolis*: in the negative: that is to say, the nullity of marriage had not been proved.

B. CONTRA BONUM SACRAMENTI

1. This court is of the further opinion that the acts of the case do not demonstrate that Paul entered marriage with an *absolute* intention against the permanence of marriage but that they do prove that, at the time of the marriage, Paul intrinsically limited his consent by attaching to the contract a *hupothetical* intention against the permanence of the marriage, namely, that if the marriage did not work out, he reserved to himself the right to get a divorce and thus terminate the relationship.

2. Paul's testimomy in this respect is far more consistent than it was as regards the *bonum prolis* and results in what may be considered a valid confession. In this preliminary testimony given before Father Lunt he repeatedly asserts his right to a divorce where the marriage is unhappy and in question 11 indicates that, as a matter of fact, he felt that this marriage would not work out (the perfect circumstance to trigger the leap from intellect to will, from theory to practice). Not only, in other words, did Paul feel that people in general enjoyed the right of divorce in unhappy situations but he felt quite sure that this particular marriage would very likely be unhappy and he therefore determined to utilize this right if his suspicions were verified. The urgency and forcefulness of his suspicions right at the time of the marriage are well expressed in Paul's answer to a question: "I was thinking of turning around and walking down the aisle and if I encountered any irate fathers or brothers of dropping them as I went."

It is, of course, Paul's answer to another question, which apparently conflicts with every other. It reads: "At the time that I married, I believed that ours was a fairy tale romance and that it had the same permanence as any other marriage, that neither of us knew that it would break up. When I was standing at the altar I believed in the permanence of marriage and I had no intention of getting out of it. You have the double conflict here of what I knew to be true and what I was doing as an individual."

The face value of these words, were they spoken by an ingenuous person, would be diametrically opposed to an intention against permanence. When spoken by Paul, however, a man whose mind is at best complicated and at worst disingenuous, they do not completely devaluate his "confession" since the conflict of this statement with others can be viewed as only apparent. Without really falsifying the sense of the words and without in any way distorting what seems to be Paul's prevailing mentality, the conflict can be composed by rephrasing the whole statement in this way: "At the time that I married, though I had many misgivings, I believed, or perhaps more accurately, hoped that ours was a fairy tale romance, that it had the same chance of success as any other marriage (25% of which end in divorce) and that neither of us knew for sure that it would break up. When I was standing at the altar, I believed, according to my own lights, in the permanence of marriage and I had no absolute intention (though I did harbor a hypothetical intention) of getting out of it. You have the double conflict here of my knowing that marriage is ideally permanent and my own hypothetical intention against permanence."

So phrased, Paul's answer seems to reflect accurately his mind at the time and does not really contravene his confession.

In this light, his answer to question 68: "I believed in the permanence of marriage not because the Catholic Church taught it but simply because we had made an agreement and I thought we should keep it," makes perfect sense. Paul had agreed to try living with Alice and in that sense marriage enjoyed some permanence but this did not exclude his right to obtain a divorce if the try failed.

In respect to Paul's confession, the court would make one final observation. Thus far the argument has been first of all, that Paul did testify to an intention on his *contra bonum sacramenti* and secondly, that in those places where he might seem to deny such an intention the denial can be considered illusory. Having concluded then that we have here a consistent confession by Paul, the question remains whether that confession has any value. Paul's ingenuousness has after all, already been called into question. This court is of the opinion that the confession does not enjoy considerable value, first of all because a person who tells a lie is not presumed to be always and everywhere lying (*"semel malus praesumitur semper malus"* may be taken, says Bartocetti, *"cum mica salis"*) and secondly because an intention on Paul's part *contra bonum sacramenti* is borne out by other facts, (e.g., his not wanting to take Alice to L.A. only three days after the marriage, his calling a lawyer within a few weeks of the marriage and his actually obtaining a divorce and remarrying), and by witnesses.

3. Indeed, some aspects of the case (e.g., Paul's admission that right at the time of marriage he wanted to back out and didn't want to marry) would seem to point to an absolute exclusion of permanence by Paul. This court, however, is of the opinion that the absolute exclusion theory is first of all not demonstrable (or at least was not demonstrated in the Acts) and secondly is less psychologically congruent with the burden of testimony. Alice K., for example, in her personal account, indicates that Paul was experimenting in playing house and that he could try marriage and if he didn't like it, could get a divorce. Didi, Paul's sister, points repeatedly to conditional permanence as Paul's marital philosophy as do Mr. and Mrs. Joseph L., his parents, in their preliminary testimony. In respect to the Laras' testimony, the court wishes to point out that it attaches greater credibility to their remarks in the *bonum sacramenti* area than it did as regards the *bonum prolis* since Mr. L.'s formal testimony on this subject, though more vague than his preliminary, is not as debilitating to the latter as it was on the *bonum prolis* question. Linda B. has nothing detrimental to offer to parallel her "not more than one child" statement in the *bonum prolis* question and as a matter of fact positively corroborates the conditional permanence theory when she says that Paul believed in the permanence of marriage as long as it suited him. Cecil K. tells us that Paul "mentioned that as far as he was concerned there were divorce courts and no man is obliged to live with a woman if he doesn't want to. I thought he was joking at the time but he did mention it and I'm still not quite sure how he meant it." That Paul

would mention this to the bride's father is, it seems, considerably more meaningful than if it were mentioned to a less interested person and is an indication of the compulsive character of the concept in Paul's mind. That it was no joke as far as Paul is concerned is obvious when this isolated instance assumes its proper position in the total contextual history of events. John A. and Kit C. are not particularly relevant witnesses in the *bonum sacramenti* investigation. Paul told Mr. A. about a year before the marriage that he never wanted to be tied down but he never really said anything explicit about the permanence of marriage and Mr. A.'s conjecture, that the ceremony was only a show and that Paul never intended to assume any responsibility, must be taken as just that—conjecture.

    4. In conclusion, the Acts of this case, suggest the following picture:

        a) that Paul entered marriage hypothetically excluding permanence, reserving to himself the right to divorce, if things didn't work out and feeling pretty sure that they wouldn't;

        b) that having entered marriage he felt trapped and felt that he had made a mistake and then formed the intention not to perpetuate the mistake with children;

        c) that at some later time Paul absolutely decided to end the marriage by divorce.

    5. Wherefore, we the undersigned judges of the tribunal, having invoked the divine name and having only God before our eyes, seated in the hall of the tribunal, having considered and weighed the law and the facts pertaining to this case, by these presence define, declare and decree answering the proposed *dubium quoad intentionem contra bonum sacramenti:* in the *affirmative:* that is to say, *the nullity of the marriage has been proved.*

    We further decree that this sentence be published according to the second method prescribed by canon 1877.

Case #5

CANON 1013 (T.R.)
INTENTION AGAINST FIDELITY
No. 25/Sheila vs Bernard

The Facts

Sheila, a Catholic, contracted marriage with Bernard, a non—Catholic, in a Catholic church, in New York, on April 1, 1955. Three children were born of this union and cohabitation ceased in 1961, when Bernard was arrested for bigamy. Subsequent to the marriage Sheila learned that Bernard had contracted four other marriages and had fathered ten other children.

On December 11, 1961, Sheila asked the Court of——to declare her marriage null on the grounds that Bernard excluded from his consent the quality of indissolubility and fidelity. The Court of——declared on December 21, 1964, that Sheila's allegation on the basis of *contra bonum fidei* had been fully proved. The Court of New York in sentence given on April 12, 1965, sustained both parts of the decision.

The Law

Canon 1013; 2. The essential properties of marriage are unity and indissolubity and these, in Christian marriage are given special support in virtue of the sacrament.

Canon 1081; 1. A marriage is made by the consent of the parties, i.e., lawfully manifested by persons qualified in the law; this can be supplied by no human power.

2. Matrimonial consent is an act of the will by which each party surrenders and accepts a perpetual and exclusive bodily right to the end that acts may be performed which as such are adequate for the generation of offspring.

Canon 1084. Mere error concerning the unity, indissolubility, and sacramental dignity of marriage does not invalidate the matrimonial consent, even if such error was the cause of the contract.

Canon 1086; 1. The internal consent of the mind is always presumed to be in conformity with the words or signs used in the contracting of marriage.

2. But if either party or both parties by a positive act of the will should exclude . . . any essential property of marriage, he contracts invalidity.

However, in deciding any case wherein the validity of a marriage s impugned on any grounds, the Tribunal must take into consideration the presumption of Canon

1014; Marriage enjoys the favor of the law; wherefore in case of doubt the marriage is to be considered valid until the contrary is proved. In case of the Pauline Privilege, however, the presumption is not in favor of upholding the marriage bond but rather in favor of dissolution as stated in Canon 1127.

According to both the natural law and canon law, marriage arises from the mutual consent of a man and a woman, who are eligible to do so, to take each other for life as husband and wife. The object of the marital consent is the mutual exchange of the exclusive and perpetual right to proper marital relations as a means to fulfilling the ends of marriage. Therefore the existence of marriage depends upon the valid consent of the contracting parties to all the essential elements of the object of marriage. Rightly does the Code of Canon Law presume that the contracting parties are sincere so that ordinarily the external expression of marital consent is accepted as sufficient indication of their internal consent. However, should the consent, contrary to the external manifestition, be actually internally withheld either altogether or even with regard to just one essential element, there would be no marriage. It would be a case of simulation.

If, in spite of the use of external expressions indicative of marital consent, at least one contractant internally withholds all marital consent, the simulation would be total. But if such consent is withheld with regard only to one or another of the essential elements of the object of true marital consent, the simulation would be partial. Traditionally the essential elements of the object of the marital consent are expressed as: *bonum prolis* (the procreation of children), *bonum fidei* (the mutual exchange of exclusive rights to each other's body) and *bonum sacramenti* (the permanence of the marital union until the death of one of the parties).

According to Canon 1086; 2, simulation is verified only when a contractant excludes some essential element of marriage by a *positive act* of the will. However, it is not necessary that the act of exclusion be explicit; an implicit act would suffice as a basis for an invalidating simulation of marital consent. Furthermore,it is not necessary that the positive act required for simulation be actual; a virtual intention contrary to the essence of marriage would suffice to render the consent invalid by reason of simulation. On the other hand, an habitual or interpretative intention would certainly not suffice.

It is also true that a purely internal act of the will contrary to the essence of marriage would vitiate the consent externally manifested. But such an internal act would not justify the declaring of a marriage to be null and void on the grounds of simulation because a purely internal act is not a juridical act. In other words, a purely internal act could not be known, much less proved, except by the admission of the simulator; and such an admission by itself does not constitute full juridical proof. Therefore, it is possible that a *de facto* invalid marriage must be considered valid in the external forum because of a lack of juridical proof.

Total simulation was neither alleged in the petition nor indicated in the subsequent investigation in this case. Again the facts of the case make it obvious that the alleged simulator never entertained any intention *contra bonum prolis*. Neither are ignorance, simple error or conditional consent pertinent to this case. Therefore, none of these possible grounds for the invalidity of marriage need be considered any further.

In her *libelus*, the plaintiff states "I maintain that Bernard did not have the intention of entering a true and permanent marriage with me . . . and that he had no intention of being faithful to me." She then petitioned the tribunal to investigate the marriage "to determine whether his intention against permanence and fidelity invalidated the marriage." The tribunal accepted her petition on those two possible grounds of invalidity and formulated the *dubium* accordingly.

The subsequent investigation, however, hardly substantiated the possibility of proving an intention *contra bonum sacramenti*; in fact the investigation clearly brought out that, in spite of his involvement with several other women, the respondent desired and attempted to continue his relationship with the petitioner on a permanent basis. Therefore, nothing more need be said concerning the law pertaining to an intention *contra bonum sacramenti*.

What remains to be considered more in detail is partial simulation because of an intention *contra bonum fidei*, that is, an intention contrary to the unity of marriage. Unity is the second essential quality of marriage as stated in Canon 1013: 2.

If a man gives external matrimonial consent, but does not include in that the *bonum fidei*, the giving of the exclusive right over his body for acts which are apt for generation, the marriage is invalid. It seems self-evident that a man does not give an exclusive right over his body to a woman when at the time of externally expressing marital consent he intends to share his body equally and concomitantly with two women. If in exchanging marital consent, a man reserves the rights over his body in the same act of the will, he does not contract a valid marriage. The refusal or failure to bestow the exclusive right over his body vitiates the act of the will in consenting to the objects of marriage. On the other hand, it is possible for a man and woman validly to exchange a mutual and exclusive right to each other's body and still intend to abuse that right by infidelity or even promiscuity. What must be demonstrated, then, in case of an alleged intention *contra bonum fidei* is that the person accused of simulation gave defective consent because by reason of at least an implicit, virtual but nevertheless positive act of the will, he did not give his partner the exclusive right over his body for the performance of acts apt for the generation of offspring.

Obviously it is difficult to prove simulation when words indicating that marital consent is exchanged have been duly pronounced; yet such proof is possible. The ordinary means of canonical proof can be used to establish the fact of such simulation. These proofs include the confession of the parties themselves; the testimony of other witnesses; documents; presumptions based on antecedent concomitant and subsequent circumstances; the assignment of a sufficient reason to explain why the simulator went through with a marriage ceremony and at the same time failed to give valid consent.

Since it is a matter of determining an internal intention, the confession of the alleged simulator could carry greater weight than in other types of cases. On the other hand, the value of his confession, as also of the testimony of relatives of the parties, can easily be vitiated because of the emotions involved. Therefore these depositions must be carefully considered by the tribunal.

The proofs offered must show that the contrary intention elicited before the marriage, perdured up to and existed at the time of the celebration of the marriage so that it can be truly said the marriage was not entered into with the intention of bestowing the exclusive right essential to marriage. Care must always be taken not to declare null a marriage which is valid because only the exercise of the right or the fulfillment of the obligation of fidelity and not the right or obligation itself was excluded. Unless the contrary positive act of the will was reduced to a unilateral or bilateral pact, the ordinary presumption would seem to be that the exclusion refers only to the use of the right or the fulfillment of the obligation; but such a presumption can be overcome by evidence to the contrary.

Finally, it must be noted that the tribunal is bound to arrive at moral certitude by considering all of the proofs; circumstances and other evidence taken together and not singly. It is possible that each item considered separately may prove little or nothing, but considered altogether they may suffice to produce moral certitude in the minds of the judges.

The Argument

As mentioned above, the alleged intention against the indissolubility, considered as possible grounds of nullity at the time of the *contestatio litis* and included in the formulation of the *dubium*, was not substantiated by the subsequent investigation of this case; and thus it is dismissed from this sentence.

The universal difficulty of proving an intention against the unity of marriage seems to be intensified in this case. Both parties were, by natural law and by canon law, apparently eligible for marriage. Both freely and willingly exchanged, at least externally, marital consent according to the canonical form. They cohabited for some three years and had three children. The plaintiff says that she continued to live with Bernard even after she had learned about his other "wives" because she hoped to hold her marriage and family together. In her deposition, she says that at the time of ceremony she thought that Bernard was giving proper consent. The respondent consistently states that he intended to give proper consent and that he had in fact given Mary up some six months prior to marrying Sheila and he had intended to give Mary up for good. He claims that he returned to Mary because Sheila proved to be a disappointment as a wife—that she was a "fast" girl and started "running around." Moreover, neither the documents nor any of the testimony in the case offer any direct proof of any invalidating intention on the part of the respondent contrary to the unity of marriage.

On the other hand, there is a large body of proof, some general, some very specific, which indicates that at the time Bernard gave external marital consent according to the proper form, he did not really consent to give exclusive rights over his body to Sheila Previn and thus he did not give marital consent because of an intention *contra bonum fidei*, i.e. against the unity of marriage.

First of all we consider the available documents. While they are not direct proofs, they do betray the attitude or mind of Bernard towards the unity of marriage and towards marriage itself as we consider Christian marriage. First of all he married Mary without any divorce from Joan, so he must have falsely stated to the officials in South

Carolina that that was his first marriage. Secondly, he also lied to the New York State officials. In his application for a marriage license to marry Sheila he did not mention his marriage to Mary. He lied about this also in the questionaire filled out by Father McHugh and again in the suppletory oath. Finally, he lied about the number of his former marriages when obtaining a license to marry Kathy C.

Actions indeed do speak louder than words. Bernard's actions, attested to by himself and by witnesses as well as by documents, and his statements show that he did not understand the unity necessary for a valid marriage and indeed indicate a mind in him contrary to a belief in the unity of marriage. This is a permanent mind and so would have been his mind at the time he gave external consent to marry Sheila.

That such was the permanent mind of Bernard towards marriage is brought out by the following points in the whole incredible life history of the man.

1) His four marriages, his many other affairs, his fathering of children indiscriminately and concomitantly by various women and his contentment with his actions paint a general picture which is in itself and in its entirety a strong proof of his faulty concept of marriage.

2) His attitude was and is that women are creatures of pleasure for him and not by any means partners in a holy contract or union.

3) His relations with Mary and Liz, marrying one and living with and having children by both at the same time, emphasizes his attitude towards women and marriage.

4) His courtship of Sheila, at a time when he was married, his casual having relations with her during that "courtship," was only a convenient means of having a "woman away from home," as it were.

5) All his lying about his marital status, even permitting the use of the untrue testimony of his mother and brother, when arranging to marry Sheila, bespeak his dishonorable imtentions.

6) His courtship and "pre-marital" relations with Kathy C. while he was still married to Sheila and was continuing his association with both Mary and Liz W., show that he hardly had it in him to be faithful to any one woman.

7) His incredible marriage to Kathy C., while still legally married to two other women, further shows that he did not consider or consent to marriage as being "one man and one woman."

8) His desire that Sheila continue to live with him as his wife, while permitting him to continue living with Mary W., his incredible arrangement whereby he brought Mary into the house in which he was living with Sheila, so that he actually was living with two wives and two families under the same roof and at the same time: his practice of alternately sleeping with Sheila and Mary (which he saw as something that shouldn't have caused trouble but sometimes did, to his annoyance), and his suggestion (after all this had become public) to re-establish his cohabitation with Sheila while reserving his "rights" to Mary—and perhaps to other women; all put together, this fantastic series of revelations of Bernard's attitude toward his marriage to Sheila, leaves little room to doubt that Bernard ever considered that he had given himself or belonged exclusively to one woman.

Looking at it from a slightly different point of view, since the development and history of Bernard's association with each of his "wives" followed the same almost invariable pattern of pre-marital sexual relations, pregnancy, marriage, infidelity, subsequent marriage without previous divorce etc., it seems reasonable to presume that he did not intend to endow Sheila with any more exclusive right over his body than he gave to either Liz or Kathy. He admits he realized that he was not eligible legally or morally to marry either of the latter; he thereby admits that these marriages were only convenient arrangements. Why should his word be taken that he was any more honorable or Christian in his intentions when he married Sheila?

It is also a help to proving simulation if there is established the fact that the party had a motive to explain the external expression of consent while withholding internal consent. Bernard had such a motive in simulating marriage with Sheila. He married her because he wanted to continue having her body and because she was pregnant. But this going through the external formality did not represent a change in his mind, which did not see unity as an essential part of marriage. To have intended to give exclusive marital rights and to be faithful to Sheila would have had to mean a complete change in his entire outlook on sex, marriage and life; the evidence at hand argues strongly against such a change having ever taken place.

Now, therefore, having considered the law and the facts in evidence, We, the undersigned judges, sitting as a tribunal, and having only God before our eyes, invoking the name of Christ, give sentence, replying to the proposed *dubium* as follows:

"To the first part, affirmative, or the nullity of the marriage in question is proved on the grounds of intention against fidelity.

"To the second part, negative, that is the nullity of the marriage in question is not proved on the grounds of intention against indissolubility."

We further decree that this sentence shall be published according to the second method prescribed by Canon 1877.

We further decree that this our definitive sentence be executed in accordance with the prescriptions of the sacred canons and that all ordinaries and ministers of tribunals, whose duty it is to execute the definitive sentences of ecclesiastical tribunals, proceed against those who refuse to obey these decrees in accordance with Title XVII of Book IV of the Code of Canon Law, using whatever means appear to be opportune or efficacious for this purpose.

Case #6

CANON 1013 (T.R.)
AGAINST FIDELITY
No. 26/Doris vs. Ron

The Facts

Doris, a baptized Catholic, originally residing in Omaha, Nebraska but now a resident of the Diocese of——attempted marriage with Ron, a baptized Protestant, before a Methodist minister in Washington, D.C., on August 6, 1941. Following the birth of their third child, Ron determined there were to be no more children and employed either contraceptives or withdrawal for this purpose. In 1952, he met Dottie,a baptized Catholic, and within a short time made her his mistress, seeing her three or four times a week. This was not the only woman with whom Ron had an affair but she was the most permanent. In an effort to save the marriage or what there was left of it, Doris urged a revalidation which took place at Our Lady of Fatima, on November 20, 1954. This did not really solve the problem, for Ron began spending more time with Dottie than before. In January of 1955, Ron moved out completely and accordingly, Doris in July of 1955, sued for divorce, which was granted on August 2, 1955. On August 14, 1957, Doris petitioned a Declaration of Nullity of her marriage with Ron from the Omaha Matrimonial Tribunal on grounds *contra bonum fidei et sacramenti.*

The Law

1) Through the concept of fidelity one assumes the obligation of being faithful, as St. Thomas teaches. (Suppl. III, q. 49a 3). By reason of this obligation, which belongs to the essence of the matrimonial contract, raised to the dignity of a sacrament, the right to those acts ordered to the generation of children is given to only one person and is accepted by only one person. (Canons 1012, 1013; 2, 1081).

For the proof of this simulation, which consists in the exclusion of fidelity, it does not suffice that the contracting party have a general intention of engaging in extramarital sexual activities, but it must be clear that he refused to accept or to give the exclusive right to fidelity, i.e. in the sense that he would give his body to others for sexual purposes.

This exclusive right is not given when: a) there is some limitation, placed on the consent, which is contrary to fidelity; b) there is no intention of contracting without a restriction, namely of giving oneself to others sexually; c) there is a positive intention of having a sexual relationship with a third party; d) there is a reservation not to observe fidelity.

For fidelity to be excluded it is not necessasry that one have the intention of entering into an adulterous relationship at the proper time, but it is enough that he decide by a positive act of the will to lead a conjugal life with his spouse and at the same time with a third party.

Simulation of fidelity is more difficult to prove than other types of simulation, for on the one hand the whole question is concerned about an internal act, and on the other hand the distinction must be made between the obligation of fidelity and the fulfillment of that obligation. As the Sacred Roman Rota teaches, the simple proposition of violating marital fidelity through adultery (which *per se* is contrary to the fulfillment of the obligation) does not substantially restrict a valid consent.

Nevertheless, this simulation of fidelity can be proven through arguments which are well known, i.e., an adequate and proven cause of simulation, the confession of the simulator, and the antecedent, concomitant, and subsequent circumstances.

The confession of the simulator ought to be examined in greater detail.

If the confession is given only in the judicial forum it does not prove the infidelity of the marriage, and generally speaking, it is of minor importance. But if it is given extrajudicially, it is for the judge to determine what value it has from the surrounding circumstances. Because of the nature of the material, more so than the other types of simulation, the confession lends itself to denial or rejection by those who have some interest in it. The prudent judge will view the confession of the simulator not only on the testimony of those accused, but will consider even more the evidence of those who have been silent about the confession or who have omitted it in their testimony, or have not averted to it. If proper attention is given to deeds and acts of unquestionable meaning, the intention, hidden in the heart of the simulator or in one who refuses to make a confession, will readily appear.

2) Concerning the permanence of marriage, the principles of law contained in Canon 1086: 2 are well known because of the number of cases which are considered under this heading.

A marriage can be invalid not only because of an absolute exclusion of indissolubility but also because of hypothetical exclusion, even though he who contracts neither knows nor foresees that the bond of marriage can be broken. As a matter of fact, where one determines to sever the bond, given an absolute or hypothetical circumstance, this intention will prevail over the general intention of contracting a true marriage. Consequently, he excludes the permanence of the bond.

For the exclusion of permanence in marriage, a positive act of the will is required. The act of the will must be actual or at least virtual. An explicit act of the will is not required, since an implicit act of the will suffices, according to the jurisprudence of the rota. He who, by a positive act of the will, intends to obtain a civil divorce, whether absolutely or hypothetically, excludes indissolubility even though he purports to contract a Catholic marriage.

Error or ignorance, concerning the means readily available for the breaking of the bond, does not affect the validity of the marriage, since at least an implicit positive act of the will is required. Thus, "simple error concerning the indissolubility of marriage even though it is the cause of the contract, does not vitiate matrimonial consent." (Canon 1084).

As noted by the rota, it is not altogether impossible to combine error with a positive exclusion of indissolubility. This is verified, for example, when one is so convinced of the right to divorce that he would not enter marriage under different circumstances.

It is easier to prove the exclusion of indissolubility if it had been reduced to an agreement rather than the consideration of the mere act of the will.

In both cases, since we are concerned with simulation, great emphasis should be given to the confession of the simulating party, especially an extra-judicial confession made at a non-suspect time. The proof can be corroborated by the trustworthiness and reliability of the parties, the character of the simulator, and all those circumstances, antecedent, concomitant, and subsequent, which surround the marriage.

The Argument

Doris Toth, plaintiff, is considered by all to be honest, sincere and truthful. Although the moral guilt of living in an invalid marriage for so many years is indicative of no great concern for the eternal welfare of her soul, it by no means diminishes the truthfulness of her character.

Ron, defendant, is on the contrary, judged by the unanimous declarations and depositions of all concerned to be completely devoid of integrity as far as truthfulness is concerned. Ron, although not wholly evil, lies in situations where he considers it in his own best interests and thus his word alone by itself is not *per se* worthy of credence.

Since, however, so much of the crucial testimony available in this case is either the very words of Ron, or intimately connected with the same, it behooves the court to give initial enunciation to a precise and clear formula whereby the truth and falsehood latent in Ron's assertions and denials can be ascertained.

Since then Ron's words alone are not worthy of credence he must be judged according to the classic rule of jurisprudence: not by what he says so much as by what he does. In other words if his words are in conformity with his deeds and the testimony of others, then his deeds give adequate indication of the veracity of his words. This is the classical way of judging a man whose word cannot be accepted on its own merit. Thus by this rule is truth distilled from a vast quantity of verbiage.

A. With regard to the charge of exclusion of the obligation of fidelity:

Proof of simulation, as was noted above, usually consists in: a) proof of an adequate cause for simulating consent; b) the testimony of the party admitting simulation; c) the proof of circumstances before, at the time of, and after the marriage, which support the fact.

1) In this case what is the adequate cause for simulating consent? In accord with the testimony at hand it is a composite of two elements: first, of course, infatuation with Dottie and secondly the pressure brought to bear upon Ron by Doris to go

through with convalidation. Since Ron considered the convalidation of small importance (as seen unmistakably by his words and deeds—not even the Defender of the Bond disputes this), it seemed to him to be a small price to pay for the cessation or lessening of the nagging and discontent of Doris, who could thus return to the Sacraments, something which seemed important to her.

To be more precise—and the duty incumbent upon the administration of justice demands this—a distinction must be made. The cause for simulating consent was infatuation with Dottie, whereas the cause for the marriage (going through the convalidation ceremony) was the pressure brought to bear upon Ron by Doris.

Thus it has been clearly established and proven in this case that there was an adequate cause for simulating consent.

2) We now proceed to the question of confession or admission of simulation on the part of the defendant, and also other direct and indirect arguments of proof in the matter.

Before proceeding further it is necessary to point out that we must keep before our eyes the proven fact that certainly the convalidation ceremony meant nothing to Ron, i.e., nothing in terms of sacredness, marital obligations and rights, etc. The officiating minister states: "He gave the impression of complete indifference to everything." The plaintiff states in response to the question: Did he agree that a Christian marriage might straighten the marriage out?: "He didn't agree to anything except to have it done." Jane Baver: "He said it didn't mean anything to him."

These statements are strengthened by the fact that Ron spent the very night of the convalidation with Dottie.

Thus in accord with the rule stated above we can say with certainty that Ron speaks the truth when he says in reply to the question: Why did you agree to go ahead with the Church ceremony?: "I finally decided that since it did not involve me (i.e., by my having to become Catholic) and would make her happy and give her peace of conscience and the right to practice her religion fully, the best thing to do would be to go ahead with it." The ceremony truly meant mothing to the defendant as regards his personal rights, duties and intentions.

Therefore, when he says that at the time of the convalidation: "At that time I had not made any decision on the matter of 'seeing' Dottie," he simply means that he had not yet decided to leave the plaintiff and marry Dottie. It would however, be wrong to say that Ron had no positive intention of retaining Dottie as a mistress as he had done up to this time and without interruption continued to do after the convalidation ceremony. Based on these facts the truth is once more distilled in Ron's admission (in reply to the statement: "It is evident from this that you had not broken up with Dottie at the time of the ceremony?: "I was still seeing her—we had not broken up."

Now if they had not broken up and he was still seeing her (sleeping with her), his positive or at least implicit intention of continuing his illicit relationship of infidelity (at least for a period of time more or less undetermined by the defendant) comes to the surface. For he can hardly continue the relationship and yet at the same time not have the positive will of doing so—unless he were forced, which is obviously not the case here. Thus when the defendant refuses to swear that he positively intended to continue his relationship with Dottie at the time of the Church ceremony, he is simply evading the issue. He is not lying; rather he is merely making his response stay within the bounds of a narrow interpretation of a question that thus does not really get to the heart of the matter. He neither affirms nor denies the real crucial question with this response.

Ron without doubt contradicts himself when at one point he affirms: "At that time (of the Church ceremony) I had not made any decision on the matter of 'seeing' Dottie," and later in the same deposition he states: "Yes. I definitely intended to stop seeing Dottie eventually. From time to time I had this in mind before the Church ceremony and quite definitely at the time of the Church ceremony." The latter statement is obvious retrospective wishful thinking. The former statement simply means, as we have pointed out above, that he had not as yet decided to leave the plaintiff permanently and marry Dottie. Ron's statements of alleged intention to stay with the plaintiff for life are likewise for the same reasons judged by us to be figments of the defendant's imagination.

Finally, then, we come to the crowning achievement of the defendant's testimony where he states: "The petition is right as to the occurrence of infidelity, but wrong as to my intention: my intention was good but my behavior was bad." This is truly beyond the shadow of a doubt a prime example of a *mera velleitas omnino inefficax* as opposed to a *vera voluntas non peccandi.* His behavior was morally wrong and culpably so, as he readily admits. Therefore, what scholastic terminology calls his mental intention in committing these acts of infidelity and allowing himself to remain in this habitual state of infidelity, was altogether bad, morally evil. This should be clear to all. The canonical distinction between the right and the abuse of the right is totally out of place here and has absolutely nothing to do with this response of the defendant.

We have already seen the circumstances at the time of the Church ceremony and how these events shed light on Ron's positive intention of continuing his illicit relationship with Dottie *just as before.* We now ask the crucial question regarding the "just as before." What precisely was Ron's intention during the time prior to the convalidation? Fran Lowe testifies to the extrajudicial confession of the defendant: "He told me he wanted Dottie and he was going to keep her. This was before the validation." Dick E. narrates regarding the birth and death of a child which took place some months before the convalidation: "Both Dottie and Ron were glad they had a child and when the child died they were looking forward to having another one." In general terms the same witness testifies: "At no time did Ron have any sincere intentions of breaking up with Dottie. He reaffirmed many times that he loved Dottie. He stated that he would be willing to lose Doris rather than lose Dottie." Now these statements attributed to the defendant can, according to the rule found in the initial portion of this judgment, be accepted as truthful utterances of Ron since they are very certainly in accord with the facts. This indicates once again a positive intention of handing over to Dottie the right to the use of his body and correspondingly the lack of exclusivity of the same for his civil spouse, the plaintiff.

What about the circumstances *after* the Church ceremony? When the convalidation took place and Dottie, having been apprised of the fact and being very angry, confronted Ron with it, what was Ron's reaction? "Ron didn't think it was so important and said the convalidation would make no difference in his relationship with Dottie." Jane B. is surely a prime witness due to her relationship with Dottie. In other words Ron informed Dottie that his intentions had not changed because of the convalidation and he quite clearly had already himself testified to the truth of this statement by sleeping with Dottie the very night of the convalidation. Nothing was changed in their relationship. He would still rather have skipped the convalidation if it would have meant losing Dottie. Of course he had not as yet come to any definite conclusion as regards long range plans, i.e. whether he should leave the plaintiff and marry Dottie. He was confused and wanted to continue his relationship with Dottie as before.

Thus it should be clear to all that: 1) Prior to the convalidation Ron did not intend to accept the exclusivity of the *jus in corpus.* 2) This intention perdured during and after the convalidation. His extrajudicial confessions together with the testimony of faithful witnesses and all the circumstances (especially Ron's staying more frequently with Dottie after the Church ceremony and even on the very night of the convalidation) adequately supply moral certitude in this regard despite the fact that there is no direct judicial confession of simulation. A decision of the S.R. Rota provides us, with its practical rule of thumb, the key to this case. "It is incumbent upon the really prudent judge to establish the confession of simulation not only from those things which the alleged simulator in or outside of court expressly affirms or denies, but also, and even more so, from those things which he is cunningly silent about, omits or does not dare to impugn, while he is quite unaware of their importance. If due attention is given to a comparison of such things with clearly established deeds and acts, the intention of simulation hidden deep within the heart will come to light, all his efforts to the contrary notwithstanding." (S.R.R., October 30, 1953). The same noted decision wisely states: "In contracting marriage a person is shown to reserve to himself the right of adultery under these circumstances: if he were faced with the dilemma of breaking up with the third party or not contracting the marriage, he would choose to renounce the marriage. Neither is it necessary for the exclusion of *bonum fidei* that he have the intention of marrying his accomplice at some future date, but it is sufficient that by a positive act he decides to retain the third party as a mistress together with his wife." (*Ibid.*)

Thus we arrive with moral certitude at this conclusion: not only did Ron fail to be faithful to his spouse but he also rejected the very obligation of conjugal fidelity. There was thus no sacramental bond because of the exclusion of *bonum fidei.*

B. With regard to the complaint of nullity on the grounds of excluding the *bonum sacramenti,* the following must be observed in accordance with the rules laid down *In Jure* above.

In this case there certainly was no evidence of a pact excluding indissolubility. Neither is there available in the evidence presented any judicial confession of the positive and absolute exclusion of indissolubility. Neither is there available in the evidence presented any judicial confession of the positive and absolute exclusion of indissolubility.

What, however, is to be said about a hypothetical exclusion? There is not available in the evidence presented any certain proof of an explicit hypothetical exclusion. But what about an *implicit* hypothetical exclusion? Now the facts in this case prove that at the time of the convalidation, Ron had a positive intention of continuing his illicit relationship with Dottie—at least for some vague undetermined period of time. On the other hand Ron had not as yet decided to leave the plaintiff permanently and marry Dottie (Cf. above in this decision).

Ron's attitude on divorce could be simple error, but can we say with certainty from the evidence presented that it had passed from the speculative to the practical field, from the intellect to a positive, if only implicit, act of the will? We do know for certain that Ron positively intended to maintain his illicit relationship with Dottie before, during, and after the convalidation. We further know that he had reached no definite decision as to his long range plans, i.e. whether to divorce the plaintiff and marry Dottie. What Ron is telling us, therefore, is: at the time of the convalidation he still had sexual relations with Dottie two or three times weekly. He intended to continue this practice for the time being, but he had not made up his mind if he was going to do this permanently—marry her, or give her up.

To admit the possibility of divorce is not necessarily the same as the positive, implicit, hypothetical intention of divorce. This is not to deny that Ron had such an invalidating intention. It is only to affirm that the evidence at hand is not adequate for moral certainty in this regard. Ron may have asked for his freedom through Dottie at some time prior to the convalidation, and thus may have had such a hypothetical intention. Furthermore this intention may have endured through the convalidation, but there is not enough evidence for this from the documents presented in the case to arrive at moral certainty.

Although it is true that Ron considered the Church convalidation a mere empty ceremony, this *per se* is insufficient for satisfactory proof of simulation of consent. At most this only proves a reason for simulating consent, "an atmosphere in which feigned consent could easily occur."

Thus there is no sufficient proof of a positive act of *contra bonum sacramenti.*

Now, therefore, having considered the law and the facts in evidence, we, the undersigned judges, sitting as a tribunal, and having only God before our eyes, invoking the name of Christ, give sentence, replying to the proposed *dubium* as follows:

To the first part, *affirmative*, or the *nullity of the marriage in question is proved on the grounds of infidelity.*

To the second part, *negative*, or *the nullity of the marriage in question is not proved on the grounds of intention against indissolubility.*

CANON 1068 (T.R.)
IMPOTENCY
No. 58/Boyle vs. Jackson

The Facts

Following a courtship of almost one year, Susan Boyle, a Roman Catholic, contracted marriage in the Cathedral Church of St. Michael, Toronto, Ontario, Canada, on May 3, 1953, with Robert Jackson, a Jew. The parties lived together until May, 1962. No children were born of this marriage. A civil dissolution of this marriage was obtained by Susan Boyle on April 3, 1964.

On June 7, 1963, Susan Boyle presented a libellus to the Tribunal of——alleging the invalidity of her marriage to Robert Jackson on the grounds that, at the time of the marriage, he was antecedently and perpetually impotent. This libellus was accepted on June 26, 1963, and at the joinder of the issue, effected on September 27, 1963, the doubt to be resolved was formulated in the usual manner; viz. "Has the nullity of this marriage been certainly proved?"

The Law

Since marriage is a contract through which the parties give and receive a perpetual and exclusive right over each other's body in the performance of acts that are of themselves suited for the procreation of children, it follows that those who are incapable of placing such acts are disqualified from marriage. It is to be noted, however, that impotence— the inability to place such acts—invalidates a marriage only when it is both antecedent and perpetual (Canon 1086; 1). The third paragraph of this same canon indicates that sterility—the inability to procreate even though capable of coition—does not invalidate marriage.

While the Code of Canon Law does not indicate what constitutes the act which, of itself, is suited for the procreation of children, a description of what does constitute such an act is found in the response of the Supreme Sacred Congregation of the Holy Office of February 12, 1941. According to this response, it is necessary that the man in some manner, even though imperfectly, penetrate the vagina of the woman and thereupon immediately deposit seed therein in a natural manner. The Sacred Roman Rota specifies the components of the act when it describes impotence as follows: "Male impotency is verified as long as the erection of the male organ, or the penetration of the same into the proper vessel, or the effusion within the same of material elaborated in the testicles—in other words, true seed—is impeded by some obstacle" (S. R. R. *Decisiones,* Vol. XLIII, Dec. XVI, no. 2). The same decision goes on to state that their inability to produce testicular material, is one cause of impotency, adding that such inability can be easily established by the absence of, or definite atrophy of both testicles.

It is to be noted, however, that in the case of atrophy of the testicles, it must be shown that the atrophied condition was complete and that it affected both testicles. Partial atrophy of one or both of the testicles would not of itself preclude the possibility of true seed being elaborated in the testicles. Again, to quote the rota: "If both testicles are either completely absent or definitively atrophied, it is clear that testicular seed cannot be produced and if the spermatic cord is absolutely and irreparably occluded the seed produced cannot be ejaculated. In each case the man is to be declared incapable of copulation in the canonical sense" (S. R. R. *Decisiones, Vol. SLIII,* Dec. XV, no. 3). "Speaking further of the inability to produce true seed, the rota states: "Therefore, attention must be given not to the ability to obtain an erection or to ejaculate . . . but rather to the site of the testicles, their size and consistency, their sensibility to heat, to touch, and to pain so that, from this consideration, it is possible to determine whether or not we are dealing with a still functioning organ in which spermatogenesis or an external secretion is produced, or with an organ which is perfectly atrophied" (S. R. R. *Decisiones,* Vol. XLIII, Dec. LXI, no. 2).

While it is true that there are canonists who disagree with this teaching, nevertheless, in view of the admonitions of the Sacred Roman Rota, such teaching may not be followed with safety in the adjudication of marriage cases.

The elements of proof, in establishing the existence of invalidating impotence, are the confession of the parties, the testimony of knowledgeable witnesses, and the reports and testimony of medical experts. The Code of Canon Law specified that in cases of impotency and non-consummation it is required that the parties present witnesses *septimae manus.* In establishing this requirement, however, the canon makes it clear that such may be omitted when the non-consummation or the impotency can be proved from other sources (Canon 1975; 1). With regard to the medical experts, while indicating that great weight is to be accorded the opinions and conclusions of the experts, the law makes it clear also that the judge alone can render sentence and by no means is he bound to follow medical opinions unquestionably, especially since experts often speak in terms of what is very probable rather than what is morally certain (S. R. R. *Decisiones,* Vol. XXXIX, Dec. LXV, no. 4). At the same time, the mere fact that the medical expert uses the term "probable" does not necessarily imply that he lacks moral certitude, for it may very well be that his use of this term indicates that he is striving for physical certitude whereas moral certitude suffices (S. R. R. *Decisiones,* Vol. XXXVI, Dec. LXIV, no. 12).

Finally, two presumptions must be borne in mind: (1) that man is presumed to be capable of functioning as a man, and (2) that marriage enjoys the favor of law. Consequently, in doubt, the man is to be adjudged potent and the validity of the marriage is to be sustained.

The Argument

In the case at hand, there is no question with regard to the determination of the fact of penetration or with regard to semination within the vagina. Granted that the testimony regarding these points is confused, the fact remains that the question to be determined by the tribunal is not the question of penetration or of semination but, rather, the qualitative content of the ejaculate, granted that some semination did take place. In other words, we are concerned here with a matter that is strictly medical, namely, whether the man was capable of producing true semen. In view of this fact, and in accordance with Canon 1975; 1, as referred to above, it is the judgment of this tribunal that the testimony of witnesses *septimae manus* may be dispensed with.

In 1929, 1930, and again in the year 1935, Robert Jackson underwent operations at the Edith Cavell Clinic in Brussels, Belgium. These operations were made necessary by reason of the fact that Robert Jackson suffered from inguinal hernias on both the right and the left side. In the report from Doctor Lopatniko, who performed the operations in 1930 and 1935, it was noted that on both sides there was an ectopic testicle. As a result of these operations, the right testicle was removed as well as also part of the left testicle. According to the testimony of the respondent, as a result of these operations he was very slow in developing the male characteristics. Accordingly, his father made arrangements for the boy to begin treatment with a doctor in South America, where he was then living. That treatment, which consisted in the administration of hormones to stimulate the male characteristics, has continued throughout his life with various doctors in the cities in which he happened to be living.

As noted in the Acts, Doctor John Eagleson and Doctor E. Dymond, whose care the respondent sought while living in Florida, failed to honor the request of the tribunal for information regarding the respondent. In 1956, three years after the marriage and after he had moved to New York, Robert Jackson consulted Doctor Edmund Pink, a specialist in endocrinology. In his testimony Doctor Pink stated that, upon examination, he found the left testicle of the respondent was missing and that there was present "a remnant of a right testicle or an atrophied testicle." He stated as his opinion that the remnant of the right testicle was not a functioning organ, and he based this opinion on the history, the size of the genital organs, and the size of the tissue on the right side of the scrotum which could be palpated.

In 1957 Robert Jackson consulted another endocrinologist, Doctor Harry E. Kaufmann. He continued under Doctor Kaufmann's care for some eight months. Upon examination, it was learned that the respondent lacked a left testicle entirely and had but a pea-sized remnant of a right testicle. A diagnosis of hypogonadism, secondary to testicular tissue loss, as well as impotence, secondary to hypogonadism and feelings of inadequacy, was rendered. In his formal deposition Doctor Kaufmann stated that he presumes, from the absence in his notes of any mention of sensitivity, that there was no sensitivity in the remnant of the right testicle. Doctor Pink continued hormonal treatment of the man and, as a result, was informed by him that on three occasions during the period of treatment he had succeeded in ejaculating during attempts in having intercourse with his wife. We might note, in passing, how consistent this is with the statement of the plaintiff regarding successful attempts at intercourse on some three occasions during this period. Doctor Pink states as his opinion that, even though the man succeeded in ejaculating, it could not have been testicular fluid of any kind that was ejaculated.

In the year 1961, Robert Jackson began treatment with Doctor James Nicholson. The medical report and testimony of Doctor Nicholson are in substantial agreement with that of the other two physicians whose testimony has been considered. In addition, Doctor Nicholson obtained from the respondent a detailed history, including the one attempt at intercourse prior to the marriage which ended in failure. It is true that, contrary to the other doctors and to the medical experts, Doctor Nicholson stated he was unable to palpate any testicular tissue on either side but, in the opinion of this tribunal, this statement does not constitute any serious problem, and especially is this so because Doctor Nicholson is an endocrinologist and would not be as concerned about this point as would a specialist in urology.

The respondent was examined during the course of the trial by two duly appointed medical experts—Doctor James H. Garvey and Doctor Philip F. Holly. While minor discrepancies may appear in the reports of these physicians, such discrepancies are of a minor nature and do not in anywise represent a difference of opinion between the experts. Both doctors are in agreement that the man lacks an entire left testicle; both are in agreement that there remains a small portion of testicular tissue on the right side; both are in agreement that this mass can in nowise be considered a functioning testicle. When confronted with the canonical concept of potency, as noted above, both agreed that they would have to consider the man impotent. It is true that Doctor Garvey refers to the necessity of a chemical analysis to determine, with absolute certitude, whether or not the man is capable of producing any testicular fluid, but it is clear that in this matter the doctor was more concerned with physical certitude than with moral certitude. Both physicians have stated as their opinion that the respondent is impotent, and in this conclusion they are morally and medically certain. Doctor Holly raised the further point that even were the remnant capable of producing testicular fluid, the fluid could never pass into the ejaculate because of the minute quality of the spermatic chord. While Doctor Garvey stated that he could not be certain of the statement made by Doctor Holly, he gave as his opinion that the chord was definitely abnormal in structure. Finally, both doctors stated as their opinion that this condition antedated the marriage and was the result of surgery during childhood; that the condition was permanent, and that hormonal treatment could never stimulate the production of testicular fluid in this man. Concerning the latter point, both doctors are in complete agreement with the endocrinologists who have treated the respondent over a long period of time.

Summing up, the findings of the two experts are fully supported by the statements of Doctor Kaufmann and Doctor Nicholson, as well as by the history of the respondent's lifelong difficulties in sexual development, especially his failure to attain a normal state of puberty, at least up to the age of eighteen, and his admitted ineptness in engaging in normal marital relations. In view of all these facts, both in law and in fact, it is the opinion of this Tribunal that the evidence in this case provides full and sufficient proof that the respondent in this case was physically impotent because of his demonstrated inability to manufacture true male seed and that, therefore, this marriage is and should be declared invalid.

Wherefore, having thoroughly examined all of these matters, both as regards the law and the facts, and invoking the Name of Christ, we, the undersigned Judges, sitting as a court of first instance and having only God before our eyes, declare, decreé, and define, in answer to the issue proposed for solution to-day (viz., *"Has the nullity of this marriage been certainly proved?"*), in the *affirmative;* that is to say, the *nullity of the marriage in question has been certainly proved.*

We further *decree* that this definitive sentence be *published* according to the second method prescribed by canon 1877.

Given at the Hall of the Tribunal, this 29th day of April, 1966.

CANON 1068 (T.R.)
IMPOTENCY
No. 66/Samson vs. Costello

The Facts

Kathleen Samson, the petitioner, contracted marriage with Harry Costello on July 6, 1959, in St. John the Baptist Church, before the Rev. John F. Smith, pastor. This marriage was entered into even though the respondent had doubts about his ability to perform the marital act. Upon the advice of the Rev. George Bardin, Harry Costello submitted to a physical examination. The physician, Doctor James Burns, stated after examination that he found no impediment to marriage.

The parties maintained common life during a period of six months and in spite or repeated efforts during this time Harry Costello was never able to maintain a sufficient erection of his penis to penetrate the vagina of his wife. The respondent consulted two doctors who attempted to stimulate his sexual activity with medicine but to no avail. Finally the petitioner was hospitalized due to the extreme nervous tension caused by this abnormal situation, and was allowed by this tribunal to live apart from her husband.

On February 28, 1960, Kathleen Samson requested that the Tribunal declare the nullity of her marriage to Harry Costello on the grounds that the latter was impotent. On March 3, 1960, the judges declared themselves competent, being the place of the contract of the contested marriage, and accepted the libellus of Kathleen Samson. The following doubt was formulated on March 12, 1960: "Is the nullity of the marriage proved on the grounds of impotence?"

Divorce proceedings have not yet been initiated, but this problem is expected to be solved in the not too distant future.

The Law

The Code in Canon 1068; 1, states: "Impotence, antecedent and perpetual, whether on the part of the man or the woman, whether known to the other party or not, whether absolute or relative, invalidates marriage by the law of nature itself."

Thus, while the Code speaks clearly of the impediment of impotence, it says nothing of the concept of impotence itself. The meaning "impotence" must be obtained from the writings of recognized authors, rotal decisions, etc.

It is admitted by all authorities that the incapacity to perform the act of sexual intercourse by which marriage is consummated constitutes the *"impotentia"* of Canon 1068; 1. True enough, the act of intercourse is not, of itself, of the essence of marriage, it is of its essence that each party give the other a body capable of performing that act (cf. Gerard Sheehy, *Male Psychical Impotence in Judicial Proceedings,* The Jurist XX, 1960).

It is also equally agreed upon by all the authorities and is consistently reiterated in the jurisprudence of the rota that, on the part of the male partner in the contract, and we are concerned only with the male partner in the case at hand, the act of intercourse by which marriage is consummated consists of three essential elements, namely, natural erection of the penis, penetration of the penis into the female vagina, and the emission therein of true human semen (cf. *S.R.R. Dec.,* XXIII, 1931, 132-133).

It stands to reason that the inability to carry out all, or any one, of these constitutent elements of the conjugal act is what constitutes the *"impotentia coeundi"* referred to in canon 1068; 1 (cf. *S.R.R. Dec.,* XXIV, 1932, 125). We need not here elaborate on the nature of true human semen. It has been shown, for the purposes of the present case, that true impotency exists if the man is incapable of either erection or penetration.

This incapacity of performing the marriage act can be caused either by the absence of, or by some anatomical defect in the genital organs themselves, and this is called organic impotence (*S.R.R. Dec.,* XXV, 1933, 206). Or again, given the case of apparently normal genitals, the impotency may result from a wide variety of factors which control or influence the function and activity of the sexual apparatus. (*S.R.R.,* 1930, 341).

This functional impotence can be caused by a number of factors: (1) organic defect or abnormality in some other part of the body, as for example, a damaged spine; (2) physiological defect, as for example, the malfunctioning of the endocrine glands, such as the thyroid; (3) psychical defect, which arises from the purely mental or psychological make-up of the individual in question (Cf. Sheehy, *op. cit.,* The Jurist XX, 1960, p. 258). For the present we need only consider the third cause, psychical deficiency which is of course admitted by the rota.

While it is not always easy to determine the specific cause of psychic impotence, medical authorities are nevertheless certain that purely psychical deficiencies can render the man unable to perform the conjugal act. "It involves the whole personality of the individual. Even when considered as a purely physiological fact, it is not a simple operation: it requires the harmonious co-operation of many organs and functions. But it is very much more than that. It is indeed a mental process and it is linked essentially to the psychical constitution of the individual" (Sheehy, *op. cit.,* The Jurist XX, 1960, p. 61; Van Duin, *De impedimento impotentiae psychicali in iuri canonico,"* Apollinanis, XXIII, 1950, 124-144). That is why, in cases of this nature, the help of an expert psychiatrist is needed, and why his judgment must be accorded a very important role.

It would be impossible here to discuss all the possible causes that lead to impotency. We are dealing here with one individual and are trying to determine whether or not the respondent is truly impotent. Suffice it to say that medical experts point to three characteristic features of psychic impotence, namely: (1) deficiency in sexual desire (libido); (2) defective erection of the penis; and (3) deficiency or abnormality in the emission of semen.

Thus far we have elaborated on the concept of impotence, namely the inability, not merely the difficulty, of sexual intercourse. A man is certainly impotent if he is unable to have sexual intercourse either with one particular woman (relative impotence) or with all women (absolute impotence).

Now, this impotence becomes a diriment impediment to marriage only if it is antecedent to the marriage and is incurable.

1. The impotence must be antecedent. Any factor which supervenes after the marriage but which did not exist at the time of the contract, cannot affect the validity of the marriage.

2. The impotence must be perpetual. This means that the malady need not be absolutely incurable, but that it cannot be cured by lawful means which do not involve a probable danger to life: *"qui per opus humanum licitum et honestum, absque mortis periculo, nequet removeri" (S.R.R. Dec.,* XVII, 1935, 42). It must be noted, of course, that the perpetual nature of the impotence must have been verified at the time of the marriage. If, for any reason, the malady is incurable at the time of the proceedings, but was curable at the time of the marriage, the impotence is not perpetual in the canonical sense and the impediment of impotence does not exist.

The perpetual nature of the malady is the most difficult point in the proceedings in cases of psychical impotence. Some authors even venture to say that the non-curability of such impotence may never, or scarcely ever, be proved (cf. Cappello, *De Matrimonio,* no. 346, p. 357; Coronata, *De Matrimonio,* no. 309, pp. 388-389). These generalities merely stress the difficulty of proof. The question to be solved is this, has the non-curability been proved in this particular case?

In fact the rota has rendered affirmative decisions in cases of this kind. This tribunal has made some relevant observations concerning relative impotence. While this condition could theoretically improve, it often becomes worse with the passing of time. If marital relations are impossible at first, very often coldness, rejection and finally, hatred will develop *(S.R.R. Dec.,* XXXIII, 1941, 901).

Formerly, the "triennial experiment" was considered necessary before concluding in favor of the incurability of psychic impotence. In recent years, however, advances in the science of medicine and psychiatry have enabled experts to reach a far greater degree of certainty in their opinions, so much so that the rota seems quite satisfied to accept their reasoned verdicts on the point (*Il Duitto Ecclesiastico, LXV, 1954, 127).*

True, the rota does occasionally refer to the "triennial experiment" but we fail to see that this period of three years is necessary for proof (S. R. R. Dec., XXXVI, 1944, 723).

The triennial experiment was sufficient years ago when medical science was less developed. Today, as shown above, the rota considers as sufficient proof of perpetuity the considered opinion of medical experts.

It must be borne in mind that moral certitude of the existence of the impediment is sufficient for a declaration of nullity. In cases of psychic impotence absolute certitude is simply impossible to obtain.

The Argument

The evidence this case brings out the following: that the Samson-Costello marriage was not consummated because of Harry Costello's inability to maintain a sufficient erection, that this impotence on the part of the man existed at the time of the marriage and that this condition was incurable at the time of the marriage.

1. Fact of Impotence:

Both the petitioner and the respondent state in unequivocal terms that there was never any penetration of Mr. Costello's penis into his wife's vagina, and that, in spite of repeated efforts on the part of the man.

Thus the petitioner states: "I know that he did not penetrate at all, because he could not have a strong enough erection of his penis to enter."

This inability perdured during all the time the spouses maintained common life. Kathleen Samson was asked if her husband was ever able to get an erection. She replied as follows: "No, he could not . . . sometimes he became erect to a certain degree and he thought he might be able to penetrate but I knew or thought that he couldn't, but I let him try anyway: but it never became erect enough to penetrate."

The respondent admits candidly that he was never successful at completing the marriage act: "No, nothing worked. My wife thought I was nervous or something like that; she told me that perhaps another night it could work, maybe I would get used to it, maybe I would not be so nervous. She tried, she caressed me to try to provoke an erection, and I caressed her a little bit too, but nothing worked."

This condition did not improve. Never was Harry Costello able to maintain a sufficient erection: "Well, once it (the penis) became rigid, and we tried to have intercourse, but it was not rigid enough, the erection did not last, the penis became soft right away. . . . That happened once, *perhaps* twice, not often."

Such were the statements of the principals. Kathleen Samson submitted to an examination by two competent and trustworthy gynecologists at Mercy Hospital, on March 12, 1960. The findings of the experts were not conclusive. Doctor Charles Skillin wrote: "From examination the marriage may have been consummated but it is my opinion that this is rather doubtful."

In other words, the physical examination neither proves nor disproves the allegations of the parties. The moral argument, however, is of the highest order in this case, and that is sufficient to bring about moral certitude. The Holy Office stated on June 12, 1942, that the physical argument was not always necessary to establish satisfactory proof (A. A. S. XXXIV, 1942, 201).

The trustworthiness of the principals is so evident that the defender of the bond is himself convinced of it. All the character witnesses speak of the excellent moral qualities, veracity and probity of the principals.

Father Bardin's words may be used to summarize the worthiness of the parties: "There is no doubt in my mind about their sincerity and trustworthiness in these matters which are related to their marriage case. . . . I can say that everything they said and did in regards to this marriage case was sincere and trustworthy. At least, that is my opinion after dealing with them and basing myself on their religious convictions."

The worthiness of the principals is enhanced by the fact that the spouses had no reason to separate, impotence excepted. Thus, there was no other cause of friction in the mind of the petitioner. The respondent also stated that there was no other reason for the separation.

2. The Impotence is Antecedent to the Marriage:

This point also is quite clear. Harry Costello had doubts, before the marriage, about his virility, and consulted Doctor Jean Bolduc on October 29, 1958, some eight months before the nuptial ceremony. The respondent returned to see Doctor Burns on Oct. 12, 1959, (less than six weeks after the nuptial ceremony), and again on Oct. 28, 1959. Later on the respondent consulted another medical man, Doctor B. M. Begin. These consultations took place on Nov. 20, 1959, Jan. 22, 1960, and Feb. 3, 1960.

Furthermore all the physicians who treated Harry Costello are of the opinion that the impotence of Harry Costello is antecedent to the marriage—Dr. David, Dr. B.M. Begin, Dr. Kirk Patrick, Dr. James Burns.

3. The Impotence is Perpetual or Incurable:

This is above all a medical problem, and the judges must rely to a great extent on the reasoned opinions of experts.

Doctor B. M. Begin who treated Harry Costello reported as follows: "It is my impression that Mr. Costello has psychogenic impotence of a degree that intensive psychotherapy would not be beneficial. There appears to be a lack of sufficient incentives or motivations to change his sexual attitude." On June 20, 1960, Dr. Begin testified thus: "It is my belief that the patient has a true, antecedent incapacity to consummate the marriage. On the basis of the past experience and the findings as of present, it is reasonable, logical and rational to expect this condition to be permanent."

Dr. Kirk Patrick, expert in psychiatry, gave the following in his report: "his heterosexual strivings are extremely weak *and are not likely* to be modified by any drug or other treatment known. His basic sexual orientation, emotionally speaking, is poorly oriented with regard to either sex."

This view was confirmed by Dr. Kirk Patrick in his deposition of June 21, 1960: "It is extremely doubtful that any treatment known today would be effective. . . . This kind of condition starts in childhood and is usually confirmed by the age of twenty. This was realized in his case."

Dr. Burns is of the same opinion: "Not being a qualified psychiatrist, I cannot tell whether the impotency is permanent but as a physician I feel that this impotency is permanent." Only Dr. David, of all those who examined Harry Costello, refuses to express an opinion: "I believe the condition is true and was antecedent. I honestly don't know if it is permanent." Dr. David's stand is quite understandable. He knows that an expert in psychiatry had examined Mr. Costello. He simply does not wish to commit himself in a field where he is not considered an expert.

Wherefore, having thoroughly examined the law and the facts pertaining to this case, and invoking the name of Christ, we, the undersigned judges sitting as a tribunal of first instance and having only God before our eyes find that Harry Costello was truly impotent on July 6, 1959, the date of the marriage to Kathleen Samson, the impotence being due to psychic factors, and that this impotence was incurable on and after the date of the marriage. We, therefore, declare, define and decree, in answer to the proposed doubt: *"Whether the nullity of the marriage in this case has been proved on account of the impediment of impotency?"* in the *affirmative,* or the *nullity of the marriage in question has been proved.*

Given at the Tribunal, December 4, 1961.

Case #9

CANON 1013 (M.J.)
IMPOTENCY
No. 60/Sharon vs. Jack

The Facts:

tSharon, a Catholic, residing in the Diocese of——petitioned the Tribunal to annul her marriage to Jack, a Catholic. She first entered a civil marriage with Jack, a Catholic, on May 7, 1958, in Seekonk, Massachusetts, which was convalidated on November 28, 1959. During the time the couple lived together, marital relations were not able to take place because of the physical inability of Jack Ball. The couple knew of this inability but were hoping that it would remedy itself in time. However, it became evident that this did not and would not occur. When Sharon Bovard became sick and also labored under the strain of the abnormal situation, the couple mutually agreed to separate.

In view of the situation, Sharon petitioned the Tribunal of——to annul the marriage on the grounds of impotency existing prior to the marriage and permanently. The tribunal found itself competent by virtue of the domicile of the petitioner and after consultation with the Diocese of Providence which requested that the case be heard by——. Sharon acquired her domicile after a legal separation. The Tribunal of—— accepted the case.

The Law:

As is evident from canon 1068, antecendent and perpetual impotence, whether on the part of the male or female, whether known or not known by the other party, whether absolute or relative, of its very nature invalidates a marriage. Quite often impotence is described as the inability of the male or female to achieve perfect copulation, i.e., copulation which is in itself apt or capable of reproduction or the generation of offspring. It is important that impotence, if it is to be a diriment impediment, be antecedent and perpetual. Whether it is absolute or relative, whether it is the result of nature or some human act, it is not ad rem. Impotence is said to be perpetual if it cannot be remedied licitly without endangering the life of the subject. Subsequent impotence, i.e., which occurs after the marriage, even though it be perpetual, does not affect the validity of the marriage. Neither does impotence which, though antecedent (to the marriage), can be remedied. This is so because in order to contract a valid marriage it is not required that the parties be actually (here and now) fit or prepared for consummation by perfect copulation; it suffices that they enjoy "habitual fitness," i.e., their temporary impotence is able to be remedied either by itself (in time) or by some legitimate operation.

Well do Wernz-Vidal reason when they write: "Four elements are required and suffice for true copulation: (1) Ejection of male semen. If this is not present, even though penetration of the vagina occurs, true copulation has not taken place. However, given the natural connection between physical sexual union and the ejection of semen, the latter is always presumed given the former, and thus in the external forum the presumption is that physiological and juridical copulation has taken place. This presumption, which can be removed only by the most persuasive arguments, is of the greatest importance in cases concerning nonconsummation. Such an argument would be had when it could be shown that there was absolutely no communication between the penis and testicles. (2) The ejection must be an ejection of true semen, whether it be sterile or not, and not some other fluid which can be produced even by those who have been castrated. An absolute lack of communication between the penis and the vasa deferentia or testicles, even though these latter organs be functioning properly in themselves, would render impossible the ejection of true semen. (3) The semen must be ejected into the female vagina, since it is the organ naturally made for receiving it. In a case where semen cannot be ejected into the vagina, impotence is present, since copulation cannot be effected. (4) The semen must be received in the vagina in the natural way, i.e., by erection of the male member and its penetration into the vagina. Thus, perfect conjugal copulation is had by the ejection of semen from the male member into the vagina. For this, on the part of the male three things are required and suffice: 1. A penis capable of erection. 2. At least one testicle capable of producing true semen. 3. Communication between the penis and testicle. On the part of the female the only requirement is a vagina which is capable absolutely and relatively of penetration by the male member." (Wernz-Vidal, *Jus Canon* V, De Matr., no. 217, p. 240. Allers, *"Some Medico-Psychological Remarks on Canons 1068, 1081, and 1087."* The Jurist, IV, (1944), 351-380. Wernz-Vidal, *Jus Canon*, V, no. 218, pp. 242, 243).

The Argument:

Both of the principals in this case narrate essentially the same story. They state that they met each other at the Massachusetts General Hospital. Jack, at that time, was a patient at the hospital because of an injury he received when he was thrown from a horse. The petitioner also about this time became a patient. Both admit that, at this time, the defendant was a paraplegic. However, despite his handicap, they kept company for a number of years and finally attempted a civil marriage on May 7, 1958. The marriage took place thus because of the parental opposition of Sharon's parents. Her father is a doctor and recognized the difficulty in marrying a paraplegic.

The evidence indicates that the couple did talk with Dr. Lead before this civil marriage and inquired if the injury of the defendant would prevent normal marital relations.

According to the defendant, he received some assurance from Dr. Lead that he could lead a normal married life. This evidently was due to the fact that, after the first operation on the defendant in 1954, he had first lost his sexual powers and then they seemed to revive until he was able to have an erection and some ejaculation.

The couple lived together after the civil union between March 7, 1958, and November 28, 1959, only with the hope that their relationship could become completely normal. However, each time marital relations were attempted, they were unsuccessful because the defendant was not able to maintain an erection. It was the defendant's belief, according to his testimony, that his difficulty possibly was psychological rather than organic. At least he seems to have so interpreted Dr. Leadbetter's remarks. Despite the unsuccessful attempts during their time together after the civil marriage, the couple finally validated the marriage in November of 1959. According to each one in their testimony, they still entertained hope that the sexual powers of Jack would be eventually normal.

However, both testified that all subsequent attempts also after 1959 were completely in vain. Relations were attempted and, on a few occasions, the best the defendant was able to do was to have an erection which immediately subsided when he attempted to enter the vagina. Most of the time, he was not able to do even this. Thus, because of his inability, the marriage was never consummated. Finally, when the petitioner became ill coupled with the abnormal strain of the marriage, they finally separated.

It is quite obvious to the tribunal that any definitive opinion about the nature and results of the injury to the defendant would have to be a medical one. The statements submitted by Dr. Lead, a nationally known authority in the treatment of paraplegics, describes the various operations to which the defendant was subjected because of his injuries. From these, it is evident that, due to the spasm of the defendant's legs, surgery was necessary. Dr. Sweet performed operations on the spine of the defendant for relief. However, after another operation, during May of 1957, was performed to relieve a continuing difficulty which the patient had with spasms of his legs, it was noted that the operation had affected the sexual powers of the defendant. From this time on, he was not able to have an erection either spontaneously or by stimulation. Dr. Lead notes that the result was regrettable but necessary to perform because of the defendant's condition. The results are irreversible and the sexual power of the defendant is permanently impaired.

The defendant himself stated in answer to the question "Were you able to effuse any seed in the vagina of Sharon Bovard?" and he said, "No. About one and one-half years or two years before we were married, ejaculations ceased and I have never had them again." Thus, before 1959, the defendant confesses that he had lost the power to ejaculate. Although, after November of 1959, he did have some power for a little while to have an erection sufficient enough for an attempt at partial penetration but no emission. As he states, "I did not have complete intercourse. I think I entered her body with a partial penetration. The erection subsided almost immediately and no emission."

Dr. Robert, an expert in Urology, was asked to evaluate the medical statements made by Dr. Lead and also evaluate the testimony given by the principals.

Dr. Robert's testimony indicates that the operation on May 21, 1957, called a "Laminectomy at L1-L2 level" was the operation which affected the erectile powers of the defendant. Dr. Robert stated, "The centers for penile erection are in the sacral segments of the cord and most think that the nerves rise from the sacral 2, 3, 4 segments. Dr. Sweet must think that Sacral 1 was concerned with erectile function since he made an attempt not to sever this nerve. The lowermost rootlet of sacral spinal nerves were left intact trying to save most of S1. That is why he stopped the operation in that area trying to preserve erectile function." Dr. Robert further testifies that, "Whatever power he (that is, the defendant) had was completely impaired by Dr. Sweet's operation." In Dr. Robert's opinion, whatever power he may have had was impaired after the operation by Dr. Sweet. In his opinion, the only thing that the defendant could have, as a result of his injury and operations, was the desire to perform the marital act but, in his opinion, he had lost his complete capacity. He states that the defendant cannot have an erection, for the penis if flaccid and he had lost this ability completely. Furthermore, he stated that the results of the operation are permanent. He agreed completely with the opinion and report of Dr. Lead.

The tribunal could draw no other conclusion from the evidence submitted by the medical men than that, from May of 1957, it is certain the defendant had lost the ability to perform a natural marital act.

Dr. B., the father of the plaintiff, testified. He stated that he was opposed to the marriage because he realized that a paraplegic offered great problems as far as a normal marriage was concerned. Because the couple knew of his opposition to the marriage, they attempted it without his consent. After their union, he made no attempt to pry into the situation but he was told by his daughter that the marriage had not been consummated. She told him that they had not been able to consummate the marriage because Jack was impotent. He said, "She told me there was never any sexual intercourse. She said that he was impotent and was unable to perform the sexual act."

There was no doubt in the mind of the tribunal that the oral testimony and the medical testimony indicate that the defendant was permanently injured and that the operations performed on him destroyed whatever little power that he may have retained after his first injury. To be considered potent, it is necessary for the male to have the ability to have an erection, maintain it, and effuse seed. It is obvious, from the testimony in this case, that the defendant did not have these capacities; thus, impotency existed prior to his marriage and is permanent.

In view of the evidence and taking into consideration all that must be considered, we, the undersigned judges, rule: *The nullity of the marriage is proved.*

Case #10

CANON 1069 (T.R.)
PREVIOUS BOND (Ligamen)
No. 15/Martha vs. John

Martha, an unbaptized woman, married John, also non-baptized, in 1941. A few years later, both joined the Lutheran Church and were baptized. In 1963 they sought to become Catholics, but were prevented from doing so because of a previous marriage of John to Louise, which had taken place in 1937. There was some doubt concerning the validity of John's first marriage. Accordingly, John sought a Document of Liberty from the Holy Office on the basis of this doubt, and on the absence of baptism at the time of the marriage. The Holy Office granted this document in 1964.

Meanwhile, Martha had separated from John because of his mental condition. In 1965 she asked that her union with him be declared invalid because of his first marriage with Louise. Because a genuine doubt concerning the validity of the first marriage had been raised, the Presiding Judge requested a formal trial in order to determine whether the subsequent marriage could be adjudged invalid. The case was therefore remanded to a collegiate Tribunal.

Canon 1069 states that "they attempt marriage invalidly who are bound by the bond of a prior marriage." In such a case as this, there arises an uncertainty concerning Canon 1014. For many years there has been uncertainty concerning the interpretation of this canon in cases where more than one marriage is in question. Which marriage enjoys the favor of law?

The Commission for the Authentic Interpretation of the Code, in a decree of June 26, 1947, stated that it is the prior marriage which has the presumption of validity. Consequently, only when such a marriage is proved to be invalid should the later marriage be judged valid. Therefore, as long as any serious probability of the prior marriage's validity remains, the subsequent marriage must be declared invalid.

In the present case, there are several possible sources of invalidity of John's first marriage: force and fear, exclusion of permanence, total simulation.

John himself, when he testified, was quite certain that his union with Louise was invalid. He said that he married under threat of jail, that he and Louise had not intended to live together, that hardly anyone knew of the marriage, and that he and Louise did not in fact live together at all. His mother confirmed that John was forced to marry because Louise's pregnancy was attributed to him, that they did not live together but parted immediately after the ceremony, and that they had not intended a lasting marriage. Both John's brother and sister corroborated these statements.

For the most part, Louise confirmed these accounts. She said that John was unwilling to marry her, and that it was a "shot-gun" marriage because she was pregnant. Louise also stated that they never lived together because John was unwilling to live with her.

Louise's mother agreed with the others that they "had to get married." She herself went to the lawyer, who put pressure on John to marry. She did not know what this lawyer told John nor what was in John's mind, since she never talked to him about this, even at the wedding. She confirmed the fact that the young people never lived together because John never returned with Louise after the wedding.

It was not certain that the marriage was invalid because of force and fear. First, John was not baptized at that time, and there is doubt that the impediment would apply to him by virtue of Louise's baptism. Secondly, there was no convincing evidence that it was the pressure brought to bear upon him by Louise's mother and the lawyer that induced him to marry. No evidence supported the belief that John offered resistance to the importunities of the lawyer. As far as the evidence is concerned, it could just as well have been John's sense of duty that led him to marry Louise.

Was the marriage invalid because of a defective intention with regard to the exclusion of marriage itself or of permanence? John seemed to say so, stating that he and Louise never intended to live together. This statement is denied at least in part by the testimony of Louise and her mother. Louise said she wanted to live with John, and her mother said that Louise hoped that John would live with her. Moreover, Louise's mother stated that John's mother would not let him live with Louise, thus raising a doubt about his reluctance. Louise said that there was an engagement for two months, and her mother expressed the belief that John was in love with her daughter. All these circumstances cast doubt upon John's assertion that he married with no intention of cohabiting with Louise.

If the marriage of John and Louise were in question here, should the decision be that it was invalid? Surely there is sufficient evidence to raise a serious doubt concerning its validity both on the score of undue pressure and concerning the exclusion of a permanent indissoluble union. This evidence is not compelling, however, and there does not appear to be any possibility of resolving the doubt. The only witnesses who knew anything of the circumstances of this marriage have testified, but the uncertainty remains. The strongest testimony favoring its invalidity is that of John himself, and his situation was such as to cause him to see most clearly all that militated against the validity of his first marriage, and to be forgetful of anything pointing in the other direction.

Thus the Court of First Instance upheld the validity of the first marriage and declared John's union with Mary invalid on the grounds of a previously existing bond. The Defender of the Bond properly appealed the case.

The Court of Second Instance interviewed the mother and sister of John a second time. However, no significant additional evidence was obtained.

The Court of Second Instance concludes:

> While admitting the possibility and even probability that the marriage
> was not a valid one, the question here is whether there remains a positive

and insoluble doubt about the validity of the marriage. If so, we must declare the second marriage invalid and presume the validity of the first marriage.

Since we do find positive and insoluble doubt remaining about the validity of the first marriage, we must declare and judge the second marriage invalid from the beginning by reason of the existing bond of the prior marriage.

DECISION: FIRST INSTANCE—AFFIRMATIVE.
SECOND INSTANCE—AFFIRMATIVE

CANON 1081
DEFECTIVE CONSENT
No. 23/Stanley vs. Stella

These two Catholics entered marriage in the depths of the economic depression in 1935. Within two years the marriage collapsed irretrievably when Stella was caught in infidelity: there had been reports from neighbors earlier that she was entertaining other men but Stanley could not bring himself to believe them. Later both parties attempted marriage civilly with other partners and these second unions survived over these many years. In 1975 the Tribunal accepted Stanley's petition which claimed the nullity of this marriage on the grounds that the Respondent Stella's consent in the wedding ceremony was inadequate to constitute the unique reality known as Christian marriage.

The Judge's sentence cited the jurisprudence reported in an English decision in 1973, in a case which involved a question of lack of due discretion (in the sense of an inability to fulfill the essential obligations of the marriage covenant) besides the question of inadequacy of consent. After quoting the texts of Canons 1081; 2, and 1086; 2, the law section of the sentence reads:

> "Unlike the heading of Lack of Due Discretion, we are here concerned with consent—a consent which, although sufficient in itself, is so necessary that while in a civil contract the absence of consent may sometimes, for certain reasons, be supplied by law, no human power can do this in the case of marriage (cf. Canon 1081; 1). If, therefore, consent is lacking, or is in some way intrinsically limited, there is no marriage. As the Canon quoted above lays down, matrimonial consent is an act of the will, and while it is presumed that 'the consent that has been externally manifested corresponds to the internal disposition of the will of each of the contracting parties' (Canon 1086; 1), it is always possible for a person to vitiate his consent by simulation. This simulation, which in a case of nullity must always be proved, can either be total in that a person excludes marriage itself, or it can be partial, in that a person has a positive intention to marry but excludes one or more of the essential properties of marriage, viz. children, fidelity or indissolubility."

> "Matrimonial consent can also fail owing to its inadequacy. What is

required on the part of the contracting parties is a human act—an act of the will, but an enlightened will, committed to and conscious of what is involved in the way of permanency, obligation and responsibility. Here again, as with simulation, it is possible to go through all the motions of giving consent—words, actions signs—and yet, because of some attitude of mind, or because of the reason for marriage or the circumstances surrounding the marriage, be totally inadequate to fulfill the requirements of a valid contract of marriage."

"In reference to what it calls the 'conjugal pact' the document *Gaudium et Spes* speaks of the 'intimate community of life and love,' and goes on to mention the permanent mutual help and service which the partners render each other in 'an intimate linking of their persons and activities.' What is created, therefore, by true matrimonial consent is essentially a relationship between the parties *as persons* in a permanent union, and it is precisely in the failure to understand what this relationship involves that we can speak of inadequate consent in the sense of a lack of commitment to marriage. Matrimonial consent, therefore to be adequate, requires that the contracting parties fully commit themselves to a lifelong partnership in a community of married life and love with all its responsibilities and obligations." (*MDEW,* VIII, pp. 389-392)

The Court noted that the Stanley-Stella marriage took place during the great depression and that these were indeed "hard times." Stella had to drop out of high school in her second year and go to work. Stanley lost his job and could not find employment. But other young married people, contemporaries of Stanley and Stella, faced the same economic hardships, yet their marriages survived. Indeed, the Court noted, most of them, facing hard times equal to those experienced by Stanley and Stella, found that the sharing of these hardships brought them closer together as husband and wife and strengthened their family life. Why did this not happen in the case of Stanley and Stella? The Court found that the unfortunate, disturbing quality of Stella's home environment during her adolescence made her inordinately anxious to say goodbye to her parental home. The depression became a factor because jobs were almost non-existent and what employment was available paid very small salaries, and she could not alone be financially independent. Marriage in effect became Stella's only usable exit from home, the only escape into what she hoped would be a better life, and Stanley happened to be on the spot as the quickest ticket to independence. The Court saw these circumstances working to curtail her freedom in the selection of a life-partner and to invite her to a less than wholehearted commitment to the partner selected under this kind of duress.

The Petitioner and the Respondent were the only source of evidence available to the Court and after forty years, during which there was some deliberate suppression of the painful memories of this broken marriage, they were unable to recapture in detail their youthful attitudes, intentions and motivations, so the Court had to put aside any kind of clinical approach to this case. But both parties came to the witness stand extremely well-recommended for their honesty and probity and for their spiritual motivation in seeking to regularize their public status in the Church now in their senior years.

According to Stanley, Stella had a very unhappy childhood: her parents did not care for her and she was left to go her own way. At age sixteen she left her parents' home and was taken in by Stanley's parents. He reports that Stella had an undesirable reputation for sexual promiscuity at the time. Despite this, he offered marriage to her which she accepted because there was "no other way out for her" on any kind of long-range basis. During the two years of their brief marriage his neighbors gave him evidences of Stella's infidelity with at least one man. She denied this, and he did not want to believe it. But at the end he returned home unexpectedly after a short vacation with his relatives and found her absent from home. This verified his suspicions; there was a heated argument and Stella stomped out to return to the unpleasantness of her parental home. She spurned all attempts at reconciliation.

The Respondent Stella admitted that she has purposely closed her mind to almost everything that happened to her up to the age of twenty, her age at the time of her separation from Stanley. "All I am able to remember," she declares, "is how miserable I was at home and how I thought being married would get me away from the misery and bring some meaning to life for me." Her real mother died when she was five years old and her father remarried. Her stepmother turned out to be a rough, tough woman who gambled, had a filthy mind, showed no affection to the children, made them toe the line and even told lies about them so their father would punish them when he came home. Stella spent almost a year in an orphanage because she could not get along with her discipline-minded stepmother. At home her life was prolonged drudgery—cleaning house, washing clothes, going to school. There was no normal model of marriage visible in the relationship between her father and her stepmother. So she had no way to comprehend what marriage really involved; to her marriage was a means of getting away from her home and finding the affection which she craved but did not find from her parents.

Stella had left home and was staying with Stanley's parents when he proposed marriage, but this arrangement could only be temporary and his proposal presented a more permanent solution. She knew that Stanley was also immature and irresponsible but she thought marriage would be an improvement of her lot; and it was this primarily which made her marry at such a young age. "My feelings now," Stella concludes, "are that I was very young when this marriage occurred. Now I know that I was very immature because of my home life. I really didn't know what life was all about. I really didn't know how much there was to married life. I had hoped to make my married life completely opposite from my home life, but I found it was too difficult. The affection in general that I thought would come with marriage just didn't happen. Now I think I just didn't understand or learn to cope with it. After this experience my stepsister helped me very much. If I compare my experience as a married woman now with then, it is like night and day."

The Auditor who interviewed the Respondent was a parish priest experienced in doing field-advocacy work for the Tribunal. He recorded these observations of Stella: "She claims to have been very immature at the time of the marriage. She thought of it as something 'better than I had at home.' She really had no idea of what marriage was about; she didn't even know what the fulfillment of sexual life was. After taking her testimony I feel that she is telling the truth. I think she has been trying to forget a very unpleasant set of circumstances—her home life and subsequent marriage to the Petitioner—and this is why she cannot recall more. She may be unconsciously blocking things out. She was definitely too unstable to enter into a marriage at that time because of her home life. Marriage was a way out for her, not a stable union of husband and wife. She had no idea of what it was all about and her intention was more to escape than anything else."

Since the obtaining of proof in this case depended almost entirely on the judicial testimony of the two interested parties, the Court was naturally concerned about the probative value of this testimony. In his sentence the Judge cited the jurisprudence spelled out in another English decision in 1971:

> "Article 117 of the Instruction *Provida* says: 'Depositio iudicialis coniugum non est apta ad probationem contra valorem matrimonii constituendam.' This does not say that the evidence of the spouses cannot prove invalidity; it merely says *non est apta*. If the only item against the validity of the marriage is the evidence of the parties as written down, then there could be no question of declaring the invalidity. A Judge should always consider other factors and not accept merely the words of the parties as given on oath. For example, the story of the parties as a whole, has it a ring of truth about it? Is it something which is so incredible that a person of this particular standard of intelligence could never have fabricated? What is the person apt to gain by telling a lie on oath? Is the attitude and demeanor of the person when giving evidence such that he seems to be speaking the truth? When all these things are added together we have something which is no longer the bare words of evidence of the parties, and if corroborative indications from witnesses are present there is no reason why a Judge cannot be morally certain in a particular case. It is not impossible to have a successful case resting on the direct evidence of only one party when the other cannot be traced or refuses to give evidence—or even when the evidence is contradictory, provided that there are some clear indications that the Respondent is lying." (*MDEW*-1971, p. 105)

The Court was convinced that the circumstances of how this marriage was entered into and how it collapsed so quickly lent support to the Petitioner's allegation and the Respondent's confession. It concluded that the Respondent's consent was inadequate for a matrimonial contract because she simply did not comprehend the reality of Christian marriage and therefore could not commit herself to it.

DECISION: FIRST INSTANCE—AFFIRMATIVE.
DISPENSATION FROM APPEAL

CANON 1081
MENTAL ILLNESS—INABILITY TO ASSUME
OBLIGATIONS OF MARRIAGE
No. 53/Anne vs. Ronald

The Facts

Anne and Ronald were married in a Catholic Church in the province of Ontario in October of 1937. Their married life was unhappy because the husband on many occasions had to receive treatment in a hospital for the mentally ill. Their common life ended and the wife brought a suit before the Tribunal of Ottawa on January 19, 1963, claiming the marriage was invalid because of the insanity of her husband. A guardian was appointed and the judicial process followed until the court of first instance reached an affirmative decision on June 9, 1967. As required by law, the defender of the bond of the Ottawa tribunal appealed to our court on June 22, 1967. The guardian of the defendant remanded his cause to the justice of our tribunal. The joinder of the issues was held on October 7, 1967, and the doubt formulated in the usual manner: Whether or not the nullity of this marriage has been proven. Today we meet to solve this doubt.

The Law

Canon 1982 warns: Even in case of defect of consent because of insanity, the opinion of experts, who have seen the patient, if possible, and examined according to medical norms the acts which suggest insanity, is necessary; moreover, others who have previously seen the patient are to be heard as witnesses.

Certainly there are times when a mentally sick person is unable to give matrimonial consent because he is not in possession of his faculties. Such cases are not too difficult. But since marriage brings into existence serious obligations which are both perpetual and irrescindible, there is required in addition that the contracting party be able to assume such obligations. A person who is suffering from a mental illness which will progressively evolve to full insanity is incapable of undertaking such obligations, even though at the time of marriage he can give his consent with the requisite licidity and deliberation. In this vein we note the following remarks in a rotal decision of Mattioli on November 6, 1956:

Reason itself prohibits that these unfortunate victims be bound to these burdens which with licud intellect and full actual deliberation they may have undertaken, but which nevertheless they are incapable of fulfilling by the very nature of a mental disorder which has already begun and cannot but worsen.

Whence in matters of this kind the salient point of the question is not to be found in the state of mind of the contracting party when he offers his consent in the form required by law. For it can be conceded from the outset that generally there is no question of full thought about all those elements which are necessary there is no question of full thought about all those elements which are necessary or of the freedom of his will and its conscious determination, or even of his valid occupation in those tasks and duties by which he could support a family.

Rather, the matter to be sedulously investigated is whether or not at the time of marriage there are already certain signs of mental weakness. This is chiefly the task of the doctor. The point to be determined is this: Is the individual, because of mental illness, already incapable of fulfilling the obligations of marriage for his whole life. If so, he cannot assume these obligations even if he has the intention to do so.

The Argument

From the Acts, it is proven that the defendant actually did progress to the state of full *dementia,* in the juridical and medical sense, after the marriage. Dr. J. testified: "By his conduct I saw that the sickness evolved slowly and progressively. . . . In the spring of 1964, I examined Ronald at the request of Social Service for the purpose of his obtaining a pension. . . . The report which I made showed his inability to work (literally, to give 100 for 100)." Dr. L. who examined the hospital report affirmed: "Ronald's admission to the hospital was on December 2, 1941. The general paralysis from which he suffered showed he was in the tertiary phase of syphillis." The witnesses, from the facts they observed, described the mental disorder of the defendant immediately or almost immediately after the marriage. "My sister, Anne, has not spoken to me about what happened between them in the early days of marriage, and I have never asked her about the subject in order not to put her through pain. But my husband and I were aware that Ronald had not been interested in his wife (at that time we were living in the same house); *All this was in the month of November, 1937.* He was doing things 'like a child would'; for example, at that time we were heating the stove with wood and when my husband was going to pick up some wood in the cellar, Ronald told him to stop making holes in the cellar because that was not the place to do that. Another example: I remember that one day in the presence of guests, in the course of a family dinner, Ronald suddenly left the table to chase flies and ran after them until he caught them. This is evidently not normal. The conversation he would have with guests was not consistent; he was munching his words. He was going from one subject to another. He was saying desperate things that did not make sense. Things were going from bad to worse after the marriage. This started in the first months after our wedding." (Therese L., wife of Samuel S., who was married the same day as the plaintiff).

"I was aware of it the New Years' day at noon following the marriage, that is,

January 1, 1938, when we went to dine at the Lavelle house. Ronald locked himself in a room and cried all during the dinner instead of joining in with the others. We asked him what was the matter but we could never find out. At that time I did not think that this was a mental illness; it is only later that I became aware that it was probably mental illness. . . .About a couple of years after the marriage, he was in the police. When I learned that Ronald was doing strange things like chasing flies in the City Hall, that impressed me. I realized his mental state myself, soon after learning this news. *What he said no longer made any sense.* I realized that he was babbling and saying things that we could not understand" (Robert T.).

The same witness asserts: "I knew him since infancy. I lost tract of him around 1951. Before his marriage Ronald never, to my knowledge, gave signs of mental illness by either doing or saying anything which would cause suspicion of some sort of mental problem."

The relatives of the defendant testify: "He had a good disposition, always happy. He had a good temperament. He was a boy who was liked by everyone and popular with his companions. . . . He went to St. James College until the seventh or eighth year where he was good in class" (Alice R. Also others).

It can be objected that when one treats of mental illness or simply of mental disorder, the affirmations of those who observe nothing are of no moment. This is true when there are other witnesses giving evident signs of illness; but it is not true when such other witnesses are lacking. It can be argued that the witnesses, especially relatives, noted nothing abnormal in the defendant immediately before the marriage. That is not strange, as those close to a person do not generally acknowledge the existence of mental disease in a loved one who always acted normally unless the signs are evident or there is simply no other way of explaining the behaviour. This latter is the case with the brother-in-law of the plaintiff who observed about the defendant: "He is a type who would drink at the end of the week; *it is probably for this reason that he lost his jobs.*"

In the case at hand, the deposition of the medical doctor, Dr. J., is of great importance. Even though Dr. J. is not a psychiatrist, he can be considered as a qualified witness. He relates: "I had the occasion to speak with Ronald many times before the autumn of 1938, because I served the family as family doctor. I remember that Ronald in particular did not reach the same level of achievement as the others. One could not hold a conversation with him; he limited himself to commonplaces, as the temperature. . . . I had him under my care for some months. I saw him on November 8 and 19, 1963. The result of the examination (Wassermann) was positive. The exact diagnosis was syphillis. He had been mentally retarded for some time, a little childish for his age. He was 25 years old at the time. He was a little automatic, always using the same phrases. One could not discuss anything with him, he always repeated the same things. He spoke of innocuous things. He was rather smug. He did not realize his real condition. He was living a rather vegetable life in the broad sense, namely, since he had to live and be sheltered, one would have to say that he was satisfied. He spoke slowly. His walking was slow, a little like an automaton who does what he has to do. To the questions that were asked of him, he answered by a yes or a no."

Considering the testimony of Dr. J., it is incomprehensible how the medical expert could report: "His almost morbid personality was characterized by a slow intelligence (low middle or borderline) and by immaturity." All the testimony cries out against such an assertion, for the defendant in adolescence and even afterwards showed no signs of mental weakness or of immaturity. The medical expert adds another statement which seems equally absurd: "I was saying rather that they (the characteristics of a premorbid personality) are acquired due to the family influence in infancy and adolescence." That is a mere hypothesis, noways proven in this case, because the family, as all the witnesses affirm, was a good and peaceful one and the parents exhibited no severity towards their children.

The expert writes: "My opinions are the following: Ronald appeared a nervous syphilitic type, general-sumptomatic paralysis, early in November, 1937, some six months after the marriage. At the moment of marriage, the condition was *asymptomatic.*"

It is a truism both in canonical jurisprudence as in medical science, that the nature of a mental disease, which is not clearly shown in the first manifestation, is known clearly and evidently from its further evolution. Another point must be added. The medical expert concludes that the specific signs of general paralysis first manifested themselves in the month of November, 1937, a month after the marriage. He draws this conclusion from the testimony of the sisters of the plaintiff. But she made the same observations as were made by Dr. J. (and his were from before the marriage).

Whence, not only was the defendant at the time of the marriage incapable of assuming the requisite obligations as required by law, but he already suffered from a mental illness in the full stage of development at that time.

Therefore, having considered all matters that should be considered in fact and in law in cases of this kind, we, the undersigned judges, sitting as a tribunal, having only God before our eyes, and having invoked the name of Christ, discern, declare, and definitely decree, responding to the proposed doubt, *affirmative* or the nullity of this marriage on account of the insanity of the defendant has been proven.

This we pronounce, commanding Ordinaries and Tribunal officers to execute this sentence and to proceed according to the norms of the law against those who oppose it.

Case #13

CANON 1081 (M.J.)
LACK OF DUE DISCRETION
No. 39/Mary vs. Walter

The Facts

When twenty and thirty-one years of age respectively, Mary and Walter contracted marriage in a Catholic Church in Philadelphia, Pennsylvania, in June of 1945. The acquaintanceship of the parties began in October of 1943. Married life lasted for three years after the marriage, at which time they separated for a period of four months. After resumed cohabitation, they lived together until March of 1959, when the final separation took place.

The respondent began to drink heavily when he was seventeen years old and in 1932, when he was nineteen years old, he required hospitalization. By the time he was twenty-one, he was considered alcoholic. From that time on, he suffered from chronic alcoholism requiring hospitalization many times over the years. Because of this condition, the petitioner presented a petition asking for a declaration of nullity "insofar as the respondent both before and after the marriage was suffering from a serious mental illness which prevented him from eliciting true matrimonial consent."

The Law

With the increasing awareness of the spread of alcoholism it is only to be expected that sooner or later the validity of marriage entered by would be subject to scrutiny. The rotal precedents have mainly concerned *"ebrietas"* or manifest drunkenness (Cf. *S.R.R. Dec.*, XXV, 1933, XXXI, no. 2, p. 265; *ibid.*, XXII, 1930, IX, no. 2, p. 88) and it is only recently the judges of lower ecclesiastical courts have a guide from the rota concerning the effect of chronic alcoholism on the validity of marriage.

In a fine decision dated February 24, 1961, Sabattani (reported in *Monitor Ecclesiasticus*, 1961, Fasc. IV, pp. 638-640) finds that chronic alcoholism can debilitate the mind sufficiently to invalidate matrimonial consent if it has progressed to the stage where maturity of judgment is impaired. He gives five criteria for determining the stage at which judgment is affected:

a) the period of time over which the disease has extended (to be judged morally not by the number of years of existence);

b) the seriousness of the disease;

c) commitments to mental hospitals for alcoholism;
d) definite symptoms of mental aberration such as delirium, hallucinations, etc.;
e) whether or not the loss of moral feeling has been affected. It is noted that this illness invariably leads to moral dysesthesia or obtuseness.

The decision points out that, if all five of the criteria cited above are present around the time of the marriage, there is full proof of mental inability to contract marriage. If the majority of these criteria are proved to have existed at the time of the marriage or even a minority of these signs, provided there are definite symptoms of mental disturbance such as delirium and hallucinations, there is likewise full proof of mental inability to enter marriage. If one of the criteria is present there is only a presumption of insufficient ability and if there is a certain diagnosis of chronic alcholism at the time of the marriage, there is a grave presumption regarding defect of proper consent.

The Argument

Walter began to drink when he was seventeen years of age. When nineteen, he required his first (at least as far as the court has been able to ascertain) hospitalization and was already considered an alcoholic when he was twenty-one years of age. This was ten years before he contracted marriage. In 1935 he had been hospitalized for ten weeks for this illness. Shortly after his discharge he was re-hospitalized with delirium tremens. Not long after that he was court committed to the Pennsylvania Hospital where he was hospitalized for chronic alcoholism for one year (July, 1936-July, 1937). At this time organic brain damage was indicated by virtue of memory impairment.

The petitioner had informed the court that there were several hospitalizations in various hospitals in the ten-year period until the marriage. However, the respondent could not recall all of the places in which he had been hospitalized. For a period of a year prior to the marriage, he did abstain from drinking; but shortly after the marriage he was back to his old habits in this regard. Subsequent to the marriage he had numerous hospitalizations for acute alcoholism with toxic encephalopathy, an unsuccessful attempt at individual psychotherapy with extensive chemotherapy, and a number of years of membership in Alcoholics Anonymous, including group psychotherapy. Walter was confined to Fairmount Farms for alcoholism four times before the marriage and twice since. As early as four months subsequent to the marriage he began a series of confinements which amounted to ten confinements.

The rota, in the decision referred to above, has established criteria whereby judges can arrive at a decision concerning the mental state of an alcoholic and as a consequence his contractual capacity. The first thing that must be examined is the period of time over which the toxic process of the disease has extended. If the toxic process effected by alcoholism is of long standing, the court can conclude that there is implied a serious disorder of the mind. In the case of Walter the court finds that he began drinking heavily at age seventeen. From then on he suffered acute and frequent eqisodes of alcoholism. Organic brain damage was apparent by reason of memory impairment as early as 1937.

The next of the criteria is the seriousness of the toxic process. The disorder in the case of Walter was so serious that his mental processes were already disturbed. Thus the second of the criteria is verified.

The seriousness of the illness can also be determined by the commitments of the patient to hospitals for mental illness. This case has uncovered some, but by no means all, of the various hospitalizations of Walter. Certainly, these in themselves are incontrovertible signs of the toxic process.

The fourth of the signs in indications of insanity. On many occasions Walter was diagnosed as suffering from delirium tremens and his acute alcoholism was diagnosed as existing toxic encephalopathy.

The last of the criteria given by the rotal decision was to discover whether or not there was any loss of the moral sense. In this case one sees no moral dysesthesia or moral obtuseness.

According to the jurisprudence given by the rota, judges can conclude that there is probably existing the lack of discretionary judgment to contract marriage if these various criteria are established. When all five of these or at least when the greater number of these criteria coalesce at the time of the marriage, the court can conclude that there is full proof that the discretionary judgment necessary to contract marriage is lacking. This is especially so when there are definite signs of insanity such as deliria and in this case the chronicity of brain damage. One also notes that the progress of the disease in Walter was rapid and severe and one of the psychiatrists who took care of him stated that as early as 1947, (two years after the marriage) Walter had reached the infantile stage of emotional performance.

The court feels that the question of brain damage is irrelevant to the merits of the case and it is only a clinical, not a juridic question. Both the advocate and the defender of the bond have mentioned this aspect of the case but with the law applicable to the case so well explained by the rota, this court consequently feels that the nullity of the Mary-Walter marriage has been fully proved.

Wherefore, having duly examined all these matters both as regards the law and facts, and invoking the name of Christ, we, the undersigned judges, sitting as a court of first instance and having only God before our eyes declare, decree, and define in answer to the following question: *("Has the nullity of the Mary-Walter marriage been fully proved?")* in the *affirmative; that is to say, the nullity of the marriage has been fully proved.*

We further decree that this our definitive sentence, be executed in accordance with the prescriptions of the sacred canons and all ordinaries and ministers of tribunals, whose duty it is to execute the definitive sentences of ecclesiastical tribunals, proceed against those who refuse to obey these decrees in accordance with Title XVII of the Code of Canon Law using whatever means appear to be opportune or efficacious for this purpose.

CANON 1081 (M.J.)
IMMATURITY
No 13/Harold vs. Anne

Harold, age 21, and Anne, age 20, both Catholics, were married in May, 1950 according to the form prescribed by law. Two children were born of this union. They were divorced in October, 1967. In January, 1976, Harold petitioned the Tribunal to consider a possible declaration of nullity of his marriage on the grounds of relative incompatibility on the part of both parties which existed from the very beginning of the marriage. The Respondent did not cooperate in the investigation.

The Law

Jurisprudence used in this case can be found in *Studia Canonica*, Vol. 6, No. 1, 1972, pp. 104-108, "Relative Incompatibility As Grounds For The Nullity of Marriage." Relative, psychic incapacity of two spouses to contract a valid marriage has been described as an essential incompatibility that is "essential incompatibility" resulting from "constitutional incapacity."

In such cases, we are dealing with fixed personality structures which, relative to each other, make it impossible for two parties in marriage to enter a valid union. The invalidity is alleged to be present because of incapabilities on the part of both, relative to each, to fulfill one or more of the essential elements or terms of the marriage contract. Invalidity is considered to result not from the personality structure of just one of parties (or of both parties, considered separately) but precisely from the interaction of both parties together—an interaction already basically present at the time of the wedding which prevents them from being able to fulfill one or more of the essential elements of the marriage contract.

This essential incompatibility must be constitutional, in the sense that it affects the personality structure of each of the parties, but in different ways; it renders them radically incapable of fulfilling the essential obligations of conjugal life, the *jus ad corpus* or the *jus ad consortium vitae*, even if they both tried wholeheartedly to correct the situation and to get along with each other.

This inability to fulfill, which we call constitutional incapacity, is itself the result of radical, constitutional and fairly permanent makeup of the persons. Thus, it is this personality, constituted as such, which permanently excludes (morally at least) such fulfillment. In this case the object of the contract is missing, and the marriage is invalid because of the incapacity of fulfilling the essential obligations of matrimony.

Thus, if essential incompatibility exists because of relative constitutional incapacity to lead a "common life," and if this relative constitutional incapacity exists at the time of the marriage and is incurable with a reasonable amount of therapy, the marriage is invalid.

The jurisprudence quoted in the above article concerns basically radical constitutional *personality defects*. It seems reasonable to the assembled court that a radical, constitutional *physical defect* would have the same consequences as a radical, constitutional personality defect, as long as the physical defect existed prior to the marriage and is incurable.

As a final condition for invalidity, it is required that (a) that both parties in the marriage have a radical, constitutional personality or physical defect. This radical deficiency in each party must not be necessarily as serious as when proof of nullity is to be based on the personality disorder of one of them. (b) The deficiencies must exist at the time of the wedding. Usually, it is not difficult to prove this point since personality structure does not easily change nor does physical structure easily change, especially without medical assistance or when medical assistance is useless. (c) The deficiencies of both parties must be permanent, in the sense that they are connaturally destined to exist in an inevitable manner, at least throughout a certain period of conugal life subsequent to the marriage. (d) Both deficient structures must meet or come into opposition in such a way that conjugal life—that is, the *omne jus ad actum conjugalem* or the *omne jus ad consortium vitae*—become connaturally, or humanly impossible.

If these provable elements exist, at least in the opinion of the judges who are experienced, a sentence of nullity might be justified.

The Petitioner stated that from the start of the marriage, "our marriage was a failure." Anne did not know how to cook or keep house. Neither of them knew real love for each other. The priest who married them said to one of their parents that the marriage would never last. From the beginning of the marriage there were fights all the time, especially about money, sex and having children. He claimed that Anne did not want either sex or children and that he wished both. He stated that Anne felt that sex was dirty. He stated that they both had different views about what marriage should be and it could never work out. He stated that the first child just came. She consented to have another child but he stated that Anne held it against him no matter what he did. He claimed that while no contraceptives were used during the marriage, she allowed very little sex relations, at the most, once a month. He believed that she did not want children because she was not grown up enough to have the responsibility to take care of children. Their first serious quarrel occurred shortly after they got back from their honeymoon and that the cause of it was her father. He stated that she had a very great dependency upon her parents. The first separation occurred when the first baby was born. Anne went to live with her parents for about two months before the child was born. She left because she felt that he was not capable of taking care of her. He admitted that he could not stay in the house all the time because he was a farmer and had to work. The petitioner stated that a great deal of their difficulties were caused by his nervousness. After they were married for about six and a half years, he was diagnosed as a victim of multiple sclerosis, an incurable disease. He stated that Anne was not able to cope with his nerves and his sickness. He needed help, but he stated that Anne did not want him to see a doctor because they would have to spend a great deal more money which they did not have much of. He stated that the reason for the divorce was that there was no cohabitation between the two of them and that the real reason for the divorce was that she did not want him anymore. He stated that with his disease, he becomes very depressed, has the blues, is nervous, suffers a great deal of pain and because of the pain, sometimes is not able to think straight. The petitioner stated that the Respondent was very immature, irresponsible, unstable, impulsive and unpredictable. Her moods would change quickly and her behavior would become very violent at times. He stated that the breakup of the marriage was as much his fault as it was hers as he should not have listened to her and should have gone to see a doctor long before he did. He stated that they were just not suitable as partners and it was a disasterous choice.

The sister of the Petitioner stated that the Respondent had a college education whereas Harold only went through the eighth grade. The witness stated that the Respondent wondered at the time of the marriage if she was making the right choice. She had planned on joining the convent and had even ordered her habit. The witness stated that the father of the Respondent gave her the impression that he was disappointed in her choice of husband. She further believed that they were both immature. Harold and Anne attempted to make decisions on their own, but Anne seemed to have more of a problem. Anne had her feelings hurt easily and Harold was always cautioning the witness not to say this or that. The witness stated that they were both responsible except that Anne could not handle the day to day problems herself without including the rest of the family. Harold was always put down in front of the children. The Respondent always talked about her own faults too. She stated that the Petitioner came down with multiple sclerosis during his marriage. She stated that the parties probably could have lived together very happily if Harold was a little more educated, had the help of a marriage counselor and if they had not been confronted with the disease. Neither of them could help each other during this time—the time that they needed each other the most. She believed that it was their personalities and immaturity which caused this. The marriage breakdown was definitely the fault of both parties, but because of their background, immaturity possibly, and being uneducated in the ways of helping and giving each other the love and attention they needed; they really didn't have much of a chance of having a lasting marriage.

The brother of the Petitioner stated that Harold finished the eighth grade, worked on area farms until he was old enough and then joined the Navy for four years where he was trained in diesel machines and mechanics. He stated that Harold had a problem of exaggerating events and told stories which had no basis in fact. The witness admitted that Harold was a hard worker, skilled in mechanics and farm machinery. He stated that Anne had a problem keeping house and did not believe that she did much work at home when she was growing up. Her family was quite well-to-do. He believed that Anne was or tended to be self-centered. Everything seemed to be going well until Harold got sick. The sickness, multiple sclerosis, had been diagnosed as service-connected. He stated that earlier in their marriage, the disease caused the Petitioner to have double vision and stumbling and that no one could figure out what was wrong. He believed that the disease had a lot to do with the breakup of the marriage.

Another witness stated that Harold was in a nursing home from April 1959 to April 1964. The witness could not provide testimony concerning the beginning of the marriage, but could speak of the reluctance of the Respondent to care for the Petitioner. She stated that due to Harold's illness, he was incapable of supporting his family and his absence from the home made the relationship strained and formal. She stated that they were not concerned about each other as they should have been and were not handling their stresses and the events of their lives constructively. At the time of this hospitalization, they were not capable of planning for life together.

Ex-officio, the Reverend Presiding Judge spoke with his own physician and questioned him about the case. It was his opinion that the disease would probably not be an invalidating factor for marriage. At his suggestion, a Catholic physician was spoken to who was a specialist in the field of multiple sclerosis. He stated that it often happens that one spouse is not able to cope with the change which might occur. It was his opinion that many times the families of the diseased person are *de facto* not able to cope with the situation. He would not be able to give any kind of medical opinion of Harold's specific case unless he had extensive interviews with both the Petitioner and the Respondent, however, there were several letters in the file from the Petitioner and from the Petitioner's present wife. Those letters indicated that the Petitioner and his present wife were able to cope with the problems of his illness. His present wife is a registered nurse and knows how to deal with the disease. She felt her accepting him as he was without question, proved that at last someone loved him with no sex strings attached which made him relax, happy and secure and then naturally took over and he was a whole man again as far as sex was concerned. Rejection by his first wife caused him to lose his potency. She stated that they are the answer to each other's prayers and they do not wish to lose each other. She is a Catholic who is free to marry and they both need and want the sacraments. They live by faith.

Conclusion

The Attorney-Advocate was present at the Plenary Session of the Collegiate Tribunal and he asked for a Declaration of Nullity. The Reverend Defender of the Bond presented his observations in writing and stated that he would accept the decision of the Court.

The Court was sad that it was not able to obtain the testimony of the Respondent, however, sufficient time was given to her to respond and indeed the case was delayed in the hope that she would respond, however, she did not.

It seemed clear to the Collegiate Tribunal that the testimony indicated that the Respondent possessed at the time of the marriage a certain amount of immaturity. She was a college graduate and the Petitioner had graduated only from the eighth grade. Surely, this should have been an indication that their backgrounds were radically different. Her expectations of life because she came from a well-to-do family were entirely different than that of the Petitioner, who came from a working farm family.

The testimony indicated that she was not a good housekeeper, nor cook, that she possessed a difficult temper, that she would talk against her spouse in the presence of others, that she did not wish sexual intercourse to any degree, that she could not act without the advice of her parents. All of these points were common points used by the Court in establishing immaturity. Further, the Court noted that she had wanted to enter a convent even to the extent of ordering a habit, whatever that might mean. However, she did not do so. The Court judged that there was immaturity on her part right at the beginning of the marriage. The Court, also, judged that the Respondent was not able to cope with the vicissitudes of life brought about by the disease of the Petitioner. This was manifested to the extent that she did not even wish him to receive medical treatment, because as she thought, they could not afford it. The evidence clearly showed that when the disease was diagnosed, the Respondent would have nothing to do with her husband. All of the above again proved to the satisfaction of the Court that she was immature.

The Collegiate Tribunal judged that the Petitioner did possess the disease, at least in its incipient stage, long before the marriage in question. The question was raised whether or not the court should have a medical specialist evaluate the testimony. However, the Court judged that since all three Collegiate Judges are experienced as trial judges, they are capable of making a decision in this matter based upon the testimony of the characteristics of the disease of multiple sclerosis.

It appears evident to the Court that the invalidity of the marriage is proven to result not from the personality structure of just one of the parties, but precisely from the interaction of both parties together. The interaction was already basically present at the time of the marriage and it prevented the parties from being able to fulfill the essential elements of the marriage contract. It is judged that essential incompatibility rendered it impossible for them to live a common life together. It is judged that the Petitioner possessed a radical, constitutional personality defect which prevented the Respondent from being able to cope with the problems of the illness of the Petitioner. This defect on the part of the Respondent resulted from the immaturity of the Respondent although she was of sufficient chronological age. Life together was connaturally, or humanly impossible.

Case #15

CANON 1081 (C.L.D.)
LACK OF DUE DISCRETION
"E" vs. "A"

Presented here is the *in iure* section of a definitive Rotal sentence *coram* Pinto.

Case

While the last world war was raging, E., 23 years old, was fighting in Tripoli and suffered a very severe misfortune on the 15th of December, 1940. He was violently attacked by a military machine and left half-dead with bones broken in his forehead, left clavicle, pelvis and right thigh. After he had been cured through a year's time in various hospitals, on the 2nd of August, 1942, he requested to fight again in Albania. He later obtained a leave of eight days and returned to the home of his family. On the 23rd of January, 1943, he entered marriage with A., 20 years old, whom he had come to know a year earlier while he was convalescing. Immediately upon completion of his leave, he returned to camp. Thereafter his wife knew nothing about him until October-November of 1945, at which time she heard that her husband had returned. When she found him in the area of Reggio, she heard from him that he already had another woman. In fact, E., right from September, 1945, lived a married life with F., whom he presented as his wife, and had three sons by her.

The deserted wife, A., on 19-VI-46 sought a separation from the civil tribunal because of the fault of the man and obtained it on 17-I-48. Then, after a prorogation of competence had been granted by the Supreme Tribunal of the Apostolic Signatura for the handling of the case in first instance before Our Tribunal (decree 7-IV-1971, P.N. 1443/71 C.P.), the said wife accused her marriage of nullity on the 4th of May, 1971, because of insanity of the man or, if not that, because of defect of discretion of judgment due to the marriage.

After the case had been instructed and discussed, it is proposed to Us today for definition by responding to the question thus agreed on:

"1) Is there proof of nullity of marriage in the instance and, inasmuch as the answer is negative,

"2) Is there proof of nonconsummation of the marriage in the instance" because the Most Excellent Dean granted (19-I-73) the faculty to look into this aspect subordinately.

The Law

Since the consent of the parties whereby they mutually give and accept the perpetual and exclusive right to conjugal copula effects marriage,[1] a party who is incapable of giving this kind of matrimonial consent, invalidly contracts marriage. A man and a woman evidence this consent when they express to one another a will to enter a permanent society between them by the exchange of the rights necessary for the procreation of children.[2]

He especially is incapable of placing matrimonial consent who *at the moment when he celebrates the marriage* lacks the use of reason, "because there cannot be consent where the use of reason is lacking."[3]

Those who habitually or actually lack the use of reason are called *insane*. The *habitually* insane, where there is question of a purely ecclesiastical law, are likened to infants who are considered as not having mastery of themselves;[4] but, when there is talk of defect of consent, they are indeed presumed incapable of placing that consent; the presumption, however, is of law only and admits of proof to the contrary.[5] After completion of the seventh year, a person, before puberty is presumed to have the use of reason.[6] This, indeed, to a certain degree is in agreement with more recent psychology: "About the seventh year is had the first manifestation of intellectual activity as knowledge of a nonsensory nature. . . . At seven years a young person can formulate elementary concepts and judgments . . . on the other hand, the logical process, intellectual activity in the true and proper sense, is had later on."[7]

The word, *insane*, is a juridical term which is employed in order to determine the legal effects of certain mental disturbances. In the science of psychiatry which is occupied rather with the study of mental disturbances under their etiological aspect, extremely different terms correspond to the aforesaid word. Nevertheless, in an extremely general manner, it can be said that the following persons must be considered as insane:

(1) Adults who have never arrived at the use of reason or, having reached it, have to a grave degree lost it. This abnormality can be found in kind rather than in quantity: as regards the first, in defective mental development (oligophrenia) or in feebleness of mind (phrenasthenia); as regards the second, in mental deterioration (dementia).[8]

(2) Adults who have a gravely disturbed use of reason which is a disorder of qualitative rank and can be found in psychotic cases.[9]

(3) Adults who habitually possess the use of reason but who have that use impeded because of actual mental disturbance.[10]

There is question, therefore, of cases in which a contracting party is incapable of eliciting a human act.

A person is also incapable of giving matrimonial consent if he, although actually possessing the use of reason, nevertheless is lacking *the discretion of judgment proportionate to the marriage to be contracted.*

In the law of the decretals discretion of judgment proportionate to the marriage to be contracted was presumed when puberty was reached for puberty was sufficient for the contraction of marriage.[11] But if the C.I.C. demanded for the celebration of marriage 14 years in the case of the woman and 16 in the case of the man, it did not set this down in order that the necessary discretion be had, but: 1) in order to avoid "the degeneration of the race"; 2) in order to foster "public morality"; 3) because "laws must be adapted to customs."[12]

According to St. Thomas, a person before puberty does not yet possess sufficient discretion of judgment "in order to obligate himself by a perpetual bond because he does not yet have a firm will."[13] Therefore, the defect is not one of the intellect but of the will.

More recent psychology has progressed further, for it holds that a person before puberty "finds it impossible to have a volitive act in which it faces the knowledge of ends between which it has to choose, and their evaluation." "With the arrival of puberty, then, there is realized that awareness of one's 'ego,' that is, of one's independence from the worlds of reality . . ."[14] But if the same author adds: "I do not intend to say that the person attaining puberty is already mature for a volitive act and that he can carry it out. . . . The same youth very often will also not be capable of this.... We can speak of the will only when the human personality has completely achieved its development,"[15] among more recent authors we find this: "There are many reasons for believing that only a psychic structure, such as is formed in puberty, creates the bases for ability to experiment with authentic decisions."[16]

Furthermore, the decision to contract marriage is of an altogether special character. This is especially because there is question of assuming a state of life to which nature herself inclines. For "in those matters to which nature inclines, such great strength of reason is not required for deliberation as in other matters. As a result, a person deliberating sufficiently on marriage can consent to it before he can handle his affairs without a tutor in other contracts."[17] The awakening of the physiological sexual function is found among boys . . . between the ages of 12 and 14, among young males between the ages of 14 and 16." "The psychic factor begins to work later . . . it manifests itself at first as a pure desire, need, sentiment of love, to love and to be loved, without inclination to the sexual act. For boys this is verified between the ages of 14 and 16; for young males, between the ages of 15 and 17. . . . Only later, in youth, are the two factors, the physiological and the psychic, found."[18] Nevertheless, consideration must be had of the different circumstances of times and persons.[19]

Next, although, when a person chooses a partner to enter into an interpersonal, perpetual and exclusive relationship with him, a wait must be had in order that steps in this direction may be taken in a tranquil manner, "not so much by a sudden decision as through an interior maturation or the accumulation of definite experiences ('growth' decisions),"[20] nevertheless, this is not the general rule. "In the 108 autobiographies of engaged persons, now married, whom we have questioned . . . Ten of those interviewed expressly deny that a decision preceded the conclusion for their marriage, and, for the others, the total description leads one to think that the start of marriage was rather an impulsive reaction than a decision."[21] The decision, however, which does not seek to satisfy particular needs but which has in view the solution of the universal question, "makes itself evident in only a few cases . . . where internal or external difficulties are found."[22]

Therefore, while the use of reason looks to the speculative knowledge of the intellect, inasmuch as he who possesses it, is capable of understanding what marriage and its essential properties are as regards their substance, discretion of judgment proportionate to marriage considers the deliberate decision of the will which necessarily supposes the evaluation of motives and the practical judgment of the intellect regarding the marriage which is here and now to be contracted. With reference to the process of the decision of the will, see, for example, R. Zavalloni: *La Liberta Personale*, 1965, pp. 90-117.

For nullity of marriage there is not required "mature consideration and prior deliberation of all the circumstances which can occur in such a matter";[23] it suffices to collate the subjective and objective motives which impel one to marriage with those which turn one away from it. This, indeed, is required "because the discursive action whereby the intellect collates a given thing with its opposite, opens the way so that, by showing to the will some aspect of good in each one of them which the will may choose, the will may be able to embrace or to repudiate that thing: consequently, where there is no such collation, there simply is no perfect freedom. No great lapse of time is, however, required for this deliberation, even when the judgment is disturbed by some passion . . . and this author (Cajetan) adds that it is possible that that deliberation take place imperceptibly."[24] "The self-determination of the subject that follows an intuitive comprehension of reality, can express a choice which is perfectly voluntary and conscious, albeit there is not question of a rationally deliberate choice."[25] However, he is incapable of making an intuitive comprehension who cannot make a choice with rational deliberation, for "an intuitive comprehension represents an immediate evaluation of the alternatives of choice."[26]

Moreover, although a person has diverse potencies, it must not be forgotten "that a person acts as a sole subject of these diverse potentialities." "The free act is the most typical expression of the person and involves his total personality."[27]

With all these points kept in view, it must be said that any person, after having attained puberty, *lacks the discretion of judgment proportionate to marriage* when he is affected by such psychic disturbances that he is rendered incapable by them of freely choosing marriage. This is evidently, although indirectly, verified when a person lacks the use of reason because the will is a rational appetite.[28] But that can also result from disease. Neither the intellect nor the will can be directly affected by any disease since they are spiritual faculties. Nevertheless, since each of those faculties needs a certain psychosomatic structure in order to function and it can be ill, their function also can, as a result, be gravely disturbed.

For the process of a voluntary act *can be disturbed*:

(1) in the phase of presentation of motives "through defect of perceptibility or of memory which do not permit the placing of all the motivating factors really existing, whether useful or necessary for such a determined act of the will."[29]

(2) in the phase of election "through defect of instinct which can be very strong, very weak, or also qualitatively deviate, that is, perverted; through defect of critical ability which does not permit a correct evaluation of each of the motivating factors; through defect of affectivity which does not furnish to the various motivating factors a coloring adequate for quality and for intensity; hence, indecision."[30]

What the C.I.C. implicitly presupposed from natural law relative to incapacity to elicit valid consent are explicitly and clearly expressed in the schema of the

Commission for the Revision of the Code, for it distinguishes: "total incapacity to elicit such consent because of mental disease or disturbance which impedes the use of reason; incapacity deriving from a serious defect of discretion of judgment regarding the matrimonial rights and obligations which are to be mutually given and accepted; incapacity to assume the essential obligations of marriage because the incapacity derives from a serious psycho-sexual disorder."[31]

The proposer, Fr. Huizing, rightly observes that in the first two cases there is question of the incapacity of the contractor to elicit a psychological act of consent but in the third case there is question of the incapacity to implement the object of the consent. Although in the second case they speak indiscriminately about defect of discretion of judgment, because of the importance which the deliberation has, actually there is question, as we have set forth above (n. 4), of defect of a free decision. As a result, the disturbances which are comprehended here are those called "impulsiveness and loss of will power (abulia)."[32] In the third case, however, the incapacity to implement the object of consent arises from a disturbance of the sexual instinct because of hyperesthesia, e.g., nymphomania, or inversion, e.g., homosexuality, which are disorders of the psycho-sexual order.[33]

Wherefore, the difficulties raised against the schema[34] can, seemingly, have an apt response.

Traumata of the brain in cases of concussion, and even of compression, once the symptoms cease, leave no sequelae, either somatic or psychic. On the other hand, in cases of *contusion*, where, namely, an anatomically demonstrable cerebral lesion has been produced, generally, not only the vegetative-traumatic syndrome but also psychic disturbance still persist for a more or less long time (regarding memory, affectivity, attention, mental discursiveness is rendered difficult and causes fatigue, etc.).[35]

"It is a fact of current observation that after a trauma of the head which has had, as a consequence, a cerebral lesion, there can occur *alterations of character*." In order that we may take into account how a trauma of the head can have as a consequence of perversion of character, we must refer to the localization of this complex mental function which . . . is composed essentially of affectivity . . . and of instinct . . . and influences the will . . . in such a way as to give a particular stamp to the finished products of the mental affectivity." "In any event it must be considered as certain that traumatic lesions of the frontal lobe, and especially lesions of the orbital portion of this lobe, certainly bring about serious disorders of character." "The phenomenon of 'disinhibition,' which is very often found in the symtomatological descriptions of ancients with trauma of the head . . . is identified especially with a state of impulsiveness, irritability, irascibility, intolerance towards sensory stimuli which are particularly intense (noises, etc.)."[36]

With these points kept in view, it appears to be unquestionable that in this kind of wounded person is found that proclivity from which the so-called "psychopathologic reaction" can burst forth. "In the psychogenesis of these reactions there are three factors: constitution, psychic trauma, and internal psychic conflict. To say it in another way: the reaction derives not only from the conditions of the milieu but from the very constitution of the subject." "The crisis, sharpened by anxiety, is a tempest of the total organism. The psychosomatic unity is profoundly troubled, at times momentarily imperilled, in a sort of unruly struggle for preservation. The most severe states go on to a dissolution, more or less profound, of the conscience and the greatest part of them involve multiple somatic manifestations."[37]

In circumstances of this kind, it is patently clear that the contractor can lack discretion of judgment proportionate to the mariage to be contracted.

The Sentence

"*In the affirmative*, that is, *there is proof of nullity of marriage in the instance.*" Rome, at the seat of the Tribunal of the Sacred Roman Rota, February 4, 1974.

(Private); Rota, decision, 4 Feb., 1974; reported in *Periodica*, 64 (1975). 517-527.

Footnotes

1. Cn. 1081
2. Cf. Cn. 1081: 2.
3. St. Thomas: *Suppl.*, q. 58, a. 3, c. Cf. X, 4, 1, 24 and Cs. 1982; 2201: 1.
4. Cn. 88: 3.
5. Cf. can. 2201: 2; G. Michiels: *Principia Generalia de Personis in Ecclesia*, 1955, pp. 78-80.
6. Cn. 88: 3.
7. A. Gemelli: *La Psicologia della Eta Evolutiva*, 1956, p. 222.
8. Cf. C. Ferrio: *Trattato di Psichiatria Clinica e Forense*, I,1970, pp. 925-975; 114-117.
9. Cf. Ferrio: *op. cit.*, pp. 976-1451.
10. Cf. Ferrio: *op cit.*, pp. 418-503, and vol. II, pp. 1650-1725.
11. X, 4, 2, chap. 2, 3, 6, 10, 14.
12. Card. Gasparri: *De Matrimonio*, I, 1932, pp. 292-293, footnote.
13. *Suppl.*, q. 43, a. 2, c.
14. A. Gemelli: *op. cit.*, pp. 280-281.
15. *Op. cit.*, p. 281.
16. H. Thomae: *Der Mensch in der Entscheidung*, 1960, Italian translation of R. P. Ronco, under the title, *Dinamica della Decisione Umana*, p. 226.
17. St. Thomas: *Suppl.*, q. 58, a. 5, ad 1.
18. A. Gemelli: *op. cit.*, p. 318.
19. Cf. Vari: *Enciclopedia della Sessualita*, 1966, ed. Borla: E. Thompson: "La Sessualita del Bambino," pp. 242-247; "Le Fasi della Puberta," pp. 261-267.
20. H. Thomae: *op. cit.*, p. 189.
21. H. Thomae: *op. cit.*, p. 205.
22. H. Thomae: *op. cit.*, p. 207.
23. Sanchez: *De S. Matrimonii Sacramento*, L. I, disp. 8, no. 3, collated with no 5.
24. Sanchez: *disp. cit.*, no. 7. Cf. B. Pontius: *De S. Matrimonii Sacramento*, L. IV, chap. 1, nos. 1-5.
25. R. Zavalloni: *op. cit.*, p. 369.
26. R. Zavalloni: *op. cit.*, p. 370.

27. R. Zavalloni: *op. cit.*, p. 367.
28. St. Thomas: I, q. 82, a. 5, c.
29. C. Ferrio: *op. cit.*, p. 240.
30. C. Ferrio: *loc. cit.*, cf. also pp. 241-245 where he explains how election is disturbed in impulsive actions; also pp. 279-280.
31. *Communicationes*, 3/1 (1971), 77.
32. Cf. C. Ferrio: *op. cit.*, pp. 242-245.
33. Cf. C. Ferrio: *op. cit.*, pp. 1538-1539, 1555-1556, 1591-1610.
34. Cf. *Periodica* 61 (1972), 69-70; *Concillium*, 9 (1973), 71-72.
35. Cf. J. Wyrsch: *Gerichtliche Psychiatrie*, 1948, Spanish trans., pp. 112-114.
36. C. Ferrio: *op. cit.*, pp. 1430-1432.
37. H. Ey, P. Bernard, and C. Brisset: *Manuel de Psychiatrie*, 1970, pp. 216-217.

Case #16

CANON 1081 (C.L.D.)
PSYCHIC INCAPACITY
Peter vs. Joanne (Serrano Decision)

The following case, often referred to as the "Serrano decision," was given a negative decision by the tribunal of first instance but that decision was reversed by the appellate tribunal. Thereupon, the case was appealed to the Rota *coram* Serrano in third instance. The decision is particularly noteworthy for the compilation of background sources on "serious psychic incapacity."

Summary of facts: marriage in 1955; lasted eight turbulent years, Joanne vainly tried to improve the situation. Finally, she petitioned for nullity on the grounds of Peter's serious psychic incapacity. First instance: negative. Second instance: affirmative.

The Law

Recent scholarly studies, including the elaborate work done in this apostolic tribunal, concerning the genuine nature or marriage usually spotlight the most characteristic element of marriage covenant, which is its interpersonality, in such a way that it is very difficult to compare it with any other juridical or moral matter, no matter how bilateral it may be.

Thus, when the law defines the act by which each partner hands over and accepts the perpetual and exclusive right to the body,[1] it already implies the interpersonal element in which marriage essentially consists and upon which its perpetuity and exclusivity depend, and from which they derive their source.

According to the norm, the mutual handing over of rights and duties does not suffice for the marriage consent. It is true that the very nature of the right of being-for-the-other creates a relationship and would sufficiently express the juridical line between the partners. But the law adds the word "Acceptance" and therefore includes the connotation of something further which is most proper to marriage. For the rights which are given and received are personal and freely exchanged just as they are in a definite subject existing and subsisting in his autonomous (personal) actuality, with the result that in no way can they be conceived and exist according to the exclusive whim and understanding of either partner, inasmuch as it is a question of accepting the other, and not merely of obligating one's self.

Furthermore, it is not enough to assert that such rights have a fixed definition and description in law, either natural or positive; for those rights which are considered only in law, whether they be stated in codes or rooted in hearts, either cannot yet be strictly termed rights or they presuppose a subject endowed with definitive psychological tendencies;[2] in this case keeping in mind the juridical relationship to be established, namely, the marriage relationship, these rights are to be understood in a strict sense. Hence, in real rights or obligations concerning material things, the "object of the right" recognized by law and distinct from the persons, may allow a kind of extra-personal objectivity with regard to certain types of rights and obligations. This is not the case in the strictly conjugal right, since one cannot prescind from the persons, each of whom is endowed with specific human qualities. The realm of persons completely encloses the ambit of conjugal rights, both in its totality and in its parts, i.e., whether from the point of view of the contracting parties, or from that of the mutual giving and accepting (the elements which would be the object of the right in question).

Recent statements of the Magisterium on matrimony often refer to such interpersonal sharing or communication. This is so whether those statements be considered independently or as bolstered by some qualification of that juridically disputed notion of 'conjugal love':

"Hence, by that human act whereby spouses mutually bestow and accept each other, a relationship arises which by divine will and in the eyes of society, too, is a lasting one.

"A man and a woman, who by the marriage covenant of conjugal love 'are no longer two, but one flesh,[3] render mutual help and service to each other through an intimate union of their persons and of their actions. Through this union they experience the meaning of their oneness and attain to it with growing perfection day by day. As a mutual gift of two persons, this intimate union, as well as the good of the children, imposes total fidelity on the spouses and argues for an unbreakable oneness between them."[4]

"Far from arising from any kind of chance or from the blind impulses of natural forces, marriage was instituted through the wisdom and providence of God the Creator with the intention of bringing to completion among people the planning of His love. Hence it is through the mutual gift of themselves, a gift which is specific to them and exclusively theirs, that spouses carry into effect that sharing of persons by which they bring one another to perfection."[5]

From the quotations just given a minimal conclusion must be drawn, that the marriage consent is exchanged by the persons as they are inadequately distinguished from the rights and duties which are handed over and accepted.

Thus, our jurisprudence, relying on such weighty authority, has in no way overlooked the importance of the matter. In recent decisions, one may read the following:

"Indeed the expert . . . cites the immature personality of the man which can hardly be reconciled with that intrapersonal and interpersonal integration required for accepting the duality essential to the married state.[6] For this consultant previously established that the reported excessive selfishness shows an 'insufficient self-giving capacity.' Consequently, an authentic interpersonal relationship becomes very hard to achieve."[7]

"Furthermore, if the history of the one about to marry convinces experts that, even before the wedding, he was seriously lacking in intrapersonal and interpersonal integration, he must then be considered incapable of the correct understanding of the very nature of that sharing of life which is directed toward the procreation and formation of children, that sharing which is called marriage. Hence, he should be judged equally incapable of correctly judging and reasoning concerning entrance into this perpetual sharing of life with another person. . . . Surely, however, he can remain able to fulfill other responsibilities which do not involve this intrapersonal and interpersonal integration."[8]

Let it suffice to cite just one more decision, before Anne,[9] in which he skilfully brings out the strictly juridical character of these principles in the light of which jurisprudence proceeds: "This proposition of Vatican II has juridical meaning, for it treats, not the mere fact of the beginning of a shared life, but rather the right and obligation to that intimate sharing of life, the most specific element of which is that close union of the persons by which a man and woman become the one flesh toward which that sharing of life tends as towards its climax. This means that marriage is a most personal relationship and that the marriage consent is an act of the will by which the spouses 'mutually give and accept each other'. . . . Thus, the state of marriage, in its essential elements, at least implicitly and mediately, must be intended as the substantial formal object of the act of marrying. For in every juridical matter, it depends on the formal object, whether, through the mediation of an act of the will, this or any other juridical action be verified. It is on the object concerning which the wills of the contracting parties give and receive promises that depends the truth of whether such a consent constitutes one juridical matter and not another. Surely, the sharing of life can be lacking from the state of marriage, but the right to such sharing can never be lacking."[10]   If further study is given to that interpersonal relationship which is said to be and truly is most special to marriage, then one easily discovers what may be termed the two-fold formality which constitutes marriage. For sometimes it seems, that attention is paid rather to the "object" of the marriage consent, which is rightly considered to be the very relationship considered under the aspect of its exclusivity, perpetuity, and orientation toward the children. Yet, according to traditional teaching, this means that the spouses mutually give and accept one another. Hence, one necessarily considers the persons of the spouses inasmuch as they give their consent. The matter can be put another way: the interpersonal relationship, or sharing of life, begun by spouses on the analogy of a habit (surely, it ought to be this, though at times it fails: thus, the right involved is appropriately termed a "perpetual right"), arises from that singular definite act which is the consent given of themselves by the spouses.

But since one is treating incapacity, and not a simulated or restricted object of consent, it would be evaluated more fittingly and more in harmony with current jurisprudence if one spoke of the incapability of the subjects rather than of an object which is either essentially imperfect or completely defective. One who simulates or excludes his consent is aware that he is excluding a requirement for marriage, whether he does not properly give himself or accept his partner. One, however, who is incapable of properly giving himself or accepting another in marriage, even though he had thought he was properly entering marriage inasmuch as he was marrying in consequence of his correct intellectual concept of marriage, could perhaps correctly understand and even desire, to the extent of his powers, the object of his consent, without having to be considered capable of true marriage, because some subjective defect has disqualified him.

For years our jurisprudence has followed a similar teaching in dealing with invalidity "due to abnormality in matrimonial matters" (*propter insaniam in re uxoria*).[11] . . . In this phrase, the word "abnormality" refers more to the capacity or, better, to the incapacity of the subject; "matrimonial matters" refers to the application or the object of such capacity or incapacity. Hence, one would not do wrong in speaking of "the incapacity for interpersonal conjugal consent."

Thus, one can understand that, in dealing with individual cases, to claim or to deny ability to marry, it is not enough to establish either the absence of any mental abnormality taken in its restricted sense or a lack of freedom, if these two are viewed in themselves in isolation from any specific relationship to the other person just as he must be accepted in marriage. For, though the imtimate interpersonal relationship depends on the powers mentioned, still the personality can be seriously disturbed precisely in that it ought to be directed to another person who exists with his own individuality and ought to accept him as he is so that in some way he makes him master of himself in some matters. Thus, it is possible to imagine a person who not only sees marriage as a complexity of rights and duties which intrinsically carry an obligation, but obliged himself only objectively without any reference to his partner as a person with independent existence. In such a case, whether this happens consciously or not, I do not know whether there would arise a juridical 'bilateral personality' relationship; it certainly would not be an interpersonal marriage covenant.

Hence, at least in many cases, capacity for marriage is less appropriately treated by analogy with subjective moral imputability. As a result, special attention should be paid to the famous words of Aquinas: "It must be said that, to commit a mortal sin, consent for a present act suffices. But for an engagement, the consent concerns the future" (n.b. and for marriage, the consent concerns perpetuity).[12] "But greater discretion is required to plan for the future. . . ."[13] These words must be understood not only in the sense of the "greater degree" of discretion requisite for marriage, but also in the sense of that "different kind" of discretion. If such a kind of distinction is regarded as logical in any act of a spiritual power, surely it is seen to be necessary in marriage according to what has been said.

Similarly, one must not always press any analogy either with the ability to perform any juridical-contractual act (matters concerning objects or rights attaching to those objects) or with the ability to undergo a penalty.

In a decision before Fiere, we read these wise words: "Setting aside historical discussions, the measure of discretion required for a marriage consent is determined by two boundaries . . . the lesser limit is that required for a mortal sin, the greater is that needed for other contracts.[14] But this rule, like any rule, falls short because it is abstract, either because one is dealing with contracts which are too common . . . or because it depends on limits which themselves need to be defined, or finally because the difference indicated admits of a greater or lesser degree even within itself, while the object of the inquiry is the minimum required for giving a valid marriage consent."[15] And we read: ". . . and one could still emphasize the interpersonal nature of marriage, just as has happened very well in each case of recent jurisprudence. . . ."

Hence, the examination of the personalities of the parties is not to consist merely or even primarily of the separate investigation into each of them in relation to the mental acuity or strength of will in each one's personal actions, thoughts, and intentions; in marriage cases, the most attention must be given to that area of psychic life in which an interpersonal relationship is established and developed. I speak of an interpersonal relationship which, in every respect, is concrete and singular, endowed with that individuality which modern scholars usually term 'incapable of repetition,' and which is special to a human person who develops himself, gives himself, and accepts another as a person, just as he is in the existential order of his particular culture.

But this statement may be regarded as too subtle and, as it were, too refined for the nature of this elemental subject which Nature has taught all kinds of people, even the simplest, namely, that marriage has an uncomplicated essence and is generally desirable.[16] Therefore, one must state that it often seems very difficult to ascertain whether absolutely no right to one's person is given to another, or whether one experiences in himself what is proper to the other, or whether there is present at least some beginning of all of these elements as a type of sharing. As a result, one who is only doubtfully capable, cannot be deprived of his certain right to marry. Furthermore, one must strongly maintain this truth lest, after the appearance of serious discord in married life when the interpersonal relationship clearly breaks down, too easy an excuse be offered for opening a case for nullity which should rather be termed developing divorce.[17]

Though the interpersonal relationship can reach greater or lesser perfection in different couples, yet in no way can it be said that this relationship completely belongs to the "more perfect" or "desirable" ideal marriage, since, in fact, according to what has been said, it constitutes an essential property of any marriage consent. If this relationship is completely lacking, the consent itself is missing. Hence, no value attaches to a discussion of "the interpersonality of marriage in the sense in which such discussions are sometimes had about the 'knowledge' of the object of the consent, discussions which more or less minimize that knowledge to preserve the essence of the marriage."[18]

"Interpersonality" consists in the "quality" more than in the "extent" of the marriage consent, and it is enough for it to be present in a minimal or, rather, in an imperfect degree for that consent to be marital. Hence, in examining such a subtle question, as in others proposed about the incapacity of subjects, one must carefully proceed, following the lead of science, in no way setting aside any new study of human existence and behavior. To fulfill this responsibility, we are constantly moved by the authoritative statement: "it would be quite useful toward this end to plumb the depth of the idea of 'equity' which has already been mentioned, either in the development of Roman law or in the total complex of canon law; such a concept implies a demanding evaluation of the subject awaiting a judicial decision. Thus we have the modern process, be it canonical or civil, which takes into account the psychology of the partners in the case and of the subjective elements involved, evaluating also the environmental, familial, sociological circumstances, etc. . . ."[19]

The analysis of interpersonal relationship has been perceptively approached by the philosopher Merleau-Ponty, whose authority even psychiatrists often invoke. He offers no little help for the diagnosis of the specific nature of "interpersonality" as it appears in human behavior, even though his description bears traces of a philosophical system which makes no distinction between the essential and the accidental, and which, in this case, completely prescinds from the elements of supernatural Christian ethics.

Merleau-Ponty distinguishes three stances which a person takes relative to the outside world: first, a stance for the world nature; second, one for the social order; third, one for another person precisely as such. In the first two kinds of relationship, the "other" is found as something determined and, as it were, predictable even without experiencing it; but in the third, which concerns us: ("The grief and the anger of another have never quite the same significance for him as they have for me. For him these situations are lived through, for me they are displayed. Or in so far as I can, by some friendly gesture, become part of that grief or that anger, they still remain the grief and anger of my friend Paul: Paul suffers because he has lost his wife, or is angry because his watch has been stolen, whereas I suffer because Paul is grieved, or I am angry because he is angry, and our situation cannot be superimposed on each other. If, moreover, we undertake some project in common, this common project is not one single project, it does not appear in the selfsame light to both of us, we are not both equally enthusiastic about it, or, at any rate, not quite in the same way, simply because Paul is Paul and I am myself. Although his consciousness and mine, working through our respective situations, may contrive to produce a common situation in which they can communicate, it is nevertheless from the subjectivity of each of us that each one projects this "one and only" world.) The difficulties inherent in considering the perception of other people did not all stem from objective thought, nor do they all dissolve with the discovery of behavior, or rather objective thought and the uniqueness of the *cogito* which flows from it are not fictions, but firmly grounded phenomena of which we shall have to seek the basis. The conflict between myself and the other does not begin only when we try to *think ourselves into* the other and does not vanish if we reintegrate thought into non-positing consciousness and unreflective living; it is already there if I try to live another's experiences, for example, in the blindness of sacrifice. I enter into a pact with the other person, having resolved to live in an interworld in which I accord as much place to others as to myself. But this interworld is still a project of mine, and it would be hypocritical to pretend that I seek the welfare of another *as if it were mine*, since this very attachment to another's interest still has its source in me. (This sharply differs from the Christian concept of love for the other which derives from the grace of the spirit.)

"In the absence of reciprocity there is no alter Ego, since the world of the one then takes in completely that of the other, so that one feels disinherited in favor of the other.

This is what happens in the case of a couple where there is more love felt on one side than on the other: one throws himself, and his whole life, into his love, the other remains free, finding in this love a merely contingent manner of living. The former feels his being and substance flowing away into that freedom which confronts him, whole and unqualified. And even if the second partner, through fidelity to his vows or through generosity, tries to reciprocate by reducing himself, or herself, to the status of a mere phenomenon in the other's world, and to see himself through the other's eyes, he can succeed only by an expansion of his own life, so that he denies by necessity the equivalence of himself with the other that he is trying to posit. Co-existence must in all cases be experienced on both sides. If neither of us is a constituting consciousness at the moment when we are about to communicate and discover a common world, the question then is: who communicates, and for whom does this world exist? [And if someone does communicate with someone else, if the interworld is not an inconceivable *in-itself* and must exist for both of us, then, again, communication breaks down, and each of us operates in his own private world like two players playing on two chessboards a hundred miles apart. But here the players can still make known their moves to each other by telephone or correspondence, which means that they are in fact participants in the same world. I, on the other hand, share no common ground with another person, for the positing of the other with his world, and the positing of myself with mine are mutually exclusive.] Once the other is posited, once the other's gaze fixed upon me has, by inserting me into his field, stripped me of part of my being, it will readily be understood that I can recover it only by establishing relations with him, by bringing about his clear recognition of me, and that my freedom requires the same freedom for others."[20]

Though the concluding words clearly refer to a generic interpersonal relationship and so cannot be adapted to the indissolubility of the marriage covenant, nonetheless, they harmonize well with that interpersonal freedom with which one must approach his wedding (*matrimonium in fieri*), at which he must in the very act of marriage concede to his partner, precisely as to another person, whatever he himself intends to have for himself through the marriage.

Laing, Phillipson and Lee exert still more pressure on the basis for the interpersonal relationship: "The aspect of the question which interests us is that of being aware and not being aware. Effective and undistorted interaction is possible only if each partner approaches the wedding attuned to the point of view of the other partner. Granted that interpersonal perceptivity can take place at many levels, so can obtuseness; and it is possible that, for every level of perceptivity, there is an analogous level of obtuseness or failure to perceive. Whenever there is a failure to be acutely aware (when there is insensitivity), there always appear pseudo-problems to which the partners take recourse. . . . There exists a presumed harmony which lacks any true foundation and which the partners attain. There also arise disagreements based on presumptions without any concrete basis. On these disagreements, their arguments take fire."[21]

These references, besides making a great contribution to a deeper examination of that class of human relationship which we call a right and which exists in every treatment of rights—"for justice is orientated toward *the other*"[22]—deserve the main attention in that area, both juridical and, in the strictest sense, interpersonal, which is called and is "the marriage consent."

Hence, we are not surprised if psychiatrists are studying more and more closely the existential situation of the individual, and so give much weight to conclusions like those just drawn.

Thus, Callieri-Castellani-De Vincentiis: "The block to dialogue essentially consists in the inability to give witness, to arouse in the other a similar form of mutual presence. In the last analysis, this block is the inability to make tangible and enjoyable the meeting of two persons. It is as if, through a depressing influence, the genuine 'thou' were failing, not simply to attempt, so much as to achieve concentration on its peculiar interpersonal essence. A polarity is set up between the subjective and objective expressions of the consciousness of the ego. As a result, the composition of the other precisely inasmuch as that other is a person who offers and seeks free interchange, becomes slippery and unbalanced."[23]

In this instance, the scholarly Professor Gozzano writes: "As is known, there is a huge literature, especially recently, about the problems of communication, whether they may be considered from the structural or the phenomenological point of view. . . . Even when one is dealing with mere information, that (the common link between communicating people) happens through the codification and decodification of the message. But when one deals, not with mere information, in other words, a merely conceptual communication, but with a message which contains an emotional element, the relationship between the source and the receiver of the message is much more complex and deep."[24]

It is clear to all that the "message" or "import" of the marriage consent implies a two-fold meaning (giving-accepting) in each spouse, a meaning giving room to several human inclinations.

Therefore, from a close study of the essential elements of the marriage consent, the conclusion must be drawn that such consent is indeed readily possible, according to the law of nature and the disposition of God, for every person who truly enjoys the power to deliberate and to decide and who is not legitimately prevented on some other count. Yet another conclusion must also be drawn: that this consent 'in itself' involves a process which is difficult and complex, a process produced by several weighty powers of the human spirit, for example, the use of reason, the free play of the will, strong affective and emotional drives, all of which can seriously influence the consent in one direction or another.

There is no valid objection from the fact that people of sound mind perform this important process almost connaturally without seeming to pay any heed to the subtle implications which are many and difficult, for example, knowing, willing, considering, all of which one freely does; from the merely habitual performance of these functions, no one will argue that they are less complex. Something similar is true for marriage: if the partners are more or less sufficiently aware when they exchange consent in marriage (and this awareness would not be said to be the same for everybody), and if this consent were to be ascribed to mere naivete, or levity, or inadvertence in the act of marrying, then it will be easier to defend the validity of a natural bond, especially since it enjoys the presumption of the law, which favors the marriage. For in the case of those who, so to speak, give potential consent—a potency which, on another count, harmonizes well with the essence of the right which is being given and received—other elements are present, though they do not yet actually exist; but if a serious failing in an interpersonal relationship really is a characteristic of the subject's incapacity, then nothing further need be sought since he fundamentally lacks the very power to consent. But, whether this incapacity has completely prevented the consent or merely deprived it of a desirable degree of perfection (one becoming such an undertaking) is a question of fact, to be determined, in each case, as is clear, with the help of experts.

Therefore, the question arises about the radical incapacity of people in whom one encounters all these personality disorders which, according to psychiatrists, are not so serious as to be classified as illnesses, and yet cause a psychopathic abnormality which can influence the very power which the subject should have to enter into an interpersonal relationship by which the rights of another over him and his rights over the other are correctly understood, deliberately pursued, and exchanged by mutual giving and accepting.

In this case, we must deal either with a personality which is called paranoid or with one which is marked by some paranoid characteristics. Thus Ian Gregory: "The characteristics of the paranoid personality include egocentrism, narcissism, and the excessive use of the device of projection, because of which everything which is not emotionally acceptable to the ego is unconsciously rejected and attributed (projected on to others)."[25]

Professor Gozzano: " 'Pure paranoia,' which represents the simplest and most typical form of this class of psychoses, is not strictly a disease, but rather a constitutional anomaly which remains latent in youth and becomes manifest later, slowly evolving with the creation of a form of imbalance which is well organized and firmly riveted to an unshakable faith and to a capacity for criticism which can indeed be sharp, but is always one-sided. Even before the imbalance appears, the psychopathic composition of the future paranoid is almost always marked by a tendency to quibble, to reason sophistically, and, on the affective side, by a lofty self-image which is sometimes masked by continuous lack of self-confidence in dealing with others."[25a]

H. Ey, P. Bernard, and C. Brisset seem to touch the heart of the question when they write: "To grasp the sense and import of this fundamental symptomatic aspect of personality disorders, we should try to specify that these disorders bear essentially upon the conception of the world implied, as we have seen, in the notion of the I. The I is in effect bound to his World, and this existential thinking is constitutive of the Reality of the being in the world inasmuch as it is the order in which his existence is manifested. Naturally, by reality we do not simply mean the physical world, but the human world of the environment and also the psychic or interior world of the subject. It is thus that the I appears in this respect as the Subject which systematically develops the values of reality which link it to its World. This bond is essentially constituted by the beliefs which give to all the phenomena of the World their degree of reality for the I . . . the alienation of the Person, which psychiatrists term the psychotic I, manifests itself clinically by certain symptoms: dogmatic convictions and judgments, ideoverbal formulations, behavior and attitudes governed by irreducible beliefs which form for the subject a sort of truth and ideal which corresponds neither with reality *nor with the coexistence with the other* (emphasis added) and which manifest the work of the germination and construction of delirious ideas. Soon they form a system, then a fantastic conception, finally, an impenetrable labyrinth . . . All of this occurs as a form of pathological existence assigning itself to an inferior level of personality pathology which implies superior levels (character troubles and nervous disorders) by adding only a more profound deformation of the structure of the I, delirium, as a falsified conception of existence. Delirium, we repeat, is here in a sense less strong than that of the perception of 'delirious experiences' as it is less intensely lived in a sense and sensibility, but it is more radical insofar as it does not suppress vicissitudes of the perceptions but commands them.

"A first type of delirious alienation of the persòn is characterized by the erroneous development of the personality (Jaspers). It is manifested sometimes by passionate frenzies which polarize the I in a mode of erotomania, jealousy, revenge, or anger; sometimes by systematized deliria of persecution or influence. This type of delirious personality (Paranoia) is characterized by clarity and order in the psychic life, by polarization in the sense of one or several auxiliary delirious beliefs, by the systematic and 'reasoning' structure of fiction. The mechanisms of intuition and interpretation are prevalent."[26]

In light of this medical testimony, it is clear that such people are fundamentally incapable of accepting another as such; moreover, there is grave doubt that, in giving consent, they can give over anything of themselves, since their perception of themselves seems essentially distorted and 'alienated' from the actual truth.

To help the evaluation of specific facts, we wish to add the medical testimony of the doctors who have studied the respondent regarding what they have said in a generic fashion about abnormalities.

Dr. Christopher: "Those who have this kind of personality . . . start with the principle that everybody is aware of what they are thinking, even though on the part of the sick person, there is no communication of private thoughts. Hence, the reactions of this kind of individual are based, not on what others can think or know, but rather on what these sick people are waiting for others to know, and these sick people feed and show their contempt and resentment for anyone who does not know something which the sick are waiting for them to know independently of whether these others have or have not had the chance to learn the matter in question" (p. 158).

Dr. Knight: "[The paranoid personality is] . . . rigid, chained to a fixed idea, stubborn, a person who thinks that the world is colored only black and white, without any shading of gray. A thing is either right or wrong; for no reason can there be an extenuating circumstance. A question is either black or white; for that reason, the person has an idea of being persecuted, but the paranoid personality is not necessarily accompanied by any idea of persecution which is not based on facts.

"The paranoid personality is more or less a character construct, as I have described above, a construct due to distortion and perhaps to the rigid method in which the person has been brought up" (p. 202).

Dr. Morris: "[Paranoid personality]: People like this are not ordinarily hospitalized; they can function on certain levels, but this is a serious disturbance inasmuch as the patient could not function on the emotional level" (p. 213).

All this testimony indeed deals with the behavior of the subject rather than with its cause. Yet the testimony gives much help to the judicial interpretation of the case, since it is not the province of the judge to investigate its interior and remote causes.

Much depends also on the consideration of the person of 'the other' when one seeks to determine the validity or invalidity of any specific marriage consent on the grounds of abnormality in interpersonal relationships. This is so especially in the case of a paranoid personality, where so much weight must be given especially to the 'reactionary' nature of the illness[27] and also to the intrinsic importance of the unconscious habit of projecting on to the other ["mechanisms of projection"].[28]

Let no one object that such abnormality can arise or at least can become serious only after lengthy association of the partners, and hence that the initial wedding consent is easily free of such abnormality. For, though no one denies that a condition which, in the course of time, has worsened, may be foreseen, still two elements must be carefully established in the investigation by the judge: the part played by the genetic constitution in the psychic disorientation of the person and the way in which the premarital association began and developed.

For it is clear that a movement of violent rejection of a person, arising from unconscious mental imbalances, can arise without reflection or delay, if the person is burdened by a demagoging weight of projection.

Finally, as has just been said, a few words should be added about the time at which one proves this incapacity for interpersonal relationship to have existed.

Certainly, from the mere proof that the interpersonal relationship was broken off after the wedding, it would be wrong to conclude that the marriage is null, since that break could have been caused by several factors, even by those extrinsic to the partners, or by a psychic incapacity which is not serious, or even without any psychic incapacity.

But we must maintain the principle which states that the impossibility of leading any true married life, when that life cannot be harmonized with the giving and receiving of the right to that life, renders impossible the very marriage consent. "For we must recall that no one can oblige himself to do or give what he cannot, even if this block occurs apart from or against his free will, because no one can oblige himself to the impossible."[29] We have strenuously tried to show how the incapacity of the partners is studied precisely in the very expression of the consent, and that the consent is examined under the formality of an act, that is, as an interpersonal relationship complete in itself. If this interpersonal relationship is essentially defective, the marriage is rightly attacked as null on the grounds of the antecedent moral incapacity of either or both partners [we used this term which is as vague as "psychic" and this psychic impotence refers more often to the capacity for intercourse, preexisting the marriage].[30]

The question can and ought to be seen from a different, namely, procedural point of view. For the judge will never reject any means of proof, if he is free of prejudice and anxious for the truth. But if, moved by the correct principle that it is impossible to declare a marriage null which was initially valid, he does not turn his attention with the same and, sometimes, with even greater care to the post-wedding events, he would without reason reject a valid and, perhaps, unassailable support for truth. For what is later clearly recognized can throw light on what was previously dimly presumed, and thus also it can establish with moral certainty circumstances, for example, the origin of the illness, the effects of certain happenings, etc., which offer much help toward a clear description of personality development.

Furthermore, our jurisprudence has never been branded with the censure of excessive liberality in granting declarations of nullity; yet, using the same method, this jurisprudence usually proceeds in almost all cases where validity is questioned and especially in those concerned with defective consent,whether due to the radical incapacity of the subject or to a deliberate exclusion or simulation—and it usually places great weight on the circumstances, including those after the marriage. So, though neither the breakup of the common life nor the serious difficulties in the marriage relationship are enough to demonstrate nullity, nonetheless, they cannot be easily rejected as supports to proof in the light of which the judge can more clearly estimate the personality of the spouses.

The Argument

The Fathers thought it pointless to delay in showing the unusual nature of the respondent, for this is abundantly clear not only in the reports of the doctors but also in the concordant depositions of the witnesses and the parties concerned. Hence, it is right to conclude that the case hinges on the careful consideration of the power and degree of the abnormality of Peter in regard to giving a genuine marital consent. Hence, we see the importance of the opinion of experts who examine the minutes and the documents beneath the penetrating light of their science.

Besides other doctors whose testimony is available, four experts, three of whom were court-appointed, helped the judges in successive stages of the case.

To Dr. Christopher, fresh from his ministration to the respondent, is due the detailed and thorough examination of the personality of the man. In his personality he found, among other discoveries:

> A) Such an abnormal isolation within himself that he judges the thinking of others according to his own and allows no chance for the affirmation of another: "They start with the principle that everybody is aware of what they are thinking, even though on the part of the sick person, there is no communication of private thoughts. Hence, the reactions of this kind of individual are based, not on what others can think or know, but rather on what these sick people are waiting for others to know and these sick people feed and show their contempt and resentment for anyone who does not know something which the sick are waiting for them to know independently of whether these others have or have not had the chance to learn the matter in question" (p. 158).
> B) A constant urge toward self-destruction, which seriously damages

his personal freedom: "His whole concept of life in self-destructive . . . All of his life has been notably dedicated to self-destruction in regard to his mother. Now all of this can seem obscure, but one must understand that Peter does what he does because it ought to be done, or because in so doing, he thinks he is helping someone; but, in fact, he does suddenly whatever is completely contrary to what was set before him to do" (pp. 166-167).

C) Concerning his marriage, such a poor picture of his relationship with the petitioner that it is completely foreign to interpersonal marriage: "When he married her, the first thing he said to Joanne was, not a word of love or of joy in seeing her again (he was then in the Air Force), but an expression of anger because she had failed to invite somebody to the wedding. At this point one must note that he had not let her know that he wanted this person to be invited, but in some way he expected her to know what he had in mind, and he became angry and furious with her because she had not invited this person" (pp. 157-158). ". . . Turning now to their married life, he started to form for himself the same portrait (to build the same idea) of Joanne, which, as far as I can determine, did not correspond to the facts. But he simply saw Joanne somehow as a projection of his mother" (p. 166). ". . . Thus he came to married life. It seems to me that his unconscious intention (of which he is not consciously aware) was simply to express his resentment against his mother, to feel oppressed and trampled; in other words, to relive his childhood in a different way—and this is what he has continued to do" (p. 167).

These words, which are further illuminated both by the past history of the man's disorder which was traceable even to his earlier childhood, and by his manner of acting in other situations of their life together, convincingly indicate the true essence of the respondent's personality. "Whatever he does is not done or seen with consideration for the feelings of others, or with regard for what others can think or need, or even in reply to one of his own needs or to help himself and feel better. It is done solely because he is absorbed in himself, and usually in a destructive way" (pp. 170-171).

Thus, according to the Doctor's opinion, a person with a paranoiac character— or, better, paranois— ". . . we can basically classify him as a paranoid personality" (p. 159)—who is insensitive to any interpersonal relationship properly so-called— "he gives the general impression that everybody knows what he knows; he communicates a deep feeling of diffidence or distrust of those who come into contact with him; moreover, he gives a deep impression of being preoccupied with a concern which also concerns others, but only insofar as they affect him; this is a preoccupation which concerns himself" (p. 159)—such a person, precisely insofar as he is abnormal, is rightly considered incapable of the marriage covenant: "I think he would have some concept on the intellectual level, but not on the emotional. . . . Essentially, insofar as he is aware of it, he does not foster any direct feeling for anybody" (p. 157); "No, in my opinion, no" (p. 158: namely, he was not able to fulfill matrimonial duties).

It must be admitted that the official expert, Dr. Knight, threw the weight of his opinion in favor of the validity of the marriage: "I do not think I can say that he did not have a correct understanding of his duties, of his conjugal obligations. . . . I do not see that one can say this. Perhaps he perceived these matters only on the intellectual level; but at least at that level, it seems that he comprehended them; on the intellectual level he was aware of them. Perhaps he had some emotional distortion due to his upbringing, but who does not have that?" (p. 189).

However, in regard to this opinion, it is worthwhile to make a few comments. First, Dr. Knight, together with Dr. Christopher, holds that the case concerns a paranoid personality: "You know that this man has a paranoid personality" (p. 187). But the point at issue is to determine whether the degree of abnormality is such that it incapacitates the person for a marriage consent: "I think that, given the structure of the personality of this man, he would have trouble in any conjugal relationship" (p. 188).

To defend the capacity of the man, this expert has used norms which are not very clear:—Thus, when he turns to matters which occur often and without deliberation, he writes: "In my opinion, one must take things as they seem. . . . It is presumed that these people—and perhaps the supposition is false—but one ought to presume, for reasons of convenience, that these people know what they are doing, that they have the correct evaluation of what they are doing, and that the covenant is valid, at least because it is not clear to all that the partners are psychotic, which means that their behavior is so psychotic that anyone could diagnose it as such. Just so: one must take matters of fact as they seem. I do not see how one can proceed any other way" (pp. 194-195), This manner of speaking must be termed at least unusual for an expert!

According to what was said in the section, "The Law," it is not right to draw analogies either with the ability to enter a contract in civil law or with criminal imputability: ". . . Certainly, the Church and anyone concerned in an agreement or contract follows such reasoning (I presume that this is so), because we do not examine each individual from a psychiatric point of view before we come to enter the contract . . ." (ibid). ". . . As far as civil court is concerned, I have no doubt about my statement: I would say that this man was capable of making a valid contract. . . . have observed that this man had troubles with the federal government and that he was under federal indictment. Apparently, the government holds him responsible" (p. 205).

When one gives special consideration to the unique nature of marriage, one sees that too much insistence is being placed on "merely intellectual" capacity, to the consequent neglect of the emotional: "I think that the composition of his personality at the emotional level would have blocked his capacity to fulfill the obligations of which he had an intellectual understanding" Tp. 191). "There seems to be no doubt that he is extremely hostile to his mother. . . . There is no doubt that he came to the marriage with a twisted mentality. . . . This relationship with his mother undoubtedly colored and twisted his attitude towards women in general" (p. 193).

Hence, even though the experts admit a degree of uncertainty in their interpretation £an uncertainty which does not necessarily derive from their words), the undersigned essentially agree with the judges called in the second instance, who say: "In judging the respondent, Dr. Knight describes well what is usually called a lack of proper judgment, or psychic incapacity. Even if the judges disagree with the conclusion of Dr. Knight, it is indeed because of his deposition, rather than in spite of it, that they judge that this marriage was invalid due to the psychic incapacity of the respondent."[31]

Dr. Morris, the second official expert, unhesitatingly favors incapacity. Though his report seems rather brief, by no means does it lack the same clarity; nor was there any reason why his report should be lengthened by more extended explanations, because he had made his own the conclusions of the preceding experts and approved the opinion of Dr. Christopher.

It helps to give the opinion of Dr. Morris concerning the aptitude of Peter: "Because of a personality block at the emotional level, I doubt that he could fulfill the duties of marriage" (p. 213). However, lest anyone should want to press too hard the literal meaning of a translated opinion, in which no one should minimize the difficulty of translating from a spoken language with distinctive characteristics ("the spirit of the English language") we have taken the correct and certain force of the words from the experts who answered the clear-cut questions of the judges: "Was he able to enter a marriage contract and to observe the obligations of such a contract for life?"—To this I have already replied above: "No" (p. 213). "In general, I believe that this marriage could in no way be healed or workable, granted that he (Peter) does not put up with a shared life" (p. 214).

Similarly, Dr. Gozzano, court-appointed expert, votes for incapacity: "The behavior of Peter toward Joanne, and probably toward any other wife, clearly shows his lack of more than one of those qualities (love, sharing, deep understanding) which make two spouses into one true couple harmoniously linked in a genuine marriage, qualities which are needed to be able to fulfill the conjugal duties. . . . This lack existed from the beginning of their relationship and, therefore, at the time of the wedding" (p. 21).

It is true that this expert gives a different diagnosis of the disorder of the respondent, whom he considers a 'fanatic,' but not 'paranoid.' But, whatever may be said about the importance which he gives to the signs of personality (that is, whether one should expect insanity from a person who is simply paranoid), nevertheless, "Peter lacks that tendency toward value-judgments which urge the paranoid toward insane imaginings" (p. 13)—the conclusion is the same as that of the preceding reports: "It is precisely what we find in Peter: rigidity of judgment, a vision of reality which is painted in clearly contrasting colors without shading an abnormal feeling of certainty; as a result, there is a kind of contentiousness and an inability to communicate with his neighbor in a way that is not merely logical, but especially emotional, affective, and genuinely human . . ." (p. 15).

Moreover, it is important to note how the expert discovers the psychopathic condition of Peter operative even at the time of the wedding, and this condition need not be attributed, as matrimonial failures are, to subsequent marital conflicts: "Rather far more acceptable and appropriate in relation to the act of the wedding consent, is the hypothesis of projection of his mother upon his wife" (p. 24). "A commercial or financial contract or transaction is a very different matter from the moral agreement termed marriage; to be valid, the first types require the ability to intend, that is, to undertake on the intellectual level the contents of the contract; whereas to assume and fulfill that special contract or responsibility called marriage, far more is required: one needs also participation on the emotional and ethical level" (p. 27). "On the 'abnormal level,' i.e., on the temperament and character of the respondent, I would say that the wife had had very little influence. . . . The wife must certainly have influenced the behavior of her husband by exacerbating some points of his personality which certainly antedated their marriage" (pp. 27-28).

This quotation from Prof. Gozzano is of great service in defining the extent and nature of the incapacity of the respondent. For it would not be enough to find Peter unsuited for building a happy married way of life, or that he was a person for whom married life would not have been reasonably recommended, or even, finally, that he is a person devoid of true feeling for his wife. Although all of this is true of this case, our statement goes further, and we think it is proved by the facts: The man is completely incapable of interpersonal communication, in other words, unable to incorporate into himself any of the feelings of his partner; hence, it is judged morally certain that his marriage consent was invalid.

It is not necessary to maintain that this man is incapable of any possible marriage. Whatever may be the case for other interpersonal relationships which he could have or will have formed, nonetheless, from what has been said about his dealings with the petitioner, it is sufficiently clear that we must judge that this concrete marriage was null from the beginning.

This conclusion, from the philosophical point of view, is sufficiently explained by psychologists, just as psychiatrists, who, in diagnosing the psychopathic personality of this man, clearly examine the case from the medical viewpoint. And we, too, involved in the field of law, and studying the same case under another formality, are moved by the reasons mentioned, to declare the man incapable of accepting his partner's rights, precisely as those of his partner, at least as those of this petitioner, through a marital consent which was only apparent and verbal, but not real.

The arguments used thus far lay open the main avenue toward a decision, inasmuch as they are based on the sciences. Now we must turn to the impression the man gave at the wedding.

His very own words are most helpful for our purpose:

In a letter written to the petitioner before the wedding, Peter clearly revealed his abnormal self-esteem and his unbelievable disregard for the judgments of his beloved bride: "If you have any complaints or dissatisfaction, for the sake of our love and your love, keep them to yourself" (note how his manner shows the excessive force of his emotions in that, among the other words, he writes these in capital letters!) . . . "I appreciate and love your wonderful Catholic qualities (thus, his feelings are directed toward ideas, and indeed his own ideas, rather than a person) but you cannot make me so angry and make me believe that I could never live with you when you act this way" (p. 136). "I love you, Joanne, and I want to be able to say that you are the girl for me. I want to be able to know that I can follow my heart and marry you and live a happy married life and make you happy. This is the only reason why I have taken time to mention matters which my kind of personality would not be able to take" (p. 242).

"I will not go through (I will not live) a married life of unhappiness just because I love you. I want a girl who believes that the husband is the head of the house and of the family—a girl who will not behave in such a way as to treat him as discourteous and naughty, e.g., because he says that his point of view is correct after he has thought about it.

"This is my last word on the matter. Either some changes will be made, or you do not love me enough" (p. 243).

Everything above was written by hand in printed letters; hence, it shows the dominant feeling spontaneously arising from the personality of the man. Let no one say that these expressions are common among those about to marry, and that these words do not exceed the bounds of what can and usually does happen in similar cases. Let us pass beyond the forcefulness with which he has expressed his feelings. "In my opinion, this is not a normal point of view concerning marriage, and it is certainly not normal at the beginning of a conjugal union. Such a way of thinking can come about later, but the entirety of his thinking even before the wedding consisted precisely in that marriage was a sacrifice which he would make" (cf. Dr. Christopher, p. 164). Considering the personality of Peter, these words form a symptom of great importance.

Consider also the description which the respondent gave of the way in which he approached his wedding and of the attitude which led him to marry: "I remember, and I laugh when I remember, the time when a young man said that he did not want to marry, and I said 'my God, you should not have married' . . . and he said 'Yes, but we had already sent out the invitations and ordered the beer.' I suppose the same would hold true for me, because my way of doing this is . . . ; well, I will simply say that what pleases you does not please me, I do not want to do what all women like to do" (pp. 67-68). "I am what I am, and if I am sufficiently attractive and pleasant—such as she likes, then do not try to change me" (p. 72).

". . . But if I were asked why I married or why I wanted to marry, my answer would be: because I wanted a family. If I could have the baby, something which is naturally impossible, but if I had the baby, I would feel at ease. I can say I have washed as much linen as any other woman, and I have washed the dishes, and I have always stayed at home, and I have always enjoyed staying with the babies" (pp. 76-77).

More serious, however, are those assertions concerning a kind of fixation toward a single object in marrying like the 'solipsism' of his expression of desire for the ends of marriage, which are essentially interpersonal. And add to this the disruptive preoccupation with his planning concerning the smallest details of the wedding and honeymoon, which so deeply disturbed the newlyweds because of the man's way of acting (pp. 50 ff.). An expert has thus interpreted this: ". . . he brought up some points which upset him concerning the invitations, some clothing, concerning what they were wearing and how he was in a hurry and preoccupied and upset with her because he was in a rush to return to his military base—as I have said, at that time, he was in military service. All this instead of being concerned about the marriage. He appeared as a totally passive participant during the preparations for the wedding" (p. 161). ". . . During the honeymoon, there was a kind of mad reaction on the first night of their marriage due to a complete misunderstanding between them about the reason why he had been angry . . . but he had an idea completely different from what was happening, and he maintained that he was not truly angry. According to his way of seeing things, he maintains that in the marriage he had never been truly angry, even though he made threats, for example, to want to strangle her, but he is not conscious that these threats were made in a state of rage" (p. 162).

In her statement, the petitioner fully confirms what the respondent has said. Moreover, she reports other matters, of which the man is perhaps unaware or which are somehow hidden from him, though they shed much light on the case. Thus she speaks of this relationship with his family and especially with his mother: "I noticed a strange animosity, a strange relationship with his mother. . . . In fact, he hated her. When we were hardly married, I started to put together all these matters and I concluded that I was dealing with an abnormal situation. Nobody hates his mother so violently as to call her dreadful names" (p. 23). About these words the specialist writes: "There is no doubt that Peter identified his mother with his wife and hence transferred to his wife the hatred which he had for his mother. Because it is worth our trouble to dwell on this subject, it is now only too easy to see the meaning of one of his letters from which I quoted earlier. If a man hates a woman, even if it be through a mechanism of projection, can he have the full ability to fulfill his conjugal duties?" (p. 24 of Dr. Gozzano).

This expert quotes from a pre-matrimonial letter from the man: "Baby, I love you, but I would like to be able to think that I could beat you and abuse you, and that you would still love me" (p. 224). This excerpt is important for us to grant what must be granted, namely, that the incapacity of the man to enter into a truly conjugal relationship antedated the wedding. This is true even if after the wedding, his psychopathic dealings with his wife were aggravated by her behavior ('I am still quite close to his family and I deeply love all of them' (petitioner, p. 24). "The behavior of the wife had contributed to the symptoms of abnormality in her husband. Hence, we say the proof is legitimate because it is drawn from the abnormal mutual relationship of the partners. But though her behavior contributed something, this fact does not deny that there remains the nucleus of his clearly psychopathic personality."[35]

Out of the group of witnesses, those were chosen who are truly commendable and eminent for their long-standing and close knowledge of Peter, for their professional abilities, and for the objectivity which they manifested in the case.

Dr. Shaw: "In retrospect, the relationship of Peter with his mother was not normal. This fact has decisive consequences for the capability of a young man to love a woman and subsequently to love a wife" (p. 181). "In the context of his experience, I do not believe he was able to respond normally to the duties or demands of marriage (p. 182).

Dr. Irwin; ". . . but we deny it (that is, we say that the respondent was incapable of giving a true marriage consent). The young man is exceedingly rigid. In marriage, there is give and take, and he cannot see the seriousness of this" (p. 209).

"In view of my earlier statements, I would have to say yes (namely, that his consent was invalid) . . . He was extremely rigid in his points of view, and he was making life impossible for this girl. . . . And from the way in which his wife described the situation, this was to be attributed to his psychotic nature rather than merely to a normal disagreement" (p. 209).

Fr. A: "I have always maintained that he had psychological problems. He could understand the mechanics of marriage—religion, children, fidelity, but beyond this, I seriously doubt that he was capable of observing the obligations which are part of the marriage. . . . I do not see how one can contract marriage with someone who is incapable of permanently continuing that union; for this reason, I do not believe that, on his part, there was complete and total consent, nor that this would be a valid marriage" (pp. 151-152).

Fr. B: "In my view, the view of a person unversed in psychology, I would say that Peter shows signs of misogyny, a fact that could have prevented him from giving a true marriage consent" (p. 179).

In what has already been said in the reports of experts and the statements of the partners and witnesses, the circumstances of the marriage have already been sufficiently described. If anyone still needs further arguments, from them the judges draw further strength for their moral conviction. It has seemed good, at the end of the decision, to summarize the changing course of this marriage.

As far as the pre-matrimonial period is concerned, the doctors unanimously pronounce the man a psychopath; they bring to light family conflicts even from early childhood, especially with his mother, and they show that these conflicts seriously wounded the personality of Peter. Concerning the marriage, writings are available and facts proven which easily show abnormal mental and emotional upsets together with the clear influence of so-called "psychic projection" of the mother upon the future wife. All this certainly prevented that peculiarly human and intimate interpersonal giving and accepting which true marriage implies.

The respondent behaved similarly in preparing for and entering the marriage and in the period after the wedding. Due to his remarkable psychic make-up—which, for other reasons, he was unable to overcome—he concentrated solely on himself. In no way did he consider any of the slightest desires and plans of the woman (which often express legitimate rights), and since he had reserved for himself the whole of his unusual personality, which was either consciously or unconsciously completely divorced from her rights, he came to a kind of marriage which was essentially defective.

Thus far, for the most part, a painstaking investigation has gone into all the elements which unfold the personality of the man as he was before marriage. The logic of our law indicated this procedure lest we open the door to doubtful conclusions and lest the fundamental failure of the marriage be illegitimately derived merely from the proven disaster of their cohabitation. The difficulty must be untangled more carefully, in that we must frankly admit that, at least on first sight, the man fulfilled his duties as father and head of his family: he had children and he merited praise for his frequent delight in them; he earned the daily bread for his family by working at different jobs— even though he did this with an uncertain mental balance and consequently, with a suspicious lack of success—at home he helped in many undertakings.

Yet in all this, one clearly sees concordance, not only with the information already stated about the psychopathic quality of this man, but also with his circumstances before his wedding. Thus, Peter can easily be said to have indeed satisfied those rights and obligations which he considers personally his own; but this he did, not as a husband, but as a person, in every case making his own rules without admitting the slightest right of his wife in regard to him. Nor could any other outcome be foreseen, granted the nature of the personality disorder which undoubtedly afflicted him.

But if the woman for her part must be blamed for the failure of the marriage, let us, in passing, consider the difference between the make-up of each of them and the difference of her effect on the nullity. No blame is to be attached to her for any abuse of his conjugal rights. Indeed, she received no recognition from her spouse. Blame rather may be put on the way, plausible, though often too forceful and insufficient for such a husband, in which she resisted the subjective and strictly selfish manner in which Peter envisioned and lived his marriage and his marriage relationship.

Finally, from the partners, strong proof is derived in support of the evidence, in that they, and especially she, sincerely tried to maintain the marriage. Hence, since Peter cannot be accused of base intentions, and since his wife is endowed with a serious awareness on the indissolubility of a sacred covenant, it is clear that the respondent was incapable of the interpersonal covenant of marriage, at least, of that which he entered with Joanne.

Decisions:

Affirmative; Peter forbidden to remarry unless the Ordinary has been consulted.

Footnotes

1. C. 1081: 2.
2. Cf. *S.T.*,II-II, q. 57, art. 1, ad 2.
3. Mt. 19:6.
4. Cf. Vatican II: *Gadium et Spes*, no. 48.
5. Cf. encyc. *Humanae vitae* by Paul VI, no. 8, in *AAS*, 60 (1968), 485-486.
6. *Supplement*, no. 14 init.
7. Cf. the decision of Lefebvre, 1 March, 1969, in a Malta case, Prot. no. 7236, no. 12
8. Cf. Quebec decision before Anne, Prot. no. 8971, 22 July, 1969, no. 4.
9. Montreal, Prot. no. 9325.
10. Cf. *Il Diritto Ecclesiastico*, an. 81, nn. 3-4 (1970), 226-227, no. 13.
11. Cf. the decision before Prior, 10 July, 1909 (1, 87, no. 3); before Teodori (34, 467, no. 2); before Jullien (34, 776, no. 2).
12. Cf. *S.T.*, q. 58, art. 5, ad 4.
13. *Ibid.*, Supplement, q. 43, art. 2, ad 2.
14. Literally; more is required than for sinning mortally, less suffices than for other contracts.
15. 53, 233, no. 2.
16. Cf. *S.T.*, Supplement III, q. 43, art. 2, ad 2.
17. Cf. the Montreal Case before Anne quoted above: "Treatment of such marriage cases would resemble breaking a marriage rather than declaring it null." *Ibid.*, no. 19.
18. Cf. controversy about "the manner of intercourse," e.g., in a decision before Sabattani; 22 March, 1963 (55, 196, ff.)—reported in *C.L.D.*, 6, pp. 612-616.
19. Cf. "Allocation of Paul VI to the Holy Roman Rota," *AAS*, 62 (1970), 112.

20. Cf. Merleau-Ponty: *Phenomenology of Perception*, Colin Smith, Trans. [New York: Humanities Press, 1972], pp. 356-357.
21. Cf. citation in Watzlawick, Helmick, Jackson: *Pragmatica della Communicazione Umana*, Roma, 1971, p. 83, no. 11.
22. *S.T.*, II-II, q. 58, art. 8.
23. *Op. cit.*, p. 267.
24. Cf. *Suppl. Instr.*, vol. 22-23.
25. Cf. *Psiquiatria Clinica*, Mexico: Editorial Espanol De Bengio, 1970, p. 459.
25a. *Compendio di Psichiatria*, (Torino, 1970), pp. 175-176.
26. Cf. *Manuel de Psychiatrie*, (Paris, 1970), pp. 126-129.
27. Cf. Schneider K.: *Klinische Psychopathologie*, (Stuttgart, 1973), p. 108.
28. Cf. Ian Gregory, *loc. cit.*
29. Cf. the Viviers decision before Pompedda, Prot. N. 9419, no. 2.
30. Cf. a decision before Anne [52, 271, no. 2].
31. P. 237, no. 18 of the Chicago Decision.
32. Cf. the report of Dr. Gozzano, an expert in his field, p. 33.

CANON 1081 (M.J.)
HOMOSEXUALITY
No. 17/Ellen vs. Walter

During the courtship of three years and engagement of nine months Ellen noticed nothing abnormal about Walter: he seemed conventionally affectionate and loving; in fact, he tried to have premarital sex with her several times, but she rebuffed him. One question-raising incident occurred during the prenuptial examination: the priest, who apparently had sacramentally-sealed knowledge of Walter's homosexual tendencies, warned him in Ellen's presence that he should always be completely honest and open with Ellen and not conceal anything from her. The priest also tried to warn Ellen's mother in a general way that Walter was not the right man for Ellen, but he would give no reason and managed only to peeve these people. The marriage took place as scheduled; it lasted fourteen years during which two sons were born. The only unusual thing which Ellen noticed during these years is that Walter seemed uninterested in sex for long periods; otherwise they seemed to her to have a good sexual relationship which she thought Walter enjoyed. During the last three years of common life Walter, who had always got along well with everyone, began to have trouble with his bosses at work. The family moved out to California the last year and here Walter began staying out late at night, refusing an explanation and avoiding sexual contact with his wife. When Ellen finally demanded an explanation for his late hours, Walter simply said that he was tired of marital responsibilities and wanted a divorce. Ellen took the children away for a thinking period; she returned a month later and Walter immediately confessed that he was a homosexual and had always been, and that he was involved with another man in a relationship which he wanted to make permanent.

    The Court formulated the grounds of nullity as the Respondent's incapacity to fulfill the essential obligations of the permanent covenant of marriage due to a psychosexual anomaly—in his case, homosexuality. The papal Commission for the Revision of the Code of Canon Law has pointed up this incapacity in *Communicationes-1971*, noting that it derives from the law of nature and is therefore usable before the promulgation of the revised Code. The incapacity touches not on the act of matrimonial consent as such, but on the ability of an individual to carry out or deliver the substance of his commitment in marriage on a permanent or perpetual basis. This incapacity is sometimes called *moral* impotence, as distinguished from physical impotence; and the Judge in his sentence cited three paragraphs from L.

Wrenn, *Annulments*, Ed. 2, pp. 55-56, in which homosexuality is considered in this light. Wrenn's work is so available that a complete citation seems unnecessary here.

The point of jurisprudence is that a person is morally impotent when he or she is radically unfit for marriage due to some incurable defect of personality which makes it impossible for this person to fulfill, and therefore to assume, the essential obligations of marriage on a permanent basis. It is impossible, in the interest of truth, to generalize and say that *all* homosexuals are incapable of marriage; but fixed homosexuals, and even some facultative inverts, do lack this basic fitness demanded by the matrimonial state. The object of marriage, which must be mutually given and received in the contract if it is to be valid, is a *perpetual* right to the conjugal act and to the communion of conjugal life. So at the time of contract a homosexual must be able to sustain marriage in its essential elements not just for a year or ten years, but until death; and if his or her sexual inversion is not reversible or redirectable before it has effectually destroyed the marital relationship, the incapacity relative to this marriage is considered legally incurable in our jurisprudence. Evidence of this is sought in the predominent etiology of the homosexual drive (although this Court thought the origin or cause is scientifically unknown and not crucial to a decision about the validity of a particular marriage), the chronological date of its appearance, the exclusivity of the attraction to one's own sex, the motives for entering marriage, the homosexual's adjustment to the heterosexual relationship, and the duration of the cohabitation. And in an annulment process the question confronting the Court is: Is this homosexual, by reason of his personality makeup, incurably incapable of fulfilling the spiritual, emotional and physical needs of his particular spouse over a long-range period of time?

The Petitioner Ellen testified that during fourteen years of married life she never suspected that her husband was a homosexual. He seemed to love her and the children. He enjoyed the sexual act with her, as far as she could tell; he seemed also to enjoy the other aspects of the conjugal relationship. "When we had sex, we had very good sex" Ellen recalled; "the only thing was that there were times when we didn't have sex very often." She thought this strange for a young man, but she attributed it to the fact that Walter was tired from overwork. Not until the end did she learn the truth: "He used the word 'gay' and he said he had been gay all his life, since before we were married. He said he had been living a double life all his life, and he just couldn't live it any more. He told me that there was a time, before we were dating, when he was seriously ill and even had the last rites; and at that time he prayed that the Lord would take him because he was right with the Lord then. He knew that he was homosexual at the time and he just wished that he had died instead of going on into the life. He told me that this was the reason he wanted a divorce—that he had been a homosexual since before we were married, that he had been so through our marriage, and at the time of telling me this he was involved with a man and wanted to continue the relationship."

The Respondent Walter, questioned by a priest-Auditor under rogatory commission, made this confession: "I was aware that I was drawn to a homosexual way of life prior to my marriage. My dad died when I was two and a half years old; I was close to my mother. The tendency was there; who knows what causes it? I entered marriage because society expected it. I did love Ellen (even now I love her as the mother of my children, not as a wife). We were from a small town and when you graduated from high school, you did one of two things—marry or go to college. I got married . . . I feel that I deceived Ellen; she knew nothing of my problem. I felt that I had done a bad thing to a nice person, but I thought that marriage might be some cure." Asked about the parish priest's attempt to warn Ellen before the wedding, Walter says: "I don't think he tried to warn her, but I do think he tried to warn me. He wanted us to make a general confession; I would not do this. He knew about my problem from confession, but I knew that his hands were tied. I wanted to prove him wrong."

Walter described his experiment with the conventional relationship of marriage in these words: "I wanted to cope with a heterosexual relationship, but as time went on I realized that there was no way. I was losing a battle with myself. Sex was a chore; it was distasteful. I really didn't desire it. I was not being honest with myself. However, I tried and fought the problem. I went into debt so that I would have to work harder and harder and stay busy and thus keep my mind off the problem. We had everything, except that I did not have a clear mind . . . I realized almost right away that it would not work. It was phony. I was not being truthful to myself. If there had not been children I would probably have divorced the first year." Asked whether he had been leading a bisexual life throughout most of the marriage, Walter answered: "Yes, I was having sex with males throughout my marriage. I was leading a double life. I was a good actor. She knew nothing about this; she was totally surprised when she found out after our separation." Finally, to the question of why he did not seek professional help or therapy, Walter replied: "I have talked to people about my homosexuality; I have consulted with priests. My information is that professional help would not solve the problem. There is no way to reverse the trend. It remains a mystery . . . I will never marry again" the Respondent concluded.

The priest—Auditor who interviewed the Respondent considered him truthful and cooperative, and passed along this eye—witness description: "His appearance was interesting. He wears three rings. He is a small fellow, well dressed, hair styled, dark glasses resting in his hair. He sells jewelry and drives a Cadillac. He currently lives with a fellow who is his lover. He is quite open about this. They have lived together for over two years. He says that if the civil law would permit it, they would probably get married. He says that this fellow has been very faithful to him, sticking by him throughout the turmoil of the divorce."

The Petitioner's present parish priest, who counselled her after the final separation, thinks there is no doubt that Walter deceived Ellen before their marriage, that he married her because at that time homosexuality was something which was swept under the rug or hidden in a closet, so it was common for a man with this proclivity to marry in the hope of leading a normal married life. But in the end it was impossible, the homosexual tendency was too strong to resist. "I don't think there was any hope for this marriage," the priest concluded. "I don't think there is a hope in the world for this couple to ever get together and live together in a compatible union as husband and wife."

The Judge concluded his sentence with this paragraph:

"In the Court's opinion this is conclusive evidence that the Respondent was emotionally and psychically unable to fulfill the essential obligations of the heterosexual relationship of marriage due to his perverted sex drive. The Court does not feel called on to point up the etiology of this condition; what is clearly proven is that the Respondent's homosexuality predated the marriage and was continuously practiced throughout married life. Marital relations were distasteful, a chore, done out of obligation and to carry on the act of being a husband until the point in time arrived when the Respondent could not tolerate his double life any longer. His homosexual bent was the sole cause of the breakup of this marriage; since then he has lived exclusively a homosexual way of life and has no intention of ever marrying again. The court has no doubt that this Respondent was incurably incapable of fulfilling the basic spiritual, emotional and physical needs of a wife on a long-term basis, and that the Petitioner was led into this marriage by his deceit in concealing his basic perversion."

DECISION: FIRST INSTANCE—Affirmative
DISPENSATION FROM APPEAL

CANON 1082 (C.L.D.)
IGNORANCE

No. 18/Monica vs. Ernest

Facts

This marriage was celebrated in 1944 between Monica and Ernest, both baptized Anglicans, before an Anglican minister. In 1954 the parties separated because of desertion on the part of the woman. The man afterward obtained a divorce and remarried. In 1957 the woman entered the Catholic Church, and in 1959 she brought suit for nullity on the ground that she was ignorant of the nature of marriage. The judgment, 10 March, 1961, was adverse to her claim, but it was reversed by an appellate tribunal, 8 March, 1962, and so the case is brought to the Rota on appeal.

At the time of the marriage the woman was 24 years of age, of at least average intelligence and culture, had attended public schools, made elementary studies in biology, was fond of music. For six months before the marriage the parties had had the normal relations of an engaged couple, with the usual signs and gestures of endearment, but without sexual intercourse.

That with this background and at the age of 24 she could remain ignorant of the conjugal right is explained by an extraordinary combination of facts. Her mother and father had, since her early childhood, occupied separate apartments in the house. Not only were "the facts of life" never revealed to her, but her mother consistently misinformed her and misled her with false principles. Sex was something intrinsically evil and unmentionable. At her first menstruation, when she went in some alarm to her mother, she was simply told that this would happen every month. At the birth of her little brother she was told that "the doctor brought him." In her reverence for her mother it never occurred to her to doubt her word. Questions on the subject were not permitted. Thus she not only remained in complete ignorance, but she developed an instinctive abhorrence for everything connected with sex, a sentiment which her natural simplicity and purity of heart tended to accentuate. There is much more to the same effect in the evidence and in its discussion by the Court, but it must be omitted, especially as the chief interest of the case lies in the Court's clear and forthright exposition of the law regarding ignorance of the conjugal right.

The Law

Some authorities consider canon 1082 as standing by itself, apart from canons 1081 and 1013, as if it alone purported to state absolutely the degree of knowledge that is *sufficient* for valid matrimonial consent: *"necesse est ut contrahentes saltem non ignorent matrimonium esse societatem permanentem inter virum et mulierem ad filios procreandos."* The Court actually cites an earlier Rota decision in which this canon is quoted with emphasis on the word *"saltem,"* which is interpreted parenthetically as ("ideoque *satis* est"); whereas on the contrary *"saltem"* clearly indicates that *this knowledge at least is required*, without any intimation that it is also sufficient. It cannot be sufficient without some knowledge of the *"ius in corpus"* which is conferred by mutual contractual consent (c. 1081:2).

The Court calls attention to the extraordinary reticence and obscurity with which many authorities treat of this essential matter. This decision clearly holds that valid consent requires more than the mere knowledge that marriage is a permanent society between a man and a woman for the purpose of "having" children. The words of canon 1082 are *"ad filios procreandos."* *"Procreare,"* in this context implies sexual cooperation. There must be knowledge that by the marriage contract the parties mutually confer the right to mutual bodily cooperation by means of sexual organs. *"Sufficiens haberi debet praevisus mutuus concursus physicus, ponendus per quaedam organa specifica, huic operi aptata et propria, quamvis a contrahente non clare perspecta et cognita in eorum identitate.*

Because of this clear and forthright statement of the law, the present decision deserves to be classed as a "leading case" on the subject of the nullity of marriage because of ignorance of the substance of the contract.

The Decision

Affirmative, seu constare de matrimonii nullitate in casu.

CANON 1083 (C.L.D.)
ERROR OF PERSONS

No. 19/Auxiliatrix vs. Espedito

The following case was tried *coram* Canals and is of special interest because of its teaching on error regarding a quality of the person redounding into error as to the person.

The Facts

1. On the 19th of October, 1965, Auxiliatrix contracted marriage and its civil effects with Espedito in the cathedral church of Niteròi, Brazil, without knowing or suspecting that this man was held by a purely civil bond to Astrogild by whom he fathered three children. Auxiliatrix found out this fact two months after her marriage when Astrogild charged the man with bigamy and he was thrown into prison (for two years). Shortly after the sentence of condemnation on 16 August, 19——, Auxiliatrix, without any delay, sought from the Tribunal of Niteròi a declaration of nullity of her marriage on the grounds of error of quality redounding into error as to the person. By decision on the 9th of March, 1967, the Niteròi Tribunal acknowledged that kind of error and declared the marriage null. However, on appeal, the Tribunal of Sao Sebastiao do Rio de Janeiro, by its decision on the 30th of September, 1968, declared nullity of the marriage, not on the grounds of error but on grounds introduced later, namely, on the incapacity of the man to hand himself over to his wife in marriage, that is, on the grounds of exlusion of fidelity.

Finally, the case was referred to this Apostolic Tribunal and there remains to be resolved the usual formula of question: "Is there proof of nullity of marriage in the instance?"

The Law

2. The notion of error regarding a quality redounding into an error as to the person (c. 1083:2, 1°) is manifold. The strictest notion, indeed, is that in which the quality is understood as the only characteristc which identifies a physical person who is otherwise unknown. This error, it seems, is an error regarding quality in name but in reality is an error regarding the person. Another notion is less strict since the quality

rather than the person is looked to, for example: "I wish to marry a person of noble blood, such as I think Titia is; then the error redounds into a substantive because it is the quality which is directly and mainly looked to and secondarily the person" (Alphonsus Liguori: *Theologia Moralis,* Bassani, 1832, Lib. VI, Tract. VI, cap. III, n. 1016). Giacchi (*Il consenso nel matrimonio*, 1968, p. 73) explains this thus: "In the case of 'error giving cause,' which is excluded by canon 1083:2 as a basis for nullity, the person entering marriage primarily intends to espouse the other contractor, even if this decision has been arrived at only because he supposes that the other party has a quality without which he would not have espoused her. On the other hand, in the case of "error redounding," the person entering marriage wishes to espouse, so to say, the quality under consideration, that is, to say it better, an abstracted type of person which has been constructed by the abstraction of that quality (for example, virginity, nobility, musicianship, diplomatist, American, etc." The third notion is that the moral, juridical, social quality is so intimately connected with the physical person that, if that quality is absent, the physical person also turns out to be utterly different. Therefore, if a person contracts marriage with another person who is married purely civilly, although thought to be free of all bonds, there is an invalid contract according to this third opinion, not because of any implicit or interpretative condition, but because of an error regarding a quality redounding into an error as to the person considered in a more complete and integral manner. For a purely civil marriage cannot be confused with concubinage. Such marriage between non-believers and between baptized non-Catholics is recognized by the Church as valid. Between two Catholics or between a Catholic and a non-Catholic such marriage is not recognized as valid because of defect of form. Nevertheless, even in canon law, it is recognized as regards certain juridical effects, for example, for a radical sanation, for providing the basis for the impediment of public propriety and crime, for the infliction of certain penalties. Moreover, where an absolute separation of civil and religious marriage obtains because of civil law, the Church is accustomed to exhort, admonish, and order the faithful to enter into civil marriage first and then into a religious marriage so that the religious marriage may be strengthened by indirect sanction arising out of the civil laws relative to indissolubility, legitimacy of children, and property rights. Consequently, although civil marriage must be rejected as a matter of principle, it cannot be denied that it constitutes a status of the person and, as a result, that an error implying that kind of status redounds into an error as to the person. In this regard the rejection which the Church makes of civil marriage within the stipulated limits, does not prevent this conclusion because the Church also rejects slavery in the strict sense of the term and yet an error in its regard, by express prescription of the law, certainly invalidates a marriage. We also note that a strict interpretation of error regarding a quality redounding into the person is redolent of the pre-Tridentine discipline when marriages could take place without observance of any form and were decided upon by the parents. Referring to the Italian civil law (art. 122 c.c.) which, in the matter under consideration, coincides with canon law, Jemolo (*Il Matrimonio*, Utet, 1961, pp. 122 ff.) thus explains the point: "The formula, which maintains the same stance presented in the canonical tradition, does not correspond to the realities which can occur. This same tradition, as appears from reading through the jurisprudence of the ecclesiastical tribunals, is a dead thing, reflecting the pre-Tridentine period when there were no acts of the civil state; when normal marriages were imposed by the parents, practically without an engagement period and without acquaintance with the other party; when marriages in the upper classes were frequently proxy marriages; when there could have been a meeting between reality and the supposition that a man would have espoused Bertha without interesting himself whether she was beautiful or deformed, cultured or illiterate, virtuous or not, but only intending to marry her insofar as she was the daughter of the King of Cyprus, identifying her as the daughter of the King of Cyprus. But this is outside the real order of our world of today. . . . We should ask ourselves what are those qualities which are commonly considered as delineating the figure of a person without thereafter resorting to investigate (as long as the ignorance or error is certain) what would in reality be the reaction of the spouse faced with the discovery of a mistake into which he had fallen. . . . If we place ourselves in this avenue, it is almost impossible to deny the relevancy of error not only in the hypothesis mentioned above (the case of a Catholic priest, or of a man or a woman bound by solemn vows, or of a man or a woman who has married civilly a person he/she did not know was bound by a religious bond) and also in the more remote case in which marriage is contracted with a countrified person who has admitted polygamy, but also in the case of another error which consists is believing that one is marrying an honest person when, instead, one had married a person who has a long history of criminal convictions, or marrying a virgin when, instead, he has given his hand to a prostitute." Finally, we think that it must not be forgotten that the teaching and jurisprudence up to the present have followed the restrictive interpretation of Sanchez (*De S. Matrimonii Sacramento Disputationes,* Lib. VII, disp. XVII, nn. 27 and 31) who, however, does not seem to have correctly interpreted the teaching of St. Thomas (*Summa Theol.,* Supplementum Partis 3, q. Ll, art. 2, ad 5). Inasmuch as the times have notably changed after so much scientific progress, the world wars, the universally vindicated liberty and dignity of men, and especially, after Vatican Council II, we cannot still relate invalidating error as to quality *only* to those matters which are recognized as looking to a given physical person such as the name or those matters which perhaps substitute for the name.

[Numbers 3-6 examine the appellate court's introduction of the grounds of exclusion of fidelity.]

7. Consequently, there can be no argument but that Auxiliatrix fell into error when marrying Espedito on the 19th of October, 1965. That this error centered on a quality redounding into an error as to the person is likewise beyond doubt from what has been developed *in the Law,* because, although the plaintiff had known the defendant through an engagement period of fourteen months, nevertheless, she did not know of his civil union and, as a result, she thought she was actually marrying a single man when, as a matter of fact, she married a married man. This man had already civilly married Astrogild on 17 September, 1960, and from that marriage had fathered three children. When he contracted the second religious marriage, that first marriage was still in full existence inasmuch as it had not been dissolved either by the death of his wife or by divorce which is prohibited by civil law in Brazil. The criminal conviction with which the man, not Auxiliatrix, was saddled, confirms the error. As a matter of fact, this error was produced by deceit on the part of the man who, in order to win the

marriage, simulated a state of freedom, presented himself under a false name, and by means of this false name—Espedito C. in place of Espedito S.—furnished himself with documents of freedom: but this fact does not create any difficulty because of the nullity of the marriage does not emanate simply from deceit but from the effect of the deceit which was the error concerning the true status of the person. To be sure, the plaintiff did not set a condition regarding the freedom of the civil status of the man: but the error regarding the person or redounding into an error as to the person produces an invalidating effect by its own force without the quality needing to be reduced into any form of condition. In her deposition, among other things, Auxiliatrix said: "If I had known before the marriage that Espedito was married, I would not have agreed even to becoming engaged to him and in no wise would I have given consent to the marriage." From these and similar words by the witnesses Mary C., Elizabeth, Aeneas, the conclusion can certainly be drawn against a stipulated condition or for an interpretative condition but not against error which consists in a false mental representation which happened in this case. Moreover, words of that kind directly reveal the mind of the persons who made the error after they discovered the error.

[Number 8 rejects the grounds of exclusion of fidelity.]

9. After having weighed and considered everything both in fact and especially in law, we, the undersigned auditors of the turnus, having invoked the name of Christ, decree, declare and definitively pronounce sentence: *In the affirmative, that is, proof is had of nullity of the marriage in the instance because of error regarding a quality redounding into error as to the person of the man, the defendant.*

Case #20

CANON 1083 (M.J.)
ERROR OF PERSON (FRAUD)
No. 44/Vincent vs. Jane

Vincent and Jane engaged in sexual relations since the Petitioner was age 16. A year later, Jane became pregnant. Vincent left for military service, and apparently, had no intention whatever of marrying Jane. One day, Jane appeared in the Commander's office and Vincent was called in. Jane said that she wanted to marry Vincent so that the child would have a name. Vincent wanted to hold off on marrying but Jane was crying and created quite a scene. The Commander did not involve himself in the situation and the matter was turned over to the Catholic chaplain. The chaplain discussed the whole situation with the parties and did raise the question of paternity of the child. Jane insisted that Vincent was indeed the father. Vincent agreed to marry Jane. In his testimony he stated: "The one and only reason I married Jane was because she swore that she was pregnant with my child." The baby was born some three months later and was obviously black even though Vincent and Jane were both caucasian.

There were psychological factors involved which suggest that one or both parties were consentually incapacitated at the time of the marriage. The Court noted: "Very often this would simply be the beginning of an unhappy marriage and the allegation regarding incapacitating psychological factors would be the only *caput nullitatis* worth considering. However, the allegation of substantial error regarding Vincent's paternity of the child became a key factor.

The Court draws on a summary of current jurisprudence on error and deceit as found in *Handbook for Marriage Nullity Cases*, Hudson et al., Ottawa (St. Paul University) 1975; pp. 79-80. Commenting on Canons 1083, 1084, and 104, it is noted that the error under consideration is a false judgment about a fact, and not about the law. Furtermore, the type of error must be substantial. Substantial error is present when the quality or attribute about which a spouse errs is a true quality, is present at the time of the marriage, subjectively grave, unknown to the other party, and is fraudulently concealed for the purposes of obtaining marital consent. In addition to the above-mentioned points, when the deceived person learns about the presence of the quality after marriage, a real crisis must result if the error is substantial. That is, the discovery of the quality must give rise to serious consideration of terminating the marriage then and there. (Cf. Wrenn, *Annulments*, pp. 100-101)

Worthy of note are the proposed new canons on error and deceit, and, in particular, canon 300, which has no corresponding number in the Code of Canon Law.

It reads: "The person who enters into matrimony deceived by fraud, perpetrated to obtain consent, on some quality of the other party, which could seriously disrupt the community of conjugal life, contracts invalidly." This is interesting because it takes into consideration in cases involving fraud a consequence which flows from the teaching of the Second Vatican Council. *Gaudium et Spes* teaches that the object of matrimonial consent is the partnership rather than the *jus in corpus*. (For a discussion on the formal object of matrimonial consent taking into consideration the teaching of *Gauidium et Spes*, cf. decision *coram* Anne, February 25, 1969, *Ephemerides Juris Canonici*, 1970, pp. 419-442).

The allegation of the Petitioner is set forth clearly and unequivocally by him in three simple sentences: "The one and only reason I married Jane was because she swore that she was pregnant with my child. This turned out to be totally false. She used deceit in order to coerce me into marriage." The Respondent herself is very frank in telling the Court how the marriage took place and confirming, by her own confession, the allegation of the Petitioner. (She freely came forth to testify after reading the citation in the diocesan newspaper). She stated that the parties "hung around in a group of kids" when they were 14, 15, or 16. Vincent had no plans for marriage, and marriage had not been discussed before the pregnancy. He wanted to establish himself in life before marriage. Jane freely admitted that she had sexual relations with others. She testified: "We made the decision to get married because I was pregnant. I wasn't pregnant by him. I didn't know that at the time . . . He was probably convinced that he was the father of the child. Well, I didn't—I was kind of hoping it was his, and I thought if I opened my mouth and it wasn't, then he would know I wasn't faithful, you know, you know what I mean, like if I told him I was with somebody else and it happened to be his baby, then I would be letting out a bunch of stuff that was unnecessary, so I thought I'd kinda let things roll and see what happens, and as it was, it wasn't his baby and he knew it and that was it, we split."

The witnesses also substantiated the allegation of the Petitioner and the confession of the Respondent. For example, one witness stated: "Jane was not honest with him about her pregnancy and broke up when he found that he not only was not the father of the child but the child was of a different race.

The Court then noted that the Petitioner, the Respondent, and the witnesses all testified that knowledge of this deceit precipitated a crisis. The Petitioner testified: "When the child was born, it was obviously Negro . . . I tried to talk her into giving the child up, but she refused . . . if she had been willing to do that, I would have been willing to try to put the relationship back together. But I could not bring myself to accept that child." The Respondent testified: "It was obvious that it wasn't his child . . . Next, we went to some marriage counselling, and well, we decided, you know, that if we were going to stay together that I had to give up the baby, and I could see his point, and I didn't want to give up the baby, that's my baby, you know, so we just—I let him be . . . so I said, okay, Vincent you go your way and I'll go mine." One of the witnesses stated: "The breakup came when Vincent found out the baby was not his . . . He became quite emotionally upset . . ."

The Court then addressed the allegation of psychological factors on the part of either or both parties. The report of the Court expert focused primarily on the problems then suffered by the Respondent, but it does provide the setting in which the Court considered the alleged grounds:

The total accumulated testimony, plus the admission of the respondent herself leads to the inevitable conclusion that at the time of the marriage she was far too unstable and emotionally immature to have accepted and fulfilled its basic responsibilities.

These circumstances themselves, that is, her illegitimate pregnancy, were the occasion of her pressure on the Petitioner to marry, and yet at the same time, when the child was born it was discovered to be the child of a Negro father. One can argue obviously simulation and deception and fraud in this case. However, it is obvious that the primary problem was that of emotional immaturity and general personality instability. The Respondent as a teen-ager had serious discipline problems in high school, and was known as the neighborhood whore. It is further stated that she had made a suicidal attempt in her teens and had been under psychiatric treatment. The family of origin of the Respondent was equally pathological, one which would have been a fruitful ground for the development of her sociopathic and delinquent behavior."

"Given the level of immaturity as well as the hostile resentment and sexually acting out behavior at the time of the marriage, there is no reasonable possibility that the Respondent could have been sufficiently objective and capable of true freedom of choice at the time of the marriage. The whole affair was nothing more than another opportunistic and manipulative act on her part in a series of attempts to compensate for her very disordered and disturbed emotional existence."

DECISION: AFFIRMATIVE on both counts.
    DISPENSATION FROM APPEAL

CANON 1086
EXCLUDING RIGHTS AND OBLIGATIONS OF MARRIAGE
No. 4/Jim vs. Nancy

The Facts

Jim, a non-Catholic, was stopped from presenting this case by Article 36 of the Instruction *Provids Mater* and even could be charged with being a direct cause of the alleged nullity. He appealed to the Supreme Sacred Congregation of the Holy Office and was granted the legal right to act as plaintiff. Since both parties to the contested marriage live in the Archdiocese of——and since the marriage was contracted in the territory of this Archdiocese, the plaintiff's petition was accepted and the trial proceeded with full observance of all procedural requirements. Hence definitive answer is now given to the the *dubium* established in the *contestatio litis:*

Has the nullity of the marriage in this case been proved on the grounds of total simulation?

The Law

Canon 1086 establishes the legal presumption that the parties of any marriage give full consent to the marriage contract itself, as indicated by the words and signs used in the marriage ceremony. The plaintiff, therefore, has the obligation to prove the contrary fact that full consent was not given. The process of proof includes, first, the production of documents. In cases of this kind, the record of the marriage ceremony gives documentary proof that the ceremony itself took place and thus supports the presumption established by Canon 1086. Proof can also be produced in the form of testimony by those who had immediate knowledge of the words, actions and omissions of one or both parties in connection with the marriage, before, during and after the ceremony. In the present case, testimony was given by the two parties and by three other witnesses.

It is here necessary to add that a further element of proof derives from the "judicial cognizance" by the judges of the background of the society in which the parties live. Even though there are no witnesses who testify explicitly concerning this background, the judges have the right and duty, based on their own experience, to consider the judicial depositions in the light of the social, ethical and religious principles which govern people of the present day in the matter of marriages which are later charged with total simulation. It is obvious that the bare words of the recorded testimony should be understood in the sense which they have in the thinking and speech of the present day. This sense is often considerably different from the literal meaning of the words themselves.

It will be noted below that marriages "to give the child a name" have a specific social meaning which the judges themselves know and which they must take into account when weighing the testimony before them. This is mentioned at the present time to indicate that this "judicial cognizance" is a proper and necessary part of the process of reaching a decision, and has always been recognized as in full agreement with Canons 1868ff., and Canons 1825ff.

The Argument

The plaintiff testified that he married the respondent in 1946, under the following circumstances. They had been friendly, and even sexually intimate, but had not contemplated marrying each other. She became pregnant. The plaintiff knew he was responsible, but did not wish to marry her because he was still in school, had no income and felt no real love for her. They first tried, ineffectually, to procure an abortion. Later they went to New York City, still with no definite plans. Very few knew of the pregnancy: her parents did not, nor did the plaintiff's parents.

After living for some time as man and wife, and after consultation with an uncle of the respondent, they agreed to go through a civil marriage, but live separately. The expected child would be given up for adoption and there would be no common life thereafter. Actually, after the ceremony, the plaintiff spent a year in California, while the respondent returned to her home. The respondent secured a divorce in 1948.

This is the plaintiff's averment. He admits the marriage ceremony, which is proved by civil records. He claims there was a formal pact, before the marriage, in which he and the respondent agreed that there would be no common life, that they would not keep and rear the child of their illicit relations, and that a divorce would be obtained at an early date. He therefore claims that the marriage ceremony would not, in his case, mean the assumption of the obligations (and rights) of a husband, and that to the respondent, the ceremony would not entail the duties and rights of a wife. The motivation for this pact, was the desire to provide for the respondent's social reputation and to establish a legal background for the expected baby. The affirmative agreement to enter a civil marriage was limited to purely external, social and legal arrangements. It was accompanied by an agreement to exclude any duty to establish common life, to live in marital union and to accept the obligation of mutual fidelity on a permanent basis, that is, until one or the other died.

The plaintiff's averment must be proved. His case is strengthened by the judicial deposition of the respondent. She confesses sexual intimacies before there was any marriage even in contemplation, the fact that she became pregnant, and that she and the plaintiff agree. "He made it clear that he did not want to marry and agreed only on the terms that a divorce be obtained as soon as possible and the baby adopted . . . and I agreed. This was in late September. . . . It was discussed only with my mother and Ann H. by mail."

Article 117 of *Provida Mater* states that the depositions of the two parties to a contested marriage are not adequate proof of the alleged nullity; but there is universal agreement that they furnish "valuable corroborative evidence, which may help in the ascertainment of the entire proof" (Doheny, *Canonical Procedure, Formal Procedure*, p. 339).

Three witnesses gave judicial deposition, Roberta G. stated: "When she found herself pregnant, they decided to marry. They married, not of love, but merely not to bring an illegitimate child into the world. They wanted to give the baby a name. . . . If she were not not pregnant, he would not have married her. All he wanted was a good time. . . . He told my husband and me this even before the marriage. She said the same. They both told my husband and me, before the marriage, that they would marry to give the baby a name and then, after the baby was born, they would divorce. They had no intention of living together after the marriage ceremony."

Art G., husband of the previous witness, and brother of the plaintiff, testified to the same effect, except that he dated his knowledge as coming from what he heard only after the marriage. Later, in more specific testimony, he reported a conversation about a week before the marriage, during which the plaintiff told the respondent: "I'll marry you but I will not live with you as a husband." They planned on the marriage and then a divorce. He said to her, "When the baby comes, you can get a divorce." She agreed to this. Ted Riley, first cousin of the plaintiff, stated: "I heard (from Jim G. about 1949 or 1950) that this marriage of convenience, was to be terminated at the birth of the child."

This is the supporting testimony provided by the plaintiff. It indicates the motive for a marriage ceremony, the respondent's pregnancy; and the mutual agreement that the marriage be only a temporary arrangement, to be quickly dissolved by a complete civil divorce. The tribunal, however, notes with regret that the plaintiff did not secure the testimony of the respondent's uncle and her mother. According to the parties, these relatives intervened in the arrangements for the contested marriage and dealt directly with the parties in the formulation of the alleged pact. The absence of this testimony removed what would have been, presumably, a strong corroboration of the plaintiff's case.

The tribunal further notes the divergence of the two depositions given by Mr. and Mrs. Art G. The wife intimated that she and her husband had exactly the same information, prior to the marriage. The husband at first dated his knowledge after the marriage, but later described an interview, at which his wife seemingly was not present. Ted R. dates his knowledge from 1949 or 1950, some three or four years after the marriage. Admittedly, the depositions in the Acts are not beyond criticism.

All this notwithstanding, the judges of the Metropolitan Tribunal are convinced, with moral certainty, that both parties consented to a premarriage agreement or pact whereby their performance of a civil marriage ceremony did not bind them to a permanent and exclusive giving and acceptance of the rights and duties of husbands and wives. Even with the limited testimony in the case, it cannot be doubted that the respondent was pregnant, that neither felt any strong desire (so-called love) for a permanent and exclusive marital partnership, that the parties separated completely after the marriage, that the wife obtained a complete divorce (in 1947), very shortly after the marriage, and that both thereafter entered new marriages. There is not the slightest divergence or questioning about this background of the case. There is the further element that the parties left Boston and went to New York for privacy and even secrecy. The respondent's family (apparently) knew of the development, but the plaintiff managed in such wise that, according to his brother, his parents even now do not know that the contested marriage even took place. This secrecy is itself an indication that the parties wished something much less than a publicly known and publicly recognized status as husband and wife. It also serves as explanation for the limited number of available witnesses.

The Metropolitan Tribunal notes that both parties and the three witnesses are non-Catholic, reared in and accustomed to the present day non-religious concept of marriage. The Rota has, in various decisions, noted that it is almost unthinkable that a party would fraudulently dissimulate such a holy and sacred contract as marriage. The tribunal however, has judicial cognizance that much of our society conceives of marriage as neither holy nor sacred, and certainly as always dissoluble: in this background a merely temporary assumption of marriage is not immoral or unethical, and it is not fraudulent when the parties agree to such an arrangement. With the background of this case, a simulated civil marriage is entirely probably. The parties wished to provide legal legitimacy for their child and for the respondent's social respectability. The civil ceremony, merely as a recorded civil act, took care of these needs. On the other hand, the plaintiff had various reasons not to desire a real marriage and felt no "love" for the respondent; and she for her own reasons was content with a speedy ending of their relationship. This attitude does not seem to mean aversion or hate, but it does indicate a readiness to accept a nominal temporary but not real status as husband and wife. At this point simulation was more than a mere possibility or probability; it was the obvious prudent and necessary course of action, socially and legally permissible, not affected by any conscientious scruples or worries. The depositions given by the parties are not, in canon law, complete proof; but in this case they are supported by three respectable witnesses, each of whom knew the background of the marriage and the reaction of the parties to this background. It was a marriage "to give the baby a name." This popular phrase, seen in its present day American usage, means a nominal, but not a real marriage; a temporary, not a permanent association; freedom to seek elsewhere for a spouse, not a vow of exclusive fidelity.

Wherefore, we, the judges of the Metropolitan Tribunal of——duly constituted to give judgment, having invoked the Divine Name and having considered before God the law and the facts, in first instance, define, decree and issue this definitive sentence, answering the proposed *dubium* in the *affirmative, that the nullity of the marriage in this case has been proved on the grounds of total simulation.*

We order that this sentence be promulgated to the parties and the Defender of the Bond in accordance with Canon 1877.

So we decree, ordering all local ordinaries and tribunal officials to carry into effect this sentence, and to take action against any disobedience in accordance with the Sacred Canons, using those executive and coercive measures which, in the circumstances, shall appear to be most opportune and efficacious.

CANON 1086 (T.R.)
TOTAL SIMULATION
Excluding Indissolubility

No. 7/Ann vs. Jim

The Facts

Ann was born on September 1, 1940 and was baptized in New Orleans, Louisiana on September 20, 1940. Jim was born on October 4, 1941 and was baptized in New Orleans, Louisiana on October 20, 1941. Plaintiff and defendant were both reared in the Catholic faith.

Sometime, about October of 1960, the defendant was introduced to the plaintiff. This was about six months prior to the marriage here in question. Plaintiff and defendant began dating. By December of 1960 or January of 1961 the parties were quite serious with each other and began to think of marriage. In February of 1961 defendant gave plaintiff a ring and they were engaged, but no definite plans were made relative to a future marriage.

It appears that the defendant began his association with the plaintiff with the view of satisfying his lust, and he says that he met with "pretty good success." However, he soon began to get attached to the plaintiff, and he started pressing her about her associations with others. At first she denied any indiscretions with others, but about January of 1961 she admitted to having been intimate with an older man just after she got out of high school. She denied all other contacts. Not too long after the parties had become engaged the defendant pressed the plaintiff more and more to admit that she had been intimate with a Mr. Doyle. Finally she admitted it. This upset the defendant to the point that he called off the engagement and asked that the ring he gave the plaintiff be returned to him.

In spite of the broken engagement there were times when the parties dated. As the defendant states: "I just about hated her; I couldn't stand her. . . . She wouldn't leave me alone. And the only time I would go out with her was to have intercourse with her." The plaintiff got pregnant by the defendant around the end of March, 1961.

The plaintiff avers: "He gave me my ring in February. Then he found out about the second man, so he took my ring back, and he told me that he didn't want to go out with me any more. So off and on we were seeing each other, making up and then breaking up, until finally we did get intimate. He still didn't want to marry me, but then after he found out that I was pregnant, he changed his mind."

Both parties were jolted by the fact of pregnancy. The defendant was "very shocked" and even "speechless." The plaintiff says, "He felt cornered. He felt that I was pushing him into a corner that he couldn't get out of, and he wanted to save face in front of his family and friends. He said he wanted to do the right thing, which would be getting married in the Church." However, the defendant gives a different view of this matter. "After I found out that she was pregnant, the deal was—we were both ashamed, of course, and we didn't want anyone to know about it, either of our parents. The plan was that we were to say that we went to Alabama and we got married there in a civil marriage, and we'd come back, and that we had been married for some time and upon her getting pregnant, we figured we had better have the marriage blessed. That was the story that we had planned on telling everybody—our parents and our friends."

Hasty preparations were made for a quiet celebration in St. John's Church in New Orleans. Two days before the marriage the defendant proposed that the plaintiff have an abortion, but she revolted at the idea. However, she proposed an alternative, viz., to have a civil marriage instead of one in Church. Defendant objected to this because it would disrupt the devised scheme.

The marriage took place at St. John's Church before the Reverend Smith, the required witnesses, and a few members of the immediate families. There was no honeymoon, and after a brief celebration at the home of the bride's parents, the parties took up common life in their own apartment.

The very first night there was a serious quarrel between the parties because the defendant was obsessed with the thought that the plaintiff had been intimate with others, particularly, with defendant's friend. After five days of married life the parties separated and returned to their respective families. For the next six months there were repeated efforts on the part of the parties to make something of the marriage, but matters continued to get worse until the defendant reached the point where he could no longer abide the sight of the plaintiff. He ordered her out. This final separation took place around October, 1961.

The child, a son, was born on December 2, 1961 and was baptized at a Catholic church on December 30, 1961.

The plaintiff obtained a decree of divorce from the civil courts of Orleans Parish on February 2, 1963. Subsequently, on May 20, 1964 the plaintiff entered a second union, a civil marriage.

On September 28, 1964 a petition was presented in this tribunal seeking a declaration of nullity on the grounds of total simulation (or) intention *contra bonum sacramenti* on the part of the defendant. The parties to the marriage and the witnesses were heard, the briefs on the procurator-advocate, the animadversiones of the Defender of the Bond were thoughtfully considered, and the process of law having been duly fulfilled, we proceed to resolve the doubt proposed under the formula: *whether the nullity of the marriage under consideration has been proven on the grounds of total simulation or an intention against indissolubility.*

The Law

Canon 1086: 1. "The internal consent of the mind is always presumed to be in agreement with the words or signs which are used in the celebration of the marriage." 2. "But if either party or both parties by a positive act of the will exclude marriage itself, or all right to the conjugal act, or any essential property of marriage, the marriage contract is invalid."

Canon 1081: 1. "Marriage is effected by the consent of the parties lawfully expressed between persons who are capable according to law; and this consent no human power can supply." 2. "Matrimonial Consent is an act of the will by which each party gives and accepts a perpetual and exclusive right over the body, for acts which are themselves suitable for the generation of children."

Canon 1013: 2. "The essential properties of marriage are unity and indissolubility, which acquire a peculiar firmness in Christian marriage by reason of its sacramental character."

The intention to really marry (the consent) must be both internal, and externally manifested. And where there is a presumption that the internal consent of the mind and will conforms to the expressed words. If, in reality, the internal consent is absent, even though the external manifestation is given, then the contract would be null and void in itself and before God.

Thus we have the Church's law: "If either party or both parties, by a positive act of the will, exclude marriage itself, or any essential property of marriage, the marriage contract in invalid" (Canon 1086: 1). This canon (and the specified essential property of indissolubility of Canon 1013: 2) covers both grounds on which the present case is being tried, namely, total simulation of consent, and an intention against the essential property of indissolubility.

Simulation (total) is present when a party pronounces words which express willingness to contract marriage, while internally he excludes it by a positive act of the will. Such simulation renders the marriage invalid as there exists a total lack of matrimonial consent. Proof of simulation is difficult. However, "canonists hold that, ordinarily, the existence of complete simulation is sufficiently established if four things coexist: first, a confession of the party simulating consent, especially if this is made under oath and immediately after the marriage ceremony; second, a plausible reason for the simulation; third, if the circumstances surrounding the case seem to point to simulation; and fourth, if the testimony of witnesses or documentary evidence proves the contentions of the parties" (Doheny, p. 860).

Indissolubility is an essential quality of marriage (Canon 1013: 2). Consequently, in order to contract a valid marriage the parties must intend at least in a general or an implicit manner to become spouses for the duration of their lives. So if one, or both, positively determines to enter a marriage which will be terminable before the death of one of the parties, or to contract a marriage which is temporary, such a marriage is invalid.

To prove a marriage invalid on the grounds of the exclusion of an essential element (such as indissolubility) it must be clearly established that this essential element was excluded from the mutual consent by a positive act of the will. While we normally expect persons who contract marriages to do so in the manner instituted by God—one that will find its termination only in the death of one of the parties—still, in an exceptional case, it is possible for us to find that the element of indissolubility is deliberately excluded from the intention of a person contracting marriage. In such a case the marriage would be null and void.

A person whose understanding of the necessary qualities of marriage is correct can still enter a marriage with the intention of terminating it before the death of one of the spouses, if there is sufficient motive (subjectively considered) for doing so. It is not a matter of knowledge, it is a matter of what a person wills and intends. Once indissolubility is effectively excluded from the matrimonial contract by positive and express acts of the will, an essential element is ruled out and there can be no true marriage within the provisions of Canon 1013: 2. (Doheny).

The Argument

On Simulation: a) *Confession.* Defendant gives a clear judicial confession under oath. When asked if he intended to enter a valid marriage, he answered: "No sir, I did not." Further, Father Smith states that the defendant told him, *tempore non suspecto,* that he had simply lied in filling out the questionnaire and answering the marriage ceremony.

b) *Proof by witnesses.* The principals in the case give concordant evidence. The Defender of the Bond makes too much of apparent contradictions in the story that Jim, the defendant, would never be satisfied to marry a woman who had been to bed with another man. The defendant knew about the plaintiff and Doyle, but at first, he wasn't sure. Doyle had been known to lie and the plaintiff denied his story. The disclosure about the older man who had taken advantage of her youth, and whom she put entirely out of her life, brought out the forgiving urge in the defendant. But when he finally learned from the defendant herself about her affair with his friend, Doyle, then he found her a liar and a "whore" and an unworthy companion in marriage, although not in pleasure. Defendant had quite a few double standards.

The witnesses, six of them, give it as their opinion or as their observation of fact that the defendant did not intend a true marriage. Not one witness avers that he *did* intend a true marriage, not even the defendant's mother, who says, "Yes, he wanted to marry her, on account of the baby." She is neither theologian nor canonist, and does not express herself as either, but the totality of her testimony shows that in the passage alluded to she is merely indicating *why* the defendant simulated consent. The plaintiff's mother and father, as well as her maternal grandmother, all state—in one or another—that the defendant went through with the marriage to save face—to give the child a name—without any idea of binding himself to the responsibilities of marriage. Among the things spoken of by the witnesses there seem to be contradictions. But these contradictions are more apparent than real. The testimony is concordant along its main lines, and variant reports and recollections show a singular absence of any sign of collusion. The depositions of the parties, and the testimony of the witnesses, when they are considered as a whole, supplement and complement each other rather well.

c) *Cause of simulation.* First of all there was the pre-marital pregnancy which made the defendant feel that he was trapped into marriage. Then the necessity of saving face—of doing what was right—of giving the child a name—without any idea of entering into a true and binding contract. Finally there was the added necessity of upholding the story of the supposed marriage in Alabama.

d) *Circumstances.* The circumstances before the marriage are recited at considerable length in the petition and the testimony of parties and most of the witnesses. The preparations for the ceremony, and the ceremony itself, are also recited in several places in the Acts. The story of the circumstances after the marriage, beginning with the first night, are given prominence in the statements of the principals and witnesses. It was a strange courtship, conceived in lust and nurtured in jealousy. The broken engagement, the frequent quarreling, and the shock of the announcement of the pregnancy hardly point to what would be called a normal, happy courtship. Then the planned story to cover up, the suggestion of abortion as a way out, the constant protestations of the defendant to his confidant that the marriage would never work—all this gives reason to believe that any marriage ceremony would hardly have been unsuspect. They came to the altar confused, feeling trapped, frustrated and unsure. The ceremony went off according to script, but appears to have been a lie. After the wedding the fights continue, even on the very night of the wedding. The frequent separations and attempts at reconciliations, give evidence that the defendant did not want to make the marriage work. That he begged her to come back could be explained by his wanting to give the appearance of respectability, though, as he avows, he knew it wouldn't work. He finally gave up the sham entirely, even before the baby was born. Such evidence points to the fact that he never really intended to be truly married.

Concerning the Intention Against Indissolubility

This seems to be an alternative plea. The defendant states explicitly that he did not intend to stay married. "I had no intention of living with her or staying with her (except) until the baby was born. I guess I had that on my mind, because I couldn't stand to live with her. I hated her. And there was no other way out but to get married in Church. The story wouldn't work out." He called the marriage in Church "a foolish move . . . knowing that I wasn't going to live with her. I had no intention of living with her. I knew I couldn't. I knew that." The plaintiff avers that for the week prior to the wedding the defendant repeated his intention of not living with her permanently after the ceremony . . . only until the baby was born. Donald Ross declares that the defendant told him prior to the wedding and at the reception immediately afterwards that the marriage would never work out. The plaintiff's father testified that the defendant declared to him, just a week after the wedding, that he would only live with her until the baby was born. His testimony of the defendant's dating of other girls soon after the wedding indicated to him that he never intended to be married to the plaintiff. The defendant's mother testified that the defendant, before the wedding, declared to her that he did not want to be married: "I cannot do that; I cannot live with her." In her opinion he went through the ceremony because of the baby—because he wanted to give the baby a name. When the maternal grandmother of the plaintiff was asked whether the defendant was sincere in his marriage before the priest, she answered: "No, Father, because right then he had intentions of leaving her as soon as the baby was born."

If we examine the testimony of all these witnesses, as a whole, we see that the defendant was more interested in saving face than in getting married—he wanted to give the baby a name—do the "right thing"—but not bind himself to a true marriage as God intends. He said the words, but did not intend to bind himself by them. In this area, he specifically did not intend to enter an indissoluble union, only one that would last until the baby was born—and in fact, it did not even last that long.

Wherefore, having thoroughly examined all of these matters, both as regards the law and the facts, we, the undersigned Judges of the Sacred Tribunal of New Orleans, having invoked the name of Christ and having only God before our eyes, hereby declare, define and pronounce the definitive sentence in response to the doubt: Whether the nullity of the marriage under consideration has been proven on the grounds of total simulation or an intention against indissolubility, in the *affirmative*, e.g.: *The nullity of this marriage has been proved.*

We determine and command that this our sentence be published according to the second method indicated in Canon 1877 of the Code of Canon Law. Given at New Orleans, 22 March, 1967.

The Argument in Court of Second Instance

Certainly the evidence presented in this case has been subjected to very penetrating analysis by the Procurator-Advocate and the Defenders of the Bond in the first and second instance.

It is abundantly clear from the Acts of the case the defendant asserted in a number of ways over and over again that he had his mind set on positively going through the wedding ceremony, but internally denying genuine consent. This is both a confession of simulation and a firm declaration of a positive and fixed attitude to simulate consent at the time of the marriage. Under oath the defendant confesses that he first went out with the plaintiff, Ann, because he thought she was the kind of girl with whom he could have a "good time," having heard that she had been free with others. But it was not long before he began to like her and became attached to her. It was then that the indiscretion of the plaintiff with a friend of his, Pete D., began to prey on his mind and when this was shown to be true to his internal satisfaction, his affection began to turn to hate. As he put it: "I just about hated her; I couldn't stand her; I couldn't stand to be around her." Then when he found out that she was pregnant he became terribly confused and upset. He felt that there was no other solution than getting married. "There was no way of getting out of being married as far as we were concerned. The both of us just had to get married, that was it. She was pregnant and there was no other way out."

Then he goes on to explain, "There was no other way I could see. The story would (not) work out unless we got married in the Church. I had no intentions of living with her or of staying with her, (but) until the baby was born. I guess I had that on my mind.

It was the only thing I could have on my mind, because I could not stand to live with her. I hated her. And there was no other way out but to get married in Church. The story wouldn't work out." The defendant confesses that he really did mean what he said when he stated he did not want to marry the plaintiff. Then in the very next question he states that at the very moment he was filling out the premarital questionnaire he did not intend a valid and permanent union. He goes on to explain his dilemma: "It was the most foolish move I've ever made in my life—to get married in Church knowing that I wasn't going to live with her, that I wasn't even going to stay with her. Like I said the only way that I thought the story would work out—that is the whole deal—if we got married in Church. I had no intention of living with her. I knew I couldn't; I knew that." Again the defendant gives a most clear confession of simulation. He deposes that at the time he was asked whether or not he would take Ann as his lawful wife, he answered "yes" but meant "no." He goes on to explain: "I will explain why I said 'yes,' and why I really didn't mean it. The deal was that everything had to go along. When the priest said: 'Do you take Ann to be your lawful wedded wife?' I would have to naturally say 'yes,' I couldn't say 'no' or I never should have in the first place. Everything was going along as planned, that's all there was to it—fooling everybody else except myself."

The witnesses clearly and emphatically state that the defendant went through this marriage ceremony before the priest only to save face with his friends; only to give the child a name, without any idea of binding himself to the marriage responsibilities.

Donald R. who is the defendant's fourth cousin and "over the years Jim had confided in me about everything he does . . . we are really very close," when asked if the defendant really intended to get married, answered: "No, Father, he didn't. In fact, the very day of the wedding when we were both in the kitchen, he said: 'This will never work out. It will never work.' The only reason he did it was because of the baby, because she was pregnant." In this same question the witness goes on to say that the defendant told him that not only on the wedding, but "almost every day I talked to him before the wedding."

Mrs. Rose G., the plaintiff's mother, deposes that after her daughter become pregnant, the daughter suggested a civil marriage, but Jim insisted on a Church marriage; and "I realized after why he wanted the Church marriage, because he had told all his friends and family that he had been married in, I think, Alabama a month or so before, and evidently it was to save himself embarrassment." When asked if Jim was really sincere in getting married, this witness answered: "At that time I din't really believe he did want to get married; he was just frightened and scared, I think, at that time." In this same question this witness goes on to give the reason why the defendant acted in this way: "What are my friends going to say?" And so he had that all planned, (that) he was married previously in Alabama. It seemed his friends were uppermost in his mind—in Jim's mind. He was so frightened what his friends would think of all the time." This testimony is clarified and amplified by this witness, in answer to why the defendant wished a marriage before a priest: "Well, the way I understand, he wanted everyone to be under the impression that they were married in a civil ceremony before she got pregnant."

Michael G., the plaintiff's father, deposes under oath that, "He claimed that he didn't want the baby . . . he wanted to have an abortion. He told us that after she left him (that is one week after the wedding) he said that the only way he would live with her was until she had the baby, and then he would leave her because he didn't want to lose face with his friends. He told his friends that he had been married in Alabama, and he had the marriage in the Church to prove that he was married in Alabama, and he said that as soon as she had the baby, he would leave her." This witness further deposes why he thinks that the defendant never considered himself really married to his daughter: "First, I don't think he tried at any time to make a go of the marriage." Then as to considering himself really married to the plaintiff, this witness said: "I'd say no, for the simple reason that he even told her when she was six-months pregnant that he went out on dates with other girls, and he even made it a habit to be sure that, when he was with other girls, it would get back to Ann."

Mrs. Mary, the defendant's mother, deposes that, "When this thing happened in March (the pregnancy), he (defendant) wasn't the same—it upset him." Then when they were hastily searching for an apartment about a week before the marriage, she remarked: "From the way they were going around looking, I said, 'Gee whiz, why do you have to be in such a hurry? This looks like a shotgun wedding.' That's the words I said." Then speaking about the marriage itself she says: "To tell the truth, Father, I think Jim was very much ashamed. He only went through this thing because of the baby. So it was a very sad wedding." When this witness was asked why the parties planned a Church wedding instead of a civil ceremony, she states, "I don't know much about these things (plaintiff's pre-marital pregnancy). It's never happened in my immediate family, but they could have got married by a judge. That's what Jim tells me he wanted to do, get married by a judge, and have their wedding blessed after. But it seems like they couldn't get married in Alabama or some place he said, and so they agreed on the Church wedding." And she goes on to say: "When this thing happened (plaintiff's pregnancy), I said, 'Jim, you know you took the vows in front of the Church, in front of the altar. You have to take her for better or for worse.' Jim answered, 'Mother, I cannot do that; I cannot live with her. I don't love her; I don't want to live with her.' "

The defendant's grandmother deposes that, "He said he only wanted to marry to save face with his friends." Then a little later she testifies: "He said that he wouldn't marry her unless they married in Church. But he had no intentions of keeping it, because he told her that after the baby was born he had no intentions of living with her. He made all his friends believe that he had been married months before by a judge." His motives for the Church wedding are as follows: "He had said that he wanted to have a good face before his friends. He didn't want his friends to know that he was a rat. These were his exact words." Then when she was asked whether the defendant was sincere when he married before the priest, she replied: "No, father, because right then he had intentions of leaving her as soon as the baby was born."

Father Smith, who conducted the pre-nuptial inquiry testifies that, "He told me after this when they came about the annulment to the marriage that he had lied to me about all these things." He goes on to testify: "But now he tells me that he was lying to me, that he never intended to make the marriage."

The confession of the defendant and the depositions of the witnesses are further corroborated by the sworn deposition of the petitioner. She deposes that the defendant gave her the ring in February, but then found out about the second man and took the ring back, and at that time he told her he did not want to go out with her any more. However, they did go out on and off, but "he still didn't want to marry me." However, she became pregnant and "then he changed his mind." She goes on to say that he told her he did not want to marry her "practically every time I saw him . . . he would start off hollering at me, telling me he didn't want to marry me." She goes on to say that the defendant's cousin, Donald Ross, knew that the defendant did not want to marry her but he tried to conceal from her the fact "that Jim really didn't want to marry me." All this is confirmed by the defendant's repeated declaration the week before the marriage that he would leave the plaintiff immediately after the birth of the child, and by the suggestion made to the plaintiff two days before the marriage that she have an abortion. In answer to the question: "When did he first speak of leaving you immediately after the birth of the child?" the plaintiff answered: "That week before we got married, off and on, so finally when he did suggest that I have an abortion that Saturday before we got married, that's when I suggested that we have a civil marriage for the baby's name, and then we would part company. But then he said: "No, it was going to be a ‛Church marriage or no marriage."

The Acts of the case reveal that there were several very powerful and operative motives that compelled as it were, the defendant to go through the externalization of a marriage before the Church while he simultaneously denied genuine internal consent. The first cause or reason proposed is the plaintiff's pre-marital pregnancy. Although the defendant had already made up his mind he would not marry the plaintiff, still when she got pregnant by him, he felt that there was no other way out of the situation than marriage. So intense did he feel this pressure that he felt he was trapped into this situation.

Secondly, repugnance, and even hatred, arose from his incapacity to accept the fact that the plaintiff had been intimate with at least two previous men, especially Pete D., who was a friend of the defendant. This preyed on the defendant's mind so intensely that he could not expel it, and psychologically impeded him from internally accepting the plaintiff as his wife. Be it noted that this gnawing anxiety, repugnance, and even hatred of plaintiff arose in the defendant before the pregnancy and before the "forced marriage." The fact of pregnancy did not soften his repugnance for the plaintiff, but it did put him in a position where he felt he had to go through a marriage ceremony before the Church in order to save face.

The third and last cause is the unusually strong feeling that the defendant had to save face before his family and friends. That is why he devised the story of the previous civil ceremony in Alabama which made it necessary for him to go before a priest in order to validate the marriage and give the full appearance of uprightness before his family and friends.

The circumstances before, during and after the marriage lend adminicular evidence to the contention of simulation. There was the broken engagement, broken by the defendant because he learned definitely from the admission of the plaintiff that she had been intimate with the second gentleman, the defendant's friend. Then there was the pregnancy which created in the defendant's mind a feeling that he was trapped into an unwanted marriage. The shock of the defendant and there is the suggested abortion by the defendant two days before the marriage as a last ditch effort to avoid the horrors of the up-coming marriage. The plaintiff suggested civil marriage as an alternative, but the defendant could not agree to this because he had already spread the story about the celebration of a civil marriage in Alabama which was to be followed by validation in Church.

The marriage itself was very hastily prepared (little over a week of preparations) and was celebrated on the first occasion permissible by Church law after the disclosure of the pregnancy, i.e., the Monday after Easter. It was truly a "closed" marriage in the sense that only the parties, the witnesses, and the immediate family on both sides were present. There was a very small celebration for this group with only a cake at the home of the plaintiff's parents. There was no honeymoon.

There was a violent, even physical, quarrel the very first night of the marriage prompted by the defendant's inability to forget about the plaintiff's past intimacies. The first separation occurred only five days after the marriage and there were frequent attempts at reconciliation during the next six months only to be followed by separation. After six months common life became so intolerable because of the defendant's gnawing hatred of the plaintiff's past imtimacies with other men, that common life was terminated never to be resumed again. The defendant showed no interest in the child that was subsequently born, and ultimately gave his approval that it be legally adopted by the plaintiff's present husband.

In conclusion, two points should be noted: 1) Father Smith could not understand how Jim could respect Ann before the marriage, when he certainly knew of her past, then after the marriage lose respect for her, precisely because of her past life. There is no indication in the case that Jim did in fact respect Ann before the marriage. All evidence in fact points to the contrary. 2) The Defender of the Bond in the Court of Second Instance has, it seems, quoted out of context the vital testimony of Donald R. "After learning of the pregnancy did Jim ever say that he did not intend to stay with Ann?" Donald did not answer "no," as the defender of the bond stated. Rather Donald replied, "No, I don't remember Jim saying that. I am trying to think now. I know that he had already said it was just to give the baby a name, but I just don't remember the identical words. He might have—I see something in the picture but I can't exactly remember to quote him saying something like that. I really can't comment on that, Father." Donald did reply, "I know that Jim really loved Ann and I think he would have liked it to work," but he immediately continued, "but, you see, he just couldn't forget about Doyle, and I imagine he wanted to give it a try, but every time something came up, I knew that he threw that up constantly to Ann—I'm sure of that. He might have wanted to give it a try, but he probably figured he could never overcome the situation.

It is interesting to note that the plaintiff, who had ceased practicing his religion, was actually the one who insisted on the Church marriage. Such insistence serves to confirm our opinion, that the circumstances were almost exactly as described in the Acts of this case, namely that the defendant would go to almost any lengths to "save face" before his family and friends.

Wherefore, having carefully weighed and considered all elements in law and in fact, we the undersigned Judges of the Sacred Tribunal of Chicago, having invoked the name of Jesus Christ, relying on our own consciences and having only our obligation to God, hereby define and pronounce the definitive sentence in response to the doubt as formulated above:

In the affirmative. The sentence of the Court of First Instance is to be confirmed.

No. 6/Millicent vs. Waldo

The Facts

In a letter to the promoter of justice of the Archdiocese of——, on February 13, 1963, Millicent accused her marriage to Waldo of invalidity on the ground of simulated consent. In accord with the nature of such cases in which the culpable party is canonically stopped from impugning the validity of marriage (Cn 1971:1), the promoter of justice, on the same date, February 13, 1963, formally accused the marriage to the————Tribunal.

On October 24, 1956, Waldo and Milicent, both baptized Catholics domiciled in the Archdiocese of ——, had gone through a marriage ceremony in a Catholic church in New Jersey. There is testimony of some uncertainty in Millicent's mind before the ceremony; the marriage itself was an unhappy one. A civil divorce was granted in Reno, Nevada to Milicent on the grounds of extreme cruelty, October 24, 1958. A civil divorce on the grounds of desertion was granted to Waldo on December 7, 1961 in Newark, New Jersey.

The *libellus* of the promoter of justice was accepted at a meeting of a duly constituted court of the Archdiocese of —— on March 25, 1963. Of note in the Acts is the fact that no testimony was given by Waldo; he is believed to be institutionalized in a mental hospital in New Jersey because of a recurring illness. The confession and further testimony of Milicent, together with the testimony of eleven witnesses, are offered in the Acts as the basis for judgment as to the soundness of the accusation of the invalidity of the marriage of Milicent-Waldo on the grounds of total simulation of consent *ex parte mulieris.*

The Law

True and internal consent is essential to the validity of marriage. The contract is valid only if both parties consent by acts of the will to give and receive rights over their bodies, perpetual and exclusive, to acts apt for the generation of children (Canon 1081). Internal consent is presumed to be present in conformity to external acts (words or signs) used in the celebration of marriage. If either or both parties by a positive act of the will, exclude marriage itself or all rights to the conjugal act, or some essential property of marriage, the contract is invalid (Canon 1086).

The consent required for a valid marriage may be vitiated by simulation, total or partial. Acceptance of the contract but exclusion of one or all of its essential obligations is *partial* simulation. Rejection of marriage, i.e., the contract, itself, is *total* or complete simulation. The case in question is based on a claim of total simulation, proof of which depends on the presentation of conclusive testimony and documentation of the contrary will of the culpable party. In doubt, the validity of marriage enjoys the favor of the law (Canon 1014).

The Argument

The Acts offer elements for judgment in the four areas to be explored as to the existence of total simulation, as found in Rotal precedents and canonists' recommendations. (Cf. e.g., Doheny, Canonical Procedure in Matrimonial Cases, I, p. 860): 1. The confession of Milicent; 2. Presentation of alleged grounds for the total simulation; 3. Description of the circumstances of the case before, at and after the ceremony; 4. The testimony of eleven witnesses.

The Confession, Testimony and Motivation of Milicent

Her letter and testimony under oath claim that Milicent "did not give full and complete consent . . . Did not intend to marry," intended to divorce even before marriage; on the actual day of marriage did not want to marry Waldo; that she never changed her mind on this point. Corroboration of this intention to simulate and the alleged simulation is sought from the sworn statements of witnesses—her mother, Angelene, John G., her cousin and Marie S. Further indications of the uncertainty of her mind is sought from the maid of honor, Anna C., Anna's mother and Loretta P.

The motivation for simulated consent is given by Milicent "to avoid the gossip and embarrassment." She set the final date of marriage "because I was begged to do so." Her parents indicated at first that she should not marry Waldo. After the engagement was cancelled, the embarrassment was manifested to her parents and "they advised me to go ahead with the marriage." "Different people advised both for and against the marriage." "Those who advised in favor of the marriage based their judgment on the fact that I would avoid embarrassment." Besides the advice of her parents and others, the desire to avoid embarrassment, and to end gossip, a further motive is indicated in the interrogation, i.e., "If I did not marry him, he would get sick," presumably a plea for marriage not from Waldo but vaguely from "everyone."

The grounds for the alleged total simulation therefore appear to be the avoidance of gossip and embarrassment to the parties and their families arising from the cancellation of the marriage planned by Milicent and Waldo. To that might be added the suggestions of pressure from some vague "forces unknown" and the lessening of any attraction to Waldo because he was not "all there," "and did not want to work."

The most important circumstance before the marriage seems to be the cancellation of the marriage and return of the ring by Milicent Smith. While supposing there may have been more than one such dispute, it is clear that one cancellation, that of the June 14, 1956 date noted by Waldo, is almost one month before both parties gave sworn answers as to their intentions to marry freely (July 9, 1956).

That there was widespread "gossip" is testified to by several parties; frequent arguments are also cited.

During the ceremony, Milicent "did not seem happy" (according to her mother), she herself alleges she actually cried, and the maid of honor felt Milicent might even say "No" instead of "Yes." Afterwards, there are the reception in which the couple greets the guests, a honeymoon of two weeks, cohabitation for several months broken by frequent disputes and finally separation and civil divorce.

Aside from the testimony of Inez (Mother of Waldo) whose veracity is called into question by the auditor, the depositions of the witnesses seem to fill out credibly the outline of the facts as given above. It remains to assign a weight to the total presentation and to render a judgment as to whether total simulation has been proved.

The judgment is in favor of the validity of marriage, i.e., in spite of the evidence of uncertainty and indecisiveness on the part of Milicent before marriage, *total simulation has not been convincingly proved*:

1. The confession and testimony of Milicent, considered separately and together with the testimony of the witnesses, contain admissions of conduct implying the will to marry and to exchange the essential rights and privileges of marriage:

a) She is the principal in arranging the marriage, both before and after the cancellation(s); b) she swears that she intends to enter the marriage of her own free will, without conditions affecting consent; c) she went on a honeymoon with Waldo, lived with him as his wife for several months, had marital relations with him even after two separations due to arguments; d) she consummated the marriage by intercourse, at least once, without contraceptives.

It is hardly credible that she could do all these acts without both the intention to marry and the belief that she was properly married, especially in the light of the pre-marital instruction given by Father Bailey and the pre-Cana Conference which the couple attended. We add what may also be somewhat significant: There is no evidence of any other man to whom Milicent is attracted before the marriage; no social or financial advantage is apparently to be gained by marriage to Waldo. Milicent's confession is uncorroborated by the groom, Waldo, and by the lack of testimony of Loretta and Nicholas, who were the witnesses who swore to the freedom to marry, at the pre-nuptial interrogation before Father Bailey on July 9, 1956. In the light of the importance paid to the cancellation of the marriage at least once, it is noteworthy also that the date for the wedding indicated in the July 9, 1956 interrogation of the parties was the date of the actual marriage, October 24, 1958. Again the confession of Milicent is given after a lapse of five and one-half years since the marriage, and almost five years since the separation of the parties.

2. The *motivation* alleged for the simulation—"to have peace of mind and to avoid embarrassment" i.e., to go through the ceremony but "not spend my life with him" is rendered less plausible by the actual honeymoon and cohabitation. Again, it would

appear that the major "embarrassment" was already complete by the cancellation; the advice of parents previously reluctant to have her marry Waldo at all and the "gossip" might create some persuasion or fear but improbably so as dictating marriage as the alternative. The choice for Milicent was not confined to marriage or continued embarrassment. At the time of marriage she was twenty years of age, reasonably well educated, and thoroughly American in outlook; as one alternative, she could simply have gone away for a while to remove herself from the problems as described. Nor does even reverential or other fear seem present to the serious degree needed to offer some analogy to the *metus* envisaged by Canon 1087, in view of the ambivalent attitudes of her parents in regard to the marriage.

3. The chronology of the circumstances before marriage makes them less than totally persuasive as indication of the likelihood of simulation. One cancellation (the major one?) is of a June date for marriage; afterwards, there are the pre-nuptial interrogation, the new preparations directed by Milicent, presumably the pre-Cana Conference and the wedding rehearsal, in connection with none of which are there major external signs of other than some disputes and uncertainty.

4. The testimony of the witnesses deals with a variety of conversations and incidents, no one of which is itself indicative of a completely contrary will to marry on the part of Milicent Smith. *Cumulatively, the testimony corroborates the presence of uncertainty but hardly constitutes evidence, conclusive enough to offset the presumption of validity (C. 1014) and the lack of convincing proof as noted above.*

Therefore, all the facts and circumstances having been carefully considered, and having invoked the name of God, we the undersigned Judges, having only God before our eyes, define, determine, and declare in response to the doubt proposed negatively, *Non constare de nullitate matrimonii.*

We further declare that this sentence be published in the third way permitted by Canon 1877.

CANON 1087 (T.R.)
FORCE AND FEAR
No. 31/Betty vs. Joseph

The Facts

Betty, a baptized Catholic, married Joseph, a baptized Catholic, on March 4, 1953, observing the required form of marriage in the Catholic Church. After a short and unhappy common life, the parties separated. The respondent obtained a civil divorce in 1958. On September 14, 1964, Betty Johnson presented a petition to the tribunal, alleging the nullity of her marriage on the grounds of force and fear, afflicted on her by her parents. The petition was accepted for trial on January 15, 1965. All the solemnities established by law were duly observed. On April 6, 1965, the point at issue was officially determined and the parties, duly cited, gave their judicial depositions. Thereafter, seven witnesses were heard and, with the plaintiff's advocate and the defender of the bond acknowledging that no further testimony was available or useful, a decree of publication issued on June 2, 1965 and a decree of conclusion on June 12, 1965. The plaintiff's advocate submitted a carefully worked out statement concerning the law and the facts and the defender of the bond added his animadversions. Hence, answer is now to be given to the usual *dubium*: Has the nullity of the Johnson-Clark marriage been proved on the grounds of force and fear inflicted on the plaintiff?

The Law

The basic law governing this case is found in Canon 1087: 1: That marriage is also invalid if it is entered into because of grave force or fear that is externally and unjustly imposed, from which one is forced to choose marriage as the only way of freeing himself. In canonical jurisprudence a distinction is made between ordinary and reverential fear. The plaintiff has acted in the case under the second heading.

Ordinarily, reverential fear is not serious and can be readily resisted by the parties to a marriage. Hence, the plaintiff in this case must prove that the alleged reverential fear was, for her a really serious constraint. In accordance with the canon, she must prove that her parents acted unjustly, depriving her of her right to make an independent decision as to whether she would marry or not marry. Finally, the plaintiff must prove that the parents' actions made it impossible for her to take any course of action other than submit to the marriage which they required of her.

These basic principles of law are familiar, well known, and entirely clear. The difficulty of the case is found not in the law but in the evaluation of the evidence which is presented in the Acts. It suffices to note that the sworn statements of the plaintiff and the respondent, even though they are in complete agreement, do not provide full proof of the alleged nullity. There must always be corroborative testimony from qualified and truthful witnesses. The judges must weigh this evidence to discover whether or not the alleged nullity has been proved with moral certainty. If sufficient proof is not found, the validity of the marriage must be upheld. If, however, moral certainty of the nullity exists in the minds of the judges they must give an affirmative answer, namely, that the nullity of the marriage has been proved.

The Argument

The gravity of reverential fear can be evaluated by considering the character and personality of each of the parents or the dominant parent, where only one intervenes, the forcefulness or weakness of the personality of the child in question, and the relationship which exists between the child and the parents.

In this particular case, Betty was the youngest of several children and at the time of the marriage was less than fifteen years of age. Her older sisters testified that she probably enjoyed greater privileges and more freedom than did they at the same age. Betty appeared to be happy at home and seemed able to relate well with her parents with one exception of her father's serious drinking problem. It is agreed upon by all of the children that the plaintiff's father, usually of mild manner, could and did become cruel and abusive, and a force to contend with, when drinking. From the testimony, one gathers the impression that the father was responsible as a husband and father as regards employment and support of the family, but one to be feared when drinking. The plaintiff's mother is described as a woman who had much concern for her family, was unusually mild-mannered and gentle but one who, by force of circumstances, had to assume the leadership, the decision-making and the planning in the family.

The evidence clearly indicates that there was a friendship between Betty and Joseph in the months prior to their marriage and there is indication that the petitioner enjoyed this association with a young man who was older than she and who enjoyed the popularity of an athlete. The witnesses state that they had met the respondent, while he was visiting at Betty's home, on a casual basis and on only a few occasions. No one of the witnesses thought that this friendship or relationship was a serious one or one that would culminate in marriage; it was accepted as a passing episode. The testimony clearly reveals that the plaintiff's mother considered the defendant as an attractive young man and seemed to be impressed with his athletic prowess. Her husband, on the other hand, had certain misgivings about him, primarily because of his nationality. Any encouragement for calling on Betty was given by her mother. It would appear that the petitioner had no thoughts of marriage and particularly no plans for marriage with Joseph at this time because of her youthful age and also because of her desire to continue her education.

The pregnant condition of Betty was verified by Dr. Arthur and the responsibility for her condition was accepted without doubt or reservation by the defendant.

On verifying the pregnancy, Dr. Arthur recommended and advised Betty's mother to consider seriously allowing Betty to go to a home for unwed mothers, await the delivery of her child and then possibly arrange for its adoption. The doctor stated very forthrightly that he could make the necessary arrangements and reservations for the confinement.

Betty herself, protested that she did not wish to marry and that she favored the suggestion of her doctor. Even privately and on her own, she consulted with a girl friend who had been in the same difficulty and solved it by going to a confinement home and placing the child for adoption.

Betty's mother, however, refused to consider this solution because an older daughter, deceased at the time of the present difficulty, had gone to such a home and both the mother and daughter were unhappy with the prevailing conditions. The mother protested to members of her family that the original episode was a nightmarish experience and that she did not wish to expose her youngest child to this same inhuman situation. On this point the mother was stubbornly adamant.

The father was insistent that a marriage ensue in order to protect the reputation and respectability of the family name.

One of the daughters was not consulted concerning the problem or its solution and knew nothing of the situation until she was hastily invited to the marriage reception, the very night of the marriage. Another sister of the plaintiff and her husband lived in the same family dwelling and were apprized of the pregnancy on the evening of the day it was verified by Dr. Arthur. This daughter and her husband, considering the situation and the future welfare of Betty, felt that a marriage would not be the ideal situation and tried to prevail on the mother but to no avail. Her determined and positive decision that a marriage was the best solution could not be effectively countered by alternate proposals.

Betty's father was friendly with the pastor of their local parish and relying on this friendship, Betty's mother approached him and suggested, without any discussion of its advisability, that he make the necessary preparations for a speedy marriage.

During the brief interim period, the plaintiff was held as a captive hostage by her parents in their home and was not available for communication, in person or by telephone, with any outsiders.

Dr. Arthur tried to intervene further, when the plaintiff appeared for the usual pre-marital blood test but, again, could not and did not succeed in altering what, by now, was the definitive planning for a marriage.

Within a few short days, the marriage between the plaintiff and the respondent took place in the local parish in the evening and was followed by a small family gathering at the home of the bride's parents.

There is some confusion as to whether the bride and groom lived together for a short period in the Brockton area before Joseph reported for baseball practice in the South, or whether the young couple immediately began their trip to the South. This is not a matter of substantial importance. In any event, the bride returned to her home in Brockton within a few months to await the birth of her child and the respondent ultimately was sent overseas on a Service assignment. During his absence, Betty

Johnson appears to have accepted her new duties and responsibilities in a mature and adult fashion but found it too difficult to live compatibly with the defendant after his return from the Service because of his immature attitudes and irresponsible behavior. There can be no question that the young plaintiff, at the time not even fifteen years of age, was caught in a very difficult and serious situation. On the one hand, she did not wish marriage with Joseph and on the other hand, both of her parents in a very positive, determined, adamant and unrelenting manner insisted that she marry and that marriage was the only solution to the existing problem.

There appeared to be no way in which Betty could free herself from this situation that kept closing in upon her. She could not stay at home pregnant and unmarried; a civil marriage would not have been acceptable to her parents; she could not receive the permission or the cooperation of her parents to go to a home for unwed mothers, which is what she preferred, and she could not leave the household—she was young, inexperienced, without a completed education, without a job and unemployable because of her age and no place to live. The home of her sisters and brother could not be a haven for her since they did not wish to incur the wrath of their parents by cooperating with their youngest sister in defying the arrangements and decisions of the mother and father.

Marriage was the one remedy for Betty if she were to free herself from the fear-inspiring situation.

The situation and chain of events clearly testify to the fact that the parents far exceeded their right to advise, counsel, direct and guide their daughter in seeking a solution for the predicament in which she found herself. The good faith and well-meaning of the parents can still be the cause of objective injustice to their own daughter.

The fear of the child must be considered grave and serious; the intervention from an outside force, by the parents, must be considered unjust and marriage must be realized as the only choice without alternative that was presented to Betty. The free and voluntary decision to marry, which is the right and prerogative of any contractant and which is required and essential for the validity of consent cannot be considered to have been present.

Wherefore, having carefully examined all of these matters of law and of facts, and having invoked the Divine Name, we, the undersigned judges, duly empowered to give decision, in first instance, with God before our eyes, declare, decree and define the answer to the proposed *dubium* in the *affirmative*, that is, the nullity of the marriage has been proved.

We decree that this definitive sentence be published according to the second method authorized in canon 1877.

We finally decree that this our definitive sentence be executed in accordance with the Sacred Canons, and that all local Ordinaries and officers of tribunals proceed against any who refuse to obey our decrees, using those executive and coercive measures which are most opportune and efficacious.

Case #25

CANON 1087 (T.R.)
FORCE AND FEAR
No. 30/Rita vs. Alan

The Facts

The petitioner, Rita and the defendant, Alan, both Catholics, met around July, 1955. Although there had been no promise of marriage the petitioner became pregnant. Because of the pregnancy the petitioner and defendant decided to marry civilly on November 24, 1955. The baby was born in July, 1956. They went to the parish of the defendant's parents where they had been attending church, St. James, to make arrangements for the baptism. Both the petitioner and the defendant understood that the pastor of St. James would baptize their baby only on the condition that they were first married in church. Both the defendant and the petitioner were reluctant to be married in church because they still had their doubts about the ultimate success of their marriage. However, grave concern regarding the spiritual welfare of the baby motivated them to accept the pastor's condition, and their marriage was revalidated on August 10, 1956, at St. James Church.

Another child was born of this marriage. In June of 1959, the couple separated, and a divorce was obtained in 1961. Rita, the petitioner in this case, attacked the validity of her marriage before the Tribunal of the Archdiocese of —— on August 10, 1966, because of force and fear on the part of the defendant and/or the petitioner. It is now incumbent upon the judges of this tribunal to respond to the following doubt: Whether the nullity of the marriage under consideration is proven.

The Law

Canon 1087: 1: "That marriage is also invalid if it is entered into because of grave force or fear that is externally and unjustly imposed, from which one is forced to choose marriage as the only way of freeing himself."

2: "No other fear, even though it is the cause of the contract, causes the contract to be null."

Extrinsic fear is that fear which is brought to bear by a free cause or by one human being against another. Therefore, in this distinction it is not a question of whether the cause is internal or external; for internal fear is able to have an external cause, as for example, fear of a bad reputation, death, or imprisonment, etc. The only question is whether it comes from a free cause. A necessary cause is not able to produce external fear. It can be said that fear is produced necessarily by the threatening evil itself; but external fear comes from a free person.

Fear can be either grave or light. That fear is said to be grave which fulfills these two conditions: the evil which threatens must be serious for that person who is threatened, or who experiences the fear; secondly, that same person must perceive the evil as grave and must be convinced that it is threatening him. If one of these conditions is lacking, the fear is light.

The gravity of the fear is not taken only from the nature of the evil that is feared, but also from the certainty by the one who experiences the fear thinks that he will undergo evil, from which arises the trepidation of mind which constitutes the fear itself. Therefore, very often the Roman Rota has held that a just suspicion of fear suffices for fear itself, since one must be free not only from compulsion, but also the fear of compulsion.

As regards the second requisite, namely, that the person experiencing fear conceives of it as an evil threatening himself and is convinced that it is threatening him, we wish to make the following points:

1. I am said to be threatened not only by that evil which personally threatens me, but also that evil which threatens my relatives, my in-laws, and the members of my household.

2. It is necessary that the one who is experiencing the fear, knows for certain that the person who threatens the grave evil really intends to execute it. In other words he is able, he wants to, and he is accustomed to making demands. For if there is a question of a person who threatens who does not have the power to or who does not usually fulfill his grave threats, even though the threats are thought to constitute a very grave evil, the fear is not considered grave.

3. It is also required that the one who experiences the fear cannot escape the threats directed against him in some other way except by entering marriage *(De Sacramentis*, P. A. Coronata, Marietti, 1947, Vol. III, pp. 631-633).

The Argument

To prove the allegation of the petitioner it must be canonically shown that the force inflicted upon the party was external, grave, and unjust; that the party was unable to extricate herself from this situation except by marriage, that the party considered the pressure to be grave, and had an aversion to the marriage.

It is a fact that in the Archdiocese of ——, until September 20, 1955, it was the understanding of some priests of the archdiocese, that it was the policy of the chancery office to demand that the parents, invalidly living a married life, would have to have their marriage validated before baptism would be administered to their child. Priests believed that they were expected to exhort and encourage validations as a condition for the baptism of children. Such a policy was believed to be maintained because of a claim that infants could not be baptized unless their Catholic education was assured. It was further alleged that such education was not assured if the parents continued to live in a civil marriage that could be validated. It was further reasoned that if parents insisted on continuing to live in such an invalid marriage, depriving themselves of the sacraments, their promise to raise their children as Catholics could not be trusted. This condition in the archdiocese was so prevalent that on September 20, 1955, at a Clergy Conference the policy of the Archdiocese of —— had to be clarified. Couples who were living in a marriage that could be validated were to be encouraged to validate such a marriage but it was not to be insisted upon as a condition for the baptism of a child born of such a union. It was further declared that the selection of good Catholic sponsors for such a child was sufficient to be assured of the Catholic education of such a child. The responsibility was thus transferred from the priest baptizing to the sponsors at baptism.

The two cases treated read as follows:

1. John and Mary, who are validly married, and who were at one time Catholics but are now heretics, seek the administration of the sacrament of Baptism for their infant from Robert, a Catholic priest. May Robert licitly baptize their infant? Ought he to do so?

2. Thomas and Anna, Catholics, living in an invalid marriage, at present refuse a Catholic education for their children, but from the same pastor, Robert, they request the sacrament of Baptism for their newly born infant. Is Robert licitly able to and ought he to baptize their new infant.

It was at the end of the discussion on these cases that Monsignor George Casey, presiding at the Conference, made the statement that contrary to the understanding of some priests in the archdiocese, it was not the policy of the chancery office to demand that the parents, invalidly living a married life, would have to have their marriage validated before baptism would be administered to their child.

It is an established fact in the archdiocese that despite this clarification many priests continued to refuse baptism because of the former misunderstanding.

Thus, theoretically at the time of this marriage the priests of the Archdiocese in — — could justly encourage, exhort and insist on the parents to validate their marriage but in effect and in reality a priest would unjustly refuse to baptize a child if the parents refused to validate the marriage. He did not give the parents the theoretical alternative of assuring the Catholic education of the child. The laity of the archdiocese were not aware of the *monitum* given by the Vicar General on September 20, 1955, to the priests of the archdiocese. They knew only of the former practice of the priests of the archdiocese.

The Acts of this case abundantly prove that this threat of non-baptism of a child was used either in substance or at least in the manner it was applied or understood by the parties involved.

Rita tells that the civil marriage took place because of her pregnancy and the church marriage because of the baptism of the child. There was an interval of 8-12 months before the civil marriage was rectified in church. She maintains that the monsignor to whom they spoke about having their child baptized insisted they be married first. She maintains she knew the marriage would not work and did not want it. No course was left open to them but to be married to have the child baptized. The

Church marriage lasted two and a half years and was never happy. Another child was born and baptized.

After the birth of the child arrangements were being made for its baptism, when Father Stanislaus informed them that they would have to marry in the Church before the child could be baptized. They were not sure whether they were ready to make a lifetime commitment to one another in a Catholic narriage. Both knew the other did not want a church marriage. Rita's own mother had been involved in a very unpleasant situation, because her own church marriage lasted only a few months and then she had to live in a marriage outside the Church for many years. So they were apprehensive about entering a church marriage, since they were not sure they were ready to marry for life. The marriage was a quiet one in a dark church with only a few persons present.

Susan is a sister to the defendant. The marriage did not last because both were immature. The couple married in church because the pastor said, "they had to marry so that the baby could be baptized." The couple felt that they had no other choice. The marriage broke up because of the instability of both parties.

Donna, the mother of the defendant, tells that the priest would not baptize the baby unless the couple married in church. They did not want the church marriage. She was present when the priest said this. They married as a favor to her and to have the baby baptized.

Marie, mother of the petitioner, heard that the priest told the couple they could not have the baby baptized unless they married in church.

Father Stanislaus mentions in his letter to the matrimonial tribunal and in his formal testimony, he had no strict obligation in justice to attend to the spiritual needs of this couple who came to him with their baby for baptism. It was out of his priestly zeal and charity that he took the time and effort to tend to the spiritual needs of this couple. The defendant's parents who lived in his parish and were his parishioners asked for his spiritual help and assistance; he agreed to give it. The pastor was concerned about using this occasion to help this young couple be married in church so that they might return to the sacraments, and become truly Christian parents. He admits that he persuaded the couple to have their marriage validated, but points out quite correctly that they were free to go to see their own parish priest. But unfortunately all the persons involved in this baptism misunderstood the efforts of this zealous priest. They understood his efforts at "persuasion" to be a real threat that was forcing them to do something they did not want to do. This is evident from the testimony of the petitioner; the testimony of the defendant; the testimony of the defendant's sister; the testimony of the defendant's mother, and the testimony of the petitioner's mother.

The parties could have gone to another priest, but they were under the impression that the decision of Father Stanislaus would be equally upheld by another priest.

That the parties considered the refusal of baptism to their child a grave harm and evil is evidenced by their sworn deposition.

The petitioner deposes that she was afraid of the spiritual harm that might come to her child if the child died without baptism. The defendant testifies that he was concerned about a mild outbreak in polio that summer and, ". . . the danger that something of that sort might happen to our boy without baptism did stick in my mind. So I was prepared to sacrifice myself in a sense to have the baby baptized. . . ."

The circumstances prior, during and consequent to the marriage definitely indicate that they did not contract marriage freely. There was definite evident aversion to the marriage. The defendant deposes: ". . . there was still an element of doubt in our minds about the marriage. We had been getting along well to the extent that we were not at each other's throats. We were not sure if we wanted a life-long commitment, which we knew a church marriage meant. . . ." The defendant also testifies that both he and the petitioner had additional reasons for hesitation regarding the church marriage because of the unhappy examples in their own families. The petitioner's mother had been married outside the church for twenty-five years to a divorced man. The defendant's sister was divorced by her husband and was not free to remarry. The defendant says: "So these factors were in the back of the minds of myself and Rita when presented with the church marriage, realizing what we were getting ourselves into."

The petitioner describes very vividly how angry and upset she became, when she first received the news that the pastor of Saint James would not baptize her baby, unless she was first married in church. She even became violently sick to her stomach. The defendant's sister also substantiates the fact that up until the time of the baptism of the baby, no plans had been made for a church revalidation.

The defendant's mother testifies: "They agreed to get it (the church marriage) over with and have the baby baptized. They did not want to be married by the priest. They were fussing about it even on the day of the marriage. . . . They were hesitant about the marriage. It is the truth that they did not want to marry in church. . . ." She also testifies that immediately after the ceremony on the way home there was no sign of any happiness on the part of the petitioner or defendant.

After the church marriage both parties tried to make the marriage work, even to the point of having a second child. However, the petitioner testifies that the marriage was never happy from the very beginning. While there were never any big fights, there was never any communication or sharing things in common. They managed to stay together for only two and a half years.

Although the baptism of a child is a salutary thing, it is unjust to force people to marry to obtain that salutary thing; it should be accorded the child freely. Marriage should not be a compelled condition. This couple was not one that merely neglected to validate a marriage that was wanted anyway; the couple definitely would not have married otherwise and even under that pressure of refusal to baptize the child, got married only because so forced.

Wherefore, all these points both in law and in fact having been duly weighed, we the undersigned judges, sitting in the Sacred Tribunal of the Diocese of Chicago, mindful of our duties before Almighty God, and having invoked the sacred name of Christ, do now in consideration of the question proposed, *(viz,. "Whether the marriage contracted between Rita and Alan be invalid on the grounds as envisioned in canon 1087 C.I.C.)* adjudge and order published our definitive sentence in the a *affirmative* to the affect that *the nullity of the marriage in question has been proven.*

Case #26

CANON 1092 (M.J.)
CONDITION IN MARRIAGE
No 21/John vs. Alice

John and Alice married in 1967. They had known each other for three years, and were both twenty years of age. There were two facts that precipitated the marriage:

a) The fact of her pregnancy prior to the marriage.

b) The considerable opposition of Alice's parents, and John's subsequent defiance.

They were quickly united in 1967. In due course, the child was born, but unfortunately, died a few days later. Cohabitation ceased a few momths later and a civil divorce was granted in 1972.

a) An intention *contra bonum prolis.*

b) An intention*contra bonum sacramenti.*

c) Lack of *"communio vitae."*

The ground that was finally accepted was "the absence of communio vitae due to psychic irregularity on the part of one or both parties." In 1976, the Court came to a negative decision on this ground.

A Court of Second Instance was constituted and the grounds were in this request to add a new ground, "conditioned consent on the part of the Petitioner."

There were, therefore, two issues before the Court:

a) Should the decision of the Court of First Instance be upheld?

b) Should the marriage be declared null on the ground of an implicit condition contrary to the nature of marriage?

Concerning the first issue, the Court took into consideration the statement of the Medical Witness who indicated that the difficulties of the Petitioner were not strictly speaking incapacitating. This same Court realized what was the constant teaching of the Sacred Roman Rota that the simple capacity to live out and fulfill matrimonial responsibilities is not sufficient for considering a marriage valid. The Rota, however, has always taught, even before the title of "psychic irregularity" came to be, that adequate discretion and internal liberty be present on the part of both parties in order to enter into a marriage with binding consent. What the Court proceeded to do is show that, due to John's personality character he found himself prior to the marriage (i.e., the difficult courtship, the pregnancy, the bride's parental opposition, the Petitioner's defiance), that John's consent to marry Alice lacked internal freedom and the proper evaluation required. The Court, therefore, found the marriage in question to be null and void because of an invalidating lack of discretion and reversed decision of the Court of First Instance.

Concerning the second issue, that of implicit condition, the Court demonstrated that John did in fact so condition his consent as to make implicitly an "intention contra bonum sacramenti." This allegation was mentioned in the original petition but unfortunately it was not carefully examined. The ground stated that if there were any doubt of paternity, he would be free to leave her. Both Petitioner and Respondent attested to the fact that this condition had been verbalized some days prior to the marriage.

The Court then proceeded to indicate from the personal history of John and Alice that there was, in fact, a predisposition to such a ground being realized. The Court agreed that the Respondent was suffering from an immature personality. She had a known record for being sexually aggressive and had relations with others by her own admission. She had enticed the Petitioner to relations, but he had for a long time refused. Finally, he succumbed and this resulted in John becoming very confused and feeling guilty. The condition, then was really in the Petitioner's mind prior to the date of the marriage.

The Court therefore concluded that "The Acts indicate clearly that he was willing to accept responsibility for the child solely if it were his. Due to his state of mind and personality characteristics, this condition truly entered into the consent he was giving."

What finally confirmed this condition in the mind of the Court was the breakdown of the marriage and the extreme reaction of the Petitioner upon discovering that his paternity of the child was not certain. With the death of the baby and his parental uncertainty, the Petitioner felt almost internally compelled to leave Alice. John fulfilled the condition which had always been present.

The Acts of this case concluded:
"It is to be carefully noted that this type of condition vitiates the contract from the outset, independently of its possible fulfillment or lack thereof. The Petitioner was effectively reserving to himself the right to terminate the marriage, which was an intention contrary to an essential property of marriage, namely permanence. This is not a condition regarding a past event (Canon 1092, paragraph 4) but rather a future condition contrary to the substance of matrimony (Canon 1092, paragraph 2). The Petitioner was not conditioning his consent on the parentage of the child, a past event whose actuality is no longer verifiable. His condition rested rather on his certainty of his parenthood. His statement indicates clearly that this certainty was a future event, constantly verifiable. If his certainty were somehow shaken, he would feel free to leave. His insecure, compulsive nature required that he be certain. Thus, this marriage must be seen as invalid."

The Court, therefore, safeguarded the tenets of Canon 1092 and concluded that the ground contrary to the nature of the sacrament had been proven. The marriage of

John and Alice was subsequently declared null and void on the ground of lack of due discretion, and secondly, on that of implicit condition.

DECISION: FIRST INSTANCE—AFFIRMATIVE
        DISPENSATION FROM APPEAL
                INTENTION AGAINST PERMANENCE

Documents of the Holy See
on Marriage

Appendix: Documents of The Holy See

Vatican Council II is an historical event; more than ten years have elapsed since it was completed. Laws and directives have been promulgated as the need required it, through Decrees, Motu Proprios, Instructions, etc. We still do not have a New Code of Canon Law. The proposed code has been found inadequate among the hierarchy, Canonists, and others. Suggestions were offered to promulgate the new law at present in the manner of Motu Proprio whereby the laws would prove their worth or be abrogated. This is an excellent suggestion. For example, the Norms of Procedure for the U.S.A., of 1970, were issued in such a manner and have proven to be very successful for justice sake and the salvation of souls. Due to the fact that we have no new code, and although it may seem very bold and ironical to publish another book on marriage while the new laws on marriage are being formulated, nevertheless, during the interim we might find it helpful to include here various important documents of the Holy See. After all, these will be utilized in formulating new laws for the New Code of Canon Law. These Motu Proprios originate through the requests from various countries of the world for special circumstances existing in those countries. Because of these various aspects, the Holy See decided it was necessary to standardize these laws. One such law was that on procedure. Thus came about in 1971, a special document: Motu Proprio: *Causas Matrimoniales* for the entire world, even though it allowed variations from this procedure for the United States and Canada because of the special circumstances (Norms of 1970) existing in these countries. Both Motu Proprios will be found in this appendix. For the same reason the Holy See standardized the procedure on non-consummation cases, March 7, 1972. There were different reasons for the natural bond petitions. About 1968 the S.C. of the Doctrine of Faith began examining the procedures being used which created a doubt whether the Holy Father even had the power to grant such favors. For example, a Catholic party who was married to a non-baptized party with a despensation from disparity of cult, after a dissolution of this natural bond, now wanted to marry another unbaptized person. This meant the Catholic party was entering into a series of dissoluble unions. This procedure was suspended and a special commission of theologians was established by the S.C. for the Doctrine of the Faith. After a study of this question, the same Congregation issued an instruction December 6, 1973, on the proper procedure now required for natural bond cases. This document is also in the appendix. The most important documents are incorporated in this appendix for the convenience of the reader. Cases herein will cover Canons on Diriment Impediments and Consent of Marriage.

Document I

Special Faculties & Privileges to Local Ordinaries

The Motu Proprio, *Pastorale Munus* of Pope Paul VI, given December 3, 1963 grants special faculties and privileges to all local ordinaries on a permanent basis.

The bishops, though hindered by many obstacles, have nonetheless given an example of special charity in all times and dedicated themselves to the pastoral office to which Jesus Christ assigned the very important task of teaching, of leading to holiness, of binding and loosing.

With the increase through the centuries of the Church's concerns and labors, the Apostolic See has always replied promptly and eagerly to the requests of the bishops regarding pastoral care and not only has it added to the extraordinary authority and jurisdiction of the heads of dioceses but also endowed them with singular faculties and privileges which appropriately met current needs.

Now, moreover, while the second session of the Second Vatican Ecumenical Council approaches its end and since we wish nothing more dearly than to express to the council Fathers the very great esteem we have for all the venerable brothers in the episcopacy, it seemed good to us to accept their requests willingly and grant them things which may place their episcopal dignity in the proper light and at the same time render their pastoral function freer and more effective. We think this is very fitting to our office as universal Shepherd. In bestowing these things most willingly on the bishops, we at the same time request that they all, moved by the breadth of flaming charity and joined closely with Christ and with us, His vicar on earth, should seek through their collaboration to lighten *that care for all the churches* (cf. 2 Cor 11; 28) which weighs upon our shoulders.

Since it is a matter of faculties of the utmost importance, we grant them in such a way that they cannot be delegated by the bishops except to a coadjutor, auxiliaries and vicar general, unless expressly noted in the concession of an individual faculty.

According to the prevaling norm of law, however, such faculties, which we declare belong by law to residential bishops, also belong by law to vicars and prefects apostolic, permanent apostolic administrators, abbots and prelates *nullius*, who in their territory enjoy the same rights and faculties that residential bishops have in their own dioceses. and although vicar general, they nevertheless can legitimately delegate to their vicar delegate the faculties treated here.

Having maturely considered everything from our reverence and charity toward each bishop of the Catholic Church, of our own initiative (motu proprio) and by our apostolic authority we decree and establish that from the eighth of December of this year 1963, the bishops may immediately and legitimately use and enjoy the following faculties and privileges:

I. *Faculties* which by right belong to a residential bishop from the moment that he takes canonical possession of the diocese. Unless it is espressly stated in the faculties, he may not delegate them to others except to coadjutor and auxiliary bishops and a vicar general.

1. Proroguing for a just cause, but not beyond a month, the lawful use of rescripts or indults which were granted by the Holy See and have expired, without a request for their renewal having been sent at the proper time to the Holy See. There is an obligation to apply at once to the Holy See for the favor, or to seek a reply if the petition has already been submitted.
2. Permitting priests, because of scarcity of clergy and for a just cause, to celebrate Mass twice on weekdays, and even three times on Sundays and Holy Days of obligation, provided genuine pastoral necessities so demand.
3. Permitting priests, when celebrating two or three Masses, to take liquids even though there be not an interval of an hour before the next Mass.
4. Permitting priests, for a just cause, to celebrate Mass at any hour of the day and to distribute Communion in the evening, with due observance of the other prescriptions of law.
5. Granting the faculty to priests who suffer from poor eyesight or are afflicted with some other infirmity, to offer daily the votive Mass of the Blessed Virgin or the Mass of the dead with the assistance, according to their needs, of a priest or deacon and with due observance of the Instruction of the Sacred Congregation of Rites of April 15, 1961.
6. Granting the same permission to priests who are totally blind provided they are always assisted by another priest or deacon.
7. Granting priests the faculty to celebrate Mass outside a sacred place, but in a reputable and decent place, never in a bedroom, on an altar stone: in an individual case for a just cause but habitually only for a graver cause.
8. Granting also the faculty to celebrate Mass for a just cause at sea and on rivers, with observance of the required precautions.
9. Granting the faculty to priests, who enjoy the privilege of the portable altar, that, for a just and grave cause, they may use instead of an altar stone, the Greek antimension, or the cloth blessed by the bishop, in the right corner of which are placed relics of the holy martyrs authenticated by the bishop, with due observance of other requirements of the rubrics, particularly regarding altar cloths and the corporal.
10. Granting to infirm or elderly priests the faculty of celebrating Mass at home, but not in a bedroom, daily and even on the more solemn feasts, observing the liturgical laws, but with the permission of sitting if they are unable to stand.
11. Reducing because of a decrease in income, as long as the cause obtains, Masses from a legacy (which per se remain fixed) at the rate of the stipend lawfully in effect in the diocese, provided that there is none who is obliged and can rightfully be expected to increase the stipend; likewise, of reducing the obligations or legacies of Masses which burden benefices or other ecclesiastical institutes, if the income of the benefice or institute becomes insufficient for the suitable sustenance of the beneficiary and for fulfilling the works of the sacred ministry

attached to the benefice or for attaining in a fitting manner the proper end of the ecclesiastical institute.

12. Granting the chaplains of all hospitals, orphanages and prisons the faculty, in the absence of the pastor, to administer the sacrament of Confirmation to the faithful in danger of death, with due observance of the norms of the Sacred Congregation of the Discipline of the Sacraments established by the decree, "Spiritus Sancti munera" of September 14, 1946, for priests administering the sacrament of Confirmation.

13. Granting to confessors the faculty, in individual cases, of absolving any of the faithful in the act of sacramental confession from all reserved sins, with the exception however of the sin of false denunciation in which an innocent priest is accused of the crime of solicitation before ecclesiastical judges.

14. Granting confessors distinguished for knowledge and prudence the faculty, in individual cases, of absolving any of the faithful in the act of sacramental confession from all censures even reserved, with the following exceptions: (a) "ab homine" censures; (b) censures reserved in a most special way to the Holy See; (c) censures which are attached to disclosure of the secret of the Holy Office; (d) the excommunication incurred by clerics in sacred orders and all presuming to contract marriage with them, even only civilly, and actually living together.

15. Dispensing for a just cause from the defect of age for ordination provided that it does not exceed six full months.

16. Dispensing from the impediment to orders by which the sons of non-Catholics are bound as long as the parents remain in error.

17. Dispensing those already ordained, for the purposes both of celebrating Mass and obtaining and retaining ecclesiastical benefices, from any of the irregularities, whether ex dilicto or ex defectu, provided that scandal does not arise thereby and provided that the ministry of the altar is correctly performed, with the exception of those mentioned in Canon 985: 3 and 4 of the Code of Canon Law. In the case of the crime of heresy or schism, there must be a prior abjuration in the hands of the one absolving.

18. Conferring sacred orders outside the cathedral church and "extra tempora," including weekdays, if this is useful from a pastoral point of view.

19. Dispensing for a just and reasonable cause from all the minor matrimonial impediments, even if there is question of mixed marriages, but with observance in this latter case of the prescriptions of Canons 1061-1064 of the Code of Canon Law.[1]

20. Dispensing when a just and grave cause urges, from the impediments of mixed relgion and disparity of worship, even in the case of use of the Pauline Privilege, with observance of the prescriptions of Canons 1061-1064 of the Code of Canon Law.

21. "Sanandi in radice," provided the consent perdures, marriages that are invalid because of a minor impediment or defect of form, even if there is question of mixed marriages, but in this case there must be observance of Canon 1061 of the Code of Canon Law.

22. "Sanandi in radice," provided consent perdures, marriages that are invalid because of the impediment of disparity of worship, even if they are also invalid because of a defect of form, with observance of prescriptions of Canon 1061 of the Code of Canon Law.[2]

23. Permitting for a grave cause, that the interpellations of an infidel spouse may be done before the baptism of the party who is being converted to the faith; and dispensing, also for a grave cause, from the same interpellation before the baptism of the party who is being converted: provided, in this case that it is clear from a summary and extra-judicial process that the interpellation cannot be made or it would be useless.

24. Reducing, for a just cause, the obligation by which cathedral chapters and colleges of canons are obliged to perform ritually the daily Divine Office in Choir, by granting that choral service may be satisfied either only on certain days or merely by a certain determined part.

25. Entrusting where necessary, certain canons with the tasks of the sacred ministry, of teaching or of the apostolate, with a dispensation from choir, while preserving the right of receiving the fruits of the prebend, but not the distributions, whether *inter praesentes*, as they are called, or daily.

26. Commuting for reason of weak eyesight or other cause, as long as the condition persists, the Divine Office into daily recitation of at least a third part of the Rosary of the Blessed Virgin Mary or other prayers.

27. Deputing in particular cases, or for a time, the vicar general or another priest with ecclesiastical dignity, to consecrate portable altars, chalices and patens, according to the rite prescribed in the Pontifical and using the Holy Oils blessed by the bishop.

28. Allowing minor clerics, lay Religious and also pious women to wash with the first ablution, palls, corporals and purificators.

29. Using the faculties and privileges, while observing their extent and intent, which religious communities having a house in the diocese enjoy for the good of the faithful.

30. Granting to priests the faculty by which, with the rites prescribed by the Church, they may erect the Stations of the Cross, even in the open air, with all the indulgences that have been granted to those who make this pious exercise. The faculty cannot be exercised in parochial territory where there is a house of religious who by apostolic grant enjoy the privilege of erecting the Stations of the Cross.

31. Admitting illegitimate sons into the seminary if they show the qualities required for admission into the seminary, provided it is not a question of offspring of an adulterous or sacrilegious union.

32. Granting permission that, for a legitimate cause, ecclesiastical goods may be alienated, pledged, mortgaged, leased, redeemed from a long-term lease, and that ecclesiastical moral persons may contract on indebtedness to an amount proposed by the national or regional conference of bishops and approved by the Holy See.

33. Confirming even to a fifth triennium the ordinary confessor of Religious women if another provision cannot be made because of the scarcity of priests suitable for this office, or if the majority of the Religious, even those who in other matters do have the right to vote, agree in secret ballot to the confirmation of the same confessor. Another provision must be made for those who disagree, if they so desire.

34. Entering, for a just cause, into a pontifical cloister of monasteries of nuns situated in his diocese, and permitting for a just and grave cause, that others be admitted into the cloister, and that the nuns go out from it—for a truly necessary period of time.

35. Dispensing, on the petition of the competent superior, from the impedimeents which prevent those who have adhered to a non-Catholic sect from being admitted into Religion.

36. Dispensing, on the petition of the competent superior, from illegitimacy of birth, those to be admitted into Religion who are destined for the priesthood, and also others who are forbidden admission into Religion by a prescription of the Constitutions. In neither case can adulterous or sacrilegious offspring be dispensed.

37. Waiving in whole or in part, on the petition of the competent superior, the dowry which postulants should bring to be admitted to a monastery of nuns or another religious community, even of pontifical right.

38. Permitting religious to transfer from one to another community of diocesan right.

39. Dismissing from the diocese, in the presence of a most serious cause, individual Religious, if their major superior has been warned and has failed to provide; moreover, the matter is to be referred immediately to the Holy See.

40. Granting, also through other prudent and capable men, to the individual faithful subject to himself, the permission to read and retain, with care however less they fall into the hands of others, prohibited books and periodicals, not excepting those which purposely defend heresy or schism, or attempt to overturn the very foundations of religion. However, this permission can be granted only to those who need to read the forbidden books and periodicals either to attack them, or to meet properly their own obligations or to follow lawfully a course of studies.

II. *Privileges*, which, besides those enumerated in their titles in the Code of Canon Law, belong to all bishops, residential or titular, as soon as they have received the authentic notification of canonical election.

1. Preaching the word of God—everywhere in the world, unless the Ordinary of the place expressly denies it.

2. Hearing the confessions of the faithful and of Religious women anywhere in the world, unless the Ordinary of the place expressly denies it.

3. Absolving any of the faithful anywhere in the act of sacramental confession, from all reserved sins, except however the sin of false denunciation in which an innocent priest is accused of the crime of solicitation before ecclesiastical judges.

4. Absolving any of the faitful anywhere in the act of sacramental confession from all censures, even reserved, except however: (a) censures "ab homine"; (b) censures reserved in a most special way to the Holy See; (c) censures which are attached to disclosure of the secret of the Holy Office; (d) the excommunication incurred by clerics in sacred orders and all presuming to contract marriage with them, even only civilly, and actually living together. Residential bishops can also use this faculty for their subjects in the external forum.

5. Reserving the Blessed Sacrament in their private oratory provided that the prescriptions of the liturgical laws are fully observed.

6. Celebrating Mass at any hour of the day, for a serious reason, and distributing Holy Communion even in the evening, observing all norms enjoined.

7. Blessing anywhere by a single sign of the Cross, with all the indulgences usually granted by the Holy See, rosaries and other beads used for prayers, crosses, medals, scapulars approved by the Holy See and imposing them without the obligation of inscription.

8. Blessing for the faithful, who because of infirmity or other lawful impediments cannot visit the sacred Stations of the Cross, images of the Crucified with an application of all the indulgences attached by the Roman Pontiffs to the devout exercise of the Way of the Cross.

We with pleasure grant these faculties and privileges to Our Brothers in the Episcopacy with the intention and purpose we have noted above: that all these may particularly be for the glory and advantage of the Church of Christ to whom We and Ours are indebted for all things.

Nothwithstanding anything to the contrary, even worthy of special mention.

Given at Rome, at St. Peter's on November 30, 1963.

PAUL PP. VI

1. Cf. C. 1063, New Decree on Mixed Marriage.
2. Cf. C. 1063.

DOCUMENT II—NORMS FOR MIXED MARRIAGES

APOSTOLIC LETTER ISSUED "MOTU PROPRIO" DETERMINING NORMS FOR MIXED MARRIAGES

Pope Paul VI

Mixed marriages, that is to say marriages in which one party is a Catholic and the other a non-Catholic, whether baptized or not, have always been given careful attention by the Church in pursuance of her duty. Today the Church is constrained to give even greater attention to them, owing to the conditions of present times. In the past Catholics were separated from members of other Christian confessions and from non-Christians, by their situation in their community or even by physical boundaries. In more recent times, however, not only has this separation been reduced, but communication between men of different regions and religions has greatly developed, and as a result there has been a great increase in the number of mixed marriages. Also a great influence in this regard has been exercised by the growth and spread of civilization and industry, urbanization and consequent rural depopulation, migrations in great numbers and the increase of exiles of every kind.

The Church is indeed aware that mixed marriages, precisely because they admit differences of religion and are a consequence of the division among Christians, do not, except in some cases, help in re-establishing unity among Christians. There are many difficulties inherent in a mixed marriage, since a certain division is introduced into the living cell of the Church, as the Christian family is rightly called, and in the family itself the fulfillment of the gospel teachings is more difficult because of diversities in matters of religion, especially with regard to those matters which concern Christian worship and the education of the children.

For these reasons the Church, conscious of her duty, discourages the contracting of mixed marriages, for she is most desirous that Catholics be able in matrimony to attain to perfect union of mind and full communion of life. However, since man has the natural right to marry and beget children, the Church, by her laws, which clearly show her pastoral concern, makes such arrangements that on the one hand the principles of Divine Law be scrupulously observed and that on the other the said right to contract marriage be respected.

The Church vigilantly concerns itself with the education of the young and their fitness to undertake their duties with a sense of responsibility and to perform their obligations as members of the Church, and she shows this both in preparing for marriage those who intend to contract a mixed marriage and in caring for those who have already contracted such a marriage. Although in the case of baptized persons of different religious confessions, there is less risk of religious indifferentism, it can be more easily avoided if both husband and wife have a sound knowledge of the Christian nature of marital partnership, and if they are properly helped by their respective Church authorities. Even difficulties arising in marriage between a Catholic and an unbaptized person can be overcome through pastoral watchfulness and skill.

Neither in doctrine nor in law does the Church place on the same level a marriage between a Catholic and a baptized non-Catholic, and one between a Catholic and an unbaptized person; for, as the Second Vatican Council declared, men, who, though they are not Catholics "believe in Christ and have been properly baptized are brought into a certain, though imperfect, communion with the Catholic Church."[1] Moreover, although Eastern Christians who have been baptized outside the Catholic Church are separated from communion with us, they possess true sacraments, above all the Priesthood and the Eucharist, whereby they are joined to us in a very close relationship.[2] Undoubtedly there exists in a marriage between baptized persons, since such a marriage is a true sacrament, a certain communion of spiritual benefits which is lacking in a marriage entered into by a baptized person and one who is not baptized.

Nevertheless, one cannot ignore the difficulties inherent even in mixed marriages between baptized persons. There is often a difference of opinion on the sacramental nature of matrimony, on the special significance of marriage celebrated within the Church, on the interpretation of certain moral principles pertaining to marriage and the family, on the extent to which obedience is due to the Catholic Church, and on the competence that belongs to ecclesiastical authority. From this it is clear that difficult questions of this kind can only be fully resolved when Christian unity is restored.

The faithful must therefore be taught that, although the Church somewhat relaxes ecclesiastical discipline in particular cases, she can never remove the obligation of the Catholic party, which, by divine law, namely by the plan of salvation instituted through Christ, is imposed according to the various situations.

The faithful should therefore be reminded that the Catholic party to a marriage has the duty of preserving his or her own faith; nor is it ever permitted to expose oneself to a proximate danger of losing it.

Furthermore, the Catholic partner in a mixed marriage is obliged, not only to remain steadfast in the faith, but also, as far as possible, to see to it that the children be baptized and brought up in that same faith and receive all those aids to eternal salvation which the Catholic Church provides for her sons and daughters.

The problem of the children's education is a particularly difficult one, in view of the fact that both husband and wife are bound by that responsibility and may by no means ignore it or any of the obligations connected with it. However the Church endeavors to meet this problem, just as she does the others, by her legislation and pastoral care.

With all this in mind, no one will be really surprised to find that even the canonical discipline on mixed marriages cannot be uniform and that it must be adapted to the various cases in what pertains to the juridical form of contracting marriage, its liturgical celebration, and, finally the pastoral care to be given to the married people, and the children of the marriage, according to the distinct circumstances of the married couple and the differing degrees of their ecclesiastical communion.

It was altogether fitting that so important a question should receive the attention of the Second Vatican Council. This occured several times as occasion arose. Indeed, in the third session the Council Fathers voted to entrust the question to us in its entirety.

To meet their desire, the Sacred Congregation for the Doctrine of the Faith, on the 18th of March, 1966, promulgated an Instruction on mixed marriages, entitled *Matrimonii Sacramentum*,[3] which provided that, if the norms laid down therein stood the test of experience, they should be introduced in a definite and precise form into the Code of Canon Law which is now being revised.[4]

When certain questions on mixed marriages were raised in the first General Meeting of the Synod of Bishops, held in October 1967[5] and many useful observations had been made upon them by the Fathers, we decided to submit those questions to examination by a special Commission of Cardinals which after diligent consideration, presented us with its conclusions.

At the outset we state that Eastern Catholics contracting marriage with baptized non-Catholics or with unbaptized persons are not subject to the norms established by this Letter. With regard to the marriage of Catholics of whatsoever rite with Eastern non-Catholic Christians, the Church has recently issued certain norms,[6] which we wish to remain in force.

Accordingly, in order that ecclesiastical discipline on mixed marriages be more perfectly formulated and that, without violating divine law, canonical law should have regard for the differing circumstances of married couples, in accordance with the mind of the Second Vatican Council expressed especially in the Decree *Unitatis Redintegratio*[7] and in the Declaration *Dignitatis Humanae*,[8] and also in careful consideration of the wishes expressed in the Synod of Bishops, we, by our own authority, and after mature deliberation, establish and decree the following norms:

1. A marriage between two baptized persons, of whom one is a Catholic, while the other is a non-Catholic, may not licitly be contracted without the previous dispensation of the local Ordinary, since such a marriage is by its nature an obstacle to the full spiritual communion of the married parties.

2. A marriage between two persons, of whom one has been baptized in the Catholic Church or received into it, while the other is unbaptized, entered into without previous dispensation by the local Ordinary, is invalid.

3. The Church, taking into account the nature and circumstances of times, places and persons, is prepared to dispense from both impediments provided there is a just cause.

4. To obtain from the local Ordinary dispensation from an impediment, the Catholic party shall declare that he is ready to remove dangers of falling away from the faith. He is also gravely bound to make a sincere promise to do all in his power to have all the children baptized and brought up in the Catholic Church.

5. At an opportune time the non-Catholic party must be informed of these promises

which the Catholic party has to make, so that it is clear that he is cognizant of the promise and obligation on the part of the Catholic.

6. Both parties are to be clearly instructed on the ends and essential properties of marriage, not to be excluded by either party.

7. Within its own territorial competence, it is for the Bishops' Conference to determine the way in which these declarations and promises, which are always required, shall be made; whether by word of mouth alone, in writing, or before witnesses; and also to determine what proof of them there should be in the external forum, and how they are to be brought to the knowledge of the non-Catholic party, as well as to lay down whatever other requirements may be opportune.

8. The canonical form is to be used for contracting mixed marriages, and is required for validity, without prejudice, however, to the provisions of the Decree *Crescens Matrimoniorum* published by the Sacred Congregation for the Eastern Churches on 22nd February, 1967.[9]

9. If serious difficulties stand in the way of observing the canonical form, local Ordinaries have the right to dispense from the canonical form in any mixed marriage; but the Bishops' Conference is to determine norms according to which the said dispensation may be granted licitly and uniformly within the region or territory of the Conference, with the provision that there should always be some public form of ceremony.

10. Arrangements must be made that all validly contracted marriages be diligently entered in the books prescribed by canon law. Priests responsible should make sure that non-Catholic ministers also assist in recording in their own books the fact of a marriage with a Catholic.

    Episcopal Conferences are to issue regulations determining, for their region or territory, a uniform method by which a marriage that has been publicly contracted after a dispensation from the canonical form was obtained, is registered in the book prescribed by canon law.

11. With regard to the liturgical form of the celebration of a mixed marriage, if it is to be taken from the Roman Ritual, use must be made of the ceremonies in the *Rite of Celebration of Marriage* promulgated by our authority, whether it is a question of a marriage between a Catholic and a baptized non-Catholic (39-54) or of a marriage between a Catholic and an unbaptized person (55-66). If, however, the circumstances justify it, a marriage between a Catholic and a baptized non-Catholic can be celebrated, subject to the local Ordinary's consent, according to the rites for the celebration of marriage within the Mass (19-38), while respecting the prescription of general law with regard to Eucharistic Communion.

12. The Episcopal Conferences shall inform the Apostolic See of all decisions which, within their competence, they make concerning mixed marriages.

13. The celebration of marriage before a Catholic priest or deacon and a non-Catholic minister, performing their respective rites together, is forbidden; nor is it permitted to have another religious marriage ceremony before or after the Catholic ceremony, for the purpose of giving or renewing matrimonial consent.

14. Local Ordinaries and parish priests shall see to it that the Catholic husband or wife and the children born of a mixed marriage do not lack spiritual assistance in fulfilling their duties of conscience. They shall encourage the Catholic husband or wife to keep ever in mind the divine gift of the Catholic faith and to bear witness to it with gentleness and reverence, and with a clear conscience.[10] They are to aid the married couple to foster the unity of their conjugal and family life, a unity which, in the case of Christians, is based on their baptism too. To these ends it is to be desired that those pastors should establish relationships of sincere openness and enlightened confidence with ministers of other religious communities.

15. The penalties decreed by Canon 2319 of the Code of Canon Law are all abrogated. For those who have incurred them the effects of those penalties cease, without prejudice to the obligations mentioned in number 4 of these norms.

16. The local Ordinary is able to give a *sanatio in radice* of a mixed marriage when the conditions spoken of in numbers 4 and 5 of these norms have been fulfilled, and provided that the conditions of law are observed.

17. In the case of a particular difficulty or doubt with regard to the application of these norms, recourse is to be made to the Holy See.

We order that what we have decreed in this Letter, given in the form of "Motu Proprio," be regarded as established and ratified, notwithstanding any measure to the contrary, and is to take effect from the first day of October of this year.

Given at Rome, at St. Peter's March 31, 1970.

PAULUS PP. VI

ROMAN CATHOLIC—ORTHODOX MARRIAGE DECREE

The Sacred Congregation for the Oriental Church issued this decree on mixed marriages between Latin Rite Catholics and the Orthodox, February 22, 1967.

The increasing frequency of mixed marriages between Oriental Catholics and non-Catholic Oriental Christians in the eastern patriarchates and eparchies as well as in the Latin diocese themselves and the necessity of coping with the inconveniences resulting from this, were the reasons why the Second Vatican Ecumenical Council decreed: "When Oriental Catholics enter into marriage with baptized non-Catholic Orientals the canonical form for the celebration of such marriages obliges only for lawfulness; for their validity, the presence of a sacred minister suffices, as long as the other requirements of the law are observed" (Decree on the Eastern Catholic Churches, n. 18).

In the exceptional circumstances of today, mixed marriages between the Catholic faithful of the Latin rite and non-Catholic Oriental faithful are taking place the variety in canonical disciplines has brought about many grave difficulties both in the East and the West. For this reason petitions from various regions have been addressed to the Supreme Pontiff asking that he be pleased to unify canonical discipline in this matter by also permitting to Catholics of the Latin rite what has been decreed for Catholics of the Eastern rite.

His Holiness, our Lord Paul VI, by divine providence Pope, after mature reflection and diligent investigation, has resolved to agree to the petitions and desires addressed to him and, as a means of preventing invalid marriages between the faithful of the Latin rite and the non-Catholic Christian faithful of the Oriental rites, of showing proper regard for the permanence and sanctity of marriages, and of promoting charity between the Catholic faithful and the non-Catholic Oriental faithful, he has kindly granted that, when Catholics, whether they be Orientals or Latins, contract marriage with non-Catholic Oriental faithful, the canonical form for the celebration of these marriages obliges only for lawfulness; for validity the presence of a sacred minister suffices, as long as the other requirements of law are observed.

All care should be taken that under the guidance of the pastor such marriages be carefully entered into the prescribed registers as soon as possible; this prescription also holds when Catholic Orientals enter marriage with baptized non-Catholic Orientals according to the norm of the conciliar decree "On the Catholic Oriental Churches."

In conformity with the holiness of marriage itself, non-Catholic ministers are reverently and earnestly requested to cooperate in the task of registering marriages in the books of the Catholic party, whether of the Latin or Oriental rite.

Ordinaries of the place, who grant dispensation from the impediment of mixed religion, are likewise given the faculty of dispensing from the obligation of observing canonical form for lawfulness if there exist difficulties which, according to their prudent judgment, require this dispensation.

This same Supreme Pontiff has ordered the Sacred Congregation for the Oriental Church, of which he himself is the prefect, to make known to all this resolution and concession. Wherefore, the same sacred congregation, after also consulting the Sacred Doctrinal Congregation, at the order of His Holiness, has composed the present decree to be published in the *Acta Apostolicae Sedis*.

Meanwhile, in order that his new statute may be brought to the attention of those whom it concerns, whether they be Catholics of any rite whatever or Orthodox, the present decree will go into effect beginning from March 25, 1967, the feast of the Annunciation of the Blessed Virgin Mary.

Notwithstanding anything which in any way may be to the contrary.

EPISCOPAL FACULTIES

The most important single faculty granted to bishops is that described in the motu proprio *De Episcoporum Muneribus* (June 15, 1966). The Latin text is found in the Acta Apostolicae Sedis, LVII (1966), 467-472. An English translation is in the *Canon Law Digest*, 1966 Supplement, under Canon 329. This faculty, based on the Decree *Christus Dominus* of the council (Vatican II), gives to the diocesan bishops the faculty to dispense their faithful in particular cases from the general laws of the Church whenever they judge that it would be for their spiritual good, unless a special reservation has been made by the Supreme authority. For each new case that arises all that will be necessary is to consult this motu proprio to determine whether the particular faculty is there. A Handbook on all these faculties had been prepared by a special committee of the Canon Law Society of America. Copies can be obtained by writing to the headquarters of the CLS.

 1. Decree on Ecumenism *Unitatis Redintegratio*, 3, AAS 57, 1965, p. 93; Cf. Dogmatic Constitution on the Church *Lumen Gentium*, AAS 57, 1965, pp. 19-20.
 2. Cf. *Decree on Ecumenism* pp. 13-18, pp. 100-104.
 3. Cf. AAS 58, 1966, pp. 235-239
 4. Cf. *ibid.*, p. 237.
 5. Cf. *Argumenta de quibus disceptabitur in primo generali coetu Synodi Episcoporum, pars altera, Typis Polyglottis Vaticanis,* 1967, pp. 27-37.
 6. Cf. Decree on Eastern Catholic Churches *Orientalium Ecclesiarum*, 18, AAS 57, 1965, p. 82; Sacred Congregation for the Eastern Churches: Decree *Crescens Matrimoniorum*, AAS 59, 1967, pp. 165-166.
 7. AAS 57, 1965, pp. 90-112.
 8. AAS 58, 1966, pp. 929-946.
 9. AAS 59, 1967, p. 166.
10. 1 P 3:16.

Document III

Norms for Mixed Marriages in USA (Private)

The following "statement of the National Conference of Catholic Bishops on the implementation of the apostolic letter on mixed marriages" in the United States of America was issued on 16 November, 1970 and given the effective date of 1 January, 1971.

Introductory Principles

The Fathers of the Second Vatican Council requested the Holy See to provide for the application of conciliar teaching to marriages which unite Catholics and those of differing religious convictions. Following discussions of this matter by the Synod of Bishops in 1967, the Holy See, after collegial consultation with the episcopal conferences, prepared a response to that request. And on March 31, 1970 Pope Paul VI issued *motu proprio* the Apostolic Letter Determining Norms for Mixed Marriages. The provisions of this apostolic letter, effective October 1, 1970, open the way to an improved pastoral approach in support of couples united or to be united in such marriages.

The National Conference of Catholic Bishops welcomes the apostolic letter and encourages its ready application within our country. We call to mind the principles upon which it is based and the values it seeks to uphold. Our statement is to be understood only with a view to the complete text of the *mortu proprio*.

First of all, the apostolic letter recognizes the natural right of man to marry and beget children, and to exercise this right, free from undue pressure (cf. *Pacem in Terris*, no. 15).

Within marriage the Church seeks always to uphold the strength and stability of marital union and the family which flows from it. For "the well-being of the individual person and of human and Christian society is intimately linked with the healthy condition of that community produced by marriage and family. Hence Christians and all men who hold this community in high esteem sincerely rejoice in the various ways by which men today find help in fostering this community of love and perfecting its life, and by which spouses and parents are assisted in their lofty calling." (*The Church in the Modern World*, no. 47).

As the apostolic letter observes, the "perfect union of mind and full communion of life" to which married couples aspire can be more readily achieved when both partners share the same Catholic belief and life. For this reason, the Church greatly desires that Catholics marry Catholics and generally discourages mixed marriages.

Yet, recognizing that mixed marriages do occur, the Church, upholding the principles of Divine Law, makes special arrangements for them. And recognizing that these marriages do at times encounter special difficulties, the Church wishes to see that special help and support are extended to the couples concerned. This is the abiding responsibility of all. For "Christians should actively promote the values of marriage and family, both by example of their own lives and by cooperation with other men of good will. Thus when difficulties arise, Christians will provide, on behalf of family life, those necessities and helps which are suitably modern." (*Ibid.*, no. 52).

In a particular way, priests with a pastoral ministry to families and all persons engaged in the family life apostolate are to be commended for their attention to the specific needs of individual couples. Since these will vary, the apostolic letter stresses the importance of individualized support for diverse situations. It recognizes that ". . . . the canonical discipline on mixed marriages cannot be uniform and must be adapted . . ." and "the pastoral care to be given to the married people and children of marriage" must also be adapted "according to the distinct circumstances of the married couple and the differing degrees of their ecclesiastical communion." Consequently, pastors, in exercising their ministry in behalf of marriages that unite Catholics and others will do so with zealous concern and respect for the couples involved. They should have an active and positive regard for the holy state in which the couples are united.

In such marriages, the conscientious devotion of the Catholic to the Catholic Church is to be safeguarded, and the conscience of the other partner is to be respected. This is in keeping with the principle of religious liberty (cf. *Declaration on Religious Freedom*, no. 3).

In all valid marriages the Church recognizes sacred and abiding values. For "the intimate partnership of married life and love has been established by the Creator and qualified by His laws. It is rooted in the conjugal covenant of irrevocable personal consent. Hence by that human act whereby spouses mutually bestow and accept each other, a relationship arises which by divine will and in the eyes of society too is a lasting one. For the good of the spouses and their offspring as well as of society, the existence of this sacred bond no longer depends on human decisions alone." (*The Church in the Modern World*, no. 48). So the sacred character of all valid marriages, including those which the Church does not consider as sacramental, is recognized. For those, too, manifest the hand of God, Who is the author of marriage, and should lead the couple to holiness of life. In preparing couples for mixed marriages, pastors should make clear to the partners the deep significance which the Church perceives in their intended union as "two in one flesh." (Mt 19:16).

In this regard, the broad areas of agreement which unite Christians and Jews in their appreciation of the religious character of marriage should be kept significantly in mind. (cf. *Joint Statement on Marriage and Family Life in the United States*, issued by the United States Catholic Conference, the National Council of the Churches of Christ, and the Synagogue Council of America, June 8, 1966).

In this context, it should be clearly noted that while Catholics are required to observe the Catholic form of marriage for validity, unless dispensed by their Bishop, the Catholic Church recognizes the reality of marriages contracted validly among those who are not Christians and among those Christians separated from us.

In addition to the sacred character of all valid marriages still more must be said of marriages between a Catholic and another baptized Christian. According to our Catholic tradition, we believe such marriages to be truly sacramental. The apostolic letter states that there exists between the persons united in them a special "communion of spiritual benefits." These spiritual bonds in which couples are united are grounded in the "true, though imperfect, communion" which exists between the Catholic Church and all who believe in Christ and are properly baptized. (*Decree on Ecumenism*, no. 3). Along with us, such persons are honored by the title of Christians and are rightly regarded as brothers in the Lord. In marriages which unite Catholics and other baptized Christians, the couple should be encouraged to recognize in practical ways what they share together in the life of grace, in faith, and charity along with other interior gifts of the Holy Spirit, and that in service to the same Lord they await the salvation which He promised to those who would be His followers.

A number of the particular difficulties faced by Catholics and other Christians in mixed marriages result from the division among Christians. However successful these marriages may be, they do not erase the pain of that wider division. Yet this division need not weaken these marriages, and given proper understanding, they may lead to a deep spiritual unity between the spouses. Such couples should accept the painful aspects of Christian division insofar as these affect their lives together as a sharing in the suffering of the Church. Thus they should regard their personal efforts at understanding and patience as symbolic of and a participation in the broader efforts toward unity among the separated churches. Their own love as it reaches out to relatives and friends should have a healing effect in establishing closer relationships between groups of Christians who have been estranged due to divisions among them. In this way, such marriages, while encompassing within one home the divisions among Christians, nevertheless, like all sacramental marriages, should be seen as compelling signs of the mystery of Christ's abiding love for His Church, a love which continually seeks to reconcile. Finally, such couples, should they achieve such a perspective in regard to their marriage, can do much to intensify the longing among Christians, nevertheless, like all sacramental marriages, should be seen as compelling signs of the mystery of Christ's abiding love for His Church, a love which continually seeks to reconcile. Finally, such couples, should they achieve such a perspective in regard to their marriage, can do much to intensify the longing among Christians for the day when all shall be one.

In order to aid these couples to come to this deep understanding of their married life together, when possible, their Catholic and other Christian pastors should jointly do all that they can to prepare them for marriage and to support them and their families with all the aids their ministry can provide. They can, for example, enliven the couple's appreciation of the virtue of fidelity, mutual trust, forgiveness, honesty, openness, love and responsibility for their children. In this way the past of the different Christian communities can best bring the couple to a keen awareness of all that they have in common as Christians as well as to a proper appreciation of the gravity of the differences that yet remain between their churches.

In their homes, these couples should be encouraged in practical ways to develop a common life of prayer calling upon the many elements of spirituality which they share as a common Christian heritage and expressing their own common faith in the Lord, together asking Him to help them grow in their love for each other, to bless their families with the graces they need, and to keep them always mindful of the needs of others. The example of parents united in prayer is especially important for the children whom God may give them. In regard to public worship together in each other's churches, pastors may explain to the couple the provisions made for this by the Holy See in the *Ecumenical Directory*.[1]

Beyond this, parents have the right and the responsibility to provide for the religious education of their children. This right is clearly taught by Vatican II: "Since the family is a society in its own original right, it has the right freely to live its own domestic religious life under the guidance of the parents. Parents, moreover, have the right to determine, in accordance with their own religious beliefs, the kind of religious education that their children are to receive." (*Declaration on Religious Freedom*, no. 5). It is evident that in preparing for a mixed marriage, the couple will have to reach decisions and make specific choices in order to fulfill successfully the responsibility that is theirs toward their children in this respect. It is to be hoped for their own sake that in this matter, the couple may reach a common mind. If this issue is not resolved before marriage, the couple, as sad experience has shown, find a severe strain in their marital life that can subject them to well-meaning but tension-building pressures from relatives on both sides. If this issue cannot be resolved, there is a serious question whether the couple should marry. In reaching a concrete decision concerning the baptism and religious education of children, both partners should remember that neither thereby abdicates the fundamental responsibility of parents to see that their children are instilled with deep and abiding religious values. In this the Catholic partner is seriously bound to act in accord with the faith which recognizes that, "This is the unique Church of Christ which in the Creed we avow as one, holy, catholic, and apostolic. After His resurrection our Savior handed her over to Peter to be shepherded (Jn 21:17), commissioning him and the other apostles to a propagate and govern her (cf. Mt 28:18f). Her He erected for all ages as 'the pillar and mainstay of the truth' (1 Tm 3:15). This Church, constituted and organized in the world as a society, subsists in the Catholic Church, which is governed by the successor of Peter and by the Bishops in union with that successor, although many elements of sanctification and of truth can be found outside her visible structure. These elements, however, as gifts properly belonging to the Church of Christ, possess an inner dynamism toward Catholic unity." (*Constitution of the Church*, no. 8). This faith is the source of a serious obligation in conscience on the part of the Catholic, whose conscience in this regard must be respected.

Specific Norms

This apostolic letter on mixed marriages leaves to episcopal conferences the further determination of specific questions. (The norms of *Matrimonia mixta* are not repeated here, nor are the special norms affecting the marriages of Eastern Catholics and marriages of Catholics with Eastern non-Catholic Christians. They are found in the

Document IV

Decree on Catholic-Orthodox Marriages, of February 22, 1967).[2] In order to implement this mandate, the NCCB sets forth the following for the dioceses of the United States.

I. Pastoral Responsibility

1. In every diocese, there shall be appropriate informational programs to explain both the reasons for restrictions upon mixed marriages and the positive spiritual values to be sought in such marriages when permitted. This is particularly important if the non-Catholic is a Christian believer and the unity of married and family life is ultimately based upon the baptism of both wife and husband. If possible, all such programs should be undertaken after consultation with and in conjunction with non-Catholic authorities.

2. In every diocese there shall be appropriate programs for the instruction and orientation of the clergy, as well as of candidates for the ministry, so that they may understand fully the reasons for the successive changes in the discipline of mixed marriage and may willingly undertake their personal responsibilities to each individual couple and family in the exercise of their pastoral ministry.

3. In addition to the customary marriage preparation programs, it is the serious duty of each one in the pastoral ministry, according to his own responsibility, office or assignment, to undertake:

(a) the spiritual and catechetical preparation, especially in regard to the "ends and essential properties of marriage (which) are not to be excluded by either party" (cf. *Matrimonia mixta*, no. 6), on a direct and individual basis, of couples who seek to enter a mixed marriage, and

(b) continued concern and assistance to the wife and husband in mixed marriages and to their children, so that married and family life may be supported in unity, respect for conscience, and common spiritual benefit.

4. In the assistance which he gives in preparation for marriage between a Catholic and non-Catholic, and his continued efforts to help all married couples and families, the priest should endeavor to be in contact and to cooperate with the minister or religious counselor of the non-Catholic.

II. Declaration and Promise (M.P., no. 7)

5. The declaration and promise by the Catholic, necessary for dispensation from the impediment to a mixed marriage (either mixed religion or disparity of worship), shall be made, in the following words or their substantial equivalent:

"I reaffirm my faith in Jesus Christ and, with God's help, intend to continue living that faith in the Catholic Church.

"I promise to do all in my power to share the faith I have received with our children by having them baptized and reared as Catholics."

6. The declaration and promise are made in the presence of a priest or deacon

either orally or in writing as the Catholic prefers.

7.   The form of the declaration and promise is not altered in the case of the marriage of a Catholic with another baptized Christian, but the priest should draw the attention of the Catholic to the communion of spiritual benefits in such a Christian marriage. The promise and declaration should be made in the light of the "certairect, communion" of the non-Catholic with the Catholic Church because of his belief in Christ and baptism. (cf. *Decree on Ecumenism*, no. 3).

8.   At an opportune time before marriage, and preferably as part of usual pre-marital instructions, the non-Catholic must be informed of the promises and of the responsibility of the Catholic. No precise manner or occasion of informing the non-Catholic is prescribed. It may be done by the priest, deacon or the Catholic party. No formal statement of the non-Catholic is required. But the mutual understanding of this question beforehand should prevent possible disharmony that might otherwise arise during married life.

9.   The priest who submits the request for dispensation from the impediment to a mixed marriage shall certify that the declaration and promise have been made by the Catholic and that the non-Catholic has been informed of this requirement. This is done in the following or similar words:

"The required promise and declaration have been made by the Catholic in my presence. The non-Catholic has been informed of this and obligation on the part of the Catholic."

The promise of the Catholic must be sincerely made, and is to be presumed to be sincerely made. If, however, the priest has reason to doubt the sincerity of the promise made by the Catholic, he may not recommend the request for the dispensation and should submit the matter to the local Ordinary.

III. Form of Marriage (M.P., no. 9)

10.   Where there are serious difficulties in observing the Catholic canonical form in a mixed marriage, the local Ordinary of the Catholic party or of the place where the marriage is to occur may dispense the Catholic from the observance of the form for a just pastoral cause. An exhaustive list is impossible, but the following are the types of reasons: to achieve family harmony or to avoid family alienation, to obtain parental agreement to the marriage, to recognize the significant claims of relationship or special friendship with a non-Catholic minister, to permit the marriage in a church that has particular importance to the non-Catholic. If the Ordinary of the Catholic party grants a dispensation for a marriage which is to take place in another diocese, the Ordinary of that diocese should be informed beforehand.

11.   Ordinarily this dispensation from the canonical form is granted in view of the proposed celebration of a religious marriage service. In some exceptional circumstances (e.g., Catholic-Jewish marriages) it may be necessary that the dispensation be granted so that a civil ceremony may be performed. In any case, a public form that is civilly recognized for the celebration of marriage is required.

IV. Recording Marriages (M.P., no. 10)

12. In a mixed marriage for which there has been granted a dispensation from the canonical form, an ecclesiastical record of the marriage shall be kept in the chancery of the diocese which granted the dispensation from the impediment, and in the marriage records of the parish from which application for the dispensation was made.

13. It is the responsibility of the priest who submits the request for the dispensation to see that, after the public form of marriage ceremony is performed, notices of the marriage are sent in the usual form to:

(a) the parish and chancery noted above (12);

(b) the place of baptism of the Catholic party.

The recording of other mixed marriages is not changed.

V. Celebration of Marriages Between
Catholics and Non—Catholics

14. It is not permitted to have two religious marriage services or to have a single service in which both the Catholic marriage ritual and a non-Catholic marriage ritual are celebrated jointly or successively (cf. no. 13 of *Matrimonia mixta*).

15. With the permission of the local Ordinary and the consent of the appropriate authority of the other church or community, a non-Catholic minister may be invited to participate in the Catholic marriage service by giving additional prayers, blessings, or words of greeting or exhortation. If the marriage is not part of the Eucharistic celebration, the minister may also be invited to read a lesson and/or to preach (cf. the *Ecumenical Directory*, Part I, no. 56).

16. In the case where there has been a dispensation from the Catholic canonical form and the priest has been invited to participate in the non-catholic marriage service, with the permission of the local Ordinary and the consent of the appropriate authority of the other church or communion, he may do so by giving additional prayers, blessings, or words of greeting and exhortation. If the marriage is not part of the Lord's Supper or the principal liturgical service of the Word, the priest, if invited, may also read a lesson and/or preach (cf. *ibid.*).

17. To the extent that Eucharistic sharing is not permitted by the general discipline of the Church (cf. no. 11, *Matrimonia mixta*, and the exceptions in no. 39 of the *Ecumenical Directory*, Part I, May 14, 1967), this is to be considered when plans are being made to have the mixed marriage at Mass or not.

18. Since the revised Catholic rite of marriage includes a rich variety of scriptural readings and biblically orientated prayers and blessings from which to chose, its use may promote harmony and unity on the occasion of a mixed marriage (cf. *Introduction to the Rite of Marriage*, no. 9), provided the service is carefully planned and celebrated. The general directives that the selection of texts and other preparations should involve "all concerned including the faithful . . ." (*General Imstruction on the*

Roman Missal, no. 73; cf. 313) are especially applicable to the mixed marriage service, where the concerns of the couple, the non-Catholic minister and other participants should be considered.

VI. Place of Marriage

19.   The ordinary place of marriage is in the parish church or other sacred place. For serious reasons, the local Ordinary may permit the celebration of a mixed marriage, when there has been no dispensation from the canonical form and the Catholic marriage service is to be celebrated, outside a Catholic church or chapel, providing there is no scandal involved and proper delegation is granted (for example, where there is no Catholic church in the area, etc.).

20.   If there has been a dispensation from canonical form, ordinarily the marriage service is celebrated in the non-Catholic church.

Document V

Norms for Orientals with Orthodox in Orthodox Church. Decree: *Orientalium Ecclesiarum* Vat. II. Pope Paul VI, November 21, 1964. Effective: January 21, 1965 for Ruthenians, April 7, 1965 for Ukrainians.

This new marriage form is found in Article 18 of *Orientalium Ecclesiarum*, the Decree on the Eastern Catholic Churches of Vatican II. Article 18 states the following:

"To obviate invalid marriages when Eastern Catholics marry baptized Eastern non-Catholics, and in order to promote the stability and the sanctity of marriage, as well as domestic peace, the Sacred Council determines that the canonical form for the celebration of these marriages obliges only for liceity; for their validity the presence of a sacred minister is sufficient, provided the other prescriptions of law are observed."

The introduction of this new marriage form for Orientals affects the validity of a marriage, therefore it is very important that the date (January 21, 1965) be kept in mind when dealing with cases involving *a Byzantine Catholic and a baptized non-Catholic of an Eastern rite.* Chancery and tribunal officials must keep this new legislation in mind when dealing with cases involving individuals of this category.

Liceity: The liceity of such marriages remains in effect as found in the former law (*Crebrae Allatae* - May 2, 1949) whereby censures and other penalties are incurred if the regular prescriptions of the law are not observed. Neither can ordinaries dispense from this marriage form whereby they would grant permission for a Catholic to contract marriage *solely* or *first* before a non-Catholic minister (*communicatio in sacris*). It must be noted that Pospishil gives his opinion and makes a fine distinction when he states that although *communicatio in sacris* is forbidden, nevertheless, after such a couple has exchanged the marriage vows before a Catholic priest, thereby becoming recipients of the sacrament of matrimony, the rites performed in the Eastern dissident church cannot lead to a sacrament; therefore this is an extra-sacramental *communicatio in sacris*, which is permissible according to the above mentioned principle.

Document VI

Norms for Romans with Orthodox

The Sacred Congregation for the Oriental Church issued this decree on mixed marriages between Latin Rite Catholics and the Orthodox, Feb. 22, 1967.

The increasing frequency of mixed marriages between Oriental Catholics and non-Catholic Oriental Christians in the eastern patriarchates and eparchies as well as in the Latin dioceses themselves and the necessity of coping with the inconveniences resulting from this, were the reasons why the Second Vatican Ecumenical Council decreed: "When Oriental Catholics enter into marriage with baptized non-Catholic Orientals the canonical form for the celebration of such marriages obliges only for lawfulness: for their validity, the presence of a sacred minister suffices, as long as the other requirements of the law are observed" (Decree on the Eastern Catholic Churches, n. 18).

In the exceptional circumstances of today, mixed marriages between the Catholic faithful of the Latin rite and non-Catholic Oriental faithful are taking place and the variety in canonical disciplines has brought about many grave difficulties both in the East and the West. For this reason petitions from various regions have been addressed to the Supreme Pontiff asking that he be pleased to unify canonical discipline in this matter by also permitting to Catholics of the Latin rite what has been decreed for Catholics of the Eastern rite.

His Holiness, our Lord Paul VI, by divine providence Pope, after mature reflection and diligent investigation, has resolved to agree to the petitions and desires addressed to him and, as a means of preventing invalid marriages between the faithful of the Latin rite and the non-Catholic Christian faithful of the Oriental rites, of showing proper regard for the permanence and sanctity of marriages, and of promoting charity between the Catholic faithful and the non-Catholic Oriental faithful, he has kindly granted that, when Catholics, whether they be Orientals or Latins, contract marriage with non-Catholic Oriental faithful, the canonical form for the celebration of these marriages obliges only for lawfulness; for validity the presence of a sacred minister suffices, as long as the other requirements of law are observed.

A New Marriage Form for the Latin Church

The Decree *Orientalium Ecclesiarum*, Art. 18, was promulgated only for the Orientals, but the Latin bishops requested the same privilege for their subjects. It was granted three years later and went into effect March 25, 1967. Therefore this date is important because all marriages between a Latin Catholic and an Orthodox person in the Orthodox Church, *with* or *without* the Latin Ordinary's permission, is considered valid. The marriage would be considered only illicit if no permission was granted.

All care should be taken that, under the guidance of the pastor such marriages be carefully entered into the prescribed registers as soon as possible; this prescription also holds when Catholic Orientals enter marriage with baptized non-Catholic Orientals according to the norm of the conciliar decree "On the Catholic Oriental Churches."

In conformity with the holiness of marriage itself, non-Catholic ministers are reverently and earnestly requested to cooperate in the task of registering marriages in the books of the Catholic party, whether of the Latin or of the Oriental rite.

Ordinaries of the place, who grant the dispensation from the impediment of mixed religion, are likewise given the faculty of dispensing from the obligation of observing canonical form for lawfulness if there exist difficulties which, according to their prudent judgment, require this dispensation.

The same Supreme Pontiff has ordered the Sacred Congregation for the Oriental Church, of which he himself is the prefect, to make known to all this resolution and concession. Wherefore, the same sacred congregation, after also consulting the Sacred Doctrinal Congregation, at the order of His Holiness, has composed the present decree to be published in the Acta Apostolicae Sedis.

Meanwhile, in order that his new statute may be brought to the attention of those whom it concerns, whether they be Catholics of any rite whatever or Orthodox, the present decree will go into effect beginning from March 25, 1967, feast of the Annunciation of the Blessed Virgin Mary.

Notwithstanding anything which in any way may be to the contrary.

Norms of Procedure on Nullity Cases
Motu Proprio, *Causes Matrimonialis*

Pope Paul VI, March 27, 1971, AAS 1971, Vol. 63, p. 441. Special Faculties were given, at different times, to England, Wales, Canada, USA, Australia, Belgium, Spain and other countries, so this special document was issued to standardize these laws, which was the purpose of this Motu Proprio-*Causas Matrimonialis*.

Marriage cases have always been given special care by Mother Church, and through them she endeavors to safeguard the holiness and true nature of the sacred bond of matrimony. The ministry of ecclesiastical judges shows forth clearly—though in its own special way—the pastoral charity of the Church, which is well aware how much the salvation of souls is sought in marriage cases.

Since the number of these cases is greatly increasing at the present time, the Church cannot but be very concerned about this matter. This increase of cases, as we said to the Prelates of the Sacred Roman Rota, "is a special sign of the decrease of the sense of the sacred nature of the law upon which the Christian family is based; it is a sign of the restlessness and disturbance of present-day life, and of the uncertain social and economic conditions in which it is lived. It is a sign therefore of the danger which may threaten the solidity, vigor and happiness of the institution of the family" (cf. *AAS*, LVIII, 1966, p. 154.

Mother Church trusts that the attention given by the recent Ecumenical Council to explaining and fostering the spiritual good and pastoral care of marriage may produce results with regard also to the firmness of the marriage bond; she moreover desires at the same time by the laying down of opportune norms that the spiritual well-being of many of her sons and daughters may not be damaged by the excessive lengthiness of matrimonial processes.

Therefore, while awaiting the fuller reform of the marriage process which our Commission for the Revision of the Code of Canon Law is preparing, we thought it well to issue certain norms on the constitution of ecclesiastical tribunals and on the judicial process, which will expedite the matrimonial process itself.

While other canonical norms concerning processes remain unchanged, we therefore on our own initiative and by our apostolic authority decree and lay down the following norms, which are to be faithfully observed from 1 October 1971 in all tribunals, including apostolic tribunals, until the new Code of Canon Law is promulgated.

Competent Forum

I.   The marriage cases of the baptized by proper right pertain to an ecclesiastical judge.

II.   Cases concerning the merely civil effects of marriage are the concern of the civil authorities, unless particular law lays down that such cases, if they are dealt with in an incidental and accessory manner, may be examined and decided by an ecclesiastical judge.

III.   All marriage cases concerning those persons mentioned in the *Code of Canon Law*, Canon 1557; 1, no. 1, are judged by the Congregation, Tribunal, or special Commission to which the Supreme Pontiff entrusts them in each case.

IV.   1. In other cases concerning the nullity of marriage the competent body is:

   a)   the tribunal of the place in which the marriage was celebrated; or

   b)   the tribunal of the place in which the respondent has an abode which is not transitory, which may be proved from some ecclesiastical document or in some other legitimate manner; or

   c)   the tribunal of the place in which *de facto* most of the depositions or proofs have to be collected, provided the consent is obtained both of the Ordinary of the place where the respondent habitually lives and of the Ordinary of the place in which the tribunal approached is situated, and of the president of the tribunal itself.

   2.   If the circumstances mentioned in 1.c) above occur, the tribunal, before admitting the case must inquire of the respondent whether he or she has any objection to the forum approached by the petitioner.

   3.   Should there occur a substantial change in the circumstances, places or persons mentioned in 1, the cause, before its closure, may be transferred in particular cases from one tribunal to another equally competent one, provided both parties and both tribunals agree.

Constitution of Tribunals

V.   1. If it is impossible either in a diocesan tribunal or, where one is set up, in a regional tribunal, to form a college of three clerical judges, the episcopal conference is given the faculty of permitting in the first and second instance the appointment of a college composed of two clerics and one layman.

   2.   In the first instance, when a college as described in 1 cannot be set up even by adding a layman, in individual instances, cases concerning the nullity of marriage may be entrusted by the episcopal conference to one cleric as the sole judge. Such a judge where possible will choose an assessor and auditor for the case.

   3.   The episcopal conference can, in accordance with its statutes, grant the above mentioned faculties either through a group of members or at least one member of the conference, to be chosen for this purpose.

VI.   For the office of assessor and auditor in tribunals of any instance laymen may be used. The office of notary may be accepted by both men and women.

VII.   Lay people chosen for these offices should be outstanding in their Catholic faith and good character as well as their knowledge of canon law. When it is a question of conferring the office of judge upon a layman, as laid down in V, 1, those who have legal experience are to be preferred.

Appeals

VIII. 1. The Defender of the Bond is obliged to appeal to the higher tribunal, within the time laid down by law, against a first sentence declaring the nullity of a marriage. If he fails to do this, he shall be compelled to do so by the authority of the president or the sole judge.

   2. Before the tribunal of second instance, the 'defender of the bond' shall produce his observations stating whether or not he has any objection to make against the decision made in the first instance. The college shall, if it thinks it opportune, ask for the observations of the parties or of their advocates against those made by the 'defender of the bond.'

   3. Having examined the sentence and having considered the observations of the Defender of the Bond and, if they were asked for and given, those of the parties or of their advocates, the college by its decree shall either ratify the decision of the first instance, or admit the case to the ordinary examination of the second instance. In the first of the two cases, if no one makes recourse, the couple, provided there is no other impediment, have the right to contract a new marriage after ten days have elapsed from the publication of the decree.

IX. 1. If the decree of the college ratifies the first-instance sentence, the Defender of the Bond or a party who believes himself to be aggrieved has the right to make recourse to a higher tribunal within ten days from the date of publication of the decree, provided he presents new and serious arguments. These arguments must be placed before the third-instance tribunal within a month from making recourse.

   2. The Defender of the Bond of the third instance, after hearing the president of the tribunal, can withdraw from the recourse, and in that case the tribunal shall declare the case terminated. If it is a party who makes recourse, the tribunal having considered the arguments adduced, within a month from the making of recourse shall either reject it by decree or admit the case to ordinary examination in the third instance.

Special Cases

X. When there is proof from a certain and authentic document, not subject to any contradiction or exception, that a diriment impediment exists, and when it is also equally certain and clear that no dispensation from this impediment has been given, in these cases the formalities laid down in law can be omitted and the Ordinary, after the parties have been summoned and the "defender of the bond" has intervened, can declare the marriage null.

XI. With the same provisions and in the same manner as in X, the Ordinary can declare a marriage null also when the case was entered into on the grounds of lack of canonical form or lack of a valid mandate on the part of the proxy.

XII.   If the Defender of the Bond prudently considers that the impediments or defects mentioned in X and XI are not certain or that it is probable that there was a dispensation from them, he is bound to appeal against this declaration to the judge of second instance. The proceedings are to be transmitted to him and he is to be notified in writing that the case is a special one.

XIII.   The judge of second instance, with the sole intervention of the Defender of the Bond, shall decide in the same way as in X whether the sentence is to be confirmed or whether the case is to be proceeded with through the ordinary channels of law. In this latter case he shall send it back to the tribunal of first instance.

Transitional Norms

1.   On the day on which the present apostolic letter comes into force, a marriage case which is proceeding before a higher tribunal by reason of lawful appeal after a first sentence declaring the marriage null shall be temporarily suspended.

2.   The Defender of the Bond of the tribunal of second instance shall make his observations on all that concerns either the decision given in the first instance or the proceedings completed in the second instance up to that date, and thereby state whether or not he has any objection to make against the decision made in the first instance. The college shall, if it thinks it opportune, ask for the observations of the parties or of their advocates against these observations.

3.   Having considered the observations of the Defender of the Bond and, if they were asked for and given, those of the parties or of their advocates, and having examined the sentence of the first instance, the college by its decree shall either ratify the first-instance decision or decide that the case must be proceeded with by examination in the second instance. In the former case, if no one makes recourse, the couple have the right, provided there is no other impediment, to contract a new marriage after ten days have elapsed from the publication of the decree. In the latter case the instance must be proceeded with until the definitive sentence is given.

We order that all that is decreed in this letter issued by us *motu proprio* be valid and firm, anything to the contrary notwithstanding, even if worthy of most special mention.

Given in Rome at St. Peter's, on March 28, 1971, Paulus P.P. VI.

Matrimonial Cases in the
Eastern Churches

In an apostolic letter issued *moto proprio* by Pope Paul VI on September 8, 1973, norms are established for matrimonial procedure in the Eastern Churches. These norms were prompted by the same circumstances as those for the Latin Church (*Causas matrimoniales*, March 28, 1971), namely, the pastoral need to simplify procedures for the more expeditious resolution of cases.

The prescriptions of the apostolic letter *Sollicitudinem Nostram* of Pius XII (January 6, 1950) remain in effect where they are not changed by the present document. The specific provisions follow those of *Causas matrimoniales*.
(Excerpts from the commentary given by Reverend Raymond Bidagor, S.J., Secretary of the Commission for the Revision of the Code, on *Causas Matrimoniales*. This commentary was given during the publication ceremony of C.M. It is found in *Communicationes*, 1971, vol. III, no. 1, pp. 98-99. This is a translation from the original Italian.)

The most notable changes from the *Motu Proprio Causas Matrimoniales* can be found in the chapter dealing with Appeals. As is well known, Sentences of nullity of the marriage never become *res iudicata*. Since such cases deal with the state of the person they can always be re-examined for serious reasons, even after two Sentences have declared the nullity of the marriage. But the double conforming Sentences produce the effect that the married couple who have obtained them have the right to contract a new marriage. In order for this right to become an actuality, the two steps of judgment must be pursued by the two distinct Tribunals, the ordinary Tribunal and the Tribunal of Appeal. Both these courts, in order to pronounce its own Sentence, are required to follow the same procedure—from the citation of the parties up to the publication of process and the actual discussion of the case. It is, therefore, a repetition of the judicial process before new judges.

After today's *Motu Proprio*, the Tribunal of Appeal which receives a Sentence from First Instance declaring the nullity of the marriage, has to proceed in a different manner. The Sentence of First Instance is immediately examined by the Defender of the Bond from the Tribunal of Second Instance; this Defender of the Bond must explain his observations before his Tribunal in order for him to declare if he has or has not anything against the decision pronounced in First Instance. The college, if it thinks it opportune, could request counter-observations from the parties or from their respective Advocates. After having examined the Sentences of First Instance, which must contain the motivations upon which it is based, and after having given thought to the observations of the Defender of the Bond and those of the parties and their Advocates—if asked—the college, by a decree, will either ratify the decision of First Instance or will submit the case to the ordinary examination of Second Instance. If the first course is pursued, says the Motu Proprio, and if no one makes an appeal, the spouses, who are not prevented by any other reason, have the right to contract a new marriage after ten days from the p-lication of the decree.

Let no one be ignorant of the importance of this new method. Matrimonial cases which are well founded when they are presented to ecclesiastical Tribunals can be concluded in a relatively brief time, and with every guarantee of full justice. Indeed this change, dictated by the personal interest of the Holy Father in order to supply a remedy for the actual difficulty which he has seen—as we said in the beginning—to exist in almost every diocese of the world, should move the members of the Tribunals to a greater solicitude towards expediting their proper duty and to an increased responsibility for the eternal salvation of souls which are depressed by problems so intimate and pressing, and which disturb the peace of family life and impede the spiritual peace to which they have a right.

Permit me to point out the great responsibility which, under this new proceedure, is carried by the Defender of the Bond. Just as are the Judges, so the Defender of the Bond and in a way also the Advocates, are all bound to the unity of purpose of the Matrimonial process, that is, to ascertain with authority and to carry into practice truth and the right which corresponds to it as both relate to the existence or to the continuation of the marriage bond.

The Defender of the Bond, for his part, certainly must openly present all which in the process speaks in favor and not just that which speaks against the existence or the continuation of the marriage bond, but he, as anyone else who has any part in the process, must, without any exception as Pius XII said in one of his famous discourses to the Roman Rota, work to bring together all their actions to a single purpose: to establish truth.

The Motu Proprio has given to the Defender of the Bond or to party who believes himself to be unjustly treated, the option to have recourse to a higher Tribunal against the decree of the college which ratifies the Sentence of First Instance. But this option must be pursued only within the limitations of existing law which limits have been fixed concerning a third appeal after two conforming sentences, that is, only by inducing new and grave arguments which must be quickly at hand. The right to have recourse must be exercised within ten days of the publication of the decree. Such a disposition was thought necessary by the legislator, and it emanates naturally from the very nature of cases which deal *de statu personarem*; since such is the case with matrimonial cases, as we have said before, that never pass *in rem iudicatam*.

DOCUMENT VII-a—NORMS FOR MIXED MARRIAGE IN CANADA

Motu Proprio, "Matrimonia Mixta"
Pope Paul VI, August 1, 1970
Formulated by Canadian Catholic Conference
June 5-6, 1970. Effective August 1, 1970.

I. The Canonical Form

General Principle: A Catholic should normally contract marriage in and before the Catholic Church (cf. note 1).

A. The Ordinary of the Catholic party, or the Ordinary of the place where the marriage is to be celebrated, may dispense from the canonical form. In cases where the marriage is celebrated in a diocese other than that of the Catholic party, the "nihil obstat" of the Ordinary of the place where the marriage is to be celebrated, should be given.

B. In order for the dispensations to be granted legitimately, the reasons for doing so should concern *in an important way* the good of the parties, especially their spiritual well being and the tranquility and peace of their personal and family relationships (cf note 2).

II. Promises to be made by the Catholic Party

A. The promises to be made by the Catholic party will be made orally (not in written form), and the presence of a witness is not necessary; the priest who prepared the couple for their marriage will certify to the Ordinary that these promises were sincerely made, and that he is morally certain that the Catholic party will be faithful to them (Cf. Annex "B").

B. The celebration of a mixed marriage will not be authorized in those cases where:
   a. it is clearly evident that the Catholic party is not sincere in making the promises;
   b. the Catholic party refuses to promise to do his or her best to safeguard the Catholic faith and to see to the Catholic baptism and education of children to be born from the marriage.

III. Preparation of the Non-Catholic Party

The priest who prepares the couple for marriage will inform the non-Catholic party of the promises made by the Catholic party and will certify to the Ordinary that this has been done. He will see to it that the couple accept the ends and essential properties of Christian matrimony. He can make use of the formula given in Annex "B" for this purpose.

IV. Annotation of the Marriage

A marriage celebrated with dispensation from the canonical form will be recorded at the place where the marriage was celebrated (v.g., church, court house, etc.

A marginal annotation will be made in the baptismal records of the place where the Catholic party was baptized (see Annex "A").

Record of the granting of the dispensation from the canonical form will be kept in the Chancery Office of the diocese granting the dispensation

V. Celebration of the Marriage

A. The celebration of a mixed marriage in the Catholic Church should be presided by the Catholic priest. It is desirable that the non-Catholic minister be invited to take part in the ceremony in some way, according to norms to be drawn up in an Ecumenical Directory.

B. The celebration of a mixed marriage outside the Catholic Church—with dispensation from the canonical form—should be presided by the non-Catholic minister. It is desirable that the Catholic priest be invited to take part in the ceremony in some way.

C. Thus, the celebration of the marriage of a Catholic with a non-Catholic will be accompanied by various sacred rites; this will depend on whether the non-Catholic party belongs to a given Church, ecclesial community, or religion, and on the personal religious convictions of the parties.

The marriage could be celebrated during Mass, or within a Liturgy of the Word, or simply, by fulfilling the rites of the ceremony itself, but always *according to certain principles*, such as those of "Matrimonia mixta" which allows the celebration of Mass only when the marriage is taking place between two Christians.

D. In each case, it is the priest who will decide, after having consulted the couple, and in accordance with the directives given in Annex "C".

VI. Marriage Banns

In order to ensure greater cooperation between the ministers of both Churches, it is recommended that the practice be introduced of publishing the marriage banns in both Churches (Catholic and non-Catholic); this applies in places where it is customary to have such publications.

VII. Witnesses

Non-Catholics may be invited to act as witnesses to such a marriage or to assist the spouses in some other capacity.

Notes

1. Reasons in favor of maintaining or using the canonical form for mixed marriages:

    a) greater facility in ensuring that appropriate instructions have been given for the preparation of the marriage;
    b) possibility of avoiding the celebration of premature and hasty marriages;
    c) greater order in parish records.

2. Among the many reasons for which the Holy See has granted dispensations from the canonical form since 1966, are the following:

    a) to keep the non-Catholic partner from breaking with his/her Church or religious body;
    b) to avoid the danger of having an invalid or illicit marriage celebrated outside the Church;
    c) promotion of better relations between the two families so that both may offer better support for the newly-married couple;
    d) *active* participation of the non-Catholic party in the life of his or her Church; for example, if the party were a Sunday School Teacher, Warden, Trustee, etc.
    e) local customs (e.g., in Canada the marriage is traditionally celebrated in the bride's Church).

The other canonical reasons previously recognized in law for the dispensation from the impediments of mixed religion and disparity of worship (canon 1061) also apply in certain cases.

Concerning the procedure to be followed for the celebration of a marriage with dispensation from the canonical form, see Annex "A".

3. Notation in the Marriage Register

The following considerations seem to justify the proposed procedure:

a) avoid unnecessary administrative work;
b) the Catholic priest cannot attend to a marriage which took place elsewhere;
c) the registration of all dispensations in the Chancery office which grants the dispensation and assigns a protocol number to it;
d) the plural used in the Latin text of the Motu Proprio is to be interpreted according to the general rules of Canon Law and, in certain cases, applies only to baptismal registers.

Annex "A"
Procedure for the Celebration of a Mixed Marriage with a Dispensation from the Canonical Form

1. The pastor (or the curate) of the Catholic party makes the prenuptial inquiry and completes the dossier which remains in the archives of the parish.
2. Using Form "V", the pastor or curate of the Catholic party requests from the Ordinary the dispensations required for a mixed marriage (mixed religion or disparity of worship, as the case may be), dispensation from the form, the nihil obstat, and, if necessary, the dispensation from other impediments. He indicates on the reverse side of Form "V", along with the reasons for requesting the other dispensations, the reasons for which he requests a dispensation from the canonical form, and mentions before what Church or civil institution the marriage is to be celebrated.
3. The pastor receives the regular rescript from the Chancery Office together with two copies of a document authorizing the celebration of the marriage outside the Catholic Church. The rescript is placed in the dossier, together with one copy of the authorization
4. When advising the Catholic party that the dispensation has been granted, the pastor gives him or her one copy of the document authorizing the celebration of marriage before a minister other than a Catholic priest. The Catholic party is requested to forward a certificate of marriage as soon as possible after the ceremony.
5. When the marriage certificate is received, the pastor will advise the parish where the Catholic party was baptized. The following text may be used:
X_____, a Catholic baptized on
_____in_____Church,
_____married Y _____
on_____19____in _____
(Church, temple, Courthouse) after receiving a dispensation from the canonical form of marriage (Prot. No____)

Please make this annotation in your Baptismal Register and return this notice, certifying that the annotation has been made as requested.

Annex "B"

Declaration Concerning the Preparation of the Parties to a Mixed Marriage

(This form must be filled out by the priest who conducts the prenuptial inquiry. One copy is sufficient. It is to be sent to the Chancery Office with the petition for the nihil obstat, and will be returned to the parish to be included in the dossier.)

Names of the parties:
The Catholic party _____
The non-Catholic party _____
Member of _____
(Name of Church)

YES

    1. *Promise of the Catholic party*

The Catholic party has been carefully instructed concerning his responsibility to live according to his faith, to give witness to his faith, to avoid anything that could weaken his faith, and to do his best to have the children who will be born of the marriage baptized and educated in the Catholic faith. The Catholic party has explicitly promised to be faithful to these responsibilities.

YES

    2. *Preparation of the non-Catholic party*

The non-Catholic party has been instructed on the doctrine of the Catholic Church with regard to Crhistian marriage and recognizes that the marriage he wishes to contract is too be one and indissoluble. The non-Catholic party is aware of the responsibilites of the Catholic party with regard to religious practice and to the Catholic baptism and education of the children.

Describe briefly the non-Catholic party's attitude:

YES

    3. *Preparation for marriage*
Both parties have been adequately prepared for their forthcoming marriage.

YES

    4. *Opinion of the priest*
I am morally certain that the Catholic party will be faithful to these obligations.
Date   Signature of the priest

Liturgical Celebration

General Principles

1. For all marriages celebrated in the Catholic Church, it is normal that the exchange of consent be accompanied by sacred rites which help the spouses to turn their minds and hearts to God, to discover God's love in their mutual love and to give thanks to Him.

2. However, no matter how keen our desire to share with non-Catholics the Church's means of grace, participation in the same sacred actions must always be respectful of truth. To avoid any ambiguity unworthy of an action which is directed to God and unbecoming of the persons who perform that action, the words, the acts, the chants and the responses of the ceremony must be in accord with the religious beliefs of both spouses. This respect for truth and for the convictions of the persons involved in *communicatio in sacris* is a primordial principle of ecumenism.

Though it may be painful to the spouses that the divergence of their respective convictions appear at a time when they join together in marriage, they should be invited by the priest to acknowledge in humility this distressing reality and to accept the suffering that it brings instead of seeking to cover it up with false pretenses.

3. No one should be surprised that the Catholic Church should consider itself closer to one Church than to another and that, as a consequence, it should invite certain Christians to participate more fully in its worship. This difference of attitude does not stem from a judgement on persons but rather from the fact of a greater unity in faith and sacramental life.

The marriage of a Catholic with a non-Catholic will therefore be differently accompanied by sacred rites depending on what Church, what community, what religion, the non-Catholic partner belongs to, as well as upon the personal religious dispositions of those who are contracting marriage. This marriage could be celebrated within the Holy Sacrifice or even in the framework of the Celebration of the Word, or simply using the rites for marriage alone.

This decision will be made for reasons in the religious or pastoral order and not for reasons foreign to faith, or to the spiritual good of the persons such as, for example, the desire of underlining the celebration of a marriage celebration or of following social conveniences.

In some cases it will be necessary to recall that the sacred rites are not favors and consequently the decision to not accompany the marriage with a Mass is not because of an intention of penalizing those contracting a mixed marriage.

Catholic and Orthodox

A marriage of a Catholic to a Christian of an Oriental Church separated from the Roman Catholic Church may be celebrated within Mass; in this particular circumstance, the Orthodox Christian may, if he has the required dispositions and *his own Church has no objections*, take part with the Catholic partner in the blessed Eucharist.

Catholic and Protestant

The differences in doctrine and the sacrament of life which exist between the Catholic Church and the churches and church communities in the West, generally lead one to celebrate the marriage of a Catholic with a Christian Protestant outside the ceremonies of Mass. Since Christian fiancees have nevertheless in common their faith in the Word of God, their marriage naturally fits into the framework of a Celebration of the Word.

Nevertheless, it may sometimes be desirable that the marriage of a Catholic with a Protestant Christian be celebrated within the Mass. This would particularly be the case when the spouses have requested it for motives which flow from a living and educated faith. The non-Catholic spouse nevertheless is not permitted to receive communion at this Mass and the priest will take care to inform the non-Catholic partner of this disposition and if necessary during the preparatory meetings for the marriage indicate the reasons for such a law.

Document VIII

Procedural Norms For United States

Granted 28 April 1970; renewed and in force until the promulgation of *De Processibus* of the new *Code of Canon Law*.

The Canon Law Society of America initiated a study on procedural law (1968) whereby Tribunals in the United States would operate in a manner that would be meaningful and effective for the benefit of Christian people in the circumstances of our present age. It was presented to the National Conference of Bishops for approval; it was adopted by this body and submitted to the Holy Father with the request that the rules be authorized for use in the United States.

In response to the request from the National Conference of Catholic Bishops at its plenary session of November 1969, the Holy See issued a series of twenty-three norms to be used on an experimental basis for three years beginning July 1, 1970, for matrimonial cases. The following are the norms with a brief commentary, preceded by the rescript from the Council for the Public Affairs of the Church:

The Rescript

CONSILIUM PRO PUBLICIS ECCLESIAE NEGOTIIS

N. 3320-70

Attentis precibus Conferentiae Episcopalis Statuum Foederatorum Americae Septemtrionalis, quibus petitur ut, consideratis peculiaribus sui territorii necessitatibus, normis quibusdam, quae precibus adnectuntur, ad expeditiorem reddendum causarum de nullitate matrimonii cursum, in eodem territorio, tribunalia utantur, Ss.mus Dominus Noster PAULUS Papa VI supradictis precibus annuere dignatus est, ad triennium et experimenti causa, concedendo facultates omnes necessarias et opportunas et derogando, quatenus opus est, iuri vigenti; cauto tamen ut de cetero, cum praedictis normis totus processus non exhauriatur, serventur iuris canonici praescripta. Idem Summus Pontifex statuit ut supradictae normae a die 1 Iulii 1970 valere incipiant.

Velit autem Praeses Conferentiae expostulantis mittere quotannis Supremo Tribunali Signaturae Apostolicae relationem de causis in unoquoque Tribunali propositis, vel desertis, vel appellatis.

Ex Aedibus Vaticanis, die 28 Aprilis A.D. MCMLXX.

J. CARD. VILLOT
Praefectus Consilii pro Publicis Ecclesiae Negotiis

Procedural Norms

1. The Diocesan Tribunal will consist of judges, a defender of the bond, a promoter of justice and notaries and all will be appointed to their offices by the Ordinary. The judges, defenders of the bond and promoter of justice shall be priests; all, however, shall be endowed with those qualities required by law.

2. The Ordinary will appoint a chief judge who will direct the work of the Tribunal and assign judges and defenders of the bond for individual cases.

3. A collegiate Tribunal must be constituted for each case. The Episcopal Conference, in accordance with faculties to be sought from the Holy See, may permit the competent ecclesiastical Tribunal to derogate from this norm for a specified period of time so that a case may be handled by a single judge.

The conditions are that: 1) there be a grave reason for granting the derogation; and 2) no formal opposition be expressed prior to the definitive sentence by either the judge, the defender of the bond, the promoter of justice or either of the parties.

4. If both parties are desirous of a declaration of nullity, one advocate may represent both. Unless a party decides otherwise, the advocate in first instance will also be the advocate in second instance. Advocates representing the parties will be those approved to work with marriage cases by the Ordinary or his delegate.

5. The notary for the Tribunal will preserve a written record of all procedural and substantive acts, with special regard to names, dates and places as well as the authenticity of documents and depositions. While acts not authenticated by the notary are null, it suffices that copies of these acts be authenticated by a single statement of the notary at the termination of the case.

6. The Ordinary will provide sufficient judges, defenders and advocates so that all petitions for declaration of nullity may be accepted or rejected promptly and decisions given within six months following acceptance of the petition.

7. The first competent Tribunal to which a party presents a petition has an obligation to accept or reject the petition. The competence of a Tribunal of first instance shall be determined by the residency of either party to the marriage, the place of the marriage or the decree of the judge to whom the petition is presented that his Tribunal is better able to judge the case than any other Tribunal. In this last instance, however, the judge may not issue such a decree without first obtaining the consent of his Ordinary and the consent of the petitioner's Ordinary and chief judge.

8. Any spouse, without qualification, may seek a declaration of nullity of his marriage. To do so, he will employ the services of an advocate. The petition for the declaration of nullity indicating the basis for nullity and the sources of proof is to be accepted or rejected by the judge within the thirty days following the presentation and after consultation with the advocate and defender. Recourse against the rejection of a petition may be made to the Tribunal of second instance. Within thirty days of recourse, rejection of the petition is to be sustained or the case is to be remanded for prompt instruction by the Tribunal of first instance.

9. The promoter of justice may petition that a marriage be declared null when he decides this will be for the public good.

10. If he is available and cooperative, the respondent will be given the opportunity to

choose an advocate prior to the determination of the precise basis of nullity. If the respondent is not available and cooperative, the judge will proceed to this determination in accordance with the following rule.

11. Within a month after the acceptance of the petition, the judge, after consultation with the advocate and defender, will determine the precise basis or bases for the nullity of the marriage, the documents to be obtained, and the witnesses to be heard. During the course of the trial the judge may add an additional basis or bases for nullity.

12. At any time in the course of the trial, the petitioner may request that the case be transferred from one competent tribunal to another competent tribunal. This permission will be granted provided that a grave reason warrants it, that the defender of the bond has been heard and that it is agreeable to the other party, the Ordinary *a quo* and the chief judges of both tribunals.

13. The testimony of the principals and the witnesses will be taken by the judge as soon as available, either at the Tribunal or elsewhere. A person will be asked to take an oath before testifying unless the judge determines othersise. The advocate (unless the judge determines otherwise) and the defender have the right to be present at the hearing of the principals and witnesses. In the event that the advocate is present, the defender of the bond must always at least be cited. The question proposed by the judge will be based upon the information and questions supplied by the advocate and the defender. The principals and witnesses may also be questioned directly by the advocate and the defender under the direction of the judge. When a judge is personally unable to take the testimony of a witness, he will appoint a competent delegate to do so.

14. Following consultation with the advocate and defender, the judge will determine the significance of the unwillingness of a principal and-or witnesses to testify and will, if necessary, proceed to the conclusion of the case without their testimony.

15. The advocate and the defender may examine the acts of the case at any stage of the process unless in particular cases the judge decides otherwise.

16. The judge will carefully weigh the depositions of each witness. Testimonials concerning the credibility of the principals and witnesses will be required if, in the opinion of the judge, they seem necessary or useful.

17. In cases involving physical or psychic impotence and lack of consensual capacity, the judge, after consultation with the advocate and the defender shall designate one or more experts to study the acts of the case and submit a written report thereon. When advisable, this expert will examine the party or parties to the case and will include in his report the results of his examination. The oral testimony of the expert is to be taken only if his report requires clarification or implementation. Following consultation with the advocate and the defender, the judge may appoint additional experts.

18. When, after consultation with the advocate and the defender, the judge has decided that all necessary and available evidence has been obtained, the principals will be permitted to read the acts unless, in the opinion of the judge, there is danger of violation of the rights of privacy. The judge will consider the requests by the principals for further instruction before bringing the case to the conclusion.

19. The advocate and the defender will submit written briefs independently within one month after all evidence has been presented and will be given the opportunity of a rejoinder to be made within two weeks.

20. Following whatever consultation with the advocate and the defender which is allowed by law and which he deems necessary, the judge will render a decision within one month after the presentation of the briefs and rejoinders.

21. The judge will render his decision according to moral certitude generated by the prevailing weight of that evidence having a recognized value in law and jurisprudence.

22. Any instance of nullity as defined in positive law with regard to acts or processes is considered sanated by the sentence itself provided that it was not previously challenged.

A sentence is irremediably null only when: 1) Its presuppositions were lacking grounds; 2) the right of defense has been denied; 3) the judge was coerced either by violence or grave fear to render his decision; 4) the sentence fails to address itself to the controversy in question.

The nullity described in the paragraph above may be perpetually proposed either as an action or as an exception.

23. I. Once an appeal has been made to a higher Tribunal and the Tribunal itself has been constituted in accord with Norm 3, the citation of the parties and the joining of issues shall take place within one month.

At the time of the joining of issues, if further investigations are requested either by the parties or the defender of the bond or the Tribunal itself *ex officio*, the case shall be heard in the ordinary manner of second instance. This instance, however, should not if possible exceed the limit of six months.

If further investigations are not required, the judge will immediately decree the case concluded. Within a month from the date of this decree, the Tribunal, taking into account the briefs and animadversions of the advocate and defender of the bond, shall issue a new sentence according to the norm of the law.

II. In those exceptional cases where in the judgment of the defender of the bond and his Ordinary an appeal against an affirmative decision would clearly be superfluous, the Ordinary may himself request of the Episcopal Conference that in these individual cases the defender of the bond be dispensed from the obligation to appeal so that the sentence of the first instance may be executed immediately.

Document IX

Norms For Processing Non-consummation Cases

Special instructions of the Congregation of the Sacraments dealing with alterations in the procedure for Non-consummation cases, dated 7 March 1972. AAA Vol. 64, p. 244 ff.

I. General Faculty to Conduct the Process Super Rato et Non Consummato

It pertains exclusively to the Congregation of the Sacraments to examine the fact of non-consummation of marriage not only between Catholic parties, whether of the Latin or Eastern Churches, but also between a Catholic party and a non-Catholic party and between baptized non-Catholics, as well as to examine the existence of a just or proportionately serious cause for the granting of the pontifical favor of a dissolution.

By force of this instruction all diocesan bishops have the general faculty, for their own territory, to conduct the *super matrimonio rato et non consummato* process from the day when this instruction comes into effect until the promulgation of the revised *Code of Canon Law*, so that they no longer need to seek this faculty from the Apostolic See. In using this faculty the bishops should take into account articles 7 and 8 of the *Regulae Servandae* and carefully observe the following prescriptions:

a   The process is not judicial but administrative, and therefore it differs from the judicial process for cases of nullity. In the process a simple petition is made for a favor to be obtained from the concession of the Supreme Pontiff. Nevertheless, in view of the gravity of the matter, the truth of the fact of non-consummation is to be sought no less religiously and diligently than in strictly judicial matters, so that the Pope may use his supreme power with full knowledge of the case. It is for the properly deputed Instructing Judge, therefore, to gather proofs of non-consummation and of the existence of a just or proportionately serious cause for the concession of the favor. If from an examination of the acts of the process insufficient proofs are found, the Congregation may suggest to the bishop, according to circumstances, that the proofs be completed in accord with appropriate instructions.

b)   Only the spouses may seek the dissolution; both may seek it or either one, even against the will of the other. Although it is the right of any member of the faithful to send the petition (which is always to be addressed to the Supreme Pontiff) directly to the Apostolic See it is expedient and always recommended that it be presented to the bishop. After considering the matter, he will see to the conduct of the process. Whenever it is a petition of one party alone, the other is to be heard extra-judicially before the process is begun, unless in particular cases another course seems opportune.

c) Before the process is conducted the bishop must be certain of the juridical basis of the petition and the opportuneness of undertaking the process. Likewise he should not fail to encourage the reconciliation of the parties, if this is possible, through the removal of the reasons for aversion and dissension, unless the facts and personal circumstances indicate that such an attempt would be useless.

d) The bishop should refer to the Congregation complicated cases or those with special difficulties of the juridical or moral order. The Congregation will weigh carefully all the circumstances and will communicate to the bishop the steps to be taken.

e) If it happens that a prudent doubt arises, from the examination of the petition, concerning the validity of the marriage, then it is for the bishop either to counsel the petitioner to follow the judicial order (or a declaration of nullity, in accord with the law) or—provided the petition is based on a solid and juridical foundation—to permit the *super rato et non consummato* process to be conducted. When, however, a case of nullity has been prosecuted on the grounds of impotence and, in the judgment of the tribunal, proof not of impotence but of non-consummation has emerged from the acts and evidence, then, upon the petition of one or both parties for an apostolic dissolution, all the acts should be sent to the Congregation together with the animadversions of the 'defender of the bond' and the *votum* of the tribunal and the bishop, based on legal and especially factual arguments. With regard to the *votum*, the bishop may follow that of the tribunal and add his signature to it, with the assurance of a just or proportionately serious cause for the dissolution, and the absence of scandal. If in the judgment of the tribunal, insufficient proofs of non-consummation have been obtained up to this point, in accord with the *Regulae Servandae* of May 7, 1923, the proofs should be completed by the instructing judge and the completed acts sent to the Congregation with the animadversions of the 'defender of the bond' and the *votum* of the tribunal and the bishop. If it is a question of another ground of nullity (e.g., defect of consent, force and fear, etc.) and in the judgment of the tribunal the nullity cannot be established but incidentally a very probable doubt emerges about non-consummation, it is the right of one or both parties to present a petition for the dissolution to the Supreme Pontiff and the instruction judge has the right to conduct the case in accord with the norms in the *Regulae Servandae*. Then all the facts, as above, should be sent to the Congregation together with the usual animadversions of the 'defender of the bond' and the *votum* of the tribunal and the bishop.

f) The bishop must be vigilant lest the parties, witnesses, or experts give false depositions or withhold the truth. He knows—and through him all interested persons should know—that the favor of dissolution cannot be granted unless two things are proved: that the marriage was actually not consummated and that a just or proportionately serious cause exists; in the absence of either or both the rescript is affected by *obreptio* and can in no way work to the advantage of the one who obtains it. It is clear that the pontifical dissolution never becomes definitive and a new marriage which may be entered after an invalid dissolution can always be declared null, if it later becomes known that the first marriage was actually *ratum et consummatum*.

II. Conduct of the Case and the Acts

With regard to the conduct of the case, the inquiry to establish accurately and expeditiously, whether it is true that the marriage was not consummated should foster the holiness and indissolubility of marriage. It therefore seems that the following emendations should be introduced in the norms for these processes in the *Code of Canon Law* and the *Regulae Servandae* of the Congregation for the Discipline of the Sacraments:

a)   If, because of the size of the diocese or eparchy and especially because of the lack of priests who are expert in canon law, it is difficult to conduct the *super rato* process in the *curia* or tribunal, the bishop may, after prudent consideration and especially in more difficult cases, transfer his competence to conduct the process to the ministers of the regional, provincial, interdiocesan, or interritual tribunal (if any) or of the tribunal of a nearby diocese or eparchy which is capable of undertaking the process.

b)   In cases of non-consummation both spouses must present witnesses who can testify to their probity and especially to their truthfulness with reference to the asserted non-consummation; the instructing judge may add other witnesses *ex officio*. A few witnesses may suffice, provided their concordant testimony can give valid proof and moral certitude. This is the case if they are persons above suspicion, agree among themselves, and testify under oath: indicating when, how, and what they heard from the spouses or their close relatives about the non-consummation. It should not be forgotten that in these cases the moral argument is of great weight in attaining moral certitude concerning non-consummation.

c)   The physical examination is to be employed if necessary for juridical proof of the fact of non-consummation. If, however, in accord with the decree of the Congregation of the Holy Office of June 12, 1942, the bishop judges there is full proof in view of the moral excellence of the parties and witnesses, after serious consideration of their spiritual disposition and other supporting arguments, the medical examination may be omitted; all these matters should be weighed before the examination is decreed to be useless. If the woman refuses the physical examination should not be insisted upon. Finally, with regard to this examination, patriarchal synods and episcopal conferences have the faculty to establish additional norms according to local and other circumstances.

d)   The procedural acts must be in writing and must be certified by notaries. With the bishop's consent the *curia* or tribunal may use tape recorders, in accord with current practice and technical progress, if their use seems to be useful and suitable for making a more accurate and certain record of the acts. The acts, however, may be given credence only if, although taken down by tape recorder, they satisfy the prescriptions expressly required by the law.

e) Differently from cases of nullity, because of the special nature of the *super rato* process, the assistance of advocates and procurators may not be sought. In response to. the recommendations and the desires of some pastors, however, it is decreed that the parties—at their own request or by *ex officio* decree of the bishop— may use the services of counsellors or experts, especially ecclesiastics, in these cases. These may assist in drawing up petitions, in the conduct of the case, or in completing the acts of the process. Thus the good of souls may be assured more certainly, while the truth of non-consummation is protected. The designation of counsellors or experts, whether chosen *ex officio* or at the request of the parties, pertains to the bishop after he has heard the Defender of the Bond and informed the counsellors or experts beforehand. This is done by a special decree and with the requirement of secrecy lest the procedural acts become known to outsiders.

f) In writing the *votum pro rei veritate*, bishops should weigh the nature and qualities of the case in a concrete and practical manner, that is, by considering the special circumstances of the persons, the fact of non-consummation, and the opportuneness of the concession.

In cases of nullity, when the acts are sent to the Congregation for a dissolution (cf. no. I, e), or of non-consummation which are conducted with an extension of competence (cf. no. II, a), the archbishop or metropolitan of the regional, provincial, interdiocesan, interritual, tribunal or the bishop of the neighboring diocese or eparchy should before writing his *votum*, consult with the bishop of the petitioner who knows the conditions of his diocese or eparchy, at least with regard to the scandal which may arise from a pontifical dissolution. If the bishop judges that the scandal arises or has arisen without basis or reason, then he should try to prevent it or contain it with pastoral care and appropriate means.

g) All the procedural acts, both of the case and of the process, together with other documents which are not in Latin, may be drawn up in those vernacular languages that are widely used. Judicial acts and documents drawn up in a language that is not well known may be translated into one of the above languages.

The procedural acts and documents are to be sent to the Congregation in three copies, which may be photostatic copies, with certification of authenticity, the original manuscript shall be preserved in the archives of the *curia* or tribunal and is to be submitted, with appropriate precautions, only if this is expressly required by the Congregation.

Since it will contribute greatly to a more careful and expeditious solution of cases, it is hoped that copies of all judicial acts and documents will be typed and that the individual pages of the process, numbered and bound in a folder, will be guaranteed as to integrity and authenticity, with the certification of the actuary or notary of their faithful transcription.

III. Clauses Attached to Rescripts

After the pontifical dissolution of the bond of a non-consummated marriage has been granted, it is proper for the spouses to enter new marriages, provided this has not been prohibited. Such a prohibition may be expressed in two ways: an *ad mentem* clause (and in this case the *mens* can be of different kinds and is appropriately explained) or a *vetitum* clause.

a)   The clause with the words *ad mentem*, which is prohibitory, is usually added when the fact of non-consummation depends on reasons of lesser significance, its removal is entrusted to the bishop, so that he may provide more suitably for pastoral needs. The bishop should not permit the remarriage of the party who asks for the removal of the clause unless after the prescribed regulations have been observed, the party is found to be truly ready to undertake the burdens of marriage and has promised that in the future he will fulfill his matrimonial duties in an honest and Christian manner.

b)   In special cases, however, when the reason for nonconsummation is a physical or psychic defect of major significance and seriousness, a *vetitum* for remarriage may be attached. Unless it so states in the rescript, this is not a diriment impediment but only a prohibiting impediment, the removal of which is reserved to the Apostolic See. Permission to remarry is granted if the petitioner, after making a petition to the Congregation and fulfilling the prescribed conditions, is shown to be capable of properly performing conjugal acts.

It is left to the bishop's judgment and pastoral consideration to inform the party with whom the second marriage is to be entered concerning either clause added to the rescript and later removed.

15

Document X

Procedure of Natural Bond Case

Special Instruction of the Congregation for the Doctrine of the Faith concerning the procedure of natural bond cases, dated 6 December 1973.
(Sac. Cong. Doct. of Faith (Prot. no. 2717/68)

As is well known, this Congregation has subjected to lengthy investigation and study the question of the dissolution of marriage in favor of the faith. At length, after this careful investigation, His Holiness, Pope Paul VI, has approved new norms which express the conditions for the grant of the dissolution of marriage in favor of the faith whether the petitioner is baptized or converted or not.

I. The following three conditions *sine qua non* are required for the valid grant of the dissolution:

a) absence of baptism in one of the spouses throughout the entire period of conjugal life;
b) non-use of marriage after baptism, if the sacrament is received by the party who was previously non-baptised;
c) that the unbaptised person or the person baptized outside the Catholic Church leave to the Catholic party the freedom and opportunity to profess his or her own religion and to baptise and bring up the children as Catholics. This condition, in the form of a promise *(cautio)*, is to be kept safely.

II. The following are required in addition:

1. That there be no possibility of restoring conjugal life, in view of the continuing radical and incurable separation.
2. That there be no danger of public scandal or serious wonderment from the grant of the favor.
3. That the petitioner be shown not to have been the culpable cause of the failure of a legitimate marriage and that the Catholic party, with whom the new marriage is to be contracted or validated, was not the guilty cause of the separation of the spouses.
4. That the second party in the prior marriage be questioned, if possible, and not be reasonably opposed to the granting of the dissolution.
5. That the party who seeks the dissolution sees to the religious formation of any children from the prior marriage.

6. That equitable provision be made, according to the norms of justice, for the previous spouse and any children.

7. That the Catholic party with whom the new marriage is to be entered lived in accord with his or her baptismal promises and is concerned for the welfare of the new family.

8. If it is a question of a catechumen with whom marriage is to be contracted, there should be moral certainty of the baptism which is to be received in the future, if the baptism itself has not taken place (which is preferable).

III. The dissolution is more easily granted where there is a serious doubt concerning the validity of the marriage, arising on other grounds.

IV. It is also possible to dissolve the marriage between a Catholic and an unbaptised person which was entered into with a dispensation from the impediment of disparity of cult, provided the conditions established in nos. II and III are verified and it is established that the Catholic, because of the particular circumstances of the region, especially the small number of Catholics, could not have avoided marriage and lead a life proper to the Catholic religion in that marriage. It is necessary, in addition that this Congregation be informed concerning the public knowledge of the marriage celebrated.

V. The dissolution of a legitimate marriage entered into with a dispensation from the impediment of disparity of cult is not granted to a Catholic petitioner in order to enter a new marriage with an unbaptised person who is not converted.

VI. The dissolution of a legitimate marriage which was contracted or validated after a dissolution from a previous legitimate marriage is not granted.

In order that these conditions may be properly fulfilled, new procedural norms have been drawn up, and all future processes are to be carried out in accord with them. These norms are attached to the present Instruction.

With the establishment of the new norms, the earlier regulations for the conduct of these processes are entirely abrogated.

Dissolution of the Natural Bond of Marriage With No Conversion (S. C. Doct. Fid., .30 Aug., 1976) **Private.**

The reply is of interest because, after years of denying that the privilege of the faith could be applied to cases in which no conversion was had, the S. C. for the Doctrine of the Faith is back to the practice of earlier years.

In your letter of August 10, of the current year, Your Excellency proposed the following question to this S. Congregation: whether a marriage which was entered into by a Catholic party and a non-baptized party after a prior dispensation from disparity of cult had been granted and the promises had been made, can be dissolved so that the Catholic party can contract a new marriage with a validly baptized non-Catholic party.

To the proposed question this S. Dicastery believes the response must be: *In the affirmative*. However, the Catholic party must do everything to bring about the conversion of the non-Catholic party by word and example.

Document XI—*Norms for Processing Privilege of the Faith Cases*
S.C. for Doctrine of the Faith, Prot. N. 2717/68, 1973*

Procedural Norms for the Process of Dissolution of the Bond of Marriage in Favour of the Faith

Art. 1: The process which is to precede the granting of the favour of a dissolution of a legitimate marriage is conducted by the local Ordinary who is competent in accord with the prescription of the Apostolic Letter *Causas Matrimoniales*. IV, 1, either personally or through another ecclesiastic delegated by him. The Acts to be sent to the Holy See must contain proof of the fact of delegation or commission.

Art. 2: Allegations must not be simply asserted but proved in accord with the prescriptions of the canon law, either by documents or by trustworthy depositions of witnesses.

Art. 3: Both original documents and authentic copies must be certified by the Ordinary or by the delegated judge.

Art. 4: 1. In the preparation of questions to be asked of the parties and witnesses, the services of the defender of the bond or of some other person delegated for this function in individual cases must be employed. This delegation is to be mentioned in the Acts.

2. Before the witnesses are questioned they must take an oath to speak the truth.

3. The Ordinary or his delegate should ask the questions already prepared. He may add other questions which he judges appropriate for a better understanding of the matter or which are suggested by the responses already given.

When the parties or witnesses testify concerning facts not of their own knowledge, the judge should question them also concerning the reason for or the origin of their knowledge.

4. The judge must take great care that the question and the responses be accurately transcribed by the notary and signed by the witnesses.

Art. 5: 1. If a non-Catholic witness refuses to present himself or to testify before a Catholic priest, a document containing a deposition on the matter given by the witness before a notary public or other trustworthy person may be accepted. This is to be expressly noted in the Acts.

2. In order to decide whether this document is to be given credence, the Ordinary or the delegated judge should introduce sworn witnesses, especially Catholics, who know the non-Catholic witness well and are willing and able to testify to his truthfulness.

3. The judge himself should also express his opinion concerning the credence to be given to this document.

Art. 6: 1. The absence of baptism in one of the spouses is to be demonstrated in such a way that all prudent doubt is removed.

2. The party who says that he was baptized should be questioned under oath, if possible.

3. Moreover, witnesses and especially the parents and blood relatives of the party should be examined, as well as others, especially those who knew the party during infancy or throughout the course of his life.

4. Witnesses are to be questioned not only concerning the absence of baptism but also concerning the circumstances which make it believable or probable that baptism was not conferred.

5. Care should be taken to search the baptismal registers of places where the person who was said to be unbaptized lived during infancy, especially in churches which he frequented to acquire religious instruction or where the marriage was celebrated.

Art. 7: 1. If at the time the dissolution is sought the unbaptized person has already been admitted to baptism, at least a summary process must be conducted, with the intervention of the defender of the bond, concerning the non-use of marriage after reception of baptism.

2. The party should be questioned under oath concerning the kind of contract he or she may have had with the other party after the separation and especially asked whether following baptism he or she had matrimonial relations with the other person.

3. The other party is also to be questioned, under oath if possible, concerning the non-consummation of the marriage.

4. In addition, witnesses, especially blood relatives and friends, are to be questioned, likewise under oath, not only concerning what has taken place after the separation of the parties and especially after the baptism, but also with regard to the probity and truthfulness of the parties, that is, concerning the credence which their testimony deserves.

Art. 8: The petitioner, if converted and baptized, should be questioned concerning the time and the intention which led him to receive baptism or to be converted.

Art. 9: 1. In the same case, the judge should question the parish priest and other priests who participated in the doctrinal instruction and in the preparation for conversion concerning the reason which led the petitioner to receive baptism.

2. The Ordinary should never direct any petition to the Congregation for the Doctrine of the Faith unless every reasonable suspicion concerning the sincerity of conversion has been removed.

Art. 10: 1. The Ordinary or judge should question the petitioner or the witnesses concerning the reason for the separation or divorce, namely, whether the petitioner was the cause or not.

2. The judge should include in the Acts an authentic copy of the divorce decree.

Art. 11: The judge or the Ordinary should report whether the petitioner has children from the marriage or other union and how he has provided or intends to provide for their religious upbringing.

Art. 12: The judge or the Ordinary should likewise report how the petitioner will make or intends to make equitable provision for the spouse and the children if any, in accord with the laws of justice.

Art. 13: The Ordinary or judge should gather information concerning the non-

Catholic party from whom he may determine whether the restoration of conjugal life can be hoped for. He should not fail to report whether the non-Catholic party has attempted a new marriage after divorce.

Art. 14: The Ordinary should report expressly whether any danger is to be feared of scandal, *admiratio*, or calumnious interpretation if the dissolution were to be granted, either among Catholics or among non-Catholics, as if the Church in practice was favourable to divorce. He should explain the circumstances which makes this danger probable in the case or exclude it.

Art. 15: The Ordinary should express the reasons which support the granting of the favour in the individual cases, at the same time always adding whether the petitioner has already attempted a new marriage in any form or is living in another union. The Ordinary should also report the fulfillment of the conditions for the grant of the favour and whether the promises mentioned in no. I, c), were given. He should transmit an authentic document, with these promises.

Art. 16: The Ordinary should send to the Congregation for the Doctrine of the Faith three copies of the petition, all the Acts, and the information concerning which he is bound to report.

*A commentary on *Instructions and Norms for the Resolution of Marriages in Favor of the Faith* (A Practical Guide for Canonists) was published, February, 1979, by N.C.C.B. of Wash., D.C., and distributed to all bishops of the U.S.A. Since the commentary is not for publication, this information is available in your respective chancery.

- JURISPRUDENCE

The jurisprudence of the Sacred Roman Rota provides the tribunals of the Church more than interpretative rules of law as decisional guidelines for particular cases. It serves also as a working exemplification of a methodology of canonical development through the rigorous discipline of the judicial process. This process is of inestimable value to the Church, particularly in these times when pastors and ecclesiastical judges are under such great pressure to apply the best of contemporary scholarship to meet the practical pastoral needs of the people. The logical analysis of law and facts, careful argumentation that thoroughly discusses the fruits of scientific investigation, the balancing of reasons for and against—these are the elements of a living and growing jurisprudence. More than merely conclusive in stated instances, such a process is assimilative, critical and in the precedents it offers contributes greatly to confidence in the Church's judicial wisdom and stability in its law. In the words of Archbishop Aurelio Sabattani, formerly an Auditor of the Rota:

> *Renewal is usually brought about by jurisprudence* sensim sine sensu. *Ordinarily, jurisprudence "renovat iuventutem iuris" not through noisy interventions or destructive propositions, not even by entirely new constructions, but slowly and surely, by humble labor, as that of the sea which imperceptibly sweeps away sand and pebbles from the beach so that the coastline is eventually modified. Thus jurisprudence imposes itself not* ratione imperii sed imperio rationis. *Jurisprudence covers cases not foreseen in the law, it perfects the rules of law by taking into account the progress of auxiliary sciences. . . . It can also correct previously accepted principles and maxims formulated at a time when a reality was insufficiently known and understood.*

The Church needs its great tribunals where that law which must embody the Savior's sanctifying mission among men will not only be applied, but also interpreted, developed and grow. We need a living, contemporary jurisprudence and the assurance born of a judicial methodology truly attuned to the needs of Christians in this age.

Notes on Canonical Jurisprudence

Definition: Canonical jurisprudence is the science and art of utilizing, interpreting, and supplying for the codified law by rescript and by judicial sentence.

Utilizing means the fitting of a clear law to a corresponding situation. An example might be the fitting of C. 1081 (the canon which says that consent makes marriage) to the marriage of a severe schizophrenic, who, obviously, lacks the degree of discretion that would be necessary to give free consent to marriage.

Intepreting means explaining the sense of a law that is obscure, at least as it applies to a particular situation. An example would be extending C. 1081 to the marriage of a sociopath, who probably, but not so obviously, lacks the due discretion for marriage.

Supplying means creating a new norm where there is no express law. An example would be judging invalid the marriage of a sociopath or homosexual, not because he lacked due discretion (the consent required by C. 1081) but because he lacked due competence (the ability to function in marriage—not expressly required in the Code).

Significance of Definition: The general significance of defining jurisprudence as an art is that it gives to the local judge a degree of autonomy. One that must be used responsibly, of course, but still, it lifts the judge above the level of a mere enforcement officer. The local judge is not one who merely applies the judicial principles determined by higher courts. More specifically:

Utilization—Occasionally a perfectly clear law goes unutilized. C. 1134, for example, says that, in a convalidation ceremony, the parties must personally recognize the former ceremony as invalid. It is only recently, however, that this law has been widely utilized in the United States to declare invalid ceremonies where a party viewed the convalidation as a mere blessing of an already valid marriage.

Intepretation—C. 17 points out that there are two interpreters of law: the legislator and the judge. When the legislator officially interprets a law, the interpretation has the same force as the law itself but when a judge interprets a law it does not have the force of law and affects only the parties involved in the case.

This is true per se. But per accidens, namely by the force of consuetudinary law, the interpretations of judges can become law. If in other words, all judges hand down like decisions over a period of forty years, the interpretation is then tantamount to law. Or, to put it another way, the original law, at that point, may no longer be regarded as obscure. Later judges should view it as a clear law to be utilized according to the generally accepted sense.

The Code (C. 18) recommends that, in interpreting a law, the judge should look to various sources: other similar laws, the purpose of the law, the circumstances, and the mind of the legislator. Interestingly, it does not recommend that he look to the interpretations of other judges, even rotal judges.

Supplementation—When there is a lacuna or deficiency in the law, the Code views this situation as somewhat more urgent and delicate than it does an unclear law that needs interpreting. To fill the lacuna C. 20 suggests four sources, one of which is the practice of the Curia, which in our case means the jurisprudence of the Rota.

Rotal supplementation does not, of course, have legal force but only suppletive force. A Rotal supplementation, in other words, is a priori recommended as safe. It has something more than its own intrinsic wisdom (which is all a supplementation by any other court has) to recommend it. This "Goodchurchkeeping Seal of Approval" awards a certain dignity to the Rota. On the other hand, it should not rob the local court of its independence, or make it excessively reliant on the Rota, because ultimately the real value of jurisprudence is not extrinsic (based on authority) but intrinsic (based on the merits of the legal argument).

There would seem to be only one occasion where a Rotal supplementation would be binding on a lower court and that would be when the following three conditions are verified: 1). some suppletory norm is required. 2). the lower court, using the other sources mentioned in C. 20, cannot supply its own norm and 3). the lower court cannot disprove the legitimacy of the Rota's norm.

Development: Like any other science, jurisprudence is dynamic and always evolving. It does this in many ways: by newly utilizing forgotten laws, by finding new applications for old laws, by restoring laws or principles which were once in effect but were not included in the Code, by expanding the sense of a principle to include new situations, and occasionally by giving a more restrictive interpretation to a law. In recent years, the behavioral sciences, with their insights into psychic disorders and the effect of those disorders on the consensual and functional capabilities of people, have been widely utilized by jurists in the development of jurisprudence.

The Roman Rota: The Roman Wheel, as this great Tribunal is called, is most likely referred to as "The Wheel" either because the judges originally sat in a circle, or because there was a circle on the chamber floor at Avignon where the title is first known to have been used (circa A.D. 1350), or because the cases under consideration were moved from judge to judge on a bookstand which was on wheels. At any rate, the Rota has not only retained the name but still uses the wheel as its logo.

History: The Rota dates back at least to the twelfth century, though in those days the auditors, who were the Pope's chaplains, were only auditors and not judges as they are today. In the early days, in other words, the Pope's chaplains sat in an auditorium and took or audited the testimony, but only the Pope judged the cases. Today a judge on the Rota is still referred to as an auditor, but he has, of course, full judicial power.

There are twenty such auditors today. Eleven of them are Italian; and there is one from each of the following countries: Belgium, Canada, Colombia, France, Lebanon, Poland, Spain, Switzerland and the United States. They are listed in the *Annuario Pontificio* according to the date of their Rotal appointment and are assigned cases according to that listing in turns or boards of three in such a way that what might be called the first case would be heard by the three senior auditors, the next case by the second, third and fourth auditors and so on. The senior man on each turn is the Ponens or Commissioner and the sentence is frequently cited by referring to him: one might, for example, refer to a case "before Wynen" or "coram Wynen."

In 1870 when the Italian army invaded Rome the doors of the Rota were closed and they did not open again until 1908 when the Rota was revived by Pope Pius X. This marks, as it were, the beginning of the Rota's modern era.

Published Sentences: Volume I of the Rota's published sentences contains the decisions of 1909, the year following the Rota's revival. Each volume number, therefore, always lags eight numbers behind the year, so that Volume 50, for example, contains the decisions for the year 1958.

The Work Load: The Rota as might be expected, took on an increasing number of cases during the first several decades of its modern era. The 1923 volume contains 36 decisions, the 1933, 77 decisions, the 1943, 93 decisions and the 1953, 126 decisions (though 178 cases were actually sentenced that year).

Around this time there seems to have occurred a kind of marriage case explosion. In one year the Rota increased its decision load by better than 40%, and it published 251 decisions in 1954. This, in itself, was a dramatic jump, but was even more impressive because there was no proportionate increase in the number of auditors judging the cases. From the beginning of 1950 to the end of 1954 the number of auditors increased only from fourteen to seventeen. Bonet came to the Rota in May of 1950 and Pinna was appointed early in 1952. Lamas became an auditor early in 1954 but he was the only judge added to the Rotal staff during that expansive year of 1954.

On October 16 of that same year, the Holy Father issued a rescript (A.A.S. XXXXVI, 614) by which he derogated C. 1599 1,1° as it applied to Italy, thus disallowing the Italian Tribunals to appeal their cases to the Rota in second instance, as had been their right along with the other Tribunals of the world. In that same rescript Pope Pius XII suggested that Italy begin to make use of its regional Tribunals for second instance and he also ordered that a court of appeal be established in Rome to hear cases on appeal from the Vicariate and a couple of other dioceses.

This rescript apparently had the desired effect of lightening the Rota's work because the Rota issued only 236 sentences in 1957 and just 224 in 1968.

In the 1970's interest in bringing a case to the Rota diminished. Special procedural laws were granted to several countries facilitating a more local settlement of marriage cases. In some individual instances, where a third instance judgment, usually provided by the Rota, was needed, another court, closer to home, was appointed in the Rota's stead. The result of all this is that the work load of the Rota is now less than it was in 1953. In 1976 the Rota judged only 155 cases.

Citing a Rotal Decision: The year 1954 also introduced a new way of citing rotal decisions. Up to 1953 the decisions were numbered in Roman numerals both in the Table of Contents and in the text, and a citation would include the volume number, the decision number and the page number. In 1954, however, the decision number was dropped altogether from the text, and received an Arabic number in the Table of Contents. Since it was dropped from the text it has also commonly been dropped from the citation and a sentence formerly referred to as XX, XXXV, 323 is now generally cited simply as 20, 323. In formal citations, the numbers are preceded by S.R.R.D. (Sacrae Romanae Rotae Decisiones).

Indexing: The indexing of rotal decisions also saw a change in 1954. Up until 1953 each volume of decisions contained two indexes. One was a long summary (it comprised 32 pages in the 1953 Volume and 66 pages in the 1950 Volume) of all the jurisprudence contained in the volume. This was called the *Index Rerum Notabilium* and amounted to a cursillo in jurisprudence. The other index was called the *Tabula Rerum* and was a brief listing (a page and a half in 1953) of all the sentences under each principal ground for nullity. In 1954 and 1955 the Index was discontinued and only the Tabula retained.

In 1956 a new system was introduced, namely the *Index Rerum Analyticus* which was a kind of expanded tabula listing both the generic and specific grounds with references to the pertinent sentences. Under the heading of amentia, for example, the 1956 index (which was four pages long) listed the following subheadings: homosexuality, lucid interval, paralysis, phrenasthenia and moral imbecillity, psychasthenia, manic-depressive psychosis and schizophrenia.

In 1957 the *Index Rerum Analyticus* was retained but was lengthened to twenty pages in order to include a precis of the specific point of law under each subheading.

This is by far the best indexing system to date. Under the old system neither the index nor the tabula was of much use, the first being too long and the second too short. The analytical index of 1956 was a definite improvement and the 1957 edition offers us finally a highly functional system of indexing. In 1962 the word "Analyticus" was dropped, but otherwise the Index remained unchanged. The *Index Rerum* of 1967 still contained about twenty pages, and followed the format of the 1957 volume.

Value: The Rota is certainly the chief source of canonical jurisprudence for all other courts. It has set the tone and established virtually singlehandedly the traditional jurisprudence to which all other Tribunals turn. And it has done so with masterly finesse and thoroughness, especially in the area of utilizing the law.

In the areas of interpreting and supplying, rotal auditors, as might be expected, often take divergent positions on a given question. Generally, however, they are thorough, excellent theoreticians, and especially considering their distance from the people involved, remarkably empathetic. Local judges, on the other hand, though sometimes inferior as theoreticians, nevertheless have their own pragmatic strengths. Their understanding of the capacities of people, an understanding gained from broad, clinical experience, seems especially acute and real; and they have a high awareness and sensitivity to local conditions and their importance.

The challenge, at any rate, is the same for every judge, both rotal and local. He must know his own culture and his own times. He must be able to perceive, and to weigh, and to create suitable, enlightened norms by which justice can be rendered. He must avoid the extremes of being insensitive on the one hand, and pandering on the other; of being too theoretical on the one hand, and too intuitive on the other. He must be neither too legalistic nor too romantic, neither too demanding nor too excusing. He must, above all, show forth the ability of the Church to treat people as individual persons of the community and not just as cases or sterotypes. Only in this way can jurisprudence continue to be the "ars boni et aequi" for each succeeding generation.

Also Cf. "Jurisprudence in Canon Law" by Arthur Caron, *The Jurist*, Vol. XVIII, 1. Jan. 1958, pp. 88-97; and *A Survey of Recent Rotal Jurisprudence on Psychological Cases*, James A. McEnerney, S.J., 1973.

XII — THE DIOCESAN TRIBUNAL

The common complaint among laymen who have a marriage case is that the pastor or assitant does not understand them or their case. They fail to realize that the life of a pastor is one of manifold dimensions: instructing, administering the sacraments, building, financial worries, etc., so much so that it is impossible for him to be an expert in the matrimonial field. The pastor of souls is not expected to understand all the details of matrimonial procedure, nevertheless, there are certain fundamental principles that every priest should know and understand in matrimonial procedure. The following is a brief resumé of some of these fundamentals:

Personnel

The personnel of the diocesan tribunal are the following: Officials, Judges, Promoter of Justice, Defender of the Bond, Notary, Procurator and Advocate.

The Officials

The bishop or archbishop is the Presiding Judge of the tribunal; however, according to the Canon Law prescription the bishop appoints one to take his place. This person is called the Officialis who shares with the bishop all the powers on judicial matters. Therefore, the Officialis is also the Presiding Judge of the Tribunal and in this capacity he functions as one person with the bishop. He may also exercise the delegated powers which the bishop grants to him upon his appointment.

The Judges

Besides the Presiding Judge, Canon Law requires that the Ordinary appoint other Judges to the Tribunal who help to decide the cases that come to their attention. Three Judges are required for deciding formal cases. Some cases of a criminal nature require five judges. (If judges are selected in a Synod, they are called Synodal Judges; if chosen outside the Synod they are called pro-synodal judges. They should not number more than twelve in a diocese).

The Promoter of Justice

The Promoter of Justice may be considered the diocesan attorney. He has the responsibility to uphold the common good. Thus, if it is known publicly that a certain marriage is invalid, and that scandal has resulted from the parties cohabiting, it is the duty of the Promoter of Justice to petition the nullity by bringing forth witnesses and other proofs to substantiate his claim; or, he can enter a cause for nullity to a Tribunal when the parties involved are prohibited by law from acting as Plaintiffs (e.g., non-Catholics) and the Promoter of Justice is convinced that the public good requires the intervention of the Tribunal. Moreover, among his other duties, he must follow the progress of a case during a trial and see to it that the proper procedure is followed in the case. Usually this office is filled by the Defender of the Bond.

The Defender of the Bond

The Defender of the Bond is the attorney for the Church; his office is similar to that of the State Attorney or Prosecuting Attorney in a criminal case. He is a very important member of the Tribunal. He is the defender of the law, insofar as he sees to it that the law is always upheld. For example, when a certain marriage is attacked to be invalid, he defends the marriage bond by the application of the proper canons. He also prepares the questionnaires for the examination of the witnesses. These questions, in turn, are proposed to the witnesses by one of the judges (or by the Auditor-appointed by the Officialis) in the judicial examination. He also points out the flaws in the evidence offered by the plaintiff, by calling witnesses of his own, etc.

The Notary

The Notary is an official who, in a formal trial, puts into writing the replies of the witnesses. He must put to writing either the exact words of the witnesses or the substance of them as dictated by the judge or auditor. The Notary keeps a record of the entire trial. His name and seal attest to the authenticity of a very judicial act or deposition. If his signature is not on the judicial act, this act is considered null. It is also advantageous for the Notary to take shorthand.

Procurator-Auditor

The Procurator or Auditor is appointed by the Ordinary, to serve as lawyers for the parties in the case. One is appointed for each of the parties—namely, the Plaintiff and Defendant. If the Defendant does not select one, the Presiding Judge will appoint one or leave the defense to the Defender of the Bond.

The Procurator-Auditor assists in contacting witnesses; he takes the necessary steps during the trial to promote the cause of the client, without however, jeopardizing the truth in any way; when the case is closed he will, by a written brief, seek to advance the case of his client. This brief will be answered in writing by the Defender of the Bond. If necessary he may write a second brief which is handled in the same manner. The Procurator-Auditor may leave the defense of the marriage to the Defender of the Bond.

XIII—MARRIAGE PROCEDURE

The fourth Book of the Code of Canon Law gives the procedure on handling marriage cases. Some are simple, others are complicated and require more study. In summary, we have the following types of procedure:

I. Simple Administrative Procedure

This procedure is called simple because there is *no court procedure* of any kind here. It consists merely in a judgment made by the Ordinary or his delegate based upon the documents or affidavits presented. For example, in deciding questions of nullity based on the *lack of canonical form* (Defect of Form). Pauline privilege cases are decided in the same way. Here again the Ordinary or his delegate makes a judgment on the proof of both parties in the marriage in question based on the evidence presented to them.

II. The Formal Procedure

The formal process is more complicated than the others. The case is usually admitted for trial by three judges. In all such cases, (1) careful investigation must be made to determine whether a particular court is competent[1] to handle it; (2) the judges must determine whether there is a case according to the law (an impediment) as a basis of nullity in this particular case; (3) that there is a possibility of proving the case by competent witnesses, documents, testimony, etc. Following the acceptance of the case and after the Procurators are appointed, the session is held for "joining the issues" (*litis contestatio*). At this meeting the Presiding Judge (Officialis) together with the Defender of the Bond and the Procurator of the parties, determine the exact point in question to be solved in the case.

The testimony of the parties and the witnesses are then taken. All the witnesses are heard in the presence of the three judges of the court (or auditor), the Defender of the Bond and Notary. When all the testimony has been taken and all the proofs submitted, the case is declared closed. Afterward, the Procurator and the Defender of the Bond must submit their written briefs. These together with all the testimony gathered, are submitted to the three judges. (Copies are made for each).

The decision of the Judges is based entirely upon the facts contained in the case. Judges are reminded here to remember the well-known axiom *"Quod non est in actis, non est in mundo."* If the Judges uphold the validity of the marriage, their decision will be considered: "Negative." If the Judges declare the marriage null, the decision of the Judges will be considered: "Affirmative."

In either the affirmative or negative decision, the case is not considered settled as yet, because the law requires two concordant decisions.

For example, (1) the decision of the Judges is "Affirmative" the law requires the Defender of the Bond to appeal the case to the higher court (Court of Appeal or Court of Second Instance). If this Appellate Court likewise gives an "Affirmative" decision, the marriage case in question is considered null and the case is considered settled. If (2) the decision of the Judges of the First Court is "Negative," the plaintiff has the right to appeal the case to the Court of Appeals, but is not obliged to do so. He may abide by the decision. If the Plaintiff does appeal, his case to the Appellate Court and this Court would reverse the decision (i.e., First Court: "Negative"—the Second Court: "Affirmative"), the case has to be appealed further (for two concordant decisions) to the Court of Third Instance, namely to the highest court, the Roman Rota.

III. Summary Procedure

The Summary Process, in brief, means that the testimony is heard by the Ordinary or his delegate after the Defender of the Bond has reviewed the case and the parties to the marriage in question have been notified or cited. This procedure is used in all cases that come under Canon 1990, namely, disparity of cult, Order, solemn vows, ligamen, consanguinity, affinity and spiritual relationship. If any of these cases become too complicated, then it is processed according to the Formal Procedure mentioned above. The Defender of the Bond has the right to appeal the decision of the Judge to the court of appeal. Courts of appeal are selected by the Holy See for each diocese. The court is also called the Appellate Court.

IV. Special Procedure

The Special Procedure pertains to cases which are sent to Rome for a decision:

I. *Non Consummation Cases*

1. The Ordinary no longer needs permission from the Holy See to begin such a case. Cf. Document IX, Appendix.

2. The decision is not made by the local Ordinary or Tribunal, but the case is sent directly to Rome and the decision is made by the Sacred Congregation.

II. *Privilege of the Faith*

These cases also follow this formal procedure, except that (1) the Defender of the Bond need not be present at the hearings of the witnesses; however, he prepares the necessary questionnaire in the case, (2) neither Judges nor Procurators are appointed, and (3) the decision is not given by the Ordinary or the Tribunal but by the Sacred Congregation.

1. A Tribunal is competent if it (1) is the diocese in which the marriage in question took place or (2) is in the diocese of the defendant, or (3) in the case of a mixed marriage, is in the diocese of the Catholic party; and (4) a woman who has separated with ecclesiastical approval may choose the diocese in which she is, otherwise, she must follow the domicile of her husband. There are some other exceptions.

XIV—HOW TO BEGIN A FORMAL CASE

Between 1940-1950 Canon Law was at its peak. Every seminary had a comprehensive course in this field. Scripture was in the background. Since then Scripture assumed the place of priority in seminaries. Canon Law has not only a second place in the curriculum today but seems to occupy the lowest place on the rostrums.

Scripture rightfully belongs where it is. Unfortunately, Canon Law has been put in the background, as if it had no importance in the seminary curriculum. Some feel that since the Code Commissions are still (after twelve years since the Vatican Council II), revising the law, Canon Law has no place in the curriculum, but they are wrong.

Revising the code, does not mean that the Church has abandoned Canon Law on Marriage altogether. The laws on marriage are substantially the same as they were. Yet it seems as if this important subject has been put in a vacuum.

Fortunately, despite this indifference the Canon Law Society of America and some Societies of other countries are holding the lifeline to this all important subject. I regret to express this comment, but the many inquiries I have received from priests and chanceries since the end of Vatican Council II, indicates a lack of knowledge among many ecclesiastics of the basic elements of Canon Law on marriage.

Pope Paul VI was also alarmed about this situation of apathy and ignorance of the law when he issued several instructions on this subject. He said in the Motu Proprio, *Causas Matrimoniales,* "Marriage cases have always been given special care by Mother Church . . . The Ministry of the ecclesiastical judges shows forth clearly . . . the pastoral charity of the Church. Since the number of these cases is greatly increasing at the present time, the Church cannot but be very concerned about this matter."

Due to the lack of proper pastoral instructions on marriage in the seminaries, it seems that many newly ordained priests do not know how to go about introducing a marriage case to their tribunal. Therefore, for justice, charity, and the salvation of souls, which is our concern, I wish to propose the following to those who need such guidance. It is very simple and is not time consuming.

Every person has a right to be heard by the Church in matrimonial problems. Especially so when he or she seeks an annulment. After a brief interview, all one must do is to give the person the following guidelines, putting the burden on him or her, and have them submit this in writing to some responsible person in the tribunal for evaluation.

The Priest should also give some information on what an annulment really is, and the procedure involved. The following is the guideline and annulment information which is used by our Metropolitan Archdiocese of Pittsburgh (Byzantine Rite):

XV — PREPARING A MARRIAGE CASE HISTORY

Matrimonial Tribunal
Metropolitan Archidocese of Pittsburgh

OUTLINE OF A CASE HISTORY

This is not a questionnaire. It is an arrangement of topics which are of concern in a Tribunal process. Please give specific information on the points which follow. Omit any item which does not pertain to your case. Number your responses according to the number given each item. It is suggested that you prepare a preliminary draft and then revise it for clarity. A typed resume would be appreciated if at all possible. Please try to contain your statement to six pages. You should keep a copy for yourself. When returning the resume by mail, use the address given above.

A. Identification and Background:

For the writer:

1. Present legal name, (maiden name), complete address, phone, birthday, religion of baptism, religion presently practiced, present marital status.
2. Education, religious education, professional training, present employment.
3. Name of parents, essential facts about parents, description of home-life.
4. Description of personality, medical history which has a bearing on the marriage.

For the other party to the marriage:

5. Present legal name, (maiden name), complete address, phone, birthday, religion of baptism, religion presently practiced, present marital status.
6. Education, religious education, professional training, present employment.
7. Name of parents, essential facts about parents, description of home-life.
8. Description of personality, medical history which has a bearing on the marriage.

B. Courtship:

1. Meeting, length of acquaintanceship before the marriage, basis of interest, development of serious relationship, degree of intimacy.

2. Intention to marry: who proposed, willing acceptance by the other party, length of engagement-period, objections to the engagement from other parties, preparations for the marriage.
3. Discussion between parties about: the nature of marriage, obligations of marriage, of life-long, faithful marriage.
4. Discussion between parties about children: how many, when, agreement to delay children.
5. Problems in courtship: disagreements, personality clashes, involvement with other parties; family interference, any breaking of the engagement.
6. Presence of pregnancy before marriage.
7. Any pressures impelling either party to enter marriage.

C. Wedding:

1. *For a Catholic party who attempted marriage before a civil official or minister of another religion:* date, reasons, circumstances of this attempted marriage.
For validation of this type of marriage: reasons which brought the couple to have the marriage rectified in the Church, any pressure to do so, attitude of the priest toward the validation, attitude of the couple to each other at time of this validation, their attitudes toward marriage at the time of validation.
2. *For marriage of two non-Catholic parties*: date, place of celebration, type of official who witnessed the marriage.
3. *For a marriage celebrated in the Catholic Church*: details on arrangements, instructions for marriage, consent of the parents, priest's attitude toward the marriage, date and place of marriage.
4. Anything unusual in connection with wedding rehearsal, ceremony, reception.
5. Honeymoon: where, how long, consummation by physical union, reactions of both parties.

D. Married Life:

1. Life-style: residence, with whom, first adjustments to married life, financial situation.
2. List the problems which arose in the marriage: nature, cause, efforts to overcome the problems.
3. Situations of personality-change, drinking, associations with others, attitudes toward each party's family.
4. Children born to the marriage: number, when, attitude toward children, treatment of them.
5. Sickness caused by problems in the marriage, medical consultations, psychiatric treatments, marriage counselling.

E. Separation and Divorce:

1. Length of time lived together, number of separations, length of separations,

what brought about any reconciliations.

2. Cause of final separation: date, who initiated the separation.

3. Divorce: who filed, grounds, contested, date divorce was granted, where.

4. Re-marriage: *For the writer*—have you married again, when, to whom, where, children born of this marriage.

Re-marriage: *For the other party*—has the other party married again, when, to whom, where, children born of this marriage.

5. Witnesses who can support allegations: complete names, addresses, relationship to parties in the case.

(Please sign and date your statement.)

XVI — THE ANNULMENT PROCEDURE

CANON NO. 1 (Crae. All.), 1012 (CIC) OF THE CODE OF CANON LAW

Christ the Lord has raised to the dignity of a sacrament the matimonial bond contracted between baptized persons.

For this reason then there can be no valid marriage contract between baptized persons unless the same is also a Sacrament.

Paragraph 48 of the Church in the Modern World:

The intimate partnership of married life and love has been established by the Creator and qualified by His laws. It is rooted in the conjugal covenant of irrevocable personal consent. Hence, by that human act whereby spouses mutually bestow and accept each other, a relationship arises which by divine will and in the eyes of society too is a lasting one. For the good of the spouses and their offspring as well as of society, the existence of this sacred bond no longer depends on human decisions alone.

For God Himself is the author of Matrimony, endowed as it is with various benefits and purposes. All of these have a very decisive bearing on the continuation of the human race, on the personal development and eternal destiny of the individual members of the family, and on the dignity, stability, peace, and prosperity of the family itself and of human society as a whole. By their very nature, the institution of Matrimony itself and conjugal love are ordained for the procreation and education of children, and find in them their ultimate crown.

Thus a man and a woman, who by the marriage covenant of conjugal love "are no longer two, but one flesh," render mutual help and service to each other through an intimate union of their persons and of their actions. Through this union they experience the meaning of their oneness and attain to it with growing perfection day by day. As a mutual gift of two persons, this intimate union, as well as the good of the children, imposes total fidelity on the spouses and argues for an unbreakable oneness between them.

What is an annulment?

In the CATHOLIC CHURCH (Byzantine and Roman) a marriage is considered valid when:

1. It is celebrated in a Marriage Ceremony which is legally accepted in the eyes of the Church;

2. Both partners in the marriage were free to marry each other;

3. Each partner intended from the beginning of the marriage to accept God's plan for married life as that plan is taught by the Church;

4. Each partner had the physical and/or psychological ability to live up to the consent initially given to the marriage;

If any one of these requirements is lacking from the beginning of the marriage, then the Church Tribunal, acting as the Bishop's representative, can declare that marriage to have been invalid from its very beginning.

It must always be kept in mind however, that merely because a marriage case is accepted for consideration by the Tribunal that fact *does not mean that a Church Annulment will always be granted.*

What is the Archdiocesan Tribunal?

Somewhat like civil governments, the Church has a system of Courts. These Church Courts are called Tribunals.

s   In each diocese the Bishop is the chief Teacher and chief Priest for that portion of God's People over whom he has been placed as Shepherd. At times in his role as Teacher and Priest it becomes necessary for the Bishop to give judgment whether the teaching and sanctifying mission of the Church is correctly being carried out in practice. This necessity then gives the Bishop the role also of being the Chief Judge concerning the practice of the Christian Gospel as the Church intends it to be practiced.

Since the Bishop of a diocese, however, cannot personally act as Judge in all these matters, he delegates certain priests to set up a Tribunal to handle this aspect of the Bishop's work.

Most of the problems presented to the Tribunal for judgment are those which deal with the validity of the Sacrament of Marriage. Persons will contend that their marriages were not really sacramental christian marriages in the eyes of the Church. Their contention is that these marriages never really existed, that they are null and void. The work of the Tribunal, therefore, for the most part exists in an attempt to arrive at the truth of such contentions. To do so requires that such marriages be proved *null and void* before the Judges of the Tribunal.

To help the person present such proof, a priest or priests is assigned to each case as an Advocate to build up evidence for the case. Because of the long-standing teaching of the Church concerning the holiness of married life, however, another priest called the Defender of the Bond of Matrimony is also assigned to each case. His function is to see to it that the teaching of the Church is preserved in practice.

During the annulment process, then, several priests will be involved in each marriage case. The final decision—whether or not this particular marriage is to be considered valid in the eyes of the Church—is made by the priest or priests delegated as

Judge by the Bishop. Before any case comes to this final judgment stage the following usually happens in each case:

1. The person petitioning for the annulment is interviewed by one of the priests on the Tribunal staff, or the Pastor.

2. The other partner of the marriage in question likewise is interviewed if this is at all possible;

(These two steps are taken for the Tribunal to determine the "grounds" on which the validity of the marriage is to be "attacked.")

3. When sufficient evidence is gathered, the case is then presented to one or more Judges who decide whether or not to accept the case;

If the case is accepted, the priest who acts as Advocate then formally petitions the Tribunal to accept this case for consideration based on the evidence contained in the acts of the case;

If the case is not accepted at this stage, then more evidence must be gathered, if this is at all possible;

4. When so accepted and after both the Advocate and the Defender of the Bond of Matrimony have asked for the Tribunal's judgment, the case then goes to the Judge or Judges who give the final decision;

The evidence spoken of above is gathered by the Tribunal from witnesses who have been supplied by the person asking for the annulment. These witnesses must be able to give their testimony concerning the alleged grounds for the invalidity of the marriage.

The above description of the Tribunal gives a mere outline of what the Tribunal is and how it operates. The time involved in this process may be long due to several reasons—e.g., the difficulty met in contacting witnesses, the difficulty met in obtaining certain Church, Civil, or Medical records which may be needed, or the large number of similar cases gathered before the Tribunal. Whatever can be done to arrive at the truth in such matters will be done.

How much money is involved

It is often said by persons who know little or nothing of Church Tribunals that someone has to have a lot of money in order for their marriage case to be considered by the Church. What is even sadder is that more people believe such rumors. The fact, however, is that such is not true.

But as would be expected, expenses are incurred in the running of the Tribunal. There are salaries to be paid to the Tribunal staff. There are costs incurred by the Tribunal office for mailing letters and other material, stationery, stamps, and telephone bills. Heating and electricity, etc., are also costly to run such an office operated for annulment procedures. This is all done for people whose marriage has been a failure. Therefore, the person asking for the annulment is expected to bear some of this burden.

The total average expense incurred by the Tribunal in each trial case are approximately $1000.00. The Tribunal would expect an offering, not of $1000 but $200.00 for the ordinary case. Of this amount $200 covers only the minimal expenses. If medical experts, such as psychiatrists, psychologists, etc., are employed by the Tribunal court, this must be borne by the Petitioner. If the Petitioner is financially unable to assume these minimal expenses, arrangements can be made through the pastor of the Petitioner. Installments are also possible. When the case is introduced into the Tribunal by the Pastor, the Petitioner is asked to make a deposit of $25.00 toward Court costs.

Certain cases cannot be judged by the Archdiocesan Tribunal, but must be referred to Rome. This does not happen frequently, but when it does, the person is asked to pay the amount of tax which is asked by Rome. This amount is somewhat greater than that asked by our Tribunal.

What Documents or Records are Needed

For each marriage case under consideration the Tribunal needs the following documents:
1. *Recent copies* of the Baptismal Certificate of each partner in the marriage, if each partner was baptized in the Catholic Church;
2. A copy of the Marriage License;
3. A copy of the Civil Divorce Decree.

These documents should be sent in to the Tribunal by the person as soon as possible after the initial interview. This will help save time in the processing of the case since no final decision will be given unless these documents have been presented to the Tribunal. The only exception to this is the case in which no Civil Divorce has been obtained.

At times it may be necessary for the Tribunal to have certain Medical Records concerning treatment given previously to one or both of the marriage partners. In order for the Tribunal to obtain such Records it will be necessary for the party concerned to sign a Release from Professional Secrecy.

What is expected in the Testimony?

After the initial interview the party interviewed will be asked to send to the Tribunal a short report on why he or she thinks the marriage should be declared invalid. This report should be no more than three pages in length. In this report should be given only those facts of the marriage which would have a bearing on the alleged invalidity of the marriage. (Such facts would be details concerning the courtship and the preparations made for the marriage, the details of the marriage itself, details concerning separations which may have occurred in the marriage, and the reasons for the final break-up of the marriage.)

Witnesses to these facts must be supplied by the person asking for the annulment. These witnesses should be persons who have first-hand knowledge of these facts. These witnesses should also be contacted beforehand by the person asking for the annulment and informed that they may be contacted for their testimony by the Tribunal. Unless such witnesses are supplied the Tribunal, there is very little that can be done in the annulment process.

XVII — CANONICAL BASES FOR DEFERRAL OF MARRIAGE

Anthony J. Bevilacqua

Two major problems areas:
1. Lack of faith commitment: Though baptized Catholics, couples at times seem to bring no spiritual dimension to the marriage. Frequently they are either grossly ignorant of Catholic teaching or have rejected important doctrines or hold them in contempt. Except for the absence of the religious dimension, they often possess sufficient psychological maturity to give otherwise adequate consent. Motives for their request for a Catholic marriage run the gamut from wanting to please parents or grandparents to a nostalgia for the interior artistic design of the Church. Priests instinctively find it difficult to accept such couples as worthy candidates for Catholic marriage. Yet it is equally difficult for such priests to find and articulate the legal grounds for denying or deferring marriage in these instances.
2. Immaturity with consequent inability to fulfill the obligations of marriage: Priests frequently intuit that one or both prospective marriage partners are so immature that the prognosis for a lasting marriage is very poor. This intuition of the priest is one derived from the behavior, age, remarks, background, etc. of the couple, the product of the knowledge and experience of the priest, and can approach moral certitude. Usually this evaluation of the priest involves teenagers, though not limited to them. The blatant immaturity can or cannot be accompanied by lack of faith commitment. Though instinctively certain of the eventual failure of the marriage in such cases, the priest often cannot support with canonical authority his judgment to refuse or postpone the marriage.

Cautions
A. In prescribing and utilizing canonical bases for the denial or deferral of marriage, we must be aware that there are various tensions to be considered.
B. The tensions arise primarily from the following rights and interests which must be protected and balanced: Rights and interests of parties themselves, natural right of all to marry, interests of institution of marriage, rights and interests of the Church, rights and interests of Society, and rights and interests of children either born or to be born.
C. The major tension seems to be between the natural right to marry and the preservation of the institution of marriage.

D. In all problems of deferral or refusal of marriage, the major concern should be pastoral not canonical. Opportunity should be used to instruct persons, retain pastoral contacts even in denials or postponements, explain reasons for the refusal or deferral.

E. A priest cannot canonically "forbid" marriages. He can declare that parties do not have a present right to marry.

F. Where dioceses have established marriage guidelines such as "Teenage Marriage Policies": Policies should provide some sort of recourse for parties if they feel that the decision of the priest is arbitrary, whimsical, capricious or unreasonable. Policies should not set down such absolute, rigid prohibitions that in effect they are establishing impediments or permanent barriers to marriage in contravention of C. 1038:2 and C. 1039. e.g., "No one under 18 can give valid consent." The purpose of policy should not be solely to prevent invalid marriages but it should provide the couple with reasonable opportunity to seek expert aid in achieving the required maturity and faith commitment.

G. Note that in most cases of possible deferral of marriage, the law prescribes that the Bishop must be consulted before priest can make the decision.

Required Certitude of Freedom of Parties

A. Before a priest can officiate at a marriage, he must be certain that there are no legal obstacles to its valid and licit celebration. If there are reasonable doubts about either the valid or the licit celebration, then he cannot proceed until the doubts are removed. What degree of certitude for freedom must the priest acquire?

B. Authorities indicate that moral certitude is required: C. 1019: — "Before a marriage is celebrated it must be *certain* that nothing stands in the way of its valid and licit celebration."

   a. Latin is "debet constare." "Constare" is generally used by tribunals to mean "moral certitude."
   Instructions of S.C. Sacraments in 1921 and 1941 make it very clear that the freedom to marry must be established beyond all reasonable doubt. This is equivalent to reaching moral certitude.
   Bouscaren-Ellis-Korth commenting on C. 1019:1: "Before a marriage is celebrated it must appear with *moral certainty* from a careful investigation, that there is no obstacle to its valid and licit celebration."

Canonical Bases

A. General Canonical Bases—The legal grounds on which a marriage can be deferred or denied fall generally into the following three areas: Impediments, religious instruction or commitment and consent. A few bases cannot be fit into any of the above categories, such as C. 1034 on marriage of minors; C. 1067:2 on customary age.

B. List of specific canonical bases with brief evaluation. This list will attempt to give all the possible grounds even though some are tenuous and without much force.

  1. Religious Instruction C. 1020:

  1. The pastor who has the right to assist at the marriage shall, a suitable time beforehand, carefully investigate whether there is any obstacle to the celebration of the marriage.

  2. He must ask the man and woman, even separately and cautiously, whether they are under any impediment, whether they are giving their consent freely, especially the woman, and whether they are sufficiently instructed in Christian doctrine, unless in view of the quality of the persons this last question should seem unnecessary.

  3. It is the province of the Ordinary of the place to lay down special rules for this investigation by the pastor.

  According to this canon, a marriage can be deferred until the couple receive sufficient instruction in Christian doctrine if the priest determines such is needed. According to 3 of this same canon, the Ordinary can set down regulations on the number and content of instructions. If parties lack sufficient knowledge of Christian doctrine and refuse to take instructions, what can be done? This question was asked of the Code Commission on June 3, 1918:

Question: "If either of the parties to a prospective marriage be found ignorant of Christian doctrine, should the priest refuse to marry them, or postpone the marriage until he has instructed them?"

Reply: "The Pastor should observe the prescriptions of C. 1020:2, and while he does what the Code prescribes, he should carefully teach the ignorant parties at least the first elements of Christian doctrine. If, however, they refuse, he should not refuse to marry them as is prescribed for other cases in C. 1066."

This same policy is repeated in the Instruction of the S.C] Sacraments of June 29, 1941 (N° 8): "If he finds them ignorant of Christian doctrine, he must carefully instruct them a least in its first elements; in case they refuse, however, this is no reason for refusing to marry them, as is prescribed for other cases in Canon 1066.

Evaluation—This basis can frequently be used to delay a marriage for as long as the priest wants to give them sufficient instruction. If the couple happen to have knowledge of the Code Commission reply or happen to be defiant in this regard and refuse instructions, the basis loses all of its force in virtue of the 1918 reply and 1941 instruction.

  2. Reception of Confirmation

  C. 1021: 2. "Catholics who have not yet received the sacrament of confirmation should receive it before being married, if they can do so without grave inconvenience."

Evaluation—One does not ordinarily resort to this canon as a basis for deferral. However, it can be utilized if a priest is looking for a peg to hang on his postponement of marriage especially in cases where a person lacks a faith commitment or is inadequately instructed. The priest must determine according to the circumstances what constitutes "grave inconvenience."

3. *Instruction on Marriage*

C. 1033. "The pastor must not fail, with due regard to the condition of the persons concerned, to instruct the parties on the sanctity of the sacrament of matrimony, the mutual obligations of husband and wife, and the duties of parents toward their children; and he must earnestly exhort them to make a careful confession of their sins before the marriage, and to receive with devotion the Most Blessed Eucharist."

Evaluation—This would not be a very strong support for refusal or deferral. However, it can be used indirectly if the priest senses in the parties an ignorance of the responsibilities and nature of marriage. It can serve as a basis for delaying the marriage especially if the Bishop, in virtue of C. 1020:3, has set down regulations on such instructions as part of the investigation.

4. *Minors*

C. 1034. "The pastor must seriously dissuade minor sons and daughters from contracting marriage without the knowledge or against the reasonable wishes of their parents; in case they refuse to obey, he should not assist at their marriage without having first consulted the Ordinary." Minors include both male and female under 21 years of age.
C. 1034 does not require consent of parents. It requires that they be aware of the marriage or that it not take place against their reasonable objectives. Note the need for consultation with the Ordinary in the event they refuse to abide by the directives of the canon.

Evaluation—This canon could serve as a formidable basis for deferral of marriage until the age of 21 if the parents would cooperate. Unfortunately its strength is frequently depleted since, in spite of objectively good reasons against the marriage, the parents acquiesce in the wishes of the children to marry.

5. *Vetitum of Ordinary*

C. 1039 1—"Only Ordinaries of places can forbid marriage in a particular case, but only temporarily, for just cause, and as long as such cause continues, to all persons actually stopping in their territory, and to their subjects even outside their territory."
This canon can serve as one of the strongest supports for postponement of marriage since the required "just cause" covers a multitude of possibilities. The "just cause" includes all the other canonical bases for deferral such as possible presence of impediments, possible defect of consent, lack of

knowledge of faith or marriage. But it is not limited to these grounds. The Ordinary may in accordance with the nature of his diocese consider other circumstances as a "just cause" for a temporary ban.

Waterhouse, in his thesis, enumerates "scandal" in the broad sense as a "just cause" within C. 1039. Thus it would iclude "notions of enmities, quarrels, and dissensions among the faithful, and even bewilderment, shock and wonderment when these are detrimental to the welfare of the Church." Waterhouse seems to be saying that the obligation of the Ordinary to seek the common good and preserve public order justifies him in individual circumstances to use C. 1039 to restrict the rights of certain individuals in regard to marriage.

Evaluation—One of the most formidable and inclusive bases if properly used.

6. *Attempted Marital Consent Before Non-Catholic Minister.*
   C. 1063 1. "Even though a dispensation from the impediment of mixed religion has been obtained from the Church, the parties may not, either before or after the celebration of the marriage before the Church, apply also, either in persn or by proxy, to a non-Catholic minister in his religious capacity, in order to express or renew matrimonial consent."
   C. 1063 2. "If the pastor knows for certain that the parties intend to violate or that they have violated this law,.he must not assist at their marriage except for the gravest reasons, on condition that scandal be removed, and after consulting the Ordinary.

Evaluation—In mixed marriages, this can serve as a strong basis for delaying a marriage in Church should the priest judge this necessary. The strength of this basis can be seen in the three conditions set down for assisting at such a marriage: gravest reasons, removal of scandal, consultation of Ordinary. However, the force of the canon has waned in recent years because of the growing desire for "ecumenical marriages." Today marriage outside the Church before a non-Catholic minister is not seen in the same forbidden light as in yesteryear. Much less would there be opposition voiced against a second ceremony. Nevertheless, the canon still remains in force to be used when needed.

7. Notorious Abandonment of Faith; Members of Condemned Societies
   C. 1065 1. "The faithful must also be deterred from contracting marriage with persons who have either notoriously abandoned the Catholic faith, even without having gone over to a non-Catholic sect, or have notoriously become members of societies which are condemned by the Church."
   C. 1065 2. "The pastor must not assist at the above-mentioned marriages without having consulted the Ordinary, who may in view of all the circumstances of the case permit him to assist at the marriage, provided that there be a grave reason and the Ordinary judges that adequate measures

have been taken to insure the Catholic education of all the children and the removal of danger of perversion from the other party."
There would not be too much call for use of this canon in the case of members of condemned societies. Today, Catholics in the United States are no longer prohibited from joining the Freemasons which is the most known of the "condemned societies.
It is not neglect in the practice of the Faith which is grounds for the prohibition of this canon. Rather it is a public profession by a person that he no longer considers himself a member of the Church or publicly and habitually derides or rejects Catholic teaching.

Evaluation—In the case of parties without a Faith commitment, this canon is a strong support for postponemt of the marriage provided the definition of "notorious abandonment of faith" is fulfilled. The severity of the prohibition can be gleaned from the conditions set down for assistance at the marriage: grave reasons, consultation and permission of Ordinary; guarantees for Catholic education of children; removal of danger of perversion.

8. *Public Sinner; Notoriously Under Censure*
   C. 1066 "If a public sinner or one who is notoriously under censure refused to go to sacramental confession or to be reconciled to the Church before marriage, the pastor must not assist at his marriage unless there be a grave reason regarding which he should if possible consult the Ordinary."
   Ordinarily, there would be little occasion to resort to this canon for anyone "notoriously under censure." Some canonists consider a public sinner one who is publicly known to have been away from the sacraments for years. Cappello, for example, lists among public sinners one who is publicly known not to have made his Easter duty.

Evaluation—A priest can use this canon to delay a marriage until the party reforms his way of life. At first sight, this canon seems to be a strong basis since it calls for a grave reason and consultation with the Ordinary before a priest can assist at the marriage. However, the effectiveness of the canon is diminished by the response of June 3, 1918 given above on the question of religious instruction. The reply states that if the parties refuse to take religious instructions, the pastor "should not refuse to marry them as *is prescribed for other cases in C. 1066.*"

9. *Customary Age*
   C. 1067 2. "Although a marriage contracted after the aforesaid age is valid, yet pastors of souls should try to deter young people from marrying before the age at which, according to the received customs of the country, marriage is usually contracted." The first paragraph of C. 1067 states the age for validity, i.e., 16 for boys and 14 for girls.

Evaluation—The force of the canon itself is weak since it can only exhort pastors to "try to deter" young people. Teenage marriage guidelines in various dioceses have proved much more effective and acceptable.

10. *Impediments*

The impeding and diriment impediments are enumerated in Cs. 1058-1080. If there is certitude of the existence of an impediment, a priest cannot officiate at the marriage until the impediment is dispensed from or ceases. If there is reasonable suspicion of the presence of an impediment, a priest cannot officiate at the marriage until the investigation removes the suspicion.

Evaluation—All the force of law prevents the performance of a marriage when an impediment exists or is reasonably thought to exist.

11. *Defect of Consent*

—The following is an enumeration of various defects of consent, which if there is reasonable suspicion of their existence, would be a canonical basis for refusal or deferral of marriage.

a. *Amentia*—This would be a total lack of required consent. In effect, there would be no human act. The total absence of consent in amentia would stem either from a psychological or pathological ailment or from a temporary incapacity, such as, intoxication. The present legislative articulation of the consent which is required for validity is contained in C. 1081:

1. "Marriage is effected by the consent of the parties lawfully expressed between persons who are capable according to law; and this consent no human power can supply."

2. "Matrimonial consentis an act of the will by which each party gives and accepts a perpetual and exclusive right over the body, for acts which are of themselves suitable for the generation of children.

b. Ignorance that marriage is a permanent society of man and woman for procreation of children.

C. 1082: 1. "In order that matrimonial consent may be possible it is necessary that the contracting parties be at least not ignorant that marriage is a permanent society between man and woman for the procreation of children."

2. "This ignorance is not presumed after puberty."

3. Exclusion of marriage itself, or of the right to the conjugal act, or of any of the essential properties of marriage.

C. 1086: 2. "But if either party or both parties by a positive act of the will exclude marriage itself, or all right to the conjugal act, or any essential property of marriage, the marriage contract in invalid."

d. Consent obtained through force or fear.

C. 1087: 1. "Likewise invalid is a marriage entered into through force or grave fear unjustly inspired from without, such that in order to escape from it a party is compelled to choose marriage."

2. "No other fear, even if it furnish the cause for the contract, entails the nullity of the marriage."

e. Lack of Due Discretion—

Involves a defective judgmental appreciation concerning the rights and obligations exchanged in marriage. Because of this judgmental impairment affecting consent, a party is incapable of marital consent.

f. Inability to fulfill the obligations of marriage;

Exclusion of right to community life—This category will be considered separately in the next section.

Fuller examination of the two major problem areas

A. Lack of Faith Commitment, Though Otherwise Mature

1. This is becoming more and more an occasion of frustration for parish priests. It is also injurious to the law which seems anachronistic in this problem. It is very difficult for priests to see how a couple, often without any comprehension of or regard for the Catholic Faith, can be said to be entering Christian marriage and receiving the sacrament. It if were not for the fact of their baptism, they would be labeled pagans.

2. In these cases, priests instinctively feel that they should deny marriage, presuming all pastoral means were in vain. Yet they often feel a sense of guilt since they know the couple will marry invalidly outside the Church. They are more reluctant to give the couple a positive directive to marry before a civil official since they feel they would be cooperating in a sinful act and would be advocating trial marriage.

3. The problem has been largely complicated by two legislative norms: That all baptized Catholics are subject to the canonical form of marriage. For Catholics, either the marriage takes place before the Church, or it is invalid. This must not be construed to be a suggestion to abrogate the canonical form but merely a statement of reality.

Even more by C. 1012:2 which states: "Therefore it is impossible for a valid contract of marriage between baptized persons to exist without being by that very fact a sacrament." In other words the marriage between two baptized persons is automatically a sacrament even though the parties do not intend to receive the sacrament, even though they are indifferent to the sacrament, even though they are not even aware they are baptized. For baptized persons, the only condition seems to be that they do not positively exclude the sacrament.

How a marriage between baptized parties is automatically a sacrament becomes more difficult to comprehend when we recall our theology that to receive a sacrament one must have at least a virtual intention to receive the sacrament. The Church teaches that in infant Baptism, the faith and intention of the parents and godparents supplies. But one may ask where is the requisite minimal intention for the sacrament of baptism in persons who do not even know that marriage is a sacrament and could not care less.

Some have suggested that the Church consider the possibility that marriages between baptized without a faith commitment be considered valid but not sacramental. In present legislation, this is not possible. In these cases of couples without faith commitment, it is often possible to delay the marriage on the basis of lack of knowledge of marriage, lack of religious instruction, public sinner prohibition of C. 1066, use of just cause vetitum of C. 1039:1. It may be even possible to deny the marriage because of a reasonable suspicion of the exclusion of one of the essential properties of marriage.

But in the long run, presuming all other requirements are present, it is difficult to see how one can refuse marriage to a couple solely on the lack of faith commitment. In virtue of the 1918 response and 1941 Instruction that a priest may not refuse marriage when a couple refused to take instructions in the teachings of the Faith, the Church does not seem to consider this a formidable obstacle to marriage. In this instance, the Church seems to favor the natural right to marry over the need for a faith commitment.

B. Immaturity which renders parties incapable of fulfilling obligations of marriage: Exclusion of right to community life.

1. *General Observations*: The experience of priests has underlined the widespread immaturity which exists among couples, especially teenagers, who want to be married. By their words, actions, attitudes, background, style of life and in many other ways, these parties reveal almost a certitude that they are incapable of carrying out the heavy obligations and responsibilities of life involved in marriage.

If a priest has a reasonable suspicion that a couple is so immature that they are incapable of fulfilling the obligations of marriage and therefore, incapable of giving and receiving the right to community of life which is an essential element of marital consent, then he has a legitimate basis to postpone the marriage. It should be emphasized that when the essential element of the right to community of life seems to be clearly lacking in the consent that a couple is required to make, the priest should provide the opportunity for the parties to receive expert counseling. In other words, the priest's main function is not to prevent marriage but to assist persons to become capable of happy and successful marriages.

When a couple requests marriage, it is not their burden to prove that they are capable of fulfilling the obligations of community of life in marriage. To refuse marriage in the case of this immaturity, the priest would have to see positive signs that they lack the minimal maturity needed for the responsibilities of community life. This is in conformity with the prescription of C. 1035 that: "All persons who are not prohibited by law can contract marriage."

2. Authority that marriage is a communion of life and that the right to this communion of life is an essential element of marital consent.

a. Vatican Council II

Gaudium et Spes, No. 48: "The *intimate partnership of married life and love* has been established by the Creator and qualified by His laws. It is rooted in the conjugal covenant of *irrevocable personal consent*".
. . By their very nature, the institution of marriage itself and conjugal love are ordained for the procreation and education of children and find in them their ultimate crown."

Gaudium et Spes, No. 50: "Marriage to be sure is not instituted solely for procreation. Rather, its very nature as an *unbreakable compact between persons*, and the welfare of the children, both demand that the mutual love of the spouses, too, be embodied in a rightly ordered manner, that it grow and ripen. Therefore, *marriage persists as a whole manner and communion of life*, and maintains its value and indissolubility, even when offspring are lacking."

b. *Humanae Vitae*, No. 8:

"Marriage is not, then, the effect of chance or the product of evolution of unconscious natural forces; it is the wise institution of the Creator to realize in mankind His design of love. By means of the reciprocal personal gift of self, proper and exclusive to them, husband and wife tend towards *the communion of their beings* in view of mutual personal perfection, to collaborate with God in the generation and education of new lives."

c. *Pope Paul VI's Address to Sacred Roman Rota* (February 9, 1976)

". . . marriage has become better known and understood in its *true nature as a community of love* . . ."

d. *Pope Paul's Address to the Equipes Notre-Dame* (September 26, 1976):

"Marriage—let us constantly recall is a *communion founded on love* and made stable and definitive by an irrevocable covenant and commitment."

    Understood in this way, this interpersonal communion, widened by the birth of children, is a mark of God's love and goodness."

e. *Sacred Roman Rota Decisions*: Coram Anne, February 25, 1964

"The formal substantial object of matrimonial consent is not only the exclusive and perpetual bodily right to acts suitable for the generation of children but also embraces a right to a *community of life* which is properly called marriage together with its correlative obligations."

    Coram Anne, July 22, 1069 (unpublished)

"Marriage consists in an *interpersonal relationship* underlying which there is a healthy orientation of two persons toward each other. If from the history of the common life, in the opinion of experts even before the marriage there was seriously lacking that necessary internal and interpersonal integrity, such a person must be considered incapable to undertake that *community of life* for the procreation and education of children, and incapable likewise, of judging and reasoning correctly, about instituting a *community of life* with another person. There is lacking that discretion of judgment which would be necessary for a valid judgment about marriage."

Coram Serrano, April 15, 1973: "Thus, one can understand that, in dealing with individual cases, to claim or to deny ability to marry, it is not enough to establish either the absence of any mental abnormality taken in its restricted sense or a lack of freedom, if these two are viewed in themselves in isolation from any *specific relationship to the other person* just as he must be accepted in marriage. For though the *intimate interpersonal relationship* depends on the powers mentioned, still the personality can be seriously disturbed precisely in that it ought to be directed to another person who exists with his own individuality and ought to accept him as he is so that in some way he makes him master of himself in some matters. Thus, in no way is it impossible to imagine a person who not only sees marriage as a complexity of rights and duties which intrinsically carry an obligation, but obliged himself only objectively without any reference to his partner as a person with independent existence. In such a case, whether this happens consciously or not, I do not know whether there would arise a juridical 'bilateral personality' relationship; *it certainly would not be an interpersonal marriage covenant.*"

"Though it must be granted that the *interpersonal relationship* can reach greater or lesser perfection in different couples, yet in no way can it be said that this relationship completely belongs to the 'more perfect' or 'desirable' ideal marriage, since, in fact, according to what has been said, it *constitutes an essential property of any marriage consent. If this relationship is completely lacking, the consent itself is missing.*"

"Therefore, the question arises about the radical incapacity of people in whom one encounters all these personality disorders which, according to psychiatrists, are not so serious as to be classified as illnesses, and yet cause a psychopathic abnormality which can influence the very power which the subject should have to enter into an *interpersonal relationship* by which the rights of another over him and his rights over the other are correctly understood, deliberately pursued, and exchanged by mutual giving and accepting."

f. Draft of Proposed Code: C. 295 (revision of C. 1081)

1. "Marriage is effected by the consent of the parties lawfully expressed between persons who are capable according to law; and this consent no human power can supply.

2. Matrimonial consent is an act of the will by which a man and a woman, by means of a mutual covenant constitute with one another a *communion of conjugal life* which is perpetual and exclusive and which by its very nature is ordered to the procreation and education of children." C. 303:2 (revision of C. 1086:2)

"But if either party or both parties by a positive act of the will exclude marriage itself or the *right to the community of life*, or the right to the conjugal act, or any essential property of marriage, the marriage is invalid."

3. Some argue that the "right to community of life" may be an essential element of marital consent in the new code, but it is not yet the law and therefore cannot be considered part of marital consent until the new code goes into effect. The answer to this lies in the fact that community of life as a constitutive element of marital consent is not a creation of ecclesiastical law but a product of the natural law. There are many authorities to corroborate this conclusion but the following Rotal decision is reflective of the accepted position that even now a marriage would be invalid if the parties were incapable of giving and accepting the right to communion of life.

Coram Fagiolo, January 23, 1970: "There are some today who think that there should be included explicitly in the new code a new matrimonial impediment which should be called moral impotency. This new impediment would declare as incapable of contracting marriage one who suffers from a mental debility such that he is not capable of assuming the burdens and responsibilities of marriage."

"Whatever the status of the new code, it can no longer be doubted that anyone who is incapable of assuming the essential burdens of marriage is likewise incapable of contracting marriage, and the basis for this is the natural law itself . . . This capacity is not only that which spelled out in positive law but primarily is that which the natural law determines. According to this natural law, those parties are certainly incapable of marriage who are not capable of perceiving, accepting and giving the right to that intimate community of life which by its very nature is ordained to the procreation of children and which is correctly termed matrimony."

"We do not have to wait for a new and explicit statute of the Code since we already know from our traditional principles and from our jurisprudence that all habitual mental defects and mental disturbances can cause serious defects in the use of reason which can relate to defects of consent or to lack of discretionary judgment . . . Among the defects of consent can be included all classes of inability to assume the essential burdens of marriage."

"In weighing the evidence of the exclusion of the bonum prolis, the judge should not waste time solely on the statements of the parties and witnesses concerning the words spoken by the one who simulated if it is seen that the exclusion stemmed from some incapacity of the party to assume the essential burdens, such as the duty of intimate community of life which is ordered to the procreation of children."

XVIII — PROPOSED LEGISLATION ON DEFECTIVE MATRIMONIAL CONSENT

Francis G. Morrisey, O.M.I.

On January 22, 1974, Professor Pietro Agostino d'Avack, an advocate at the Tribunal of the Roman Rota, startled canonists around the world with his straight-forward condemnation of the current matrimonial legislation and jurisprudence of the Church.[1] It did not take long for a reaction to be felt against these feelings. Even the Holy Father, in his annual address to the Rota, one week later, referred indirectly to this address when he urged Catholics to have trust in the legislation of the Church. The Pope then went on to say that neither he nor others could hide their surprise at some of the excessive criticisms that were levelled against the juridical system presently in effect throughout the Church.[2]

Pope Paul VI did not refer in his address to any specific point in Professor d'Avack's paper that he found unsatisfactory. This would have been quite helpful for our purposes here in trying to study the proposed legislation on defective matrimonial consent, because some of the points raised in d'Avack's address will be considered in the following pages, and the Holy Father would have provided us with an authorized commentary on the legislator's intentions in the matter. Nevertheless, we must keep the Pope's observations foremost in our minds as we proceed with this study.

My intention in this seminar is quite positive: to explain some of the proposed changes presented by the Pontifical Commission for the Revision of the Code on the question of defective matrimonial consent, and, indirectly to show that a correct understanding of these important modifications will answer many of d'Avack's propositions, some of them almost to the letter. Naturally, he too had access to the *Relatio* presented by the Code Commission and was able to make good use of it in his talk.

The field is not completely new since commentaries have already been published on the whole of the proposed marriage legislation,[3] as well as on particular aspects of the proposed changes.[4]

We intend to study some of the points involved in the new legislation on defective consent and determine the object of sufficient consent. We will then, in a second part, be able to see what will be required for matrimonial consent if the proposed changes in the legislation are carried through, and, finally, we will refer to some of the practical applications that arise from these proposed changes.

I. THE NATURE AND OBJECT OF MATRIMONIAL CONSENT

The Church's teaching on Christian marriage

Most canonists are familiar with the developments in the Church's teaching on the nature of Christian marriage and of matrimonial consent. At the second Vatican Council, Christian marriage was redefined as an "intimate partnership of life and love, established by the Creator and qualified by His laws". The Council did not state how the partnership was to be lived or what was necessary for its existence. Completing the teaching of *Gaudium et Spes,* Pope Paul VI clarified the notion in his encyclical letter *"Humanae Vitae"* when he gave the characteristics of Christian love, as found in marriage. The love of the couple of each other must be human, moral, total, and fruitful.[5]

Marriage is no longer presented in terms of primary and secondary ends, but rather as a partnership of married life and love. Consequently, matrimonial consent— whose object is necessarily the partnership—is no longer said to consist exclusively in the acceptance and giving of the rights by which both partners join "in one flesh".

This presentation of the Church's teaching does not seem to be simply the result of individual canonists' theorizing. Indeed, it is re-echoed constantly in many of the important documents of the Church and of its highest Tribunals. In his very learned and scholarly study on conjugal love and the juridical structure of Christian marriage, Father W.J. LaDue shows how this teaching was incorporated after the Council into the decisions of the Rota as of 1968, if not sooner.[6] The famous decision of Msgr. Lucien Anne, February 25, 1969, was the first instance, it seems, of a case where marriage was presented as a *"consortium totius vitae."* Anne proceeded to show the juridical implications of the Conciliar pronouncement, but stopped short of saying what specific rights and corresponding duties were involved in this *consortium totius vitae.*

Msgr. Anne's sentence was written some months after the date of the decision. From all appearances, it seems as though he was waiting for the Code commission to proceed in its work of reviewing the legislation on marriage, since he uses the same expressions in the *relatio* on the subject. Indeed, the subcommission's report proposed a new wording of Canon 1013: 1, so that henceforth it would read as follows:

> *Marriage is that intimate partnership of the whole of life between a man and a woman which by its very nature is ordered to the procreation and education of children.*[7]

No reference is made to a hierarchy of ends of marriage, nor to the mere biological functions involved. Rather, the emphasis is rightly placed on the community of life, or the "partnership" as it is called. Msgr. Anne used almost the same definition in his landmark decision.

Matrimonial Consent

Since marriage is defined as a partnership, the consent to marriage must necessarily include the consenting to the partnership and to all that it entails. The present canon 1081: * of the Code calls for consent to cover those acts apt for the generation of children. It is now proposed to describe consent as that act of the will whereby a man and a woman by means of a mutual covenant constitute with one another a communion of conjugal life which is perpetual and exclusive and which by its very nature is ordered to the procreating and education of offspring.[8]

A number of very significant points could be mentioned concerning this new wording. The first is the use of the word "covenant" rather than "contract." Indeed, in his oft-quoted study, "Christian Marriage: Contract or Covenant,"[9] Father Paul Palmer analyzed the significance of this change of emphasis: covenant is seen as a relationship of mutual trust and fidelity, as opposed to contract which is used of things, of property or of personal belongings.[10] The importance of the change is that we must now take into account the long-range dimensions of marriage, and not limit ourselves to the event and the situation occurring at the time of the actual ceremony itself (what could be called the "contract"). Consequently, in the consent to marriage, we must now find this element of life-time commitment.

As a parenthesis to this last remark, we could quote from an unpublished decision of the Rota, February 28, 1973, *coram* Agostoni, which seems to ignore totally the existence of this change of perspective. We read as follows: "The matrimonial consent gives and accepts only the obligations which make up the object of the consent, not, however, the carrying out of these obligations."[11]

This principle seems completely unacceptable at this time because it means that we do not in any way take into account the capacity of fulfilling the obligations of the matrimonial state, which is generally accepted by the majority of the judges of the Rota. The new description of consent incorporates the notion of a perpetual and exclusive community of conjugal life. It is to be noted that the word "conjugal love" does not appear in the text. The reason for this is rather simple: love, being a passion, is not one of the elements that can be rightly evaluated by law, since by its nature it is not of the external forum. Instead, the law, with the help of the psychiatric sciences, can evaluate—and indeed must in many cases—the aptitude of a person to carry out and fulfill the obligations of the matrimonial state.

This definition states clearly that the community of conjugal life is orderd by its very nature to the procreating and education of offspring. These various elements: covenant, perpetual and exclusive community of conjugal life, and ordering toward offspring recall somewhat the characteristics laid down by Pope Paul to describe true and authentic Christian love: it must be human, moral, total and fruitful.[12]

The definition that Professor d'Avack proposed of consent in his celebrated address is similar, but with some striking differences:

> *"Consent is the act of the will by which each party acquires and accepts, in perpetuity and exclusively, both the right to a community of life and love and the right to perform those acts which lead to procreation"*[13]

We see from this proposed definition consent is reduced to a simple *act of the will* without reference to a covenant, the element of *conjugal love* is included as a right, and no reference is made to the *education* of children.

It is certain that conjugal love, or *"amor coniugalis"* as it is frequently called, has been accepted by a number of Rotal judges, especially Archbishop Fagiolo, as a juridical element.[14] However, this notion was not universally received, and I personally would prefer limiting our court inquiries to the judicial investigation of the existence of the aptitude for undertaking and fulfilling the obligations of the *consortium vitae* without direct reference to love itself.

It might well be for this reason that Pope Paul VI did not accept d'Avack's proposals. Moreover, the same line of thought is evident in the letter of the Apostolic Signatura to Cardinal Alfrink on December 30, 1971.[15]

The Object of Matrimonial Consent

Given the new presentation of the *nature of* matrimonial consent, it was necessary to propose a revision of the canons concerning the *object* of matrimonial consent.

The present law, in canon 1086:2, refers to the exclusion of the conjugal act or of any essential property of marriage as necessary and sufficient for the invalidity of the marriage. Since consent now is said to consist in a mutual covenant for a communion of conjugal life, it follows that the willful exclusion of the community of life or of one of its essential elements, renders the covenant void. Consequently, if the *right* to an intimate, lifelong conjugal partnership is not mutually given and accepted, there is no marriage.[16]

In positivs terms, then, the parties must offer each other: 1) the right to the community of life; 2) the possibility of living this community of life; 3) the right to conjugal acts; 4) the other essential properties of marriage: unity, fidelity, indissolubility.

It must be asked what is the extension of each of these terms. What are, for instance, the essential rights to which a partner in the community must have access? Father G. Lesage has grouped these rights under five headings which could be listed as: 1) the balance and maturity required for a truly human form of conduct, 2) the relationships of interpersonal and heterosexual friendship, 3) the aptitude to cooperate sufficiently for conjugal assistance, 4) mental balance and the sense of responsibility required for the material welfare of the home, and 5) the psychic capacity of both spouses to participate in their own normal way, in promoting the welfare of the children.[17]

What is meant by the second item: the possibility of living the community of life? This is now generally taken to mean that the partners are able to bind themselves to long range commitments and fulfill the obligations of the marriage state. This is the counter-part of the first section: the rights to which the parties should have access; here we are dealing with the corresponding duties.

By the right to conjugal acts we usually now understand the right to all moral acts, without any restriction in time or space. In former jurisprudence, it was considered sufficient for any right to be given; today, if any part of the right is reserved, it is understood that the right itself was reserved. A different meaning is given to the expression "*omne ius*" of the Code.

The other essential properties of marriage—its unity and indissolubility—are to be interpreted as they are now received in the common jurisprudence of the Church, with which most canonists are familiar.

Consequently if the proposed legislation is accepted as such, we will have to admit that the four elements mentioned above are essential for matrimonial consent and constitute its object.

The problem that must be considered as this time is what is required in the person to be able to give sufficient consent for marriage. The consent may be defective for many reasons: a) a defect of the will, b) a defect of knowledge, c) a defect of mental capacity. This latter is distinguished into three categories: 1) defect of human responsibility, which usually constitutes insanity and is a permanent disability, 2) defect of contractual capacity, usually resulting from a temporary incapacity which affects one of the parties at the time of the wedding, and 3) defect of capacity to fulfill the long-range obligations of the matrimonial state, which defect usually arises from some permanent psychic cause that renders a person inept for marriage.

This presentation is not covered directly in the present Code, although ample provision is made for defects of knowledge and defects of the will. How does the new Code plan to overcome this deficiency? This is the object of the second part of our paper.

II. THE REQUIRED CAPACITY FOR MATRIMONIAL CONSENT

Even though the principles governing the incapacity to give valid matrimonial consent are implicit in the prescriptions of the Code it was considered expedient to express them more distinctly and clearly in the new law.[18]

Consequently, in the new Code, it is proposed to distinguish three categories of incapacity: 1) the total incapacity to elicit consent because of a mental illness or disturbance that impedes the use of reason; 2) the incapacity arising from a serious lack of discretion of judgment concerning the matrimonial rights and duties to be mutually given and accepted; 3) the incapacity of assuming the essential obligations of matrimony caused by a serious psycho-sexual anomaly.[19]

These three incapacities correspond to the division mentioned above: *incapacity of personal responsibility, incapacity of contractual act, incapacity of fulfilling obligations.*

The incapacity of personal responsibility or insanity, is the same as the total incapacity to elicit consent because of a mental illness or disturbance that impedes the use of reason. It should be mentioned that some courts, operating on this division, are using the psychic causes for invalidity as the grounds of nullity. The most common psychic causes that would intervene in this category are schizophrenia, pure paranoia mental debility and constitutional immaturity. I have already mentioned elsewhere[20] that for the safeguarding of the doctrine of indissolubility and eventually, the protection of Tribunal personnel, it is advisable that the Tribunal require the presence of a specifically diagnosed illness before proceeding to a declaration of nullity on these grounds.

The new Code will provide directly for cases of this nature, it seems, by admitting as grounds of nullity the total *incapacity* to elicit consent.

The *second* category of incapacity proposed by the Code Commission is also the same as what is expressed in the term "incapacity of conctractual act." The serious lack of due discretion concerning the matrimonial rights and obligations, may, of itself, be only temporary in nature. This means that at the time of the wedding, one of the parties (or both, for that matter) was unable to perceive the object of consent. This could arise from a psychic cause that could eventually be cured or arrested and allow the person to enter into another marriage where he or she would be able to give and know the essential rights and obligations of the matrimonial state. Examples of such causes might be found in cases of depressive neurosis, anxiety neurosis, and some instances of homosexuality. The situation could also arise, however, from a temporary disturbance or perturbation without being caused by an illness of the psychic order. Two illustrations come to mind here. The first is the case of the young pregnant girl who wishes to get married simply to protect the child. Her physical state prevents her from perceiving clearly the object of her consent. If these marriages break up shortly after the birth of a child, it seems that there is no difficulty in introducing the case on these grounds. A competent psychiatrist will be able to evaluate quite easily the fact that the young girl was not free to consent at the time and bind herself to a community of life and love with all that this entails. The second case would be that of a young person who felt compelled to leave his home because of parental pressure and entered matrimony simply for the purpose of freeing himself from a desperate situation.

The court should not impose a *vetitum* in these instances because of the strong possibility of obtaining a cure when an illness is involved. It would not always seem as neccessary to insist in these cases upon a specifically-diagnosed psychic cause because of the transitory nature of the situation, although it will be easier for the court to reach moral certitude with a strong medical report to support its decision. It seems that a number of courts are unwilling to make use of this important distinction, and are rejecting sound cases that could be accepted quite easily on the grounds of temporary incapacity. I do not believe that we have, as yet, reached a full understanding of what is meant by the necessary "discretion of judgment" to accept the rights and duties of the matrimonial state. Could the courts not establish a series of practical presumptions to help them in their work? One of these might be that if a marriage lasts less than six months (or possibly even a year) the presumption favors nullity; another presumption might be that if a girl is pregnant at the time of wedding and it breaks up shortly after the birth of the child, the simple facts, combined with good psychiatric opinion, indicate that the marriage was null and void. Naturally, these presumptions are not included in the proposed text of the new law—nor could they be because it is meant to be law for the universal Church. Nevertheless, in our North American context could we not look into this matter more seriously, and, consequently, be able to administer true justice more quickly and efficaciously in cases which, in many instances, are clear illustrations of invalid marriages?

The *third* type of incapacity proposed by the Code Commission is described as that of being unable to assume essential obligations of the matrimonial state because of a serious psycho-sexual anomaly. Upon further reflecion and discussion with other canonists, I would like to modify somewhat the opinion I expressed in an article published in the Jurist in 1973.[21] This concerns the meaning of the expression "psycho-sexual anomaly." It seems now that the expression "sexual" is used, not in the sense of matters relating to genital activities, but rather to those aspects of complementarity of the spouses. Consequently, a psycho-sexual anomaly would be understood to mean a disorder that prevented the couple from giving and accepting the basic obligations of the *consortium vitae.*

As most canonists know today, these disorders are quite frequent. While the person is able to perceive and even accept the rights and obligations of the marriage state, he is completely incapable of fulfilling them throughout his lifetime. In cases of this nature, we are speaking of the long-range obligations we referred to when considering the nature of consent. Some instances, among many, of psychic causes giving rise to an incapacity of this nature are forms of psychosis, antisocial personality or sociopathy, and hyperaesthesia.

One important consideration to be made at this time is that it is not necessary to await the promulgation of the new Code before using this threefold division of incapacities. This classification is simply the result, it seems, of a post-factum analysis of decisions already granted by the courts and applied in practice in the large Tribunals.

As a result of this proposed legislation, which, again, is simply a codified existing practice, we are now able to reach some type of positive formulation on what is required for valid matrimonial consent. A person wishing to have a covenant for a community of married life and love, must be of sound mind, be free of abnormal pressures preventing him from accepting the rights and duties of matrimony, and must be able to fulfill these obligations throughout the normal course of his life.

Having studied the nature and object of matrimonial consent, and the capacity to give this consent, let us now proceed to the third and final section of this paper where we will examine some of the practical applications arising from the changes proposed in the law.

III. APPLICATIONS OF THE PROPOSED NEW LAW ON CONSENT

We began this paper by referring to some remarks made by Professor Pietro d'Avack and showing how he was calling for a reform of the Church's law on marriage. We then proceeded to examine some of the proposed changes in the law.

Subsequently, we examined certain forms of defective consent, especially as they were related to incapacities preventing valid consent from being given. When referring to these incapacities we also mentioned in passing that consent can be invalid for other reasons, namely, a defect of the will or a defect of knowledge. It would be worth our while to take a few moments to consider these other two aspects of the defect of consent and see how the new Code proposes to cover them.

Defects of the Will

By defects of the will we mean that a person's outward consent does not correspond to his interior feelings and intentions. These intentions can be verified either in implicit or explicit conditions, or in internal rejection of the marriage itself (as, for instance, in cases of force and fear) or of one of its properties such as unity or indissolubility. A new type of defect of the will that would be recognized would be found in willfully excluding one of the essential elements of the community of life.

A question that arises when speaking of excluding one of the essential elements of the community of life is to what extent is the desire to provide for the Catholic education of children born of the marriage essential to the matrimonial community. It is generally admitted that providing for the education and well-being of the children is as important a part of the community of life as providing for the relationships of hetero-sexual and interpersonal friendship. We may ask whether providing for the Catholic education of children (not necessarily being the equivalent of sending them to Catholic schools) is truly one of the essential obligations of the community of life taken in its full sense. If so, would the systematic refusal to provide for this form of education—taken in its minimal sense—provide grounds for nullity: a defect of consent due to an intention against one of the essential obligations of the community of life?

This could easily happen in some mixed marriages where a person might not express his true feelings until after the children are born, or might not express them before the priest to avoid having "difficulties" in getting married. An interesting affirmative sentence was given on these very grounds by the Portsmouth Matrimonial Tribunal in England on the 29th of May, 1974. This decision followed a very lively discussion held at the annual meeting of the Canon Law Society of Great Britain near Dublin in May, 1974. I personally believe we should look into this matter more deeply. Three remarks should be made, however, on this topic: 1) the systematic refusal to allow or provide for Catholic education must have been the cause or one of the causes of the break-up of the marriage; 2) the judges must still determine whether education of offspring can be considered as an essential component of the *consortium vitae;* 3) we must be able to agree on what would constitute Catholic education.

A distinction would also have to be made, it seems, between an intention that was present at the time of marriage, and an intention that was only expressed later in the course of the conjugal life, for instance, if one of the partners left the Church and subsequently became very hostile to all her teachings. I do not think that in this second case we would be able to make use of the refusal to provide a Catholic eduation as grounds of nullity, but the opposite could be true in the first case.

Since, as we have already seen, the new Code will most likely include the provision that the exclusion of the community of life would amount to a defect of consent, it seems as though we are on solid canonical grounds in proposing this new aspect. And since the Code Commission is simply incorporating the teaching of the Council, there is no reason why we could not proceed to apply this now.

The new Code proposes to tighten the present legislation on conditional marriages by excluding the possibility of contracting marriage with a future condition.

This would apply to invalidating conditions against the substance of marriage and to conditions relating to licit matters. Conditions concerning the past or the present will be admitted with the written permission of the Ordinary.

No changes are mentioned in the *Relatio* concerning intentions against children, fidelity or indissolubility.

Defects of Knowledge

Many changes are proposed in this category, especially on the notions of error and fraud. Speaking of "error in the person" Pio Fedele published a long study on this aspect in 1973.[22] He stated explicitly that we can even now say that a marriage entered into because of an error on the quality of the person is invalid if the error were caused by grave deceit in order to elicit consent.[23]

Another type of error that is quite common and at the same time is difficult to evaluate is what is known as *simple error* on the unity or indissolubility of marriage. The Code Commission proposes to change the wording of Canon 1084 so that it would read: error on the unity or indissolubility of mariage, as long as it does not affect the will, does not invalidate the marriage. However, in the case of error concerning indissolubility (which in many cases could also lead to a defect of the will) it now seems that new principles are being devised by the Rotal judges: the presumption that a person wishes to contract marriage like all other persons becomes weaker as the error on indissolubility becomes stronger: the error can easily influence or affect the will, and consequently cause invalidity.[24] The recognition of the existence of error created by a divorce mentality is now something accepted in Rotal jurisprudence.[25]

The Latin Code Commission also proposes accepting a canon on the invalidating effect of fraud.[26] Certain conditions would be laid down: the fraud must be perpetrated in order to obtain consent, and it must concern a specific quality in the other person that would render the community of life impossible. This would probably cover cases where prgnancy or paternity were falsely alleged in order to have the proposed partner accept to have a wedding celebrated.

Canonists will have to decide when a deficiency or a state that was fraudulently hidden was of sufficient magnitude to prevent the community of life from taking place. We might be faced with a complete scale of cases, ranging from one extreme to the other. It will, nevertheless, be important to avoid subjective criteria in applying this new norm—which was badly needed—if the Church is to avoid what could appear to be widespread granting of divorce.

Footnotes

* Seminar presented at the 36th Annual General Meeting of the Canon Law Society of America, Minneapolis, Minn., October 7-10, 1974.

1. Cf. *The Tablet,* February 2, 1974, p.114.
2. Pope Paul VI, "Address to the Tribunal of the Rota," January 31, 1974, in A.A.S., 66 (1974), p. 84-88; cf. *The Tablet,* February 9, 1974, p. 139.
3. Cf. U. Navarrete, S.J., "Mutationes et praevisae innovationes on iure matrimoniali," in *Prawo Kanoniczne,* 15 (1972), pp.3-17; Francis G] Morrisey, O.M.I., "Preparing Ourselves for the New Marriage Legislation" in *The Jurist,* 33 (1973), p. 343-357; U. Naverrete, S.J., "Incapacitas assumendi onera uti caput autonomum nullitatis matrimonii", in *Periodica, (1972),* pp. 47-80.
4. Cf. Pio Fedele, "A proposito della innovazioni proposte della Commissione per la revisione del C.I.C. intema di consenso matrimoniale," in L'Annee canonique. 17 (1973), p. 365-412; William J. LaDue, "Conjugal Love and the Juridical Structure of Christian Marriage," in *The Jurist,* 34 (1974), pp. 36-67.
5. Cf. Pope Paul VI, Encyclical letter "Humanae vitae," July 25, 1968, Nos. 7-10, in A.A.S., 60 (1968) pp. 485-488.
6. Cf. W.J.LaDue, *op. cit.,* pp.41-43.
7. Cf. *Communicationes,* 3 (1971), p. 70; translation by W.J. LaDue, *op. cit.,* p. 46.
8. Cf. *Communicationes, op. cit.,* p. 75; W.J. LaDue, *op. cit., p. 46.*
9. P. Palmer, S.J., "Christian Marriage: Contract or Covenant," in *Theological Studies,* 33 (1972), pp. 617-667.
10. *Ibid.,* pp. 618-619.
11. S.R.R. Dec., C. Agostoni, February 28, 1973, Prot. No. 9565, par. 3.
12. Cf. Pope Paul VI, *Humanae vitae, op. cit.,* Nos. 7-10.
13. Text in *Informations catholiques internationales,* No. 450, February 15, 1974, p. 30; *The Tablet,* February 2, 1974, p. 114.
14. Cf. Cyril Murtagh, "The Judicial Importance of 'Amor Conjugalis,' " in *Studia Canonica,* 7 (1973), pp. 49-57.
15. Cf. English translation in *The Jurist,* 33 (1973), pp. 296-300.
16. Cf. W.J. LaDue, *op. cit.,* p. 48.
17. Cf. G. Lesage, O.M.I., "Evolution recente de la jurisprudence matrimoniale," in Societe Canadienne de Theologie, *Le Divorce, Montreal,* Fides, 1973, pp. 47-48.
18. Cf. *Communicationes, op. cit.,* p. 77.
19. *Ibid.*
20. Francis G. Morrisey, O.M.I., "The Incapacity of Entering Into Marriage," in *Studia Canonica,* 8 *(1974).*
21. *ID., "Preparing Ourselves for the New Marriage Legislation," op. cit., p. 353.*
22. *Op. cit.,* pp. 391-396.
23. *Ibid.,* p. 391.
24. Cf. I. Parisella, "De pervicaci seu radicato errore circa matrimonii indissolubilitatem. Iurisprudentia rotalis recentior," in *Ius Populi Dei, Romae, P.U.G.,* (1972), pp. 511-540, esp. p. 539.
25. Cf. S.R.R. Dec., C. Ewers, May 18, 1968, in *Monitor Ecclesiasticus,* 94 (1969), p. 398 ff.
26. *Communicationes, op. cit.,* pp. 76-77.

XX—BIBLIOGRAPHY

Books

American Handbook of Psychiatry Ed. by Silvano Arieti. Vols. 1-2, New York: Basic Books, Inc., 1959 Vol. 3, 1966.

Ayrinhac, Henry, *Marriage Legislation in the New Code*, 4th rev. ed., rev. & enl. by P.J. Lydon, N.Y., Benziger, 1959.

Bartoccetti, Victorius, *De Causis Matrimonialibus*. Romae: 1950.

Bassett, William, ed., *The Bond of Mariage; an Ecumenical and Interdisciplinary Study*, Notre Dame, Univ. of N.D. Press, 1968.

———— and Peter Huizing, *The Future of Christian Marriage*, N.Y. Herder, 1973 (vol. 86 of Concilium Religion in the Seventies).

Bertocci, Peter, *Sex, Love and the Person*, N.Y., Sheed & Ward, 1967.

Bevilacqua, Anthony, "The History of the Indissolubility of Marriage," *Proceedings of the Twenty-Second Annual Convention: The Catholic Theological Society of America*, Chicago, 1967.

Bockle, Franz, ed., *The Future of Marriage as Institution*, N.Y., Herder, 1970 (vol. 55 of Concilium/Theology in the Age of Renewal).

Boff, L., "The Theology of Marriage," *Concilium, the Future of Christian Marriage*, ed. by Bassett & Huizing, vol. 87, N.Y., Herder, 1973.

Brown, Ralph, ed., *Matrimonial Decisions for England and Wales for 1968, 1969, 1970*, vols. 2, 3 & 4, London, Canon Law Society of Great Britain, 1969-71.

Cavanagh, John R., *Counseling the Invert*, Milwaukee: Bruce, 1966.

Chatham, Josiah G., *Force and Fear as Invalidating Marriage: The Element of Injustice*, Washington: Catholic University, 1950.

Cloran, Owen M., *Previews and Practical Cases on Marriage*, Milwaukee: Bruce, 1960.

Detroit (Archdiocesan) Tribunal, *A Practice Guide for Marriage Cases prepared by the Tribunal for the private use of the Priests of the Archdiocese of Detroit*, Detroit, The Tribunal, 1963.

Diagnostic and Statistical Manual of Mental Disorders, Washington: American Psychiatric Association, First edition 1952; Second edition 1968, Third edition expected to be available in late 1979.

Goldstein, Joseph and Jay Katz, *The Family and the Law*, New York: The Free Press, 1965

Haring, Bernard, *Marriage in the Modern World*, Westminster: The Newman Press, 1966.

Haring, Bernard, "Pastoral Work among the Divorced and Invalidly Married," Concilium, *The Future of Marriage as Institution*, ed. by Bockle, vol. 55, N.Y., Herder, 1970.

Hellwig, Monica, *The Meaning of the Sacraments*, Dayton, Ohio, Pflaum, 1972.

Hertel, James, *When Marriage Fails*, N.Y. Paulist Press, 1969.

Hudson, Edward, *Handbook for Marriage Nullity Cases*, Ottawa: St. Paul University, 1975.

Joyce, George, *Christian Marriage: An Historical and Doctrinal Study*, 2nd ed. rev. & enl., London, Sheed & Ward, 1948.

Keating, John Richard, *The Bearing of Mental Impairment on the Validity of Marriage*, Roma: Gregorian University Press, 1964.

Kelleher, Stephen, *Divorce and Remarriage for Catholics?*, N.Y., Doubleday, 1973.

Kilmartin, E., "When is Marriage a Sacrament?" *Theological Studies*, 34:2, June 1973.

Kindregan, Charles, *A Theology of Marriage: A Doctrinal, Moral and Legal Study*, Milwaukee, Bruce, 1967.

Kohut, Nester, *A Manual on Marital Reconciliations; a Social-Legal Analysis of Divorce*, Chicago, Adams, 1964.

Lesage, Germain and Francis Morrisey, *Documentation on Marriage Nullity Cases*, Ottawa: St. Paul University, 1973.

Mackin, T., "Consummation: of contract or of covenant?" *Jurist*, 32:2, 1972 and 32:3, 1972.

Maida, Adam, *The Tribunal Reporter*, Huntington, Ind., Our Sunday Visitor Press, 1970.

Marriage Annulment: A Practical Guide for Roman Catholics and Others, London, G. Chapman, 1970.

Matrimonial Jurisprudence, United States, 5´vols. covering years 1968 to 1978, Toledo, CLSA, published annually beginning in 1973.

McCormack, R., "Theology and Divorce," *Theological Studies*, March 1971.

McHugh, James, *Marriage in the Light of Vatican II*, Washington, Family Life Bureau, 1968.

————— *Mixed Marriages: New Directions*, Washington, Family Life Division, U.S.C.C., 1971.

Montserrat-Torrents, José, *The Abandoned Spouse*, Milwaukee, Bruce, 1969.

Noonan, John, *Power to Dissolve: Lawyers and Marriages in the Courts of the Roman Curia*, Cambridge, Belknap Press of Harvard U., 1972.

O'Callaghan, D., "Marriage as Sacrament," *Concilium, The Future of Marriage as Institution*, ed. by Bockle, vol. 55, N.Y., Herder, 1970.

Orsay, Ladislas et at., *Law, Conscience and Marriage*, Washington,

School of Canon Law, C.U.A., 1970 (Reprinted from *The Jurist*, 30, 1970).

Packard, Vance, *The Sexual Wilderness; the Contemporary Upheaval in Male-Female Relationships*, N.Y., McKay, 1968.

Pospishil, Victor J., *Divorce and Remarriage; towards a new Catholic Teaching*, N.Y., Herder, 1963.

Schillebeeckx, E., *Marriage: Human Reality and Saving Mystery*, N.Y][Sheed & Ward, 1966.

Schleck, Charles, *The Sacrament of Matrimony; a Dogmatic Study*, Milwaukee, Bruce, 1964.

The Bond of Marriage, Ed. by William Bassett, University of Notre Dame Press, 1968.

The Future of Marriage as Institution, Ed. by Franz Bockle, New York, Herder and Herder, Vol. 55 of the Concilium Series, 1970.

Tobin, William, *Homosexuality and Marriage*, Rome, Catholic Book Agency, 1964.

Van der Poel, Cornelius, *God's Love in Human Language; a Study of the Meaning of Marriage and Conjugal Responsibility*, Pittsburgh, Duquesne University Press, 1969.

Van Ommeren, William M., *Mental Illness Affecting Matrimonial Consent*, (Canon Law Studies #415) Washington, D.C.,: Catholic University of America Press, 1961.

Articles

Abate, The Dissolution of the Matrimonial Bond in Ecclesiastical Jurisprudence (Rome: Desclee, 1962).

Ahern, "Psychological Incapacity for Marriage," Studia Canonica, 7/2 (1973), pp. 227-252.

Ambrozic, "Indissolubility: Law of Ideal?" Studia Canonica 6 (1972), pp. 269-288.

American Procedural Norms, (Washington: USCC Publications, 1970).

Bassett, "Divorce and Remarriage: The Catholic Search for a Pastoral Reconciliation," 162 *Amer. Eccl. Rev.* (1970), pp. 20-36; 92-105.

Bauer, "Relative Incapacity to establish a Christian Conjugal Union," 6 *CSLA Proceed.* (1974).

Bevilaqua, "The History of the Indissolubility of Marriage," 22 *CTSA Proceed.* (1967), pp. 253-308.

Brown, "The Natural Law, the Marriage Bond and Divorce," *The Jurist* 15 (1955), pp. 21-51.

Carr, "The Invalidly Married and the Sacraments," *Homil. and Pastoral Review*, 71 (1971), pp. 316-318; 72 (1972), pp. 67-71; 71-74.

Catoir, "When the Courts Don't Work," 125 *America*, (1971), pp. 254-257.

Conway, "Psychiatric Immaturity and its Implications for the Marriage Contract," *(The Australasian) Cath. Rec.*, 50 (1973) pp. 152-162.

Crogham, "Is Baptism the Decisive Factor?" 118 *America* (1968), pp. 222 ff.

Dolicamore, "Interpersonal Relationships and their Effect on the Validity of Marriages," 5 *CSLA Proceed.* (1973), pp. 84-100. Also published in *Origins* (Vol. 3 No. 18), dtd. Nov. 1, 1973 under the tile of "Annulments: The Psychology in Marriage."

Farley and Reich, "Toward an Immediate Internal Forum Solution for Deserving Couples in Canonically Indissoluble Marriage Cases," *The Jurist*, (1970) 30, pp. 45-74.

Finnegan, "Spiritual Direction for the Catholic Divorced and Remarried," *Chicago Studies,* 13 (1974), pp. 54-64. Also, cf., 5 *CSLA Proceed.* (1973) pp. 70-83.

Finnegan, "The Current Jurisprudence Concerning the Psychopathic Personality," *The Jurist* 27 (1967), pp. 440-453.

Finnegan, "When is a marriage Indissoluble?" *The Jurist* 28 (1968), pp. 309-329.

Haring, "Pastoral Work Among Divorced and Invalidly Married," *Concilium*, 55 (1970), pp. 123-130.

Hertel, "Save the Bond or Save the Person?" *America*, Feb. 17, 1968.

Huizing, "Law, Conscience and Marriage," *The Jurist*, 30 (1970), pp. 15-20.

Huizing, "The Indissolubility of Marriage and Church Order," *Concilium* 39 (1968), pp. 45-57.

Keating, *The Bearing of Mental Impairment on the Validity of Marriage* (Rome: Gregorian Univ. Press, 1964).

Kelleher, "The Problem of the Intolerable Marriage," *America*, Sept. 14, 1968. For a reaction to this controversial article cf., Marion Reinhardt, "Updating Marriage Tribunals," *America*, Nov. 9, 1968.

Kelly, "The Invalidly Married and Admission to the Sacraments," *Clergy Review*, 55 (1970), pp. 123-141.

Kenny, "Homosexuality and Nullity: Developing Jurisprudence," *The Cath. Lawyer*, 17 (1971), pp. 110-122.

Kuntz, "The Petrine Privilege: A Study of Some Recent Cases" *The Jurist*, 28 (1968), pp. 486-496.

LaDue, "Conjugal Love and the Juridical Structure of Christian Marriage," 34 *The Jurist* (1974), pp. 36-67.

Lasage, "Pour une renovation de la procedure matrimoniale," *Studia Canonica*, 7 (1973), pp. 253-280.

Leguerrier, "Recent Practice of the Holy See in regard to the dissolution of marriages between non-baptized persons without conversion," *The Jurist*, 25 (1965), pp. 458-465.

Lesage, "The Consortium Vitae Conjugalis: Nature and Applications," 6 *Studia Canonica* (1972), pp. 99-113.

Lesage and Morrisey, *Documentation on Marriage Nullity Cases*, (Ottawa: St. Paul Univ., 1973).

Maloney, "Oeconomia: A Corrective to Law," *Cath. Lawyer*, 19 (1971), pp. 90-109.

Matrimonial Jurisprudence: USA 1968-1971 (Hartford: CSLA, 1973). A second volume was published in 1974 for the year 1972. Also cf. Maida, *The Tribunal Reporter* (Huntington, Ind.: OSV Press—Vol. I, 1970).

Morrisey, "Defective Consent: Toward a New Church Law," *Origins*, Vol. 4 No. 21 dtd. Nov. 14, 1974, pp. 322-328. Also published in 6 *CSLA Proceedings (1974)*.

Morrisey, *"Preparing ourselves for the new Marriage Legislation,"* *The Jurist*, 33 (1973), pp. 343-357. Also published in *The Catholic Lawyer*, 20 (1974), pp. 30-43.

Murtagh, "The Juridical Importance of Amor Conjugalis," 33 *The Jurist* (1973), pp. 377-383.

Noonan, "Papal Dissolution of Marriage: Fiction and Function," *CSLA Proceed.*, 1 (1969), pp. 89-95.

O'Callaghan, "How far is Christian Marriage Indissoluble?" 40 *Irish Theolog. Qtrly.* (1973), pp. 162-173.

Orsy, "Intolerable Marriage Situations: Conflict between External and Internal Forum," *The Jurist*, 30 (1970), pp. 1-14.

Provost, "Church Tribunals and the Sacrament of Matrimony," *Chicago Studies* (Fall 1972), pp. 319-328.

Rahner, "Marriage as a Sacrament," 10 *Theological Investigations*, pp. 199-221.

Ryan, "Survey of Periodicals: Indissolubility of Marriage," *The Furrow* 24 (1973), pp. 150-159; 214-224; 272-284; 365-374; 524-539.

Sattler, "Divorce and Remarriage in the Church," *Americ. Eccl. Rev.*, 165 (1973), pp. 553-573.

Seal, "Marriage: Psychiatric Incapacity," *(The Australasian) Cath. Rec.* 50 (1973), pp. 140-151.

Wrenn, *Annulments* (Hartford: CSLA, 2nd ed., 1972).

INDEX